P9-AFT-792

The Social History
of Imperial Russia, 1700–1917
Volume Two

The Social History of Imperial Russia, 1700–1917 Volume Two

Boris N. Mironov

with

Ben Eklof

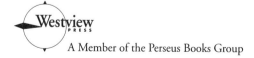

Westview
PRESS

A Member of the Perseus Books Group

Boris Mironov is the sole author of this text. Ben Eklof participated in its collective translation into English, supervised the project and the graduate assistants taking part, edited the translations at all stages, and also, by prior arrangement with the author, deleted, altered, or rewrote passages to adapt the text for an English-speaking adudience. Eklof assumes full and exclusive responsibility for the English text.

Copyright © 2000 by Westview Press, A Member of the Perseus Books Group

Published in 2000 in the United States of America by Westview Press, 5500 Central Avenue, Boulder, Colorado 80301-2877, and in the United Kingdom by Westview Press, 12 Hid's Copse Road, Cumnor Hill, Oxford OX2 9JJ

Library of Congress Cataloging-in-Publication Data
Mironov, Boris Nikolaevich.
    A social history of Imperial Russia, 1700–1917 / Boris Mironov with Ben Eklof.
      v. <2>. cm.
    Includes bibliographical references (p.) and index.
    ISBN 0-8133-3665-1 (v. 2)
    1. Russia—Social conditions—To 1801. 2. Russia—Social conditions—1801–1917. 3. Social structure—Russia—History. 4. Social classes—Russia—History. 5. Social change—Russia—History. 6. Russia—Politics and government—1689–1801. 7. Russia—Politics and government—1801–1917. I. Eklof, Ben, 1946– . II. Title.
HN523.M547 1999
306'.0947—dc21   99-19884
                                                                             CIP

The paper used in this publication meets the requirements of the American National Standard for Permanence of Paper for Printed Library Materials Z39.48-1984.

10 9 8 7 6 5 4 3 2 1

To my parents,
Nina Yakovlevna Mironova and
Nikolai Alekseevich Mironov

Contents

Tables

1

Patterns of State-Building

The argument that imperial Russia suffered from weak legal development is commonplace in both Russian and Western historiography. Indeed, there seems to be every reason to agree that Russia was ruled "not by law but by people." This view first emerged in prerevolutionary liberal historiography, whose proponents sought to make a transparent political critique of autocracy and to juxtapose an ideal of Western democracy. In critiquing the extralegal character of the Russian state, the liberal thesis undeniably had a progressive import. For that very reason, however, one should be cautious: Whenever politics is muddled with scholarship, the latter is bound to suffer. This is especially true with regard to scholarly analyses of Russian state-building. In this chapter I reconsider and modify the thesis of the "extralegal" character of the Russian state order. I give particular attention to the role of imperial administration, law, and public institutions in the central government as I delineate the main stages and formative factors in the development of the Russian state.[1]

The most promising way to approach this problem is to examine the state as a juridical relationship in which the object of law is state authority (its use and execution) and all of the subjects are integral elements of the state (from the monarch to the lowliest subject). Obviously, the role of a given subject will depend upon the relative power among different subjects as well as upon law, custom, and tradition. One very persuasive argument holds that restraints on the authority of the sovereign, his or her government, and other organs of imperial administration could come from three

Translated by Gregory Freeze, Brandeis University, with Deborah Howard, Indiana University.

sources: representative institutions; laws issued by the sovereign but obligating all, including the state institutions and the sovereign; and competition for power among different organs (as when several independent government bodies perform the same or related functions, or when a single organ performs different functions in various ways).[2]

My analysis is based on two assumptions. First, "real authority" in a country is vested in the individual or institution that the majority of the population deems to be the real holder of state power. Second, throughout its history the Russian state held *legitimate* authority and rule, for the general populace recognized its right to rule and govern (and, in turn, their own duty to submit and obey). Support for these assumptions may be found in events such as the church schism after Patriarch Nikon's reforms in the 1650s; the Razin uprising (1670–71) after the final enserfment of the seigniorial *(chastnovladel'cheskie)* peasantry in 1649; the Pugachev rebellion after the intensification of serfdom in the 1750s and 1760s; and the Revolutions of 1905–1907 and 1917, not to mention innumerable local disorders. All of these events clearly demonstrate that the people were passive and submissive only so long as they were satisfied with the existing regime. The upper strata of society also raised their voices in protest when they were dissatisfied with the ruling authorities. They were particularly vocal in the eighteenth century: Whenever the nobility was dissatisfied with the reigning sovereign, or whenever various claimants to the throne appeared, the result was a palace coup aimed at bringing a more desirable figure to the throne.

Legitimacy, and hence power, rests upon a variety of foundations. These include formal law (legal claims to authority), belief in the legality and sacrality of the existing order (traditional authority), and leadership charisma (charismatic authority).[3] To elucidate these elements as they developed through history is an extraordinarily interesting problem, the solution of which will determine how one evaluates state-building in a particular case. Legitimate rule presupposes, at a minimum, the existence of a state based on law *(pravomernoe gosudarstvo*, to use nineteenth-century Russian terminology)—that is, a state limited by laws that cannot be transgressed. But one can distinguish between two types of states based on law. In the first type, state rule is executed in accordance with the law, through the exertions of a bureaucracy, and the personal and political rights of the state's subjects, in contrast, are severely restricted. In this kind of regime, the lack of individual rights is maintained under the law. The second type of state provides for rule under law through the active participation of citizens, who have personal and political rights. Let us call the first type a "state limited by law" and the second a "state governed by law." Historically, most countries have experienced a transition from the first to the second type as their rulers realized that the absence or deprivation of legal rights was hindering the development of state order; for people tend to violate laws that infringe upon what they view as their rightful private or personal actions.

The realization of true legality necessarily implies a prior recognition of personal rights—the rights to private property; to freedom of religion, movement, and social mobility; to a profession, entrepreneurial activity, and education; to judicial protection of one's person, honor, and property, and of one's right to petition; and to freedom from corporal punishment. In short, in order for a state to be ruled and not just limited by law, it is not enough to institute laws that precisely and definitively limit the rights of the state's subjects. It is also essential that those subjects have personal and political rights.

Patriarchal, Popular Monarchy in the Seventeenth Century

Of crucial importance in determining the character of a state is the role that law plays in its governance—that is, the legal foundation for the continuity of the state's authority and for the definition of its subjects; and the popular assumptions about the character and foundations of authority. This analysis begins with the seventeenth century in order to make clear what the Petersburg empire inherited—and what it repudiated—from the legacy of medieval Muscovy.

The Foundations of Legitimacy

After the death of Ivan the Terrible, in 1584, the traditional, hereditary monarchy—for all practical purposes—became elective. This new, elective monarchy lasted until the end of the seventeenth century; all seven tsars between Ivan and Peter were either elected or confirmed by an assembly of the land *(zemskii sobor)*. The same order, it should be noted, obtained for Peter himself, who was elected to accede to the throne on 27 April 1682. Election was confirmed each time by an "election charter" *(izbiratel'naia gramota)*—a legal document signed by the electors that was deemed mandatory for confirming the tsar's right to rule.[4] The subjects confirmed their duty to obey the new tsar through an oath sworn on the cross *(krestnoe tselovanie)*, the text of which varied according to the social group. Thus the aristocratic elite *(boiarstvo)* took a vow of political loyalty (with a promise not to emigrate to other states), and together with the lesser nobility *(dvorianstvo)* agreed to serve the tsar. The townspeople and peasantry swore that they would fulfill all the duties required of them as subjects.

The legitimacy of the new tsar was also determined by his direct blood kinship with the deceased ruler and by the sacred ritual of coronation, including consecration by the Orthodox Church, with the attendance and participation of the people. The coronation was deemed "holy" and was regarded by the people as such, for it included a special sacrament of anointment *(miropomazanie)*. According to Orthodox teachings, the anointment conferred the strength and wisdom to wield power over the state and church but did not imply ordination to holy orders or convey the power to dispense the sacraments or to expound on theological matters (in contrast to the ritual anointment of Byzantine emperors). The rites of coronation unquestionably contained religious and magical elements: Just as a marriage without a church wedding lacked legality, the tsar's rule gained legal force only if he received these religious rites. Indeed, the rites of marriage and of coronation had a similar root *(venchanie)*. This ritual fused the tsar with the people in a sacred and indelible union that laid obligations on the tsar as well as on his subjects. The sovereign assumed the obligation to rule justly and in a Christian manner (that is, in accordance with Christian morality); and the people assumed the duty of obedience.

Oaths of fealty, and popular participation in the coronation, were obligatory, but not because they signaled the people's delegation of power to the tsar. Rather, these rituals affirmed the people's willingness to obey and their acceptance of the new monarch's right to rule.[5] Legitimacy gave the emperor a certain freedom to act. This freedom was not regarded as dangerous, however, since the sovereign's authority was legitimate and all of his actions were assumed to be dictated by God and intended for the well-being of his people.

The Role of the Boyar Duma, Zemskii Sobor, and Church Council

In the seventeenth century the sovereign shared his power to rule with four other institutions: the Boyar Duma (a council comprised of boyars); the *zemskii sobor* (assembly of the land, or national assembly); the church council *(osviashchennyi sobor)*, headed by the patriarch; and the people. Each of these groups played a role in state governance.

Article 98 of the Law Code *(sudebnik)* of 1550 stipulated the order for adopting laws: Laws were to emanate from the tsar's initiative; to receive the collective approval of the boyars; and then to receive final confirmation by the tsar.[6] In the seventeenth century the range of those participating in legislation steadily widened to include the lesser nobility, the merchantry, and other service categories of the population *(chiny,* or "service ranks"), who sent collective petitions to the sovereign and also to the *zemskie sobory.* This process is evident in the formula used in tsarist decrees in the seventeenth century, which states that each decree is a response to a petition from the people, or the result of the tsar's consultations with the Boyar

Duma, church council, or *zemskii sobor*.[7] It is important to examine more closely the role played by each of these institutions.

Neither the Law Code *(Ulozhenie)* of 1649 nor other legal acts defined the legal rights of the Boyar Duma (or, for that matter, the rights of the sovereign). One can, however, deduce the Duma's legal status from its activity, which was reflected on the pages of the *Ulozhenie* and in other sources. The Boyar Duma was, above all, a legislative organ working together with the tsar and under his aegis. The Law Code points to the fact that many important laws were adopted jointly by the tsar and the Boyar Duma. An analysis of legislative acts issued after 1649 shows that the most important decrees included a resolution by the Boyar Duma, whereas less significant matters were treated by edicts from the tsar alone, without a resolution from the Boyar Duma. The Duma was, after the tsar, the highest judicial and appellate instance, and it bore exclusive legal competence for a great number of matters.[8] Acting in its adjudicatory capacity, the Boyar Duma played an extrabureaucratic role, imposing limits on the tsar's authority.

The membership of the Boyar Duma gradually increased during the course of the seventeenth century—from 29 in 1613, to 66 in 1675, and to 131 in 1682. The Duma included boyars (19, 23, and 66, respectively) as well as "duma nobles" *(dumnye dvoriane)* and "duma clerks" *(dumnye d'iaki)*. The primary role fell to the boyars, many of whom were descendants of appanage princes who had entered Muscovite service in the fourteenth and fifteenth centuries. In the judgment of V. O. Kliuchevskii, the boyars regarded themselves as the true proprietors of the Russian land. The only difference was that whereas the boyars previously had governed Rus individually, in many small, independent fragments, they now gathered in Moscow as a single group to govern the entire state.[9] The boyars had power over central and local administration, and the titled elite of the boyars—descendants of the princely clans of medieval Rus—dominated the Boyar Duma. All matters of significance were decided by "resolution of the boyars and decree of the Sovereign"; that is, once the tsar had directed that a particular question be considered and resolved, the Boyar Duma then adopted and promulgated a resolution, which had to be approved unanimously.

The relations between tsar and Duma were determined primarily by custom and tradition but also could be affected by other factors, such as the real balance of power between tsar and Duma, the personality of the sovereign, and the general conditions prevailing in the country. As the significance of these factors varied from reign to reign and from year to year, the significance of the Boyar Duma rose and fell accordingly. This variability has impelled some researchers to ascribe only a consultative role to the Duma. Yet, even when the Duma's power demonstrably had declined to a consultative role, it still imposed a limit on the authority of the tsar. And under conditions more favorable to the Duma, it wielded important and clearly discernible political rights.[10] For example, Tsar Michael (the first representative of the Romanov dynasty) gave the boyars a written assurance *(zapis')* that the Duma would participate in running the state, and the tsar in fact upheld this promise. The Duma limited the sovereign's power throughout the seventeenth century.[11] It is precisely for this reason that Peter the Great felt burdened by the authority of the Boyar Duma and seized the first opportunity to disband it.[12]

Throughout the sixteenth and seventeenth centuries, the tsar acting without the Boyar Duma—or vice versa—created a highly abnormal situation. The Law Code of 1649 formally recognized a resolution by the Duma as equivalent to the tsar's decrees. The inseparability of joint action by the tsar and the Boyar Duma was expressed in the general legal formula: "The sovereign has decreed, and the boyars have resolved. . . ."[13] The Duma and sovereign were so closely linked that they even shared the daily rituals of life (for example, attending church services and dining together).

The power of the sovereign was limited by yet another institution—the system of service appointments based on clan status *(mestnichestvo)*. This institution guaranteed boyars (and to some degree, the other two "orders"—nobles and the merchant elite) the right to occupy a place in the civil or military hierarchy according to their social origin, determined by the status and rank of their predecessors. The assignment within the hierarchy was commensurate with the "honor" *(chest')* ascribed to the individual and the clan. The assignment of a place in the service hierarchy lower than that mandated by one's "honor" was deemed the greatest possible insult and degradation. Until this institution was finally abolished in 1682, it severely limited the sovereign's choice in making appointments, protecting the boyars from arbitrary treatment by the sovereign.[14]

At critical junctures in the history of the state, the activity of the Duma was augmented by that of the assemblies of the land, which had no less significance than did the Duma, except that they were limited to the particular period for which they were convoked. The assemblies of the land were not juxtaposed to the tsar, the Boyar Duma, or the church council; rather, they included all three, as well as a number of "elected members" *(vybornye)*. The phrase "elected members" refers not only to those elected by the population but also to the so-called better people *(luchshie liudi,* a term denoting local elites).[15] The elected members represented various service orders of the population (not estates, which did not yet exist) and specific geographical areas.

The presence of peasants has been established at only two of the fifty-seven assemblies. With respect to peasant representation, however, two additional circumstances must be taken into account: The city, in an administrative sense, was not separate from the countryside; and the common townspeople (*posadskie*, a term denoting the taxable urban population as distinct from the merchant elite) were barely distinguishable from peasants, even in their economic activity, for like peasants, they derived their main source of support from agriculture. Because both groups had similar interests, the townspeople's elected delegates partly represented the peasantry.

The assemblies of the land were not generally representative bodies: Rarely did they include delegates from all strata of the population and all geographic areas. Yet according to the popular conception in Muscovy, the assembly was legitimate if it sufficiently expressed the thinking and will of the "Russian land." The "elected deputies" were sometimes elected by the population, and at other times, appointed by the local governor *(voevoda)*. In the former case, the voters compiled a written act confirming the election, as well as an instruction *(nakaz)* for their deputy.

The rights of the assembly of the land, like those of the tsar and the Boyar Duma, were determined by custom and tradition. The assemblies were summoned either at the initiative of the tsar, or during an interregnum, by the servitors themselves. There was no regularity in the summoning of assemblies, but the Soviet historian L. V. Cherepnin has identified a total of fifty-seven assemblies of the land—eleven in the sixteenth century, and forty-six in the seventeenth.[16] The assemblies' competence was very broad: They elected or confirmed the sovereign; sanctioned the adoption of major reforms (judicial, administrative, financial, and military); and examined questions of foreign policy and taxation. Petitions from assemblies of the land represented, for the sovereign, the indisputable voice of the people, and they invariably led to the promulgation of corresponding laws. The "elected" deputies functioned as advisers to the sovereign, supplying information and counsel, expressing public opinion, and performing supervisory and regulatory functions.

In the opinion of contemporaries, a decision could be legal and hold force for the whole country only if it were made public. The presence of the people provided a guarantee that every act of state—including election to the throne, the coronation, the compilation of a law code, and the declaration of war—was executed in accordance with tradition and with the observance of the requisite rituals. For the seventeenth century and earlier periods, it was characteristic for the people to participate actively in the life of the sovereign's court. Weddings, christenings, elections to the throne, coronations, name days, and funerals all proceeded in the presence of the people, including not only the church council members, the Boyar Duma, and elected representatives of every rank from each town but also members of the lower classes *(chern')*, which were not represented at the assemblies. These events were accompanied by feasting and an exchange of gifts as well as by prayer services and pilgrimages of the tsar and tsaritsa to monasteries, churches, almshouses, and prisons. On such occasions, the sovereign pardoned criminals and dispensed alms, money, and gifts amounting to huge sums from the state treasury. The coronation and wedding were attended by the same people, the same elected deputies and in the same number, as was the assembly of the land, only now in the capacity of guests.[17] Their presence during these rituals was mandatory and was deemed an essential condition for the legitimacy of the given event.

As is apparent from these customs, however much the Russian assembly of the land differed from the States General in west European countries, it was a representative organ that limited the authority of the sovereign. The assembly of the land was not a direct successor to the ancient city assembly *(veche)*, although it did take root at a time when the city assembly was declining. Sources refer to city assemblies in Moscow in 1547, and in Pskov in 1534 and in the early seventeenth century. The tradition of city assemblies was still making itself felt during the urban disorders of the mid-seventeenth century.[18] It would not be an exaggeration to say that popular representation existed for many centuries in medieval Russia.

Participants in state governance included the patriarch of Moscow and the church council, which was made up of ranking prelates in the Orthodox Church. Because the entire life of Russians (including those at the tsar's court) was ritualized to a very high degree, the church council was a regular participant in all the important events of the life of the tsar's family, the court, and the entire country. Clergy surrounded the tsar every day, virtually around the clock. The tsar did not undertake a single enterprise, complete a single act, or take a single step without their active—and not merely their formal—participation. The patriarch performed an exceptionally important role. His significance is reflected in the official form of address used by the tsar, who addressed the patriarch as "father." In the conventions of the time, this title connoted the patriarch's superior authority and the tsar's dependence and subordination to him.

The patriarchate, as an institution, was a very great force; it rested on the moral authority of Christianity and stood at the head of the enormous organization of the Russian Orthodox Church. It also governed the white clergy and monasteries, which played a major role in the social and economic life of the country. The patriarchate had enormous material resources at its disposal, including its own court and service people, a vast domain of land, and 12.5 percent of the entire peasantry.[19] The patriarch was no servant or subject of the tsar; only other patriarchs of the Eastern church could sit in judgment over him. In a word, the patriarchate was a state within a state. The supreme status of this institution conferred on the patriarch, as head of the church, enormous weight in society and the state.[20] If the patriarch himself had a strong personality, his role in state affairs was all the greater, hardly less than that of the tsar—as indeed was the case under Patriarchs Filaret (1619–1633) and Nikon (1652–1658). Both patriarchs even bore the title "Great Sovereign"—that is, the title used by the tsar himself. Although the tsar participated in the selection of the patriarchate, the decisive vote rested with the hierarchs of the church. The tsar appointed certain candidates, whose names were inscribed on paper, which was sealed and transmitted to a church council; but the latter made the final selection. Tsar Alexis conceded that without a church council, on his own authority, he could not replace the patriarch—even if the latter were guilty of heresy.[21]

Custom, Tradition, and Law in State Administration

Both customary and written law played a significant role in the life of Russian society in the sixteenth and seventeenth centuries. Custom nevertheless dominated. Muscovy still did not recognize the idea of creative, positive law; the inviolability of tradition continued to dominate the thinking of people inside and outside the government. The will of the sovereign, however expansive and powerful, was restricted by custom. The autocrats themselves subordinated their authority to tradition and conceded that they could not create law. This mentality was manifest in the fact that the sovereign did not issue general laws to establish the state order on new foundations but modified the old order gradually and incrementally, through a long and tortuous path of successive measures and through changes in daily praxis. This approach gradually generated new customs that in time found their way into law. New phenomena in daily life emerged under the mask of old formulas. Given the slow pace of change in law, custom, and tradition, most changes went unnoticed.

Given the dominant view among both the populace and the elites that custom and tradition were unalterable, it would not have been possible for the Muscovite state to develop or for any other far-reaching social changes to occur. The obvious solution to this contradiction was to invent tradition—to justify innovations in the state order by referring to an imaginary past. References to fictitious traditions, for example, were used in the mid-sixteenth century to justify a new type of autocratic tsardom, the emergent assemblies of the land. In the seventeenth century a make-believe tradition was used to justify legislative activity (by the tsar, Boyar Duma, and assemblies of the land) to crowd out custom and play a significant role in the process of state-building. The source of legislative creativity was the new Law Code adopted by the Assembly of the Land of 1649. This legal code was the first compilation that included legislation from virtually every sphere of contemporary law and was both known and comprehensible to the general populace. During the second half of the seventeenth century it was published twice (with press runs of 2,400 copies) and was distributed to all official institutions, to serve as a solid juridical foundation for administration. The Law Code also proclaimed the principle of universal and equal subordination to court and law. The introduction of a single legal code—printed and applicable to the entire country—made it possible to unify and bring order to legal norms, as well as to both court structure *(sudoustroistvo)* and legal proceedings *(sudoproizvodstvo)*, and to the judicial system as a whole. As research has shown, all spheres of life in Russian society developed in the second half of the seventeenth century in close conformity with the legal norms of the Law Code of 1649.[22] This reveals the great significance of law in the life of Muscovite society.

For example, in the seventeenth century the tsar's daughters could not marry Russian boyars, since this would be tantamount to a derogation of "honor." Yet the tsars often married women of inconsequential social origin. The explanation for this paradox rests in the fact that according to law, the status of a woman was determined by that of her husband, but a husband's was not affected by that of his wife. As a result, immediately after a tsar had married a woman from a modest clan, he would issue a decree conferring on all her relatives new service titles, landed estates (benefices and alods), and official appointments that elevated them to the upper elite.[23] It would seem that in order to ensure the happiness of his daughters, a tsar needed only to make an exception to the rule and to permit them to marry Russians. But in fact tsars made no such exceptions: The law and custom were stronger than personal desires. Hence the tsar's daughters were fated to remain unmarried.

Because Muscovite custom and tradition carried greater force than the will of the sovereign, the tsar could not realize the ideal of unlimited autocratic authority. To be sure, in the eyes of foreign observers, his real power appeared greater than that of all the monarchs of Europe. However, as V. O. Kliuchevskii aptly observed, the magnitude of the tsar's power derived from personal relations, not from the existing order. The state system stood under the protection of tradition and custom; it was deemed beyond the reach of the tsar's will. The clan-based system of service appointments *(mestnichestvo)*, for example, was in many instances deleterious to state interests, and it imposed limits even on the sovereign's power over individual subjects. Nevertheless, for two centuries the tsars submitted to lineage-based claims to service appointments—until this system was abolished by the Assembly of the Land of 1682.[24] Hence, the sovereign could not confer the title of prince, "because there was no custom for doing this."[25]

Political Ideology and Mentality

The Russian people—from the educated elites to the lowliest illiterate bondsman *(kholop)*—shared a common political mentality in the seventeenth century. The core of this mentality consisted of three main ideas: the legitimacy and sacrality of ancient orders and authority because of their very antiquity and divine origin; the universal obligation to serve the sovereign; and the identity of the will of the sovereign with the will of God. The notion of secular service derived from spiritual, religious service to God. The idea of state service consisted essentially of the following: The "earthly God" was placed on his throne by the "heavenly tsar" to perform the will of the latter; hence the heavenly tsar took part in governing the country through the worldly tsar, who was in "divine service." Thus, "matters concerning God" *(delo bozhie)* and "matters concerning the sovereign" *(gosudarevo delo)* were related in the most intimate fashion: The people served the tsar as the servant of God; hence, by serving the sovereign, they were serving God. The result was the obligation of the tsar's servitors and other subjects to render service "in the cause of God and the sovereign."

The universal obligation of secular service, which applied equally to the tsar and to his subjects, bore an essentially religious character: It was believed that one's service would lead to one's salvation. In renouncing their own will in favor of that of the monarch, the people were submitting to a higher, divine will. The tsar himself renounced his own personal will, performing his service as a form of obedience to God. The authority of the sovereign was regarded as an obligation imposed by God, which he had no right to evade.

The sovereign's authority was not only divine but also paternalist: The sovereign's relations to his subjects were to be "paternal"; he was to punish the sinner, encourage the loyal and diligent, and heed the counsel of wise advisers. From this emanated the practice of referring to subjects as "orphans" *(siroty)*—that is, helpless, homeless, isolated, and poor. Likewise, those in state service were called "bondsmen" *(kholopy)*—submissive and obedient servants. This unique configuration of the sovereign's power was particularly striking to foreigners in Russia. S. Herberstein (the ambassador of the Holy Roman Emperor Maximilian) wrote in 1549 that the tsar's advisers openly proclaimed the sovereign's will to be the will of God and believed that whatever the sovereign did was in accordance with God's will. Therefore, they also referred to the tsar as the personal servitor of God (*kliuchnik* and *postel'nichii*), and believed that he performed the will of God.[26]

It should be observed that in recognizing the divine right of the tsar to rule, the people of Muscovy saw an emanation of divine will when an assembly of the land elected a tsar or performed another act of state-building. This is how Tsar Alexis (1629–1676), the father of Peter the Great,[27] perceived the secular service and duties of the monarch. Similar views were shared by Alexis's children's tutor, Simeon Polotskii (1629–1680),[28] and other Russian intellectuals as well as by the general public.[29]

As the foregoing suggests, a special form of statehood existed in seventeenth-century Russia. Public authority was shared by the sovereign, the Boyar Duma, the patriarch and church council, and the assembly of the land. The people participated in state administration through the assembly of the land, through petitions, and through mass movements. An essential attribute to ensure that these decisions and procedures were legitimate and valid was that they had to be both public and collective. True, the populace was often represented by certain ranks of townsmen, as were the provinces by Moscow.[30] Still, the people were not walled off from the life of the court; both the sovereign and the government had to take the people into account.

Just as the antiquity of customs and government institutions was a sign of legitimacy and perfection, a long genealogy served as the basis of a person's dignity and honor. The tsars were purported to have descended from the Roman emperor Augustus, and the Muscovite state to be the heir of the Roman empire. Antiquity as a criterion of perfection was firmly embedded in popular consciousness. "There are many states in the West that are older and have more honor than the Muscovite state," wrote G. Kotoshikhin, who evidently believed that the older European states (such as France, England, and Austria) held a higher and more honored place than Russia in the hierarchy of states.[31] In contrast to the various social estates in west European monarchies, which represented the people's interests before the state in matters of governance,[32] social estates as such did not exist in Muscovy and hence could not share power. Nevertheless, the relationship between the Russian state and people, even if it lacked a contractual juridical foundation, was based on custom, tradition, and ad hoc circumstances. Although there are no known instances when the Boyar Duma or the assembly of the land came into open conflict with the tsar, they nevertheless did impose limits on his autocratic power: The tsar needed their counsel and approval both in the conduct of routine administrative tasks and in deciding more weighty matters of state. Obviously, the Boyar Duma and the assembly of the land embodied and defended tradition; this placed the sovereign firmly within the restraints of custom. And the tsar—even so imperious a ruler as Ivan the Terrible—could not extricate himself from the clutches of tradition.

From this historical evidence one can assuredly conclude that in Muscovy, society existed as a distinct entity, separate from the state. Given that the Russian tsar felt it necessary to convoke the assembly of the land on a regular basis and to invite sundry ranks of the population to give him counsel and to approve important state decisions, there must have been social pressure—if not explicit popular demand—for this action. Yet a master or proprietor does not need the advice of his slaves, nor will he bother to hear their opinions. If the tsar's decrees referred to the participation of the Boyar

Duma or church council in a decision, or to the resolutions of an assembly of the land on the conduct of domestic or foreign policy, then clearly the sovereign did not wield absolute, unlimited power. Significantly, historians have found no justification for the theory of absolute tsarist authority in the entire corpus of Russian texts written before the end of the seventeenth century. As Russian historian V. E. Valdenberg concluded, "The notion of absolute power is unknown in [medieval] Russian literature."[33]

Nor was monarchy in Muscovy "patrimonial." The Russian monarchy was distinguished from a patrimonial monarchy in four respects: the presence of institutions limiting the authority of the tsar; the existence of a professional bureaucracy; the role of a printed secular law code (the *Ulozhenie* of 1649), which had been confirmed by an assembly of the land and which all state institutions were obliged to observe; and the fact that the source of law was not only the will of the sovereign but also the statutes and edicts of the Boyar Duma, central administrative offices *(prikazy)*, collective petitions from various social groups, and ecclesiastical law.[34]

At the same time, the Russian monarchy had a strong theocratic element.[35] First, the sovereign was considered the representative of God, who conferred power and thus endowed the monarchy with a divine character. Second, the church as an institution was one of the pillars of public authority. The type of Russian state that existed in the sixteenth and seventeenth centuries can perhaps be called a popular-patriarchal monarchy, which was limited externally by the aristocracy, a representative institution (the assembly of the land), and the church as an institution, and united internally by its own complex of Orthodox values and ideas. The sovereign exercised patriarchal rule, which was based on religious faith, tradition, custom, and law.[36] The elements of rudimentary democracy are plainly apparent in the Muscovite state and society of the time.[37]

Paternalist, Noble Monarchy in the Eighteenth Century

The foundations of the sovereign's legitimacy underwent a fundamental change in the eighteenth century.[38] The traditional basis of the tsar's right to rule—the legality and sacrality of the order existing from time immemorial—gave way to a new, rational, formal, juridical foundation of authority.

The New Foundations of Legitimacy

At the instigation of Peter the Great, Archbishop Feofan Prokopovich reformulated the official view of authority in his commentary to the "Statute on Succession." Entitled *The Truth About the Monarch's Will in Appointing an Heir to the Throne*, Feofan's theoretical argument for the tsar's authority was in accord with the idea of the contractual origins of power that then prevailed in western Europe, which ascribed the monarch's power to a contract with the people, for their benefit. The latter, in effect, had surrendered power to the monarch forever and unconditionally. A second basis of the tsar's authority was the church's teaching about the divine origins of power, now modified—in accordance with the spirit of the time—to give the well-known biblical passages a modern interpretation: "Every sovereign who obtains his scepter by inheritance or by election receives it from God."

To reconcile the contractual theory with the doctrine of divine right, Feofan declared that "the voice of the people is the voice of God." That is, all power emanates from God, because popular will is controlled by the divine will. Thus Feofan proclaimed a dual foundation for the legitimacy of power: the traditional, religious justification for popular consumption, and a more modern, rationalist justification for the educated noble elite. The change in the fundamental legitimacy of power bore considerable significance for the new state, for it liberated the sovereign from the fetters of tradition and custom. It was thus no longer true that tradition was sacred and that the antiquity of state institutions was the criterion of their perfection; the revised political justification for autocracy enabled the monarch to make basic changes in the state and social order.

This definition of legitimacy in turn generated three rules for the behavior of subjects. They were obliged to fulfill all the demands of the state without resistance or complaint, never to pass judgment on their sovereign, and not to instruct the monarch as to what he should do. It is readily apparent how unacceptable these requirements would have been for the subjects of seventeenth-century Muscovy, who still elected the sovereign and many of whom still gave him advice and instructions. At the same time, the sovereign was obliged to ensure the well-being of the people and the needs of the "fatherland."[39] To be sure, this conception did appear among individual writers in the seventeenth century (for example, Iurii Krizhanich), but Peter the Great was the first to attempt to apply the notion to actual practice. Peter personally observed a new rule of service—namely, that each man must work his way up through the ranks. In 1711 Peter also changed the form of the oath: Henceforth, subjects swore fealty not only to the tsar but also to the state.[40] The very same year, as he took part in a military campaign on the Prut, Peter sent the Senate an order stating that if he were taken prisoner, it should disregard any command he might send, and that if he perished, it should choose a worthy successor to the throne.

Under Peter the Great, the monarchy also acquired an autocratic character in a formal, juridical sense. The juridical definition of autocracy emerged from a number of decrees, especially the Military Charter of 1716: "His Majesty is an *autocratic* monarch, who is obliged to answer to none and who is to rule his own state and land as a Christian sovereign, according to his own will and good judgment."[41] The ecclesiastical statute of 1721, promulgated as the fundamental charter for the governance of the Russian Orthodox Church, similarly described the monarch's power as "autocratic."[42] As these declarations indicate, Peter implicitly renounced the old formula justifying power, which had limited the sovereign's power by morality, religion, and tradition; he now embraced in toto the second half of the formula, which left the sovereign free to act as he saw fit.

This new concept was explicitly articulated by Empress Anna when she acceded to the throne in 1730, proclaiming the "unlimited autocracy" *(samoderzhavstvo)* of imperial authority.[43] In her Instruction *(Nakaz)* to the Legislative Commission of 1767–1768, Catherine the Great, emulating the spirit of enlightened absolutism, offered two rational justifications for unlimited autocracy in Russia: first, the enormous expanse of the Russian state, where only the prompt decision of the monarch could compensate for the great distances (an argument borrowed, like much else in the Instruction, from Montesquieu); and second, the advantage for subjects to submit to a single master rather than many (i.e., aristocratic or democratic systems of governance). Catherine pronounced the goal of autocratic rule to be that of enlightened absolutism—that is, "not to take away the natural liberty of people" but to ensure that "their actions be directed toward obtaining the maximum good for them." In 1797, under the rule of Paul I, the autocratic authority of the sovereign acquired a formal legal formulation.[44]

There were also changes in the sovereign's official title. In 1721 the tsar assumed the title of "emperor," thereby proclaiming Russia's resolve to follow European traditions. The new title stood in stark contrast to the title of tsar, which was identified with ancient Russian sovereigns and Byzantine rulers. Moreover, as the territorial expanse of the state gradually was extended, the emperor acquired additional descriptors signaling a boost in imperial status ("most august," "most powerful"). The people's manner of addressing the sovereign also changed. In 1701 Peter ordered that petitioners sign their full names rather than the derogatory, humiliating short forms (for example, Ivan, not Ivashka) that had been used in the past. The same decree also directed that petitioners not refer to themselves as "bondsmen" *(kholopy)* but as "slaves" *(raby)*, which Catherine the Great in turn changed to "subjects" *(poddannye)*. Both *kholop* and *rab* had the same meaning of "unconditionally devoted and most humble servant"; but in 1701 *kholop* referred to the social group with the lowest status, whereas *rab* had only the general meaning of someone who was personally dependent. The purpose of these changes, given the norms of Russian linguistic etiquette, was to confer more dignity on the person. At the same time, Peter forbade petitioners to fall on their knees and to remove their hats when entering his court—a custom that was also commonly practiced upon entering a church—with the explanation that the court was not a church.

To the traditional state regalia (the scepter, orb, and the cap of Monomakh—reputed to have been sent to the Great Prince of Kiev, Vladimir, by the Byzantine emperor in the eleventh century), Russian rulers added a crown in 1724 (porphyry lined with ermine), a state sword, and a state banner of yellow satin with the state coat of arms in the middle and the coats of arms of the various regions along the side (1742). Beginning in 1724, the male sovereign's wife (in this case, Catherine I) was crowned alongside her husband, in a ceremony that followed European rather than Muscovite ritual. The secularization of power was expressed, asserted, and reinforced by means of these new symbols and practices,[45] which served a dual purpose: to place Russian emperors on a par with west European emperors and yet to keep them as far above their subjects as possible—as though comparability with the West would compensate for the autocrat's loss of divinity.

The sovereign now could claim the right to rule at will, without anyone else's approval. The basis for the legal transfer of power in the eighteenth century thus was the will of the previous monarch as expressed in his or her testament, followed by the ritual of coronation (which was strongly secularized) and the oath of loyalty. In 1797, however, Emperor Paul I changed the law on succession that had been promulgated by Peter in 1722. According to the new law, the succession would not be determined by the arbitrary designation of the last ruler but by a statutory prescription for succession through the male line of the ruling family. This law remained in force until the end of the Russian empire in 1917.

The participation of the populace in coronation ceremonies during the eighteenth century was severely curtailed. Accession to the throne was accompanied instead by the promulgation of a manifesto to the people and by an oath of fealty that was uniform for all subjects. In 1741, Elizabeth forbade seigniorial serfs (48 percent of the population) to take the oath,[46] with the explanation that their squires had already taken the oath on their behalf.

In the eighteenth century the formula for tsarist decrees also underwent significant changes, and the ancient phrasing "the sovereign has decreed, and the boyars have resolved" (gosudar' ukazal i boiare prigovorili) disappeared. Laws thereafter referred simply to "the will of the monarch," reinforced by allusions to state interests: "We, Peter the First, tsar and autocrat of all Russia, etc. etc. etc., proclaim this decree to all the subjects of our state." "We, Peter the Third, through the authority divinely conferred on us, . . . grant to all the Russian wellborn nobility freedom and liberty." Gone were the Muscovite references to the supplication of subjects, meetings of the Boyar Duma, and the decisions of an assembly of the land.

Peter the Great was the first tsar who was willing to violate tradition in favor of rational considerations. Hence, at the first opportunity, he moved to rid himself of the patriarch, Boyar Duma, and church councils, and he ceased to convoke assemblies of the land. The last assembly of the land met in 1683; the Boyar Duma disappeared in 1700; and the church councils were nominally replaced by the Synod in 1721, but in fact ceased to exist after the death of the last patriarch in 1700. The autocratic sovereign, with all his enormous will and energy, feared these institutions—in itself a serious demonstration of how significantly they had limited the power of past tsars. Even as late as 1730—five years after Peter's death—in electing Anna to the throne, the aristocracy attempted to impose "conditions" on her rule. This last attempt by the noble elite to recover their former political significance failed, as the majority of lesser nobles rose in defense of the autocracy.[47]

The state also gained eventual control over the church. Although the church was administratively governed by the Synod (comprised of ranking clergy), it operated under the supervision of the chief procurator, a layman appointed by the emperor. The Synod was the highest body for legislative, administrative, and judicial affairs of the Russian Orthodox Church, and in this domain it exercised considerable autonomy. It suffered a serious blow to its economic power in 1701, however, when Peter established the Monastery Bureau *(Monastyrskii prikaz),* which assumed responsibility for all administrative, financial, and judicial matters involving the church's landed estates and the peasants attached to them. In this regard, two seemingly minor but highly revealing details suggest how much the status of the church had changed and how secular the character of the emperor's power had become. During her coronation ceremonies in 1730, Empress Anna walked into the altar area (despite the fact that ecclesiastical law strictly forbade laymen—especially women—from entering this inner sanctum) to receive communion, as though she were a cleric instead of a layperson. This action was a radical violation of tradition. Significantly, all subsequent emperors followed the new ritual. Beginning with the coronation of Elizabeth in 1742, sovereigns also placed the crown on their own heads instead of accepting it from the highest-ranking prelate.[48]

Despite the church's declining power, some members of the clergy were tapped by the autocrat to help articulate and promulgate the new ideology. Feofan Prokopovich, archbishop of Novgorod, served both Peter the Great and Anna in this capacity. He developed the first theoretical justification for autocracy in Russia, combining scholarly and religious argumentation in a way that was fundamentally uncharacteristic of Orthodoxy. Feofan had studied at a Jesuit college in Rome (which necessitated his nominal conversion to Catholicism for several years), although in his own views he was actually much closer to Protestant theologians. As a rule, the Orthodox clergy ignored the fruits of Catholic enlightenment, and they had adumbrated a paternalistic conception of autocracy. This perspective was articulated in the model sermons compiled by synodal and diocesan authorities (for parish priests to read during services). It also informed the official doctrine of the church, clearly expressed in the teaching of leading Orthodox theologian Metropolitan Filaret Drozdov (1783–1867). In Filaret's view, the authority of the tsar was like that of a father: "Since the power of the father is not created by the father himself and is not given to him by his son but is derived (together with man) from Him who created man, it is clear that the most profound source and real foundation of authority comes solely from God." From God too came the power of the tsar: "On the model of His own heavenly monocratic power God has put the tsar on earth—an autocratic tsar after the example of His omnipotence, a hereditary tsar after the example of His eternal rule." The holy coronation to the throne made the tsar's power sacred and instilled love in the union between tsar and people. Filaret taught: "With autocracy Russia stands firm. According to the true understanding of the Tsar, he is the head and soul of his tsardom. Law, which is a dead letter in books, comes alive through his acts; the tsar is the supreme statesman and inspires the people subordinate to him." The activity of the tsar was inextricably linked to the realization of the divine will, "the welfare of the people and state, in which the tsar stands as the common and bright central point and freely limits his autocracy to the will of the Heavenly Father." The subordination of the tsar's authority to God created a union between church and state, an accord that moved in the same direction, leading the people toward well-being: "The Orthodox Church and state in Russia stand in harmony and union."[49] This view of autocracy was not substantially different from that of the seventeenth century; it was clearly compatible with the popular view at that time.

It is noteworthy that throughout the imperial period, the rulers continued to adhere to this paternalistic view of the sovereign's power. A number of decrees by Peter the Great candidly expressed his relationship as similar to that between a father and his children. In one case, for example, he wrote that "our people are like children, who will never begin to read if they are not forced to do so by their master."[50] Therefore the title "father of his fatherland," which Peter I assumed in 1721, aptly expressed how the tsar, his entourage, and his subjects regarded his power. Similarly, both Elizabeth and Catherine the Great assumed the title "mother of the fatherland." And many state decrees in the eighteenth and nineteenth centuries contained references to the paternalistic quality of the emperor's authority. All Russian emperors—including Nicholas II—were reared in the spirit of paternalism; from childhood they were taught to believe that "the Russian tsars, as the defenders and bearers of the country's national spirit, must appear to the people as the final bastion of *paternal* goodness and infinite justice."[51] Paternalistic ideas also prevailed in the Russian army until the 1860s; officers looked upon their soldiers as children, and soldiers regarded their officers as their father-commanders.[52]

In sum, paternalism was the general paradigm for social relations throughout Russian society in the eighteenth century; in the first half of the nineteenth century, it was the model for relations primarily between the upper and the lower classes; and in the second half of the nineteenth century, it served as the ideal for relations between the tsar and the people. The operative sphere of paternalism in social relations was steadily contracting.

The Nobility's Role in State Administration

In a relatively short time, Peter the Great eliminated the Boyar Duma, church councils, patriarchate, and assembly of the land. How was he able to do this? Several factors helped to make it possible. First, after adoption of the Law Code of 1649, in the second half of the seventeenth century the lower townspeople *(posadskie liudi)* and peasantry were gradually transformed from free social groups into serfs; and the nobility, having succeeded in satisfying its own interests, lost interest in assemblies of the land. Muscovite society had neither estates *(sosloviia)* nor estate organizations. The rights of the Boyar Duma, the church council, the assembly of the land, and the tsar himself were not fixed in law but depended on the correlation of forces among them. In the concrete circumstances of the late seventeenth and early eighteenth centuries, the tsar proved more powerful.[53]

Second, although Peter abolished the Boyar Duma, he did not eliminate the aristocracy. Rather, he transformed the boyar class into a new elite that continued to dominate the upper echelon of power, but henceforth on terms dictated by the tsar himself. The new conditions included an obligation of state service, either military or civil. Each member, independently of social origin, had to begin service from the lowest ranks; and promotions were determined not only by social background but also by competence, education, and suitability. The aristocracy lost its organization in the form of the Boyar Duma and became totally dependent on the monarch. In addition, although the aristocracy remained a closed social group, at the emperor's will some outsiders did manage to penetrate its ranks. Unwilling to sacrifice the privileges that came with state service, the aristocracy accepted these terms and thereby preserved its position as the ruling group in the upper administration through the mid-nineteenth century. To be sure, it did not have the political significance of the seventeenth-century boyars who had ruled jointly with the sovereign.[54] Evidence for the gradual transformation of the old elite is provided by the fact that until the mid-eighteenth century, the old bureaucratic ranks were preserved, embellished by new titles. The result was a medley of ranks that included the old *boyarin* and *okol'nichii*, along with new titles like *deistvitel'nyi tainyi sovetnik* ("actual privy councillor") and *statskii sovetnik* ("councillor of state").[55]

Third, Peter the Great and his successors found a firm base of support in the lesser nobility, especially in its upper strata,[56] which had been transformed into a service estate on the same terms as the aristocracy and occupied a dominant position in the second echelon of power. Under Peter the Great the preconditions were laid for the transformation of the state into a nobility-dominated monarchy, and after Peter's death this possibility became a reality. Why did this happen? One can point to several circumstances of great significance.

In the first half of the eighteenth century, with the support of the autocracy, the nobility became consolidated into an estate. In 1762 it obtained its emancipation from obligatory state service, and from 1775 to 1785 it acquired the legal right to have an estate organization at the provincial level and to participate actively in governing the country. The nobility exercised this power to the fullest possible extent. Before the abolition of serfdom, the nobility held a monopoly over the commanding positions in civil and military administration; it controlled all the main branches of central administration, the courts (except the lowest instance), local administration, and police. The nobility supplied the core of the administrative staff and the entire officer corps; only city government lacked a noble element. Nobles formed powerful patron-client networks: Those living in Moscow were linked to their provincial brethren in a peculiar political lobby that functioned to further the group interests of the nobility. The emperors had no choice but to take into account the demands of the more powerful interest groups.[57] After the consolidation of this privileged estate and the emergence of a distinctly noble estate consciousness,[58] and until the mid-nineteenth century, the nobility was the only source of public opinion. Only nobles had the formal right and the practical capacity to express an opinion and to exert an influence on autocratic decisionmaking, which they did through the provincial assemblies and through participation as officials in the state administration. In both cases this was a matter of the noble elite—that is, those with wealth and estates.

Peter the Great's successors were either weak rulers or people who lacked a clear legal claim to the throne and had usurped power through a palace coup. Of the eight rulers who came to the throne between 1725 and 1801, four—Catherine I, Elizabeth, Catherine II, and Alexander I—came to power through a palace coup by the noble guards' regiments. Anna, the exception, had been elected by the nobility. Their dependence on the nobility inspired some of these autocrats to confer special favors, especially in the period immediately after the coup that brought them to power. For example, when Catherine the Great was preparing her Instruction to the Legislative Commission of 1767–1768, she heeded the advice of her advisers and deleted all the more liberal passages—particularly those critical of serfdom. So far as the sovereign was concerned, the nobility not only constituted a solid pillar of autocracy but also represented all Russia before supreme authority, insofar as it remained a landowning estate closely tied to the other groups of the population (especially the peasantry), to life in the provinces, and to local and public administration. Accordingly, public opinion was equivalent to the opinion of the nobility.[59] Hence the decision of emperors to rely on the nobility was pragmatic and reasonable, especially for those who did not have a legal claim to the Russian throne.

But neither in the eighteenth nor in the nineteenth century were emperors mere mouthpieces of noble interests—the nobility did not supplant the emperor. Autocracy demonstrated sufficient autonomy in its policy, which more often than not was determined more by state interests and objectives than by the strength of noble opposition. Of course, the government could not completely disregard the nobility. As Carol Leonard has shown, Peter III—precisely because he carelessly ignored the noble elite—was promptly deposed, despite the fact that he had promulgated two laws very popular among the nobility: the manifestos on the emancipation of nobles from obligatory service and on the secularization of church lands and peasants.[60] The same fate awaited Paul I, who similarly attempted to ignore the noble patronage cliques.[61] The nobility had turned into a "ruling class" in the sense that it had become a partner in state administration, and simultaneously, the transmission belt that linked supreme authority with society. The administrative reforms adopted by Catherine the Great between 1775 and 1785 represented a certain compromise between the autocracy and the nobility: The latter acquired significant power in local governance (the right to elect about one-half of district officials and one-third of provincial officials),[62] but the sovereign strengthened her power in the center. In other words, the nobility acquired its rights as an estate, but paid for them in terms of loyalty and devotion to Catherine.[63] This reform also permitted the autocracy to ameliorate the critical shortage of officials, which had made it impossible to govern the provinces efficiently. The weakness of administration at the district level was in part offset by involving the nobility. In the future, relations between the emperor and the nobility were based on compromise. Autocracy, however, remained an independent political force, laying complete and sole claim to leadership of the nation.[64]

The Role of Law in State Administration

Formal law was the only recognized source of rights and status from the reign of Peter the Great to 1917. Custom, which previously had played this central role in state administration, vanished. To a significant degree, it also lost force in urban society, although it did remain strong among peasants in the village commune. As a consequence, the character and purpose of legislation in imperial Russia underwent substantial change. In Muscovy legislation had been based primarily on customary law and was therefore distinguished by its traditional character. In imperial Russia law broke with custom and drew primarily on foreign legislation (for example, under Peter the Great or Alexander II), or was the result of theoretical, rationalist thinking (for example, under Catherine the Great and Alexander I); it bore primarily a reformist character. As a consequence of this, legislation formulated in the eighteenth century (and to a significant degree thereafter) was fundamentally at odds with earlier law. Autocracy endeavored to establish new legal norms among the people with the aid of new laws, on the assumption that law need not incorporate popular custom but only the will of the lawmaker. Thus the main goal of law fundamentally changed: Its aim in Muscovy was to conserve, whereas in imperial Russia its purpose was to improve social relations (although, to be sure, in both cases it also was aimed at upholding the social order).

One tradition in prerevolutionary and contemporary Russian historiography has categorized the eighteenth-century Russian state as a police state, on the grounds that it attempted to regulate a mass of minor matters (especially in the economic and everyday sphere) and to correct them through the use of law.[65] Indeed, commencing with Peter the Great, the government did bombard subjects with a massive number of decrees—for example, what materials to use in constructing houses and fireplaces, how to build coffins, which implements to use in tilling the soil, what materials to use in making shoes, how many horses a man of each rank might use for his carriage, what model to use in constructing ships, and so forth. Such policies were common among a number of eighteenth-century European states, where they accorded well with monarchical paternalism.[66] The distinctive feature of the Russian state in this period was its specific paternalism, which was not ornamental and decorative (as in the West) but extremely active and central to state policy. The state's effort to regulate everything arose from its awareness of the people's cultural backwardness and their blind devotion to various superstitions and prejudices, which necessitated paternal oversight by wise and enlightened masters. In addition, the state's practice of invading the private lives of subjects had a firm tradition in sixteenth- and seventeenth-century Muscovy.[67]

Paternalism was not new to eighteenth-century Russia, but its form and scale were. For example, whereas police functions had been performed by general administrative bodies at the central and local levels in Muscovy, under Peter the Great specialized police organs were created in St. Petersburg and Moscow. It remained for Catherine the Great to extend these to provincial Russia (in her provincial reform of 1775 and in the Statute on Good Order, *Ustav blagochiniia*, in 1782). The new system included a senior chief of police *(ober-politseimeister)* in the capitals; a mayor *(gorodnichii)* and police board *(uprava blagochiniia)* in provincial cities; and a constable *(kapitan-ispravnik)* and lower courts *(nizhnie zemskie sudy)* at the district level, elected by the local nobility. As for the scale of the police system, it should be noted that the attempt to regulate private life remained, to a significant degree, on paper (not only in Russia but in the West as well) and could never be fully realized. This limited implementation was due to the overt and clandestine sabotage of state decrees by the populace and to the weakness of the state apparatus.[68] Isabelle de Madariaga is correct in arguing that a police state could never be the model for Russian autocracy (except, perhaps, during the reign of Nicholas I), and that under Catherine II the attempt to regulate private life gradually abated.[69] These attempts persisted until the mid-nineteenth century, however, as reflected in the frequent reprinting of *The Rights and Duties of the City and Rural Police* under Nicholas I (1825–1855).

Although the concept of "police state" might have been appropriately applied in and to eighteenth-century Russia, the phrase has become a political label with tremendous negative connotations that severely undermine the appearance of scholarly objectivity. *Police state* now implies strict rule, coercion, and violent repression—not merely a paternal concern about everything and everyone and a desire to improve administration and social relations. It is in this newer sense that the term is used in the historical literature.[70]

A second, fundamental change in eighteenth-century legislation was the fact that the autocrat became the sole source of law and retained this monopoly until the establishment of the State Duma in 1906. As a result, law came to be understood as an expression of the sovereign's will. The very process of compiling a law—from its initiation to its publication—was subject to a strictly controlled procedure. The initiative could come from the sovereign; from central institutions (Senate, Synod, colleges, ministries, and so on); or from local provincial bodies (after 1775), provincial assemblies of the nobility (after 1785), or various groups in the population (for example, the instructions to deputies at the Legislative Commission of 1767; the proposal to reform city administration in 1828, submitted by the merchants of St. Petersburg; and various proposals to abolish serfdom, submitted by the provincial committees in the late 1850s). But each law was to be confirmed by the sovereign and published by the Senate.[71] It should be pointed out that legislative initiative by private groups had incomparably lesser significance in imperial Russia than it had in the preceding, Muscovite period, when a plethora of fundamental laws derived from petitions by various classes of the population. The decline of public initiative commenced with

Peter the Great and persisted until the middle of the nineteenth century. Indicative here was the failure of several attempts by the government in the first half of the eighteenth century to assemble deputies from the populace to compile a new law code (*ulozhenie*): The problem was simply the unwillingness of the public to participate in lawmaking. For example, in 1728, local authorities were forced to resort to coercion (arrest of deputies' wives and confiscation of their property) to compel the deputies to journey to the capital.[72]

Finally, a third substantial difference concerned the implementation of law, which now applied to everyone and was to be executed precisely and literally. Under penalty of punishment, a subordinate was not to obey an illegal order of his superior; rather, he was to denounce the offender to the next highest authority. The last rule had great significance for the development of Russian society as a monarchy based on law, for it created the juridical basis for an official to adhere strictly to the letter of the law.

Although the autocracy established the written decree as the sole source of law, it did not promulgate a Digest of Laws *(Svod zakonov)* until 1835—after many attempts to do so had miscarried (in 1700, 1714, 1720, 1726, 1728, 1730, 1754, 1761, 1767, and 1809). Virtually every new monarch, without effect, endeavored to compile a new law code. Failure to do so meant that in the course of the eighteenth and early nineteenth centuries, law became unstable, voluminous, and contradictory—indeed, a complex of numerous directives, instructions, orders, laws, and statutes.[73] Given that legislation was not systematized and that the level of moral and legal development in the state administration and in society was low, progress toward a state based on law was slow. To some degree the lack of an official law code was offset by the publication, beginning in the late eighteenth century, of a number of private handbooks and collections of previous legislation (for example, the works of M. Chulkov, F. Pravikov, L. Maksimovich, and S. Khapylev).[74]

Why was the autocracy unable to compile a new law code? Several factors helped to account for this: the strength and vitality of customary law, which governed the life of the peasantry (more than 90 percent of the population); the exceptional difficulty of reconciling customary and written law, and old and new legislation; the instability of Russian life because of rapid and contradictory modernization, which would quickly turn a new law code into an outdated one; and the vacillation of Russian legislators between two different goals as they worked on a law code in the eighteenth and early nineteenth centuries—to compile a digest of current laws, or to compose an entirely new code that was not limited to existing laws. This last (but not least important) factor was due to the influence on Catherinean lawmakers (including Catherine the Great herself) of certain naive ideas derived from contemporary French philosophy. Such ideas led them to believe that simply by heeding common sense and love for the father-land, they could easily compile a new law code that in short order would transform the Russian state and society.

Substantial changes also occurred in the definition of law and the duties of different strata of the population. These changes affected all social groups, but were particularly felt by the nobility and urban inhabitants. The manifesto for the nobility's emancipation from obligatory service (1762) and the charters to the nobility and the cities (1785) established their rights on a solid juridical basis and defended them against arbitrary actions by the imperial administration. These laws also gave the cities and the nobility the right of self-government. The recognition of civil rights, even if only for a few categories of the population, was a major factor in the autocracy's evolution toward a state limited by law.

In the course of the eighteenth century, important changes also took place in the state apparatus. Between 1718 and 1720 the Muscovite *prikaz,* a central office acting on direct orders from the sovereign, was replaced by a new type of state institution, the college *(kollegiia),* a permanent organ operating on the basis of a secure juridical foundation and under the con-trol of the procuracy. The latter was established in 1722 to exercise super-vision over the central imperial institutions (the Senate and colleges), with only limited responsibility for provincial administration. From 1775 to 1785, the reform of local administration (in accordance with the "Statute for the Administration of Provinces in the Russian Empire") separated the judicial and executive branches; as a result, for all practical purposes, the courts became more or less independent of the administration and police. At the same time, the nobility, townspeople, and peasantry received their own courts of lower instance. The reforms also established the appellate procedures for judicial cases, making the Senate the highest instance of ap-peal. The competence of the procuracy was extended to local administra-tion. This included the obligation to ensure the legality of activities by provincial and district offices and to explain the meaning of new laws to state officials. Financial administration became an independent bureau-cracy subordinated to special institutions at the local and national levels.[75]

To summarize the role of law in state administration, it is clear that the eighteenth century marked the "foundations of legality in the Russian state order."[76] Autocracy thus became, to a large degree, closely linked to legality,[77] as the state system was evolving in the direction of a monarchy limited by law. Three pieces of evidence support this conclusion: First, the significance of law steadily rose in Russian society in the eighteenth cen-tury. Second, day-to-day administration of the country was performed by professional officials who, under the impact of precise instructions and su-pervision, showed a tendency to rule according to law rather than indi-vidual whim. Third, all classes of society acquired the features of estates—

(nobility, clergy) to a greater degree than others (peasantry, lesser towns-people, and merchants).

Political Ideology and Mentality

Compared to the preceding period, in the eighteenth century all classes of Russian society changed their political attitudes, but the change was greater among the upper classes than the lower ones. In the early eighteenth century the idea of universal service to the sovereign (for divine blessing and salvation) was replaced by the idea of universal service to the state for the sake of the general welfare. The civil service of the tsar and his subjects for the sake "of the general popular benefit" or "general well-being" was the basic path to salvation.[78] This idea was fully shared by Peter the Great and his "learned circle" of contemporary intellectuals—Feofan Prokopovich, V. N. Tatishchev, and A. D. Kantemir.[79] Thus, during the first quarter of the eighteenth century, the idea of the state as primarily religious gave way to a predominantly secular idea.[80]

A comparison of the diverse justifications offered by intellectuals for autocracy at the time of Ivan the Terrible and under Peter the Great clearly demonstrates the enormous import of the change in consciousness among elites if not among the lower classes. The autocracy of Ivan was supported by legends about his descent from Pruss (brother of the Roman emperor Augustus) and from the Byzantine emperor Constantine, who in the eleventh century allegedly gave the "cap of Monomakh" to his grandson, the Kievan prince Vladimir Monomakh—Ivan's forebear. These legitimating legends bear traces of the magical (folk) mentality in their implicit resort to the assumptions that like begets like and the consequence always resembles the cause. In contrast, the Petrine justification—the social contract—bears a markedly rationalist character.

A new factor in popular political consciousness in the eighteenth century was the separation of the sovereign and the state (that is, the administrative apparatus), which were now conceived of as two distinct entities. Prior to the late seventeenth century, popular consciousness did not distinguish between the two. In the eighteenth century, as the state apparatus expanded, as the sovereign separated himself from the people, as serfdom intensified, and as the nobility formed a separate privileged estate, the people gradually began to distinguish between the sovereign and the state—an apparatus of coercion, an aggregate of officials standing between the tsar and the people. The conception of the "state" as something distinct from the "sovereign" had appeared in official consciousness and documents in the late sixteenth century—as reflected, for example, in the distinction between the court and state administrations and their respective budgets.[81]

The appeal from the Senate and Synod to Peter in 1721, requesting that he assume the title of emperor, clearly reflected the changing ideas about the sovereign, state, and society. The document expressed gratitude to Peter "for his great kindness and paternal concern and effort, which he deigned to reveal—throughout his most glorious reign and especially during the past Swedish war—with respect to the well-being of his state." The Senate and Synod therefore requested that he "deign to accept the title: Father of the Fatherland, Russian emperor, Peter the Great."[82] The tsar had been transformed from God's servant into the leader of his people, whom he ruled not for the sake of spiritual salvation but for the well-being and glory of the state. It should be noted that in the eighteenth century, as before, the subjects and the sovereign, society and state, were no more viewed as opposing sides than they were as a single unit. The sovereign was the ruling entity, and the people, the ruled entity; and together they were believed to serve a common cause.

Let us summarize the situation of the Russian state in the eighteenth century: Autocracy (that is, unlimited monarchy) emerged only in the first quarter of the eighteenth century—after Peter the Great abolished the patriarchate and Boyar Duma in 1700 and ceased to convoke assemblies of the land. During Peter's reign, autocracy not only became a fact of political life but also received a juridical formulation in law. The tsar's efforts at state-building had a contradictory impact on the fate of Russian statehood. On the one hand, they contributed to the secularization of supreme authority and its transformation from a patriarchal monarchy into absolutism—through Peter's definition of monarchical authority, his trampling on tradition and custom, his changes in the ideological basis of legitimacy, and his undermining of the traditional moral-religious basis of the monarch's power. In creating the system of estates, constraining imperial administration with law and statute, and emphasizing service to the fatherland rather than the tsar, Peter contributed significantly to the development of an enlightened monarchy based on law. At the same time, his reign retained a tie to Muscovy in its preservation of the paternalistic view of supreme power.

The new foundations of the state continued to develop during the remainder of the eighteenth century. As a result, by the end of the century, imperial Russia had broken with the patriarchal monarchy of seventeenth-century Muscovy, which had been based on religious faith and tradition. A new political system had emerged in which an unlimited autocracy realized its power through institutions regulated by law and statute, which protected the subjects' personal and property rights. The state conferred these rights on the nobility and townspeople in 1775 and 1785; they were ensured by the principle that only the formal statute was recognized as a source of law.

The eighteenth century thus witnessed the formation of a new type of state institution, a permanent body that functioned on firm juridical foundations. At the same time, the various branches of governance became partly distinct from each other. Altogether, these changes transformed the Russian state into a paternalistic, noble monarchy in which governing institutions were limited by administrative law and by estate rights.

Toward a Monarchy Limited by Law

The patterns of state-building that emerged in the eighteenth century continued to be strengthened in the ensuing half century. At the same time, the new period was marked by several new elements. The establishment of the State Council (*Gosudarstvennyi sovet*) in 1810 as an advisory legislative body gradually but inexorably pointed the Russian state in the direction of a state limited by law and a constitutional monarchy. The State Council was a bureaucratic rather than a representative institution; hence it placed no formal limits on the Russian autocracy. The emperor selected its members from among the most influential officials—frequently those who had recently retired from active service. Current ministers also served ex officio as members of the State Council.

Most importantly, from its very inception, the State Council had the responsibility to conduct a preliminary review of all draft laws before they were submitted for the emperor's approval. This fact served as the criterion for distinguishing between statutory law and administrative orders; whatever passed through the State Council became law; other measures had a higher juridical status. It should be noted that although the emperor was not bound to accept the majority opinion and in some instances endorsed the minority opinion, in two-thirds of cases he approved the majority view.[83]

The State Council subjected drafts of new laws to serious, systematic discussion, and often introduced substantial amendments. During the reign of Alexander III, this impelled the conservative press to denounce the State Council as a self-styled parliament. As M. N. Katkov (editor of *Moskovskie vedomosti*) wrote in a lead editorial printed on 6 May 1886:

> Do we really want this parliamentary game-playing, with the majority versus the minority, creeping into the State Council? And members of the State Council (summoned by the monarch's trust, to serve him with their counsel) trading their high calling for roles as members of "parties," "groups," or "coalitions" that heed the dictates of their leaders rather than their own reason [*razum*]?

After the formation of the State Council, the sovereign began to use a new formula in granting official approval to new laws: "Having received the opinion *(vniav mnenie)* of the State Council, We decree or confirm"—a phrasing that was abolished by Nicholas I in 1842. Some historians of law (A. D. Granovskii, V. I. Sergeevich, A. V. Romanovich-Slavatinskii, I. E. Engelman, M. F. Vladimirskii-Budanov, and V. G. Shcheglov) saw this phrasing as indicative of a limitation of the sovereign's legislative authority. Others (N. M. Korkunov and V. N. Latkin) argued that it meant nothing more than that the sovereign had heard the State Council's opinion.[84] In my judgment, the former view is more persuasive, for it was first put forth in 1810 (by M. M. Speranskii), at a time when Alexander I was attempting to establish an autocracy based on law. Creation of the State Council was the first reform in a series that was prematurely interrupted. Contemporaries understood the new formula as signaling a limitation of the autocracy. Thus, N. M. Karamzin commented scathingly in 1811: "I congratulate the author of this new legislative preamble—'Having received the opinion of the Council. . . . ' However, the autocracy requires no [prior] approval for laws; the sovereign's signature alone suffices. He has total authority."[85]

In the first half of the nineteenth century the mechanism for promulgating laws acquired a precise and obligatory procedure. The first stage included a preliminary review of the draft law not only by ministries but also in special committees. The latter could request expert opinion from particular social groups (as happened in 1860, when the law to abolish serfdom was being drafted) or from the estate organizations of nobles and merchants (as occurred during the preparation of a new city statute for St. Petersburg in 1846). In addition, the state in some cases collected opinions from private individuals and estate organizations—for example, during the reform of state peasants in 1837 to 1841.

In 1801 to 1803 the Senate acquired the status of an institution for administrative justice, a procuracy, and a court. It had several major responsibilities: supervision of administrative-judicial cases and of the administrative apparatus (through provincial and district procurators, independent inspections of individual senators, and formal complaints); juridical duties of the highest appellate instance; and defense and confirmation of the special rights for various classes. Gradually, the functions of supreme court and of overseer of imperial institutions became the Senate's primary functions. In the course of the nineteenth and early twentieth centuries, the Senate received complaints against all imperial institutions, with a few significant exceptions: several ministries (foreign affairs, war, navy, court); the Council of Ministers *(Sovet ministrov)*; the Committee of Ministers *(Komitet ministrov)*; the State Council; the Synod; the Office for the Charitable Institutions of Empress Maria *(Vedomostvo uchrezhdenii imperatritsy Marii)*; and His Imperial Majesty's Own Chancellery.[86]

Particularly effective was the Senate's role in conducting an inspection *(reviziia)* of local offices of state administration. During the first half of the nineteenth century, the senators conducted eighty general inspections. In the second half of the nineteenth and the early twentieth centuries, they carried out another forty-five. As a result, they investigated all the provinces of Russia at least once, and thirty provinces underwent two or more inspections.[87]

These inspections contributed to the improvement of local state administration in two ways. First, the senators were able to combat specific shortcomings, and as representatives of the central government (they were empowered with executive authority in 1819), to react directly to complaints from the populace about the actions of the local administration. After Senator S. I. Mavrin investigated complaints in Vyatka province in 1800, 186 officials were dismissed and put on trial.[88] From 1843 to 1846, Senator I. N. Tolstoi conducted a massive inspection of eastern Siberia and then dispatched a formal report to Nicholas I that exposed the inertia, malfeasance, and nonfeasance of local authorities. As a result, Governor-General V. Ia. Rupert was dismissed and a large number of lower officials were put on trial.[89] Later, to verify whether the provincial administration had corrected these deficiencies, the Senate conducted multiple inspections in these same provinces.

The revisions also helped prepare the way for reforms of local administration, especially in the borderlands. An inspection by Tolstoi generated extensive information that was essential to the central government, for designing measures that would improve administration and promote development in the extraordinarily rich areas of eastern Siberia. The Senate's activity as an organ of administrative justice and a procuracy was particularly significant in ensuring that the local organs of state administration continued to function within the bounds of the law.[90] On the basis of the inspectors' reports filed between 1825 and 1855, the Committee of Ministers issued 189 reprimands to governors for nonfeasance—an average of three per province.[91] In the 1870s, the senators' reports were published, providing ammunition for political opposition to the autocracy.[92] The senatorial inspections, although encouraged by the emperor, did not enjoy much support in the ministries, which perceived the senators as mere competitors for power and feared their exposés of shortcomings in subordinate institutions.

In 1810, the government established a special commission within the State Council to receive petitions and complaints sent (in the name of the emperor) to the Senate and to state institutions not subordinate to the Senate. In 1836 this commission was subordinated directly to the emperor, and in 1884 it was reconstituted as the Chancellery of Petitions to the Emperor. With the formation of this commission, all imperial institutions were placed under the supervision of either the Senate or the emperor.

Between 1802 and 1811, the colleges were replaced by ministries whose activity was grounded in the General Statute on Ministries of 1810. This law determined the scale and limits of power for ministers as well as their relationship to supreme administrative, legislative, and judicial bodies and to subordinate institutions. It also defined the duties of officials and established uniform standards for paperwork, record keeping, and reporting. A comparison of the General Statute on Ministries with the General Regulations on Colleges (1720) shows that the activities of ministries were more precisely defined and that their entire activity was more carefully considered.[93] The annual reports of ministers from the 1830s were published in journals and monographs, and copies were distributed to public libraries.[94] The central apparatus of each ministry, together with its local offices and agencies, constituted a separate domain with its own staff of officials, its own budget, and its own administrative order. Notwithstanding the formation of a Committee of Ministers in 1802 to coordinate the activity of individual ministries, state administration revealed an ever-growing *vedomstvennost'*—a self-serving preoccupation of each ministry with its own interests and needs. This lack of harmony and unity in administration had a negative impact on governance but favorable consequences for citizens: The authority of the bureaucracy was limited by competition among its branches for power and influence at court. Some of these battles for influence are particularly well known, especially the conflict between the Ministry of Finance and the Ministry of Internal Affairs, and that between the Ministry of Education and the Holy Synod. The ministerial reform was yet another step in the direction of erecting a state limited by law, in which every action of an imperial institution had to be based on law.[95]

The Waning Influence of the Nobility

An important new element in the political life of Russia in the first half of the nineteenth century was the marked decline in the emperor's dependence on the nobility. Alexander I, during the first years of his reign, was to some degree dependent on the nobility, since he had come to the throne through a palace coup during which the participants had assassinated his father. That Alexander I sought to abolish serfdom and to impose limits on the autocracy immediately after coming to the throne confirms his dependence. At his initiative several draft statutes were prepared; but not one of them was ever promulgated, because the overwhelming mass of nobles opposed these proposals.[96] Alexander renounced his plans and exiled the author of the reforms, M. M. Speranskii. The emperor did succeed, however, in establishing representative institutions in Poland and Finland and establishing the State Council in Russia. Later during his reign, buoyed by his defeat of Napoleon (1812), the emperor became more independent of the nobility. His heir, Nicholas I, was even less dependent on the nobility, especially after some of its members attempted in December 1825 to carry out a coup d'état (to establish a parliament, obtain a legal claim to political rights, and take over governance). The revolt of the Decembrists (as they came to be called) miscarried, but it had a profound impact on the emperor, who lost his trust in the nobility and thereafter relied more heavily on the bureaucracy. The Nikolaevan government adopted measures to limit the authority of serfowners and to an unprecedented degree began to intervene in the relations between squires and their serfs. One can fairly say that the nobility was transformed from a ruling class into a dominant class. To be sure, the government always took into account the opinions of the nobility,[97] but it placed the power to govern securely in the hands of the bureaucracy. This tendency persisted until the end of the ancien régime.

When the *Digest of Laws of the Russian Empire (Svod zakonov Rossiiskoi imperii)* was compiled in 1832, for the first time the state gave a full juridical definition of the state order in the Russian empire (in articles 1 and 47). Article 1 described the emperor's authority as "supreme, autocratic, and unlimited."[98] As these words make clear, the emperor held absolute authority and was answerable to no one. Article 47 indicates that in exercising his autocratic power, the emperor was bound by the principle of legality *(zakonnost')*: "The Russian Empire is ruled by the firm principles of positive laws, institutions, and charters, which emanate from the power of the autocrat." Thus the law proclaimed that a legal order was the basis of the Russian state system—in contradistinction to arbitrary despotism, which is governed not by the rule of law but by the unlimited personal willfulness of the ruler. Such is the interpretation Russian jurists have given to this article.[99] Articles 1 and 47 reappeared in subsequent editions of the *Digest of Laws,* unchanged until the early twentieth century.

During the reign of Nicholas I (and after 133 years of abortive attempts), in 1830 to 1832 the government issued the forty-five-volume set titled *The Complete Collection of Laws of the Russian Empire* and the fifteen-volume systematic *Digest of Laws of the Russian Empire* (on laws then in force). Thus came into being the long-awaited code of laws, which placed all state administration on a firm legal footing. From this point until 1917 the government regularly added new laws to the *Complete Collection of Laws* and periodically issued an updated version of the *Digest of Laws.*

The last third of the eighteenth century witnessed the emergence of intellectuals among the nobility who were critical of certain aspects of the existing social order; these individuals laid the foundations of conservative nationalism, constitutional liberalism, and revolutionary radicalism. At the same time, a so-called official conservatism emerged, supported by those whose views were in sympathy with those of the government. As the general line of the autocracy wavered, so too did the views of its exponents. Conservatives—who had nothing in common with reactionaries—sought a peaceful fusion of the people, society, and monarch by removing certain negative features of the existing order. Many also wanted to establish a representative body with consultative legislative powers. Liberals aspired to effect a peaceful evolution from autocracy to constitutional monarchy. Radicals simply wanted to overthrow the autocratic order. All of these strands of political thought survived until 1917.

But these critical views of the autocracy, shared among a small group of intellectuals, represented the thinking of learned elites and did not have roots in the popular mentality. The broad masses of the population did not understand or accept these views. The monarchical paradigm remained firmly embedded in popular thought. A well-known French historian and writer who journeyed through Russia in 1839, A. de Custine, was astonished to find that "for the Russians the monarch is God." Comparing his own observations with those of Herberstein in the sixteenth century, Custine concluded: "This letter by Herberstein, written more than three centuries ago, depicts the Russians of that time exactly as I see them now."[100] Until the end of the nineteenth century, all classes of Russian society continued on the whole to uphold the monarchical paradigm, and the peasantry did so virtually up to 1917.

Thus, during the first half of the nineteenth century, the state system continued to evolve in the direction of a monarchy limited by law, since the autocracy set limits on its own power insofar as it agreed to observe the laws that it had generated. In 1810 the emperor created a consultative organ, the State Council (*Gosudarstvennyi sovet),* which henceforth was to consider all new laws. This rule of law was clearly embedded in the Fundamental Laws and was observed, in the first instance, by the emperors themselves. Nicholas I was perhaps the most scrupulous in observing this principle. In its report for 1827, the secret police (the Third Section of His Imperial Majesty's Cabinet) recommended that Nicholas make changes "in both the system and in the people," while relying on law and justice.[101] Nicholas followed this advice. One example is provided by his order in 1832 (immediately after the *Digest of Laws* was completed) banning requests for an exemption from the laws. Nicholas saw here the danger that "the law and rule themselves could become the exception."[102]

The actions of Alexander I and Nicholas I with regard to Poland and Finland, which had constitutions and parliaments (Poland, until 1831), are very revealing. Both emperors, in the capacity of constitutional monarch of the Polish Kingdom and the Grand Duchy of Finland, conducted themselves in strict accordance with these constitutions. Despite Nicholas's autocratic inclinations, he confirmed the Polish supreme court's acquittals of members of Polish secret societies linked to the Decembrists. At his coronation in 1831, difficult as it must have been for him, Nicholas swore the following oath: "I promise and swear before God that I will preserve and demand observance of the constitutional charter with all my power."

Nicholas reacted with indignation to news that the French king Charles X had violated the constitution in his country.[103] The prominent Russian historian A. A. Kornilov thus had grounds to conclude that "the government system of Nicholas I was one of the most consistent attempts to realize the ideas of enlightened absolutism."[104]

A second tendency in the development of the Russian state was the formation of a bureaucratic administration that was based on law and that acted in accordance with administrative law and under the control of administrative justice and of a procuracy. The Russian official did not correspond completely to the ideal official who is subordinate only to the law and who acts impartially regarding the individuals involved. But in the course of the eighteenth century and first half of the nineteenth century, Russian bureaucracy evolved in precisely this direction, and operational administration was in its hands. The head of the gendarmes, A. Kh. Benckendorff (in his "Overview of Public Opinion" in 1827) gave the emperor this evaluation of Russian officialdom: "Unfortunately, it is they who govern, and not only the low-ranking or the most prominent of them, but in essence all of them, for they know all the subtleties of the bureaucratic system."[105]

Evolution of the state toward a monarchy based on the rule of law demanded the formulation of a new official doctrine for Russian autocracy that could take into account changes in the state order. This doctrine was formulated by Minister of Education S. S. Uvarov between 1832 and 1834 and came to be known as the theory of "official nationality." Its essence was the triadic formula "autocracy, Orthodoxy, and nationality [narodnost'']," in which the autocracy was conceived of as the highest form of state power, Orthodoxy as the only truth faith, and nationality as the "inviolable sacred treasure of our popular ideas."[106] The tsar exercised his power in the interests of the people and in accordance with moral and juridical law: "Russia is strong, with an unparalleled unanimity. Here the tsar loves the fatherland in the form of its people and rules them like a father and in accordance with the laws, and the people cannot separate the fatherland from the tsar, and see in him their own happiness, strength, and glory."[107] The lawful character of the monarchy is the novel element here, distinguishing the new doctrine from the old one that Feofan Prokopovich had formulated in the early eighteenth century (in which the monarch's will, rather than the law, was dominant). The theory of official nationality remained the ideology of Russian autocracy until the early twentieth century. In the 1840s and 1850s this ideology was carefully elaborated in the works of the Slavophiles; but in the second half of the nineteenth century and in the early twentieth century its main exponents were conservatives such as N. A. Berdiaev, S. L. Frank, L. A. Tikhomirov, K. N. Leontev, and I. A. Ilin.

The All-Estate Monarchy Limited by Law: 1860s–Early Twentieth Century

In the 1860s and 1870s, during the reign of Alexander II, the political order acquired new elements of a state based on the rule of law: The Great Reforms included the creation of all-estate organs of local self-government—the zemstvos (1864) and the city *dumas* (1870). The government conferred on them a significant part of its own plenipotentiary powers. Much as Catherine II, almost a century earlier, had conferred part of her power on the provincial nobility (to distract them from palace coups and from demands to participate in supreme administration), Alexander II employed the same maneuver to divert public opinion from politics writ large. Both cases illustrate the same general pattern: In moments of weakness, the autocracy made tangible concessions to society; but once it had recovered, it sought to minimize these concessions.[108] As a consequence of the abolition of serfdom and noble privileges, all classes of the population acquired personal (but not political) rights. The new regulations on censorship (1865) permitted society, through publicity and the press, to exercise control over the administration. Universities were granted academic autonomy (1863). In the 1860s the government also reformed its budget, accounting, and fiscal control; these changes permitted proper oversight for government finances by both the government and public opinion, as the budget and the report of the state comptroller were published annually in the press.[109]

The introduction of new judicial statutes in 1864 also strengthened the role of law in administration and served to separate the courts from administrative and legislative authority. Prior to the reform, judicial cases frequently came before the State Council, were then resolved by the emperor, and acquired the form and authority of law without really becoming law. The judicial reform provided a new support for the rule of law by drawing, more clearly than ever, a distinction between law and the emperor's administrative orders.[110]

In addition to the Senate, the supreme organ of administrative justice, the reform established organs for local administrative justice at the provincial and district levels. These organs included representatives from the administration, courts, procuracy, and local self-government, as well as marshals of the nobility. The provincial commissions for local (zemskii) and urban affairs were the most important organs of local administrative justice; the others specialized in various branches of administration (the commissions for military affairs, for taxes, for manufacture, and the like).[111]

Taken together, the new laws, institutions, and organs led to the formation of a monarchy limited by law and by an administration that included representatives of all social estates. Under this system the emperor's legislative power was limited by an objective factor—law; the executive authority of central imperial institutions was limited by administrative law and administrative justice; and local administrative authority was limited by administrative law, administrative justice, and the organs of self-government. Russia was therefore developing a form of governance based on limits set by law.

These changes in the state order were preceded by changes in the political mentality of educated society. By the middle of the nineteenth century the political consciousness of educated society had undergone substantial change. As early as the end of the eighteenth century, individual representatives of educated society had come to express dissatisfaction with their role as servants and with the activities of the government. During the first half of the nineteenth century this attitude became more widespread and more intense. By midcentury a significant part of educated society shared the new political conception that society should have the right to participate in state administration. That demand derived from the view that the sovereign and his government were failing to cope (and, in principle, could not cope) with the function of governing society and running the state without the assistance of society. Public opinion became ever more insistent in expressing its wish to participate in state administration, and a number of political concessions eventually were wrested from the government. This process was slow and painful, however, for Russian society was extremely fragmented both in social and in cultural terms. More than 95 percent of the population—the peasantry, petty townspeople, and workers—lacked the right to vote, a fact that appears to have fostered widespread political indifference. The small proportion of citizens (about 5 percent) who were granted electoral rights through the urban and zemstvo reforms also showed a high degree of absenteeism. In the 1870s and 1880s, only 12 to 14 percent of those with the right to vote actually participated in the elections to city *dumas*.[112] The voting proportions were not much higher in the case of zemstvo elections: Only 19 percent of private landowners, 21 percent of townspeople, and 48 percent of peasants exercised their franchise rights.[113]

The relatively high rate of participation by the peasantry is explained by the peasants' loyalty to the state and by the fact that the authorities took measures during elections to the peasant curiae to ensure that the electorate turned out to vote. The Russian bourgeoisie showed an exceptional devotion to autocracy, since it had grown through the support of the state.[114] The politically active liberal public, which was exceedingly small in size, fragmented into dozens of political groups, all warring against each other as well as against autocracy. Given the political silence of the people (who were monarchists by conviction), the autocracy naturally did not hasten to make concessions to the oppositionist minority.

Yet educated society demanded more—a constitution and a parliament. Liberals wanted to complete the construction of the new state edifice that had been started by the reforms of the 1860s. Conservatives sought to defend themselves from new assaults by the state and to be compensated for the loss of their former economic and political significance; and liberals wanted to correct the reforms, which in their opinion were not sufficiently democratic. Noble assemblies and zemstvos appealed to the emperor on several occasions in the 1860s with appropriate petitions but were rebuffed. Alexander II, seeking to prevent constitutional encroachments on his power, issued a law in 1867, titled "On the Order for Conducting Business in Estate and Public Assemblies." In the words of Minister of Internal Affairs P. A. Valuev, this new law put "a damper on constitutional declarations."[115] Notwithstanding, some quarters in the government prepared and submitted to Alexander II and Alexander III proposals to establish an elected, consultative legislative body. Such proposals came from P. A. Valuev (1863); Grand Duke Konstantin Nikolaevich (1866); the head of the Third Section (secret police), P. A. Shuvalov (1874); and Minister of Internal Affairs M. T. Loris-Melikov (1881). The first two proposals were rejected by the emperor and a majority in the government; the last proposal was approved by Alexander II for consideration by the State Council on 4 March 1881 but withered after Alexander was assassinated on 1 March. The sole result of governmental constitutionalism was a law of 1874, which, at the emperor's discretion, proposed to invite representatives of the nobility and institutions of self-government to discuss certain draft legislation. The decree, although never published, was invoked on two occasions (1875 and 1881). In 1882, the new minister of internal affairs, N. P. Ignatev, undertook a last constitutional attempt (to summon an assembly of the land), but his proposal met the same fate as had the earlier attempts.[116]

The assassination of Alexander II proved critical for determining the fate of representative institutions under his son, Alexander III. The new emperor and conservative circles in the government concluded that revolutionary terrorism was a consequence of the Great Reforms and that liberal circles in society with demands for a constitution and parliament were intent on depriving the emperor of his unlimited power. Until then there had been a series of partial concessions on the part of the autocracy—the inclusion of public opinion in administration at the local level, affirmation of a rule of law, and strengthening of supervision over administration on the part of administrative justice and of the public. As long as these were the issues, the autocracy made concessions to public opinion, for it too was interested in consolidating the legal basis of the state. But as soon as public opinion began to demand a constitution and a parliament—that is, a fundamental change in the state order of Russia—the attitude of the autocracy toward public opinion underwent a radical change. The government now gave serious consideration to how it might "freeze Russia" (in the words of K. P. Pobedonostsev, an ideologist for unlimited autocracy)—how it might avert the transformation of Russia from a law-abiding state to one based strictly on the rule of law and recognition of individual rights. That is why Alexander III, the unwavering advocate of autocracy, put to rest hopes for a constitution and went on the offensive against educated society.

In August 1881 his government adopted the Statute on Intensified and Extreme Security, which the government could put into operation in the event it was needed. This statute provided for placing the administration of a given territory under the complete control of the imperial administration and military authorities. This statute was followed by the so-called counterreforms. Although they did not abolish institutions created by the Great Reforms, they did weaken the democratic element and strengthen the representation of the nobility (through changes in franchise for the zemstvo in 1890 and city *dumas* in 1892). A new censorship statute (1882) tightened control over the press, and consequently, diminished publicity and the opportunities for the public to express its opinion and to control the activity of the administration. A new statute of 1884 significantly curtailed the autonomy of universities. A statute of 1889 reduced the civil rights of the peasantry and made peasants more dependent on a new official, the land captain *(zemskii nachal'nik)*, who was appointed by the governor from among hereditary nobles and endowed with administrative, police, and judicial powers. These counterreforms altered the state system, strengthening the role of imperial administration at the expense of public self-government.

Activities at the top level of state institutions also revealed a retreat from the existing order. At the outset of the reign of Alexander III, the Council of Ministers began to consider laws and to bypass the State Council, which counted among its members many liberal officials appointed by Alexander II; simultaneously, the Committee of Ministers assumed the role of supreme judicial instance.[117] Nevertheless, the State Council—indeed, the entire bureaucracy—continued to impose significant restrictions on the power of the emperor. Opposition in government circles forced the emperor to renounce a number of proposed counterreforms, such as the abolishment of bureaucratic ranks.[118] In addition, some local officials, such as the provincial governors, acquired greater autonomy during this time,[119] leading one historian to describe autocracy under Alexander III as "bureaucratic absolutism."[120]

Nonetheless, the Russian autocrats endeavored to reinforce the principle of the legitimacy of imperial administration, in which they had a vested interest. Alexander III personally dealt with any officials who violated the rules of state service, meting out harsh punishments. In 1893, for example, the emperor dismissed the director of the Department of Police, P. N. Durnovo, for conducting a search of the Brazilian emissary in order to seize the letters of his lover. Durnovo complained: "What an amazing country! For nine years I was director of the secret police and entrusted with state secrets. Then one day some Brazilian secretary lodges a complaint against me, and without even being asked for an explanation, inside of twenty-four hours I am dismissed."[121]

Despite the political reaction against reform, a liberal press and liberal public opinion continued to exist and make themselves felt. F. M. Dostoevskii once said that even if he had had prior knowledge of the assassination plot against Alexander II, he would not have denounced the conspirators to the police—despite the fact that he regarded the assassination as a horrible crime. Why? "Fear of being known for making a denunciation. They would print that Dostoevskii identified the criminals. The liberals would never forgive me for this. They would torture me and reduce me to complete despair."[122]

Under Alexander III the government attempted to retreat from the earlier process of transforming the state into a *Rechtsstaat,* with a constitution and parliament. This attempt had no chance of success, however. Despite the conservative political course, the government continued to evolve (if at a slower pace) in the direction of a constitutional monarchy, and society continued to develop in the direction of a civil society—which inexorably drew the two sides into direct confrontation.[123]

Dualistic Monarchy, 1906–1907

The order established by the counterreforms of Alexander III lasted without change until 1905, when Nicholas II—under pressure from revolution at home and defeat in the Russo-Japanese War—was forced to agree to a constitutional monarchy. The first tsarist manifesto on the subject, that of 6 August 1905, proclaimed only the establishment of a consultative assembly (*Duma*); but the subsequent manifesto, of 17 October 1905, announced the establishment of a constitutional system. On 23 April 1906 the government published the Fundamental Laws, whose juridical force and content were entirely analogous to what in the West is known as a constitution.[124] Four days later the country witnessed the meetings of the first State Duma and of a restructured State Council (an upper house in which half of the members were elected and the others were appointed by the tsar). The people of Russia thus came to possess a constitution, political freedom, and a bicameral parliament.

The majority of prerevolutionary Russian and Western Slavists (such as G. T. Robinson, J. Walkin, and M. Szeftel) regarded the Fundamental Laws as a constitution and the State Duma and State Council as a bicameral parliament. Soviet Marxist historians employed V. I. Lenin's ironic phrase *monarchical constitution* and treated the State Duma as a pseudoparliament marching in step with the new state order of "absolutism draped in pseudoconstitutional forms."[125] The intent of the Soviet approach was to denigrate progress in Russian state-building before 1917, in order to justify the state's overthrow by the Bolsheviks in the October Revolution. It is possible that the deliberate vagueness in the terms they employed also contributed to an undervaluation of the State Duma and the State Council in contemporary scholarship generally.

In terms of the relationship between their governments and parliaments, European monarchies at the beginning of the twentieth century can be divided into two basic types (with several intermediate forms in between): constitutional (or dualistic) monarchies and parliamentary monarchies. In a dualistic monarchy, the ruler and his government retained executive power; they could remain in power without enjoying the support of a parliamentary majority. Legislative power was divided, belonging both to the monarch and to the popularly elected parliament. Prussia exemplified this type of state order. In contrast, the composition of the government in parliamentary monarchies depended on the confidence of the elected representative body; this type of state order was called parliamentarism, and it existed in both monarchies and republics.

The word *parliament* therefore had two potential meanings: a representative institution with legislative functions, elected by the people and expressing its will; and a form of state order wherein the government is chosen by the parliament and accountable to it. In the early twentieth century, Russia had a parliament only in the first sense, whereas several other countries (England, France, Italy, and some others) had a parliament in both senses.[126] When the chairman of the Council of Ministers, V. N. Kokovtsev, exclaimed, "Thank God, Russia does not have a parliament!" he had in mind precisely the absence of a parliament in the second sense of the term, not the absence of a representative institution with legislative functions.[127] Although the Russian parliament did not participate in designating members of the government, it did have oversight powers through interpellation—that is, an official request that a minister explain illegal actions by his ministry, mandated by a vote of thirty or more members of parliament. Of course, the parliamentary form of rule is more democratic than the dualistic form. But virtually all the European states began as a dualistic monarchy, which gradually, as the popular representative body gained strength through the support of society, was transformed into a parliamentary monarchy or a republic.

Russia's transition from an autocratic to a constitutional regime can be dated to 27 April 1906, when the State Duma convened for its first session. Thereafter, changes in the Fundamental Laws could be made at the emperor's initiative *only* with the approval of the parliament. Thus Russia became a dualistic monarchy based on the rule of law: Legislative power rested with the parliament, whereas executive power at the center still belonged to the emperor and the bureaucracy, and at the provincial and local levels, to the bureaucracy and the organs of public self-government.

The new set of Fundamental Laws differed from the previous set in the inclusion of three additional sections: The first defined the limits to the emperor's authority; the second clearly articulated the civil rights of the people; and the third established the place of the popular representative body in the system of state institutions. These new sections, which were typical of and essential for all constitutions, made Russia's new Fundamental Laws in essence a "constitution," although this word was not employed at the time.[128]

In adopting a constitution and a parliamentary institution, Russia made a decisive step in the direction of becoming a state based on the rule of law. Prior to 1906, Russian law had recognized only individual rights,[129] which the autocrats did not confer on all subjects or all categories of the population simultaneously but only gradually and partially, over the course of two centuries. The nobility, the upper stratum of the merchant class, and the upper stratum of the clergy acquired basic individual rights in the last quarter of the eighteenth century; and the general population, the lower stratum of the urban estate, the lower stratum of the clergy, and the peasantry were granted basic individual rights in the 1860s. However, before the early twentieth century, these rights were subject to a number of restrictions. The personal freedom of an individual was not unconditional; it could be violated by the police, through clandestine surveillance and the interception of private correspondence. Freedom of confession was not equivalent to freedom of conscience, since the law did not recognize freedom of religion but only the equality of all faiths, or religious tolerance; that is, one's civil rights did not depend on one's free confession (except in the case of Jews, who lacked certain personal rights possessed by other Russian subjects). Each person was obliged to belong to some confession and did not have the right to change his faith; the sole exception was the right of conversion to Russian Orthodoxy. Such limitations were especially onerous for citizens who opposed the existing order—mainly the intelligentsia.[130]

As for political rights, prior to 1906 the Fundamental Laws made no reference at all to these. In the course of the Great Reforms, the autocracy granted limited rights to "qualified citizens" to participate in elections and to serve in local zemstvos and on juries. Freedom of speech was limited by the requirement to obtain permission to open a new periodical; by general censorship and imperial court censorship (on all information pertaining to the emperor or imperial family); by ecclesiastical censorship (for religious literature); and by administrative repression. To elect and serve in organs of local self-government or to serve as foreman of a jury one also had to satisfy certain qualifications of property and education. Under the conditions that prevailed in Russia until 1906, the right to enter state service determined access to state administration; that is, state service was the sole avenue by which an individual could participate in state administration, and consequently, in political life. The right to enter state service can therefore be regarded as a kind of political right. It depended on social origin, education, gender, age (a minimum of 16 years), and personal integrity (imprisonment or the imposition of certain other penalties deprived an individual of the right to enter state service).

From 1906, with the transition to a constitutional form of rule, the conception of law changed. To begin with, the elements of law were more precisely and explicitly defined: The text of a law was to be established jointly by the State Duma and the State Council, with confirmation by the emperor. Second, laws *(zakony)* were more strictly distinguished from administrative directives in terms of their juridical force: The administrative directive was now subordinate to the law.[131]

In 1905 to 1906 the people of Russia acquired basic political rights: They ceased to be the emperor's subjects and became instead citizens of their country.[132] Of course, one should not ignore the fact that the franchise was not universal (only 2.4 percent of Russian citizens had the right to vote); that the government was not accountable to the parliament; that the emperor still wielded enormous power; that there were significant obstacles to the realization of formal political rights; and that the new political order in Russia encountered a host of other difficulties. The Russian state order was distinguished from the ideal *Rechtsstaat* (in the Weberian sense of that term) found in the United States, England, France, or even Prussia. Still, beginning in 1906, Russia entered the circle of states with a legal foundation for its legitimacy, since the constitution and parliament had become integral institutions in Russian life.

With the establishment of a constitutional monarchy, the struggle between society and tsarism became even more acute. Nicholas II was an adamant supporter of autocratic monarchy and sincerely believed that a constitution and parliament would inflict harm on the people and state. By exploiting his enormous authority as well as the divisiveness in the camp of those opposed to autocracy, he attempted to deprive the parliament of its legislative functions and transform it into an instrument of his own will. It was with this intent that in 1907 he dissolved the State Duma, which had been dominated by liberals, and promulgated a new franchise that was tantamount to a coup d'état, although the Fundamental Laws themselves remained intact (at issue was a new statute on elections to the State Duma). The new statute deliberately altered the composition of the Duma in favor of conservative members. But Nicholas II's refusal to honor his public promises, in conjunction with his attempts to return to the old methods of rule, caused society to shift leftward, negating the stabilizing effect of the conservative majority in the State Duma. Put simply, society was no longer willing to live as it had in the past.[133] Contrary to the will of the emperor, changes in the state order after the establishment of the Duma and adoption of the constitution proved irreversible. The Duma became a central element in the general structure of the Russian state.[134] The idea of parliamentarism penetrated ever more deeply into the mentality of society. The emperor himself, even in his wildest dreams, could not imagine the state without the State Duma, although in his opinion it should have had only consultative power. Under a favorable confluence of circumstances, it was entirely realistic to anticipate that the dualistic monarchy would be transformed into a parliamentary order. This scenario, in fact, was advanced by World War I.

After the Great Reforms, the role of public self-government steadily grew, whereas that of imperial administration declined. During peacetime this process proceeded gradually and unobtrusively, and the autocracy accommodated this development. But the war brought a significant increase in the burdens on the state apparatus, which was unprepared for the strain. What was secret became public: The war exposed the inability of the imperial administration to govern the country entirely on its own. The emperor should have turned to society for assistance. Nicholas II and the bureaucracy instead attempted to muddle through and avoid appealing for aid even from the existing public organizations, and in every conceivable way resisted letting them participate in governance. When at last the tsar and his officials were forced to accept their assistance, it was too late: The country was already in the throes of a full-blown crisis. The people were fed up with war and its sacrifices; they reacted to the summons and leadership of the antigovernment opposition in February 1917 to overthrow the tsar.[135]

After the February revolution the development of the state proceeded in a contradictory manner because of the continuing war, the economic crisis, and the so-called dual power. On the one hand, the Provisional Government was sanctioned by the Provisional Duma Committee (as part of the members of the State Duma) and supported by the leadership of the Petrograd Soviet (which had been elected by the workers and soldiers of the Petrograd garrison). On the other hand, the soviets that sprang up across the entire country on popular initiative had very little sympathy for true parliamentarism. Pending the convocation of a new parliament elected on the basis of universal franchise (that is, the Constituent Assembly), the Provisional Government gradually arrogated to itself full legislative and executive authority. It proclaimed a complete political amnesty and democratic freedom, replaced the police with a people's militia, democratized local administration, and declared the equality of soldiers and officers. However, it deferred resolution of the fundamental questions—the state order, the agrarian question, and Russia's exit from the world war—until the Constituent Assembly could be convoked. But the broad masses of the people demanded immediate withdrawal from the war, confiscation of noble estates, an eight-hour day in the factory, and worker control over production. When the Provisional Government failed to fulfill these demands, it lost its legitimacy, and the peasants, workers, and soldiers withdrew their support. The balance of power shifted in favor of the soviets, in which the extreme left-wing parties—the Bolsheviks and Social-Revolutionaries—enjoyed great popular support. On 25 October 1917 the Bolsheviks overthrew the Provisional Government and soon thereafter established their dictatorship over the country.[136]

Between February and October 1917, the country had a state system that does not fit easily into any existing scholarly definitions. Russia was a democratic republic, but it was one with a parliament; the old state system had been demolished, but the new one had yet to be erected. As a result, the level of legality in governing the country, compared to prerevolutionary times, gradually declined to the point where it disappeared altogether and made the overthrow of the Provisional Government possible. The only prospects for recovery followed the convocation of the Constituent Assembly: Given the composition of the parliament (the Bolsheviks accounted for approximately 25 percent of members), Russia had some chance of turning into a legal state. One can say that the Provisional Government sacrificed itself in the name of law: If it had agreed to initiate agrarian and certain other reforms without waiting for the Constituent Assembly, it would not have disintegrated after eight months.

Conclusions: From Popular Monarchy to Rule of Law

The facts previously adduced make it possible to conclude that between the seventeenth and early twentieth centuries, Russian statehood was in a condition of constant change and development. Russia had a popular monarchy or representative patriarchal monarchy in the second half of the seventeenth century; absolutism in the first quarter of the eighteenth century; a paternalistic, petty aristocratic monarchy in the second half of the eighteenth century; an all-estate monarchy limited by law in the nineteenth century; a dualistic monarchy based on the rule of law from 1906 to February 1917; and a democratic republic from February to October 1917. By the mid-nineteenth century the Russian state had essentially become a law-governed monarchy insofar as the monarchy as a whole functioned within the framework of law, but the majority of the population was still without civil rights.

In the ensuing decades, the state gradually moved toward monarchy based on the rule of law, insofar as it made the transition to a constitutional conception of law and inasmuch as the population obtained a constitution, parliament, and civil rights. Thus, in the course of a little more than two centuries, Russia made the transition from popular monarchy (traditional legitimate rulership) to a state based primarily on the rule of law. Russia acquired the main features of a *Rechtsstaat,* as well as the instrumental basis for its administration—a bureaucracy acting in accordance with the norms of administrative law and with formal and rational rules (believed by political sociologists to signal legal rule and a state based on law).[137] Western countries, as pioneers, required more time to form a state based on law. Russia drew on the Western experience and traversed this path in a relatively short period of time. In disputes about the role of succession and other transitions in the history of the Russian state, I share the view of those who regard change as a dominant feature of the political development of Russia.[138]

To describe the Russian state from the mid-nineteenth century to 1906 as having been limited by law, and from 1906 to 1917 as based on the rule of law (or very close to that), may seem forced and misleading if one evaluates the state in late imperial Russia according to the contemporary criteria of a *Rechtsstaat,* forgetting that any ideal type is remote from the real world. Indeed, the laws that governed Russian society in the second half of the nineteenth century were far from perfect: They gave too much power to the state, invariably failed to satisfy one or another social group (especially the intelligentsia), and did not assure Russians of a life commensurate with that of their counterparts in western Europe then or now. Nevertheless, one cannot gainsay the fact that Russian society lived according to the law and that the monarch and his government essentially subordinated themselves to this law as well.

To be sure, corruption existed, and violations of lawful order (not to mention legal loopholes) occurred under Nicholas I,[139] Alexander III, Nicholas II, and even Alexander II.[140] But violations of the law were subject to prosecution and punishment. Each year thousands of state officials (as well as those elected to public service and having the status of officials) were subjected to criminal prosecution for official offenses by various judicial bodies. The apogee of this struggle against officials who violated their service duty came under Nicholas I. Beginning in 1834 the government began to publish data on crimes in the annual reports of the Ministry of Justice; after 1874 (for the thirty-three provinces where the new judicial system of 1864 had been introduced), data were published in the annual *Digest of Statistical Data on Criminal Cases.* Prereform and postreform data are not comparable, insofar as they embrace different territories; but they nonetheless permit one to gain some idea of the scale of crime committed by those in state and public service as well as the struggle to combat it. From 1834 to 1840, approximately 6,000 people were prosecuted each year in all of Russia for malfeasance; this represents about 4 percent of the number of people in service. In the 1840s the number prosecuted fell to 4,800 per annum (3.4 percent of those in service); in 1855 the annual number prosecuted was about 5,000 (or 2.2 percent of those in service, assuming that the numbers of those in imperial service and in public service were approximately the same).[141] The number of individuals subjected to criminal prosecution for malfeasance was large; but in relative terms (as a proportion of all those in state and public service), it was gradually decreasing. These data give grounds to conclude that in the second third of the nineteenth century, violations of the law by the bureaucracy were on the decline. From 1846 to 1857, crimes committed by the government comprised about 4.5 percent of all offenses committed in the empire.[142] Table 1.1 provides a dynamic view of the incidence of bureaucratic crimes between 1874 and 1913.

In the last third of the nineteenth century the absolute number of crimes reportedly committed by state officials increased, but the frequency of such crimes (the proportion of state officials accused of committing them) declined. Compared to the total number of crimes, there was no significant change. In the early twentieth century the number of offenses by state and public officials (both the absolute number and the proportion of officials involved) did increase; but as a proportion of total crimes, official offenses declined. Hence Russia's entry into the turmoil of the early twentieth century led to a sharp growth in the total number of crimes, but the share of offenses by state and public officials remained low and did not increase.

Supervision over officials was no mere formality: As the nomenclature of service offenses demonstrates (Table 1.2), it encompassed all aspects of their service. Officials were prosecuted by order of the emperor (1 to 2 percent of all cases), by order of the Senate (8 to 9 percent), and by ministers and office heads (5 to 6 percent), but primarily by provincial authorities

TABLE 1.1   Average Annual Number of Individuals Prosecuted for Official Crimes in Russia, 1874–1913 (various years)

	1874–1883	1884–1893	1899–1903	1904–1913
Number of people prosecuted	3,576	4,027	6,093	11,122
Percent of those in service	3.8	4.5	2.1	2.7

Data for 1874 to 1893 apply only to thirty-three provinces; data for 1899 to 1913 encompass the entire Russian empire (with the exception of Finland).

SOURCE: *Svod statisticheskikh svedenii po delam ugolovnym za [1874–1913] god* (St. Petersburg, 1876–1916).

TABLE 1.2   Officials Convicted of Crimes Involving Official Duties in 1847, 1883, and 1913

	1847		1883	1913
Category of Offense	Imperial State Officials	Other Public Officials		
Nonfeasance (failure to perform official duties)	126	208	350	807
Abuse of authority, illegal acts	556	867	—	—
Illegal possession and disposition of property and money	846	924	897	2,401
Falsification of official documents	239	338	316	1,304
Injustice	35	22	3	
Bribery and extortion	220	983	303	1,071
Violation of rules for entering or leaving service	16	17	8	19
Violation of rules governing relations between superiors and subordinates	40	71	43	184
Red tape, negligence, failure to perform service regulations	857	1,031	966	144
Crimes and offenses in criminal investigations	192	65	50	—
Crimes and offenses involving land surveys	11	2	—	88
Crimes and offenses involving police officials	203	55	—	—
Crimes and offenses of officials involving notary publics	61	29	4	—
Violation of laws on contracts, delivery, receipt and sale of state property, or on transactions involving spirits and excise taxes	132	103	73	1,302
Violation of statutes of recruitment, customs, forestry, and construction	24	58	—	3,272
Torture, physical abuse, insults, and illegal deprivation of liberty	—	—	660	2,821
Other	—	—	—	710
TOTAL	3,558	4,773	3,673	14,123

SOURCES: *Otchet ministra iustitsii za 1847 god* (St. Petersburg, 1849), p. 84; *Svod statisticheskikh svedenii po delam ugolovnym, proizvedennym v [1883, 1913] godu* (St. Petersburg, 1887–1916).

(83 to 86 percent). Officials in all provinces, including the most remote, were caught in malfeasance. Most violations by officials involved persons disloyal to the regime. In their contacts with ordinary, loyal citizens (99 percent of the population), as a rule officials did observe the law.

The question naturally arises: Why was the revolutionary opposition to the monarchy so intractable? In essence, liberals and revolutionaries fought at first for individual and political rights, and then later against limitations on these rights—that is, they fought for laws that contradicted existing laws. When the intelligentsia fought for a state based on the rule of law, it had political rights in mind above all: It saw no difference between a lawless or arbitrary state *(bespravnoe gosudarstvo)* and an unlawful or illegitimate state—that is, a state lacking a foundation in constitutional law and in civil rights *(nepravovoe gosudarstvo)*. Although the two types of state are not exactly the same, the confusion in terminology has left its imprint on the Russian language and even on the specialized juridical literature.[143] This confusion in turn has contributed to a general underestimation of the degree to which the Russian state did in fact adhere to legal norms.

It should be emphasized also that after the second third of the nineteenth century (we do not have corresponding data for earlier periods), imperial Russia recorded fewer crimes than did the developed states of the West (see Table 1.3).[144] This fact supports two important propositions: that Russians were more law-abiding than were other Europeans, and that the state authorities in Russia at that time had a claim to legitimacy.

It is important to observe that changes in the Russian state order from the seventeenth to the twentieth century were clearly reflected in the Russian language. The word *sovereign* (*gosudar'*) in the ordinary language bore two connotations in the sixteenth and seventeenth centuries: The proprietor of someone or something, the master, the landowner; and the

TABLE 1.3   Criminality in Russia and Three Other European Countries, 1835–1913 (annual averages, various years, per 100,000 population)

	1835–1845	1876–1884	1891–1900	1909–1913
Russia	218	177	205	274
England	–	234	183	280
Germany	–	898*	1,006	976
France	443	469	499	756

*1882–1890

SOURCES: *Entsiklopedicheskii slovar' russkogo bibliograficheskogo instituta Granat,* 7-e izd. (Moscow, 1922), tom 36, chast' 5, pp. 628–659; M. N. Gernet, *Moral'naia statistika (Ugolovnaia statistika i statistika samoubiistv)* (Moscow, 1922), pp. 50–97; ibid., *Prestupnost' za granitsei i v SSSR* (Moscow, 1931), pp. 7–85; E. N. Tarnovskii, "Itogi russkoi ugolovnoi statistiki za 20 let (1874–1894 gg.)," *Zhurnal Ministerstva iustitsii,* nomer 7 (1899), prilozhenie; Tarnovskii, "Dvizhenie prestupnosti v Rossiiskoi imperii za 1899–1908 gg.," *Zhurnal Ministerstva iustitsii,* nomer 9 (1909); *Materialy dlia statistiki Rossii, sobiraemye po vedomstvu Ministerstva gosudarstvennykh imushchestv,* vypusk 6, *Ugolovnaia statistika gosudarstvennykh krest'ian po dannym za desiatiletie 1847–1856* (St. Petersburg, 1871), Statisticheskie vedomosti, nomer 1.

supreme ruler. The word *state* (Russ. *gosudarstvo*) meant primarily "rule" or "reign" but also the authority of the sovereign. In the nineteenth century the word *sovereign* came to designate the monarch, king, or other monocrat; the word *state* referred to any country the population of which was under a single rule. The dictionary definition of *state* in the eighteenth century was "a society based on the recognition of supreme authority and law applicable to all." By the end of the nineteenth century, the term denoted "a social union of free people, with a coercively established peaceful order whereby the exclusive rights of coercion are conferred only on state organs."[145] The history of these words' definitions bears witness to the origin of the state, in the contemporary meaning of this term, from the estate, and of state authority from estate authority.

The evolution of Russian statehood was determined by many factors, the key among them being social change brought about by alterations in political mentality, together with the new demands on administration made by society and by members of the government. In accordance with the political mentality of the seventeenth century, society did not juxtapose itself to the state or endeavor to subordinate it. Rather, society saw its civic and religious duty in serving the sovereign, or more precisely, in cooperating in state administration on behalf of the sovereign (all of which was regarded as a form of service to God). Within the framework of eighteenth- and early nineteenth-century political mentality, society was viewed as the target ("object") of administration; the state was the only active agent ("subject"), which through its wise decisions could lead society toward well-being. The second half of the nineteenth century marked the emergence of a political mentality that ascribed to society the right and duty to participate in state administration. In keeping with the new mentality, public opinion began more and more insistently to express a desire to participate in running the state. The Russian autocrats gradually acceded to the demands of public opinion and delegated a part of their power. They did this reluctantly, however. One must admit that they had strong moral and political grounds for their misgivings. Whom did the radicals or liberals represent? Until the early twentieth century, for the most part, the oppositionists represented only themselves, not the popular masses. And only when public opinion succeeded in enticing the peasants and workers into rebellion did the autocracy make serious concessions, leading to the appearance of a constitution and parliament in 1906.

The evolution of the Russian state from the seventeenth to the twentieth centuries was primarily in response to changes in Russia itself. First, the principle of legality gradually penetrated state administration, as this was absolutely necessary for the effective operation of the state apparatus; with the expansion of state administration, personal control by the sovereign had become impossible. Second, state authority could be reinforced and affirmed only if it recognized the foundations of law, since only in this case would its citizens develop respect for legality: If the government observed the law, so would its citizens.[146] This was perfectly clear, above all, to the monarchs themselves. In the words of Alexander I (whose sentiments were shared by other emperors):

> The law must be the same for everyone. As soon as I permit myself to violate the laws, who will deem it their duty to observe them? Even if I could, I would not wish to be above the law, for I do not recognize on earth justice that does not emanate from law; on the contrary, I feel myself obliged to be the first to see that the law is implemented, even in those cases where others could be more lenient, but I can only be just.[147]

Nicholas I shared this view entirely, as did later emperors, including Nicholas II.

Hence, a *Rechtsstaat* developed in Russia along several paths simultaneously: subordinating supreme authority to the law by imposing limits on itself, at the same time as it left the monarch's authority untrammeled; limiting the authority of imperial institutions and officials by means of mutual competition for influence, administrative law, administrative justice, procuracy, and organs of local and estate self-government; separating legislative, executive, and judicial powers among different bodies; and conferring group and individual rights on the populace—first granting various classes estate rights and institutions (the right of estate and public self-government), and eventually conferring civil rights on the entire population. The first three processes represented action by the autocracy to satisfy its own internal needs, since public opinion primarily aimed to participate in administration, not to subordinate the autocracy and its administration to the laws that autocracy itself had promulgated. Here the gains were constant and significant even before 1905. The fourth process was due to the pressure of public opinion; its gains were significant from the 1860s on, especially between 1905 and 1917.

In the seventeenth century the authority of the sovereign was limited by the assemblies of the land, the Boyar Duma, the patriarch, and church councils, and also by custom, tradition, and law. When in the early eighteenth century Peter the Great eliminated the role of these public institutions and curtailed that of tradition and custom, he was keenly aware that to avoid chaos in state administration, he must place himself and the activity of all institutions within the framework of the law—or more precisely, of administrative law. This was the source of his feverish legislative activity aimed at giving every imperial institution instructions, guidelines, and regulations and at placing them under the control of the procuracy that had been established.[148] One finds the same issue in the work of

Nicholas I. In strengthening his own personal power, he simultaneously increased his control over imperial institutions by subordinating their activity to administrative law and administrative justice. It was precisely during the reign of Nicholas I that the *Complete Collection of Laws* and the *Digest of Laws* were prepared; the principle of placing autocracy under the law was not merely proclaimed (as in the reigns of Catherine II and Alexander I) but was also embodied in existing legislation. Under Nicholas I an enormous effort was made to create a firm legal grounding for the life and conditions of state peasants; such was the purpose of the Ministry of State Domains, which prepared legislation for state villages and scores of instructions on every facet of life. This was not simply an excess of bureaucracy but an attempt to combat shortcomings with the assistance of instructions and laws. It was a manifestation of what was perhaps a rather naive belief in the creative power of written law.

As the Russian state developed in the direction of a state based on the rule of law, Russian society was gradually transformed from an object of state rule into an active agent of governance. In other words, Russians were changing from "subjects" into "citizens." This process was strongly helped by the fact that from the seventeenth to the twentieth centuries, the state was forced to share its power with society and to admit the existence of a rather strong municipal self-government, because it never had the apparatus to govern by itself.

Progress along the long and difficult road toward creation of a *Rechtsstaat* halted in February 1917 and was stopped entirely in October. The people overthrew democracy, destroyed the foundations of a state based on the rule of law, and allowed the Bolsheviks who had seized power to establish a dictatorship and to deal summarily with their political opponents. How can these developments be explained? Clarification can be found in the fact that the ideas of democracy and the *Rechtsstaat* had become a paradigm for educated society but had not yet reached the populace. The relationship of different classes of Russian society to the Constituent Assembly from the end of 1917 to the beginning of 1918 illustrates this point very well. The peasants and workers, who for the most part at all points in history remained on the sidelines of state and political activity, modeled the future Constituent Assembly on the pattern of their rural communal gathering. They thought that once the Constituent Assembly convened, it would solve all existing problems to the people's general satisfaction, peacefully and for the long term if not for all time. They hoped that these changes would bring about a new, happier life. The real work of a parliament, with the struggle between different interests and the necessity for compromise between parties, was not understood and was alien to the people. The Constituent Assembly seemed to the people to be a simple but effective means of exiting the present crisis.

This conception of the Constituent Assembly is reminiscent of how people in the sixteenth and seventeenth centuries viewed the assemblies of the land *(zemskie sobory)* in times of anarchy, sedition, and social conflict. However, by twentieth-century standards of parliamentarism, this view was naive, bearing witness to the fact that although twentieth-century Russia had moved far ahead of the Russia of the seventeenth century, the mentality of the peasantry and of a significant part of the workers remained archaic. The populace's naive vision of parliamentarism reduced the Constituent Assembly in their conceptions and hopes to absolute power, likening its functioning to that of autocracy. It is possible to say that the idea of the Constituent Assembly forced out the idea of autocracy but preserved all the characteristics of autocracy—universality, comprehensiveness, absolutism, and omnipotence. Not without reason did the popular title for the Constituent Assembly become "Master of the Whole Land," which is clearly in the same vein as "Autocrat of All Russia." As the people had believed not long before that the monarch could instantaneously make all his citizens happy, they now transferred this faith to the Constituent Assembly. Consequently, we cannot avoid considering the preservation of the traditional mentality and the traditional political paradigm.

Inasmuch as the Constituent Assembly occupied in the popular mind-set the place of supreme autocratic power, to which the people had previously addressed their petitions and complaints, it is only natural to expect that the people would not miss the opportunity to appeal to the new supreme power with many solicitations. In fact, it was not long before a stream of petitions gushed forth. From October to December 1917, the Constituent Assembly received thousands of solicitations and requests to solve local problems, such as to prohibit home-brewing of vodka, to correct a mistake in the calculation of a pension, to wage a campaign against speculation, to redivide or to annex land, and so on.[149]

These petitions differ greatly from the 242 peasant mandates *(nakazy)* received by the Constituent Assembly, which became the main source for historians' judgments about the requests of the peasants and about their political conceptions. How can these differences be explained? In the mandates, the peasants' conception of political problems is not clearly expressed. What is instead plain is how the parties with whom the peasants were in sympathy understood the issues. This is evident because, first of all, the mandates bear an obvious party slant. At that time, because of their inexperience in political contests, the peasants did not have and could not have possessed such clarity of expression. Second, the mandates were written in turns of phrase uncharacteristic of peasant locutions and out of keeping with the typical peasant's level of education. The peasantry supported the basic aspirations of the left socialist parties; hence the peasants accepted mandates and resolutions which were written by literate agitators, without inquiring more deeply into the party programs.

Educated society presents a different picture. It understood very well that the Constituent Assembly must work as a parliament with a constitutive function, and that after the new constitution was adopted and the form of the new state system was decided, a long and laborious task still would lie ahead: Many questions about the structure of Russia's political life, which at that moment was in chaos, would yet await resolution. The political parties of Russia were prepared to tackle these questions, and were it not for the tyranny of the Bolsheviks, they might have resolved them all.

However, it would be incorrect to state that the Bolshevik dictatorship alone was responsible for the catastrophe of Russian parliamentarism. After the Constituent Assembly was dissolved, the people en masse kept silent. The opponents of Bolshevism, who had accounted for 75 percent of the vote in the elections to the Constituent Assembly, were unsuccessful in organizing any type of mass protest against the dissolution of the Assembly—whether in Petrograd or other cities, or in the provinces.[150] Why? It is unlikely that this popular inaction was due to fear, because before 5 January 1918, to all appearances there was no great fear of the new power, at least in the provinces. The new regime had been in existence for only about two months and held firm support only in the capitals and in the largest cities. The main reasons for the people's inertia were their indifference to the fate of the Russian parliament; their incomprehension of the necessity of the parliament's existence as a guarantee against a return to the old regime in a new form; their complete lack of interest in political organization; and their unfamiliarity with west European countries' experiences with democracy. The revolutionaries' decrees on peace, land, and worker control satisfied the basic aims of soldiers, peasants, and workers. Hence, from the point of view of the masses, the Second Congress of Soviets, having accepted these decrees, had fulfilled the function of the Constituent Assembly and rendered it unnecessary. Not having even the slightest understanding of constitutional and institutional guarantees of the irreversibility of the political process, the people concerned themselves with the organization of their way of life—that is, the expropriation of private land, factories and plants, estates, and palaces.

The peasants showed an interest only in local authority with which they came into direct contact. Peasants were not interested in administrative organs beyond the district level, because they considered the higher powers to have origins alien to the peasants. In the words of one observer:

Democratic rights and constitutional guarantees on a national scale have no meaning for peasants. Let power be organized by whomever, any which way, as long as it does not touch the material interests of the peasantry too painfully. Ordinary peasants have no inclination to participate in the actual construction of power. If they did harbor any inclinations one way or the other, it would be of the sort that encourage political passivity.[151]

Such were the political views of the peasantry even in the early 1920s, by which time one would expect that they should have learned a lesson or two from the Revolution and from war communism.

As concerns the workers, they were few in number, and the majority supported the Bolsheviks at the end of 1917 and the beginning of 1918. They believed that the soviets were the highest form of democracy and that the Constituent Assembly was a remnant of the old landowner-bourgeois political structure.

The educated part of Russian society, devoted to the ideas of Western liberalism, attempted to protest, but its voice was too weak to change anything.[152]

Notes

1. For a review of American literature on the development of the Russian state, see Ronald G. Suny, "Rehabilitating Tsarism: The Imperial Russian State and Its Historians; A Review Article," *Comparative Studies in Society and History*, vol. 31, no. 1 (January 1989). See also the interesting discussion (with contributions by Edward Keenan, Robert Crummey, Richard Hellie, Robert Daniels, and Richard Wortman) in *Russian Review*, vol. 45, no. 2 (April 1986), pp. 115–208; vol. 46, no. 2 (April 1987), pp. 157–210.

2. This view of the state is found in the so-called realist school of state thought, whose adherents include several Russian juridical scholars of the late nineteenth and early twentieth centuries: N. M. Korkunov, *Russkoe gosudarstvennoe pravo* (St. Petersburg, 1908), tom 1, pp. 38–51; N. I. Lazarevskii, *Otvetstvennost' za ubytki, prichinennye dolzhnostnym litsam* (St. Petersburg, 1905), pp. 234, 289–293. See also V. V. Mshvenieradze, *Vlast': Ocherki sovremennoi politicheskoi filosofii Zapada* (Moscow, 1989), pp. 65–80.

3. Max Weber, *The Theory of Social and Economic Organization* (London, 1947), p. 318; idem, *Staatssoziologie* (Berlin, 1964), pp. 99–105.

4. L. V. Cherepnin, *Zemskie sobory russkogo gosudarstva v XVI–XVII vv.* (Moscow, 1978), pp. 60–61.

5. Michael Cherniavsky, *Tsar and People: Studies in Russian Myths* (New Haven, 1961), pp. 1–100; E. V. Barsov, "Drevnerusskie pamiatniki, posviashchennye venchaniiu tsarei na tsarstvo, v sviazi s grecheskimi ikh originalami, i s istoricheskim ocherkom chinov tsarskogo venchaniia, v sviazi s razvitiem idei tsaria na Rusi," in *Chteniia v Obshchestve istorii i drevnostei rossiiskikh*, kniga 1 (1883), pp. i–xxxv; V. M. Zhivov and B. A. Uspenskii, "Tsar' i Bog: Semioticheskie aspekty," in B. A. Uspenskii, *Iazyki kul'tury i problemy perevodimosti* (Moscow,

1994), pp. 47–71; A. I. Filiushkin, "Terminy 'tsar" i 'tsarstvo' na Rusi," *Voprosy istorii*, no. 8 (1997), pp. 144–148.

6. R. B. Miuller and L. V. Cherepnin, *Sudebniki XV–XVI vv.* (Moscow, 1951), p. 176.

7. A. G. Man'kov, ed., *Sobornoe ulozhenie 1649 goda: Tekst, kommentarii* (Leningrad, 1980), p. 17; see also pp. 69, 90.

8. A. G. Man'kov, *Ulozhenie 1649 goda: Kodeks feodal'nogo prava Rossii* (Leningrad, 1980), pp. 163–165.

9. V. O. Kliuchevskii, *Boiarskaia duma drevnei Rusi* (St. Petersburg, 1918), p. 239.

10. In the opinion of Edward Keenan, the Boyar Duma played such a significant role in administration that the Russian state in Muscovy can best be characterized as an oligarchy resting on four basic principles: tradition and informality, oligarchic limitations on the monarch's power, a ruling structure based on kin and clan, and confidentiality and secrecy of administration. This traditional Russian state remained essentially unchanged until 1917, except that the clan principle of elite formation gave way to a bureaucratic system. See Edward L. Keenan, "Muscovite Political Folkways," *Russian Review*, vol. 45, no. 2 (1986), pp. 115–181.

11. Kliuchevskii, *Boiarskaia duma*, p. 520.

12. N. I. Lazarevskii, *Lektsii po russkomu gosudarstvennomu pravu* (St. Petersburg, 1910), tom 2, pp. 79–82.

13. M. F. Vladimirskii-Budanov, *Obzor istorii russkogo prava* (Kiev and St. Petersburg, 1900), pp. 179–181.

14. A. I. Markevich, *Istoriia mestnichestva v Moskovskom gosudarstve XV–XVI vv.* (Odessa, 1888); N. P. Pavlov-Sil'vanskii, *Gosudarevy sluzhilye liudi: Proiskhozhdenie russkogo dvorianstva* (St. Petersburg, 1898), pp. 79–92, 145–165; Iu. M. Eskin, *Mestnichestvo v Rossii XVI–XVII vv.: Khronologicheskii reestr* (Moscow, 1994).

15. *Slovar' russkogo iazyka XI–XVII vv.* (Moscow, 1976), tom 3, p. 181.

16. Cherepnin, *Zemskie sobory*, pp. 382–385; V. N. Sergeevich, *Lektsii i issledovaniia po istorii russkogo prava* (St. Petersburg, 1883), pp. 609, 702, 733–734, 749; V. N. Latkin, *Zemskie sobory Drevnei Rusi, ikh istoriia i organizatsiia sravnitel'no s zapadoevropeiskimi predstavitel'nymi uchrezhdeniiami: Istoriko-iuridicheskoe issledovanie* (St. Petersburg, 1885), pp. 282–286. For a historiography of this subject, see S. L. Avaliani, *Zemskie sobory: Literaturnaia istoriia zemskikh soborov* (Odessa, 1916); Cherepnin, *Zemskie sobory*, p. 554.

17. G. Kotoshikhin, *O Rossii v tsarstvovanie Alekseia Mikhailovicha* (St. Petersburg, 1840), pp. 1–17.

18. Cherepnin, *Zemskie sobory*, pp. 60–62; N. P. Pavlov-Sil'vanskii, *Feodalizm v Drevnei Rusi* (Moscow, 1923), pp. 164–175.

19. V. M. Kabuzan, *Izmeneniia v razmeshchenii naseleniia Rossii v XVIII–pervoi polovine XIX v.* (Moscow, 1971), pp. 64–65.

20. Lazarevskii, *Lektsii*, tom 1, pp. 78–79.

21. N. Markevich, *Istoriia Malorossii* (Moscow, 1842), tom 4, no. 39, p. 175.

22. Man'kov, ed., *Sobornoe ulozhenie 1649 g.*; Man'kov, *Ulozhenie 1649 goda*.

23. Kotoshikhin, *O Rossii*, pp. 12, 21.

24. M. A. D'iakonov, *Ocherki obshchestvennogo i gosudarstvennogo stroia Drevnei Rusi* (St. Petersburg, 1912), pp. 7–15, 196–200, 399–400.

25. Kotoshikhin, *O Rossii*, p. 22.

26. Iu. A. Limonov, ed., *Rossiia XV–XVII vv. glazami inostrantsev* (Leningrad, 1986), p. 53.

27. Philip Longworth, *Alexis: Tsar of All the Russians* (New York, 1984); *Sobranie pisem tsaria Alekseia Mikhailovicha* (Moscow, 1856), pp. 173, 180, 185, 230, 232.

28. I. P. Eremin, "Simeon Polotskii: Poet i dramaturg," in S. Polotskii, *Izbrannye sochineniia* (Moscow and Leningrad, 1953), pp. 245–246.

29. A. S. Lappo-Danilevskii, *Istoriia russkoi obshchestvennoi mysli i kul'tury XVII–XVIII vv.* (Moscow, 1990), pp. 26–42; A. V. Gadlo, "Bytovoi uklad zhizni pervykh Romanovykh i russkaia narodnaia kul'tura," in I. Ia. Froianov, ed., *Dom Romanov v istorii Rossii* (St. Petersburg, 1995), pp. 109–123; A. K. Leont'ev, "Gosudarstvennyi stroi," in A. V. Artsikhovskii, *Ocherki russkoi kul'tury XVII veka* (Moscow, 1979), chast' 1, pp. 297–322.

30. Marc Raeff, *Understanding Imperial Russia: State and Society in the Old Regime* (New York, 1984), p. 14; *Dnevnik Mariny Mnishek* (St. Petersburg, 1995), pp. 61–62; F. V. Taranovskii, *Entsiklopediia prava* (Berlin, 1923), pp. 357–358; idem, "Sobornoe izbranie i vlast' velikogo gosudaria v XVII stoletii," *Zhurnal Ministerstva iustitsii*, no. 5 (May 1913), pp. 1–34.

31. Kotoshikhin, *O Rossii*, p. 30.

32. H.-J. Torke, "Tak nazyvaemye zemskie sobory v Rossii," *Voprosy istorii*, 1991, no. 11 (1991).

33. V. E. Val'denberg, *Drevnerusskie ucheniia o predelakh tsarskoi vlasti: Ocherki russkoi politicheskoi literatury ot Vladimira Sviatogo do kontsa XVII veka* (Petrograd, 1916), p. 438.

34. A. G. Man'kov, ed., *Rossiiskoe zakonodatel'stvo X–XX vekov*, tom 3, *Akty zemskikh soborov* (Moscow, 1985), pp. 77–78.

35. D'iakonov, *Ocherki obshchestvennogo i gosudarstvennogo stroia*, p. 392.

36. Marc Szeftel, *Russian Institutions and Culture up to Peter the Great* (London, 1975); Pavlov-Sil'vanskii, *Feodalizm v Drevnei Rusi*, pp. 155–184.

37. In the opinion of Richard Pipes, the Russian state during the entire period of Muscovy and the Russian empire (until 1881) was essentially "patrimonial." The sovereign was the supreme "proprietor"; he alone held total power. This political system did not allow for any formal limits on the power of the sovereign; laws were nonexistent, personal freedom was absent, and the state had essentially subsumed society under its control. Richard Pipes, *Russia Under the Old Regime* (New York, 1974), pp. 19–24.

38. Raeff, *Understanding Imperial Russia*, pp. 45–50.

39. F. Prokopovich, "Slovo o vlasti I chesti tsarskoi," in F. Prokopovich, *Sochineniia* (Moscow, 1961), pp. 76–93; Cynthia Whittaker, "The Reforming Tsar: The Redefinition of Autocratic Duty in Eighteenth-Century Russia," *Slavic Review*, vol. 51, no. 1 (Spring 1992), pp. 79–98.

40. *Polnoe sobranie zakonov Rossiiskoi imperii*, pervoe sobranie (hereafter, *PSZ 1*), tom 4, no. 2329 (St. Petersburg).

41. *PSZ 1*, tom 5, no. 3006 (St. Petersburg).

42. *PSZ 1*, tom 6, no. 3718 (St. Petersburg), chast' 1, punkt 2.

43. *PSZ 1*, tom 8, no. 5509 (St. Petersburg).

44. *PSZ 1*, tom 24, no. 17906 (St. Petersburg), paragraf 71.

45. V. N. Latkin, *Uchebnik istorii russkogo prava perioda imperii (XVIII i XIX stoletiia)* (St. Petersburg, 1909), pp. 270–278; O. A. Omel'chenko, *"Zakonnaia monarkhiia" Ekateriny II: Prosveshchennyi absoliutizm v Rossii* (Moscow, 1993), p. 70; Richard S. Wortman, *Scenarios of Power: Myth and Ceremony in Russian Monarchy*, vol. 1, *From Peter the Great to the Death of Nicholas I* (Princeton, 1995).

46. Kabuzan, *Izmeneniia v razmeshchenii naseleniia Rossii*, p. 81.

47. Brenda Meehan-Waters, *Autocracy and Aristocracy: The Russian Service Elite of 1730* (New Brunswick, 1982), pp. 131–160. For an overview of attempts to limit autocracy before 1861, see B. B. Glinskii, *Bor'ba za konstitutsiiu, 1612–1861 gg.: Istoricheskie ocherki* (St. Petersburg, 1908).

48. P. V. Verkhovskii, *Uchrezhdenie Dukhovnoi kollegii i Dukhovnyi reglament: K voprosu ob otnoshenii tserkvi i gosudarstva v Rossii (Issledovanie v oblasti istorii russkogo tserkovnogo prava)* (Rostov-on-Don, 1916), tom 1, pp. 684–686; Latkin, *Uchebnik istorii russkogo prava*, p. 278.

49. Filaret (V. M. Drozdov), Khristianskoe uchenie o tsarskoi vlasti i ob obiazannostiakh vernopoddannykh (Moscow, 1891); idem, *Gosudarstvennoe uchenie Filareta, mitropolita Moskovskogo* (Moscow, 1881); idem, *Monarkhicheskoe uchenie Filareta, mitropolita Moskovskogo* (Moscow, 1907); idem, *Prostrannyi khristianskii katekhizis pravoslavnoi katolicheskoi tserkvi, rassmotrennyi i odobrennyi Sviateishim Pravitel'stvuiushchim Sinodom i izdannyi dlia prepodavaniia v uchilishchakh i dlia upotrebleniia vsekh pravoslavnykh khristian*, 1-e izd. (Moscow, 1829); 72-e izd. (St. Petersburg, 1903). See also V. V. Nazarevskii, *Gosudarstvennoe uchenie Filareta, mitropolita moskovskogo* (Moscow, 1888).

50. *PSZ 1*, tom 7, no. 4345 (St. Petersburg), and tom 6, no. 3781.

51. N. M. Karamzin, *Zapiska o drevnei i novoi Rossii v ee politicheskom i grazhdanskom otnosheniiakh* (Moscow, 1991), p. 102; A. A. Mosolov, *Pri dvore poslednego imperatora: Zapiski nachal'nika kantseliarii ministra dvora* (St. Petersburg, 1992), p. 69; Richard Wortman, "Images of Rule and Problems of Gender in the Upbringing of Paul I and Alexander I," in E. Mendelsohn and M. S. Shatz, eds., *Imperial Russia, 1700–1917* (DeKalb, 1988), pp. 58–75; Andrew M. Verner, *The Crisis of Russian Autocracy: Nicholas II and the 1905 Revolution* (Princeton, 1990), pp. 7–44.

52. Elise K. Wirtschafter, "The Ideal of Paternalism in the Prereform Army," in Mendelsohn and Shatz, eds., *Imperial Russia*, pp. 95–114.

53. N. Khlebnikov, *O vliianii obshchestva na organizatsiiu gosudarstva v tsarskii period russkoi istorii* (St. Petersburg, 1869), pp. 355–356.

54. I. Iu. Airapetian, *Feodal'naia aristokratiia v period stanovleniia absoliutizma v Rossii* (Moscow, 1988), p. 21; Kliuchevskii, *Boiarskaia duma*, pp. 520–526; Meehan-Waters, *Autocracy and Aristocracy*, pp. 161–167.

55. E. Karnovich, *Russkie chinovniki v byloe i nastoiashchee vremia* (St. Petersburg, 1897), pp. 36–37.

56. John P. LeDonne, *Absolutism and the Ruling Class: The Formation of the Russian Political Order, 1700–1825* (New York and Oxford, 1991), pp. viii–ix,

308–309; A. Kahan, "The Costs of 'Westernization' in Russia: The Gentry and the Economy in the Eighteenth Century," in Michael Cherniavsky, ed., *The Structure of Russian History: Interpretive Essays* (New York, 1970), pp. 244–245.

57. David L. Ransel, "Character and Style of Patron-Client Relations in Russia," in A. Maczak, ed., *Klientelsystem im Europa der frühen Neuzeit* (Munich, 1988), pp. 19–21, 65, 75, 87, 94, 211–231; LeDonne, *Absolutism and the Ruling Class,* pp. 19–21, 65, 75, 87, 94.

58. In the opinion of LeDonne, the hereditary nobility was the "ruling class" in the eighteenth century and the first half of the nineteenth century; he describes the Russian state itself as a "command structure" controlled by the nobility as the ruling class. See John LeDonne, *Politics and Administration in the Age of Absolutism, 1762–1796* (Princeton, 1984), pp. 343–344; idem, *Absolutism and the Ruling Class,* pp. viii–ix, 308–309. Paul Duke similarly identifies the nobility as the ruling class: See his *Catherine the Great and the Russian Nobility: A Study Based on the Materials of the Legislative Commission of 1767* (New York, 1967), pp. 144, 155–156, 165; and idem, *The Making of Russian Absolutism, 1613–1801* (London and New York, 1990), pp. 201–220.

59. A. I. Markevich, *Istoriia mestnichestva,* p. 572.

60. Carol S. Leonard, *Reform and Regicide: The Reign of Peter III of Russia* (Bloomington, Ill., 1992); see also A. S. Myl'nikov, *Legenda o russkom printse* (Leningrad, 1987), pp. 110–122.

61. David L. Ransel, "Bureaucracy and Patronage: An Eighteenth-Century Russian Letter-Writer," in Frederic C. Jaher, ed., *The Rich, the Well-born, and the Powerful: Elites and Upper Classes in History* (Urbana, 1973), p. 164.

62. N. P. Eroshkin, *Krepostnicheskoe samoderzhavie i ego politicheskie instituty* (Moscow, 1981), p. 27.

63. Isabel de Madariaga, *Russia in the Age of Catherine the Great* (New Haven, 1981), pp. 277–301, 585–586; LeDonne, *Absolutism and the Ruling Class,* pp. 3–9, 297–309; A. B. Kamenskii, *"Pod sen'iu Ekateriny . . . "* (St. Petersburg, 1992), pp. 296–309.

64. Robert E. Jones, *The Emancipation of the Russian Nobility, 1762–1785* (Princeton, 1973), pp. 180–187, 196–209, 293–299.

65. Vladimirskii-Budanov, *Obzor istorii,* p. 279; LeDonne, *Ruling Russia,* p. 279; B. I. Syromiatnikov, *"Reguliarnoe" gosudarstvo Petra Velikogo i ego ideologiia* (Moscow, 1943); Marc Raeff, *The Well-Ordered Police State: Social and Institutional Change Through Law in the Germanies and Russia, 1600–1800* (London and New Haven, 1983); B. A. Anan'ich, ed., *Vlast' i reformy: Ot samoderzhavnoi k sovetskoi Rossii* (St. Petersburg, 1996), p. 146.

66. Derek B. Heater, *Order and Rebellion: A History of Europe in the Eighteenth Century* (London, 1964), p. 226.

67. V. N. Sergeevich, *Lektsii i issledovaniia po istorii russkogo prava* (St. Petersburg, 1883), pp. 57–59.

68. Marc Raeff, "Seventeenth-Century Europe in Eighteenth-Century Russia," *Slavic Review,* vol. 41, no. 4 (Winter 1982), p. 226.

69. De Madariaga, *Russia in the Age of Catherine the Great,* pp. 582–584; idem, "Sisters Under the Skin," *Slavic Review,* vol. 41, no. 4 (Winter 1982), pp. 624–628; Vladimirskii-Budanov, *Obzor istorii,* p. 279.

70. Pipes, *Russia Under the Old Regime*, p. xxi; Anan'ich, *Vlast' i reformy*, p. 146; Omel'chenko, *"Zakonnaia monarkhiia*," p. 101.

71. It should be noted that the Senate had exercised considerably more authority earlier, during Peter the Great's absences from the capital, and throughout the reign of Elizabeth. But that role was exceptional and did not survive in later reigns. See Latkin, *Uchebnik istorii russkogo prava*, p. 4.

72. Ibid., pp. 49, 58.

73. Vladimirskii-Budanov, *Obzor istorii*, pp. 281–288.

74. M. D. Chulkov, *Slovar' iuridicheskii ili svod rossiiskikh uzakonenii, vremennykh uchrezhdenii, suda i raspravy* (Moscow, 1792–1796); F. Pravikov, *Pamiatnik iz zakonov, rukovodstvuiushchego k poznaniiu prikaznogo obriada, sobrannogo po azbuchnomu poriadku* (Vladimir, 1798–1827); L. Maksimovich, *Ukazatel' rossiiskikh zakonov, vremennykh uchrezhdenii, suda i raspravy* (Moscow, 1803–1812); S. Khapylev, *Sistematicheskoe sobranie rossiiskikh zakonov s prisovokupleniem pravil i primerov iz luchshikh zakonouchitelei* (St. Petersburg, 1817–1819); M. A. Dmitriev, *Glavy iz vospominanii moei zhizni* (Moscow, 1998), p. 288.

75. Iu. V. Got'e, "Sledstvennye komissii po zloupotrebleniiam oblastnykh vlastei v XVIII veke," in *Sbornik statei, posviashchennykh V. O. Kliuchevskomu* (Moscow, 1909), pp. 103–152; idem, "Iz istorii oblastnogo upravleniia v XVIII v.," in *Sbornik statei v chest' D. A. Korsakova* (Kazan, 1913), pp. 194–201; S. M. Kazantsev, *Istoriia tsarskoi prokuratury* (St. Petersburg, 1993), pp. 12–54; V. Leshkov, "Cherty upravleniia v Rossii po ukazam XVIII veka, 1725–1762," *Russkii vestnik*, tom 46 (1863), pp. 168–190; A. Liutsh, "Russkii absoliutizm XVIII veka," in A. Liutsh, V. Zommer, and A. Lipovskii, eds., *Itogi XVIII veka v Rossii: Vvedenie v russkuiu istoriiu XIX veka* (Moscow, 1910), pp. 250–254.

76. A. S. Lappo-Danilevskii, *Ocherk vnutrennei politiki imperatritsy Ekateriny II* (St. Petersburg, 1898), p. 62.

77. Korkunov, *Russkoe gosudarstvennoe pravo*, tom 1, pp. 161–171; A. N. Makarov, "Uchenie ob osnovnykh zakonakh v russkoi iuridicheskoi literature XVIII i pervoi treti XIX v.," in *Sbornik statei, posviashchennykh S. F. Platonovu* (Petrograd, 1922), pp. 370–381; B. E. Nol'de, "Zakony osnovnye v russkom prave," *Trudy Iuridicheskogo obshchestva pri St. Peterburgskom universitete*, tom 7 (1913), pp. 4–15.

78. L. A. Chernaia, "Ot idei 'sluzheniia gosudariu' k idee 'sluzheniia otechestvu' v russkoi obshchestvennoi mysli vtoroi poloviny XVIII–nachala XVIII v.," in A. L. Andreev and K. Kh. Delokarov, eds., *Obshchestvennaia mysl': Issledovaniia i publikatsii* (Moscow, 1989), vyp. 1, pp. 28–42; Zhivov and Uspenskii, *Tsar' i Bog*, pp. 47–153.

79. N. I. Pavlenko, *Petr I* (Moscow, 1975), p. 264.

80. A. S. Pavlov-Sil'vanskii, "Idea gosudarstva i glavneishie momenty ee razvitiia v Rossii so vremen smuty do epokhi preobrazovanii," *Golos minuvshego*, no. 12 (1914), pp. 5, 38.

81. P. N. Miliukov, *Gosudarstvennoe khoziaistvo Rossii v pervoi chetverti XVIII stoletiia i reforma Petra Velikogo* (St. Petersburg, 1905), p. 25.

82. *PSZ 1*, tom 6, p. 444.

83. P. N. Danevskii, *Istoriia obrazovaniia Gosudarstvennogo soveta v Rossii* (St. Petersburg, 1859), p. 82; Korkunov, *Russkoe gosudarstvennoe pravo*, tom 2, pp. 12–20.

84. See the discussion in Latkin, *Uchebnik istorii russkogo prava*, pp. 10–12.

85. N. M. Karamzin, *Zapiska o drevnei i novoi Rossii v ee politicheskom i grazhdanskom otnosheniiakh* (St. Petersburg, 1991), p. 60.

86. Lazarevskii, *Lektsii*, pp. 449–457, 471; idem, "Pravitel'stvuiushchii Senat kak organ nadzora," *Pravo*, no. 15 (1901), pp. 765–776.

87. "Spisok gubernii i gorodov, v kotorye posylalis' revizuiushchie senatory," in *Istoriia Pravitel'stvuiushchego Senata* (St. Petersburg, 1912), tom 4, pp. 513–516.

88. *Istoriia Pravitel'stvuiushchego Senata*, tom 2, pp. 596–600.

89. E. S. Paina, "Senatorskie revizii i ikh arkhivnye materialy," in I. N. Firsov, ed., *Nekotorye voprosy izucheniia istoricheskikh dokumentov XIX–nachala XX vekov* (Leningrad, 1967), pp. 162–164.

90. S. A. Korf, *Administrativnaia iustitsiia v Rossii* (St. Petersburg, 1910), tom 1; Korkunov, *Russkoe gosudarstvennoe pravo*, tom 2, pp. 378–388; Paina, "Senatorskie revizii," pp. 147–175.

91. I. Blinov, *Gubernatory: Istoriko-iuridicheskii ocherk* (St. Petersburg, 1905), pp. 242–247; idem, "Istoricheskie materialy, izvlechennye iz Senatskogo arkhiva: Senatorskie revizii," *Zhurnal Ministerstva iustitsii*, nos. 2, 4, 6, 7, 10 (1913); N. M. Druzhinin, "Senatorskie revizii 1860–1870-kh godov (K voprosu o realizatsii reformy 1861 g.)," *Istoricheskie zapiski*, tom 79 (1966), pp. 139–176.

92. For details on the senatorial inspections, see the pertinent sections in *Istoriia Pravitel'stvuiushchego Senata*, toma 2–4.

93. *PSZ 1*, tom 6, no. 3534, pp. 141–160; tom 31, no. 24307 (St. Petersburg), pp. 687–711.

94. I. S. Bliokh, *Finansy Rossii XIX stoletiia* (St. Petersburg, 1882), tom 2, p. 78.

95. S. P. Pokrovskii, *Ministerskaia vlast' v Rossii* (Yaroslavl, 1906), pp. 329–332; Latkin, *Uchebnik istorii russkogo prava*, pp. 356–366.

96. M. M. Safonov, *Problema reform v pravitel'stvennoi politike Rossii na rubezhe XVIII i XIX vv.* (Leningrad, 1988), pp. 238–239.

97. Gary Hamburg has described the Russian state as "a consultative bureaucratic system." See his *Politics of the Russian Nobility, 1861–1905* (New Brunswick, 1984), pp. 13–15, 67–68.

98. *Svod zakonov Rossiiskoi imperii* (St. Petersburg, 1832), tom 1, chast' 1, stat'i 1, 47.

99. A. D. Gradovskii, Nachala russkogo gosudarstvennogo prava (St. Petersburg, 1876), tom 1, p. 3; Korkunov, Russkoe gosudarstvennoe pravo, p. 158; P. E. Kazanskii, *Vlast' vserossiiskogo imperatora: Ocherki deistvuiushchego russkogo prava* (Odessa, 1913), pp. 645–658.

100. A. de Custine, *Nikolaevskaia Rossiia: Rossiia v 1839 g.* (Moscow, 1990), p. 72.

101. "Graf A. A. Benkendorf o Rossii v 1827–1830 gg.: Ezhegodnye otchety III otdeleniia i korpusa zhandarmov," *Krasnyi arkhiv*, 1929, tom 37, p. 153.

102. *Opis' del Arkhiva Gosudarstvennogo soveta*, tom 16, *Dela Gosudarstvennogo soveta i Gosudarstvennoi kantseliarii* (St. Petersburg, 1912), pp. 77–78.

103. A. A. Kizevetter, "Imperator Nikolai I kak konstitutsionnyi monarkh," in *Istoricheskie ocherki,* idem (Moscow, 1912), pp. 402–418.

104. A. A. Kornilov, *Istoriia Rossii XIX veka* (Moscow, 1912), tom 2, pp. 112–113.

105. Quoted from I. Trotskii, *III-e otdelenie pri Nikolae I* (Leningrad, 1990), p. 29.

106. Nicholas V. Riasanovsky, *Nicholas I and Official Nationality in Russia, 1825–1855* (Berkeley, 1959), p. 32; A. L. Zorin, "Ideologiia samoderzhaviia, pravoslaviia i narodnosti, i ee nemetskie istochniki," in E. L. Rudnitskaia, ed., *V razdum'iakh o Rossii (XIX v.)* (Moscow, 1996), pp. 105–128.

107. S. S. Uvarov, *Desiatiletie Ministerstva narodnogo prosveshcheniia, 1833–1843* (St. Petersburg, 1864), pp. 3–4; Iu. B. Solov'ev, "Samoderzhavie v osade: Vnesoslovnaia universal'naia ideologiia kak otvet na vyzov epokhi (1825–1855 gg.)," in *Sosloviia i gosudarstvennaia vlast' v Rossii: XV–seredina XIX v.: Chteniia pamiati L. V. Cherepnina* (Moscow, 1994), chast' 2, pp. 113–126.

108. S. F. Starr, *Decentralization and Self-Government in Russia, 1830–1870* (Princeton, 1972), pp. 352–354.

109. A. I. Koniaev, *Finansovyi kontrol' v dorevoliutsionnoi Rossii* (Moscow, 1959), p. 78.

110. Korkunov, *Russkoe gosudarstvennoe pravo,* tom 1, pp. 169–171; T. Taranovskii, "Sudebnaia reforma i razvitie politicheskoi kul'tury tsarskoi Rossii," in Larisa G. Zakharova, John Bushnell, and Ben Eklof, eds., *Velikie reformy v Rossii, 1856–1874* (Moscow, 1992), pp. 301–317.

111. Korkunov, *Russkoe gosudarstvennoe pravo,* tom 2, pp. 388–393.

112. Calculated from V. A. Nardova, *Gorodskoe samoupravlenie v Rossii v 60-kh–nachale 90-kh godov XIX v.* (Leningrad, 1984), pp. 61–63, 80–81.

113. *Sbornik svedenii po Rossii 1890 goda* (St. Petersburg, 1890), pp. 48–51.

114. Thomas C. Owen, *Capitalism and Politics in Russia: A Social History of the Moscow Merchants, 1855–1905* (New York, 1981); A. J. Rieber, *Merchants and Entrepreneurs in Imperial Russia* (Chapel Hill, 1982); Jo Ann A. Ruckman, *The Moscow Business Elite: A Social and Cultural Portrait of Two Generations, 1840–1905* (DeKalb, 1984); I. F. Gindin, *Gosudarstvennyi bank i ekonomicheskaia politika tsarskogo pravitel'stva* (1861–1892 gody) (Moscow, 1960); V. Ia. Laverychev, *Krupnaia burzhuaziia v poreformennoi Rossii, 1861–1900* (Moscow, 1974); L. E. Shepelev, *Tsarizm i burzhuaziia vo vtoroi polovine XIX veka: Problema torgovo-promyshlennoi politiki* (Leningrad, 1981); Anan'ich, ed., *Vlast' i reformy,* pp. 559–563.

115. P. A. Valuev, *Dnevnik P. A. Valueva, ministra vnutrennikh del* (Moscow, 1961), tom 2, p. 139.

116. V. G. Chernukha, *Vnutrenniaia politika tsarizma s serediny 50-kh do nachala 80-kh gg. XIX v.* (Leningrad, 1978), pp. 15–135; B. G. Litvak, "Reformy i revoliutsii v Rossii," *Istoriia SSSR,* no. 2 (1991).

117. P. A. Zaionchkovskii, *Rossiiskoe samoderzhavie v kontse XIX stoletiia* (Moscow, 1970), pp. 98–99.

118. B. B. Dubentsov, "Vopros ob otmene grazhdanskikh chinov v pravitel'stvennoi politike 80-kh gg. XIX vv.," in A. G. Man'kov, ed., *Sotsial'no-politicheskaia istoriia SSSR* (Moscow, 1974), pp. 104–131.

119. Heidi W. Whelan, *Alexander III and the State Council: Bureaucracy and Counter-Reform in Late Imperial Russia* (New Brunswick, 1982), pp. 248–251; R. G. Robbins, Jr., *The Tsar's Viceroys: Russian Provincial Governors in the Last Years of the Empire* (Ithaca, 1987), pp. 248–251.

120. Whelan, *Alexander III and the State Council*, p. 198.

121. A. S. Suvorin, *Dnevnik* (Moscow, 1992), pp. 22, 26–27.

122. Ibid., p. 16.

123. Terence Emmons and Wayne S. Vucinich, eds., *The Zemstvo in Russia: An Experiment in Local Self-Government* (New York, 1982), pp. 1–4; S. E. Allen, Jr., "The Zemstvo as a Force for Social and Civic Regeneration in Russia: A Study of Selected Aspects, 1864–1905" (dissertation, Clark University, 1969), pp. 259–266; T. E. Porter, "The Development of Political Pluralism in Late Imperial Russia: Local Self-Government and Movement for National Zemstvo Union, 1864–1917" (PhD. dissertation, University of Washington, 1990), pp. 368–379; Marc Szeftel, "The Form of Government of the Russian Empire Prior to Constitutional Reforms of 1905–1906," in J. S. Curtiss, ed., *Essays in Russian and Soviet History: In Honor of Gerold Tanquary Robinson* (Leiden, 1965), pp. 105–119.

124. Lazarevskii, *Lektsii*, pp. 105–113.

125. G. S. Kalinin and A. F. Goncharov, eds., *Istoriia gosudarstva i prava v SSSR* (Moscow, 1972), chast' 1, pp. 574–581; N. P. Eroshkin, *Istoriia gosudarstvennykh uchrezhdenii dorevoliutsionnoi Rossii* (Moscow, 1983), pp. 252–260; V. S. Diakin, ed., *Krizis samoderzhaviia v Rossii, 1895–1917* (Leningrad, 1984), p. 298; A. N. Medushevskii, *Demokratiia i avtoritarizm: Rossiiskii konstitutsionalizm v sravnitel'noi perspektive* (Moscow, 1998), pp. 198–201, 455–468.

126. Lazarevskii, *Lektsii*, pp. 171 179; V. M. Gessen, "Teoriia pravovogo gosu-darstva," in P. D. Dolgorukii and I. I. Petrunkevich, eds., *Politicheskii stroi sovre-mennykh gosudarstv* (St. Petersburg, 1905), tom 1, pp. 117–186.

127. V. N. Kokovtsev, *Iz moego proshlogo: Vospominaniia 1903–1919 gg.* (Moscow, 1992), chast' 1, pp. 140, 269–274.

128. Lazarevskii, *Lektsii*, pp. 105–113.

129. P. Guliaev, compiler, *Prava i ob'iazannosti gradskoi i zemskoi politsii i voobshche vsekh zhitelei Rossiiskogo gosudarstva v otnoshenii k politsii*, chast' 2, *O pravakh i obiazannostiakh zhitelei* (Moscow, 1827), pp. 1–51.

130. Olga Crisp and Linda Edmondson, eds., *Civil Rights in Imperial Russia* (Oxford, 1989).

131. Lazarevskii, *Lektsii*, pp. 413–415.

132. W. E. Butler, "Civil Rights in Russia: Legal Standards in Gestation," in Crisp and Edmondson, eds., *Civil Rights in Imperial Russia*, pp. 1–12.

133. Geoffrey Hosking, *The Russian Constitutional Experiment: Government and Duma, 1907–1914* (Cambridge, 1973), pp. 243–246; A. Levin, *The Second Duma: A Study of the Social-Democratic Party and the Russian Constitutional Ex-periment* (Hamden, 1966), pp. 350–359; A. Ia. Avrekh, "O prirode rossiiskogo samoderzhaviia," in L.V. Danilov, ed., *Sistema gosudarstvennogo feodalizma* (Moscow, 1993), pp. 254–331; Iu. B. Solov'ev, *Samoderzhavie i dvorianstvo v 1907–1914 gg.* (Leningrad, 1990), p. 239; "Sovetskie i amerikanskie istoriki o politicheskom krizise samoderzhaviia," *Istoriia SSSR*, no. 2 (1991), pp. 85–128; B. Vittenberg, "Politicheskii opyt rossiiskogo parlamentarizma (1906–

1917): Istoricheskii ocherk," *Novyi zhurnal*, no. 1 (1996), pp. 166–192; Anan'ich, ed., *Vlast' i reformy*, pp. 536–546.

134. V. I. Gurko, *Vospominaniia* (Paris, n.d.), p. 511; A. A. Kizevetter, *Na rubezhe dvukh stoletii: Vospominaniia, 1881–1914* (Prague, 1919), p. 466; V. N. Kokovtsov, *Iz moego proshlogo: Vospominania 1903–1919 gg.* (Moscow, 1992), chast' 1, p. 254; V. A. Maklakov, *Vlast' i obshchestvennost' na zakate staroi Rossii (Vospominaniia)* (Paris, 1936), pp. 599–600; idem, *Vtoraia gosudarstvennaia duma* (Paris, 1942), p. 28; P. N. Miliukov, *Vospominaniia, 1859–1917* (Moscow, 1990), tom 2, p. 11.

135. B. V. Anan'ich and R. Sh. Ganelin, "Krizis vlasti v Rossii: Reformy i revoliutsionnyi protsess, 1905 i 1917 gody," *Istoriia SSSR*, no. 2 (1991), pp. 96–106.

136. Alexander Rabinowitch, *The Bolsheviks Come to Power: The Revolution of 1917 in Petrograd* (New York and London, 1976); A. K. Uaildman [Wildman], "Armiia i vopros o zakonnosti vlasti v Rossii," *Otechestvennaia istoriia*, no. 26 (1994), pp. 19–30; V. I. Startsev, *Vnutrenniaia politika vremennogo pravitel'stva* (Leningrad, 1980), pp. 230–237.

137. M. Weber, *Wirtschaft und Gesellschaft*, vol. 2 (Cologne and Berlin, 1964), p. 165.

138. Jeffrey W. Hahn, "Continuity and Change in Russian Political Culture," in Frederic J. Fleron, Jr. and Eric P. Hoffmann, eds., *Post-Communist Studies and Political Science: Methodology and Empirical Theory in Sovietology* (Boulder, 1993), pp. 299–330; Alexander Dallin, "The Uses and Abuses of Russian History," ibid., pp. 131–146. Another school of historiography has held the view that continuity has dominated in the development of the Russian state, which preserved the basic characteristics of Oriental despotism over the course of many centuries. See Karl A. Wittfogel, *Oriental Despotism: A Comparative Study of Total Power* (New Haven and London, 1964). In the opinion of others, the Russian state preserved a patrimonial regime over many centuries, right up to 1881 (see Pipes, *Russia Under the Old Regime*). A third view holds that from pre-Petrine times until the end of the Soviet period, the Russian state bore an essentially oligarchical character (see Keenan, "Muscovite Political Folkways").

139. Pipes, *Russia Under the Old Regime*, p. 290.

140. G. A. Dzhanshiev, *Epokha velikikh reform* (Moscow, 1900), pp. 354–362.

141. Calculated on the basis of data in *Vsepoddaneishii otchet Ministra iustitsii za [1834–1860] god* (St. Petersburg, 1835–1862).

142. Calculated on the basis of data in *Vsepoddaneishii otchet Ministra iustitsii za [1846–1857] god* (St. Petersburg, 1847–1858).

143. B. N. Chicherin, *Kurs gosudarstvennoi nauki*, chast' 3, *Politika* (Moscow, 1898), pp. 405–406.

144. *Entsiklopedicheskii slovar' russkogo bibliograficheskogo instituta Granat*, 7-e izd. (Moscow, 1922), tom 36, vyp. 5, pp. 628–669; M. N. Gernet, *Moral'naia statistika (ugolovnaia statistika i statistika samoubiistv)* (Moscow, 1922), pp. 50–97; idem, *Prestupnost' za granitsei i v SSSR* (Moscow, 1931), pp. 7–85.

145. *Slovar' russkogo iazyka XI–XVII vv.* (Moscow, 1977), tom 4, pp. 108–109; *Slovar' russkogo iazyka XVIII v.* (Leningrad, 1989), vyp. 5, p. 199; V. N. Dal', *Tolkovyi slovar' velikorusskogo iazyka: V chetyrekh tomakh* (Moscow, 1955), tom 1, p. 187; Korkunov, *Russkoe gosudarstvennoe pravo*, tom 1, p. 27.

146. Richard S. Wortman, *The Development of a Russian Legal Consciousness* (Chicago, 1976), pp. 8–50; G. L. Yaney, *The Systematization of Russian Government: Social Evolution in the Domestic Administration of Imperial Russia* (Urbana, 1973); Taranovskii, *Entsiklopediia prava*, p. 421.

147. This was the motivation cited for denying a petition not to exact debts from the husband of A. N. Golitsyn: "Pis'mo Aleksandra I k kniagine M. G. Golitsynoi ot 7 avgusta 1801 g.," *Russkaia starina*, tom 1 (1970), p. 447.

148. N. I. Pavlenko, "Idei absoliutizma v zakonodatel'stve XVIII v.," in N. M. Druzhinin, ed., *Absoliutizm v Rossii (XVII–XVIII vv.)* (Moscow, 1964), pp. 398–403.

149. *Neizvestnaia Rossiia: XX vek* (Moscow, 1992), vyp. 2, pp. 176–199. The petitions are preserved in the State Archives of the Russian Federation, fond 1781, op. 1, dd. 20, 42.

150. M. V. Vishniak, *Vserossiiskoe uchreditel'noe sobranie* (Paris, 1932), pp. 75–90; N. A. Shaveko, *Oktiabr'skaia revoliutsiia i uchreditel'noe sobranie* (Moscow, 1928), pp. 172–178; I. G. Protasov, *Vserossiiskoe uchreditel'noe sobranie: Istoriia rozhdeniia i gibeli* (Moscow, 1997), pp. 205–262, 320–326, 364–366; O. Radkey, *The Election to the All-Russian Constituent Assembly of 1917* (Ithaca and London, 1954), pp. 51–60.

151. M. Ia. Fenomenov, *Sovremennaia derevnia* (Moscow, 1925), chast' 2, pp. 93–94; O. Figes, *Peasant Russia, Civil War: The Volga Countryside in Revolution, 1917–1921* (Oxford, 1989); idem, "The Russian Peasant Community in the Agrarian Revolution, 1917–1918," in Roger P. Bartlett, ed., *Land Commune and Peasant Community in Russia: Communal Forms in Imperial and Early Soviet Society* (New York, 1990), pp. 237–254; Figes, "Social Relations During the Russian Revolutions, 1917–1921," in E. Kingston-Mann and T. Mixter, eds., *Peasant Economy, Culture, and Politics in European Russia, 1800–1921* (Princeton, 1991).

152. B. F. Sokolov, "Zashchita Vserossiiskogo uchreditel'nogo sobraniia," *Arkhiv russkoi revoliutsii* (Berlin, 1924), tom 13, pp. 31–63.

2

The Evolution of
Servile Relations

Historians disagree about the extent to which servile relations characterized and influenced society in imperial Russia. Their analyses likewise diverge concerning the factors that generated the institution of serfdom as well as those that contributed to its abolition after two and a half centuries. Space does not permit me to set forth in detail the positions that various historians have taken on these matters. Therefore I have reduced the variety of historical perspectives to their common denominators, classifying them in three primary groups.[1]

Prior to the Revolutions of 1917, Russian non-Marxist historians perceived a difference between state-sponsored serfdom and servile relations that derived from contracts between individuals. They linked the emergence of serfdom to the state's need to bind all classes to a particular place of residence, a particular social group, and a particular occupation. This was done in order to facilitate the levying and collection of taxes and other obligations to the state: government service, labor service *(barshchina)*, monetary taxes and rents *(obrok)*, and conscription. They related the emergence of serfdom under private law to the growing indebtedness of the peasantry, on the one hand, and to the need to secure a guaranteed labor force for the class of military servitors *(sluzhilye liudi)*, on the other. In the last analysis, the primary motive for imposing bondage was the state's need

Translated by Daniel Field, Syracuse University.

for social order and a means of defense. Bondage was abolished for one class after another, beginning with the nobility in the eighteenth century and culminating in the 1860s with the emancipation of proprietary peasants, or serfs. The state's interests and imperatives were also the precipitating factor in the disenserfment of all classes.[2]

Marxist historians consider it possible to speak of bondage only with respect to the peasantry, and in a more limited sense, to the lower orders of the city population, the so-called *posadskie liudi* or obligated townspeople; in essence, they limit the concept of bondage to serfdom in the narrow sense. Furthermore, some Marxist historians explain the genesis of serfdom as a strengthening of extraeconomic compulsion and of the rise of *barshchina* in particular; others stress the flight of peasants and obligated townspeople from villages and towns due to increased levies there of taxes and dues; still others stress the interests of the servitor class.[3] Marxist historians link the abolition of serfdom to a crisis of the servile economic system, to the inefficiency and unprofitability of servile labor, and to the rise of capitalism.[4]

Present-day non-Marxist historians emphasize the general dependence of all classes on the state; but serfdom is a particular manifestation of dependence that applies only to peasants. According to the prevailing view, two factors—the indebtedness of the peasantry and the need of the servitor class for labor power in light of the development of the internal market and the rise of *barshchina*—facilitated the enserfment of the peasantry.[5] Among the causes of serfdom's abolition, they emphasize fear of peasant rebellions, the needs of the state, cultural factors, military requirements, and the crisis of the economy based on serfdom.[6]

All historians agree on one point: Serfdom had a negative effect on all aspects of Russian life. But for Marxist historians, serfdom, together with the Mongol Yoke, was the key factor in Russia's economic and cultural backwardness relative to western Europe.

Who Was in Bondage?

To establish who was in bondage in imperial Russia, we must first examine serfdom as a concept. Serfdom *(krepostnoe pravo)* was a complex of legal norms that prescribed the personal dependence of a person on his master. It could take mild or severe forms, and it could include all or only some varieties of extraeconomic compulsion. The severe forms of serfdom, which existed in the sixteenth, seventeenth, and eighteenth centuries in many nations of central and eastern Europe besides Russia, meant the deprivation of all personal and civil rights, virtually converting a person into the property of his or her master. Serfdom's milder forms, which prevailed in western Europe from the eleventh through the fifteenth centuries, lacked such restrictive and crude aspects as the prohibitions against acquiring real estate and concluding contracts or buying and selling persons, as well as other restrictions imposed on Russian serfs. Furthermore, in Russia there was also *patriarchal dependence,* which meant that the person in bondage entered into his master's family and lived under his roof but had no family rights and did more onerous work than other family members. Apprenticeship is an example of patriarchal dependence. According to the Statute on Trades of 1785, apprentices should be obedient, assiduous, and faithful and respectful to their masters; and the latter had the right to punish their apprentices or to have the police do it. Over time, the concept of "serfdom" embraced a very wide variety of forms, ranging from mild forms of personal dependence to complete subjugation. The basic feature of serfdom was the extraeconomic dependence of the serf on the master, either in the form of direct dependence or by virtue of living on the master's land.

By formulating the traits of bondage that were found in Russia, we can define clearly the extent to which different classes were in bondage. These traits were extraeconomic, personal dependence, which had administrative, juridical, and other aspects; ascription (*prikreplenie,* literally "fastening") to a place of residence, with strict controls on migration, including a system of internal passports; assignment to a civil status ("estate" or *soslovie*) and strict controls on social mobility; imposed varieties of social inferiority, such as mutual or community (rather than individual) responsibility before the authorities,[7] payment of a capitation ("soul") tax, and liability to conscription and to corporal punishment; limitations on property rights; limitations on the choice of occupation and profession; and incapacity to defend personal dignity—that is, the possibility that the lord or the state administration could arbitrarily and with impunity deprive a person of dignity, honor, or property.

Let us now look at the particular situation of the four principal classes (or *sostoianiia*—literally, "conditions") at the beginning of the eighteenth century: the nobility (*dvorianstvo* or *shliakhetstvo*), the clergy, the townsmen (merchants and *meshchane*—a category consisting mostly of petty traders), and the peasantry.

The Nobility

Under Peter I, all nobles were obliged to serve the state. Service, whether civil or military, began at age 15 and always began at the lowest rank—in the army, as a common soldier. There were no leaves or terms except for illness or death. Two-thirds of the members of each family had to serve in the military, one-third in the civil service. Nobles preferred military service, which was supposed to carry more prestige and to guarantee more rapid advancement. Because service was compulsory and lifelong, a noble was ascribed to a particular landed estate (i.e., manor, not estate of the realm), regiment, or government agency where he fulfilled his service. The harshness of service provoked large numbers of nobles to evade musters and summonses to serve (a phenomenon called *netstvo,* from the word for "no"); the government responded with severe punishments, beginning with fines and corporal punishment and culminating in the confiscation of property and in *shel'movanie*—that is, depriving a person of all rights and putting him outside the law. For example, in 1711, fifty-three officers who failed to appear when they were sent to a regiment in Kiev province were deprived of their manors, from which their wives and children also were expelled.[8] According to a decree of 1720, nobles who evaded service were subject to beating with the knout, slitting of the nostrils, and hard labor for life; the names of such nobles were to be fastened to a scaffold to the beat of drums, so that everyone would know their crimes. Those who denounced deserters from service were rewarded with the deserter's property, and those found to be harboring deserters were liable to severe punishment. Military service was so harsh that a few nobles sought transfer to the rolls of merchants or even peasants in order to escape it.[9]

In preparation for fulfilling their service obligation to the state, nobles were to acquire an education. Education was essential for appointment to higher posts and for elevation to higher ranks. To provide an added incentive, illiterate nobles were forbidden to marry. The nobleman was also obliged to maintain his own readiness for service and to prepare his sons for service; the latter were periodically mustered for examination.[*] He had, in addition, to exercise administrative and economic oversight of his peasants through manorial police and justice, the collection of state taxes, the provision of social services, and other functions. Nobles received furloughs to see to the administration of their estates, with the obligation to report back as soon as they were ordered to return. The sovereign could order any nobleman to change his place of residence, and Peter I took advantage of that right; for example, in order to populate the new city of St. Petersburg, he required dozens of noble families to move from their old homes to tracts of land set aside for them in the new city, on which they were obliged to build a dwelling within a certain period.

Nobles were no more exempt from corporal punishment than were other estates of the realm. They were subjected to beatings, clubbing, whipping, and all the other delights of Petrine justice. In 1722, during the

---

*The goal of these examinations, called *iavki,* was to determine a young man's fitness for potential service. The primary criterion of fitness was the appropriateness of a youth's education; but physical condition probably also was taken into account.—*Trans.*

census of the population in Velikie Luki *provintsiia*,* in strict conformity to the tsar's decree, eleven nobles and eighty-five peasants suspected of evading registration were tortured and beaten with a knout or a cudgel, after which one of the nobles and ten of the peasants died; in addition, seven nobles and six noblemen's wives and daughters were arrested, and one of the noblemen died because of the terrible conditions of his confinement.[10] Nobles were punished as cruelly as peasants were. However, unlike the orders of society subject to taxation—the so-called vulgar people—nobles were not subject to any state or local taxes in cash or kind, for it was supposed that nobles rendered service instead of taxes.[11] I am inclined to agree with the historian of the Russian nobility who asserted that under Peter I, nobles "stood in almost the same relationship of servile dependence to the government as peasants did to nobles."[12] Bear in mind that even though under Peter I the bondage of the nobility as of all other classes to the state reached its apogee, by and large this kind of bondage prevailed in the sixteenth and seventeenth centuries as well.

The Clergy

The situation of clergymen was worse still. This estate consisted of the *black* or monastic clergy and the *white* or parish clergy. The latter category included the *ordained* clergy (priests and deacons), who constituted the *senior clergy* in a parish, and various *lesser clergy*, such as junior deacons, vergers, sextons, and cantors. In 1711, the black clergy lost their freedom of movement and were ascribed to the monasteries in which they were enrolled. Their numbers were strictly determined, and entry into the black clergy and departure from it were limited. In 1719, the parish clergy suffered the same fate; they were ascribed to their churches and parishes and forbidden to change parishes or take up another career without permission from the ecclesiastical and secular authorities. Just as landlords' peasants had lost their right to move from place to place in 1596, so the clergy was deprived of freedom of movement. The state limited the civil rights of clergymen in other ways, too. They were forbidden to undertake any kind of entrepreneurial activity whatsoever, whether in commerce or in industry; even renting out their houses became an indictable offense. Clergymen were forbidden to participate in meetings, to interfere in secular affairs, to submit petitions, or otherwise to act on behalf of anyone else. For its part, the church limited the rights of those in holy orders, forbidding them to

---

Provintsiia here refers to a subdivision of a *guberniia*.—*Trans.*

attend theaters, play cards, dance or watch dancers, and shave their beards or have their hair cut; they were also required to dress modestly and in dark colors—that is, to wear cassocks.

The state consistently interfered in the lives of clergymen in another way: It strictly limited the number of clergymen by forcibly transferring men in holy orders to other forms of civil status. Peter I initiated this practice. In 1722, he ordered a limit to the number of white clergy, establishing a ratio of one priest and two lesser clergy to each 100 to 150 homes in a parish. In accord with the tsar's decree, a strictly limited number of men, along with their direct descendants, were enrolled for active service in the spiritual establishment as staff clergy, and all other persons of clerical estate who were not on staff were reassigned to taxpaying status. Since the number of parishes, and therefore of parish staff positions, was strictly limited and the natural population increase among the clergy was great, until 1831 the secular administration regularly carried out purges of the clergy, which were called "sortings." In consequence, a great many persons of the clerical estate who did not have a position in a church were compelled to enroll as soldiers or in other forms of civil status, primarily as peasants or obligated townspeople, with the literate among them being assigned to government institutions as clerks.[13] Access to the parish clergy was, in effect, barred to everyone except the sons of clergymen. Clergymen were required to train their sons and prepare them for positions as priests and deacons, so that these positions became hereditary. In the second half of the eighteenth century, lesser clerical positions also became hereditary, and junior deacons and sextons went through a ritual similar to ordination, which was called "consecration to the surplice."

These practices transformed the clergy into a closed caste. Church positions, together with their revenues and the lands that went with them (from 36 to 108 hectares per parish), became family property, and could be passed along by inheritance or sold. We can say that *legally* parish church positions (and their revenues) were converted into lesser *benefices,* as in the Catholic Church in the Middle Ages; but in fact, they became *fiefs,* since without a rule of celibacy for parish clergy among the Orthodox, priests' positions passed, with the sanction of the bishop, to their sons. Retention of a position at a parish church required the fulfillment of its duties and the assent of the bishop.

The white clergy had major service responsibilities. Peter I laid on the clergy, like the nobility, the obligation to study; the clergy understood the monarch's decree on education *as the imposition of a kind of tax.* Those who had not been educated could not take church positions, for fear of punishment by the bishops, who confirmed them in office. Clergymen had to render state as well as pastoral service: They kept the registers of births and had to compile annual reports of marriages, births, and deaths; every year they had to compile lists of sectarians and of those Orthodox who failed to make confession and take communion, and they had to submit these lists to the secular authorities, who levied fines on the guilty; they had to report tax evaders; they had to combat sectarianism; they had to read aloud the decrees of the tsar during church services to the totally illiterate populace; they had to act as notaries; they had to monitor the loyalty of their parishioners (priests were obliged to report to the administration about sectarians, the spread of superstition, and failures to attend church or keep the fasts, and even about subversive plans and actions *revealed to them during confession*); and so on. The clergy fulfilled these numerous obligations without payment, out of fear of punishment. By way of compensation, ordained clergy were relieved from conscription and other direct taxes, although they were subject to various taxes in kind (involving fire fighting, police functions, and the billeting of troops) and had to pay certain exactions in cash. Lower-level clergy, who were not ordained, did not have these benefits: They had the same obligations as members of the taxable orders, the people of the *posad,* and the peasants. The ordained clergymen's sons were subject to conscription.[14] These compulsory and burdensome obligations of clergymen, which had nothing to do with their role as pastors, teachers, and servants of the church, amounted in essence to *barshchina* for the benefit of the treasury or the sovereign. Taking this into account, along with their ascription to their place of residence and of service, the clergy, like the nobility, was an estate in bondage, and the state was the beneficiary of its dependence.

The dependence of the clergy on the bishop, however, was even stronger than their dependence on the state. In his diocese, the bishop was master of the clergy in the same sense that the tsar was master of the nobility, or the squire *(pomeshchik)* master of his serfs. The bishop held special examinations to determine the suitability of clergymen for clerical office; he consecrated them and appointed them to office, and annually collected from parish clergy a sum of money (called *episkopskoe tiaglo*) corresponding to the prosperity of the parish and the number of households in it. The bishop could take a clergyman's office away and give it to someone else. He could transfer a clergyman to another parish, or strip him of holy orders. Until 1841 the administration of the diocese was conducted according to the instructions of the presiding bishop of the moment, who exercised personal authority over all the institutions of the diocese (the consistory, schools, seminaries, and so on). The clerical courts were also in his hands. All of this permits us to say that the parish clergy was enserfed—or as it was put at the time, *tiaglye*—not only to the state but also to the bishop. As Gregory Freeze aptly observed, "The Church was a mirror image of lay society: The bishop was ecclesiastical prince, the clergy his subjects."[15]

Townspeople

Townspeople—that is, craftspeople and traders (until 1721, they were called *posad* people)—were from birth ascribed to a particular town or city, a commune, and a household. They had to obtain permission from the governmental and local authorities to change their civil status, profession, or residence, or even to go on a business trip. In addition, they had to fulfill a multitude of onerous obligations, called "services to the treasury,"[16] without any compensation and under threat of severe penalties. In essence, they performed *barshchina* for the state; they "served" as *tsenovshchiki, tseloval'niki,* and *brakovshchiki* (what today would be called accountants, bookkeepers, tax collectors, and consultants) in state institutions, not only in their own towns but far away; they collected taxes, sold vodka and salt for the state's monopoly, carried out police functions in their towns, and assisted in census-taking. Wherever literate people were needed to perform some task for the state, townspeople were brought in, under compulsion and without compensation.

In the first half of the eighteenth century, about 10 percent of the ostensible number (according to the most recent census) and 24 percent of the actual number of adult male townspeople were in compulsory state service. These data may understate the real burden of *barshchina* for the sovereign, for obligations to the treasury involved finance, and all the property of people of the *posad* was surety against possible losses and a guarantee of punctual and complete fulfillment of service obligations. Frequently, townspeople's *barshchina* service to the treasury left them bankrupt. If a townsman's property was not enough to cover his debt, he was put *na pravezh*—in most cases, fastened to a pillar in front of an administrative building and flogged until relatives or friends paid his debts.[17] When townspeople were in government service, their persons, their property, and their time were completely at the disposal of the administration. No one has ever attempted to calculate the value of townspeople's *barshchina* for the state; but since about 24 percent of adult men were "in service" for the government at any one time, we can suppose that such service took about 24 percent of the townspeople's time.

In addition to direct taxes and *barshchina* for the state, townspeople had to pay *obrok* (ostensibly for the tracts of land they held in the town). In the second quarter of the eighteenth century, this *obrok* was two times less than the amount that state peasants paid and three times less than serfs paid; on average, it amounted to 71 percent of townspeople's direct taxes. Thus the total of *obrok* and *barshchina* levied on townspeople was an impressive amount; it was scarcely less than the dues levied on peasants, or at least on state peasants. I must emphasize that we cannot categorize the "service" and the *obrok* exacted from the people of the *posad* as "taxation in kind" and as "rent," respectively. "Service" was compulsory and co-erced; it did not correspond to the income, the potential, or the wishes of the *posad* people; and it was not sanctioned by any representative institution but was arbitrarily imposed by the government. As for the *obrok*, it had nothing in common with rent because the rate was not the product of free agreement between townspeople and the administration; it was an arbitrary and compulsory exaction. Townspeople could not evade either service or *obrok,* since they were ascribed to their place of residence and to their civil status. To change either without the sanction of the administration was treated as a crime, for which townspeople were punished and then returned to their former situation.

These facts support the conclusion that townspeople were serfs of the state. The celebrated historian S. M. Solovev wisely observed, "The same servile relations that until recently applied to peasants and household people [that is, serfs employed as domestics] in our country applied in the past to people of the *posad.*"[18]

Peasants

Serfdom developed spontaneously and gradually in the Russian village in the fifteenth and sixteenth centuries under the influence of peasant indebtedness. Then, at the end of the sixteenth century, a series of enserfing decrees issued by the administration of Boris Godunov, especially the decrees of 1592 and 1597, rounded out the legal aspects of serfdom throughout the territory of the Russian state. These decrees bound peasants both to the land on which they were settled when the decree was issued and to the proprietor of that land, whether a squire, the state, a monastery, or another entity. These enserfing decrees lost their effect at the beginning of the seventeenth century, during the Time of Troubles, but they were restored to full force by the Law Code of 1649.[19]

Peasants of all kinds were ascribed to the land and to its proprietors and could not, without a release from the proprietor and the permission of the state administration, change their residence and civil status. Without a passport issued by the state and local administration, a peasant could not go farther than twenty miles from home. Peasants rendered *barshchina* and *obrok* or a combination of the two for the benefit of their proprietors and were subject as well to numerous taxes in kind (conscription, billeting, cartage, road mending, and so on). Peasants who ran away or fell into arrears were treated as criminals. If they were caught, fugitive peasants were subject to severe punishments—beating, branding, cutting off of the ears, slitting of the nostrils—after which they were brought back to their proprietors.[20] Squires parodied the state's system, and every estate was like a miniature state agency.[21] There were, to be sure, some positive aspects in the administrative systems set up by squires and the state. The squire, if only in the interests of self-preservation, had to show some solicitude for his peasants; he might make loans to them, provide them with cattle and equipment on occasion, provide them with food and seed in the event of a bad harvest, defend them in court or when they were oppressed by the police, take care of the elderly and infirm, or see to peasants' education and training.[22]

Squires acquired their powers over their serfs through the force of custom, but many of these rights were confirmed by government decrees. The situation of serfs deteriorated markedly as a result of the decree of 1719 that abolished the legal boundary between *kholopy*, who were virtually slaves, and serfs, who hitherto had had much the same status as state peasants. The decree provided that *kholopy*, who until then had not been taxed, must pay taxes to the state. Squires then began to exercise rights over their serfs that formerly masters had exercised over slaves, although the law provided no warrant for this.[23]

The nobility persistently tried to get from the government a clear formulation of their powers over their peasants. For a long time, the state was unresponsive; it feared the peasants' resentment and was unwilling to delimit its own right to interfere in relations between squires and serfs. These relations were clearly set forth only in 1832, in the first *Code of Laws of the Russian Empire*.[24] Here the degree of power conferred on squires over their serfs was close to that which they already exercised in practice, and also close to the ideal that nobles had formulated eighty years previously.[25]

The situation of state peasants, which had been regulated by statute rather than by the discretion of tsarist administrators, was also clearly defined in the Law Code of 1832.[26] The discrepancies between the rights of serfs and those of state peasants have prompted some scholars to see the latter as free from serfdom,[27] but the argument does not seem convincing. First of all, in the strictly legal sense, the so-called state peasants belonged not to the Russian state as a political union of persons occupying a definite territory and subject to a single sovereign power but to "the treasury" as legal persons under private law. The colloquial phrase *treasury peasants* adequately conveys the legal situation of this category of peasants, accurately denoting the bearer of power. Treasury peasants, like serfs, had a real-life proprietor, and therefore their relationship to the treasury was that of serfdom. The difference in the situation of the treasury's peasants and the serfs, which was insignificant in the early eighteenth century but became significant subsequently, did not stem from a difference in rights but from the differing characters of these two types of proprietor.[28]

Furthermore, neither in the early eighteenth century nor later did the legal position of serfs differ in principle from that of state peasants: Both kinds of peasant rendered *barshchina* and *obrok;* were ascribed to their place of residence and civil status; were bound by mutual responsibility; were under the control of proprietors; and were limited in their personal and civil rights (they were forbidden to farm taxes [*zanimat'sia otkupami*] and conclude contracts, to carry on commerce at ports, to open factories or mines, or to issue bills of exchange). The only difference was in the extent of dependence—servile dependence was stronger and harsher for serfs, especially those in *barshchina* labor service, and milder for state peasants.[29] Therefore, when P. D. Kiselev asserted that in the 1830s the situation of state peasants did not differ in any essential way from that of serfs and that enlightened laws concerning them were a dead letter, he was absolutely correct; since Kiselev was Minister of State Properties in the administration of Nicholas I, his assertion has the significance of a confession. According to the authoritative opinion of V. I. Veshniakov, a senior official of the same ministry, state peasants, at least until the reforms of 1839–1841, considered themselves "serfs of the government or of the authorities."[30]

Corporate or Communal Serfdom

Those who belonged to taxable groups—peasants, traders, craftspeople, and other classes of the population except (perhaps) for the nobility, the clergy, and those in the military—were in bondage to the corporations of which they were a part: peasants, to the village commune; and traders and craftspeople, to the urban commune. All members of a corporation were bound by mutual responsibility and were collectively responsible to the state for punctual payment of taxes; for rendering taxes in kind (conscription, cartage, and billeting, among others); for various levies of money; for crimes committed on the territory of the commune; and for unsanctioned departures by any member.[31]

Before the eighteenth century, when the regular army had not yet replaced the noble militias, nobles were grouped into town or district corporations. These "regional nobiliary cavalry hundreds," as they were called, had elected captains and performed certain police functions. They also shared collective responsibility financially and for their service obligations to the state. Thus, the nobles were enmeshed in bondage through these corporations.[32] Although the privileged noble corporations established in 1785 by the Charter to the Nobility were free of mutual responsibility and all other traits of "burden-bearing" status, they still bore collective responsibility to the sovereign for the conduct of their members, and they interfered in the affairs of members (for example, in relations between squires and serfs, if squires were abusing their authority). Robert Jones thinks it possible to compare the collective responsibility of noble assemblies vis-à-vis the sovereign with the collective responsibility of peasant communes vis-à-vis the tsarist administration after 1861.[33]

The village commune had especially great power over peasants. It fixed the sequence and timing of agricultural work and chose what crops would be sown; it regulated the use of pastures, woodlands, and other resources; and it collected taxes, governed religious life, passed judgment on law-breakers (whom it could even exile to Siberia without involving government courts), gave permission to peasants to travel away from the village, and so on. In essence, the peasants' entire lives were under the strict control of the commune. The commune's power derived from the fact that the village's landholdings were intermingled and held on communal tenure and were regularly reapportioned among the peasants. From compulsory crop rotation followed the necessity of regulating the entire range of the peasants' work and leisure.

Town dwellers also were grouped in communes: Craftspeople and merchants were obliged to join guilds, respectively called *tsekhi* and *gil'dii*. Urban corporations did not have as much authority over townspeople as village communes did over peasants. Nonetheless, their power was great enough to prevent members from making any major decision—such as traveling away from the town, shifting to another category of the population, or disposing freely of their own time—without informing their corporations and receiving consent. The degree of a townsperson's dependence on the corporation depended on many factors, of which the most important were the size of the town and the nature of its economy. In small, agrarian towns, where most residents were primarily involved in agriculture, the corporations had greater power, and their influence was like that of village communes. In larger towns and in cities dominated by trade and manufacture, town dwellers had more freedom, and there was less social control. Since small agrarian towns with a population of 500 or less predominated in eighteenth-century Russia and the towns' land and property were held collectively, it follows that a majority of townspeople were subject to strict control by corporations and by the urban commune as a whole.

It is important to note that corporate bondage, in contrast to the bondage of serfs and state peasants, was not perceived by townspeople as onerous, and in their opinion, even performed a valuable function: Under its aegis, members were defended from the arbitrary power of tsarist functionaries and from representatives of rival communes. The commune restrained social and economic differentiation and facilitated the apportionment of taxes and dues according to income. More generally, so long as serfdom prevailed, tight communal bonds provided people with refuge from the arbitrary power exercised by squires and by the state; for corporate bondage took shape spontaneously, and it was at the request of the populace that the state gave it legal form in the middle of the seventeenth century. Regarding the towns in particular, corporate bondage was conclusively confirmed in the Law Code of 1649, in response to petitions from townspeople.[34]

It may be that corporate bondage took shape in the village in much the same fashion. This view finds support in the history of the spread of communal and repartitional land tenure in the eighteenth century among state and crown (or appanage) peasants of the Far North, the Urals, and the South, and in the late nineteenth and early twentieth centuries, also among the peasants of Siberia. At the beginning of the eighteenth century the repartitional commune was unknown among the state peasants of the North and the Urals (Arkhangelsk, Vologda, Olonets, Vyatka, Perm, and Kazan provinces). There was open traffic in land, peasants bought and sold it, and there were persons of various kinds of civil status among the landholders. Although peasants had effective control of the land, however, the state remained the ultimate owner—an owner that, for the time being, had not asserted its legal authority over the land, as if temporarily delegating that power to the peasants. Free traffic in land led to considerable inequalities in landholding among the peasants. Those with little or no land persuaded the government to forbid landholding by nonpeasants and to introduce repartitioning. The government responded positively because it was in its interest to do so. A decree of 1754 prohibited the sale of peasant land to members of other classes, confiscated the peasant land already held by other classes, and turned it over to peasants. In 1766 traffic in land was forbidden even among peasants, depriving them of control over their holdings. In 1781 repartitioning was introduced, as a result of which the form of land tenure that prevailed in the central provinces—the repartitional commune—became the model that was imposed on state peasants throughout European Russia. The government's decree was, on the whole, carried out, although gradually. Remnants of former systems of landholding were discernible for a long time, as we can see from a new decree of 1829, imposing repartition in Arkhangelsk province.

In principle, the development of peasant landholding on crown lands—the property of the imperial family in the North—followed the same course. The fate of the lands held by *odnodvortsy* (descendants of military servitors of the Muscovite state who had been settled on what was then the southern frontier) was much the same. Early in the eighteenth century the *odnodvortsy* had no communes or repartitions, and land was in effect held as property, even though legally the state was the owner. Gradually, by increments over the course of the eighteenth and the first half of the nineteenth centuries, government decrees prohibited trafficking in land, and the *odnodvortsy* themselves undertook to shift to the standard model of land tenure, the repartitional commune.[35]

So it was that in the course of the eighteenth century, rights to the land and forms of use and tenure were made uniform for all categories of the Russian peasantry, following the model of the repartitional commune with mutual responsibility, compulsory rotation of crops, and intermingled holdings. The reform of the state peasantry in 1837–1839, the reforms of the 1860s, and the counterreforms of the 1880s and 1890s all contributed to the strengthening of communal landholding and consequently of corporate bondage. It is essential to emphasize that an overwhelming majority of peasants shifted to the repartitional commune voluntarily, without any constraint by the state. As with the town dwellers, the state was responding to the wishes of the majority.

The Universality of Bondage, and Its Causes

If we consider the pattern I have outlined, it follows that in Russia at the beginning of the eighteenth century, the only free man was the tsar, and everyone else was in bondage to one degree or another. Furthermore, most people experienced more than one level of bondage: The priest was in bondage to both church and state; the member of a *posad,* to the commune and to the state; the serf, to the state; a nobleman, to the commune; and the state peasant, to the state and the commune. Only the nobleman was bound solely to the state. Bondage—we may even say serfdom—was universal. As we proceed we must bear in mind that serfdom had three forms: bondage to the state or the treasury,[36] to private persons, and to corporations.

This construction of bondage relationships may seem excessively abstract. Some discerning contemporaries, however, understood the Russian social order at the beginning of the eighteenth century as I have characterized it. In "A Dialogue of Two Friends," V. N. Tatishchev (1686–1750), a well-known historian and statesman of the reign of Peter I, distinguished "three varieties of durance" in Russia: "by nature," that is, submission to the authority of a father and the monarch; "voluntary," in consequence of a social contract or a particular bargain between persons, such as *kholopstvo* or contract labor; and "by compulsion," "slavery or involuntary servitude as a result of enslavement by force." These three varieties correspond to my construct of bondage to the state, bondage to corporations, and bondage to private persons. Tatishchev believed that the consequences of any variety of bondage were ultimately the same; for however a man is held in bondage, he "cannot rest or rejoice as he listeth, he cannot pursue or preserve honor or goods, for everything hangs on the will of him who holds sway over the will of the other." Tatishchev suggested that the cause of bondage lay in the fact that "a man even at the height of his powers and reason cannot safely rely on himself alone—a man's will is put in the bridle of bondage for his own benefit. . . . One kind of bridle comes by nature, another by free choice, and the third by compulsion."[37] In Russia, freedom is impossible for two reasons: It does "not accord with our system of monarchic government, and to alter the inveterate custom of bondage would not be safe."[38]

What were the causes of the extensiveness and intensity of human bondage in imperial Russia, especially among the unprivileged classes? One factor was political—the traditional nature of Russian state policy and the patriarchal character of sovereign power. The population saw the tsar as the ultimate owner of the land, the lord of all his subjects, the father of the nation, and the master of the country. From this understanding derived the monarch's right to dispose of the freedom, well-being, life, and property of his subjects, but only to serve public rather than personal interests.

The policy of the Petrine government in the area of landownership and property relations in general leaves no doubt that the populace and the government alike saw the tsar as the ultimate owner of land and sometimes of all the property of his subjects. In 1701, Peter I established, ostensibly as a temporary, wartime measure, the monastery chancellery. The chancellery took over administration of all church properties, whether they belonged to the patriarchate, to dioceses, or to monasteries, together with 154,000 households of peasants who lived on these properties (representing a quarter of all the nation's households). Out of the revenues from these properties, the state allocated fixed sums for the needs of the church. Church estates began gradually to pass into the hands of the nobility; in the single decade from 1701 to 1711, the tsar distributed 10,000 peasant households.[39] This effective secularization of church property was fortuitous and expressive of Peter I's despotic nature, but it also reflected the traditional view in Russian society that the tsar is the real master of the Russian land. Similarly, the Law Code of 1649 prohibited the clergy and monasteries from acquiring new lands, and in 1649–1652 the government confiscated the church's real estate in towns.

In 1714, Peter I equalized the property rights of nobles who held *pomestia* (estates on conditional tenure, in return for service) with those who held *votchiny* (patrimonial estates, essentially private property). At the same time he issued the law on single inheritance, so that only one son could inherit an estate. Here, too, we confront not so much the arbitrary power of the tsar as a consistent application of the concept of the tsar as ultimate owner of all land. We see the same thing with respect to the land occupied by state peasants. A decree of 1719 on the conduct of the census *(reviziia)* ordained that all peasants should be enumerated, including "crown peasants and *others of the sovereign's peasants [gosudarevy krest'iane]*," by which was meant various categories of state peasants, such as *odnodvortsy,* "black-plowing peasants," and so on.[40] The words in italics indicated that "treasury peasants," like crown peasants who belonged to the tsar personally, were considered "the sovereign's." But the revenues from crown estates went for the personal needs of the tsar, whereas revenues from state peasants went into the state budget. Is this a contradiction? Not in the least. It is a clear manifestation of the various rights of the tsar: on the one hand, his right as ultimate owner of the land, and on the other, his right as a private person. Therefore, while he freely disposed of state lands (in Peter's reign many tens of thousands of state peasants were distributed to the nobility as property), the tsar did not apply revenues from these lands to his personal needs. The presumption that all land belonged to the tsar as ultimate owner retained its force.

In the reign of Peter I we find many instances when the tsar disposed not only of real estate but also of personal or corporate property of other kinds belonging to his subjects as if it belonged to him. In 1700, when the Russian army was facing a shortage of artillery, Peter ordered the bells to be taken down from churches and recast as cannons, which was done. In 1714, he forbade the construction of stone buildings throughout the land, except in St. Petersburg, and ordered a certain number of carpenters and masons to be sent to St. Petersburg to hasten the development of the new capital. In 1723, Peter, now emperor, banned the tonsuring of men as monks so that, on the one hand, monasteries could accommodate more wounded veterans and paupers, and on the other, the flow of labor and of taxpayers into monastic ranks would be checked. In 1724, on the occasion of the coronation of his wife Ekaterina, Peter ordered the confiscation of sixty prime horses from Russian and foreign merchants in St. Petersburg for use by the Horse Guards who would take part in the coronation festivities, and this was duly done.[41]

A second factor in the spread of bondage was military policy. The Russian state always needed enormous resources to shore up its armed forces and to pursue an active foreign policy. The population could provide these resources only if it possessed them due to a well-developed economy. Since the national economy was backward and was developing slowly in comparison with the economies of west European countries, only extraordinary exploitation of the populace by the state—only extraeconomic compulsion—could secure the necessary resources. However, rising levels of state exploitation met popular resistance, primarily in the form of migration, resettlement, and simply running away on a massive scale. Only by putting everyone in bondage—usually, in harsh forms of bondage—was it possible to some extent to keep the population in place, extract financial resources from it, and maintain social order. That is what autocracy did. The populace responded to these objective requirements, for it saw fastening people to urban and rural communes as a means of defending themselves against the unsanctioned departure of taxpayers with whom they were linked by mutual responsibility.

The meager development of the market, together with the lack of money in the treasury to maintain the army, the church, and the state apparatus, compelled the autocracy to rely on payment in kind for its military and civil servants: They were compensated with awards of land, and the peasants on that land were obliged to pay them *obrok* or render *barshchina*. In essence, serfdom, or bondage on behalf of private persons, derived from the delegation by the autocracy of a significant portion of its authority over the person of the peasant, to the squire or to the church. Another source of bondage was self-enserfment. The causes of the *corporate* bondage discussed above related to the internal workings of the village commune and the *posad*, as well as to compulsory collectivism, a lack of self-control, and the feeble development of individualism.

The mentality characteristic of the common people fostered the development of bondage in all its guises. To men and women in the sixteenth and seventeenth centuries there was nothing unnatural in forced labor and coercion. Here are two examples in point: On 14 September 1702, about 800 Swedish prisoners—men, women, and children—were brought to Moscow and sold. At first they brought three or four guilders each, but after a few days the price rose to twenty or thirty guilders. Both Russians and foreigners bought the captives; but the Russians made them *kholopy*, or slaves, whereas the foreigners bought them as domestic servants for the duration of the war, after which they restored them to freedom.[42] The second telling example is that *self-enserfment* was forbidden by law only in 1783, and even then at the initiative of the empress rather than in response to popular demand.[43] Even after 1783, the phenomenon did not disappear, and a considerable number of persons enserfed themselves. The cultural basis of serfdom, as the noted historian of Russian law K. D. Kavelin wisely suggested, was the people's "patriarchal conceptions." According to these conceptions, a subordinate considered himself a "dark person" who deserved compulsion and for whom punishment was a form of instruction; serfdom found its source in "the customs and beliefs of the common people and was maintained not by coercion but by conviction."[44]

The common people saw freedom and social order as alternatives—only one or the other could exist at a time. Only the bandit, a favorite folk hero, was free. The bandit gained his freedom by rebelling, but thereby violated the legal order, set himself against the sovereign (or the state) and the church, and put himself outside of society. The conflict between freedom and order inevitably evolved into a conflict between society and the individual. Rebellion was always against the law, freedom always violated the social order, and perdition awaited the rebel who did not repent in time.[45]

This irreconcilable conflict between freedom and order derived from a distinctive popular ideal of social organization and from a distinctive concept of freedom. The social organization of the seventeenth- and eighteenth-century cossacks, who lived beyond the reach of the autocratic state, was conceived of as the ideal. This organization entailed complete democratic self-government apart from the state but under the aegis of the tsar; the election of all officials and judges by the people; complete equality; and the abolition of inequality in wealth by repartitioning land and other goods among the common people. The common people understood freedom as complete independence from the state and the elimination of all taxes and dues to the state and to private persons. These popular ideals were clearly manifested in popular uprisings led by folk heroes, who in the end were always executed (the uprisings of Stepan Razin in 1667 to 1671, Kondratii Bulavin in 1707 to 1709, and Emelian Pugachev in 1773 to 1775); and they were equally evident in peasant riots in the first half of the nineteenth century.[46] The popular conception of freedom was always in direct conflict with the existing social order, and those who exemplified the popular ideal became state criminals who ended their lives on the block.

The autocracy and its administration knew these popular conceptions very well and resolutely made use of extreme forms of force to maintain social order. Force became a habit, a norm, and the approved means of establishing order. We can surmise that the governed perceived departure from this norm as weakness; it disoriented them and became a cause or pretext for deviant behavior. Andrei Bolotov, a well-known agronomist, squire, administrator, and writer—and a very enlightened man, by the standards of the eighteenth century—who served for twenty-two years as the administrator of several thousand state peasants, admitted in his memoirs how necessity compelled him to apply cruel punishments to these peasants in order to maintain order.

> By nature I am not at all hard-hearted, but on the contrary, I am disposed by temperament not to want to offend anyone with words, to say nothing of deeds, and I don't find any pleasure in punishing. Yet, I saw the undoubted necessity of using cruelty with these idlers [the peasants—B.N.M.] and beating them up to restrain them from wickedness [i.e., thievery] and dissolute behavior, which made me suffer annoyance and dissatisfaction. But there was nothing else to do. It was absolutely appropriate to restrain them from thieving and other kinds of dissipation, and I soon saw that kind and gentle words, or threats and warnings, or even mild punishments accomplished nothing; it was invariably necessary to resort to all the varieties of cruelty to achieve one's end.

Bolotov described how he punished the thieves he caught: "I had them stripped naked, smeared all over with tar, and led in a procession the whole length of the village street. . . . The little children were ordered to drive them to the bridge and shout 'Thieves! Thieves!' and throw mud at them." Furthermore, Bolotov threatened the peasants that a third of them would have to stand guard at night. This punishment, together with the threat of nighttime guard duty,

> not only instilled terror in all of them but had the desired effect, and my *muzhiki* averred that they would give up all dissipation, keep a watchful eye on one another, and present the guilty for punishment. . . . From that time, it was as if all the peasants had been reborn. . . . As a result they began to love me, and full of gratitude, they were very pleased with me.[47]

The overwhelming majority of overseers and those they oversaw inclined to similar approaches and tactics, as they candidly admitted without any embarrassment.[48] "The right of corporal punishment was not only an essential attribute of serfdom under the law, but as a consequence of the understanding that prevailed at the time, it was considered unconditionally necessary to maintain authority and uphold servile relations," wrote an enlightened squire in the first half of the nineteenth century. "The understandings of household serfs of that era did not recognize any other authority" [except corporal punishment—*B.N.M.*].[49]

The level of violence varied markedly—over time, in response to the rise of gentility; according to status (taxable or exempt from taxes, noble or common); and according to the person who had the right and the power to use violence. It varied so much that it is not possible to establish, so to speak, a norm. The average level of violence was always high, however, as we will see below, even though we observe undoubted progress in attitudes toward violence and cruelty in the eighteenth century and the first half of the nineteenth. Until the 1760s, violence was considered a necessary tool for the maintenance of social order. Beginning in the era of Catherine II, a negative attitude toward violence began, little by little, to take hold in the enlightened part of society. At the end of the eighteenth century were heard the first voices of protest against violence and serfdom in general—notably the voice of A. N. Radishchev. There was a further humanization of attitudes in the first half of the nineteenth century. "What now is considered cruel," wrote a student of serfdom who had observed it firsthand, "at the time under discussion [the first half of the nineteenth century—B.N.M.] was inhumane to some, made no difference to the majority, and was considered criminal by no one; it was not included among the deeds that should unconditionally entail punishment under the law."[50]

An important economic factor in the universality of bondage was the absence of the bourgeois concept of employment. Earlier, the prevailing custom held that any free person who entered the service of another or worked for him became a dependent, and the person who hired him became his master. The master bore responsibility for the morality of his servants: "If thou be not assiduous in this matter of restraining thy servants, if thou simply set them tasks and be not mindful of their souls, thou shalt answer for their souls on the day of the Last Judgment." So prescribes the *Domostroi*, a celebrated sixteenth-century text that served as a font of wisdom for many generations of Russians.[51] Although this thinking was not inscribed in written law, in Russia at that time, as in feudal Europe, real social relations and real precedents tended to convert into norms of customary law, and sometimes into statute.

For example, a government decree at the time of the second census *(reviziia)* redefined all hired workers as serfs of their employers.[52] A hired worker who left his job in a factory in the eighteenth century or the first half of the nineteenth century was equated with a runaway serf and was treated as a criminal.[53] Here is another example: The state peasants of the North commonly practiced sharecropping *(polovnichestvo,* from the word for "half"). Sharecropping emerged before the eighteenth century and endured until the 1860s. In essence, destitute peasants would sell their plots of land (which was permitted in the North until 1754–1756) and conclude an agreement to rent other land. The sharecroppers were called *polovniki.* According to the contract, the landowners would pay the sharecroppers' taxes and dues, provide them with seed, and give them a loan to get started, and the sharecroppers would usually give the landowners half the crop (hence the name) and carry out various tasks for them in agriculture and construction. The sharecroppers had the right to move from one landowner to another, but only within the boundaries of a district and after paying the original landowner "chattel money" *(pozhilye den'gi).* Legally, sharecroppers were considered state peasants, but in reality they were serfs of the landowner on whose land they lived and worked.[54]

These are typical examples of the ways in which contractual relations turned into bondage as a result of the fusion of ownership of landed property with authority in Russian society. Property conferred power: In the early eighteenth century the tsar ruled over everyone in the state because he was the ultimate owner of all the land; a squire ruled over his peasants because they lived on his land; a factory owner ruled over his workers because they worked in his factory; and so on. Conversely, authority conferred property rights; the exercise of administrative and judicial authority and police powers entailed the conversion of the area of their exercise into the possession of the person who exercised them. The tsar became ultimate owner gradually, while carrying out military, judicial, and other functions of state. The squire became the owner of his peasants after the prolonged performance of administrative and other functions on his estate. The land and peasants that the government assigned in 1721 to the merchant owners of factories and mines, the so-called possessionary enterprises,* in time became the property of the factory owners, first in practice and then by law.[55] In bourgeois society, in contrast, employment and other contractual relations did not evolve into bondage.

There were also psychological considerations behind the development and consolidation of bondage: the lack of a developed individualism, of self-awareness and self-control; and a disposition to submit only to naked force. A. P. Zablotskii-Desiatovskii, a well-known expert on the peasant question in the period between 1830 and 1860, wrote: "Among serfs the concept of the person does not exist. Frequently the squire violates marital rights, encroaches on the chastity of peasant wives and daughters, and frequently the peasants put up with this patiently; this applies particularly to the women."[56]

Did all people in the early eighteenth century feel that they were in bondage? I think not, even in the dark days of Peter I, when the emperor put society under maximum strain and tried to impose extraordinary burdens on every last person, including himself. All layers of society, except for serfs and slaves *(raby)*, followed the thinking of the time and their own inner conviction and considered themselves free; that is, they were not serfs, although until the reign of Catherine II the greatest grandee would style himself "your slave" when he addressed the monarch. Freedom was conceived of as the opposite of slavery and serfdom, because except for serfs and slaves, the lack of freedom of all other social groups did not mean a complete lack of rights; the possibility of seeking justice from the courts, the administration, or the tsar was not foreclosed. Everyone had definite rights, confirmed by custom if not by law, and the most powerful monarch and state were obliged to reckon with these rights. It is an important point of principle that as in the West in the Middle Ages, the sovereign and the state dealt by and large not with particular individuals but with persons grouped in corporations. And however weak the corporations of nobles, clergy, merchants, craftspeople, and peasants were, compared to their counterparts in western Europe, they still had the power to defend their members from the arbitrary actions monarch and state (*arbitrary* meaning that they failed to conform to custom, tradition, or law).

Even the serfs were not so bereft of rights either legally or in practice as represented in the historical literature. Although serfs were regarded as the

---

*The owner of a possessionary enterprise, usually a mine or a factory, was permitted to buy villages and then to compel a fixed proportion of the peasants in the village (ranging from one-fourth to one-third of the total) to labor in his enterprise. Possessionary peasants were distinct from serfs in that they were attached to the enterprise rather than to its owner; they could not be assigned work outside the enterprise or be sold apart from the enterprise.—*Trans.*

property of their squires, this did not mean the complete expropriation of the peasant's person. Peasants continued to consider themselves members of a tax-paying class of society (since they paid taxes to the state); they were subject to conscription on the same footing as townspeople and other categories of peasants; they had the right to bypass the manorial court and appeal to the state courts; they could undertake contractual obligations; and with the permission of their squire, they could transfer to another status group. Serfs had the right of redress against dishonor; to dishonor a male serf verbally carried a fine levied against the offender, and to dishonor his wife carried a double fine (these fines were increased in 1842).* It is interesting that the fine for dishonoring serfs and state peasants was the same. The private relations between a peasant and his squire were also delimited by a law that required squires to be solicitous of their peasants' welfare, not to bring them to ruin, and to provide them with food in the event of a harvest failure. Squires could not abuse their authority, under penalty of confiscation or sequestering of their estates.[57] No less importantly, the serf was defended by the commune of which he was a member. Only rarely did a squire overcome resistance from the commune, and victory was never complete or conclusive.[58] I. T. Pososhkov, a self-taught economist and entrepreneur who became a serfholding squire, asserted in 1724 in his *On Poverty and Wealth:*

> Squires are not in eternal possession of their peasants, who are the immediate possessions of the autocrat of all Russia; their possession is temporary. By virtue of this it is not fitting that squires should bring them to ruin, and it is fitting that they are protected by the tsar's decree, to the end that peasants be genuine peasants, rather than paupers, for when the peasants prosper, so does the tsar.[59]

He made this assertion 127 years after the enserfment of the peasantry and twelve years after the law converted estates and the peasants living on them into the squires' property!

In medieval Western society there was much violence, but law prevailed. In Russian society at the beginning of the eighteenth century there was even more violence; yet even as the "right of the strong" had a wide scope, social relations were governed to a considerable degree by legal norms rather than by violence. Even extraeconomic compulsion was not simply a matter of force but was governed by tradition and custom.

---

*For similar dishonor to an unmarried peasant woman, the woman's father might demand and receive due compensation according to peasant custom. Such cases, however, were not explicitly addressed by the written law.—*B.N.M.*

The Abolition of Bondage

To establish the chronological limits of the liberation of various classes of the population, let us identify the criteria of personal freedom that flow logically from the traits of bondage offered above: freedom from all forms of extraeconomic, personal dependence, whether economic, administrative, or juridical in origin; freedom to choose a place of residence and an unlimited right to move—the right of geographic mobility; freedom to change social status, or the right of social mobility; freedom from all varieties of imposed social inferiority—mutual or community responsibility, the soul tax, conscription, and corporal punishment—by means either of their abolition or their extension to all classes of the population; the full and unconditional right to private property; freedom to study and to choose an occupation or profession; and the inviolability of personal dignity—that is, the imposition of penalties for dishonoring persons and depriving them of dignity, honor, property, or life only by a court of law. Just as all classes were cast into bondage only gradually, so delivery from bondage did not happen at once—it entailed liberation from bondage to the state, to private persons, and to corporations.

The Emancipation of the Nobility

The emancipation of the nobility took place in several stages and was accompanied by regression in the direction of bondage. The Empress Anna, responding to entreaties from the nobility, published on 31 December 1736 a manifesto offering three major concessions. The term of compulsory service became twenty-five years instead of perpetuity; one member of a family of sons or brothers was released from service to administer the family estate (the man released was obliged to study so as to be ready to join the civil service if summoned); and last, the age of entry into compulsory service was set at 20 years. Nobles who retired or stayed home were required to provide a number of recruits for the army proportional to their holdings of serfs. The manifesto had scarcely been promulgated when practically half of the officers retired, which is understandable, inasmuch as service began very early, at age 15, and always began at the bottom of the service hierarchy. Fearing that she would be left without officers and functionaries, the empress suspended the implementation of the manifesto for a time, but gradually it came into force. In 1737, almost simultaneously, the regime raised the requirements for a nobleman's education. Henceforth, prior to beginning service, a nobleman had to be scrutinized four times (at 7, 12, 16, and 20 years of age). The last three reviews included examinations in reading, writing, religious studies, arithmetic, geometry, geography, history, and fortification. Under Anna Ivanovna it became customary to enroll nobles in service when they were very young, so that by the time they reached the age of 20 and began their service, they would have "risen" in the ranks and could enter their regiments as officers.

On February 18, 1762, Peter III issued the Manifesto on the Freedom of the Nobility, which liberated nobles from compulsory service to the state; those currently in service could stay on or retire, with the exception of men in the military during a campaign. The manifesto also granted nonserving nobles the right to go abroad and to serve another sovereign. Education, however, remained compulsory, although the requirement was framed in the form of authoritative advice "that no one dare to raise children without imparting learning to them." The manifesto offered an interesting motive for the abolition. Compulsory service had accomplished its task: It had provided the state with many useful and informed men, it had uprooted "coarseness and ignorance" from among the nobility, and it had instilled elevated ideas. Consequently there was no longer a need to compel nobles to serve. Many nobles did retire, thanks to the manifesto. After some reflection and hesitation, in 1785, Catherine II issued the Gracious Charter on the Rights, Liberties, and Privileges of the Russian Nobility (*blagorodnoe rossiiskoe dvorianstvo*—literally the "noble Russian nobility"), which further expanded the personal rights of nobles.[60]

The Charter to the Nobility affirmed for all time "freedom and liberty." In particular, it abolished compulsory service and granted the right to serve allied *(soiuznye)* European powers; it gave nobles special privileges concerning entry into civil or military service and promotion; it gave them permission to go abroad to study; it freed nobles from personal taxes and imposts; it exempted them from corporal punishment; it guaranteed the inviolability of a nobleman's dignity—that is, a nobleman could be deprived of his property, life, or patent of nobility only by a decision of a court of nobles that had been confirmed by the monarch; and it confirmed the nobility's monopoly of land populated with serfs, although nonnobles who already held land with serfs were not deprived of them. The charter completely satisfied the nobles, since it corresponded to their understanding of freedom and liberty.

Interestingly, this understanding recalls the peasant concept of liberty as freedom from all obligations to the state. Along with liberty, the nobility gained corporate rights: the right to form a nobiliary society with the status of a juridical person in each district and province; the right to convene noble assemblies regularly; and the right to convene special courts consisting solely of nobles, with jurisdiction solely over nobles. The right to vote in noble assemblies and to be elected to nobiliary offices was limited to hereditary nobles who had served the state and had attained officer rank or the equivalent. Note that many of these corporate rights already had been conferred on the nobility in 1775, albeit in more limited scope.

We should not forget that the emancipation of the nobility from compulsory service carried a significant condition, contained in Article 20 of the charter: "At any such time as the Russian autocracy deems the service of the nobility necessary and requisite, every noble man is *obligated* [emphasis mine—*B.N.M.*] to respond to the first summons of the autocratic authority and not to spare his labor or his very life in service to the state."[61] No sooner had Emperor Paul I ascended to the throne in 1797 than he annulled the Charter to the Nobility and restored compulsory service. Under Alexander I, however, the charter returned to force—this time, permanently.

Before the nobility was freed from compulsory service, the district corporations of the nobility bore collective responsibility for fulfilling certain assigned police functions. In 1775, the new nobiliary corporations were relieved of these police functions as well and put on a fundamentally new footing, so that the last elements of corporate bondage disappeared. Thus the nobility was the first status group in Russia to gain freedom from state and corporate bondage and to acquire personal rights.

For a long time, however, most emancipated nobles continued to feel subordinate to the autocracy and did not feel independent. "Here [in Russia]," E. P. Dashkova remarked, "there is not what properly speaking is called a gentleman; everyone takes the favor of the monarch as the measure of his own worth."[62] This tendency derived, on the one hand, from social inertia, and on the other, from the nobility's continued strong dependence on the autocracy until the reforms of the 1860s and even after. For many nobles, state service was essential either because of material necessity (the overwhelming majority of nobles were poor and had nothing to live on but their salaries) or because of pride. A serving noble could not feel independent or act independently, as could an English gentleman. Nonserving nobles also stood in constant need of the monarch's charity: By 1861, two-thirds of noble estates were mortgaged to state credit institutions; the grace and favor of the monarch (in paying off a debt, extending its term, or providing other relief) could save the squire from seeing his estate sold at auction.

A nobleman who did not serve the state remained suspect in the eyes of the autocracy, and as we have seen, his rights were limited. In 1853 the governors-general received instruction from Nicholas I to be watchful "lest nobles in the provinces languish in baneful idleness rather than devote themselves to state service."[63] In matters great and small, the nobility depended upon the autocracy. The emperor could permit or forbid travel abroad, and he could put a disloyal noble under police surveillance. The autocrat also oversaw relations between squires and serfs and could call a nobleman to account for exceeding his authority. A particularly large number of limitations were introduced in the reign of Nicholas I. For example, in 1831 the emperor forbade youths younger than 18 years to travel abroad for study. In 1834, nobles were forbidden to stay abroad for more than five years, and in 1851, for more than three. At the same time, an enormous fee, equal to a year's salary for the average functionary, was imposed to discourage travel abroad. A nobleman who wanted to enter service was required to begin in the provinces. In 1837, governors were charged with supervision of new entrants into service and required to report to the emperor every six months about their conduct.

We can see that even after the Russian emperors granted freedom to the nobility, they did not entirely give up power over them. This prompted some contemporaries, and in turn some historians, to suggest that the emancipation of the nobility was a fiction. "I look on every Russian planter (*plantator,* a derisive word meaning 'serfholder') as a link in an enormous iron chain that binds this realm," wrote E. P. Dashkova at the beginning of the nineteenth century, "and when I meet with them in society, I cannot but think that they themselves are serfs of the despot."[64] In the liberal reign of Alexander I, M. M. Speranskii asserted that every nobleman was the slave of the emperor, just as the serf was the squire's slave. The legal historian V. I. Sergeevich believed that "the patrimonial-patriarchal character of autocracy" was not played out in the second half of the nineteenth century.[65] Richard Pipes takes the same view today. These views are rooted in a confusion of personal rights with political ones: The nobility did not have civil rights at the beginning of the nineteenth century, and this caused them dissatisfaction.

Nobles who were particularly rankled by the remnants of bondage and the lack of civic freedom tried to acquire the latter either through rebellion, like the Decembrists, or by fleeing abroad, like Herzen, Bakunin, and many others. One of those who went abroad was V. S. Pecherin, a nobleman who had obtained an excellent education at the universities of St. Petersburg and Berlin. In 1836, at the age of 29, Pecherin left Russia, giving up everything—a career that promised him high social status, economic sufficiency, a private estate, and so on—and fled to the West. "I have lost everything that a man holds dear in life, absolutely everything. But I have retained my worth as a man and my independence of spirit."[66] What troubled Pecherin about life in Russia was the lack of personal freedom of religion, of speech, and of the press; the impossibility of freely traveling abroad and participating in political life; and his unwillingness to serve in a Russian university as a professor-functionary. Pecherin described his attraction to the West:

> In England or America, a young man of eighteen, precociously matured by the forge of freedom, already occupies a significant place among his fellow citizens. . . . All roads are open to him: science, art, industry, commerce, agricul-

ture, and finally, political life with its glorious struggles and lofty rewards. Choose as you like! There are no barriers! Even a lazy lad without gifts cannot help developing, when the turbulent activity of the entire people cries out to him, "Forward!"[67]

What Pecherin wanted most of all was civil rights and participation in state administration.

The formal emancipation of nobles from bondage to the state gradually brought with it, despite remnants of the old bondage, a genuine emancipation. In time, the rights of nobles, far from being a fiction, became habitual and customary. Earlier, Peter I had tortured and executed conspirators by the thousand and bribe-takers by the dozen, without regard to title, rank, or wealth. A negative word about the tsar or his rule, fantasies about a plot, the intention or wish to remove the monarch from power, a romantic intrigue with the empress—under Peter I, any of these warranted execution.

The insurrection of the Decembrists in 1825 ended, after six months of investigation and trial, in the conviction and sentencing of 289 noblemen, five of whom subsequently were hanged. Among the common soldiers accused of having participated in the uprising, 201 were sentenced to corporal punishment and 4,000 were sent to the Caucasian front.[68] Contemporaries were horrified by these punishments. But compare them with the denouement of the unsuccessful revolt of musketeers *(strel'tsy)* in 1698: Those executed for their alleged participation in the conspiracy against Peter I, including nobles, numbered 1,168—some of whom were decapitated by Peter himself.[69] Under Nicholas I, it was no longer possible to impose that sort of summary judgment either on nobles or on anyone else.

The emancipation of the nobility advanced in parallel with the development of its rights to private property. Under Peter I, nobles did not hold their estates as private property, since they bore compulsory service and were limited in their rights of inheritance, disposition, and use of the land. Peter introduced new limitations: All private fisheries on nobles' estates were expropriated; all apiaries and private mills were declared to be the treasury's, and on this basis, were assessed state fees. All factories, mines, and mills also were declared to be the treasury's and were laden with fees; they were placed under the supervision of the College of Manufactures, which also gave permission for new enterprises to open. Rights to all subsoil resources were transferred to the treasury (1719); and all the forests of European Russia were declared to be state preserves (1723).

Catherine II, between 1762 and 1785, abolished the limitations on the nobility's property rights that antedated Peter I or that he had introduced, with one exception: The state retained the right to expropriate private property for state purposes in extraordinary circumstances and with compensation. The state did not abuse this right but did sometimes make use of it. For example, in 1861, despite the wishes of a majority of squires, land was redeemed from them in behalf of peasants. In the 1785 Charter to the Nobility, the right to private property was ceremonially affirmed, and thereafter it was not violated. The nobility had obtained freedom together with private property rights.[70]

The Emancipation of the Clergy

The clergy's emancipation from bondage and its acquisition of civil rights began almost simultaneously with the emancipation of the nobility but proceeded slowly. In the early eighteenth century the state began to consider the clergy a privileged status group. Under Peter I, ordained clergy (priests and deacons), like nobles, were relieved from the soul tax and from conscription; at the time, such freedoms were considered the major markers of social privilege. Toward the mid-eighteenth century, the clergy were freed from all taxes in kind (e.g., fire fighting and watchman's service), and in 1764 the clergy's *obrok,* or *episkopskoe tiaglo,* was abolished. In 1767 the Holy Synod prohibited the clerical hierarchy from applying corporal punishment to priests. In 1771 the prohibition was extended to deacons, and in 1811, to monks. Priests and deacons were exempted from corporal punishment by sentence of secular courts in 1801, their wives and widows in 1808, and their children in 1835. Underdeacons, sextons, and other lesser clergy and members of their families were freed from corporal punishment by clerical and secular courts in 1862. In 1797 Paul I granted the right to receive medals and orders to priests and monks, which opened up the possibility of their attaining hereditary nobility and hence acquiring an estate with serfs. In 1849 the clergy was granted freedom from the requirement to gain an education. Thus, by 1801 the ordained clergy, and in 1862 the lesser clergy, became a privileged class, free from all personal taxes, conscription, and corporal punishment. With respect to rights, clergymen at the beginning of the nineteenth century were on a par with personal nobles.

The emancipation of the clergy from bondage, or "burdened status" *(tiaglovoe sostoianie),* culminated in the church reforms of the 1860s and 1870s. A series of measures adopted between 1867 and 1871 completely changed the social position of the clergy as well as its legal definition. The transfer of church offices by heredity, and all family claims to church offices, were banned. As a closed caste or estate of the realm, the clergy was liquidated, first of all by abolishing the hereditary character of clerical status and church office, and second, by allowing free entry into the clergy and departure from its ranks. Children of clergy were assigned secular social status: The widows of ordained clergy had the rights of personal nobles; their children, the rights of hereditary honored citizens; and the wives and children of lesser clergy, the rights of personal honored citizens. Also abolished was the custom—which had virtually become a law—that clergymen should only marry the daughters of clergy. The reform also eliminated various limitations on a clergyman's freedom of speech and of the press. In addition, seminaries and other church schools, which had been restricted to clerical offspring, were now opened to children of all social strata.

The power of the bishop over parish clergy was seriously weakened: He lost the right to punish clergy by transferring them to remote parishes with little revenue; and clergy could take long leaves (before they had accomplished their thirty-five-year terms of service) without sacrificing their pensions, or could permanently relinquish their clerical status if they wished. The bishop's private court was retained only for minor offenses, for which there was a mild punishment in the form of penance. More serious acts of malfeasance or immorality, as well as civil suits in connection with church property and in which the plaintiff was a clergyman, were considered by a court of the consistory, which conducted a formal inquiry following established rules. When criminal charges were brought, clergy were subject to secular courts on the same footing as nonclergy. The establishment of conferences of deputies elected by the clergy, authorized to discuss the improvement of seminaries and other clerical schools in the diocese and to elect members to the boards of these schools, significantly limited the bishop's power in the sphere of clerical education. Monks also were granted the right to voluntarily renounce their holy orders, after which they would return to their previous civil status with all the rights that were theirs by birth. Former monks did not, however, regain the rank and distinctions they had personally acquired before tonsuring.

All these measures combined to create the preconditions for transforming the clergy from a closed and hereditary estate of the realm into a group of persons with a profession—serving the church—and to create realistic conditions for liberating the clergy from the power of the bishops and the state. As Gregory Freeze has shown, the church reforms were carried through by the tsarist bureaucracy, in many cases without conferring with the church hierarchy or the parish clergy. Furthermore, some reforms did not please the rank-and-file clergy, and others displeased the episcopate. The implementation of these reforms proceeded very slowly due to resistance from hierarchs and parish clergy, which led to deviations from the reformers' intentions—to modifications of some reforms and to partial retreat from others. Nonetheless, one can say that the reforms liberated the clergy from their burden-bearing status and bondage of the previous century and a half.[71]

In contrast to the nobility's situation, the private property rights of the clergy developed slowly, inconsistently, and differently for the white and black clergy. Over time, the property rights of monks were curtailed. Until the eighteenth century, enormous amounts of real estate and other property belonged to the church. In 1701, a specially created state institution, the Monastery Chancellery,[72] took over the administration of the church's estates. In 1721, control passed to the Holy Synod; in 1726, to the College of Economy; and later back to the Synod. In 1762, the church's lands and the peasants on them were transferred to state ownership. The property rights of the white or parish clergy, on the other hand, slowly expanded. The household tracts (*dvorovye mesta*) allotted to the clergy were recognized as their unequivocal property in towns in 1785 and in villages in the 1860s. Right up to 1917, clerics were forbidden to engage in entrepreneurial activity, to give surety, or to act for others in business matters. The insecurity of the clergy's property rights was a major factor in their dependence on the state.

The Emancipation of the Townspeople

At the beginning of the eighteenth century, the commercial-manufacturing class enjoyed the fundamental right of engaging in trade and manufacture. Until 1785, however, this right was not secured as a monopoly. The 1785 Charter to the Towns legally guaranteed merchants and *meshchane* a monopoly only over *entrepreneurial* commerce, for nobles and peasants could sell only products they produced. But even this purely nominal monopoly did not last long. Soon the law permitted peasants who paid a special fee to trade—at first, only in the capitals (1798–1799), and then everywhere (1812). As of 1818, peasants were officially permitted also to engage in manufacture, and this right was expanded in 1824.[73] Until that time, only merchants (in the Russian sense of the word, meaning entrepreneurs rather than traders) and nobles had the right to conduct manufacturing enterprises. In fact, townspeople never had a monopoly either over commerce or over manufacture, despite their long struggle to attain it; the nobles, who had an interest in their own enterprises and in those of their peasants, had thwarted all of the townspeople's efforts.

In other respects, the merchants, the top stratum of townspeople, attained some results. In 1721, merchants of all three guilds (about 40 percent of the registered urban population around 1750,[74] about 30 percent in 1800, and about 10 percent in 1854[75]) were personally freed from conscription in that they had the right to pay for exemption; and in 1775 they were relieved of the soul tax (instead of which they had to pay a stated percentage of their declared capital) and of mutual responsibility—which liberated the merchant estate from the *posad* commune and thus from corporate bondage. The 1785 Charter to the Towns exempted merchants of the first two guilds (about 3 percent of the townspeople in the last quarter of the eighteenth century and less than 1 percent in the first quarter of the

nineteenth century) from corporal punishment; also, the fine for dishonoring them was raised, so that the offender now had to pay a sum equal to
the annual payments due from the merchant to the state and the town. The
charter also abolished most of the taxes in kind levied on townspeople, so
that *barshchina* to the state was in effect eliminated.[76] The privileges
granted to merchants by the charter were the basis for the division of
townspeople into two groups—the privileged stratum (merchants) and the
taxable stratum (the *meshchane*). Corporal punishment was abolished for
merchants of the third guild and for *meshchane* in 1863; mutual responsibility and the soul tax were lifted from the *meshchane* only in the 1860s;
and in 1874 a universal military obligation replaced the old conscription
system. These measures, in effect, meant the end of the *posad* commune,
and with it, corporate bondage in the towns.

As had happened with other classes, the emancipation of the townspeople was accompanied by an expansion in their property rights. In 1785,
the townspeople's right to hold private property was recognized. In 1801
they gained the right to purchase land with no serfs, and in 1822, to own
homes in rural locations. Thus, by 1802, the merchants of the first two
guilds were legally free of all forms of bondage, and the merchants of the
third, from all except liability to corporal punishment. As for the
meshchane, who constituted 90 percent of all townspeople, they had to
wait until the 1860s for their emancipation.

The Emancipation of the Peasants

As the bondage of the nobles, clergy, and townspeople steadily diminished
beginning in the second quarter of the eighteenth century, the bondage of
peasants became more intense, reaching its apogee during the reign of
Catherine II. The situation of the serfs was saddest of all. The law forbade
them to file complaints personally to the emperor against their masters and
gave the latter the right to send peasants to penal exile and hard labor in
Siberia without any inquiry or court proceeding, possibly on nothing more
than a whim. Squires and their stewards interfered in the private lives of
serfs, and in particular, controlled serf marriages. Squires had the right to all
of their serfs' property. The government gave the squires the obligation of
collecting state taxes from their serfs and delivering the money to the treasury, thus eliminating any direct relationship between serfs and the organs
of state power: The squire ("the peasants' police chief," as Paul I put it) always stood between the serfs and the state. Serfs retained the right to bear
witness in court, to pay state taxes, and to serve in the army, and they were
subject to the general criminal laws. They also had a right to modest compensation if they were dishonored and to receive aid from their squire in the
event of harvest failure. We have already seen that squires were forbidden

to reduce serfs to ruin and to torture or kill them, under penalty of sequestration of the estate. Interestingly, these checks on the squire's power were in place from the middle of the seventeenth century;[77] they were not an invention of the government of the imperial period.

Prior to the Manifesto on the Freedom of the Nobility (1762), the bondage of serfs had both a state and a private character. There was a balance between these elements, giving serfdom some moral justification: The squire served the state (or the tsar), and the serfs served the squire, thus helping the state. With the elimination of the nobility's compulsory service, serfdom lost a significant portion of its state-endowed character and became primarily a matter of private law. This important consideration was reflected in the elimination under Empress Elizabeth of the serfs' oath of fidelity to the ascending monarch and his or her heirs. Although the state delegated its rights to the squires, it continued to supervise relations between squires and serfs. In particular, the state had every right to regulate the squire's power. Throughout the eighteenth century, however, little was done to alleviate the bondage of serfs. Decrees of 1721 and 1771, respectively, forbade the division of families when serfs were sold, and the sale of serfs apart from the land being sold at auction. A number of decrees of Catherine II diminished the sources of new serfs: Enserfment by the purchase and sale of Asiatic captives from other countries (1776), by marriage to a serf (1781), and by self-enserfment (1783) was prohibited. In 1764, the children of conscripts born after their fathers entered service were freed. These measures served to diminish the number of serfs.

In the late eighteenth century, the government began to make more serious efforts to limit the squires' authority and to restore to serfs some of the rights they had lost earlier. In 1797, Paul I issued a special decree to limit *barshchina* to three days per week. In 1803 the Law on Free Agriculturists permitted squires to manumit entire villages by contract with their peasants. In 1842 this law was supplemented by the so-called Law on Obligated Peasants, which permitted squires to grant peasants freedom by reaching an agreement with them, according to which the peasants would pay strictly fixed dues and the land would remain the squire's property. Decrees of 1802, 1804, 1808, 1827, 1833, and 1841 set certain limits on the squire's right to sell his serfs, give them away, or exile them to Siberia; at the same time, serfs gained the right to purchase their own freedom either by agreement with the squire or without such an agreement—but only if the squire's estate was being sold at auction. However, limitation of the squire's rights evidently was not the same as their abolition: Between 1827 and 1831, squires exiled 1,249 serfs to Siberia; and between 1842 and 1846, 2,775.[78]

The law code issued in 1832 regulated the system of punishment, and the 1845 edition clearly defined the competence of manorial justice and moderated the punishment of serfs by squires. The latter now had the right to administer the following punishments: up to forty blows with rods or up to fifteen blows with sticks; and up to two months' confinement in a village lockup, three months in a house of correction, or six months' service in a punishment battalion. Squires also still had the right to send their serfs off as recruits and to banish them forever from the estate by turning them over to local agencies of state administration.

Squires often exceeded their authority. When they went beyond established limits, the administration, availing itself of the decrees of 1827 and 1826, hauled the offending squire before a court or sequestered his estate. From the incomplete data available, we can surmise that the number of squires indicted and convicted for abuse of authority was rather large. For example, in the twelve-year period from 1834 to 1845, 2,838 squires were called to account, and 630 of them were convicted. For the year 1836, and between 1851 and 1853, the annual average of estates sequestered was 212. It is interesting to note that the state prosecuted squires for abuse of authority and serfs for insubordination to their squires in similar numbers. For these offenses, taking Russia as a whole in the period between 1834 and 1845, the proportions were 0.13 percent of serfs and 0.13 percent of squires.[79]

The serfs' entire burden of triple bondage—to the state, the squire, and the commune—endured without significant change until the abolition in 1861 of the most onerous part of their burden: bondage to private persons. From the moment in 1861 when the manifesto on the emancipation of the serfs was promulgated, serfs ceased to be considered the property of their squires; they could no longer be sold, resettled against their will, or the like, and they gained various personal rights—freedom to marry, to enter into contracts, to litigate, to engage in commerce and manufacture without impediment, to leave their place of residence, to enter any educational institution, and to change their social status. They officially gained the right of self-administration, which they had informally enjoyed before the reform. The law provided, however, that the realization of all the rights that had been proclaimed depended upon permission from the commune; for the individual peasant who was not the head of a household, permission from the head of the family was required as well. In other words, a peasant could leave for the city if he had received permission from the head of his family, from the commune, and from the local administration. Getting permission was no mere formality: It entailed the satisfaction of significant conditions such as lack of tax arrears, good conduct, and so on. A peasant could join the *meshchane* if he had permission from the head of his family, the commune, and the local administration; if the society of *meshchane* in the town in question agreed to accept him as a member; and if he completely renounced his claims to the commune's land (until 1870, because a peasant had no right to give up his allotment, he was effectively bound to the land). Only one of the three tiers of the serf's bondage had been eliminated: his dependence on the squire. The state and communal tiers endured. For serfs and appanage peasants, the legal abolition of servile bondage to private persons paradoxically went hand in hand with enhanced bondage to state and corporation (the commune), and corporate bondage became stronger in state peasant villages. This paradox derived in part from the government's more active intervention into peasant affairs because of its fiscal involvement in the redemption of land allotments and because of its wish to compensate for the weakening of manorial authority. It also derived from the expanded significance of the commune. Therefore, the abolition of serfdom did not in the least mean that peasants attained full freedom. The retention of other forms of bondage contributed to the continuity, in both social and economic terms, between the prereform and postreform villages.

It is important to emphasize that the elimination of the squire's interference in peasant affairs took many years to accomplish. The reform legislation confirmed the squire's full property right to the land that peasants had cultivated prior to 1861. If peasants wanted to redeem this land under the rules and for the price prescribed by the government, they had to strike an agreement with the squire concerning its redemption. The state provided redemption loans to peasants with a term of 49 years; that is, they were to be paid off in 1910. Until the parties agreed to the redemption contract, which required the squire's initiative, peasants were "temporarily obligated"; for the period of temporary obligation, they had, as before, to pay *obrok* or render *barshchina*, and during this period the squire retained the right of "manorial police power." That is, he could demand the replacement of the village elder and of other members of the village administration and could press various demands on the peasants concerning the maintenance of social order. By 1870, two-thirds of the ex-serfs had entered into the redemption process and consequently attained the status of "peasant proprietors," but the other third remained temporarily obligated and hence dependent upon the squire. As late as 1881, 15.3 percent of former serfs were still temporarily obligated, and not until January 1883 did the state terminate temporary obligation by compelling these remaining peasants to undertake redemption.

Because they had to repay their redemption loans, with interest, to the treasury, the former serfs became even more economically dependent upon the state than they had been prior to the reform. To a certain extent, peasants became the state's peons *(zalozhniki)*. Nonetheless, the intensity of peasant bondage to the state gradually diminished. In 1874, the universal military obligation replaced the old, caste-based system of conscription; and between 1883 and 1906, in various stages, the soul tax was abolished

throughout Russia and replaced with a tax on land *(obrochnaia podat').*
The passport regulations introduced in 1895 made it much simpler for
peasants to travel. Mutual responsibility was abolished in two stages in
1899 and 1903. In 1907, redemption debts were liquidated. Peasants were
subject to corporal punishment up to the end of the old regime, but the
scope of application was significantly narrowed by a law of April 17,
1863; henceforth, corporal punishment could only be imposed on peasants
who could not satisfy certain educational qualifications, who did not hold
any village office, who did not suffer from various specified illnesses, and
who were younger than 60 years. All peasant women were exempt. As of
1863, corporal punishment was retained only for prisoners, penal exiles,
and peasants.[80]

As for the corporate bondage of the peasantry, it remained in full force
until the Stolypin reform of 1906, when every peasant gained the right to
leave the commune, even if the commune objected. Henceforth, the power
of the commune grew weaker by virtue of the departure of some peasants;
but only about 26 percent of the peasantry did depart in the period 1907
to 1915.[81] The Revolution of 1905–1907 marks the limit of corporate
bondage, after which peasants, at least formally, attained the right to freedom. In practice, however, the 74 percent of peasants who stayed in the
commune remained in a state of corporate bondage.

The situation of state peasants deteriorated, on the whole, in the course
of the eighteenth century, but their personal rights were never so limited as
the rights of serfs. The administrators of the state peasants did not have
such broad judicial power and rights to punish or exile peasants or send
them to the army as did the squires. The person of the state peasant was
better defended, because his bondage was primarily based on state law
rather than private law. The status of state peasants was reflected in the
fact that they continued to take an oath of loyalty when a new monarch ascended the throne. In the eyes of serfs the situation of state peasants was so
much better that they dreamed of transferring to that jurisdiction.

The emancipation of the state peasants began with the reforms of P. D.
Kiselev, in 1837 to 1839. These reforms significantly improved their economic, juridical, administrative, and cultural situation and gave them more
rights of self-administration. The law conferred significant rights on state
peasants: to choose their place of residence, status, and occupation; to pursue their education; to submit petitions even to the monarch; and to make
contracts. These rights have induced some scholars to hold that Kiselev's
reform emancipated the state peasants from bondage,[82] but that seems a
hasty conclusion. First of all, the reform laws included certain limitations
on the realization of these rights and were not fully implemented. Second,
state peasants continued to bear some traits of bondage, such as liability to
conscription and mutual responsibility.[83] Emancipation from bondage to

the state was granted to the state peasantry in 1866 and to appanage peasants in 1863. Further emancipation from the remnants of bondage to the state and from corporate bondage took place gradually, on the same footing as for ex-serfs, and was still incomplete in 1917.

The development of the peasant's right to private property is a matter of particular interest. The property rights of peasants were limited by law: They had no right to buy or sell land, to enter into contracts or tax-farming, or to engage in commerce or manufacture, and they could not issue bills of exchange or stand surety. These prohibitions, to be sure, could be evaded (some peasants entered into contracts nominally concluded by another individual, who had the right to engage in contracts); but they still presented serious obstacles to the development of private property among peasants. For example, serfs concluded contracts in the name of their master, but then all the property that was acquired counted as the master's. According to custom, serfs' property, other than real estate, was completely at their own disposal, and so was all other property acquired in the master's name, including land and even serfs. To violate this custom was considered immoral. All the same, some squires, especially those in serious financial difficulties, ignored the custom. In such cases, the law stood entirely on the squire's side. In contrast, state peasants retained property rights over their possessions other than land.

At the end of the eighteenth century, the property rights of peasants began gradually to broaden. Decrees of 1798, 1799, and 1812 restored to peasants their right to engage in trade, and decrees of 1818 and 1824 did the same for manufacture. Beginning in 1827, peasants were permitted to have their own houses in towns, and in 1848, in the capitals as well. In 1801, state peasants and manumitted serfs gained the right to buy land. Not until 1848—forty-seven years after state peasants had acquired the right—did serfs acquire the right to buy land, and only with their squire's consent and in his name. These progressive developments largely concerned peasant entrepreneurs with links to the towns, where the process of privatization of state property had been gaining intensity since 1700. As for property relations in the countryside, especially concerning land, there was during this time a regression—a retreat from the progressive development of peasant property rights that could be discerned in the seventeenth century.

Early in the eighteenth century, in most regions of Russia (except among the state peasants of the North, the Urals, and Siberia), the repartitional commune had taken hold among the peasants. This consolidated, collective, communal land tenure held sway on state lands under the aegis of the state and on private lands under the aegis of the squires. During the eighteenth century the state peasants of the North, the Urals, and the southern frontier of European Russia shifted to repartitional tenure, and Siberian peasants did the same in the late nineteenth and early twentieth centuries.

We can establish that although a right to private property began to develop in the towns in 1700, in the villages, right up to the beginning of the twentieth century, collective, communal property predominated.

This pattern held great significance for the destiny of town and village and for both townspeople and peasants, inasmuch as the history of property has developed in parallel with the development of human rights: The village lagged in every sphere because it lagged in the sphere of property relations. The town moved in the direction of expanding individual freedom and civil rights, along the path of the market economy, modernization, Europeanization, and the secularization of mass consciousness; the town drew Russia into the world economy and into the association of European powers. The village, however, from the beginning of the eighteenth century, lagged ever further behind the town in both social and economic relations. Everything traditional was, by and large, retained in the peasant milieu. Only in the last third of the nineteenth century and the beginning of the twentieth do we discern a stirring among the peasants, an inclination toward new ways of life. The disastrous onset of World War I, however, impeded the process of modernization in the village.

The Significance of Bondage

Bondage prevailed in Russia for several centuries. The reforms of the 1860s dealt it a powerful blow but did not entirely destroy it, and some of its forms and remnants survived until 1917. Bondage embraced the whole of society, from top to bottom, from the patriarchal peasant household to the court of the emperor, and pervaded all state institutions. As one contemporary remarked,

> Servile relations were part and parcel of the entire structure of the state; the whole structure was permeated by them. Functionaries were in servile dependence on their bosses, and likewise their bosses were in turn dependent on each other, the junior on the senior; the clergy and the merchants were in bondage, the courts were in bondage, and bondage prevailed in the army and in schools. All of life, all human relations were permeated by bondage— everything was bound to something. It is natural, therefore, that inasmuch as peasants were serfs to their squires, the latter were serfs to the whole state.[84]

Fortunately, the various forms of bondage—or to put it more concretely, the various beneficiaries of bondage—were in competition and sometimes weakened or paralyzed one another. For example, the squires—the beneficiaries of serfdom—competed with the state for power over peasants and peasant labor. The commune, the beneficiary of corporate bondage, struggled with the squires and the state, and by manipulating the contradictions between them, defended the interests of peasants. Furthermore, bondage to the state was to some decree counterbalanced by the institutions of rural, urban, and nobiliary self-administration.

Bondage was not simply one of the institutions of the Russian state; it was, especially prior to the 1860s, the milieu in which every member of society lived out his life. It exerted a powerful influence on every aspect of life. It facilitated the emergence of the command economy, political absolutism, and authoritarian relations in society and within the family. Bondage restrained the development of towns, the bourgeoisie, private property, and civil liberties; hampered social mobility; corrupted the psychology of society with a pervasive slavishness; and instilled certain negative traits in the Russian national character.[85]

Bondage arose and developed spontaneously, on the whole; it was an organic and essential component of Russian life and the Russian character. On the one hand, bondage was the converse of the weak development of Russian individualism, of Russians' easygoing and expansive temperament—what they like to call the "broad Russian nature"—and of the popular conception of freedom. We have dozens of testimonies by contemporaries, which cannot in the least be ignored or dismissed as less than dispassionate observations, to the effect that the ordinary Russian, whether peasant or townsperson, needed supervision; that he was given to spontaneity because of a lack of self-control and discipline; and that his conduct betrayed a lack of individualism and rationality.[86] These testimonies often came from enlightened and humane persons such as Tatishchev, Bolotov, and I. V. Lopukhin.[87] On the other hand, bondage was a reaction to economic backwardness; it was Russia's distinctive but rational response to the challenge of its environment and its difficult circumstances. State and society used bondage as a means of solving pressing problems—I have in mind defense, finance, keeping the population settled in place, and maintaining social order.

Beginning in 1762, one class after another was emancipated—first from bondage to private persons, then to the state, and then to corporations. This appropriate and necessary process, however, was not fated to reach its natural culmination; the world war and the October Revolution brought it to an abrupt end.

Notes

1. The most complete surveys of the literature on the problem of serfdom are P. Scheibert, *Die Russische Agrarreform von 1861: Ihre Probleme und der Stand ihrer Erforschung* (Cologne and Vienna, 1973); Richard Hellie, *Enserfment and Military Change in Muscovy* (Chicago and London, 1971), pp. 1–20.

2. See, for example, P. N. Miliukov, *Ocherki istorii russkoi kul'tury,* chast' 1, *Naselenie: Ekonomicheskii, gosudarstvennyi, i soslovnyi stroi* (Moscow, 1918), pp. 219–287.

3. A. L. Shapiro, "O prichinakh zakreposhcheniia krest'ian," in his *Russkoe krest'ianstvo pered zakreposhcheniem (XIV–XVI vv.)* (Leningrad, 1987), pp. 223–233; S. M. Kashtanov, "K istoriografii krepostnogo prava v Rossii," in M. V. Nechkina, ed., *Istoriia i istoriki: Istoriograficheskii ezhegodnik, 1971* (Moscow, 1974), pp. 126–141.

4. P. A. Zaionchkovskii, "Sovetskaia istoriografii reformy 1861 goda," *Voprosy istorii,* 1961, no. 2, pp. 85–104; V. I. Krutikov, "Sovetskaia istoriografiia krizisa feodal'no-krepostnicheskoi sistemy v Rossii," in P. A. Kolesnikov, ed., *Materialy XV sessii Simpoziuma po problemam agrarnoi istorii* (Vologda, 1976), vyp. 2, pp. 3–21; L. G. Zakharova, *Samoderzhavie i otmena krepostnogo prava v Rossii, 1856–1861* (Moscow, 1984), pp. 3–16.

5. Hellie, *Enserfment and Military Change,* pp. 1–20; Nicholas V. Riasanovsky, *A History of Russia* (New York and Oxford, 1984), pp. 185–187; Peter Kolchin, *Unfree Labor: American Slavery and Russian Serfdom* (Cambridge, 1987), pp. 17–31.

6. Jerome Blum, *Lord and Peasant in Russia from the Ninth to the Nineteenth Century* (Princeton, 1961), pp. 612–618; Alexander Gerschenkron, "Agrarian Policies and Industrialization: Russia, 1861–1917," in H. J. Habakkuk and N. Postan, eds., *Cambridge Economic History of Europe* (Cambridge, 1965), vol. 6, part 2, pp. 706–800; Alfred J. Rieber, *The Politics of Autocracy* (The Hague and Paris, 1966), pp. 15–58; Daniel Field, *The End of Serfdom: Nobility and Bureaucracy in Russia, 1855–1861* (Cambridge, 1976), pp. 96–101; Kolchin, *Unfree Labor,* pp. 359–369.

7. In Russian, *krugovaia poruka,* a very widespread system in Muscovite and imperial Russia according to which tax obligations were levied on entire communities or corporations, usually based on the number of persons or households registered in them. When members died, defaulted, or fled, their shares of the total obligation had to be covered by the members remaining.—*Trans.*

8. *Doklady i prigovory Pravitel'stvuiushchego senata* (St. Petersburg, 1880), tom 1, pp. 175–176.

9. M. T. Iablochkov, *Istoriia dvorianskogo sosloviia v Rossii* (St. Petersburg, 1876), pp. 373, 401.

10. M. M. Bogoslovskii, "Vvedenie podushnoi podati i krepostnoe pravo," in A. K. Dzhivelegov, S. P. Mel'gunov, and V. I. Picheta, eds., *Velikaia reforma: Russkoe obshchestvo i krest'ianskii vopros v proshlom i nastoiashchem* (Moscow, 1911), tom 1, p. 56.

11. See, for example, *Doklady i prigovory Pravitel'stvuiushchego senata,* tom 1, pp. 175–176.

12. A. Romanovich-Slavatinskii, *Dvorianstvo v Rossii ot nachala XVIII stoletiia do otmeny krepostnogo prava* (St. Petersburg, 1870), p. 147. See also N. P. Pavlov-Sil'vanskii, *Gosudarevy sluzhilye liudi: Proiskhozhdenie russkogo dvorianstva* (St. Petersburg, 1898), pp. 253–255, 270–294.

13. V. N. Latkin, *Uchebnik istorii russkogo prava perioda imperii* (St. Petersburg, 1909), pp. 164–165.

14. Gregory L. Freeze, *The Russian Levites: Parish Clergy in the Eighteenth Century* (Cambridge, Mass., 1977), pp. 13–45; P. V. Verkhovskii, *Ocherki po istorii russkoi tserkvi v XVIII i XIX stoletii* (Warsaw, 1912), vyp. 1; P. V. Znamenskii, *Prikhodskoe dukhovenstvo v Rossii so vremeni reformy Petra* (Kazan, 1873), pp. 354–403.

15. Freeze, *The Russian Levites*, p. 46.

16. In colloquial Russian, "treasury" is often a synonym for "state" or "government." For example, state peasants were often referred to as "treasury peasants."—*Trans.*

17. A. A. Kizevetter, *Posadskaia obshchina v Rossii XVIII stoletiia* (Moscow, 1903), pp. 170–248.

18. S. M. Solov'ev, *Istoriia Rossii s drevneishikh vremen* (Moscow, 1962), kniga 7, p. 86.

19. See, for example, V. I. Koretskii, *Zakreposhchenie krest'ian i klassovaia bor'ba v Rossii* (Moscow, 1970), pp. 5–11, 301–304; Kashtanov, "K istoriografii krepostnogo prava v Rossii," pp. 126–141.

20. Blum, *Lord and Peasant*, pp. 386–474; P. G., "O pasportakh," *Otechestvennye zapiski,* tom 129 (April 1860), pp. 386–474.

21. Romanovich-Slavatinskii, *Dvorianstvo v Rossii*, pp. 309–310.

22. There is a tendency either (and more commonly) to minimize or else to exaggerate the positive role of the squire in the life of peasants. An example of the former is A. I. Povalishin, *Riazanskie pomeshchiki i ikh krepostnye: Ocherki iz istorii krepostnogo prava v Riazanskoi gubernii v XIX stoletii* (Ryazan, 1903); an example of the latter is E. Lodyzhenskii, "Russkii pomeshchik," *Trudy Vol'nogo imperatorskogo ekonomicheskogo obshchestva,* 1856, tom 2, no. 4, pp. 67–74.

23. Latkin, *Uchebnik istorii russkogo prava perioda imperii,* pp. 207–208.

24. V. I. Krutikov, "Zakonodatel'stvo o pomeshchich'ikh krest'ianakh doreformennogo perioda," in *Sotsial'no-ekonomicheskie problemy rossiiskoi derevni v feodal'nuiu i kapitalisticheskuiu epokhi* (Rostov-on-Don, 1980), pp. 112–120.

25. In a draft bill produced by the codification commission of the 1750s; Latkin, *Uchebnik istorii russkogo prava,* p. 206.

26. P. Guliaev, *Sistematicheskoe sobranie sushchestvuiushchikh prav i obiazannostei upravleniia kazennymi krest'ianami* (Moscow, 1825).

27. A. I. Kopanev, *Krest'iane russkogo severa v XVII* (Leningrad, 1984), p. 7.

28. M. F. Vladimirskii-Budanov, *Obzor istorii russkogo prava* (Kiev and St. Petersburg, 1900), p. 255.

29. *Polnoe sobranie zakonov Rossiiskoi imperii,* Sobranie pervoe (hereafter, *PSZ 1*), tom 7, no. 4356 (St. Petersburg, 1830), p. 329. See also N. M. Druzhinin, *Gosudarstvennye krest'iane i reforma P.D. Kiseleva* (Moscow, 1946), tom 1, pp. 23–34; Olga Crisp, *Studies in the Russian Economy Before 1914* (London, 1976), pp. 73–95.

30. Rossiiskii gosudarstvennyi istoricheskii arkhiv (RGIA), fond 911 (V. I. Veshniakov), opis' 1, delo 6 ("Sravnitel'nyi obzor polozheniia gosudarstvennykh i pomeshchich'ikh krest'ian"), listy 1–30.

31. Horace W. Dewey and Ann M. Kleimola, "Suretyship and Collective Responsibility in Pre-Petrine Russia," *Jahrbücher für Geschichte Osteuropas,* 18 (1970), Heft. 3; Dewey and Kleimola, "From the Kinship to Every Man His Brother's

Keeper: Collective Responsibility in Pre-Petrine Russia," *Jahrbücher für Geschichte Osteuropas,* 30 (1982), Heft 3; M. Veber, *Istoricheskii ocherk osvoboditel'nogo dvizheniia v Rossii* (Kiev, 1906), p. 85.

32. V. O. Kliuchevskii, *Sochineniia v vos'mi tomakh* (Moscow, 1956–1959), tom 6, pp. 402–418.

33. Robert E. Jones, *The Emancipation of the Russian Nobility, 1762–1785* (Princeton, 1973), pp. 229–239, 283–286.

34. A. G. Man'kov, ed., *Sobornoe ulozhenie 1649* (Leningrad, 1987), pp. 293–308.

35. *Istoriia udelov za stoletie ikh sushchestvovaniia* (St. Petersburg, 1901), tom 2, pp. 37–41, 190–243; N. A. Blagoveshchenskii, *Chetvertnoe pravo* (Moscow, 1899); Latkin, *Uchebnik istorii russkogo prava,* pp. 190–243; V. I. Semevskii, *Krest'iane v tsarstvovanie imperatritsy Ekateriny II* (St. Petersburg, 1901), tom 2.

36. The concept of "state serfdom" *(gosudarstvennoe krepostnoe pravo)* was introduced in 1855 by K. D. Kavelin in his "Gosudarstvennoe krepostnoe pravo v Rossii," in *Golosa iz Rossii: Sborniki A.I. Gertsena i N.P. Ogareva* (reprint Moscow, 1974), knizhka 3, pp. 114–144.

37. V. N. Tatischev, *Izbrannye sochineniia* (Leningrad, 1979), pp. 121–122.

38. V. N. Tatishchev, *Istoriia Rossiiskaia* (Moscow, 1968), tom 7, p. 315.

39. N. A. Smirnov, *Tserkov' v istorii Rossii (IX vek–1917 g.)* (Moscow, 1967), pp. 163–166.

40. *PSZ 1,* tom 5, no. 3287 (22 January 1719).

41. M. I. Semevskii, *Tsaritsa Katerina Alekseevna, Anna, i Villem Mons, 1692–1724: Ocherk iz russkoi istoriia XVIII veka* (St. Petersburg, 1884), pp. 157–158.

42. K. de Bruin, "Puteshestvie v Moskoviiu," in Iu. A. Limonov, ed., *Rossiia XVIII veka glazami inostrantsev* (Leningrad, 1989), p. 95.

43. Latkin, *Uchebnik istorii russkogo prava,* p. 211.

44. K. D. Kavelin, *Sobranie sochinenii v chetyrekh tomakh* (St. Petersburg, 1897), tom 1, stolbtsy 631–632.

45. There is a discerning analysis of popular conceptions of freedom and order in Jeffrey Brooks, *When Russia Learned to Read: Literacy and Popular Literature, 1861–1917* (Princeton, 1985), pp. 171–174, 189–191, 195–200. See also A. D. Shmelev, "Leksicheskii sostav russkogo iazyka kak otrazhenie 'russkoi dushi'," *Russkii iazyk v shkole,* no. 4 (1996), pp. 83–90.

46. N. I. Kostomarov, "Sten'ka Razin," in his *Russkaia istoriia v zhizneopisaniiakh ee vazhneishikh deiatelei* (Moscow, 1991), pp. 573–587; V. I. Semevskii, *Krest'ianskii vopros v Rossii v XVIII i pervoi polovine XIX v.* (St. Petersburg, 1888), tom 1, p. 179; I. I. Smirnov et al., *Krest'ianskie voiny v Rossii XVII–XVIII vv.* (Moscow, 1966), pp. 144–147, 202, 257–266; M. A. Rakhmatullin, *Krest'ianskoe dvizhenie v velikorusskikh guberniiakh v 1826–1857 gg.* (Moscow, 1990), pp. 227–228.

47. A. T. Bolotov, *Zhizn' i prikliucheniia Andreia Bolotova, opisannye samim im dlia svoikh potomkov* (Moscow, 1986), pp. 618–622.

48. Romanovich-Slavatinskii, *Dvorianstvo v Rossii,* p. 308.

49. Povalishin, *Riazanskie pomeshchiki,* p. 105.

50. Quoted in Povalishin, *Riazanskie pomeshchiki,* p. 105.

51. *Domostroi* (Moscow, 1990), p. 140.

52. Vladimirskii-Budanov, *Obzor istorii russkogo prava*, p. 257.

53. Reginald E. Zelnik, *The Factory Workers of St. Petersburg, 1855–1870* (Stanford, 1971), p. 30.

54. A. Ia. Efimenko, "Krest'ianskoe zemlevladenie na krainem Severe," in her *Issledovaniia narodnoi zhizni*, vypusk 1: *Obychnoe pravo* (Moscow, 1884), pp. 183–380; V. I. Semevskii, "Kazennye krest'iane pri EkaterineII (Polovniki)," *Russkaia starina*, tom 24 (1879).

55. V. I. Semevskii, *Krest'iane v tsarstvovanie imperatritsy Ekateriny II* (St. Petersburg, 1903), tom 1.

56. A. P. Zablotskii-Desiatovskii, *Graf P.D. Kiselev i ego vremia: Materialy dlia istorii imperatorov AleksandraI, NikolaiaI, i AleksandraII* (St. Petersburg, 1882), tom 2, p. 304.

57. Latkin, *Uchebnik istorii russkogo prava*, p. 211; Man'kov, ed., *Sobornoe ulozhenie 1649*, pp. 191–192.

58. V. A. Aleksandrov, *Sel'skaia obshchina v Rossii (XVII–nachalo XIX vv.)* (Moscow, 1976), pp. 315–316; L. S. Prokof'eva, *Krest'ianskaia obshchina v Rossii vo vtoroi polovine XVIII–pervoi polovine XIX veka* (Leningrad, 1981), pp. 185–209.

59. I. T. Pososhkov, *Kniga o skudosti i bogatstve* (Moscow, 1951), p. 178.

60. Jones, *The Emancipation of the Russian Nobility*, pp. 273–287.

61. O. I. Chistiakov, ed., *Russkoe zakonodatel'stvo X–XX vekov* (Moscow, 1987), tom 5, p. 29.

62. *Zapiski kniagini E.P. Dashkovoi* (Moscow, 1990), p. 472.

63. Latkin, *Uchebnik istorii russkogo prava*, p. 145.

64. *Zapiski kniagini E.P. Dashkovoi*, p. 480.

65. V. I. Sergeevich, *Lektsii i issledovaniia po istorii russkogo prava* (St. Petersburg, 1883), p. 59; M. M. Speranskii, *Proekty i zapiski* (Moscow and Leningrad, 1961), p. 43.

66. V. S. Pecherin, "Zamogil'nye zametki (Apologia pro vita mea)," in I. A. Fedosov, ed., *Russkoe obshchestvo 30-kh godov XIX v.: Memuary sovremennikov* (Moscow, 1989), p. 163.

67. Pecherin, "Zamogil'nye zametki," pp. 175–176, 161.

68. G. S. Gabaev, "Soldaty-uchastniki zagovora i vosstaniia dekabristov," in *Dekabristy i ikh vremia* (Moscow, 1932), tom 2, pp. 357–364.

69. Solov'ev, *Istoriia Rossii s drevneishikh vremen*, kniga 7, pp. 571–572.

70. Vladimirskii-Budanov, *Obzor istorii russkogo prava*, pp. 595–605.

71. Gregory L. Freeze, *The Parish Clergy in Nineteenth-Century Russia: Crisis, Reform, Counter-Reform* (Princeton, 1983), pp. 459–474.

72. On this count Peter I was no innovator. Long before, Ivan IV put church property under state control at the end of his reign (around 1580). But under the influence of the Time of Troubles, which soon broke out, this measure disappeared from the practice of the state. See Vladimirskii-Budanov, *Obzor istorii russkogo prava*, pp. 544–545.

73. P. G. Ryndziunskii, *Gorodskoe grazhdanstvo doreformennoi Rossii* (Moscow, 1958), pp. 72, 82, 116–122.

74. Kizevetter, *Posadskaia obshchina*, pp. 134–141.

75. Ryndziunskii, *Gorodskoe grazhdanstvo doreformennoi Rossii*, pp. 98–103, 260–261.

76. Latkin, *Uchebnik istorii russkogo prava*, pp. 175–190; Vladimirskii-Budanov, *Obzor istorii russkogo prava*, pp. 253–260.

77. G. Kotoshikhin, *O Rossii v tsarstvovanie Alekseia Mikhailovicha* (St. Petersburg, 1840), pp. 113–114.

78. E. N. Anuchin, "Issledovanie o protsente soslannykh v Sibir' v period 1827–1846 gg.: Materialy dlia ugolovnoi statistiki Rossii," *Zapiski Imperatorskogo russkogo geograficheskogo obshchestva*, tom 2 (1871), pp. 301–305.

79. M. A. Rakhmatullin, *Krest'ianskoe dvizhenie v velikorusskikh guberniiakh v 1826–1857 gg.* (Moscow, 1990), pp. 179–186.

80. A. Timofeev, *Istoriia telesnykh nakazanii v russkom prave* (St. Petersburg, 1897), pp. 83–129.

81. V. S. Diakin, ed., *Krizis samoderzhaviia v Rossii, 1895–1917 g.* (Leningrad, 1984), p. 358.

82. RGIA, f. 911 (V. I. Veshniakov), op. 1, d. 6, ll. 20–21.

83. Druzhinin, *Gosudarstvennye krest'iane*, tom 1, pp. 628–632.

84. Povalishin, *Riazanskie pomeshchiki*, p. 96.

85. Kliuchevskii, "Kurs istorii Rossii," *Sochineniia*, tom 5, pp. 130–185; B. N. Chicherin, "O krepostnom sostoianii," in *Golosa iz Rossii*, knizhka 2, pp. 127–229.

86. I. Lavrov, "O prichinakh neudovletvoritel'nogo polozheniia zemledeliia u krest'ian," *Zhurnal Ministerstva gosudarstvennykh imushchestv*, chast' 42 (1852), p. 145; I. O. Karpovich, *Khoziaistvennyi opyt tridtsatiletnei praktiki ili nastavlenie dlia upravleniia imeniem* (St. Petersburg, 1837), pp. 297–299; A. I. Zhukov, *Rukovodstvo otchetlivo, uspeshno i vygodno zanimat'sia russkim sel'skim khoziaistvom* (Moscow, 1848), pp. 187–189; V. Kashkarov, "O nekotorykh usloviiakh, prepiatstvuiushchikh razvitiiu sel'skogo khoziaistva v Rossii," *Sel'skoe khoziaistvo*, tom 3, no. 7 (1860), pp. 42–62.

87. Tatishchev, *Izbrannye proizvedeniia*, p. 408; Bolotov, *Zhizn' i prikliucheniia*, pp. 617–622; I. V. Lopukhin, *Zapiski senatora* (Moscow, 1990), pp. 195–196.

3

Social Sources of the Demise of Bondage

The liberation of the various social classes in imperial Russia from bondage took place gradually, at different times, and under the influence of various developments. Let us examine those factors for each class in turn.

The Nobility

Why was the nobility the first class to gain personal freedom? What factors facilitated this process? The nobility waged a long and stubborn struggle for its emancipation, taking advantage of every opportunity to wrest one concession after another from the autocracy. As Russian historian P. N. Miliukov aptly put it, "It was through participation in palace coups that the nobility acquired its corporate spirit and a sense of its own power."[1]

The autocracy awarded privileges to the nobles from time to time—usually, although not always, when its own power was weak. As an expression of gratitude to the nobility for their role in freeing her from the power of the aristocrats—who, at her accession, had compelled her to renounce her autocratic authority—Empress Anna lessened the term for which nobles had to serve the state, and abolished the requirement that a noble must bequeath his landed estate to a single heir. Empress Elizabeth further reduced the nobles' service obligations and increased their mano-

---

Translated by Daniel Field, Syracuse University.

rial rights—out of gratitude and also in response to the nobles' insistent demands. Peter III completely freed the nobility from compulsory service in 1762. As Carol Leonard has shown, Peter was not prompted by fear of the nobility or by the threat of a coup, as other historians have supposed, but by policy considerations and dynastic concerns.[2] Ironically, Peter's Manifesto on the Freedom of the Nobility did not save his life.

Catherine II was hesitant when her position as empress was less than solid, but she expanded the privileges of the nobility when her own position improved. She hesitated a long time before confirming Peter's manifesto; but eventually she affirmed the personal rights of nobles in 1785, in her Charter to the Nobility. In this sphere, the Russian monarchs generally reckoned with the needs of the state as well as the demands of the nobility.[3] Catherine II attempted, insofar as possible, to transform Russia by converting the state into a corporate structure regulated by law. In pursuit of this goal, her charters to the nobility and to the merchants conferred personal rights. She wanted to do the same for the state peasants, yet did not do so, yielding instead to the objections of her advisers and to her own fears that the serfs might demand a charter of their own.

The abolition of compulsory service made it much easier for nobles to acquire full private property rights to their estates and serfs. Once these became their unconditional property, nobles had a private means of subsistence, making them independent of the state. In the early eighteenth century, few nobles had held their land and serfs on a patrimonial (*votchinal*) basis; most had service estates. There were similarities and differences between these two forms of property. With either form, nobles were obliged to "bear service to the sovereign" in proportion to the extent of their lands and the number of their serfs. Likewise, whatever the form of tenure, the nobles' right to exploit peasant labor was limited by custom: Exactions of peasants were supposed to be moderate and feasible. In addition, all peasant transactions with the manorial administration bore the *sanction* of the state. A patrimonial estate was distinct in that its holder was entitled to dispose of it as he wished, within certain state-imposed limits. For example, a patrimonial estate was supposed to pass by inheritance through the family line and could not be bequeathed at the whim of its owner; and if such an estate passed out of the family line, then relatives had the right to buy it back (a practice known as *rodovoi vykup*). Similarly, a squire *(pomeshchik)* could sell his service estate only to other squires, because all of the previous owner's obligations passed with the estate to its new holder. The effective enlargement of the squire's property rights was not sanctioned by law, however. In strict legal terms, what the squire sold, bequeathed, exchanged, and so on was only the right to use the property. Contemporaries clearly understood this distinction between patrimonial estates and estates held on service tenure.

Various policy considerations prompted Peter I to eliminate the distinction between patrimonies and estates held on service tenure. He introduced single inheritance (often misleadingly called "primogeniture" in the English-language literature); however, the practice was unknown in Russia, and the nobles did not like it. To appease and reconcile them to the new system, Peter expanded their property rights, elevating estates held on service tenure to the level of patrimonial property. This expansion was also compensation for the increased levels of service to the state that were imposed on nobles during his reign and a reward for victory in the Great Northern War. Later, during the reign of Empress Anna, nobles secured the abolition of the law imposing single inheritance and yet retained their patrimonial rights.

So it was with the serfs. Until the first census *(reviziia)*, in 1719, nobles' powers over peasants, and their rights to peasant labor, were limited by the state. Along with serfs, however, the nobility also had slaves *(kholopy)*, who constituted about one-tenth of the peasants in noble hands.[4] All categories of slaves had a lower social status than peasants, and under the law the status of some categories was that of full-fledged slaves (*raby,* the same term used for African American slaves in the New World—*Trans.*). *Kholopy* had no obligations to the state, a situation that was advantageous to their masters. In order to increase the number of taxpayers, Peter I compelled the *kholopy* (in practice, he compelled their masters) to pay taxes. He softened the blow to the nobility by giving serfs the same legal status as *kholopy.* What they lost on the one hand, the nobility eagerly grasped with the other; now their powers over their serfs were expanded to the point where the serfs became (in Alexander Herzen's phrase) "baptized property."[5] Subsequently, between 1720 and 1785, the nobility's rights to land, serfs, and all other forms of real estate and personal property expanded.

Nobles faced one remaining obstacle to the conversion of estates and serfs into unrestricted property—the obligation to serve the state. Naturally, the nobles wanted to free themselves from compulsory service and all the limitations it imposed on them, while retaining all their rights. In 1762, the nobles attained this goal, in large part because their aspirations corresponded to the policies of the autocracy. (Until the middle of the eighteenth century, the abstract concepts of "property," "real estate," and "personal property" were unknown in Russian law; it was Catherine II who introduced them.)[6]

European influences had less impact on the emancipation of the nobility than on the emancipation of other classes, because the nobility was already free in the late eighteenth century, when European culture took root in Russian soil. But it would be wrong to dismiss these influences completely. As early as the reign of Peter I, Western culture had become an attribute of the nobility—or at least, of its top rung—and that would have significant social consequences. In the first half of the eighteenth century, the new culture finally wrenched nobles away from the other classes, producing a sharp and conspicuous divide between the "base" taxpayers and the "wellborn" nobles. In 1787, Prince Shcherbatov, a well-known historian, had every reason to write:

> I can truly say that although we are setting out on the path of enlightenment later than other peoples, all we have to do is sensibly follow the way of those who gained enlightenment before us; for indeed, as regards manners and deportment and some other matters, we have already achieved remarkable success and are advancing in measured, giant strides toward a correct appearance.[7]

This transformation played a major role in the growth of the nobility's self-consciousness, even as its participation in palace coups d'état produced in the nobility a new corporate spirit and sense of its own power.[8] The nobility could no longer accept that the "gentlefolk" still resembled the "vulgar" masses in one significant respect—that they, too, had to serve the state. For the nobility, the elimination of compulsory service became a matter of honor.

We can find evidence of this new sensibility in "On Nobles and Their Privileges," a chapter of a draft law code prepared by the nobility between 1757 and 1762, and also in the nobles' mandates *(nakazy)* presented to the Commission on the Compilation of a New Law Code in 1767. Both in the draft chapter and in the mandates we encounter the clearly expressed idea of a "corps of nobles" distinct from other, "base" classes of the population in that the wellborn had earned their privileges by long and faithful service to the state. This idea found its fullest expression in the 1785 Charter to the Nobility.[9] And the perception that other European countries provided a ready-made model of a "wellborn" estate hastened the increased consciousness of rank-and-file nobles that they must gain their emancipation and conversion into a privileged estate.

The Clergy

As we have seen, the emancipation of the clergy proceeded gradually, and different factors prevailed at various stages of this process. In the early eighteenth century the government began to see the clergy as its social and ideological bastion in society—as the estate of the realm that was destined to disseminate the ideas of autocracy and Orthodoxy among the people. But if the clergy was to be equal to this challenge, it had to be given a suitable education, and its service had to be regularized and its social status elevated. In a word, the clergy had to be transformed into a privileged estate.

Church authorities were not pleased by the obligations that the state was laying on the clergy, but they sympathized with the idea of turning it into a privileged estate. Therefore, as Gregory Freeze has shown, in the eighteenth century and the first half of the nineteenth century, the church hierarchy joined the efforts of the state and the Holy Synod to transform the clergy.[10] Gradually, members of the clergy acquired personal rights, privileges, and education. In the early eighteenth century there was virtually no one with a specialized clerical education, because there were no seminaries. By 1835, as many as 43 percent of priests had a full seminary education, and by 1860, the figure was 83 percent.[11]

The clergy was vulnerable in two respects, however. Personal rights were not conferred on a person but on an estate. Someone who left a clerical position lost his privileges. The other sore point was material well-being, which lagged significantly behind the needs of the clergy and did not correspond to its privileged social status. Members of other classes of the population who had the equivalent of a seminary education were much better off. These two circumstances tormented the clergy and prevented it from taking full advantage of the benefits that in theory followed from the enjoyment of personal rights. By the middle of the nineteenth century, the clergy was dissatisfied and striving to escape from poverty and from its humiliating dependence on tyrannical bishops, against whom clergymen had no rights. Their only way of drawing the attention of clerical and lay authorities to their plight was through petitions, which they submitted in quantity. The dissatisfaction of clerics and the petitions they submitted were an important stimulus to the reform of the church. The church hierarchs understood the institutional role of the clergy and the church in the state and in society; they too wanted freedom—not in the sense of the personal rights sought by the parish clergy but in a political sense. They wanted the church to be set free from the state and to return to the situation that had existed prior to the reign of Peter I. Impulses toward reform also emanated from the bureaucracy, which was not satisfied with the clergy's performance of its duties. Finally, enlightened laypeople of various political tendencies articulated their own designs on the clergy and the church. The church reforms of the 1860s and 1870s, carried out in response to promptings from liberal clergy, from conservative hierarchs, from enlightened bureaucrats, and from the intelligentsia, conferred personal rights on the entire clergy and effectively liberated it from its bondage *(tiaglovoe sostoianie)*.[12]

The emancipation of the clergy advanced apace with the expansion of its rights to private property. Here again we see that the personal rights of the clergy were linked to their property rights. Let us first examine the situation of the parish clergy: Church buildings, together with ritual objects and other church property, belonged to the parish and not to the priest. The houses in which clerics and their family members lived could belong to the community or to the clergy, depending on who had paid for their construction. In the early eighteenth century, in urban areas of Russia, the lands *(dvorovye mesta)* on which these houses stood belonged to the *posad* (with property rights ultimately in the hands of the state). In rural areas, the land on which the cleric's house stood belonged variously to the squire, to the state, or to the village commune—depending on the ownership of the land where the church was situated. In 1700, *dvorovye mesta* in towns were recognized as the property of the clergy who lived on them; they became the private property of the clergy fully and conclusively in 1785.

In rural areas, the fate of *dvorovye mesta* was different. Until the 1860s they remained the property of the person or community that owned the land on which the church stood. The government had decreed that instead of the fixed salary the clergy wanted, a priest should get between thirty-three and ninety-nine *desiatiny* of land from the owner of the land on which the church was situated. This land was, however, awarded to the priest only for his use and under the condition that he carry out his functions at the church. Consequently, clergy in the towns could arrange transactions concerning their land, but rural clergy could not. A law of 1804 gave all clergy the right to acquire land as private property but not to hold serfs. Consequently, rural clergymen thereafter had a right to hold land as private property; but most of them were so poor that they could not take significant advantage of that right. Not until the 1860s did rural clergy begin to acquire their *dvorovye mesta* as private property. However, the acreage set aside for the clergy's subsistence became the property of the village commune rather than the priest. Throughout the period from 1700 to 1917, clergy also were forbidden to take part in business or industry.

So it was that until the 1860s, the parish clergy enjoyed lesser property rights than did merchants, *meshchane*, and state peasants. Their property rights were superior only to those of serfs (the serf's real estate and personal property ultimately belonged to his master). And after the reforms of the 1860s, which provided that peasants of all categories could own any kind of property, rural priests lost even this relative advantage. The protracted limitation of the parish clergy's property rights and its lack of significant property in any form contributed greatly to its impoverishment. Poverty, in turn, contributed to the debased condition of the clergy, especially the rural clergy, and the lesser clergy most of all.

Whereas the property rights of the parish clergy did expand little by little, the rights of the monastic clergy gradually diminished. Prior to the eighteenth century, the church—that is to say, the patriarch, the bishops, and the monasteries—had full property rights to one-third of all the land and of all the serfs in the country, and also to an immense amount of real estate and other property. The legal owner of church property was not the entire church as an institution or the clergy as an estate of the realm. Each piece of property was at the disposal of one church institution or another—the episcopate, monasteries, and various cathedrals (especially those in the Moscow Kremlin). In fact, the church's rights to its property were essentially the same as the state's rights, although this equivalence never achieved formal legal sanction. Each church institution awarded land to its servitors as patrimony or on service tenure, and likewise alienated properties without restriction. With the passage of time, both state and society lost sight of the dependence of the church's property right on the state and forgot the role of the state in authorizing the transfer to the church of all the property it held.

Peter I did not forget. In 1701 he decreed that the state should take over the administration of church properties and provide fixed stipends to church institutions. When the Holy Synod was established in 1721, all the church's property passed to this state institution. Now the legal owner was indeed the entire church as an institution, a change that facilitated the complete secularization of the church's lands.

Peter III, who had been born a Protestant and had converted to Orthodoxy out of expediency, held the Russian church in contempt. In 1762, he issued a decree on the secularization of the church's estates. In 1764, Catherine II completed the process of secularization, thus realizing a cherished dream of the nobility. The long struggle over church property ended in a complete victory for the state. Having lost its property, the church fell into dependence on the state and was compelled to display a great deal more loyalty to the state than it wished. Insofar as the church as an institution lost its property rights to monastic lands, it became increasingly dependent on the state. Here is a striking example of the connection between property, on the one hand, and power and freedom, on the other. In western Europe the outcome was very different. There the Catholic Church defended its property against the claims of the state, and this success contributed to its autonomy.

The Townspeople

Better than any other class in Russian society, townspeople understood the importance of personal rights for the successful conduct of trade, commerce, and industry. Beginning in the seventeenth century they struggled stubbornly for a variety of goals: confirmation of their right to a monopoly on commercial enterprise; confirmation of the *posad* commune's ownership of all town property; lower taxes and dues; and confirmation of the rights of private property. They also opposed arbitrary taxation and the confiscation of personal property. The government understood the needs of townspeople very well and appreciated their "service." No less importantly, it was much more anxious about the potential for discontent among the townspeople than among the peasantry. The sources of this anxiety are obvious. Disorders in towns presented an immensely greater danger to social order than did peasant upheavals. They could easily spread to other towns and cities, since towns were not isolated from the external world as villages were. Stirrings in the towns in the late seventeenth century had emphatically demonstrated to the government that they represented a real threat to order and even to the dynasty. The government drew the appropriate lesson, and between the early eighteenth century and 1785, it satisfied all of the townspeople's basic demands.

The government was especially solicitous of the urban elite—that is, the merchant guilds—since town government, commerce, and industry were in their hands. Although intended to increase tax receipts, the tax reform of 1775 played a major role in the emancipation of the merchants. The reform substituted a specific percentage of a merchant's declared capital for the soul tax—a change with far-reaching consequences. The elimination of the soul tax meant that merchants were no longer bound by mutual responsibility, and hence, that they were free from corporate bondage. Every merchant could operate independently, using his own judgment of risk and opportunity. This fiscal measure had major social consequences and worked to mutual advantage: Merchants had to pay more in taxes, but in return they received more extensive freedom. One might say that the merchants redeemed their own freedom—not all at once or forever, to be sure, but only for a given tax year. Any member of a town corporation had the right to declare his capital—the administration did not verify the declaration—and enroll as a merchant of one or another guild. At once he gained the personal rights of a merchant for the year. If he remitted the taxes due from him in a timely manner, he could continue the arrangement for the following year, and so on. If he did not pay his taxes, he had to return to his former status and pay a fine as well as back taxes. Thus the merchants' freedom was redeemed every year.

In the 1785 Charter to the Towns, the personal rights that townspeople had gained were not only confirmed but significantly expanded. The charter established the principle that the corporate rights granted to townspeople were inalienable and could be taken away only for conviction of a major crime by a court. It satisfied all of the townspeople's basic demands and provided a firm legal basis for their rights vis-à-vis other classes of society. Townspeople appreciated this gain, cherished the charter, and struggled against attempts to modify it during the reign of Nicholas I. The measured generosity of the autocracy toward townspeople and especially toward merchants helps explain why, during the eighteenth and the first half of the nineteenth centuries, antigovernment movements in the towns were very rare; townspeople did not support peasant or cossack uprisings or even respond to the Pugachev insurrection.

The development of the concept of townspeople's private property rights had great significance for their emancipation. In the seventeenth and early eighteenth centuries, the government frequently levied extraordinary taxes on the people of the *posads* and even invoked eminent domain to confiscate their property. In response to protests from the *posads* and due to its own realization that this practice deprived townspeople of any motive to accumulate property and led to their concealment of assets and to other abuses, the state began to pursue a liberal, law-based policy toward the property of townspeople. In 1700, townspeople were permitted to carry out transactions concerning *dvorovye mesta,* which meant in effect that the lands were recognized as the property of those who lived on them. The 1785 Charter to the Towns confirmed this principle. Not only did the charter extend private property rights to *dvorovye mesta* in towns, it also included houses, shops, barns, factories, and other industrial enterprises. Townspeople with the rank of "eminent citizen" were entitled to own property such as summerhouses and gardens in the suburbs, as well. On the other hand, land, fisheries, and mills belonging to the town commune became its corporate property and were not converted into the private property of townspeople.

In 1801, merchants and *meshchane* gained the right to buy tracts of land in rural districts, provided there were no serfs living on them. As of 1822 they could own buildings in the countryside, which permitted them to live legally and to conduct enterprise in villages. However, because of these rural activities, they had to pay the taxes and dues appropriate to two different estates of the realm (to both townspeople—either merchants or *meshchane*—and to peasants).

In one respect, the aspirations of the merchants and other townspeople were not satisfied: They did not gain the right to hold serfs, either with or without land. Under Peter I, townspeople were forbidden to hold serfs or slaves, but they did not have to surrender those they already held. Later, in 1746, all townspeople were required to sell their serfs within six months. Policy regarding serfs belonging to merchants was a response to the demands of nobles, who maintained that their estate enjoyed a unique right to own serfs and property populated by serfs. But even in this respect the autocracy had to make a concession to the merchants. In 1721, Peter I permitted merchants who owned factories and mines to acquire estates or villages with serfs on what was called a "possessionary right": The peasants (prior to 1811, they were called "ascribed peasants," and afterward, "possessionary peasants") were ascribed to the enterprise, not to its owner; if a factory or mine was sold, the new owner took over the peasants, as well. The state's pressing need to develop domestic production of weapons and ammunition for the army dictated this concession.[13] By 1762, squires too had developed manorial industrial production; and at their demand, the state forbade merchants to acquire more peasants for their enterprises—although they were permitted to keep those they already had. In 1798, Paul I again permitted the purchase of peasants for enterprises. Formally, possessionary peasants were state peasants; but in fact, they belonged to entrepreneurs, although the state did regulate relations between entrepreneurs and possessionary peasants. Later, in 1863, possessionary factories became the private property of their owners, and the peasants ascribed to them were emancipated on the same footing as serfs.

In two respects the development of townspeople's property rights had immense significance for their emancipation. The protection of their property under the law made them economically independent of the state; and their enhanced property rights encouraged them to accumulate property without fear of its arbitrary confiscation by the state. Their accumulation of property, in turn, strengthened the townspeople's sense of independence and permitted the elite of the towns to exert influence on state policy, especially economic policy. With money in hand, the richest merchants could become nobles; others could form marriage alliances with noble families; and others could form close contacts with the administration by working in local government. Some won the gratitude of the emperor for their philanthropic activity. Most importantly, as commercial activity developed in the towns, townspeople—in particular, the merchants—became an economically influential class with whom both the autocracy and the nobility had to reckon. Increased wealth and enhanced influence on economic policy permitted the merchant estate to elevate its social status and to follow closely on the heels of the nobility in winning its emancipation from bondage to the state.

The struggle of Old Believer merchants for freedom of religion exemplifies the same process in a different context. Sensitive to the economic power of Old Believer communities, to their influence on domestic commerce and on the development of industry, in the 1760s the government made concessions to them. By the beginning of the nineteenth century, Old Believers had achieved effective legalization of their religion, which could not have been achieved without bribes to influential officials. Clearly, these bribes were possible only because the Old Believers had accumulated significant wealth, which was completely independent of the government, by virtue of their property rights.[14]

The Peasantry

Marxist historians have offered three broad explanations of the abolition of serfdom. According to some, the manorial economy was becoming inefficient, and was even running at a loss. By the 1830s it was in a state of permanent crisis, which meant, among other things, that the serfs were dying off. Others have emphasized the importance of the development of commercial relations and a monetary economy. Another group has focused on peasant unrest and rebellion.[15] Non-Marxist historians variously emphasize fear of peasant uprisings,[16] the nation's military requirements,[17] cultural factors,[18] and the state's concern for modernizing Russia and overcoming its backwardness.[19] In contrast, in this book and its companion volume, I have tried to show that serfholders were always able to derive an income from their estates; that this income depended significantly on the level of coercion that they employed; and that the abolition of serfdom was not the product of an economic crisis but rather of a complex of cultural, social, and political developments.

Let me begin with a note of caution. Historians still do not have accurate and comprehensive data about the profitability of serf estates and the income of peasants during the era of serfdom; nor do they have accurate data on labor time and other economic indices required to calculate the return on peasant labor. As a rule, serfholders did not keep accounts or did so very laxly; the owners of great estates were grievously deceived by their stewards and overseers. Peasants did not keep accounts because they were illiterate, feared their master would get hold of the information, or thought it was a sin to reckon the harvest, which was sent by God.[20] The historian faces the alternatives of giving up any effort to assess the efficiency of an economy based on the labor of serfs, or using the inadequate data available to produce some kind of estimate. I chose the latter alternative, which means that my conclusions on this matter will have to be tentative.

Serfholders' Revenues from Serf Labor

Between 1700 and 1850, the prices of serfs and of estates populated by serfs rose faster than the prices of grain and manufactured goods. These relative prices are an indirect measure of the profitability of serf labor; and they suggest, at least, that the serf economy was profitable.[21] The price of a single military recruit is similarly suggestive. According to the law, those who wanted to escape conscription could provide a sum of money instead; the treasury determined this sum according to the market price of serfs. Only males who satisfied specific criteria of age and of physical condition were accepted as soldiers, and more than 90 percent of these recruits were drawn from the peasantry. Consequently, the movement of recruit prices can serve as another surrogate index of the profitability of serf labor. Between the 1720s and the 1850s, the price of a recruit increased in constant rubles 4.5 times;[22] and the average price of grain increased between 1721 and 1730, and between 1851 and 1860, 3.5 times, which was more than the increase in the price of manufactured goods.[23] Since the price of a recruit outstripped other prices, we can suppose that serfholders were profiting from the exploitation of their serfs.

Firm data on the increase in *obrok* confirm that serf estates were becoming more profitable. Between 1701 and 1800, the net income of serfholders from each male peasant on *obrok* (that is, allowing for inflation and the rise in grain prices) increased by 69 percent.[24] From 1801 to 1860, it increased by approximately 70 percent to 90 percent.[25] If we lump together *obrok* and the taxes the state collected from serfs, then the net total of an *obrok* serf's payments to his master and to the state (again, allowing for inflation and the rise in grain prices) increased by 14 percent in the course of the eighteenth century and by 37 percent more in the first half of the nineteenth century.[26] It follows that income from peasant labor on *obrok* estates did not decline, since the administration of *obrok* serfs entailed minimal outlays for the state and the squires. The inference can be extended to *barshchina* estates, since the labor of *barshchina* serfs was significantly more productive (twice as productive, by some estimates) than the labor of their counterparts on *obrok*. For this reason, landowners preferred *barshchina* to *obrok* in areas where agriculture predominated.[27]

State Peasants, Serfs, and Economic Performance

If we compare the basic measures of agricultural productivity for serfs (who were in an extreme form of bondage) with those for state peasants (whose bondage was milder) in twelve central provinces[28] in the years 1842 to 1853, we find that the economic performance of the serfs was better. The state peasant, who compared to the serf had greater economic freedom, more land, and lower taxes and dues, nonetheless sowed 42 percent less land, had 16 percent lower yields, held 7 to 12 percent fewer cattle, and produced 63 percent less grain. It goes without saying that the lion's share of the serfs' extra effort accrued to their masters.

In light of the poor quality of statistics in midcentury Russia, the data for these twelve provinces should be taken as approximations, but they still accurately reflect the prevailing tendency. We can see this from the data on yields for the fifty provinces of European Russia for the period from 1851 to 1860, which show that serfs' yields were about 6 to 7 percent higher than the yields of state peasants.[29] The difference is small, of course, and may derive from inaccuracies in the raw data. But there are more persuasive data. Measured in constant rubles, the total of *obrok* and of direct taxes to the state increased about 2.8[30] times between 1719–1724 and the 1850s; for serfs the increase was fivefold. To pay these exactions, serfs had to work much harder than state peasants, and that is why they brought more revenue to their masters and mistresses than state peasants brought to the treasury. Furthermore, in some respects the living standards of serfs were higher than those of state peasants.[31]

Judging by the quality of grain cultivation and the trend in yields, progress was being made in agricultural production throughout the nation. This progress was most noticeable on *barshchina* estates, where it was achieved through improved cultivation of the fields, which in turn was the result of an intensification of labor. For example, according to some rough estimates, the intensity of labor on *barshchina* estates in various regions increased by between 20 percent and 40 percent between the mid-eighteenth and the mid-nineteenth centuries.[32] Thus we are bound to conclude that serfs, under the comparatively close supervision of their masters, not only worked harder than state peasants but worked more effectively.[33] In this light we can understand why the rallying cry of all serf uprisings in the eighteenth century and in the first half of the nineteenth century was in favor of the serfs' transfer to the jurisdiction of the treasury.

The Economic Performance of Free Agriculturists and Belopashtsy

A small category of peasants, the "free agriculturists," had existed since 1804. It was composed of entire villages that had purchased their freedom from their masters and held their land under communal tenure. They paid state and local taxes and were subject to recruitment, but they did not pay *barshchina* or *obrok*. They were not subject to the squire's will and were substantially free of supervision by the state. By 1858, free agriculturists (both men and women) numbered about 216,000. We would expect their economic performance to have been good in light of their economic freedom. And indeed, when state officials in 1847–1848 conducted a survey of the economic performance of free agriculturists in six provinces, it came to light that "the peasants are in a prosperous state as regards their productive activity and standard of living."[34] In 1858, A. I. Koshelev, a well-known landowner with Slavophile views, seemed to confirm the survey's conclusions in his memorandum on the peasant question, noting that poverty afflicted only those villages of free agriculturists that had shifted from communal to household tenure, from which it would follow that the communal villages were doing well.[35]

Why were most free agriculturists flourishing? There is no other explanation than the favorable conditions under which they were set free. For example, the land the free agriculturists had received when they were set free amounted on average to 6.9 *desiatiny* (7.5 hectares or 18.6 acres) per male peasant. In 1861, on the eve of their Emancipation, serfs held on average barely half as much.[36] The landowners who allowed their serfs to become free agriculturists were mostly liberals inspired by philanthropic rather than pecuniary motives—that is, they did not want to take advantage of their peasants.[37] Hence they granted land to their peasants on favorable terms and for moderate prices (below market rates, as a rule). Furthermore, they often sold entire estates to the peasants, with all their resources, which was advantageous for the peasants. Free agriculturists paid about 11 rubles per *desiatina*, whereas the going price was between 15 and 17 rubles.[38] The serfs emancipated in 1861 had to pay 27 rubles per *desiatina*, which was 59 percent above the market price of the land they redeemed.[39] The free agriculturists who for various reasons were in bad straits after the emancipation became state or appanage peasants.[40] Despite their relative prosperity, the free agriculturists were not enterprising; they continued to conform to the traditions that had governed the lives of their ancestors. When the law required them to liquidate their communes and shift to private property, the free agriculturists nonetheless retained communal, repartitional tenure and even restored it when it had been abolished.[41]

The category of free agriculturists existed for so short a time as to preclude any conclusions about their economic efficiency. What would have been the result if this group had emerged earlier and existed longer? Russian reality provides us with the counterfactual example we need. In 1619, Tsar Mikhail awarded the son-in-law of Ivan Susanin (the legendary hero of the Time of Troubles who was supposed to have laid down his life for the tsar) a parcel of land in his native province of Kostroma, in the village of Korobovo, and relieved him and his descendants of taxes and dues for all time. These peasants received full freedom in a form that corresponded absolutely to the peasant ideal of *volnost'*. As of 1632, the award of land amounted to ninety *desiatiny*. The descendants of Ivan Susanin came to be called *belopashtsy*. Their situation was like that of the free agriculturists. By 1767 they numbered 153 persons, and by 1834, 226.

In 1834, while Nicholas I was touring Russia, he noted the wretched state of the *belopashtsy* and formed a commission to investigate their situation and render them aid. The commission established that the main cause of the lamentable state of the *belopashtsy* was their privileges. The commission found that freedom from all obligations to the state and the community, complete independence of all authority, and abundance of land had weakened their energy and spirit of enterprise. In time the *belopashtsy* stopped trying to improve their situation. "In contrast to the enterprising spirit of the peasants of Kostroma province, the *belopashtsy* of Korobovo are on the whole passive and not at all enterprising; hence most of them are very poor."[42] A second cause of the decline of the *belopashtsy*, the commission found, was their resort to individual rather than communal land tenure: There were no repartitions, and land passed from a father to his children in equal shares, so the plots gradually grew smaller. Transactions in land took place only among the residents of Korobovo. Gradually the land became concentrated in the hands of a few peasants who got rich at the expense of the rest and had almost a hereditary claim on the position of village elder. As a result of the continual parceling-out of the land, the constant disputes about property among the heirs, and the laziness of the *belopashtsy*, their land was poorly cultivated and gave very low yields—worse than the yields of peasants in the neighborhood.

In 1836, Nicholas I decreed that a large quantity of additional land be awarded to the *belopashtsy*—eight *desiatiny* for each male—but on the basis of communal landholding. They retained all their other privileges. This new favor from the tsar did not produce significant changes in the life of the *belopashtsy*. Laziness and inertia had become almost hereditary traits and continued to prevent them from taking advantage of their uniquely privileged position. Exploiting the lack of administrative control, the *belopashtsy* seceded from the official church and became sectarians; according to official information, they converted their village into a refuge for their coreligionists and for criminals. Consequently the Appanage Administration, which formerly had exercised nominal control over the *belopashtsy*, assumed responsibility for them in the early 1860s—but to no avail. Despite all the administration's solicitude and attempts to improve their material situation, at the beginning of the twentieth century the descendants of Susanin had not yet attained prosperity. Although disparities of wealth had disappeared thanks to the imposition of communal land tenure, the entire village, numbering 267 persons of both sexes, still suffered from poverty in 1910.[43] Perhaps in time the free agriculturists would have shared the fate of the *belopashtsy*.

The Economic Performance of Russian and European Peasants, American Farmers, and American Slaves

It is instructive to compare the intensity with which Russian serfs carried out their principal agricultural tasks with the performance of free or semi-free peasants in other European countries and in the United States in the period 1820 to 1850. On average, in one working day a Russian state peasant threshed 118 kilograms of rye (which was the main crop in Russia) or wheat[44]—that is, between 39 percent and 78 percent more than Belgian, Danish, or Austro-Hungarian peasants; on a par with German peasants; 39 percent less than English farmers; and 85 percent less than American farmers. Harvesting presents about the same picture: Russians reaped around 180 kilograms of rye or wheat in a day.[45] Note that in Russia reaping was solely women's work, whereas men did the threshing. We have already seen that serfs worked more intensively than state peasants, so we can extend our comparative findings to them as well.

We should bear in mind, however, that Russian serfs worked with such intensity only in the periods of sowing, haying, and reaping. The rest of the time, compared to free western European peasants or serfs in eastern Europe, their working day was shorter and they did not work so hard.[46] An important conclusion follows: *In a purely economic sense,* a serf estate had significant reserves awaiting development. Labor time could have been increased, and the efficiency of the serfs' labor could have been improved. Indeed, according to rough estimates dating from the first half of the nineteenth century, on average a male serf on a *barshchina* estate worked 2,430 hours per year, with half of that time spent laboring on the demesne land; children did not render *barshchina*.[47] As for American slaves working in agriculture, men worked from 3,055 to 3,965 hours in a year; women, from 2,548 to 3,507 hours; and children, from 1,913 to 2,549 hours.[48] So a male serf worked between 26 percent and 63 percent fewer hours than a male slave and between 6 percent and 44 percent fewer hours than a female slave. Taking the level of exploitation of a serf on *barshchina* as 100, the level for a slave was 240. After the abolition of slavery, the ex-slaves reduced their workdays by 28 to 37 percent,[49] but still worked more than did Russian serfs.

The example of England has shown that *without any technical innovations* it was possible to increase labor productivity significantly; this was achieved primarily by the intensification of hand labor and only secondarily by improving crop selection or other agronomic change. In the second half of the thirteenth century and the first half of the fourteenth, English peasants harvested wheat at a rate of 9 bushels per acre (614 kilograms per hectare). *Five hundred years later,* in the 1860s, Russian peasants were harvesting 466 kilograms per hectare, or 6.8 bushels per acre (the rate for wheat was a little lower)—that is, 32 percent less. By the middle of the nineteenth century, before the industrial revolution had had an impact on agriculture, English farm laborers had raised yields of wheat to 26 bushels an acre (1,773 kilograms per hectare) without any mechanization, whereas American farmers in the northern states were producing 21.2 bushels an acre.[50] Even two centuries later, Russia did not achieve the yields the English had at the beginning of the nineteenth century; if we can believe Soviet statistics, grain yields in 1986 to 1990 averaged 1,590 per hectare.[51]

Finally, consider the Baltic provinces. In the first half of the nineteenth century, serf estates in Estonia surpassed their counterparts in Russia by about 20 percent for all economic indices, although, as a rule, they were less favored by nature.[52] The Estonian comparison clearly shows that in the Great Russian provinces, the servile economy had by no means reached its economic limit by 1861.

In short, I share the view of scholars who hold that estates relying on serf labor produced income for their owners, and that even by 1861 they had undergone no economic crisis.[53] The data show that in conditions of bondage (either serfdom or the bondage of state peasants to the treasury), the greater the compulsion applied, the more and better the peasants worked. Furthermore, in the last hundred years of serfdom, serf estates were more efficient and more profitable than the economies of peasants who had been granted economic freedom, such as the free agriculturists and the *belopashtsy*. This does not mean that Russian peasants worked well only under the lash: Whether peasants were free or not, they generally worked exactly enough to satisfy their minimum needs. Our data also support the view that most peasants were not yet ready to conduct entrepreneurial, efficient agriculture on their own, in conditions of freedom. In the 1870s, A. N. Engelgardt, a well-known specialist in soil chemistry, an enterprising squire, and a keen student of peasant life, wrote:

> Among the peasants are many who not only cannot be good farmers and can work only under the orders of others but who do not even know how to work well. . . . It is the middling sort that predominates; and among them the greater number, thanks to constant practice since childhood, have mechanically learned to work more or less well but are unable to work their own farms; they can only work with direction from outside, under someone else's orders. . . . One can say with confidence that it is the village and communal tenure of the land that saves many peasants of modest competence from complete ruin.[54]

Why Did Serfdom Last So Long?

What explains the poor performance of the peasant economy? There were many causes, but the most important lay in the economic mentality of the peasants, which oriented them toward the satisfaction of basic material needs. In the peasants' value system, prosperity and personal success did not rank highly. Hence it took extra-economic compulsion to produce economically significant results. The enserfment of the peasantry, the sway of the repartitional commune, and the agricultural practices it imposed on everyone compensated for the peasants' lack of initiative, spirit of enterprise, and desire (not to mention ability) to achieve optimal economic results. As Olga Crisp has wisely observed, "Russia was not backward because serf relations dominated her economy; it was her backwardness which made serf relations persist."[55] We find confirmation of this in the large number of holidays and other days off that were observed in the Russian village from the eighteenth century until early in the twentieth.

In the 1850s, on the eve of the abolition of serfdom, the total of non-workdays was 230; early in the twentieth century it was 258; these totals included respectively 95 and 123 Sundays and church holidays. The rest of the days off were due to bad weather, illness, hangovers, trips to the bazaar, and so on. Most of these holidays were not recognized by the state or the Orthodox Church; they were so-called popular, parochial, or plain holidays that were observed in a particular locale, according to custom and tradition. It was the increase of these folk holidays that caused the decrease in workdays after the abolition of serfdom. Work on Sundays or holidays was forbidden both by custom and by the church; it was considered a sin and a violation of tradition. Peasants who tried to work on Sundays and holidays were punished; they were fined—and sometimes they were beaten or their equipment was broken. The lower levels of rural administration worked in accord with the commune in such cases. A comparison of the holidays observed at the beginning of the twentieth century by Orthodox peasants with those observed by other faiths and denominations in European Russia showed that Catholics in the Baltic provinces had 38 to 48 holidays, Protestants in the same region had 13 to 23, Muslims in the Crimea and along the Volga had 13 to 15, and the Orthodox had about 90. Inasmuch as peasants lived in essentially similar socioeconomic circumstances whatever their religion, we can assume that cultural and religious factors shaped the calendar of holidays.[56]

Among cultural factors, the most important was not literacy, although it played a role, but rather the system of values—the norms and precepts that governed conduct—that were customary among various confessional and ethnic groups. The level of literacy among Russian Orthodox peasants was much lower than among Catholic and Protestant peasants and about the same as among the Tatars of the Crimea and the Volga.[57] The resort to magic in agriculture and the hostility to innovation that were characteristic of Russian peasants derived, in all likelihood, more from cultural norms than from the low level of literacy. Often the Russian government had to use its authority to introduce even modest innovations into peasant life—for example, the establishment of stores of grain as a reserve against famine in the eighteenth century; the cultivation of potatoes by state peasants in the 1840s; and a system of private property in land in the early twentieth century.[58]

Low levels of literacy did play a role. For European Russia as a whole in the middle of the eighteenth century, the literacy rate among the rural population of both sexes older than 9 years did not exceed 3 percent, and it did not reach 6 percent by the end of the century. In the middle of the nineteenth century, counting only peasants, literacy ranged between 2 percent and 5 percent.[59] In 1880, fewer than one in five rural administrators—the village and cantonal elders who represented the top rung of peasant society—were literate.[60]

The emancipation of the peasantry, beginning at the end of the eighteenth century, proceeded at a pace that corresponded not only to the needs of the state and society as a whole but also to the aspirations and the potential of the peasantry; indeed, it may have outpaced the latter. Consider such a major question as the acquisition of private property in land. State peasants gained the right to acquire land in 1801. Serfs gained the same formal right in 1848, but in fact they had exercised it in practice even earlier. Their use of this right after 1848 was insignificant. Between 1802 and 1858, about 400,000 state peasants, or 3 percent of the total, acquired landed property—on average, four *desiatiny* per male.[61] There are no aggregate data about the acquisition of land by serfs, but data from particular estates indicate that purchases of land were very sluggish. For example, on the enormous properties of the Sheremetevs (on which 200,000 serfs lived at the end of the eighteenth century, and 300,000 in 1860), during the sixty-year period from 1770 to 1830, serfs purchased 33,000 *desiatiny*, or 545 per year, on average.[62] Poverty is not an adequate explanation, since between 1801 and 1861, among the state peasants of nineteen diverse provinces, between 19 percent and 27 percent were reckoned as prosperous, whereas among serfs the figure ranged between 14 percent and 19 percent; these peasants obviously had the means to buy land.[63] A more important cause was that most, though not all, peasants lacked a desire to have their own land and to become real farmers— that is, agricultural entrepreneurs. They did not want or attempt to use their own resources and efforts to emancipate themselves or even to diminish their dependence on the commune, the squire, and the state.

Another major question is the peasants' compulsory membership in the commune. Even in the 1860s, many educated nonpeasants were drawn to the idea that it was appropriate to eliminate the commune as a compulsory institution imposed by the state.[64] The government left the question of the commune up to the peasants themselves, granting them in 1861 the right to shift from communal tenure to parceled tenure on the basis of individual households, approved by a two-thirds vote of the village assembly. The government did not wish to mandate the dissolution of the commune, and in that respect it was in accord with most peasants, a majority of whom clung to the commune even in 1917.

Causes of the Abolition of Serfdom

The capacity of Russian squires for enterprise should not be exaggerated. In 1804–1805, the Free Economic Society conducted a survey, drawing information from the administrations of twenty-nine provinces; it discovered a total of 169 innovators, mostly nobles, who applied advanced agricultural techniques on their estates.[65] The situation changed little in the ensuing fifty-six years. On the eve of the reform of 1861, only about 3 percent of all serfholders had rationalized the operation of their estates; the rest adhered to tradition.[66] Russian squires were middling businessmen and entrepreneurs who avoided outlays on production, who feared innovation and risk, and who relied primarily on administrative measures; furthermore, they were under the influence of peasant agricultural techniques.[67] Even the most profitable *barshchina* estates did not extract maximum profits and were not as lucrative as the slave plantations of the southern United States, the estates in east European countries, or the large estates in Russia that relied on hired labor. In the 1850s, in connection with preparations for the abolition of serfdom, the Ministry of State Properties conducted experiments to compare the efficiency of *barshchina* and hired-labor estates operating under similar conditions as regards size, climate, soil, and so on in nineteen provinces in the black-earth and non-black-earth regions. A comparison of the net income per *desiatina* on twenty-six pairs of estates showed that income was higher on almost half of the *barshchina* estates, but the average income of the twenty-six estates using hired labor was 25 percent higher.[68]

The investigators could not, however, take into account "invisible costs of production," by which I mean the enormous moral and psychological burden that prevailed on *barshchina* estates, so that squires had to literally beat their revenues out of their serfs, relying on strict control and severe punishment. Data on the punishment of serfs for various offenses will give some conception of this mode of operation. We have estimates of the norms of punishment on a *barshchina* estate belonging to magnate Prince Gagarin, for the period 1819 to 1858, and covering an average of 640 male serfs; we have similar data for an *obrok* estate belonging to another magnate, Count Sheremetev, for the period 1790 to 1809, covering an average of 4,334 male serfs. On the *barshchina* estate, about 25 percent of the adult male serfs were subjected to punishment per year;[69] for the *obrok* estate, the figure was only 0.3 percent,[70] which means that *barshchina* serfs were punished eighty-three times as often as *obrok* serfs. On the *obrok* estate, however, the same peasants were punished again and again, so that the total of punishments was only twenty-five times higher on the *barshchina* estate. Sometimes punishment was lethal. According to incomplete data compiled by the secret police, in 1858 there were 46 instances of death under punishment and another 15 instances of babies stillborn because of the harsh punishment of women. In 1859 the corresponding figures were 55 and 17, and in 1860, 65 and 22.[71] It is probable that maximum violence secured maximum revenues (we have already noted that *barshchina* estates were twice as profitable as those on *obrok*). Carol Leonard has shown that whenever estate owners wanted to increase their revenues, they had to intensify control and expand the administrative apparatus.[72] On plantations in the southern United States in the 1840s, corporal punishment was inflicted on between 70 percent and 100 percent of slaves every year.[73] Even taking into account that slaves were not punished as severely as Russian

serfs, it is clear that the level of violence was higher on American plantations than on *barshchina* estates. It is probably for this reason that the plantations were more profitable. But it does not follow from this that income
rose *automatically* with the level of violence; violence had its own law of di-
minishing returns.

To employ extreme cruelty toward peasants for the sake of higher revenues was never easy, and over time it became very difficult due to the rise in
peasants' self-consciousness, their sense of personal worth, and the increase
in peasant protest. When compulsion exceeded what peasants understood to
be its proper limits, they responded by filing complaints with the tsar's administrators against their squire or his steward; they rioted; and frequently
they killed their squire.[74] Practically every serfholder was attacked by his
serfs at least once in his life.[75] The statistics of the peasant movement clearly
show that in the eighteenth century and the first half of the nineteenth century, peasant protests against the abuses of their masters became ever more
frequent. Between 1796 and 1800, the average number of peasant disturbances per year was 39; between 1851 and 1856, the average was 88, or 2.3
times higher.[76] It was primarily serfs who rioted, and their central demand
was not complete freedom from bondage but rather freedom from the authority of the serfholder by means of transfer to the state or appanage peasantry.[77] A prominent police official described the mood of the serfs to
Nicholas I in these words: "In this class there are more cunning heads than
might be supposed. . . . They all know that throughout the empire it is only
Russian peasants who are in slavery; all the rest—Finns, Tatars, Latvians,
Mordvinians, Chuvash, and so on are free."[78] Furthermore, stepping up
pressure on serfs necessitated an expansion in the estate's administrative apparatus, which increased the costs of production. A vicious circle, typical of
economies based on forced labor, ensued: The greater the violence, the
greater the resistance.[79]

No less important, as customary norms became less harsh, as the
serfholders underwent Europeanization, and as their educational and cultural level rose, cruelty came to seem immoral in the eyes of the more enlightened part of society.[80] Not all nobles could handle the contradiction
between a European style of life and the necessity of following the rules
dictated by the harsh realities of serfdom; to these men and women, serfdom came to seem a moral scandal and a social anachronism.[81] The
church also held a negative view of serfdom and especially of its abuses;
it struggled against them to the extent that circumstances permitted.[82]
The most enlightened serfholders were no longer able to use violence
against their peasants, which meant that their revenues began to decline
and serfdom itself lost its economic rationale. Thus the servile economy
was in a blind alley—not because it was not profitable but because it
was impossible to maintain the former level of violence, much less to

raise that level so that the system would retain its efficiency. "I shall not lament the loss of a right that every day becomes more onerous for us," wrote one serfholder from Ryazan province. "Are there many of us who still have it in them to use this right to real advantage? And do not all the troubles and problems of our time derive from habituation to unchecked power?"[83]

In contrast, however, the squire A. I. Koshelev, who was famous for his outstanding management of his estate, described how *barshchina* peasants worked when they were not subjected to severe punishment:

> Watch how they perform *barshchina*. The peasant arrives for work as late as possible; he stands around and looks around as often as possible for as long as possible, and works as little as possible, for he does not have work to do but a day to kill. . . . The labor performed on the demesne, especially when it is not task labor *(urochnaia rabota),* reduces a zealous supervisor either to desperation or to rage. You don't want to rely on punishment, but *you resort to it as the only means of moving things forward.*[84]

This is why, long before the abolition of serfdom, some serfholders manumitted serfs for a modest fee, converted them into "obligated peasants" that is, they were personally freed and their rents were fixed), and offered the government various schemes for the abolition of serfdom.[85] Koshelev, who perceived this blind alley earlier than others, presented a plan for the Emancipation of the serfs to the Ministry of Internal Affairs in 1847. He stated:

> There can be no thought of significant changes or improvement in our economy under present circumstances. *Barshchina* is always the stumbling block for any efforts in this direction. On the other hand, serfs are so convinced that their master must and will always come to their aid that they work even worse on their own fields than on the demesne. The only way of escaping from this false position is to establish an absolute boundary between our land and the peasants' and to let the advantages of working for oneself awaken their energies.[86]

Catherine II and Alexander I did not approve of serfdom; but because of the opposition of the nobility and of influential groups at court, they did not abolish it. Nicholas I was afraid of abolishing serfdom because of the unpredictable consequences, but it was his dying wish that his son abolish it. Alexander II took the fateful step primarily because the adherents of serfdom no longer had a moral and legal basis for defending the institution that had become Russia's shame. They could no longer even dream of a palace coup, and simply tried to secure the terms of reform that would be most advantageous to themselves. The time to abolish serfdom finally came at the end of the 1850s, when public opinion was increasingly inclined to see serfdom as incompatible with the spirit of the times. "*Given the present general level of education and structure of opinion,* an order of things like ours cannot be normal," an observant contemporary rightly remarked, "and that is why the abolition of serfdom was so easy to achieve." [The italics are mine.—B.N.M.].[87]

Another contributing cause of the abolition of serfdom was a certain commercialization of the peasant economy, which gave peasants a sense of property, taught them the value of money, and imparted a love for economic freedom.[88] "For money the Russian *muzhik* will outfox an Englishman," a well-known, enterprising squire once remarked, "but the same person on *barshchina* is as clumsy as a bear."[89] Peasants' work outside the village, in towns or factories, had a similar effect.

In short, the state abolished serfdom in 1861, without waiting for serfholders to exhaust the institution's economic potential or for the servile economy to reach a crisis. It was acting in response to demands from educated Russian society and from an influential contingent of rich, liberal squires—and in view of its own needs for modernization.

Vestiges of the Servile Order

After the juridical abolition of bondage to private persons and the weakening and elimination of bondage to the state, Russian peasants were still affected by vestiges of serfdom, and as late as 1917, remained bound to the commune. To some degree, squires restored the prereform system in the form of labor rental and sharecropping. They were able to do so because peasants' geographic mobility was limited; peasants were desperately short of land and were ascribed, willingly or not, to the commune; because the peasantry bore a great burden of taxation; and because some forms of extraeconomic compulsion could still be employed. The essence of the labor rental system was that the squire's land was cultivated by the emancipated peasants using their equipment and draft animals. In return, the peasants received land for their own use, loans of grain or money, forest products, and the like. Under a form of sharecropping called *izdol'shchina*, peasants contracted to give the squire a share of the harvest on the land they rented from him; under the form called *ispol'shchina*, that share was one-half the harvest. Until 1917, labor-rental and peonage systems of cultivation prevailed on estates throughout the country, predominating in the Great Russian provinces, even though a few estate owners employed hired laborers to cultivate the land using the estate's draft power and equipment. Naturally, since the peasants were deeply involved in this semiservile system, their own economic operations were also semiservile. Against this background, the few private capitalist estates employing hired labor and advanced technology belonged primarily to nobles.[90]

Why were the vestiges of serfdom so durable? Like any important socio-economic phenomenon, serfdom was produced by the interaction of several factors. Both on the estates of the nobility and among the state peasants, the servile economy was liquidated *from above,* and not because of its own disintegration; economically, it had not reached its limit. Consequently, most peasants and squires were not prepared by experience to conduct their affairs in a new way, appropriate to a free-market economy. For example, the agricultural society in Iurev conducted a special investigation in 1860 and concluded that few serfholders were familiar with the organization of an estate operated with hired labor.[91] The government's Value Commission reached a similar conclusion in the 1870s; the commission found that the shift of private estates to a hired-labor system was frustrated by a shortage of capital, knowledge, and experience on the part of the owners and by "the laziness, bad faith, and willfulness of the workers (i.e., peasants) and the unenforceability of the contracts made with them."[92] In the nation as a whole, there was a shortage of capital, and there was no free market either for labor power or for land, inasmuch as traffic in peasant land was severely restricted until 1907.

In central and east European countries the abolition of serfdom came in two stages. In the first stage, servile relations were delimited and regulated and framed by law; not until 150 to 200 years later were they abolished.[93] This transitional period enabled both squires and peasants gradually to adapt and to prepare for full economic freedom, as the economies of these countries underwent gradual restructuring. Russian legislation did not provide for such an extended transitional period; but no economic system can move abruptly from one state to another. Therefore, Russian circumstances produced a different sort of transitional period, replete with remnants of the servile order.

In villages where ex-serfs lived, bondage to the state and to the corporation was preserved. These institutions checked peasants' initiative, limited their social and geographic mobility, and impeded the penetration of bourgeois relations among them. The partial character of deliverance from bondage meant the partial liquidation of the servile order.

We should remember that the conditions of the abolition of serfdom were onerous for squires as well as for serfs. The estate owners received only about 80 percent of the capitalized rent of the land they lost, and the greater part of this sum took the form of bonds, which if they were sold at once, brought only between 80 percent and 90 percent of their face value. Russian serfs were emancipated under more onerous conditions than, for example, the serfs of Prussia and Austria; they lost up to 20 percent of the land they had cultivated for themselves before the abolition of serfdom, and they had to pay not only for the land but for their own freedom.[94]

The retention of vestiges of serfdom was also facilitated by the fact that peasants' land allotment was not recognized as their private property and until 1907 was excluded by law from the market. Richard Wortman has shown that in prerevolutionary Russian social and political thought, in the consciousness of the common people and the intelligentsia alike, a hostile attitude prevailed toward the idea of land as property. The principle of private property, including property in land, was upheld as sacred and inviolable only after the Revolution of 1905–1907 and then only by the government and by the rightist parties that were defending the nobles' landholdings.[95] In the Manifesto of 17 October 1905, we find provisions for the inviolability of the person; for freedom of speech, assembly, and association; and for a State Duma with legislative power—but nothing about private property.[96] This was no oversight. The overwhelming majority of Russians did not view private property as a civil right, as defined by European tradition; furthermore, private property was associated with the hated estates of the nobility. The political parties contending for votes omitted mention of any policy on private property in their programs so as not to alienate peasants and workers. In preparing the October Manifesto, the government was guided by the same considerations. Further social and political experience showed that this neglect of property rights was ill-conceived. Individual freedom is secured only by the aggregate of civil rights, of which the right to private property is an essential part.

Because neither peasants nor squires were mentally ready to shift to a market economy, and because the objective conditions for this shift were lacking, many components of the prereform, servile order showed great vitality in the village after 1861. P. B. Struve understood this very well: "Postreform agriculture in the central black-earth provinces represents a tenacious recreation of the servile economy, as if it had been derived from it, with all its backward economic and social features."[97]

There was a definite continuity between prereform and postreform agriculture. Both before and after the 1861 Emancipation, the Russian manorial system was a wedge of the monetary economy, driven deeply into the flesh of Russia's prevailing natural economy. The postreform economic system was not, however, simply a regeneration of the old order. Although they suffered heavy blows, the best estates recovered and began to adapt to changing conditions; there were signs of progress in their subsequent evolution. There were also positive developments in the peasant economy: more advanced techniques, the use of machines, and rising yields.[98] The postreform village became a more active player in the market, as the data show: In the mid-nineteenth century, only about 17 percent of Russia's grain was marketed; but by 1913, approximately 36 percent of the net yield was sold.[99]

Some specialists see features of postreform agrarian development that they regard as abnormal for a market economy: The price of land grew faster than did the income derived from the land, sometimes six times as fast; and rents for land increased faster than the price of land, producing an "abnormal" ratio of rents and prices in the early twentieth century. Rents were terrifically high, sometimes reaching 40 percent of the value of the product. These specialists have assumed that from the perspective of political economy, these features violate the laws of commodity production.[100] All of these features, however, are fully compatible with a market economy, because they were generated by supply and demand. The price of land outstripped agricultural incomes because the supply of land offered for sale by landowners did not correspond to the peasants' enormous demand for land. Land rents outstripped the price of land and rose to fabulous levels because of the peasants' enormous demand for land to rent. The market created all of these "abnormalities"—with vigorous help from the squires, of course, since they profited greatly from them.

The peasantry accepted the situation because it had no other option. In 1861, however, peasants began to migrate in enormous numbers; yet neither the cities, nor industry, nor Siberia could absorb the enormous natural growth of the rural population, which consequently increased by 87 percent between 1861 and 1914. As a result, surplus labor in the countryside amounted to 23 million people by 1901, and 32 million by 1914; these figures correspond respectively to 52 percent and 56 percent of all persons of working age in the villages.[101] The solutions that might have been proposed to ameliorate this situation—such as a radical reduction in the birthrate through contraception, abortion, and celibacy—were at odds with the mentality of the Russian peasant. Furthermore, the communal-collective form of landownership facilitated a rapid population increase, since every new worker was guaranteed an allotment of land.[102] The extra hands and mouths created an enormous demand for land to buy or rent, which generated the "abnormalities." When the harvest failed, grain prices responded to unsatisfied demand by rising several times over and losing all touch with the costs of grain production. Given the tremendous overpopulation, land became a precious commodity for the peasant, as did grain when the harvest failed.

The Hard Path to Freedom

In Russia, bondage was abolished from above, as it should be in a legitimate state. It was not just the state that was involved in the fall of bondage, however, but all of Russian society. Among the factors contributing to the modification and abolition of serfdom were the developing independence from the state of all classes of the population; the consolidation of private property; demands for freedom from all groups of the population; the influence of European culture; and the objective political, military, economic, and cultural requirements of state and society.[103] One of the main architects of the abolition of serfdom, N. A. Miliutin, argued that servile relations were "disadvantageous to the advancement of the national economy, hostile to the development of morality among the common people, and incompatible with a state on firm foundations."[104] The impulse to alleviate serfdom and then to abolish it came, as a rule, both from those in bondage and from the enlightened segment of society and the intelligentsia. Each estate of Russian society, from the peasant to the noble, fought for its own emancipation by every means available to it. Russians did not struggle for universal freedom but for rights and privileges for their own estate. Because of this, the various social estates received differing levels of rights at different times, with the strongest among them gaining freedom first, and the weakest, last.

Although estates gained freedom at different times, the mightiest blow against bondage was delivered by the reforms of the 1860s and 1870s. This was no mere accident. In the mid-nineteenth century it became clear to all thinking people in Russia that the nation was in need of economic modernization and an industrial revolution, a transformation of the political and legal system, and enlightenment of the common people, who were still on the level that prevailed in western Europe in the seventeenth century. It was no less clear that the abolition of serfdom had to precede other reforms. "Long ago many people anticipated and welcomed the abolition of serfdom; many people now raise objections to it," Konstantin Kavelin, one of the leaders of the liberal movement, wrote in 1862, "but it came about without regard to the desires of some and the resistance of others, at a time when neither the mass of the people nor the government could tolerate serfdom and the phenomena that it produced in all spheres of life and in government."[105] By 1861, Russia was the only great power that still kept the greater part of its population in the complete bondage of serfdom.

Before the economic potential of serfdom was exhausted and before it had reached the stage of inner decay, the autocracy had responded to the demands of all estates of Russian society and to the state's own need for modernization and for a deeper incorporation of European cultural, political, and social standards by dealing a death blow to universal bondage. The reforms that abolished bondage to private persons, bondage to the state, and corporate bondage of town-dwellers and the clergy represented, in their substance and significance, the culmination of the present and the past; they drew on lessons from the experience of Austria, Prussia, and other German states; and they created a basis for Russia's transformation into a law-governed state with a market economy.

Many factors contributed to the survival of vestiges of serfdom and other varieties of bondage in the postreform countryside. In general, their elimination culminated only in 1907, after the cancellation of redemption payments and the abolition of the soul tax and of mutual responsibility. Corporate bondage, although weakened, retained some of its force until 1917. Throughout the entire postreform period the agrarian sector of the economy functioned in tune with the market mechanism, which played an ever greater role in the regulation of economic life. However, the numerous vestiges of serfdom, the subsistence character of the peasant economy, the continued existence of the repartitional commune, and the lack of a normal market for labor power and for land, taken together, mean that we cannot say that capitalism was entrenched in rural Russia by 1917. And since the agrarian sector was dominant, the economy of Russia at the beginning of the twentieth century was of a precapitalist or transitional type.

The remnants of bondage in social consciousness, and in social and economic relations, proved so deep-seated and so vital that the Bolsheviks were able to take advantage of them to restore some elements of the old order of bondage, and under Stalin, to bring them to a level that the serfholders of the eighteenth century never dreamed of.

Notes

1. P. N. Miliukov, *Ocherki po istorii russkoi kul'tury* (Moscow, 1918), chast' 1, p. 231.

2. Carol S. Leonard, *Reform and Regicide: The Reign of Peter III of Russia* (Bloomington, 1992). See also A. S. Myl'nikov, *Legenda o russkom printse* (Leningrad, 1987), pp. 110–122.

3. Robert E. Jones, *The Emancipation of the Russian Nobility, 1762–1785* (Princeton, 1973), pp. 240–265, 285–299.

4. Ia. E. Vodarskii, *Naselenie Rossii v kontse XVI–nachala XVIII veka* (Moscow, 1977), p. 94.

5. V. O. Kliuchevskii, "Podushnaia podat' i otmena kholopstva v Rossii," in idem, *Sochineniia v vos'mi tomakh* (Moscow, 1957), tom 7, pp. 318–402.

6. M. F. Vladimirskii-Budanov, *Obzor istorii russkogo prava* (Kiev and St. Petersburg, 1900), pp. 595–605.

7. M. N. Shcherbatov, *O povrezhdenii nravov v Rossii kniazia Shcherbatova* (Moscow, 1984), pp. 59–60.

8. Miliukov, *Ocherki po istorii russkoi kul'tury,* chast' 1, p. 231.

9. V. N. Latkin, *Proekt novogo ulozheniia, sostavlennyi Zakonodatel'noi komissiei 1754–1766* (St. Petersburg, 1893), pp. 174–188; Latkin, *Zakonodatel'nye komissii v Rossii v XVIII stoletii* (St. Petersburg, 1887), tom 1, pp. 253–424; M. M. Bogoslovskii, "Dvorianskie nakazy v Ekaterinskuiu komissiiu," *Russkoe bogatstvo,* 1897, kniga 6, pp. 46–83; kniga 7, pp. 136–152.

10. Gregory L. Freeze, *The Russian Levites: Parish Clergy in the Eighteenth Century* (Cambridge and London, 1977), pp. 13–45; Freeze, *The Parish Clergy in Nineteenth-Century Russia: Crisis, Reform, Counter-Reform* (Princeton, 1983), pp. 459–474. See also P. V. Znamenskii, *Prikhodskoe dukhovenstvo v Rossii so*

vremeni reformy Petra (Kazan, 1873), pp. 460–490; idem, *Polozhenie dukhoven-stva v tsarstvovanie Ekateriny II i Pavla I* (Moscow, 1880), pp. 145–158, 183–184.

11. Freeze, *The Parish Clergy*, pp. 156, 159.

12. Ibid., pp. 298–397.

13. The ascription of peasants to industrial enterprises dates to 1637, but be-came widespread only in the reign of Peter I.

14. N. M. Nikol'skii, *Istoriia russkoi tserkvi* (Moscow, 1931), pp. 275–281.

15. V. I. Krutikov, "Sovetskaia istoriografiia krizisa krepostnoi sistemy khozi-aistva v Rossii," in P. A. Kolesnikov, ed., *Materialy XV sessii Simpoziuma po prob-lemam agrarnoi istorii* (Vologda, 1976), vyp. 2, pp. 3–26; L. G. Zakharova, *Samoderzhavie i otmena krepostnogo prava v Rossii 1856–1861* (Moscow, 1984), pp. 3–16.

16. Alexander Gerschenkron, "Agrarian Policies and Industrialization: Russia 1861–1917," in H. J. Habakkuk and N. Postan, eds., *The Cambridge Economic History of Europe* (Cambridge, 1965), vol. 6, part 2, pp. 706–800.

17. Alfred J. Rieber, *The Politics of Autocracy* (The Hague and Paris, 1966), pp. 15–58.

18. Terrence Emmons, *The Russian Landed Gentry and the Peasant Emancipa-tion of 1861* (Cambridge, 1968), pp. 34–36; Daniel Field, *The End of Serfdom: Nobility and Bureaucracy in Russia, 1855–1861* (Cambridge, 1976), pp. 96–101.

19. Jerome Blum, *Lord and Peasant in Russia from the Ninth to the Nineteenth Century* (Princeton, 1972), pp. 612–618. All of the literature that appeared before the beginning of the 1970s is reviewed in P. Scheibert, *Die Russische Agrarreform von 1861: Ihre Probleme und der Stand ihrer Erforschung* (Cologne and Vienna, 1973).

20. S. V. Maksimov, *Izbrannye proizvedeniia v dvukh tomakh* (Moscow, 1987), tom 1, p. 422.

21. Evsey D. Domar and Mark J. Machina, "On the Profitability of Russian Serfdom," *Journal of Economic History*, vol. 44, no. 4 (1984), pp. 919–956; N. L. Rubinshtein, *Sel'skoe khoziaistvo Rossii vo vtoroi polovine XVIII veka* (Moscow, 1957), pp. 47–48.

22. *Stoletie Voennogo ministerstva: 1802–1902* (St. Petersburg, 1902), tom 4, chasti 1, 2; V. N. Latkin, *Uchebnik istorii russkogo prava* (St. Petersburg, 1909), p. 455; N. N. Obruchev, *Voenno-statisticheskii sbornik*, vyp. IV, *Rossiia* (St. Peters-burg, 1871), otdel 2, pp. 11–12.

23. Boris N. Mironov, *Khlebnye tseny v Rossii za dva stoletiia (XVIII–XIX vv.)* (Leningrad, 1985), pp. 46–47.

24. Boris N. Mironov, "Consequences of the Price Revolution in Eighteenth-Century Russia," *Economic History Review*, vol. 45, no. 3 (1992), pp. 457–478.

25. Calculated from the data in I. D. Koval'chenko and L. V. Milov, "Ob inten-sivnosti obrochnoi ekspluatatsii krest'ian tsentral'noi Rossii v kontse XVIII–pervoi polovine XIX v.," *Istoriia SSSR*, no. 4 (1966), pp. 55–80; P. G. Ryndziunskii, "Ob opredelenii intensivnosti obrochnoi ekspluatatsii krest'ian tsentral'noi Rossii v kontse XVIII–pervoi polovine XIX v.," *Istoriia SSSR*, no. 6 (1966), pp. 44–64; V. A. Fedorov, *Pomeshchich'i krest'iane Tsentral'no-promyshlennogo raiona Rossii kontsa XVIII–pervoi poloviny XIX v.* (Moscow, 1974), pp. 231–233; B. G. Litvak,

Russkaia derevnia v reforme 1861 g.: Chernozemnyi tsentr, 1861–1905 gg. (Moscow, 1972), pp. 124–127; Mironov, *Khlebnye tseny,* pp. 46–47, 54–55.

26. V. I. Neupokoev, *Gosudarstvennye povinnosti krest'ian evropeiskoi Rossii v kontse XVIII–nachale XIX veka* (Moscow, 1987), p. 35; Mironov, "Consequences of the Price Revolution," pp. 469–471.

27. For various views on the matter, see: P. B. Struve, *Krepostnoe khoziaistvo* (Moscow, 1913), pp. 154–156; I. O. Karpovich, *Khoziaistvennye opyty tridtsatiletnei praktiki ili nastavlenie dlia upravleniia imeniiami* (St. Petersburg, 1837), pp. 294–301; Rubinshtein, *Sel'skoe khoziaistvo Rossii,* pp. 82–91; I. D. Koval'chenko, *Russkoe krepostnoe krest'ianstvo v pervoi polovine XIX v.* (Moscow, 1967), pp. 60–73; S. N. Prokopovich, *Agrarnyi vopros v tsifrakh* (St. Petersburg, 1907), p. 7.

28. Vladimir, Voronezh, Kaluga, Kostroma, Kursk, Moscow, Orel, Penza, Ryazan, Tambov, Tver, and Tula provinces.

29. My estimate was derived from data in A. S. Nifontov, *Zernovoe proizvodstvo v Rossii vo vtoroi polovine XIX veka* (Moscow, 1974), pp. 96–97.

30. Calculated from data in Druzhinin, *Gosudarstvennye krest'iane,* tom 1, p. 50; Neupokoev, *Gosudarvennye krest'iane,* p. 35; Mironov, *Khlebnye tseny,* pp. 46–47.

31. Rossiiskii gosudarstvennyi istoricheskii arkhiv (hereafter RGIA), fond 1589 (5-e otdelenie Sobstvennoi ego velichestva kantseliarii), opis' 1, delo 729: "Po otchetam grazhdanskikh gubernatorov o sostoianii gosudarstvennykh krest'ian," 1847; fond 1589, opis' 2, delo 144: "Ob obnishchanii krest'ian Kazanskoi gubernii," 1831; RGIA, fond 1911 (V. I. Veshniakov), opis' 1, delo 6, listy 27–40; Ia. Kryzhivoblotskii, *Kostromskaia guberniia,* in *Materialy dlia geografii i statistiki Rossii, sobrannye ofitserami General'nogo shtaba* (St. Petersburg, 1861), p. 198; Druzhinin, *Gosudarstvennye krest'iane,* tom 1, pp. 196–206, 472–475.

32. L. V. Milov, "O proizvoditel'nosti truda v zemledelii Rossii v seredine XVIII v.," *Istoricheskie zapiski,* vol. 85 (1970), pp. 264–266; L. V. Milov and L. N. Vdovina, "Kul'tura sel'skokhoziaistvennogo proizvodstva," in A. D. Gorskii, ed., *Ocherki russkoi kul'tury XVIII veka* (Moscow, 1985), chast' 1, pp. 39–147.

33. B. N. Mironov, "Vliianie krepostnogo prava na otnoshenie russkogo krest'ianina k trudu," in V. L. Ianin, ed., *Sovetskaia istoriografiia agrarnoi istorii SSSR (do 1917 g.)* (Kishinev, 1978), pp. 119–127.

34. V. I. Veshniakov, *Krest'iane sobstvenniki v Rossii* (St. Petersburg, 1858), pp. 72, 74.

35. *Zapiski A. I. Kosheleva* (Berlin, 1884), pp. 102–105.

36. Veshniakov, *Krest'iane sobstvenniki,* p. 73; V. I. Anisimov, "Nadely," in A. K. Dzhivelegov, S. P. Mel'gunov, and V. I. Picheta, eds., *Velikaia reforma: Russkoe obshchestvo i krest'ianskii vopros v proshlom i nastoiashchem* (Moscow, 1911), tom 6, p. 90.

37. V. S. Poroshin, *Dvoriane-blagotvoriteli* (St. Petersburg, 1856), pp. 21–46.

38. Calculated from data in Veshniakov, *Krest'iane-sobstvenniki,* p. 76, and *Svedeniia o prodazhnykh tsenakh na zemliu* (St. Petersburg, 1859), vypuski 1–3.

39. D. I. Shakhovskoi, "Vykupnye platezhi," in A. K. Dzhivelegov, S. P. Mel'gunov, and V. I. Picheta, eds., *Velikaia reforma,* tom 6, p. 116.

40. RGIA, fond 1284 (Departament obshchikh del Ministerstva gosudarstvennykh imushchestv), op. 234, dd. 149, 482, 623.

41. V. I. Semevskii, *Krest'ianskii vopros v Rossii v XVIII i pervoi polovine XIX veka* (St. Petersburg, 1888), tom 1, pp. 252–281; tom 2, pp. 209–254.

42. N. Vinogradov, "Istoricheskii ocherk uslovii zhiznennogo byta belopashtsev sela Korobova," in *Kostromskaia starina* (Kostroma, 1912), vyp. 7, p. 73.

43. Vinogradov, "Istoricheskii ocherki," pp. 61–115; A. S. Pankratov, *Potomki Ivana Susanina* (Moscow, 1913), pp. 1–47.

44. Calculated from data in *Materialy dlia statistiki Rossii, sobiraemye po vedomstvu Ministerstva gosudarstvennykh imushchestv* (St. Petersburg, 1859, 1861), vyp. 2, p. 180; vyp. 3, pp. 26–27, 108, 112–113; vyp. 4, pp. 63, 84; *Khoziaistvenno-statisticheskie materialy, sobiraemye komissiiami i otradami upravleniia denezhnykh sborov s gosudarstvennykh krest'ian* (St. Petersburg, 1857), vyp. 2, pp. 20, 26, 67, 72.

45. G. Clark, "Productivity Growth Without Technical Change in European Agriculture Before 1850," *Journal of Economic History*, vol. 47, no. 2 (June 1987), pp. 427–429.

46. Milov, "O proizvoditel'nosti truda," p. 266; R. Dzhons, *Ekonomicheskie sochineniia* (Leningrad, 1937), pp. 36–40, 50–64.

47. Peter Kolchin, *Unfree Labor: American Slavery and Russian Serfdom* (Cambridge, and London, 1987), pp. 107–108.

48. Roger L. Ransom and Richard Sutch, *One Kind of Freedom: The Economic Consequences of Emancipation* (Cambridge, 1977), p. 233.

49. Kolchin, *Unfree Labor*, pp. 108, 348.

50. Clark, "Productivity Growth," pp. 419–432; *Materialy vysochaishe uchrezhdnennoi 16 noiabra 1900 g. Komissii po issledovaniiu voprosa o dvizhenii s 1861 g. po 1900 g. blagosostoianii sel'skogo naseleniia evropeiskoi Rossii* (St. Petersburg, 1903), chast' 1, pp. 176–177.

51. *Narodnoe khoziaistvo SSSR v 1990 g.* (Moscow, 1991), p. 471.

52. Iu. Kakhk, *"Ostzeiskii put'" perekhoda ot feodalizma k kapitalizmu* (Tallinn, 1988), pp. 89, 93, 343–344.

53. Struve, *Krepostnoe khoziaistvo*, pp. 154–156; Domar and Machina, "On the Profitability of Russian Serfdom," pp. 919–954; Field, *The End of Serfdom*, pp. 21–35; D. Beyrau, "Agrarstruktur und Bauernprotest: Zu den Bedingungen der russischen Bauernbefreiung von 1861," in *Vierteljahrschrift für Sozial- und Wirtschaftsgeschichte* (Wiesbaden, 1977), vol. 64, no. 2, pp. 179–236.

54. A. N. Engel'gardt, *Iz derevni: 12 pisem* (Moscow, 1937), pp. 284–287.

55. Olga Crisp, *Studies in the Russian Economy Before 1914* (New York, 1976), p. 95.

56. B. N. Mironov, "Work and Rest in the Peasant Economy of European Russia in the Nineteenth and Early Twentieth Century," in I. Blanchard, ed., *Labour and Leisure in Historical Perspective: The Thirteenth to Twentieth Centuries.* Papers presented at Session B–3a of the Eleventh International Economic History Congress, Milan, 12–17 September 1994 (Edinburgh, 1994).

57. In 1897, the average levels of literacy were: for Orthodox Christians, 19 percent; for Catholics, 32 percent; for Protestants, 70 percent; for Volga and Crimean Tatars, 25.3 percent; and for Muslims throughout the empire, 7 percent. *Obshchii svod po imperii rezul'tatov razrabotki dannykh pervoi vseobshchei perepisi naseleniia 1897 goda* (St. Petersburg, 1905), tom 2, p. xxxiv; *Pervaia vseobshchaia*

perepis' naseleniia 1897 g., tom 14, *Kazanskaia guberniia* (St. Petersburg, 1904), pp. 136–139; tom 41, *Tavricheskaia guberniia* (St. Petersburg, 1904), pp. 126–129.

58. "Kartofel'nyi bunt v Permskoi gubernii," *Russkaia starina*, tom 10 (1874), pp. 86–120; N. P. Ponomarev, *Istoricheskii obzor pravitel'stvennykh meropriiatii k razvitiiu sel'skogo khoziaistva v Rossii* (St. Petersburg, 1888).

59. B. N. Mironov, *Istoriia v tsifrakh* (Leningrad, 1991), pp. 80–83.

60. Calculated from data in Osobaia komissiia dlia sostavleniia proektov mestnogo upravleniia, *Statisticheskie materialy po volostnomu i sel'skomu upravleniiu tridtsati chetyrekh gubernii, v koikh vvedeny zemskie ustanovleniia: Svod dannykh, dostavlennykh po tsirkuliaru Ministerstva vnutrennikh del, ot 17 ianvaria 1880 g.* (St. Petersburg, 1800), tablitsa 1-b.

61. Veshniakov, *Krest'iane-sobstvenniki v Rossii,* pp. 9–11.

62. K. N. Shchepetov, *Krepostnoe pravo v votchinakh Sheremetevykh* (Moscow, 1947), pp. 16–26; N. M. Druzhinin, "Kupchie zemli krepostnykh krest'ian (Po dannym Glavnogo komiteta ob ustroistve sel'skogo sostoianiia)," in N. V. Usiugov, ed., *Voprosy sotsial'no-ekonomicheskoi istorii i istochnikovedeniia perioda feodalizma v Rossii* (Moscow, 1961), pp. 176–189; V. N. Kashin, "Zemlevladenie krepostnykh krest'ian," in *Krepostnaia Rossiia* (Leningrad, 1930), pp. 180–242; idem, *Krepostnye krest'iane-zemlevladel'tsy nakanune reformy* (Leningrad, 1934).

63. B. N. Mironov, "Sotsial'noe rassloenie russkogo krest'ianstva pod uglom zreniia sotsial'noi mobil'nosti," in V. L. Ianin, ed., *Problemy agrarnoi istorii (XIX–30-e gody XX v.)* (Minsk, 1978), chast' 2, p. 113.

64. See, for example, the discussion of this question by the Free Economic Society in 1865, in *S"ezd sel'skikh khoziaev v S.-Peterburge po sluchaiu stoletnego iubileia Imperatorskogo Vol'nogo ekonomicheskogo obshchestva* (St. Petersburg, 1866), pp. 145–200.

65. RGIA, fond 91 (Vol'noe ekonomicheskoe obshchestvo), op. 1, d. 463 (O khoziaistvakh, ispol'zuiushchikh razlichnye novovvedeniia i usovershenstvovaniia v svoikh imeniiakh i na fabrikakh, 1804–1805 gg.). See also S. B. Klimova, "Popytki pomeshchich'ego predprinimatel'stva v Rossii pervoi poloviny XIX v.," *Nauchnye doklady vysshei shkoly: Istoricheskie nauki,* no. 3 (1960), pp. 43–59; and N. I. Iakovkina, "O reorganizatsii pomeshchich'ego khoziaistva v nachale XIX v.," in V. V. Mavrodin, ed., *Voprosy istorii Rossii XIX–nachala XX v.* (Leningrad, 1983), pp. 45–56.

66. M. K. Rozhkova, ed., *Ocherki ekonomicheskoi istorii Rossii XIX–nachala XX v.* (Moscow, 1959), p. 18.

67. L. Andreevskii, *Ocherk krupnogo krepostnogo khoziaistva na severe* (Vologda, 1922), pp. 1–80; I. D. Koval'chenko, "K voprosu o sostoianii pomeshchech'ego khoziaistva pered otmenoi krepostnogo prava," in V. K. Iatsunskii, ed., *Ezhegodnik po agrarnoi istorii Vostochnoi Evropy: 1959* (Moscow, 1961), pp. 191–227; B. D. Grekov, "Tambovskoe imenie M.S. Lunina v pervoi chetverti XIX v.," *Izvestiia Akademii nauk SSSR, Otdelenie obshchestvennykh nauk,* no. 6 (1932), pp. 481–520; no. 7 (1932), pp. 623–648; A. N. Nasonov, "Khoziaistvo krupnoi votchiny nakanune osvobozhdeniia v Rossii," *Izvestiia Akademii nauk SSSR, Otdelenie obshchestvennykh nauk,* ser. 7, nos. 4–7 (1928), pp. 343–374; A. Povalishin, *Riazanskie pomeshchiki i ikh krepostnye: Ocherki iz istorii krepostnogo prava v Riazanskoi gubernii v XIX stoletii* (Ryazan, 1903), pp.

84–88. The best account of the economic conduct of *pomeshchiki* is in M. Confino, *Domaines et seigneurs en Russie vers la fin du XVIII siècle* (Paris, 1963).

68. RGIA, f. 911 (V. I. Veshniakov), op. 5, d. 29, ll. 3–8. See also P. Kislovskii, "Ocherk dokhodnosti sel'skogo khoziaistva pri svobodnom trude," *Zhurnal sel'skogo khoziaistva*, no. 4 (1858), otdel 5, pp. 2–30.

69. Steven L. Hoch, *Serfdom and Social Control in Russia: Petrovskoe, a Village in Tambov* (Chicago, 1989), pp. 162–163.

70. Shchepetov, *Krepostnoe pravo v votchinakh Sheremetevykh*, pp. 118–124, 348.

71. V. Bogucharskii, ed., "Tret'e otdelenie Sobstvennoi ego velichestva kantseliarii o sebe samom," *Vestnik Evropy*, 1917, kniga 3, p. 108.

72. C. S. Leonard, "Landlords and the Mir: Transaction Costs and Economic Development in Pre-Emancipation Russia," in Roger Bartlett, ed., *Land Commune and Peasant Community in Russia* (New York, 1990), pp. 121–142.

73. Kolchin, *Unfree Labor*, pp. 123–124.

74. R. Bohac, "Everyday Forms of Resistance: Serf Opposition to Gentry Exactions, 1800–1861," in Esther Kingston-Mann and Timothy Mixter, eds., *Peasant Economy, Culture, and Politics in European Russia, 1800–1921* (Princeton, 1991), pp. 236–261.

75. N. S. Volkonskii, *Usloviia pomeshchich'ego khoziaistva pri krepostnom prave* (Ryazan, 1898), p. 42.

76. B. G. Litvak, *Opyt statisticheskogo izucheniia krest'ianskogo dvizheniia v Rossii XIX v.* (Moscow, 1967), p. 10.

77. M. A. Rakhmatullin, *Krest'ianskoe dvizhenie v velikorusskikh guberniiakh v 1826–1857 gg.* (Moscow, 1990), p. 226; B. G. Litvak, "O nekotorykh chertakh psikhologii russkikh krepostnykh pervoi polovine XIX v.," in B. F. Porshenev, ed., *Istoriia i psikhologiia* (Moscow, 1971), pp. 199–214.

78. "Ezhegodnye otchety tret'ego otdeleniia v 1827–1830 gg.: Graf A. Kh. Ben kendorf o Rossii v 1827–1830 gg.," *Krasnyi arkhiv*, tom 37 (1929), p. 152.

79. S. Fenoaltea, "Slavery and Supervision in Comparative Perspective: A Model," *Journal of Economic History*, vol. 44, no. 3 (September 1984).

80. *Zapiski A. I. Kosheleva* (Moscow, 1991), pp. 78–83.

81. Field, *The End of Serfdom*, p. 100; Emmons, *The Russian Landed Gentry*, p. 35.

82. Gregory L. Freeze, "The Orthodox Church and Serfdom in Prereform Russia," *Slavic Review*, vol. 48, no. 3 (Fall 1989), pp. 361–387.

83. K-n, "Ob ustroistve byta u pomeshchich'ikh krest'ian Riazanskoi gubernii, *Sel'skoe blagoustroistvo* (1958), pp. 30–31.

84. *Zapiski A. I. Kosheleva* (Moscow, 1991), pp. 200–201 (the italics are mine). Similar descriptions of *barshchina* labor can be found in many other sources—for example, in N. Rychkov, *Zhurnal ili dnevnye zapiski puteshestviia* (St. Petersburg, 1770).

85. A. Zablotskii-Desiatovskii, "O krepostnom sostoianii v Rossii," in Zablotskii-Desiatovskii, *Graf P.D. Kiselev i ego vremia* (St. Petersburg, 1882), tom 4.

86. *Zapiski A. I. Kosheleva*, p. 219.

87. *Materialy dlia geografii i statistiki Rossii, sobrannye ofitserami General'nogo shtaba:* Lipinskii, *Simbirskaia guberniia* (St. Petersburg, 1868), chast' 1, p. 512.

88. Robert P. Donnoramo, *The Peasants of Central Russia: Reactions to Emancipation and the Market, 1850–1900* (New York, 1987), pp. 227–252; Melton, "Proto-Industrialization," *Past and Present*, no. 115 (May 1987), pp. 69–107; I. D. Koval'chenko, *Russkoe krepostnoe krest'ianstvo v pervoi polovine XIX v.* (Moscow, 1967), p. 384.

89. A. N. Zhukov, *Rukovodstvo otchetlivo, uspeshno i vygodno zanimat'sia russkim sel'skim khoziaistvom* (Moscow, 1848), p. 275.

90. Peter Gatrell, *The Tsarist Economy, 1850–1917* (London, 1986), pp. 105–118; A. N. Anfimov, *Krupnoe pomeshchich'e khoziaistvo evropeiskoi Rossii (Konets XIX–nachalo XX veka)* (Moscow, 1969), pp. 176–188; N. M. Druzhinin, *Russkaia derevnia na perelome, 1861–1880 gg.* (Moscow, 1978); D. Fild [Daniel Field], "1861: 'God Iubileiia'," in Larisa Zakharova, John Bushnell, and Ben Eklof, eds., *Velikie reformy v Rossii, 1856–1874* (Moscow, 1992), pp. 73–89.

91. *Zapiski Iur'evskogo obshchestva sel'skogo khoziaistva: Prilozhenie k zhurnalu Sel'skogo khoziaistva*, no. 6 (1861), p. 17.

92. *Doklad vysochaishe uchrezhdennoi Komissii dlia issledovaniia nyneshnego polozheniia sel'skogo khoziaistva i sel'skoi proizvoditel'nosti v Rossii* (St. Petersburg, 1873), prilozhenie 1, pp. 6, 1–40. See also V. G. Chernukha, *Krest'ianskii vopros v pravitel'stvennoi politike Rossii (60-kh–70-kh gody XIX veka)* (Leningrad, 1972).

93. Kakhk, "Ostzeiskii put'," pp. 354–357.

94. Steven L. Hoch, "The Banking Crisis, Peasant Reform, and Economic Development in Russia, 1857–1861," *American Historical Review*, vol. 96, no. 3 (June 1991), pp. 795–820. Evsey Domar offers some interesting ideas about the burden placed on peasants by redemption payments for their emancipation, in his *Capitalism, Socialism, and Serfdom* (Cambridge, 1989), pp. 280–288.

95. Richard Wortman, "Property Rights, Populism, and Russian Political Culture," in Olga Crisp and Linda Edmondson, eds., *Civil Rights in Imperial Russia* (Oxford, 1989), pp. 13–32; V. V. Kucher, *Politicheskie partii v Rossii v nachale XX veka: Kratkii ocherk istorii; Programmnye dokumenty* (Novosibirsk, 1993). See also K. Inusov and I. Savkin, eds., *Russkaia filosofiia sobstvennosti* (St. Petersburg, 1993).

96. *Gosudarstvennaia duma v Rossii v dokumentakh i materialakh* (Moscow, 1957), pp. 90–91.

97. Struve, *Krepostnoe khoziaistvo*, p. 159.

98. Gatrell, *The Tsarist Economy, 1850–1917*, pp. 98–140; Esther Kingston-Mann, "Peasant Communes and Economic Innovation: A Preliminary Inquiry," in Kingston-Mann and Mixter, eds., *Peasant Economy*, pp. 23–51.

99. V. K. Iatsunskii, *Sotsial'no-ekonomicheskaia istoriia Rossii XVIII–XIX vv.* (Moscow, 1973), p. 104; S. G. Strumilin, *Ocherki ekonomicheskoi istorii Rossii i SSSR* (Moscow, 1973), p. 104.

100. A. M. Anfimov, *Ekonomicheskoe polozhenie i klassovaia bor'ba krest'ian evropeiskoi Rossii, 1881–1904* (Moscow, 1984), pp. 104, 225.

101. *Materialy vysochaishe uchrezhdennoi 16 noiabria 1900 g. Komissii*, chast' 1, p. 249; *Ezhegodnik Ministerstva finansov na 1914 g.* (Petrograd, 1914), p. 3; L. I. Lubny-Gertsyk, ed., *Materialy po voprosu ob izbytochnom trude v sel'skom khoziaistve SSSR* (Moscow, 1926), p. 364.

102. B. N. Mironov, "Traditsionnoe demograficheskoe povedenie krest'ian v XIX–nachale XX v.," in A. G. Vishnevskii, ed., *Brachnost', rozhdaemost', smertnost' v Rossii i v SSSR* (Moscow, 1977), pp. 83–104. Demographers have drawn on a wide range of materials to demonstrate the connection between forms of property and population growth; see A. Sovi, *Obshchaia teoriia naseleniia* (Moscow, 1977), tom 1, pp. 202–203.

103. Gerschenkron, "Agrarian Policy and Industrialization," pp. 706–800; Blum, *Lord and Peasant in Russia*, pp. 612–618; Field, *The End of Serfdom*, pp. 96–101; Rieber, *The Politics of Autocracy*, pp. 15–58; Emmons, *The Russian Landed Gentry*, pp. 29–46.

104. Cited in Zakharova, *Samoderzhavie i otmena krepostnogo prava*, p. 48.

105. K. D. Kavelin, *Sobranie sochinenii* (St. Petersburg, 1899), tom 2, stolbets 138.

4

The State and
the Public Sphere

The concept of "the state" (*gosudarstvo*) is complex and hard to define.[1] As defined in this chapter, it includes the following generally recognized basic components: public law, or those obligatory rules of conduct established by the state to regulate the population and state institutions and to defend the rights of all members of society; the system of executive organs and social institutions that realizes public policy in the interests of society; and the population and territory over which the state exercises its authority. "The state" also includes the system of executive organs and institutions through which the governing entity realizes its public authority; hence, "the state" is the totality of the political order, organization, or system.

The word *monarchy* when used in reference to Russia describes a particular form of state in which a tsar, in one or another capacity, participates in governance; *autocracy* (Russ. *samoderzhavie*) refers to a sovereign who possesses absolute executive and legislative power and controls the state apparatus and the army; and *tsarism* refers to a monarchy in which the sovereign's power is limited by representative institutions, the state apparatus, and the army. The words *bureaucracy* and *officialdom* (*chinovnichestvo*) describe the totality of persons employed in the state's civil institutions, who hold a specific post as well as a rank in the Table of Ranks, and

Translated by David A. J. Macey, Middlebury College.

who receive a salary for their work—in other words, the body of officials who represent government authority.[2] Thus, the bureaucracy includes all officeholders with civil rank as well as office workers without rank, but only those who are employed in the crown or state administrations.[3]

The word *official (chinovnik)* describes a person in state service. This word entered the Russian language at the beginning of the nineteenth century. At first, it replaced *servitor (sluzhebnyi chelovek)* or *chancellery worker (prikaznyi chelovek)*. In Old Russian, *official* was used to refer to the book from which higher clerics read the church service. The Russian words for "official" in both senses have a common root in the Russian word for "rank" *(chin)*, meaning occupation and order. Therefore, the literal meaning of the word *official* is "agent, regulator, or guardian of order." In the nineteenth century, important officials in the civil hierarchy were called dignitaries *(sanovniki)*, and the rest were known as officials.[4]

The Development of the State Administration

First we will examine how the state apparatus developed, in order to determine its strengths and weaknesses. The sovereign's rights and prerogatives in the realm of state administration were extremely broad. From the early eighteenth century until 1906, the emperors were the sole subjects of legislative authority. To them belonged executive and judicial authority as well as the right to pardon. In addition, being considered the supreme protectors and guardians of Orthodoxy, they enjoyed a degree of religious authority, which they exercised through the Holy Synod. (In 1797, in an edict on the succession to the throne, the tsar was even referred to as the "head of the church.") The introduction of a constitution and parliament in 1906 reduced the emperor's prerogatives in the legislative sphere to mere confirmation of new laws that already had been approved by both houses of parliament—the State Duma and the State Council. However, the tsar did have the right to exercise legislative initiative during periods when the parliament was not in session. Following discussion and approval of the tsar's proposals within the Council of Ministers, they could immediately be issued as imperial ukases, although they were subject to final confirmation by the parliament. The tsar also appointed half the members of the State Council, including its chairman and vice-chairman.

The sovereign determined the country's internal and external policy in conjunction with the state's supreme political institutions, the names of which changed with almost every ruler. Until the end of the seventeenth century, the supreme political body was known as the Boyar Duma. Peter I (who ruled from 1682 to 1725) abolished this institution and in 1711 established the Senate to exercise this role. Under his immediate successors, Catherine I (1725–1727) and Peter II (1727–1730), this body was known as the

Supreme Privy Council; under Anna (1730–1741), as the Cabinet of Ministers; under Elizabeth (1741–1761), as the Conference at the Imperial Court; under Peter III (1761–1762), as the Council at the Imperial Court; under Catherine II (1762–1796), as the Imperial Council; and under Alexander I (1801–1825), at first, as the Unofficial Committee, and after 1802, as the Committee of Ministers. Nicholas I (1825–1855) transferred political decisionmaking to his personal chancellery; Alexander II (1855–1881), to the Council of Ministers; Alexander III (1881–1894), to the Committee of Ministers; and Nicholas II (1894–1917), until 1906, to the Committee of Ministers, and thereafter to the Council of Ministers. The Committee of Ministers was founded in 1802 and lasted until 1906. The Council of Ministers came into being informally in 1857 and formally in 1861, and functioned until 1917. These two institutions worked in tandem from 1861 to 1906. If in the eighteenth century the composition of these higher political institutions and their activity was determined by the will or the whim of the tsar, then the work of the Committee and the Council of Ministers was established on a firm juridical foundation.[5]

Among the most important institutions of the imperial period was the Senate. Its function and role changed several times during its existence (1711–1917). At the height of its powers, between 1742 and 1761, it functioned as an executive body. From 1802 to 1917, it was the court of highest instance, simultaneously fulfilling the public prosecutorial role. The Holy Synod (1721–1917) was the supreme government organ in charge of spiritual affairs. In 1810, the State Council was created. An advisory legislative body consisting of dignitaries appointed by the tsar, the State Council was to examine all draft laws prior to their submission to the tsar for his approval. In 1906, as indicated above, this institution was transformed into the upper chamber of parliament.

In 1906, a bicameral parliament was created and endowed with legislative functions. Deputies were elected from three curiae—of rural landowners, of urban dwellers, and of peasants. Workers were represented in the urban curia. Parliament possessed legislative rights as well as the right to discuss the budget and exercise supreme oversight over the state administration. However, the cabinet *(pravitel'stvo)* was appointed by the emperor and was responsible only to him.

The history of the central (crown) administration can be divided into three periods:

1. *The Era of the Chancellery:* From the late seventeenth century to 1721, official affairs were conducted by chancelleries, institutions whose responsibilities encompassed either specific administrative tasks or a specific territorial division. The name of these instittions, "chancelleries," accurately conveys the style and character of

administration at the time. The Russian word for "chancellery" comes from the word for "command" *(prikaz)*, which refers to a special assignment. Thus, chancelleries arose in response to special assignments by the tsar. The chancellery system had no internal consistency, no clearly defined functions, and no firm juridical basis. The very number of chancelleries reflects this. At the end of the seventeenth century, there were 44 chancelleries. Decisions within these chancelleries were collegial and unanimous. The concept of the separation of powers was absolutely alien to this system; as a consequence, legislative, executive, and judicial functions were combined. In addition to state chancelleries, there were palace and ecclesiastical chancelleries, which belonged to separate palace and church administrations that were responsible to the tsar and to the patriarch, respectively.[6] State chancelleries were directly subordinate to the tsar and the Boyar Duma and were administered by officials (boyars, *okol'nichii,* duma officials, and clerks) assigned by them, who received monetary salaries, or salaries in kind or in the form of land.

2. *The Era of the College:* Between 1721 and 1811, government was conducted by colleges that specialized in separate branches of administration. Initially there were twelve, but this number increased over time. Colleges had a uniform structure, a regular staff of officials, and activity governed by law—more specifically, by the General Regulation. Decisions within the colleges were made collegially and adopted by a majority vote. The Senate and the Procuracy supervised their activity. Beginning in 1715, but excluding the period from 1726 to 1763, officials received a monetary salary. From 1763, monetary salaries were established in all crown institutions.

3. *The Era of the Ministry:* From 1811 to 1917, government was conducted by ministries. Initially there were eight ministries; in 1861 there were nine; and by 1917 there were twelve. Ministries were distinguished from colleges in that they were organized according to the principle of one-man management; they had greater operating authority; they possessed local branches; and there was greater regulation and formalization of their activities (all in the law of 8 September 1802, establishing the ministries, the *General'noe uchrezhdenie*). Ministers were appointed by the emperor and were subordinate to him.

The central institutions ran the country's administration but always suffered from three shortcomings: First, their activities were inadequately coordinated, even though formally there were always institutions charged with this responsibility. The principal reason for this was the emperors' constant efforts to keep the reins of government in their own hands.[7] The second weakness was the confusion of various branches of administration within a single institution. The judicial function was not separated from administrative and police functions until 1775; and executive and legislative authorities were separated only with the establishment of the State Duma in 1906—and even then, only incompletely, since the emperor retained some legislative functions. The third problem was the center's inadequate control of local institutions, which persisted even after the introduction in 1775 of a special procuracy responsible for local administration.

The history of *local* administration can be divided into five periods distinguished primarily by the names of the institutions and by the greater or lesser involvement of local representatives of society in their activities.

1. *1700 to 1708:* Characterized by a combination of crown organs and institutions of local self-government, without any clear definition of their mutual relations; common institutions for town and country (*uezd* or district level); and no separation of administrative, police, and judicial functions.
2. *1708 to 1722:* A mixture of crown and elective elements in the same organs. Representatives are elected from among the nobility and townspeople to sit jointly with the crown administrator in collegial bodies organized at the levels of the province (*guberniia*), county (*provintsiia*), and city to conduct rural and urban affairs.
3. *1722 to 1775:* Exclusively bureaucratic administration, without any participation by representatives from the local population; since 1721, a separation of urban and rural (*uezd*) administrations.
4. *1775 to the 1860s:* The crown administration headed by a governor is the dominant form at the provincial level as well as in urban administration. This is supplemented by a charity board consisting of elected representatives from the nobility, townspeople, and the peasantry, which is responsible for matters of education and social welfare. The district-level Boards of Social Welfare have elected representatives only from the nobility. Judicial affairs are separated from administration and police, and at the lowest level are organized by social estate.
5. *1860s–1917:* The crown administration is slightly modified. The Boards of Social Welfare are abolished in the 1860s and 1870s and their responsibilities are transferred to the newly created organs of self-government—the city dumas. Urban and rural police are united in a single, district-level police administration headed by an officer (*ispravnik*) appointed from the local nobility by the governor.

Courts become all-class in nature, with the exception of the peasants' *volost*, or country courts, which are conducted according to customary law.[8]

Municipal organs of self-government functioned independently within the system of local government, under the formal supervision of the local administration. Affecting nobles, the urban estates, and the peasantry, municipal organs were responsible for economic, fiscal, and administrative matters.

The system of state institutions underwent continual reform from the eighteenth century through the beginning of the twentieth. The most important reforms were introduced under Peter I, Catherine II, Alexander I, Alexander II, and Nicholas II. These reforms have been thoroughly analyzed elsewhere, and there is therefore no need to examine them in great detail here.[9]

Expansion of the Bureaucracy

Parallel with the reorganization of the state apparatus there were changes in the numerical composition, education, competence, and social origin of its officials. The literature on numerical composition diverges according to the authors' definitions of an "official." Table 4.1 presents the evidence more or less according to the definition of officialdom given above.

The total number of officials rapidly increased between the end of the seventeenth century and the mid-nineteenth century, when serfdom was abolished: 2.6 times by 1755, another 1.8 times by 1796, and a further 5.6 times by 1857. The bureaucracy grew especially rapidly during the reigns of Peter I, Alexander I, and Nicholas I. Peter I's modernizing reforms demanded an expansion of the state apparatus, which led to the enlargement of the bureaucracy. The Table of Ranks, adopted in 1722, played a critical role in transforming government bureaucrats into a separate social stratum. It introduced a unified system of ranks into the military, civil, and palace administrations based on the principle of personal merit. This change conformed to the interests of the middle and lower nobility, consolidated the tsar's independence from the aristocracy, and created a firm social basis of support for the autocracy. The new law also facilitated the bureaucratization of the nobility and increased its service responsibilities. The growth of bureaucracy under Alexander I was connected with the ministerial reform, and under Nicholas I, with the emperor's striving to increase the bureaucracy's control over society.

After the abolition of serfdom, the absolute growth of the bureaucracy continued at a slower pace. By 1880, officials numbered approximately 129,000, and by 1897, approximately 145,000.[10] From the beginning of

TABLE 4.1 Number and Social Composition of Officials in Imperial Russia, Excluding Poland and Finland (various years)

	1690s	1755	1796	1857	1880	1897	1913
All officials (1,000)	4.657	12.0	21.3	119.3	129.0	144.5	252.9
Office workers (%)	–	62.0	26.0	26.0	–	30.0	–
Officials, ranks I–XIV (%)	–	38.0	74.0	74.0	–	70.0	–
Social origin (%):							
Hereditary nobles	14.0	22.0	33.0	34.0	–	26.0	–
Landowners	8.0	36.0	–	–	–	–	–
Officials	49.0	–	–	–	–	–	–
Clergy	30.0	5.0	–	–	–	–	–
Merchants	7.0	1.0	–	–	–	–	–
Total Russian population (million)	12.0	21.1	37.4	59.3	92.1	116.2	155.4
Officials per 1,000 pop.	0.39	0.57	0.57	2.01	1.40	1.24	1.63
Officials of ranks I–XIV (1,000)	–	4.56	15.5	87.2	–	100.7	–
Social origin (%):							
Hereditary nobles	–	50.0	45.0	46.0	–	31.0	–
Landowners	–	34.0	–	32.0	–	16.0	–
Officials	–	13.0	–	–	–	–	–
Clergy	–	2.0	–	–	–	–	–
Merchants	–	1.0	–	–	–	–	–

SOURCES: N. F. Demidova, *Sluzhilaia biurokratiia v Rossii XVII v. i ee rol' v formirovanii absoliutizma* (Moscow, 1987), pp. 37, 61, 77, 102–112 (data on social origin and land- and serfholdings relate only to chancellery workers in central institutions); *Russkii absoliutizm i dvorianstvo v XVIII v.: Formirovanie biurokratii* (Moscow, 1974), pp. 173, 176–177, 214–215, 300–301; P. A. Zaionchkovskii, *Pravitel'stvennyi apparat samoderzhavnoi Rossii v XIX v.* (Moscow, 1978), pp. 65–71; *Obshchii svod po imperii rezul'tatov razrabotki dannykh pervoi vseobshchei perepisi naseleniia, proizvedennoi 28 ianvaria 1897 goda,* 2 toma (St. Petersburg, 1905) [hereafter, *Obshchii svod dannykh pervoi perepisi naseleniia*], tom 1, pp. 256–259; W. M. Pintner, "The Evolution of Civil Officialdom, 1755–1855," in Walter M. Pintner and Don K. Rowney, eds., *Russian Officialdom: The Bureaucratization of Russian Society from the Seventeenth to the Twentieth Century* (Chapel Hill, 1980), pp. 210, 237, 241; B. B. Dubentsov, "Samoderzhavie i chinovnichestvo v 1881–1904 gg." (dissertation, Institute of History, Academy of Sciences of the USSR, 1977), p. 61; A. P. Korelin, *Dvorianstvo v poreformennoi Rossii, 1861–1904 gg.* (Moscow, 1979), pp. 91, 94; A. G. Korelin and A. M. Anfimov, eds., *Rossiia v 1913 g.* (St. Petersburg, 1934).

the twentieth century, the bureaucracy's rate of growth increased, and by 1913, the number of officials had reached 240,000. Comparing the changing size of officialdom with the growth in population gives a clearer picture. In the first half of the eighteenth century, the growth in the bureaucracy outstripped population growth by a multiple of 1.5, and in the first half of the nineteenth century, of 3.5. In the second half of the nineteenth century, after the abolition of serfdom, the population increased from 1.3 to 1.4 times more quickly than did the bureaucracy. At the beginning of the twentieth century, the bureaucracy again grew approximately 1.2 times faster than did the population. Thus the bureaucracy's rate of growth from the eighteenth century to the first half of the nineteenth century exceeded its rate of growth in the era following the Great Reforms.

The data in Table 4.1 on the number of officials in the nineteenth and early twentieth centuries include not only those who were directly employed in regular administrative positions but also others who, despite their classification as officials, were not (for example, doctors, veterinarians, and employees of charitable institutions). Thus, the statistics contained in Table 4.1 do not completely conform to the definition of officialdom outlined above. B. B. Dubentsov has tried to separate out from these data the actual number of officials who were directly employed in state administration in 1880 and 1903 and who conformed to a strict definition of "official." According to his calculations, this number was 81,000 and 136,000 in the respective years, or approximately 60 percent of all state employees.[11] The rate of growth in the number of officials during this period was more or less the same as that of the larger group of state employees.

The historical literature asserts that in the postreform era the bureaucracy grew continuously and that by the beginning of the twentieth century there were between 435,000 and 500,000 officials.[12] But the data upon which these studies rely include, in addition to the bureaucracy proper, gendarmes, police, school and university teachers, railroad guards, cashiers, and other ministerial employees. The descriptions "government bureaucrats" and "state employees" are not identical.

How are we to interpret this evidence? An increase in the number of officials relative to the population signifies an expansion of the state apparatus, whereas a decrease in their relative number indicates its weakening. Under serfdom, both the strengthening of the serf regime in the eighteenth century and the increasingly tense relations between noble landowners and peasants in the first half of the nineteenth century forced the autocracy to establish a powerful coercive apparatus that of necessity would lead to an expansion in the state apparatus.

As a consequence of the abolition of serfdom and the introduction of self-government in the towns and the countryside, the state's need for controls over the civil population weakened. In order to reduce the responsibilities of the local agents of the crown administration and free the central state institutions from matters that were not of general state importance, the government introduced the zemstvos and a new system of urban self-government. Its goals were in large measure achieved: The relative number of officials per thousand inhabitants declined between 1857 and 1897. Accordingly, the bureaucratic sphere of responsibility in the provinces and districts narrowed, and the sphere of local self-government expanded.

Furthermore, parallel to the decline in the relative size of state administration, public (*obshehetvennaia:* societal, non-official) administration expanded. Prior to the urban reforms of 1870, the majority of people in public, urban self-government worked on a voluntary basis, and hence were
unpaid; and no accurate figures are available as to their number. However,
they were undoubtedly fewer than in the period following the introduction
of the Urban Statute in 1870. The Zemstvo Statute of 1864, meanwhile,
created an entirely new institution of public administration, which had no
analog in the prereform era. In 1880, 52,000 people were employed by the
zemstvos.[13] This is fewer than the number of state administrators. But the
zemstvos only operated in thirty-four provinces, whereas the data on the
bureaucracy cover the entire empire, excluding Poland and Finland. If one
adds the employees of the city dumas, who, it appears from the payrolls,
outnumbered zemstvo employees by about 30 percent,[14] then it seems that
by 1880 more people were employed in public administration at the district and provincial levels than in the state administration, and that they
were accomplishing more. The Senatorial Inspections of 1880 and 1881 revealed that zemstvo, judicial, and to a somewhat lesser degree, city duma
bodies executed their responsibilities considerably more effectively than
did state institutions.[15] By the 1880s, public self-government had outper-
formed the state administration so successfully that it became the primary
force in local administration, at least in the zemstvo provinces, which in
the 1870s numbered 34 of the 50 provinces in European Russia.

But it is also necessary to take into account the so-called system of rural
self-government at the *volost* and communal levels. There, if one is to
judge by expenditures on salaries, the number of employees was three and
one-half times greater than in the zemstvo administration,[16] or approximately 180,000 more. Taking this evidence into consideration, there can be
no doubt that at the beginning of the 1880s the administration of daily life
had become the prerogative of society itself.

The increasing growth of the bureaucracy beginning in the 1880s appears to be connected with Alexander III's and Nicholas II's efforts to
strengthen the autocracy. The "Counterreforms," the struggle against social and revolutionary movements, and the increasing state involvement in
the economy all required an expansion of the bureaucratic apparatus and
especially of the police, whose numbers exceeded even those of the bureaucrats proper. These efforts were futile, however: During the years
when the number of zemstvos was increasing, the total number of employees in public administration continued to outstrip the state bureaucracy.
In 1912, there were zemstvos in forty of the fifty European provinces,
and in 1913, in forty-three provinces. In 1912, approximately 85,000 people were employed in public service in the zemstvos, and 110,000 in the
urban administration.[17] In the same year, peasant self-government in the

countryside employed almost 300,000 people.[18] Likewise futile was the attempt to expand the state sector of the economy at the beginning of the twentieth century (referred to in the historical literature as "state socialism"). This attempt foundered because private capital, both domestic and foreign, developed much more rapidly than did state capital.[19]

In the years following the Great Reforms, several contemporaries noted that the bureaucratic administration was gradually being displaced by public forms of administration,[20] thus confirming the statistical evidence presented above. In the 1880s, E. P. Karnovich, a prominent bureaucrat (director of the Prison Committee), a historian, and an increasingly well-known journalist, wrote: "The many recent reforms [referring to the reforms of the 1860s and 1870s] have considerably reduced the bureaucracy's authority and influence in matters of public concern. . . . These reforms have begun to demarcate the rights and interests of the administration from the rights and interests of the population and to create well-defined borders between the activities of officialdom and society."[21] In the early 1880s, the well-known publicist R. A. Fadeev and the Minister of the Imperial Court I. I. Vorontsov-Dashkov considered the bureaucracy to be excessively large—"much larger than service needs required." As a consequence, the bureaucracy did not have enough work to keep it occupied, and hence was becoming "a virtually useless body."[22] In 1884, Imperial Secretary A. A. Polovtsov also wrote about the superfluousness of government officials.[23] Apparently, the officials of the local organs of crown administration were even less burdened with work than were those of the central offices. For example, an official on special assignment to the administration of state properties in Podolia at the turn of the century wrote in his memoirs that "officials did not have sufficient work, and so they killed time in every conceivable way."[24]

Thus, there is reason to suppose that only in the years prior to the reforms of the 1860s did the bureaucracy's sphere of activity steadily expand such that the bureaucratization of social relations systematically increased. After the reforms were concluded, society's role in public administration and its sphere of activity steadily grew. It is important to underline, however, that in *absolute* terms the crown domain, which included the bureaucracy, army, state sector of the economy, and the state budget, grew continuously, but that in *relative* terms—compared to the scope of the private and public domains—the crown's role declined as the latter domains grew. *As a consequence, society gradually became stronger, whereas the autocracy progressively declined.*

The conventional conception of the bureaucracy's omnipotence does not conform to reality. In mid-nineteenth-century Russia, there were on average 2.0 officials per thousand inhabitants, whereas in Great Britain there were 4.1, and in France, 4.8.[25] In 1910, the number of officials employed by the state or in public non-governmental service per thousand inhabitants was 6.2 in Russia, 7.3 in England, 17.6 in France, 12.6 in Germany, and 11.3 in the United States.[26] Western Europe and the United States had more government officials and public employees per capita than Russia. Hence it is accurate to describe Russia, as did S. Frederick Starr, and earlier, D. I. Mendeleev, as "undergoverned."[27] The exaggerated conception of the power of the tsarist state apparatus is a result of the transfer of ideas about Soviet Russia to prerevolutionary Russia. This can be seen in Table 4.2. Indeed, the number of officials in the USSR generally exceeded the number in tsarist Russia by between 500 and 1,000 percent.

Changes in the Composition and Structure of the Bureaucracy

Over the course of the period under study a number of important changes took place in the structure, education, qualifications, and other characteristics of Russian officials, gradually altering the physiognomy of the Russian bureaucracy. The characteristic features of Russian officialdom and the changes that took place from the eighteenth to the twentieth centuries can be summarized as follows.[28]

1. Government officials were always oriented toward the interests of the state rather than those of society. The ennoblement of people from other social classes who entered the bureaucracy, the hierarchical organization of

TABLE 4.2   Numbers Employed in Soviet State and Economic Administrations and Cooperative and Social Organizations (various years)

	1922	*1928*	*1940*	*1950*	*1985*
Employed in the state-owned sector of the national economy (1,000s)	6.24	11.4	33.6	40.4	117.8
Employed in the administration (1,000s)	700	1,010	1,837	1,831	2,389
Economic employees as % of administration	3	3	3	3	2
Population of USSR (millions)	133.5*	147**	194	179	276
Officials per 1,000 inhabitants	5.2	6.9	9.5	10.2	8.7

*1923
**1926

SOURCES: *Trud v SSSR: Statisticheskii sbornik* (Moscow, 1988), pp. 30–31; *Narodnoe khoziaistvo SSSR: Statisticheskii spravochnik 1932 g.* (Moscow and Leningrad, 1932), p. 401; *Narodnoe khoziaistvo SSSR za 70 let: Iubileinyi statisticheskii ezhegodnik* (Moscow, 1987), p. 5.

such officials, and the strict regimentation of their activities transformed the bureaucracy into a powerful and obedient instrument of autocracy, designed to achieve the latter's goals. These officials stood outside society in the sense that every official was subordinate for the most part to another, higher official and was subject to bureaucratic regulations.[29] However, it is impossible not to see another tendency: In the course of the eighteenth century and the first half of the nineteenth, the authority of the bureaucracy was increasingly limited by the constraints of the law, by precise instructions, by bureaucratic discipline, by the competence or specialization of other institutions, and by competition from various departments for authority and influence. Formal procedures, whether for better or worse, limited the arbitrariness of government officials.

In the mid-nineteenth century, meanwhile, the bureaucracy came under the influence of public opinion, which was exercised through the press.[30] With the introduction of zemstvos and city dumas, local offices of state administration were subject to even greater oversight by local society and its institutions of self-government.[31] From 1906 on, the state bureaucracy was subordinated to the State Duma.

2. In the course of the eighteenth and nineteenth centuries, state institutions underwent a series of radical transformations. In the eighteenth century, the internal structure of the colleges and of state institutions such as the provincial administrations established in 1775 was essentially *collegial:* By law, their authority was exercised jointly by several individuals, who together constituted an administrative board. Each member of a college had an equal share in the collegial authority and each had one vote by which their opinions were taken into account. Decisions of the college were carried by a simple majority. In the nineteenth century, the ministries and other state institutions were *bureaucratic* institutions. The right of final decision belonged to one person—the minister, the director of a department, or the like; but according to law, this person's decision had to be based on a report prepared by the institution's chancellery, which was to include a draft resolution accompanied by any information pertinent to a correct and legal decision, including supporting materials and references to existing laws. Thus, decisions were adopted unilaterally, but on the basis of existing laws, documents, and rational considerations rather than the arbitrary judgment of a senior official.

The changes in the internal organization of the central state institutions following the creation of ministries between 1802 and 1810 also influenced the work of local institutions. Thus, during the first half of the nineteenth century, the authority of the governor gradually increased, giving a more independent role to the provincial administrations, which little by little were transformed into the governors' executive organs. These processes were legally consolidated in the 1837 Instruction to Governors, which declared the governor "master of the province" *(khoziain gubernii)*. In the second half of the nineteenth century, the state's provincial administration devolved into executive organs of the local governor. At the same time, the provincial administrations and all other state institutions began to conduct their affairs according to bureaucratic methods. The changeover from a collegial to a bureaucratic system reflected not so much an authoritarian impulse as a striving to reduce arbitrariness and subjectivity in administration and to base decisions on a firm juridical foundation. It is no coincidence that the initiative to introduce a bureaucratic order originated with the great reformer M. M. Speranskii.

3. Throughout the eighteenth, nineteenth, and early twentieth centuries, some 85 percent of the members of the higher bureaucratic ranks in St. Petersburg and the higher administration in the provinces were members of the hereditary nobility, and a considerable number of these were also owners of large landed estates. However, in quantitative terms, landowning nobles had only limited representation within the bureaucracy as a whole—greater in the years prior to the Emancipation, and less in the years following, but never exceeding 34 percent. At the same time, one can discern over these centuries a gradual *embourgeoisement* of a part of the bureaucracy, especially at its highest levels, that was reflected in its members' entrepreneurial activity. Prior to the Emancipation, such activity was relatively limited in scope, in large part because nobles were limited both by law and by custom. After the abolition of serfdom, however, nobles' involvement in enterprise increased. As early as the 1860s, a considerable number of officials were participating in the establishment of joint-stock companies and banks, often managing several at a time as directors or members of their boards and administrations. Such activities became increasingly widespread, and led to a number of major scandals.

In 1868, the government took action to limit such pursuits, and in 1884 a law was promulgated that prohibited the participation of officials of the top five ranks in the establishment or administration of joint-stock companies while they were in government service. Despite this new law, the link between government officials and private companies was not disrupted; it merely took on new forms. Companies now began to invite individuals with close links to influential officials, or retired officials who preserved their ties with the state apparatus, to hold administrative positions. Officials increasingly began to request transfer from state to private service. In a word, the law was evaded: Before its promulgation, 225 highly placed officials of the Ministry of Finance held 251 posts in private companies; of 1,006 engineers in state service in the Department of Railroads, 370 simultaneously served in private railroad companies.[32] At the beginning of the twentieth century, 115 officials of the four highest ranks owned industrial enterprises, and another 160 held 240 posts on the governing boards of private companies. In 1901 and 1902, the administrations of 1,788 joint-stock enterprises included officials in active government service as well as in retirement; and this situation did not change prior to 1917.[33] According to Sergei Witte, the stock of the Kursk–Kiev railroad became known as the stock of the State Council and the Senate because so many of their members were shareholders. Income from stocks constituted an important share of the private budgets of many high officials.[34] Inevitably, the *embourgeoisement* of the bureaucracy made it quite sympathetic to the development of market relations in the Russian economy and to society's needs for systemic changes both in the economy and in the state government.[35]

4. The educational level of government officials began to rise during the reign of Peter I, who was the first to open special clerical schools to prepare government officials. Another such measure was the introduction, in 1809, of minimal educational standards for officials. To receive a position at the eighth rank, an official had to have completed some form of higher education or to have passed a special exam. In 1834, although this requirement was abolished, one's position on entering government service, as well as the speed of one's advancement, continued to depend directly on one's level of education. In 1857, the requirement that advancement depend on educational level also was abolished; but education remained a criterion for an individual's rank on entrance into service. In addition, to enter service, an official was now required to have completed a district-level school that provided an incomplete secondary education. The results of these changes gradually bore fruit. In 1755, 1.1 percent of officials had a higher education, 19.3 percent had a secondary education, and 80.6 percent had an elementary or home education. By the mid-nineteenth century, the figures were 29.4, 36.9, and 33.7 percent, respectively; and in 1897, 39.5, 22.8, and 37.7 percent.[36]

5. Between 1700 and 1917, a professional bureaucracy gradually emerged. The requirement imposed by Peter I that all officials receive a professional education began to achieve results during the course of the eighteenth century. Professionalization received a further boost at the turn of the century, with the introduction of educational prerequisites for holding civil office in 1809; the declining influence of family connections in gaining admission to the civil service and for promotion up the service ladder; and the increasingly marked differentiation of civil officials from military officers such that transfers from military to civil service, so common in the eighteenth century, now became quite rare. In the eighteenth century, the typical official was a military officer; in the nineteenth and early twentieth centuries, the typical official was a legal-minded bureaucrat, schooled in the law and operating in accordance with it *(pravovoi chinovnik, chinovnik-iurist)*.

6. Improvements in the professional, educational, and material status of government officials were accompanied by their gradual consolidation into a privileged class with a strictly hierarchical structure. According to the 1721 Table of Ranks, the bureaucracy was divided into four groups: officials in positions below rank XIV (office workers or clerks), who did not and could not hold a rank or achieve noble status by promotion; officials in ranks IX–XIV, who received only personal nobility; officials in ranks VI–VIII, who received hereditary noble status; and those in ranks I–V, who constituted the highest officeholders, the *generalitet.* In the mid-eighteenth century, the relative distribution of officials among these four groups was 70:20:8:2, and in the second half of the nineteenth century, 26:60:11:2. As can be seen, the principal change over this period was the decline in the proportion of clerks and the increase in the number of officials in the lower ranks. This reflects an extremely important process taking place within the bureaucracy over this period; namely, the growth in the social status of the bureaucracy as a whole and its transformation into a noble estate. However, the internal structure of officialdom scarcely changed at all. Thus, the average rank was 9.6 in 1755, 10.1 in 1796, 10.5 in 1857, and 9.6 in 1897. In other words, the average rank dropped almost one full rank (0.9) between the mid-eighteenth and mid-nineteenth centuries and then returned to its original level by the end of the century. This suggests that during the life of the Table of Ranks, a person's chances of making a career in the civil service and achieving an appropriate degree of material security—a high degree, compared to the average income of the general population—remained fairly stable.

7. The form and amount of compensation were always important in determining a person's social status. Total compensation, which consisted of salary (38 percent), a food allowance (37 percent), and a housing allowance (25 percent), varied by rank. If clerks were compensated on a scale of 100, then officials in ranks IX–XIV were compensated at the rate of 300; V–VIII, at 700; and III–IV, at 4,300. Compensation for officials holding the highest two ranks was determined by imperial will. The compensation for clerks was close to the average wage of skilled urban workers; and the compensation of the lower ranks exceeded the latter by two or three times. The salary of officials in the middle ranks assured them the same standard of living as that of the wellborn and of members of educated society; and the income of officials of the highest ranks made them rich by Russian standards. In the era of serfdom, for example, the latter's compensation was equivalent to the income enjoyed by a middling or wealthy noble landowner who possessed several hundred serfs.[37]

Until 1763, sources of income for officials were unstable. At the beginning of the eighteenth century, a salary might be made up of several components:

money, land, products, and "respect"—that is, gifts (bribes) from petitioners. In 1714, compensation in the form of land was abolished and replaced by money and grain. A unified annual salary scale was established
for all officeholders. The salary of a capital-city official was half that of an
army officer of comparable rank, and that of a provincial official was one-
quarter. However, in 1726 and 1727, as a result of the state budget deficit,
the number of officials receiving compensation was reduced, as were
salaries. Clerks in general no longer received a salary, and like their seventeenth-century predecessors, had to survive on bribes from petitioners. In
1763, Catherine II established a monetary salary for all officials, and then
doubled it.[38] In subsequent years, salaries increased; but between the second half of the eighteenth century and the beginning of the nineteenth,
these increases were canceled out by inflation. After that interlude, salaries
began to outstrip prices or at least to keep pace with them.

  8. Until 1917, government officials constituted a special community—
one that was open to entering and departing members, but whose core was
made up of hereditary officials. In the mid-eighteenth century, hereditary
nobles constituted some 49 percent of all ranks, and a century later, 40 percent. An official's authority depended on his post and not on his social origin or wealth. The typical official served primarily to improve his social
status, not for the salary. At the same time, the bureaucracy also attracted
the most capable and ambitious youths of nonnoble origin. In the mid-
eighteenth century, half of all officials in the Table of Ranks were nonnoble by origin, and at the end of the nineteenth century the proportion had
risen to 69 percent. Officials came from all strata of the population: peasants, clergy, soldiers, merchants, artisans, and *raznochintsy*. Prior to 1816,
44 percent of the nobility had received their titles as a result of government
service. Between 1836 and 1844, 4,685 officials were made hereditary nobles as a consequence of having achieved the appropriate rank. Officials
from the *raznochinstvo*, whose sole income was the salary they earned by
service, were distinguished from noble officials by their greater competence
and loyalty to the autocracy, and they constituted the most faithful segment. Over time, the requirements for achieving hereditary nobility were
raised. From 1845, holders of ranks X to XIV were rewarded only with
honorary citizenship; of ranks VI to IX, with personal nobility; and of
ranks I to V, with hereditary nobility. After 1856, hereditary nobility was
awarded only to those in ranks I to IV.

  The ennoblement of government officials hindered the transformation of
the bureaucracy into a classless component of society, preserving it as a
privileged community with a specific subculture. However, ennoblement
also prevented the transformation of the bureaucracy into a caste, and
thus, improved its vitality. Minister of Education S. S. Uvarov, in an 1846

memorandum arguing against proposals to abolish the system of ranks, which had a decisive influence on Nicholas I, wrote:

> Russia venerates the Table of Ranks as a solemn reflection of that precious Slavic principle of equality before the law; it values the important concept that everyone in is turn can aspire to the higher virtues of service. The son of the greatest lor   ' .. ~ntering the field of state service, has no adv   from his zeal to dist

Russian Of,

One might

and increas

more effec

gradually a

Max Webe

and subor

a unified a

sponsibilit

specialized qua.........,

institutions
produced a
an officials
lescribed by
rsonally free
me a link in
realm of re-
:t; to possess
letary salary;

to regard service as his sole profession; to advance according to firm criteria based on his abilities and independent of the personal opinion of his supervisor; not to regard his service position as his personal property; to be subject to clear and strict standards of discipline; to execute his responsibilities according to clearly established procedures; and to observe "impersonal" or formal, rational modes of interpersonal relations in everything that concerned public service.[40]

The chancellery official of the seventeenth century was far from meeting this Weberian ideal: He was dependent, tied to the place of his service, and obliged to serve under pain of punishment; did not belong to a unified service hierarchy but to a special hierarchy of chancellery officials; had to execute in turn a mass of highly varied tasks involving all aspects of state administration, including military, court, and ambassadorial responsibilities, the supervision of the construction of fortresses and ships, the pursuit of fugitives, the description and surveying of land, and so on; was obligated or forced to work; had no special qualifications and acted in conformity with the needs of the administration and his superiors; received an irregular salary made up of payments in kind and monetary compensation, part of which came from statutory fees for services (or from bribes); did not see civil service as his sole profession; advanced on the basis of length of service, social origin, and the discretion of his superiors; was inclined to see his salaried post as a kind of benefice from which to derive profit; was not subject to a uniform system of discipline, since accountability depended on an official's status and position; executed responsibilities according to a prescribed procedure that was determined by custom rather than by law; and conducted interpersonal relations on a deeply personal basis. In addition, it should be noted that the average government official's position was a lowly one, when compared to the status hierarchy within the larger society; and as a result, not only could these officials not improve their general social status; they were also excluded from top positions within the bureaucracy. In the seventeenth-century consciousness, chancellery workers were not "wellborn," participation in state service was considered to damage one's "noble honor," and nobles entering the bureaucracy frequently lost their nobility. At the end of the seventeenth century, chancellery officials were an exclusive and self-reproducing social group that socialized and trained its own successors.[41]

In the course of the eighteenth century, the conditions of service and the bureaucracy itself changed significantly in a number of ways:[42] Under Peter I, the text of the oath sworn by officials required them to act only according to instructions, regulations, and ukases.[43] After the 1762 Manifesto granting the nobility freedom from service, the noble officials—that is, the 74 percent of officials who held noble rank—gained the personal freedom to work in any capacity they chose. Government service was transformed from an obligation into a privilege. However, until the nineteenth century, service retained features of servile dependence for unranked chancellery workers (some of whom were also nobles), who constituted 26 percent of all officials; in essence, they were privileged serfs serving in state institutions. Like serfs, they were tied to their place of service and could not of their own will transfer to another position or work in another institution. Their only privilege was their freedom from taxes and duties. From 1790, the clerks were gradually liberated: First, they received the right to transfer to military service; then, in 1808, to enroll in the merchant estate, artisanal guilds, or the state peasantry. Naturally, the chancellery worker, who was personally unfree, was not simply bound to service by his sense of duty. However, in the eighteenth century, even officials of rank could not act freely, without regard for superordinate authority.

In 1722, the Table of Ranks established a unified and stable service hierarchy that affected all persons holding government posts. However, until the 1760s, officials continued to be employed in various kinds of work; not until the end of the eighteenth century were they assigned clearly defined service responsibilities. After 1762, rank-holding officials and chancellery workers from the nobility were employed on the basis of freely negotiated contracts.

In the eighteenth century, as a rule, officials received no specialized training in educational institutions. Practical experience was the primary and virtually the sole source of their competence. The majority of officials transferred to civil service on retiring from the military.

Officials worked for a salary, which, for most, was their main or even sole source of income. However, there was a centuries-old tradition of exacting additional payments, or "bribes" (*vziatki*), from petitioners for service. From the seventeenth to the nineteenth centuries, aside from some kind of illegal exaction, the Russian word for "bribe" also referred to an official fee legally collected from a petitioner. This practice originated prior to the introduction of salaries in 1763, at a time when officials were legally permitted to collect such payments in lieu of a salary. In nineteenth-century colloquial language, this term referred to a payment or gift to an official to avoid difficulties and to ensure a speedy execution of business.[44]

Officials looked on service as their sole profession. In 1739, legislation set forth their working hours—daily, except Saturdays, Sundays, and holidays, from 7 A.M. to 2 P.M., and, when necessary, from 4 to 7 P.M.; and special officials were appointed to record attendance and tardiness.[45] In Petersburg, the emperors—especially Paul I and Nicholas I—liked to visit government offices at the beginning of the workday.

Advancement up the service ladder depended on an official's length of time in office, personal merit, ability, social origin, and education, and on the discretion of his superiors as well as on patronage—or more accurately, on the power of the patronage clan or circle to which the official belonged.[46]

Officials were subjected to strict discipline. For example, in 1723, Senator P. P. Sharifov, the vice president of the College of Foreign Affairs, was sentenced to death for violating Senate regulations by having failed to leave the chamber during the Senate's discussion of a matter that directly concerned him.[47] Officials executed their service responsibilities according to a strictly determined set of procedures spelled out in special instructions. In 1765, a ukase titled "On the Essential Responsibilities of Officials" was published that served to regulate conduct in the workplace. Interpersonal relations henceforth were to be conducted on a formal, rational basis rather than a personal one.

Thus, the typical rank-holding Russian noble-official at the end of the eighteenth century differed from the ideal type in five ways: He (a) had no special education; (b) had broad responsibilities; (c) did not conduct interpersonal relations on a completely formal basis; (d) could not always act without regard for the prejudices of his superiors; and (e) took bribes. As David Ransel has shown, patronage connections in the eighteenth century played a major role in service relations and hindered the development of strictly official relations among noble-officials.[48] In the course of the first half of the nineteenth century, Russian officials, including chancellery workers, gradually remedied the first two limitations and became narrow specialists. The role of personal ties was also gradually mitigated, except in the highest echelons, where such relations persisted until the monarchy's collapse.[49] It is hard to say when the bureaucracy began to govern its activity exclusively according to officially established procedures. However, on the basis of Article 838, Paragraph 3, of the statute on civil service (adopted in 1850), an official could be dismissed from service without any explanation, if in the opinion of his superiors he had failed to execute his responsibilities, was unreliable, or had made mistakes that had become known to his superiors but that were impossible to prove. This practice apparently had some influence on officials, since dismissal "under Paragraph 3" was equivalent to being blacklisted.[50] However, such dismissals were quite rare, in practice being restricted to persons found guilty of abuse of office.[51] Thus, during the eight-month period between 1 November 1894 and 1 July 1895, only 56 people were dismissed on the basis of Paragraph 3—a mere 0.04 percent of the entire body of officials.[52]

Jurists at the end of the nineteenth century wrote about the "powerlessness" of the authorities in relation to undisciplined officials. They considered the real task of judicial administration to be the "proper organization of disciplined responsibility" according to the model of German legislation.[53] Although patronage connections among officials had weakened in comparison to the eighteenth century, they were never completely eliminated, and they continued to hinder the development of rational-formal principles. Insofar as gifts were concerned (in the sense of illegal extortion or bribery by officeholders), the bureaucracy was never able to eliminate them either, although their scope probably diminished over time—especially in the second half of the nineteenth century, when the public and the press began to place limits on the activities of the state administration.[54]

Two additional circumstances favored the transformation of Russian officials into exemplars. First, prior to the reforms of the 1860s, government service was the primary if not the only field for talented and educated people to pursue a career, to serve society, and to earn a living. Even in 1897, by which time a considerable number of educated people had found work in nonstate institutions, slightly more than half (51 percent) of all men with a higher education served as government officials.[55] Thus, in the mid-nineteenth century, it is possible to say that according to contemporary conceptions, the country's best sons were concentrated in the bureaucracy; the bureaucracy also included an appreciable number of people drawn from the clerical estate.[56] Another segment of Russian society's best representatives found their calling in oppositional activity—in journalism and literature—but this group was considerably smaller in number. Second, a large number of individuals of non-Russian nationality, especially Baltic Germans, served in the Russian bureaucracy. They were particularly distinguished by their higher levels of education and professionalism and their greater diligence and devotion to the legal order. In the eighteenth century and the first half of the nineteenth, 37 percent of officials in the upper ranks were of non-Russian nationality, 30 percent of them Germans.[57]

Complaints against officials are a useful source for characterizing the nature of bureaucratic activity. Interestingly, the number of complaints increased after the Great Reforms. This was not due to any increase in bureaucratic arbitrariness but rather to society's increasing resistance to official pretensions, and to its defense of newly acquired personal rights. The composition of these complaints is also interesting. Most common were complaints about inappropriate interference by officials in matters outside their jurisdiction. Such complaints, however, came from officials themselves as well as from the general populace. The Judicial Statute described such activities as abuses of authority. Complaints against formalism and red tape came second, and in third place were complaints against rude treatment and extortion. When one official complained about another, what was usually involved was either some form of patronage or attempts to exploit their positions. Complaints about violations or evasions of the law were extremely rare.[58]

The historical literature is replete with criticisms of the Russian bureaucracy's corruption and incompetence, its violations and nonobservance of the law. Although historians have collected some evidence in support of such complaints, the question remains open. There has been no comprehensive study of this topic, and the main source of this opinion until now has been the Russian literary classics penned by writers such as Nikolai V. Gogol, Mikhail E. Saltykov-Shchedrin, Aleksandr I. Herzen, A. V. Sukhovo-Kobylin, and others, as well as by public activists. It seems to me, however, that these writers and their contemporaries intentionally exaggerated the failings of the Russian bureaucracy, after all, their goal was to discredit it and indirectly to discredit the autocracy itself. Such criticism was a form of social opposition to autocracy, which began under Nicholas I. Historians, meanwhile, joined forces with belletrists, since they, too, often shared views critical of both the bureaucracy and the autocracy.

Recently, historians have tended to renounce such stereotypes and to view the Russian bureaucracy in a less biased fashion. They have identified a new generation of enlightened Russian officials in the first half of the nineteenth century who prepared the Great Reforms of the 1860–1870s. They also have learned that these bureaucrats did not simply die out in the reign of Alexander II but were succeeded by younger generations that held office until 1917. Certainly, not all Russian officials were distinguished by their enlightened attitudes and statist mentality; but a number of such officials always occupied high positions in the state apparatus. Dominic Lieven's collective biography of 215 members of the State Council between 1894 and 1914 has given us a portrait of Russia's ruling elite—as well-educated, predominantly jurists, with a broad range of interests, holding generally moderate rather than reactionary views, and understanding the necessity of reform. Further, if we remember that the majority of these men had entered the State Council after many years' service in the Ministries of Justice, Internal Affairs, and Finance, then we must conclude that the leading ministries were not filled exclusively by stupid and uneducated reactionaries.[59] Richard Robbins Jr.'s collective portrait of Russia's provincial governors at the end of the empire also breaks with the usual image of the ignorant and corrupt tsarist satrap ready to commit any crime on the tsar's orders—although such governors certainly existed.[60]

Thus, there are at present two points of view on the development of the Russian bureaucracy in the eighteenth and nineteenth centuries. Some historians consider that the number of bureaucrats increased but that their ethos remained the same. Others argue that in the first half of the nineteenth century, especially in the second quarter, a considerable part of this bureaucracy developed a new ethos. As a result, in the nineteenth century and the beginning of the twentieth, two tendencies existed within the Russian bureaucracy—a reformist and a conservative tendency—which competed with varying degrees of success to determine the direction of government policy.[61]

The evolution of the Russian bureaucracy from a group of servile service officials who fulfilled the orders of their superiors to a body of professional, educated, and freely hired officials whose authority was limited and defined by law and by departmental instructions, and who acted in the state interest, had major significance for the development of the Russian state principle. The formation of a bureaucracy of this second type is, in the opinion of Max Weber, a necessary condition for the rule of law in society and for the transformation into a rule-of-law state, regardless of whether that state is monarchic, aristocratic, or parliamentary: "Bureaucratic administration means the rule of knowledge, and in this consists its specifically rational character."[62] Judging by the evolution of the Russian bureaucracy, the advancement of Russian society toward a legal state seems indisputable. This development was so successful that the Russian official approximated the ideal type of bureaucrat, and the Russian administration approximated the ideal type of formal-rational organization. However, while subsuming concrete examples under the ideal type, one should also bear in mind that reality always differs from the ideal.

The Growth of the Army

Now, a few words about the second most important institution of autocratic rule—the army: Until the eighteenth century, the army consisted primarily of semiregular forces. Its main force was a noble militia. Peter I abandoned the militia and created a regular and professional army. Before 1793, soldiers' service term was lifelong; between 1793 and 1833, 25 years; and from 1834 to 1854, 20 years in active service, followed by 5 years in the reserves. In 1855, active service was reduced to 12 years; in the early 1870s, to 7 years; in 1874, to 6 years; in 1876, to 5 years; and in 1905, to 3 years. In the navy, the term of active service was generally one year longer. Between 1874 and 1913, the term of reserve service was reduced from 9 years to 7 years. Officers' service before 1736 was lifelong; between 1736 and 1762, 25 years; and after 1762, at their discretion. In principle, an officer could leave the service at any time; however, most preferred to remain and collect a higher pension at their retirement as well as to take advantage of the various other benefits and privileges that accrued to officers. In addition, individuals who had received their education in the state military schools and academies were obliged to serve a specific term. In 1862, the proportion of military school graduates in the officer corps was 32.6 percent; in 1896, 51.0 percent; and in the early twentieth century, 60.0 percent.[63]

The rank-and-file soldiers were peasants or artisans (*meshchane*); officers came from the nobility. The old noble militia had made the tsar and his government closely dependent not only on the nobility but also on the numerous service classes and even the peasantry, since nobles served with their own peasants. A regular army gave the state greater independence, particularly from the various social groups that made up the population, insofar as the army was more isolated from the larger society and became a more reliable instrument of government policy. In 1874, the duty of the taxable classes to select and provide recruits was replaced by universal military service, tying the army more closely to society. The army also grew in size, as shown in Table 4.3.

TABLE 4.3   Growth of the Regular Army in Imperial Russia, 1680–1913

	1680	1725	1764	1801	1850	1897	1913
Army (1,000s)	164.0	210.0	226.0	379.0	1,118.0	1,133.0	1,320.0
Total Russian population (millions)	10.2	16.0	23.7	38.8	57.1	125.7	159.0
Army as a proportion of population (%)	1.6	1.1	0.95	0.98	1.96	0.89	0.83

SOURCES: B. A. Rybakov, ed., *Istoriia SSSR* (Moscow, 1967), Pervaia seriia 1, tom 3, pp. 116, 244; N. N. Obruchev, ed., *Voenno-statisticheskii sbornik, vyp. 4, Rossiia* (St. Petersburg, 1871), otdel 2, pp. 40–46; *Obshchii svod po imperii rezul'tatov razrabotki dannykh pervoi vseobshchei perepisi naseleniia, proizvedennoi 28 ianvaria 1897 goda*, 2 toma (St. Petersburg, 1905), tom 2, p. 256; *Rossiia v mirovoi voine 1914–1918 goda (v tsifrakh)* (Moscow, 1925), p. 97.

As the table clearly shows, the absolute and relative size of the regular army changed in parallel to changes among civilian officials: The army grew steadily in absolute numbers; but relative to the growth rate of the population, it grew only until the mid-nineteenth century and thereafter declined. Thus, we can conclude that the state machine increased in strength until the reign of Alexander II and then began to weaken.

The Development of Society from the Seventeenth to the Early Twentieth Centuries

I have chosen to use an exclusively pragmatic definition of the concept "society." Broadly defined, society consists of the totality of the various classes of the population, as well as of the social, estate, and quasi-estate organizations and institutions involved in the tasks of self-government or participating in state administration (known as "civil society" in the nineteenth century[64]). In the narrowest sense, "society" is the sum of only those social strata of the population that the state is directly concerned with and whose opinion it takes into account in setting policy. I refer to these strata as the *creators of public opinion.* Initially, society was fragmented, composed of innumerable communal organizations for peasants, merchants, traders, artisans, nobles, and so on. They were not united with the state or administration but were autonomous and to a considerable degree self-governing. Gradually and very slowly, the individual social groups began to amalgamate into legal estates or quasi-estates. The nobility was consolidated into an estate between 1775 and 1785; in the course of the eighteenth and first half of the nineteenth centuries, the clergy, urban dwellers, and the peasantry also acquired the features of legal estates. In the second half of the nineteenth century, the members of these communally organized legal estates were united into all-estate institutions known as city dumas and district and provincial zemstvos. In the early twentieth century, new forms of organization emerged at the all-Russian level, including political parties that represented the interests of specific classes, trade unions, unions of towns and nobles, and other kinds of political interest groups. This process of social consolidation was crowned by the creation of the State Duma in 1906.

The concept of the "public" or the "public sphere" *(obshchestvennost')* will be used to describe the part of educated society that was not employed in the bureaucracy. Such a definition is inadequate in that it often happened that society willingly drew educated and liberal-thinking officials into its midst. However, state service to some degree always created a barrier between society and the state, especially before the mid-nineteenth century. Public representatives participated in the life of society—including social, estate, and other activities—in the roles of writers, journalists, and others engaged in intellectual endeavors, including the "reading public." In this chapter I use *educated society* as synonymous with *the public.* By *intelligentsia* I mean only the part of educated society, from whatever class, that opposed the regime. *The people (narod),* meanwhile, describes the totality of unprivileged ranks among the population, including peasants, traders, artisans, and workers. And *class* refers exclusively to a large social group whose members have common rights and responsibilities and are linked by mutual obligations—for example, petty traders, peasants, artisans, and so on.

Society influenced the state in a variety of ways, but public opinion was one of its main means of influence. *Public opinion* here describes the attitudes of different social groups toward issues of common concern. In terms of its specific contents, *public opinion* includes only judgments shared by the majority. This idea of "public opinion" arose in England at the end of the eighteenth century and subsequently gained wide acceptance in the West. In Russia the concept began to be used widely in the 1850s,[65] though it occasionally was utilized earlier—for example, in secret police reports of the 1830s and 1840s.[66]

The Composition of "the Public"

Whom did the state consider members of society, or "the public," in the sense of creators of public opinion, between the seventeenth and twentieth centuries? In Muscovite Rus, society included individuals who had been elected to and had the right to participate in the assemblies of the land *(zemskie sobory)*; in the eighteenth century and the first half of the nineteenth, they consisted of nobles, officials, and the higher strata of the merchantry; and in the period from 1860 to the 1910s, the entire population was formally included—although in practice this meant only those property-holding citizens who qualified as "electors" and had the right to participate in elections to the zemstvos and city dumas, and beginning in 1906, to the national parliament. By law, women, young unmarried males, and children were not viewed as creators of public opinion. By social status, society in seventeenth-century Muscovy included members of the clergy, boyars, members of the hereditary service nobility, regular members of the professional army (servitors by contract), the bureaucracy (chancellery officials), urban-dwelling merchants, artisans, and sometimes the state peasantry. In the eighteenth century and the first half of the nineteenth, society included members of the army, nobility, officialdom, intelligentsia, and the highest strata of the merchant guild. Between 1861 and

1917, the entire population was formally included, although in practice this meant only those property-owning citizens who qualified to participate in elections to public office. It also did not mean women, children, or young, unmarried males.

How large was this "public"? At the end of the seventeenth century, the creators of public opinion constituted about 8 percent of the population; in the eighteenth and early nineteenth centuries, 3 percent; and by 1910, about 15–16 percent (including their families). These calculations were reached in the following manner. In 1678, the nobility and army, including family members, numbered about 300,000; the clergy, about 40,000; and officials, merchants, and urban dwellers, about 426,000—a total of 766,000 without the peasantry, compared to a population of 9.6 million.[67] Thus about 8 percent of the population (counting families) by social group were represented in the assemblies of the land.

In 1719, the regular army consisted of 176,000 persons, and the nobility, officialdom, and higher merchantry (including families, the average size of which was 7.6 persons of both sexes), of approximately 350,000, out of a population of 15.6 million.[68] In 1858, these two groups numbered 620,000 and 910,000, respectively, in a population of 59.3 million and with an average family size of 8.4.[69] These figures constituted 3.4 percent and 2.4 percent of the population, respectively (including family members). If, in addition, we consider that during the eighteenth century and the first half of the nineteenth the overwhelming majority of soldiers and officers in the professional army were unmarried, that would give us a figure of 222,000 males in 1719 and 728,000 in 1858, constituting approximately 1.4 and 1.2 percent of the population, respectively.

In 1870, 5.6 percent of the city population had the right to vote in elections to the city duma,[70] and about 1.0 percent in elections to district and provincial zemstvos.[71] The new electoral laws on elections to the zemstvos and city dumas, adopted in 1890 and 1892, respectively, reduced the number of electors to between 1 and 2 percent, mainly at the expense of those engaged in trade and industry.[72] In 1910 the electoral law governing elections to the State Duma enfranchised 2.4 percent of the population.[73] Thus, society was quite small, and the number of people who could be counted among the creators of public opinion was insignificant compared to the population at large, even if we include family members.

The State and Educated Society

Every class had its own positions on issues, both natural and local. Likewise, opinion was shaped differently from class to class, and influence upon official policy varied. Let us examine these differences, beginning with the educated segment of Russian society.

Russian society in the eighteenth century and the first half of the nineteenth had two essential characteristics: fragmentation, and dependence on the state. Fragmentation was reflected in the contradictions, conflicts, and lack of mutual understanding among various segments of the population and in the absence of any attempts by any group except the nobility to consolidate their forces in order to win greater rights and privileges from the state. Society's dependence on the state, meanwhile, was reflected in the state's decisive role in the development of social stratification and social mobility such that society viewed the state as the supreme arbiter and the real, legal, and sole source of their rights and responsibilities.[74]

These characteristics were interrelated. On the one hand, social fragmentation engendered dependence on the state; on the other hand, it was the powerful state that hindered the consolidation of social groups. This fragmentation had deep historical roots and was a product of the incomplete formation of estates in Russia. In the sixteenth and seventeenth centuries, there were many different ranks in Russian society; by the eighteenth century, these had multiplied, and numbered several dozen; and by the mid-nineteenth century, there were nearly seventy.[75] Social fragmentation also guaranteed greater independence for the autocracy, especially when it conducted a balanced social policy, as it did in the years before 1725. After the death of Peter I, however, the autocracy was not always equal to the task of maintaining independence from and dominance over all social classes. In the remainder of the eighteenth century, the state fell increasingly under the influence of the nobility, largely because the Russian throne was occupied by individuals who did not have an unquestionable right to it (Catherine I and II), or in the case of the other monarchs (except Paul I), who reigned at the courtesy of the noble guards' regiments. Some who became emperor had neither sufficient political skills nor the will to maintain a balanced social policy, and hence favored the nobility. In the nineteenth century, the emperors restored a more balanced social policy. Pro-noble social policies were accompanied by still greater social fragmentation, since the other classes of the population feared the nobility and did not wish to cooperate with them. One illustration of this is the merchants' and traders' opposition to government attempts between 1828 and 1846 to introduce representatives of the nobility into the city dumas and in the 1840s to form all-class courts. The burghers were reluctant to work with the nobility, which inevitably dominated any all-estate institution.[76]

In spite of the autocracy's noble orientation, it nevertheless maintained its sense of moderation, and over the rest of the eighteenth century, it sacrificed only a part of the peasantry to the nobility, continuing a more or less balanced policy toward the other classes. As a result, no one class in Russian society was able to oppose either the state or the emperor. We can see this by looking at the work of the Legislative Commission of 1767–1768 and at the instructions to its deputies. The deputies and the voters alike viewed society as a system based on the hereditary division of rights, responsibilities, and social functions, and ruled by harmony and stability. Their ideal was a state based on legally defined social groups that was headed by a monarch who consulted with his subjects on the important social questions. Compared with the seventeenth century, the social ideal of the second half of the eighteenth century had changed in only one respect—individual classes now wanted to become legal social estates with firm rights grounded in law, which they referred to as privileges. But only the nobility was more or less able to realize this dream at the time; and it alone succeeded in obtaining individual rights, becoming essentially self-determining in cultural terms, and adopting Western culture as a mark of superior social status and of class identity. Other classes did not succeed in consolidating their legal status until 1832, with the publication of the "Collection of Laws of the Russian Empire," even as the very idea of legal social estates was on the wane elsewhere in Europe.

At the same time, Catherine II initiated a number of other important changes that affected society. Before her reign, the state had castigated society for its devotion to the past and its lack of desire to Europeanize; the state itself had initiated all reforms in both the societal and the governmental spheres. In the last third of the eighteenth century, however, following the nobility's adoption of Western social ways and culture, an intelligentsia developed that thought independently. Some members of this social group criticized the autocracy for having deviated from Russian national traditions; others, for its inconsistent support of Europeanization.[77] As a result, the state was transformed from a critic of the existing social order into its defender, and it took the side of the majority of the nobility, who wanted to preserve the existing social and state order. From this point on, the initiative, at least for generating new ideas about the reform of Russian society, was transferred to the intelligentsia, which in spite of its insignificant size, now became a force pushing the autocracy to introduce social and political reform. In this respect, we should also remember that the Russian intelligentsia acquired its influence in large part because it shared the very same Western social thought to which the autocracy was constantly acclimatizing.[78] Yet until the mid-nineteenth century, the overwhelming majority of both society and the people as a whole supported the monarchy. Yearly "surveys of social opinion" conducted by the secret police (Third Department), beginning in 1827, confirmed the loyalty of the different social classes to the autocracy, with the exception of the youth of the noble intelligentsia. For example, in 1827, the chief of gendarmes told the emperor:

> The Youth—that is, young nobles from 17 to 25 years of age—is in general a very gangrenous part of the empire. Jacobinism, in the sense of a revolution-

ary and reformist spirit, is growing among these madcaps and takes a variety of forms, most commonly adopting a mask of patriotism. . . . All of this misfortune originates in a poor upbringing. Our exalted youth dreams about the possibility of a Russian constitution, the abolition of social orders, and freedom. In this corrupt stratum of society, we are again encountering the ideas of Ryleev [a Decembrist—*B.N.M.*]. Only their fear of discovery prevents them from forming secret societies.[79]

Thus, under the influence of Western liberal ideas,[80] critics of the existing social order appeared among the nobles.[81] Those on the right supported the conservative-nationalist principle as the main direction of social thought and development; critics on the left, the liberal principle; and radicals, various radical principles.[82] Conservatives favored a peaceful rapprochement between society and the monarchy and the elimination of negative features of the existing order. (In this discussion, I refer to those whose loyalty to the autocracy was absolute as *extreme rightists,* as opposed to *conservatives,* whose loyalty was conditional.)[83] Liberals, meanwhile, strove for a peaceful evolution of the autocracy in the direction of a constitutional monarchy;[84] and radicals supported the overthrow of the autocratic order.[85] Each party had its ideologues, who formulated these desires into political doctrines, and all tendencies were active until 1917. The conservatives were less popular in educated society and in the social arena, and their representatives were not so much organizations as individual personalities, such as M. M. Shcherbatov; N. M. Karamzin; the Slavophiles I. V. Kireevskii, A. S. Khomiakov, and others; F. M. Dostoevskii, N. A. Danilevskii, K. P. Leontev, N. A. Berdiaev, S. L. Frank, and I. A. Ilin. The liberals and radicals, in contrast, had broader social support. Breaking with the eighteenth-century model of identifying with individual activists such as S. E. Desnitskii, A. P. Kunitsyn, N. I. Novikov, D. I. Fonvizin, and A. N. Radishchev, they were represented predominantly by societies and organizations such as the Decembrists, Westernizers, populists, constitutionalists, and socialists of various shades. Thus, in addition to the noble majority's loyalty to the existing regime, alternative opinions arose at the end of the eighteenth century among other social strata—particularly the intelligentsia, which although it was almost exclusively noble in origin, later came to be filled with people from other social groups. Society had a number of institutions that formed public opinion. In the first half of the nineteenth century, literary salons, discussion circles, secret societies, and the "thick journals" were the most important;[86] in the second half of the century, it was newspapers and journals, city dumas, and zemstvos; and at the beginning of the twentieth century, political parties and the State Duma.

The conservatives were the first to make their opposition known, when early in the nineteenth century they protested against Alexander I's plans for

a liberal reform of the state order. In 1811, their ideologue, the historian
N. M. Karamzin, sent his "Memorandum on Ancient and Modern Russia"
to the emperor. Karamzin subjected the liberal approach to sharp criticism
and predicted a crisis of state if the emperor did not reconsider and return to
the traditional ways of his autocratic forebears: "The autocracy founded and
resurrected Russia; any change in the state order will bring ruin and must destroy it. . . . Any novelty in the state order is evil and must be resorted to only
in extreme necessity." State wisdom must be more "conservative than creative." A true autocracy is limited by Christian belief and conscience, not by
law. "All authority is united in the Russian monarchy: Our form of rule is
paternal, patriarchal."[87] These ideas were later developed by Slavophiles and
conservatives in the second half of the nineteenth century. In their conceptions, the ideal Russian state could only be a "true monarchy"; however,
some placed special emphasis on Russian Orthodoxy, others on autocracy,
and a third group on nationalism. Despite these differences in nuance, they
were united by a common thought: The monarch was God's servant; he expressed popular Orthodox belief, spirit, and ideals, and was subordinate to
them. The people relinquished their authority to God, who delegated
supreme power to the monarch; as a result, in a "true monarchy," arbitrariness on the sovereign's part was, in principle, impossible.[88] It is appropriate
to note, too, that Russian conservative thought, from N. M. Karamzin to
L. A. Tikhomirov, was not at all cut off from Russian life; it reflected the
population's views on authority. Conservative nationalism, according to Edward Thaden, developed out of the attempt of the Russian conservative intelligentsia to create a set of national ideals that would unify the state, educated society, and the people and would ward off the threats of radicalism,
nihilism, and socialism.[89]

The radicals soon followed the conservatives into the social arena. In
December 1825, a secret society consisting mainly of guards' officers
launched a revolt with the goal of introducing a constitutional order into
Russia, but they suffered defeat. In analyzing the Decembrist movement,
attention has focused predominantly on its opposition to the two bases of
the Russian legal order, serfdom and autocracy, and on how the uprising
was provoked by the various obstacles in the path of European-educated
people who wanted to participate in state administration and public life.[90]
According to Marxist historians, the uprising had a bourgeois character.
Others (including Herzen and V. I. Semevskii) viewed the more radical Decembrists as precursors to Russia's socialists.[91] However, the conspiracy
had another side that has received less attention. In the course of the eighteenth century, the noble guards' regiments repeatedly took on the role of
praetorian guard (most recently in 1801), interfering in the imperial succession on behalf of one or another pretender to the throne, in the name of
either the dynasty or of some other goal. This time, however, although the
revolt looked like another palace revolution, it was in essence a coup

d'état. By 1825, the nobility had been transformed into a privileged estate and, in the pretext of intervening once again in the succession, had set forth its demands for a constitution and political rights, including legal rights to participate in state administration as a ruling class.

If we examine two of the Decembrists' political programs, the moderate program of N. M. Muravev and the radical program of P. I. Pestel, then it is not difficult to conclude that the realization of either program would have transferred all power to the nobility—in the first case in aristocratic form, and in the second, to all former nobles, insofar as Pestel's project contemplated the abolition of all estates. The most popular project among the Decembrists was N. M. Muravev's, which was drafted in 1825, not long before the uprising. It proposed that all males owning immovable property valued in excess of 500 silver rubles or movable property in excess of 1,000 rubles in value be granted the right to vote. Following a twenty-year transition period, voters would, in addition, have to be literate. In 1827, between 7 and 11 percent of the population was literate; and in 1857, between 15 and 17 percent.[92] However, for those who wished to be elected to legislative or executive institutions, the property requirement was from four to sixty times greater.[93] In 1825, only nobles and a few merchants could meet the property requirements for active political participation, and passive voting rights would have been accessible only to a somewhat greater number of nobles and a handful of merchants. Given the distribution of property and education, supreme power would have been transferred into the hands of the noblility, had this project been implemented.

Pestel's project appeared the more democratic of the two, since it did not propose any property requirements for voting rights. However, in an open election, the overwhelming number of seats in the representative institutions would inevitably go to former nobles, since no other social group in Russian society could offer serious competition. It is sufficient to say that 75 percent of nobles were literate, whereas among townspeople, only 20 percent were literate, and among the peasantry, only 8 percent. As a result, even with the introduction of a democratic electoral law, authority would have been transferred into the hands of those who on the whole, both in 1825 and even thirty-five years later, during preparations for serfdom's abolition, supported serfdom and looked unfavorably on emancipation.[94]

One can agree completely with the opinion of Count N. S. Mordvinov, an enlightened contemporary whom the Decembrists intended to appoint as a minister in their interim revolutionary government, who believed that the introduction of a constitution in a country such as Russia would lead first to oligarchy and then to anarchy.[95] The nobiliary character of the Decembrist movement, or at least of its moderate wing, and its striving to give power to the nobility, are confirmed by the group's attitude toward soldiers, the people, and the representatives of other estates. Only nobles were allowed into the secret societies. The Decembrists did not trust the soldiers whom they summoned to revolt, who were peasants or traders by social origin. The soldiers knew nothing of the uprising's goals and were simply manipulated by their Decembrist officers, who exploited their authority and the soldiers' simplicity. To the soldiers it was suggested that Grand Prince Nicholas wanted to seize the throne ahead of the legal heir, Konstantin, and did not intend to honor the late emperor's decision to reduce the period of military service. Therefore, it was necessary to demand the fulfillment of his last will and testament and place Konstantin on the throne. The Decembrists likewise failed to seek support from the crowds of commoners who surrounded Senate Square during the revolt.[96]

Under the influence of the Decembrist revolt, Nicholas I became disillusioned with the nobility as a reliable basis of support for the autocracy. In the course of his reign, he sought to act as independently of noble society as possible, depending increasingly on the bureaucracy. Having never before intervened in the relationship between noble landowners and peasants, the government now attempted to place those relations within the framework of law.[97] Ironically, the liberal circles closest to the secret societies in the 1820s had not supported the Decembrists either at the time of the uprising or after. They considered the uprising frivolous adventurism and hence politically insupportable, and they saw the Decembrists as political dilettantes.[98] After the Decembrists' defeat, liberal-enlightened thought both in society and in public opinion favored the country's evolutionary development, and rejected radicalism, including that of the Decembrists, as a means of resolving social problems. People sympathized with the Decembrists as individuals but did not generally agree with their politics. Society and the autocracy were conscious of the need for reform but considered Russia ill prepared for it.

Thanks to the country's prosperity, public opinion was ready to work with the autocracy, which many, including A. S. Pushkin, considered "the sole representative of Europe in Russia."[99] However, in 1848, the government of Nicholas I, fearing the spread of revolution from western Europe, began unrelentingly to persecute the radical representatives of social thought—A. I. Herzen, N. P. Ogarev, P. Ia. Chaadaev, A. I. Polezhaev, the brothers V. I. and M. I. Kritskii, M. V. Butashevich-Petrashevskii and his followers, T. G. Shevchenko and others. Having become suspicious of all radicals and any kind of secret society, Nicholas began to act as the reactionary gendarme in Europe and at home. The equilibrium between the autocracy and the liberal public, which comprised the majority of educated society, was destroyed. Many representatives of the contemporary intellectual elite, including the brothers I. V. and P. V. Kireevskii and K. S. and I. S. Aksakov, A. S. Khomiakov, V. G. Belinskii, T. N. Granovskii, and S. M. Solovev, fell under suspicion and were limited in their creative activity and personal life. And certainly these people led the intellectual movement of their time. The emperor's hostility and suspicion toward society were repaid in spades. Representatives of the three main tendencies, known as "Westernizers," "Slavophiles," and "Revolutionary Democrats," began more and more openly to oppose the government. A chasm began to open between government and society.

Thus, the differences between educated society and the autocracy at the end of the eighteenth century became transformed into alienation in the 1840s and 1850s and led to the birth of the Russian intelligentsia as a societal group of intellectuals opposed to the existing regime. In this conflict with the autocracy, the educated public generally supported the intelligentsia. As a result, the division between society and government became stronger over time. In the mid-nineteenth century, relations between the educated public and the autocracy became warmer at times (for example, during the Great Reforms of the 1860s, or at the beginning of the twentieth century with the adoption of a constitution and the formation of the State Duma) and then cooled off, approaching open hostility (for example, at the end of the 1870s and beginning of the 1880s, or between 1905 and 1907). Little by little, the division between society and autocracy became a schism, which in February 1917 opened into a permanent breach.[100] However, because educated society was weak and fragmented, it could not eliminate the autocracy and establish a representative form of government alone.[101] When political activity was legalized at the beginning of the twentieth century, there were approximately 100 political parties.[102] This weakened educated society's ability to influence the autocracy and laid the groundwork for a long period of divided rule. In such conditions, the radical intelligentsia appeared on the political stage in alliance with the lower classes, advocating all-out war with the autocracy. The struggle with society, particularly its radical segment, exhausted the autocracy and led to its paralysis. Marxist radicals capitalized on these developments, seizing power with the support of workers, soldiers, and peasants.

In the mid-nineteenth century, the populist and prosocialist intelligentsia began to idealize the people, embracing its negativism toward the state and the autocracy and adopting an extreme form of radicalism. What was the source of this idealization of the populace? The answer to this question, in my view, lies to a considerable degree in the psychological sphere, in the existence of a unique subculture among these "lovers of the people." That many members of the intelligentsia had sprung from the clergy helps explain this phenomenon. Educated in an environment where the Orthodox-Autocratic mentality ruled, these people could not change the essentially religious consciousness that they had assimilated during their socialization in childhood and youth. Under the influence of secular education and new ideas from the West, all they could do was to shift the objects of their desires and hatreds or change the nature of their relation to them, remaining, however, within the world of religious consciousness. The people were deified and the autocracy demonized—and these now became the new absolutes in their still religious consciousness. The need to justify their antigovernmental activity also played a critical role. Struggle for the aggrieved and innocent people became the ultimate value in the eyes of the revolutionaries. At the same time, hidden behind the activities of these "lovers of the people" was a sublimated desire to defend the national idea—a traditional Russian aspiration in the face of the autocracy's policies of modernization and Europeanization.[103]

The second source of this love of the people, it seems to me, was that the people were the sole potential social force on which the populists and socialists could realistically depend in order to seize power and realize their ideals. "In the rebirth of the country in the aftermath of the Great Reforms, political life, it seemed, was held back for ever. Every attempt at independent strivings or solutions was stopped by barbaric methods," V. G. Korolenko, a writer who participated in the populist movement, wrote in his memoirs. "Meanwhile, the intelligentsia had already been awakened and keenly felt the country's lawlessness. But it could only try by one means or another to rouse the politically somnolent people."[104]

The State and the People

By the eighteenth century, the people had forgotten their earlier tradition of active participation in state life through the assemblies of the land and had become passive supporters of, rather than active participants in, monarchical authority.[105] This tendency strengthened in the nineteenth century: In the first half of the century, the peasantry placed all its hopes for emancipation in the tsar; and in the second half, it also linked its dream of expropriating the nobles' lands for its own benefit to the tsar.[106] Even sincere monarchists recognized the people's lack of political consciousness, which limited the monarchical idea to instinct or subconscious feeling. They also saw that the people had no clear concept of the state structure.[107] In the realm of policy, the tsar was inseparable from God in the popular mind because he transmitted God's will into political life. The tsar did not express the popular will but God's will, and therefore all who served as tsar inevitably acted in the people's interest.[108] In their activities, local peasants piously preserved the traditional Christian order. All authority was respected as a "gift from God." Such was the peasant's political credo as reflected in answers to the Russian Geographical Society's 1847 questionnaire gathering local ethnographic information.[109]

There is little doubt about the people's monarchism, especially the peasantry's, in the eighteenth and nineteenth centuries. We need only recall the basic factors supporting the dominance of the monarchist paradigm in the people's consciousness to recognize some of the changes that later took place in political mentalities. The entire peasant movement in the eighteenth century and the first half of the nineteenth century, which was directed against serfdom, was conducted under the flag of the pretender phenomenon[110]—or, using Daniel Field's felicitous phrase, in the name of the tsar.[111] The peasants' reaction to the Decembrist revolt and the punishment meted out to the conspirators makes this clear. The peasants were on the side of the tsar and against the nobility. According to secret police reports, "The simple people were highly indignant with the nobility."[112] Meanwhile, at the beginning of the 1860s, the radical intelligentsia failed to mobilize the people against the autocracy in opposition to the burdensome conditions under which serfdom was abolished. Even appeals to the Old Believers, a confessional group of peasants oppressed by the government, failed.[113] In the 1870s, the populists were equally unsuccessful in their efforts to organize a mass movement "to the people" (in which up to 3,000 people participated) with the goal of provoking a popular revolution against the autocracy.[114] Korolenko gave a profound explanation of the causes for their failure:

It was a tragedy for the entire Russian revolutionary intelligentsia. This situation was created by the people's staggering political illiteracy, society's inertia, and the aroused consciousness of a part of the intelligentsia, which decided alone to struggle against the power of the state. The people were still completely enveloped by the powerful myth of the merciful tsar. Even when confronted by deep injustices, the peasantry could be mobilized only by counterfeit tsarist charters. True, the workers began to awaken here and there, but these were still isolated instances, and this only increased the number of martyrs without advancing the movement as a whole.[115]

In a more recent work on this theme, Field concluded that the defeat of the populists was not at all due to the peasants' sometimes having turned the populists over to the police or remaining deaf to their propaganda, as many researchers have assumed. Rather, the populists' failure was due to the manner in which they sought to win the peasants' trust—in some cases, through the influence of their higher social status, which gave them authority over the peasantry, and in other cases, by buying influence with money. In spite of the populist prognosis, the village was not ready for revolution. The peasants were not opposed to the existing regime, and they had no revolutionary ideas or ideals. Most distressing was the way in which the populists' high social status helped them to win the peasants' trust, for the peasants respected their wellborn origins.[116] The peasants' apathy toward populist appeals sharply contrasted with educated society's sympathy for the peasants.[117]

The lower social classes in the city held the same political and social orientation as the peasantry. It is not surprising, therefore, that many scholars who have researched the working class have described a persistent monarchism among workers, artisans, and tradespeople both in provincial cities and in the capitals.[118]

At the end of the nineteenth century and the beginning of the twentieth, a number of changes took place in popular political conceptions and behavior—first of all, among the peasantry. Observers of peasant life noted that the peasantry fully understood the electoral concept as it applied to the village elders and other rural officials at communal and *volost* levels. They considered these officials responsible to them; and if they were dissatisfied with the officials' activities, they voted them out at the next elections. On the other hand, when it was a question of peasants' exercising their influence through elections to the district zemstvo, not to mention the provincial zemstvo or State Duma, the peasants had very confused notions. In the eyes of the peasants, everything that went on outside the commune or *volost* had independent causes and did not depend on their will. The idea of an all-estate form of self-government was alien to them, as was the idea that supreme political power depended on the people, or that they could delegate their trust to self-government to operate on the district, provincial, or statewide level. Peasants considered such tasks the responsibility of the tsar, his deputies, and his servants. Prior to the Revolution of 1905–1907, the peasants were persistent monarchists, and as a group they did not claim to participate either in state decisionmaking or in political authority. Moreover, their concept of the state order in Russia was extremely confused. Their range of interests and level of knowledge were insufficient to enable them to understand how authority was organized and functioned, or the role of the people in the larger society. Authority derived from God and belonged to the tsar—this was a categorical imperative; even the ideas that the tsar was an earthly god and the solicitous father of the poor maintained their currency.[119] It is natural, therefore, that the interests of the peasantry did not extend beyond economic and fiscal matters at the communal and *volost* levels. Everything beyond this was meaningless to them. Such monarchical views continued to be shared in large part by the lower urban social classes, including workers.

The peasantry's monarchism and political apathy can be explained by two typical peasant characteristics: devotion to tradition and custom, and lack of political education. The roots of communal and *volost* administration lay deep in past centuries; self-government first appeared in the districts and provinces in 1864, after the introduction of zemstvos. Elections to the State Duma became a fact of Russian life only in 1906. In these circumstances, centuries-old habits and traditions held sway, as can be seen in the relationship between the peasantry and the clergy. Peter I had abolished the right of clergy and priests to be elected to public office, although such a right had existed for eight centuries, ever since the adoption of Christianity. As a result, peasants traditionally considered priests to be communal servitors, and they conducted relations between the commune and the priest in the language of the pre-Petrine charters. One can see this in their preference for political terms drawn from the sixteenth and seventeenth centuries, such as *voevoda* instead of *governor,* *tsar* instead of *emperor, boyar* instead of *noble,* and so on. Peasant political attitudes at the beginning of the twentieth century preserved earlier conceptions of the tsar as a "personal" ruler, as the sovereign owner of all the land and of the entire state, and as the father of the whole Russian people and the wielder of absolute power in the land. This paradigm was as stable as the peasants' belief in God. Naive religiosity and naive monarchism were in essence two sides of the same coin—the peasantry's traditional, patriarchal, religious consciousness.[120] The peasants were thus unable to use their new political rights effectively—first, because there was no basis for such rights in custom, and second, because their exercise of political rights would have required a higher level of political consciousness than peasants possessed.

Marxist historians, with all their desire to modernize peasant and worker mentalities, were nonetheless forced to recognize that peasant monarchism, which they called "naive," was the "normative Weltanschauung of the time" (the eighteenth century and the first half of the nineteenth),[121] was an integral part of the peasant worldview before the Revolution of 1905–1907,[122] and remained so for a considerable part of the peasantry until 1916.[123] The monarchism of workers as a whole, apart from "conscious" workers, also remained essentially unchanged prior to the Revolution of 1905–1907 insofar as the majority of workers came from the peasantry and preserved the peasant mentality;[124] only after this did their monarchism begin to weaken. The force of the monarchist paradigm among peasants, workers, and other members of the urban lower classes can be seen in their failure to respond to a number of critical political events. Thus, the tsar's dissolution of the First Duma in July 1906 was met with absolute calm by the people, including the lower classes in the capitals. Similarly, the Duma deputies' attempt to appeal to the people, the so-called Vyborg Appeal of 10 July 1906, which called for passive resistance—"not one kopeck to the state, not one soldier to the army"—found no echo among the population. Refusals to pay taxes or to sign up for military service were isolated and did not come from the workers or peasants.[125] The dissolution of the Second Duma and the change of the electoral law in June 1907 also failed to evoke any popular protest.

By the end of 1907, various "Black Hundred"* organizations had approximately 400,000 members drawn mainly from the "common people" and were operating in some 2,208 population centers, in 66 provinces. During elections to the State Duma in 1907, 42 percent of peasant electors in 51 provinces of European Russia indicated that they belonged to right-wing parties.[126] This was a mass movement in Russia at that time.[127] After the Revolution of 1905–1907, the peasants still had not become republicans.[128] It seems to me—as to other historians—that the Black Hundreds were mistaken and myopic in locating the primary social basis of the autocracy in the people, predominantly in the provinces, right up to the end of the monarchy. One of the provincial leaders of the Black Hundreds, N. N. Tikhanovich-Savitskii, in a program draft (Fundamental Statute) in May 1916, wrote:

> The people need the tsar, the rich need a constitution and a parliament. . . . When the sovereign is limited and the ministers are dependent on the Duma, then the banks, capitalists, etc., with the help of those members of the State Duma and State Council elected from their midst or won over by them, will begin to introduce the laws they need to support their interests and views; but such laws will be completely opposed to the interests and views of the middle and lower classes among the working population, who will then fall into complete dependence on these forces. . . . In order to protect their interests, the laboring classes must therefore support the indivisibility of the sovereign power by every means. . . . The Russian sovereign authority is the property of the Russian people. . . . Popular monarchical unions, being in essence predominantly unions of the common people, are based on the latter's economic activity and above all the unions' concern for the welfare of the broad popular masses—i.e., the peasants, laborers, traders, and other workers, and in general the poor and middling person whose interests the members of the unions must support, always, everywhere, and in everything.[129]

Between 1907 and 1914, the broad popular masses gradually became disillusioned with Nicholas II, although not with the monarchy.[130] The degree of this disillusionment is often exaggerated and transferred from the personality of the individual emperor to the institution of monarchy. The participation of peasants, urban artisans, and traders in Black Hundred organizations between 1907 and 1917, and the surge of monarchical and nationalistic feeling in 1914, in connection with Russia's entry into World

---

*Extreme monarchists among the nobility, urban artisans, traders, and the peasantry were referred to colloquially as "Black Hundreds" (Russ. *chernosotentsy*).

War I,[131] suggest that the monarchist idea was still far from exhausted. During the war, however, the people gradually became disillusioned with the tsar. Prior to the war, the failure to transfer the nobles' lands to the peasantry could still be explained in terms of bureaucratic influence. But the people could not blame external factors for Russia's having lost two wars during the reign of a single tsar. The battles lost by the Russian army delivered a huge blow to the monarch's authority: The myth of his godlike power and omnipotence weakened progressively with each defeat, especially after Nicholas II personally took command of the army. The paradigm and the reality of sovereign power came into conflict. Many investigators, however, have confused dissatisfaction and disillusionment with Nicholas II with antimonarchism. The rebirth of autocracy in the guise of communism in Soviet Russia further proves the vitality of the idea of monarchy in the mass consciousness of the Russian people.

From the eighteenth to the beginning of the twentieth centuries, peasants, artisans, craftsmen, petty traders, workers, and all other members of the unprivileged orders of the population, in spite of the low rate of literacy among them, were well informed about the important events that took place in the state, including legislative changes, and discussed them in their own circles. The people developed opinions on questions that concerned them, and these opinions became known to the government by means of complaints and petitions as well as through local crown authorities and informants. The many popular uprisings also provided the government opportunities to become acquainted with what the people were thinking.

Public opinion developed differently among the people than it did in educated society. This can be seen by examining how information circulated among Old Believer organizations. First, opinion developed on an individual level. It was then discussed at gatherings (meetings) in individual communities or communes, and transmitted to other communes by direct personal contacts. Subsequently, through the exchange of opinions among different communities in various regions, a common point of view crystallized. In contrast to the relatively controlled formation of Old Believer opinion, an analysis of rumors that circulated in abundance throughout Russia in the eighteenth and nineteenth centuries shows that among the people—all of whom belonged to the official church—opinion formed and circulated *spontaneously* in response to various concrete circumstances and situations. Thus, for example, in 1773 there were widespread rumors that peasants who took part in the Russo-Turkish War would be emancipated. These rumors provoked a mass flight of peasants and forced the government to turn to local parish priests to cut them off.[132] In 1825, rumors spread through twenty provinces that peasants who migrated to the Urals and Siberia would be granted freedom; these rumors, like the earlier ones, provoked serfs into mass flight.[133] In 1839, in twelve provinces that suffered conflagrations as a result of a dry summer, rumors spread to the effect that the fires had been started by noble landowners seeking to destroy their peasants, whom the emperor wanted to give as a gift to Grand Princess Maria Nikolaevna.[134] And in 1847, up to 20,000 private serfs from Russia's central provinces became enamored of a false rumor that all who resettled along the Caucasian defensive line would be granted their freedom.[135] With the appearance of railroads, oral information began to circulate more rapidly, though the mechanism for the formation and spread of opinion remained unchanged.[136] Between 1877 and 1879, the entire Russian peasantry was influenced by rumors about an impending lowering of taxes and grant of an additional allotment of land. And in 1881 this was replaced by another rumor about the repartition of all noble lands among the peasants.[137] Meanwhile, every mass peasant uprising was preceded by a wave of rumors that was transmitted by telephone and telegraph over huge distances, affecting many provinces.[138]

The secret police who investigated the sources of these rumors came to the conclusion that popular social opinion prior to the 1860s and among the peasantry until the beginning of the twentieth century developed not in response to the printed word but through direct interpersonal contacts. However, whereas among the Old Believers, opinion was spread in an organized fashion by specific individuals of the same faith, among the peasants, artisans, merchants, and other working-class people, opinion was spread spontaneously by soldiers, clergy, migrant and factory workers, pilgrims, and other devout people, as well as by people whose profession required them to move from place to place, such as buyers, peddlers, woodsmen, shepherds, and barge haulers.[139] The poor played a major role in the transmission of information. Thus, in 1875, Russian ethnographer S. V. Maksimov wrote: "Here they are, with the universal illiteracy of the villager, living, walking newspapers carrying domestic news; the intelligent ones even bring quotations and stock market prices, and always denunciations of a highly emotional nature."[140] All kinds of information spread among the people with great speed. Officials in the first half of the nineteenth century were astounded at the speed with which peasants learned about their travel itineraries. In 1853, one official complained to the Ministry of Internal Affairs in St. Petersburg: "I cannot leave or enter a village without meeting some kind of agent" [of the peasants—B.N.M.].[141]

Fairs, bazaars, and the various markets that met regularly in each city and in every large village played the role of information centers for the lower urban social classes and the peasants. Until the middle of the nineteenth century, trade was periodic in nature. In the 1860s, urban and rural fairs accounted for 30 percent of trade throughout the empire; urban and rural bazaars, for 10 to 14 percent; and peddling and street trading, for another 9 percent. In the 1860s there were more than 11,000 petty traders buying and selling goods throughout Russia. Fairs were the most important channel for the formation of public opinion, both among peasants and among the urban lower classes, artisans, and craftsmen. At the fair, city met village, and peasants from different provinces met each other. Between 1790 and the 1860s, peasants and artisans participated in virtually all fairs; nobles and officials, however, participated in only 1 to 2 percent of them. At the end of the eighteenth century, there were some 3,000 active fairs; and in the 1860s, more than 6,000, in which more than a million people took part. As many as thirty fairs had an empire-wide scope, each one being attended by tens of thousands of people from all over the country. The most important of these were held at Makarev (Nizhnii Novgorod), Irbit, Koren, Svensk, Kiev, Riga, Arkhangelsk, Orenburg, and Irkutsk, in addition to Moscow and St. Petersburg. These fairs, scattered throughout Russia, not only controlled the entire trading life of this vast country but served as centers where popular public opinion was formed. As early as the last third of the eighteenth century, fairs had linked the country economically into a single, all-Russian market, which meant that all regions were also linked by information and culture.[142]

Opinions born in the minds of individuals were discussed in social gatherings. A gathering, operating somewhat systematically, transmitted the results of this exchange, through its members, to other communities and regions. Everything was accomplished *spontaneously*, under the influence of circumstances and frequently as a result of happenstance. Nonetheless, from such individual instances something regular and continuous was created. Thus, although they were scattered over a huge area, the lower urban social classes and the peasants were not isolated in the social or spiritual sense, for they constituted two classes, each with its own subculture and social opinions.[143]

The lower classes of town and village who held religious views other than those of conventional Russian Orthodoxy had already succeeded in creating all-Russian organizations by the end of the eighteenth century. The Old Believers are the best example. In the 1770s, the Priestists and the Priestless, the two main tendencies, created all-Russian centers at the Preobrazhenskii and Rogozhskii churches in Moscow, which coordinated their activity empire-wide, by nothing other than oral communication.[144] In the 1840s, the Preobrazhenskii center had influence over Old Believer communities in twenty-six Russian provinces and abroad.[145] And all this was accomplished despite persecution at the hands of Nicholas I's government. Among the Old Believers, a single, unified public opinion was formed that depended on which of their leaders acted on the national level. So, for example, between 1803 and 1822, Old Believer communities linked to the Rogozhskii center °petitioned the government with requests to legalize their church, and thanks to a well-organized campaign, achieved their goal.[146]

But in other cases—whether of war, changes in the succession of monarchs, or other major events that affected the autocracy's interests—the government deliberately set out to form popular public opinion, utilizing every means at its disposal: priests' sermons, interventions by local crown administrators, the authority of the tsar's name, the dissemination of rumors and legends, and the printed word. Sometimes these efforts were successful. For example, the state succeeded in creating positive popular attitudes toward the Russo-Turkish War under Catherine II as well as toward autocratic policy on the Polish question in 1830–1831 and 1863–1864, on the Balkans in the 1870s and 1880s, and on the European question at the end of the century. In this respect, it is important to emphasize that before the mid-nineteenth century, the social and family lives of the peasantry and the urban lower classes who lived in and around small and middle-sized towns with fewer than 25,000 inhabitants (96 percent of all "cities" at the time)[147] were very similar, thanks to the intensive economic, cultural, and marital links between urban and rural residents who lived in the environs of a given town. It is possible to talk of a single, unified, traditional, national culture among the peasantry and urban lower classes before the Great Reforms.[148] In the postreform period, this unity (examined more closely in Volume 1, Chapter 7) was further consolidated, thanks to huge, successive waves of peasant migration to the cities.

Little by little, beginning in the last third of the nineteenth century, the press and printed literature began to penetrate popular life; but their influence on the opinion of the urban lower classes was greater than on that of the peasantry because of the latter's lower educational levels and their distrust of the press. Until the turn of the century, peasant opinion was in large measure a product of peasants' own intellectual endeavors rather than of urban or other influences. However, outside influences did increase. The transmission of knowledge and opinion from privileged circles to the peasantry always existed, and in the late nineteenth century achieved unprecedented levels thanks to the growth of literacy, the activity of the zemstvos, universal military service, jury courts, the development of migratory labor, and the activities of the radicals. Jeffrey Brooks has shown that in the popular genre known as the *lubok*, at the end of the nineteenth century and especially the beginning of the twentieth century, new ideas began to appear, and even though they did not achieve a firm foothold, they coexisted uneasily with traditional Russian peasant values[149] and undoubtedly influenced the formation of peasant opinion.

The spontaneous or deliberate formation of public opinion among the urban lower classes and the peasantry had an *integrative* character in the sense that it was the concentrated reflection of the mass consciousness of these classes, created as a result of the exchange of opinion among their representatives. The truth of this can be seen in the absence of deep-rooted individualism among the peasants and the urban lower classes, in contrast to the situation among social elites. Among the educated, privileged classes, public opinion consisted of views that were shared only by a majority; but among the urban lower classes and the peasants until the twentieth century, public opinion reflected virtual unanimity. Popular public opinion had both positive and negative aspects when it concerned the people itself, Orthodox belief, or the tsar; but as a rule, it was indifferent when questions arose outside of the everyday round of practical concerns. In the eighteenth and nineteenth centuries, the people, and especially the peasants, were generally prepolitical.

In principle, public opinion was dynamic. However, in traditional society—which Russian society remained in large part (with the exception of the nobility, intelligentsia, and bourgeoisie)—public opinion maintained consistency and stability over several generations and became consolidated in the form of *customs, norms,* and *traditions.* Negative valuations of serfdom, recruiting, landowning nobles, officials, Jews, and foreigners, and positive attitudes toward the tsar, Orthodoxy, the commune, and customary law became traditions, changing little over time. Popular public opinion was an oral creation, reflected in popular proverbs and sayings. It also took the form of nonverbal communication (gestures, expressions) of negative and positive feelings and emotions. Spontaneity and emotionalism were characteristic features of popular public opinion.

Thus, the urban lower classes and the peasantry had their own opinions about the major questions of life; this opinion was *public* insofar as it reflected the opinion of entire social classes. But until 1905–1907, the peasants, artisans, craftsmen, petty traders, workers, and other unprivileged strata in Russian society were not *creators of public opinion.* The state only considered their opinion during times of mass disorders and revolts—in a word, only when they expressed their dissatisfaction. The inclusion of any social group among the creators of public opinion depended on the importance of its opinion to the state on a given problem; and the significance of a group depended not so much on its size as on its cohesion, influence, and its leaders' ability to mobilize members in a campaign that clearly and unswervingly reflected their opinions and interests. Until the beginning of the twentieth century, the peasantry and urban lower classes as a whole were generally passive. They did not actively pursue their interests or spread their opinions. They were, rather, observers of the struggle between the autocracy on one hand and society and the intelligentsia on the other, remaining largely on the side of the autocracy—as happened, for example, at the time of the Decembrist revolt and the "going to the people" movement. Popular public opinion was not influential because it was rarely transformed into political activity. When it did manifest itself in popular revolts, strikes, and other mass demonstrations, these activities bore a spontaneous and local character.

In the years leading up to the Revolution of 1905–1907, when the peasants and workers found their leaders—or more accurately when the leaders of the professional revolutionary parties turned to the people for support and received it—the people became creators of public opinion. Still, the autocracy continued to see its principal opponents as the nonsocialist political parties within educated society.

Society's Influence on State Policy

The practical policies introduced by the emperor and the government can be seen as the result of a dialogue between the autocracy and society—a joint product that reflected both the state's and society's interests. The idea, widespread in Marxist historical literature, that with the possible exception of the reigns of Peter I and Alexander II autocratic policy during the imperial era was isolated from the interests of society, and society from policymaking,[150] needs amending. In the eighteenth and nineteenth centuries, the government generally conducted policies both in the domestic arena and in the realm of international relations that were national in that they represented a balance or compromise between the interests of society as a whole and those of the state. The government was at the same time a leader in modernization.[151] Deviations from this path were short-lived, being curtailed and corrected by society, which bore the main burdens of modernization.

Peter I (1682–1725) broke with Russian tradition in that his reforms, which were designed to break down the wall that had stood for centuries between Russia and the West, to create a regular army and navy, to stimulate trade and industry, to give new meaning to the development of national culture and education, to create a powerful state, and to conduct a capable and active foreign policy, were both strategically correct and timely. During his lifetime, his reforms met powerful opposition from society, including the nobility, and this opposition led to changes in how the reforms were conducted.[152] But on the whole, Peter's reforms gave much to Russia, and therefore they eventually were accepted by the people as well as by society. The idealization of Peter began soon after his death. Under Elizabeth, his image had already been transformed in the people's consciousness into that of an awe-inspiring but just tsar who manifested his concern for Russia's welfare and that of the common people. Legends also spread about how Peter dealt with offenders.[153]

Peter's immediate successors followed more or less the same path, and society tolerated them. But after the death of Anna (1741), when power was seized by her favorite, Count E. I. Biren of Courland (acting as regent for the minor Emperor Ivan VI), Russian society saw this as a form of foreign domination over state administration and an abandonment of the national path in internal and foreign policy. As a result, within three weeks of his accession to power, Biren was overthrown by the guards, which effectively meant by the nobility. This patriotic upsurge on the part of Russian society brought Peter's daughter Elizabeth to the throne (1741–1761) under the slogan of reestablishing Peter's legacy in state administration.

It is possible to say that Elizabeth fulfilled her preelection pledges, for she systematically patronized everything national, moved aside all foreigners close to the throne, and in every way strove to follow her father's precepts. Her reign was marked by successes in the realms of foreign policy (victories in the Seven Years' War); military affairs (rearming the military); economy (rapid development of foreign trade and industry as a result of the abolition of internal customs barriers and protectionist tariffs); and culture and education (the opening of Moscow University and a number of other scholarly institutions, including the Academy of Artists). Her government also enacted a number of other useful measures that were popular with society, such as the convocation of a Legislative Commission in the 1750s (the prototype of Catherine II's 1767 Commission), the introduction of a General Land Survey, and the opening of Russia's first commercial banks. The nobility liked Elizabeth a great deal; under her reign, they made good progress toward consolidating their estate interests. Thanks to her conduct of a national policy that was popular in society (but not among privately owned serfs), Elizabeth ruled successfully for almost twenty years, and like Peter I, died in her own bed, surrounded by those close to her.

Elizabeth's successor, Peter III (1761–1762), was removed from the throne and murdered seven months into his reign precisely for having abandoned Russia's traditional, nationalist foreign policy. (Peter III ordered the Russian army to halt military activities against Prussia in the Seven Years' War [1756–1763], and concluded a peace treaty with Frederick II.) And this despite the fact that Peter, not Catherine, published the first ukase emancipating the nobility from compulsory service; abolished the universally hated Secret Chancellery; and announced the secularization of church properties, which the nobles had long desired.

The domestic and foreign policies adopted by Catherine II (1762–1796) responded to the interests of Russian society and the majority of the population, with the exception of privately owned serfs; therefore, she enjoyed the complete approval of the nobility and the urban estates. In social policy, the empress gave up her radical projects (in particular, her intention to abolish serfdom) after consulting with her trusted advisers, familiarizing herself with the instructions submitted to the Legislative Commission, and considering her previous experience in administration. In the realm of domestic policy, she followed the desires expressed in the instructions, attempting to create a society based on legal social estates like that in her native Germany; and she was reasonably successful in doing so.[154] It was relatively easy for her to pursue this policy, which followed the traditional path of the Russian autocracy since the beginning of the seventeenth century and especially since Peter I. In foreign policy, the empress also pursued and accomplished what several centuries of Russian rulers and Russian society had striven to achieve—the consolidation of Russian power on the shores of the Black Sea and the absorption of the Crimean khanate, which had for several centuries traumatized the Russians with its military raids.[155]

Catherine's son, Paul I (1796 to 1801), paid with his life for attempting to do what he thought correct without consideration for circumstances, public opinion, or the nobility; namely, to impose a flagrantly personal and despotic regime on Russia. Paul's case in many respects paralleled that of Peter I. The latter was also a stern, cruel, and despotic emperor; he too imposed huge burdens on society. But his contemporaries bore these burdens and forgave his despotism because his regime served the interests of society and of Russia. Behind Paul's despotism stood only his sense of outrage, for which he blamed his mother, and his excessive vanity. And society would not tolerate this. At the same time, however, Paul initiated a limitation on serfdom (I have in mind his ukase limiting labor services to three days a week). This policy was inherited by his successors and cautiously implemented in the first half of the nineteenth century. The policy conformed to the strategic interests of the nobility and prepared the ground for the abolition of serfdom.

The reign of Alexander I (1801–1825) likewise can be analyzed in terms of the relationship between autocratic policy and societal interests. In domestic affairs, the nobility forced Alexander to retreat from plans for rapid and radical reform (the abolition of serfdom, the establishment of a constitutional order, and so on) at the very height of his reformist activity and to adopt a strategy of gradual reforms that would take into account society's preparedness for them. This change of course conformed to the interests of society as a whole, for the realization of Speranskii's political reforms would in all likelihood have led to the establishment of a constitutional autocracy in Russia—one that would have been limited only by the nobility—and that would have been a great misfortune for Russia. Indeed, according to Speranskii's plans for state reform, political rights—that is to say, the right to participate in representative organs and in state administration—would have belonged only to the owners of immovable property.[156] The peasantry, which constituted approximately 92 percent of Russia's population, would not have possessed any political rights, since the law prevented landlords' serfs from owning immovable property (except, in some cases, in the name of their noble owners); and state peasants' lands belonged to the state.

Among the urban estates, meanwhile, everyone who worked for hire or who owned property below the established minimum would have been deprived of political rights (although Speranskii's project did not specify the amount required). As the elections to the city dumas in 1870 showed, because of the population's poverty, the introduction of even a very limited property requirement excluded 95 percent of the urban population—in effect, the entire artisan estate, merchants of the third guild, servants, and workers of political rights. Who remained? The nobility, merchants of the first two guilds, and possibly a few elders from state villages (the project allowed state village elders to participate in *volost* dumas, and theoretically some could be elected to district- or provincial-level dumas and thus to the State Duma). Furthermore, among potential electors of deputies to the State Duma, hereditary nobles were twenty times more numerous than merchants from the first two guilds (235,000 to 12,000 in 1811, and 610,000 to 30,000 in 1858).[157] As a result, supreme power would effectively have been transferred into the hands of the nobility, which would have become the "lawmaking estate." Speranskii himself later became aware of the threat contained in his project. In 1819, he wrote: "The possibility of creating a powerful and educated class of lawmakers is extremely remote. Therefore, one of two things is possible: Either these estates will become simply a political spectacle, or due to lack of political knowledge, they will take a wrong turn."[158] One cannot help but agree with those who consider Speranskii's plan a grandiose utopia.

In 1811, Alexander I also executed an about-face in his foreign policy. Under pressure from the nobility and due to external circumstances, he shifted from his unpopular, pro-French orientation to an anti-French orientation. That year, N. M. Karamzin, in the name of the noble opposition, presented the emperor with his "Memorandum on Ancient and Modern Russia," in which he sharply criticized the entire direction of government policy. The main ideas in the "Memorandum" subsequently became the basis for the emperor's new course in both domestic and foreign policy. From this we can see that if in the eyes of the public, especially the nobility, the policies of the autocracy became antinational in character, then society would force the emperor and his government to return to the true path, as defined by society. Of the reforms he contemplated, meanwhile, the emperor was able to introduce only those that conformed to the demands of noble society—namely, the liberal reform of education and censorship, the creation of a State Council as an advisory legislative organ, and ministerial reform. However, the institutions created by these reforms survived without essential change until 1917. The educational reforms were the most successful, creating for the first time an organized and integrated system of higher, middle, and elementary education in Russia.

The reign of Nicholas I (1825–1855) was one of the most dynamic in Russia's intellectual history. It also presents a curious example of how, following a long, peaceful coexistence, autocracy and society became alienated from each other and drew the country into catastrophe. The government of Nicholas adopted a number of major, useful, and long-awaited social measures. After 133 years of unsuccessful efforts, between 1830 and 1832, a "Complete Collection of Russian Laws" and a "Digest of Laws" were prepared for publication, thereby placing the state administration on a firm legal foundation. Between 1839 and 1843, a long-expected monetary reform was enacted with the goal of stabilizing the state's finances. As an experimental step on the path to the abolition of serfdom, a reform of the state peasantry was undertaken between 1837 and 1841 that improved their situation. This reform was seen as a model for the reform of the serf village. Partial improvements also were made in the condition of the nobles' serfs. Between 1826 and 1855, some 30,007 legislative acts concerning all categories of peasants were adopted, including 367 affecting the nobles' serfs—almost three times as many as had been passed in the preceding reign.[159] The 1846 reform of the St. Petersburg city administration, meanwhile, served as a model for the urban reforms of 1870. They did much for the country's economic progress (encouraging industrial development and the activities of agricultural and industrial villages, organizing an all-Russian exhibition for the promotion of advanced technology, establishing banks and stock exchanges, constructing railroads, opening technical schools, and so on) and for the development of middle and higher education and popular enlightenment (opening many schools prior to 1848 and enacting a quite liberal university statute). As a whole, the second quarter of the nineteenth century was a period in which literature, science, art, and education flourished, as well as a time in which a professional intelligentsia formed that not only felt the necessity for radical reforms but then realized them in the 1860s.[160]

Nicholas I's reign was an incubation period for Russian society, and this is the period's fundamental historical significance. During these years, both projects for reform, or at least their basic ideas, and the people who could realize them were being prepared. And the longer reforms were postponed, the more rapidly they would be realized once Russia's defeat in the Crimean War created favorable circumstances by provoking a social upsurge in the second half of the 1850s.[161] The new emperor, Alexander II (1855–1881), introduced reforms that answered the demands of liberal society. Conservatives who disagreed did not dare oppose the emperor, who had initiated the reforms, and the radicals were too weak to win approval for their program. Affecting all areas of Russian life, the reforms abolished serfdom, introduced all-class courts, established universal military service, created all-class organs of local self-government in the cities and rural districts, introduced liberal censorship regulations, and adopted school reforms. The one thing the emperor did not do was create an all-Russian legislative body. True, in the years leading up to 1881 he became aware of the need for an advisory legislative organ; however, he was prevented from realizing this goal when a terrorist's bomb cut short his life. In the economic sphere, the autocracy also acted in a far-sighted manner. The policy of industrial development that was adopted by the government in the 1870s was strategically correct and was conducted by means that were optimal for Russia. Redemption payments, preservation of the peasant commune, and limitations on peasant freedom of movement certainly placed limits on industrialization. But the abolition of redemption payments would have provoked a fiscal crisis; the preservation of the commune also met the needs of the peasantry and ensured a smoother transition from a traditional to an industrial society. Neither the mentality of the peasantry nor its economic condition had yet prepared it for the adoption of individual forms of agriculture.

As a whole, the reign of Alexander II was marked by cooperation between the autocracy and the various political forces within society. The autocracy adhered to a middle path between the liberals, radicals, and extreme rightists. Proof of this can be found in the 2,623 petitions that the zemstvos sent the government between 1865 and 1884, 48 percent of which expressed approval of the government.[162] Certainly, the government's centrism allowed it to realize necessary reforms. It is even possible to suppose that had there been no extreme, radical terrorist activity, Alexander II would have taken new steps toward the creation of a constitutional-parliamentary order in Russia.

Alexander III (1881–1894) was unhinged by the activities of the radicals. He saw a link between these acts and the social and political reforms undertaken by his father, whose political views he did not share.[163] He therefore not only refused to continue his father's reforms but actively pursued counterreforms. The autocracy turned away from the liberal segment of educated society and placed its wager on Russia's uniqueness, traditionalism, nationalism, patriarchal peasantry, landowning nobility, and on the forces of the state itself.[164] Alexander III, and Nicholas II after him, sought to increase societal trust and autocratic legitimacy by relying on the rituals and symbols of pre-Petrine Rus and by reanimating the political ideology of the seventeenth century,[165] with an emphasis on its religiosity.[166] Success was not forthcoming, in part because the plan was poorly executed. However, the prominent Kadet (Constitutional Democrat) E. Trubetskoi acknowledged the realism of such political calculations when he wrote in 1912:

We are being destroyed by the weak, embryonic development of those middle strata of society that could serve as the supporters of legality. . . . In other countries, they justifiably consider the most extreme projects of social and political transformation to be utopian. In Russia it is the reverse: The more moderate a project, the more utopian and unrealizable it seems.[167]

But the support of the peasantry was possible only if the autocracy decided to expropriate the nobles' land, which meant also sacrificing the landowning nobility—and that was unacceptable to the autocracy. From an economic and social perspective, the landowning nobility was an imposing force in the 1880s. At the beginning of the twentieth century, when the nobility's significance was much reduced, its share of all propertied wealth (among those with an annual income in excess of 10,000–20,000 rubles, or 5,000–10,000 1905 U.S. dollars), according to various calculations, was still between 15 and 33 percent. The nobility was also powerful as an estate organization, and its political position in the localities, zemstvos, and district administrations made it the most highly unified, educated, and politically conscious class.[168] But its strength diminished from year to year, and its significance declined, due both to its loss of land (from 1862 to 1904, the area of land owned by nobles in European Russia declined by 41 percent, and from 1905 to 1914, by a further 20 percent)[169] and to its increased indebtedness and self-isolation, leading it to adopt a defiantly antibourgeois stance by the beginning of the twentieth century.[170]

The state, however, also represented a major force. Its material base consisted of a huge fund of state land and a state-owned industrial sector;[171] its social basis lay in the bureaucracy; juridically, the fundamental state laws entrusted the central state authority to an autocracy; and psychologically, the outstanding majority of the population supported the monarchy. But as we saw after 1861, the state was weakening economically and organizationally. Thus, Alexander III made a wager on forces that had no future, and two potential allies, the landowning nobility and the peasantry, were in irreconcilable conflict. However, had the autocracy struck an intelligent compromise between nationalism and westernization, and had it combined support for traditional Russian principles with Western liberal ideas, it might have experienced greater political success and might have survived.[172]

In considering Alexander III's conservative political course, it is important to remember that he did not succeed in realizing his ideas in full measure precisely because of society's opposition. Not only did he not succeed in forcing society into silence, he also failed to silence the State Council, which rejected a number of government legislative projects. Furthermore, despite the counterreforms of the zemstvo and city organs of social self-government, and contrary to the government's intentions, liberal and oppositionist forces continued to strengthen. Alexander's effort to transfer local administration back into the hands of the landowning nobles, where it had been prior to the Great Reforms, similarly failed.[173] The tsar's attempt to turn primary education over to the church likewise was defeated. The autocracy was unable to decide whether to introduce a judicial counterreform.

Despite the tsar's conservative domestic political course, his emphasis on "nationalist industry" aided industrialization; Alexander III's reign brought an unprecedented and extremely rapid rate of industrial growth. Initially encouraging only individual sectors, the government then fostered a broad-scale program of industrial development that launched the country on its industrial revolution. Historians claim that the spurt of industrial growth in the 1890s was Russia's takeoff into self-sustaining economic development.[174] Besides encouraging industrialization, the government's economic policy—which included tariff protection, consolidation of the ruble, improvement of the tax system, introduction of worker legislation, and balancing of the budget—led to the liquidation of the budget deficit and the stabilization of the ruble and prepared the way for monetary reform in 1897.[175] Industrialization was accompanied by growth in the size and wealth of the bourgeoisie[176] and in the number of workers. The increased significance of these new classes forced the autocracy to consider their societal needs and political aspirations and thus to renew the dialogue with liberal society—and ultimately, to change political direction. In this sense, the reign of Alexander III recalls the reign of Nicholas I—it was an incubation period for the stormy changes to come during the following reign.

Nicholas II least of all wanted and least of all was prepared to introduce political reforms. He was a firm supporter of autocracy, and the concept of sovereign whose status and rights were limited did not conform to his character, education, or worldview.[177] In 1900 and 1901, a number of moderate and far-sighted monarchists, grouped around the newspaper *New Times,* issued a serious proposal for reforms that included granting free exit from the peasant commune, extending general state and civil rights to the peasantry, reforming local administration and self-government, increasing the competence of the zemstvos, abolishing the estate order, and several other propositions—all the while, maintaining the autocracy. Passing up this chance once again to take the initiative in the task of reform, the autocracy doomed society to adopt revolutionary solutions to its accumulating problems.[178] Under the pressure of circumstances—above all, defeat in the Russo-Japanese War in 1904–1905, and the ensuing revolution—as well as under the onslaught of society, with whom the peasantry and workers united, the emperor was forced in 1906 to acquiesce to a constitution and parliament.

However, from the Duma's very establishment, the tsar strove to limit its competence and turn it into a strictly advisory organ. He also retained unchanged the traditional system and methods of administration both in the center and in the localities, as well as the "juridical" basis of bureaucratic authority—the 1881 Statute on Reinforced Protection. The head of the imperial chancellery described the tsar's reaction to his first encounter with the State Duma, which solidified his resolve to steer this course: "The sovereign could not imagine that these several hundred frondeurs truly reflect the voice of the people, who until now have greeted him with great enthusiasm."[179] The struggle between the Duma and the imperial government between 1906 and 1917 can be understood as a struggle between society and the surviving remnants of the autocratic regime, although on the surface it seemed a struggle between legislative and executive authorities in a situation where the executive authority was absolutely independent of the popular will and the parliament.

By pursuing such a policy, the monarch strengthened not only the liberal and radical opposition but also the conservative opposition on the right. Within the landowning nobility, the traditional supporters of tsarism formed an influential group that wanted the country to develop further along the path of parliamentarism. In August 1915, the most influential monarchist organization, the Council of the United Nobility (which included the majority of landowning nobles within the 34 zemstvo provinces), split; and in 1916, it joined the moderate opposition in demanding a "responsible ministry" (in other words, a government accountable to the Duma). By this time, a considerable part of high society seemed to have joined the opposition to the dynasty.[180]

Isolated and opposed by the most influential segments of Russian society, tsarism sought support among the "Black Hundreds", assuming that the monarchist organizations reflected the opinion of the people and would rally them once again to the tsarist banner. The Black Hundreds and their press were generously subsidized by the government under Nicholas II's personal direction. The imperial couple believed in the people's support until the day of their abdication. Even afterward, they imagined that the soldiers were on the point of rebelling and returning Nicholas to the throne. The sources of their mistaken belief were most likely their abiding conviction of the uniqueness of Russian culture and Russia's historical path of development; their deep belief in the peasantry's monarchism, reinforced by letters and telegrams from extreme monarchists; loyalist speeches and campaigns staged by Black Hundred groups; and the impressions the royal couple formed while reviewing military parades and in encounters with the public during their frequent train trips around the country.[181]

However, the extreme monarchists' ranks were split—not along political lines but according to their estate, cultural differences, and societal interests. The Europeanized elite did not want to unite with the noble majority, which professed traditional Russian ideals. As a result, according to one of the Black Hundred leaders, "the leaders were left without an army and the army without leaders." It was no easy matter for the tsarist administration to drum up support within the peasantry. To do so, it needed a viable proposal for an agrarian program that would satisfy the peasants—but it seemed incapable of devising such a program. The peasants demanded the confiscation of noble lands; but tsarism could not comply, as it then would lose the support of the landowning nobility.

As a result, the emperor was completely isolated—from society, from the Duma, and even from the bureaucracy. On the one hand, the policy of Nicholas II was bankrupt, and society refused him support; on the other, Nicholas II lost his faith in society, the Duma, and the bureaucracy, because of their opposition. Under these circumstances, the initiative was seized by the socialists, who with the aid of soldiers, peasants, and workers succeeded in overthrowing the monarchy. In February 1917, the emperor abdicated the throne, and a democratic republic was established in Russia.[182] The emperor's refusal to engage in constructive dialogue with society on the subject of Russia's political problems had brought the semi-autocratic regime to an end.

In the social and economic spheres, however, Nicholas II and his government enjoyed some success. Industrialization continued to gather strength. In 1906, the Stolypin agrarian policy—the most radical reform since the Great Reforms—was introduced. The Stolypin reforms, which included the withdrawal of support from the commune, the development of individual peasant family farms, the establishment of private property in land in the countryside, and the resettlement of peasants from European Russia to Siberia, were, in my view, strategically correct.[183] Every fourth peasant supported the reforms—a sufficient proportion to permit the reorganization of the countryside in conformity with the principles of a farmer-based market economy. Had the Stolypin reforms been successful, a middle class might have arisen in the village, in the form of an economically independent peasant-landowner. Thus the social basis of moderate Russian liberalism would have been consolidated.[184] Between 1911 and 1913, meanwhile, zemstvos were introduced into nine more provinces; and in 1914, a reform of the archaic, "estate-based," peasant *volost* court was initiated in ten provinces.

As one reflects on the autocracy's principal internal political decisions between 1700 and 1917, one becomes convinced that it diverged relatively rarely from what the *majority* of the nobility and educated classes desired. Mistakes were common; but if the autocracy deviated from the desires of the majority and this did not in the final analysis seem beneficial to society, then the government was forced to rescind its plans and to make concessions. Beginning with Peter I, the autocracy and its apparatus held firmly to the path of modernization, although the forms and methods of its implementation changed. Dialogue between society and the autocracy was difficult, but common sense usually triumphed.[185] How did the autocracy in large part succeed in fashioning a compromise that satisfied the majority of the population?

Channels of Communication Between Society and State

How did the autocracy become acquainted with public opinion and how did it accommodate that opinion? The state apparatus was itself part of society; therefore, by following its own broadly defined interests, it could to a certain degree satisfy the interests of society.

As indicated above, the landowning nobility was the backbone of the bureaucracy. It was through the nobility that the sovereign power came into contact with the countryside. To be sure, the nobility represented its own estate interests above all else; however, it is impossible to deny that it knew and understood the life of the common man better than did professional bureaucrats, because prior to the 1860s, the nobility was intimately familiar with life in the countryside—particularly with that of the peasantry. In 1858, in the forty-nine provinces of European Russia, more than two-thirds of the nobility lived in the countryside and less than one-third in the city.[186] (By the beginning of the twentieth century, however, the situation had changed significantly: In 1897, only 43 percent of the nobility remained in the countryside, and 57 percent lived in the city.[187]) The nobility was engaged in a variety of agricultural and industrial activities and was closely linked to the market, which means that it was equally well acquainted with the general mood among merchants and tradespeople. These circumstances contributed greatly to the nobility's political conservatism in two ways: First, because of its substantial material and social interests, the nobility was naturally predisposed to preserve the existing order. Second, because nobles regularly came into close contact with peasants, merchants, and tradespeople, the nobility was familiar with the people's monarchist political ideals and was undoubtedly influenced by them. The radical and liberal intelligentsia's demands for freedom and political rights naturally seemed to the nobility to be alien to the Russian people and to have been introduced artificially into Russia from the West. The autocracy's link to the people through the loyal nobility was clearly an important factor in the supreme power's political conservatism.

Throughout the period under study, numerous and varied court celebrations and ceremonies were an ever-present feature of state life. One of their main functions was to create the opportunity for informal, non-service-related social intercourse between the emperor and his subjects—representatives from the elite strata within the military and civil bureaucracies as well as from high society who were invited to the palace.[188]

One of the most important channels linking the autocracy with society and the people was the secret police. This institution originated in the sev-

enteenth century, under the first of the Romanovs, with the emergence of
the judicial concept of crimes against the tsar—which became known as
"word and deed against the Sovereign." The secret police was significantly
strengthened under Peter I;[189] was reorganized into a regular administrative institution in 1826, under Nicholas I, as part of His Majesty's Own
Imperial Chancellery; and was again reorganized in 1880, as the Department of Police within the Ministry of Internal Affairs. Although the name
of the institution executing the secret police function changed, the main
goal of its activity remained the same: to gather information about the
state of public opinion and the moods and needs of the population.[190]
Chief of Gendarmes Benckendorff, in his annual survey of public opinion
for 1839, wrote: "Public opinion is to the authorities what a map is to the
leader of an army in wartime. But to compile an accurate survey of public
opinion is just as difficult as drawing an accurate topographical map."[191]
Through its broad network of agents, the secret police came to know the
opinion of all social classes quite well. During the reign of Nicholas I, it focused its attention on court society; high society; the middle class
(landowners, merchants of the first guild, the educated, and men of letters),
which it dubbed the "empire of the heart"; "youth"; officialdom; the army;
the clergy; and peasant serfs.[192] At the end of the nineteenth century and
the beginning of the twentieth, the center of attention shifted to the secret
societies of the revolutionaries and the intelligentsia, political organizations, and workers.[193] The police correctly understood its task as one of
gathering information on the *opinion of the majority,* and toward this end
it utilized every available means: perlustration, shadowing suspects, infil-
trating illegal organizations, employing provocateurs, bribery, and so
on.[194] Some social activists, knowing that their letters were being read, intentionally wrote sincerely about the burning political topics of the day in
the hope that their opinions would be passed on to the government. In addition, every secret police report recommended to the emperor practical
measures demanded by public opinion to improve the country's situation.
Some political reports even contained their own compilation of reform
projects in the agrarian, financial, juridical, and other spheres.[195]

The secret police did not always relay an objective summary of public
opinion. At times, they exaggerated the level of opposition in society. Thus,
for example, Benckendorff warned the emperor of the danger of a revolutionary outburst at the end of the 1820s and again in the mid-1830s. However, no such outbursts took place. At the same time, in his report for 1832,
he wrote: "Russia's past was marvelous, its present is more than splendid,
and insofar as the future is concerned, then it above all can be described
only with the boldest imagination."[196] In 1839, twenty-two years before
the abolition of serfdom, Benckendorff warned the emperor that the "entire popular spirit is directed toward one goal: emancipation" and that "the
enserfed classes are a powder keg beneath the state."[197] Again, no uprising

took place. Ironically, when social upheaval was truly a threat to public order, secret police reports often tended to embellish reality in a more positive direction, perhaps because the sovereign preferred "beautiful," soothing pictures. For example, police reports generally understated the scale of peasant and worker revolts during the nineteenth and early twentieth centuries.[198] Nicholas, "the sovereign charmed by shining accounts," wrote historian M. P. Pogodin, did not have a reliable picture of the situation.[199] At the end of 1916, on the eve of tsarism's collapse, the reports from the Department of Police painted an excessively optimistic picture of the situation in the country and influenced the emperor's and his closest advisers' assessments of the political situation.[200] In all likelihood, some secret police chiefs also sought to influence state policy in a direction harmonizing with their own interests and political sympathies. All such manipulations reduced the usefulness of the information provided.

From 1810, all social classes had the right of petition and thus could inform the emperor directly of their opinions.[201] The nobility and its estate organizations had had this right since 1775. (A special Commission for the Receipt of Petitions addressed to the emperor was created in 1810; in 1884, it was renamed the Office of Petitions, and in 1895, the Office for the Receipt of Petitions.) Between 1810 and 1884, the commission received 75,000 complaints and 600,000 petitions, of which 26 percent were satisfied. The remainder were transferred to the appropriate institutions for consideration; the most important of these (6.3 percent) were forwarded directly to the sovereign. The number of petitions grew every year: In 1825, 11,582 were received; in 1893, 21,382; in 1899, 32,336; and in 1908, 65,357. In 1908, the proportion of petitions personally seen by the emperor increased to 12 percent, and all of these were satisfied. Twenty-six percent were refused, and 48 percent were transferred to other institutions. The composition of these petitions was varied and complex, but complaints against decisions by courts and higher administrative institutions and requests for pardons predominated. For example, in 1908 there were 331 complaints against decisions of the Senate, 27 against decisions made by ministries, and 96 against decisions of other officials. Thanks to the broad scope of its activity, the Office for the Receipt of Petitions to the emperor not only contributed to the oversight of the administration of justice and the observation of the law but also served as an important channel of communication between society and the autocracy.[202]

Public opinion also reached the autocracy through experts summoned by the government to serve on various commissions for the study of certain vital problems, and expert opinions were often utilized in preparing legislation. Thus, representatives from society participated in formulating all of the Great Reforms.[203] After the Great Reforms, the zemstvos and city dumas turned to the government with petitions of various kinds, many of which were taken into consideration and were satisfied.

Often, illegal means such as demonstrations and meetings were utilized to "contact" the authorities. The powerful campaign to reform the state order that was launched by society between the spring and fall of 1905 is a good example of the pressure society could bring to bear on the autocracy. Under its pressure, Nicholas II first issued the Manifesto of 6 August 1905 agreeing to the introduction of a State Duma as an advisory legislative body, and then, on 17 October of the same year, authorized the introduction of a genuine parliament.[204]

These different channels of communication between society and the sovereign functioned simultaneously, but each emperor tended to favor one over the others. In the seventeenth century, the main channel of communication was through petitions to the tsar and through the assembly of the land. In the eighteenth century and the first half of the nineteenth, communication between the autocracy and society was relayed mainly through nobles who were in state service but were at the same time landowners and rural dwellers (i.e., people familiar with local life). By the last third of the eighteenth century, the press had begun to acquire some significance, and its role continued to expand thereafter. Catherine II personally participated in polemics on the burning topics of the day that were discussed in the press, and she even tried to lead public opinion by publishing her own journal.[205] In order to gather ideas about the needs and desires of the population, she skillfully utilized the instructions to the deputies of the Legislative Commission of 1767: On her orders, all of the instructions were carefully studied, and the opinions they contained were systematized; the resulting assessment was more thorough and possibly more relevant than many studies of public opinion conducted by present-day sociologists. Based on the desires expressed in these instructions, the empress compiled a program of social reforms that she subsequently enacted.

Alexander I was similarly sensitive to public opinion, which always interested him. After wavering for a long time, he adopted a program that had been put together in the salon of his sister, Ekaterina Pavlovna, around whom the Moscow nobility had united. (The program was written by N. M. Karamzin.)

Nicholas I stumbled on an unusual means of acquainting himself with public opinion: He began his reign by attentively studying the testimony of the Decembrists, which on his orders was systematized by the investigating commission. The conclusions to which he subsequently came served as the basis for his conservative political course. He also attached great significance to the information provided him by the Russian secret police. During his reign the quality of their work rose to the level of the secret police services in west European countries.

In the second half of the 1850s, following the accession of Alexander II to the throne, the press became the autocrat's primary source for discerning public opinion.[206] Certainly at this time the concept of "public opinion" became popular and commonplace, and both government and society considered the press the main vehicle reflecting it. It is no accident that the concepts of "the press" and "public opinion" became synonyms. Under the pressure of opinion from all political orientations, the government allowed a limited degree of openness *(glasnost')* in the press; but this compromise only emphasized the autocracy's lack of answerability to society. However, despite their proclaimed independence from public opinion, the emperor and his government became increasingly dependent on the press: They needed it, first, as a source of information about the current state of affairs and about public opinion; and second, to win the trust and support of society.[207] To accomplish the first task, the government encouraged the press to discuss all of Russia's problems, except political matters and affairs of state administration. The liberal reforms that Alexander II subsequently introduced were the autocracy's response to liberal public opinion communicated by the press. The government achieved the second task by studying everything in the press that concerned social problems and the work of the administration. In the 1860s, the Ministry of Internal Affairs initiated regular surveys of the press for all critical observations directed at the government. These were then compiled by the Chief Administration for Press Affairs in the form of so-called ministerial reviews. Every press report citing improper activities by the crown administration was taken note of and verified. If the report was confirmed, the guilty were punished; but if it was not confirmed, then a denial was published in the official press. Other ministries operated in analogous form. M. N. Katkov, the popular right-wing journalist, was so powerful that he forced the Minister of Internal Affairs, P. A. Valuev, to resign. Alexander II, meanwhile, paid great attention not only to domestic public opinion but also to European public opinion.[208]

Public opinion also began to influence foreign policy. For example, one could say that public opinion in 1877 forced the autocracy into war with Turkey "to defend our Slavic brothers in the Balkans."[209] F. M. Dostoevskii remarked in his notebooks for 1880, "Public opinion in Russia is worthless, at 'sixes and sevens,' but in some places it is feared, and consequently it has come to be a unique and possibly even useful force."[210]

In the liberal reign of Alexander II, the government paid great attention to liberal opinion and its press; but in the conservative reign of Alexander III attention was turned instead to conservative opinion and its press. A. D. Pazukhin, an extreme, right-wing, noble, social activist, was the author of the program of counterreforms. His ideological inspiration and support came from the aforementioned Katkov (until his death in 1887) and thereafter from V. P. Meshcherskii, editor of the other right-wing newspaper, *The Citizen*.[211] However, liberal opinion did not lose its influence entirely, as can be seen from the following example. In 1883, in Irkutsk, the populist

K. G. Neustroev was executed for slapping the governor-general of Siberia, D. G. Anuchin, in the face. Public opinion in Irkutsk came out against Anuchin. On his journeys around the city, people cried out: "Murderer!" The gate to his home was smeared with blood on several occasions. After Neustroev's execution, the Irkutsk newspaper, *Siberia,* printed a story in its chronicle of recent events, about the completely scandalous murder of an innocent man. The governor-general was forced to resign.[212]

In the reign of Nicholas II, public opinion acquired still greater influence over policy. The press became even stronger than before, and the zemstvos and city dumas began to play a role in the formation and expression of public opinion. Public organizations, especially the zemstvos, deliberately distanced themselves from the state administration.[213] This was clearly manifested when several categories of zemstvo employees rejected an 1894 proposal to transfer them into state employ.[214]

In 1906, the State Duma became the primary mouthpiece for political parties of all tendencies, from the extreme right to the extreme left. Society now had the legal right to influence the legislative work of the parliament. A good example of such action can be seen in society's successful struggle for a new law on divorce, which was adopted in 1914.[215] Public opinion became a political force in the provinces as well as the capitals, and governors were forced to take heed. In order to cope successfully with their responsibilities, governors had to exercise great diplomatic skills, since they not only had to take into consideration the center and the representatives of other ministries in the province but also had to "get around" and "win over" the leaders of the zemstvos, city dumas, noble assemblies, and the press.[216]

Prior to 1905, people had two ways of expressing their opinions: by complaints or petitions, and by revolts.[217] Complaints to the administration were processed according to a hierarchical order, from the lower administration to the higher, and from the higher administration to the Senate. As has already been indicated, the right of petition to the emperor was officially confirmed in 1810. (It had existed de facto for some years previous, under Paul I,[218] and had been actively exercised throughout the eighteenth century despite its prohibition.[219]) Popular revolts in both city and village, meanwhile, served as an important channel for the expression of the people's negative reaction to autocratic policy, which the people linked not with the sovereign but with the administrative apparatus. At the same time, it should be noted that the autocracy in large measure responded to such revolts by adjusting its policy.[220] For example, after the Pugachev revolt in 1773–1795, the government stopped raising taxes for twenty-five years, despite inflation, and noble landowners refrained from increasing rents.[221] After the Revolution of 1905–1907, the government abolished redemption payments and permitted workers to form unions.

Popular revolts were moments of truth for the autocracy, and in fact, they promoted the regime's consolidation rather than its disintegration.[222] First of all, revolts served as a kind of safety valve that permitted the public expression of popular dissatisfaction, although at the same time they resulted in property destruction and in the murder of officials, landowning nobles, and others who appeared guilty in the eyes of the people and whom it blamed for its burdensome situation. Such acts temporarily assuaged the people's hostility toward the existing order, the bureaucracy, and the nobility, and created the prerequisites for advancement to a new stage of toleration and anticipation. Second, the administration eliminated the most active of the malcontents through exile, prison, and execution, thereby intimidating the rest and depriving them of leaders. Last, the autocracy introduced alterations into the system of administration and the social structure, strengthening both. For example, after the 1648 revolt, the government issued a new collection of laws and other reforms; after Pugachev, a reform of local administration; after the Decembrist revolt, a reform of the state peasantry, preparations for the abolition of serfdom, and a change in economic policy; and after the Revolution of 1905–1907, the Stolypin agrarian reform and various political reforms. Similarly, the factory legislation of the 1880s and 1890s was the government's answer to the growing workers' movement. In 1905, workers were granted the legal right to express their opinion by means of strikes, meetings, and demonstrations—methods they had used illegally long before 1905.

Conclusion

From the point of view of the state's rights, prerogatives, and responsibilities, it is possible to divide the period under examination into two parts: the first, proceeding from the end of the seventeenth century to 1861, during which time these rights, prerogatives, and responsibilities began to increase as the state's jurisdiction expanded and absorbed some of the functions of local self-government; and the second, from 1861 to 1917, when the state's prerogatives were reduced as part of the state's authority was delegated to local public self-government. The balance of forces between state and society changed in tandem with changes in the strength of the state apparatus: Prior to 1861, the strength of this apparatus grew; after the Great Reforms, it declined. This was reflected in changes in the relative sizes of the bureaucracy and the army. In the seventeenth century, these forces were in equilibrium. From the late seventeenth century to the mid-nineteenth century, the balance shifted in favor of the state. The balance was reestablished between 1861 and 1881, and then shifted back to the state from 1881 to 1905. Finally, between 1905 and 1917, the balance again favored society. The nature of the relationship between the autocracy and society also changed significantly over time. Prior to the end of the seventeenth century, the sovereign looked on society as a handmaiden and servant; from the beginning of the eighteenth century to 1762, society was seen exclusively as a servant; from 1762 to the 1860s, as an object of tutelage; from 1860 to 1881, as a rival; from 1881 to 1905, as a competitor for power; and after 1905, as an enemy. This trajectory demonstrates that for Russia, from the eighteenth to the early twentieth centuries there was a constant asymmetry in the development of society and the state, which resulted in continual conflict.

During the period under study, society never merged with the state and never identified with the people as a whole. The makeup of "society" changed over time—which social groups agreed with the ideas of the sovereign and his government; which groups were included in society; which groups created public opinion; and whose opinion the autocracy regularly took into account when framing its policies. In addition, some societal groups developed a corporate consciousness and attempted consciously to influence state policy.

Until the late seventeenth century, the autocracy took the views of the entire population into account: With the exception of noble landowners' peasants and slaves, all ranks of the population were invited to participate in the assemblies of the land. These groups made corporate demands, and the autocracy listened. Therefore, one can say that society at this time included all social estates except privately owned peasants and slaves, and that all were creators of public opinion. Utilizing the same criteria, one can say that in the eighteenth and first half of the nineteenth centuries, society contracted to include only the nobility, the bureaucracy, the army, and the wealthy merchantry; and in the second half of the nineteenth century, with the abolition of serfdom, society again expanded to include all social groups of the population, aside from hired laborers and anyone who did not have the right to participate in elections to local organs of self-government. After the Revolution of 1905–1907, society included all ranks of the population.

Society was always engaged in a dialogue with the autocracy and was more or less successful in influencing policy. As a result, the autocracy, in the main, conducted a balanced and national policy. The degree to which it responded positively to society's demands depended on its attitude toward society at any given time. Before the 1820s, mutual understanding and a positive relationship existed to a considerable degree between society and the autocracy; then, under Nicholas I, there was a cooling-off, while under Alexander II, mutual understanding was reestablished. Following the accession of Alexander III, this relationship was again violated; and under Nicholas II, it was finally lost. Although society gained much during Nicholas's reign, he yielded only to force. As a consequence, the relationship between society and autocracy became more and more negative, eventually breaking into open hostilities, which led to revolution and the destruction of tsarism.

From the beginning of the eighteenth century until 1917, the Russian state evolved from an autocracy to a parliamentary republic, and society, from an object of state administration to a subject thereof. The notion of society expanded beyond the privileged social groups to include all the people, and "the people" developed a public identity. However, society in imperial Russia never acquired the capacity to spontaneously determine its own development, due to the state's inability to respond adequately to society's political demands, to develop the skills necessary to resolve problems peacefully, and to adapt to the changing conditions of life.[223] In this sense, Russia's society lagged behind its economy, which by 1914 had reached the level of self-sustaining growth. It is possible that this lack of harmony had its roots in the grandiose pretensions of the Russian state dating from the mid-sixteenth century—first, to become the "Third Rome," and later, a great power. Because the state lacked sufficient material resources to realize its ambitions, it became preoccupied with the country's economic development, to the detriment of social relations.

Why did Russia's modernization end in the collapse of the monarchy— its initiator and longtime champion? Until approximately the second half of the seventeenth century, society, the people, and the state had developed fairly harmoniously; the conflicts that arose were of a temporary character and were more or less successfully resolved. At this time, society and the people shared a fairly uniform cultural and political mentality: They did not oppose the state, nor did they identify with it; however, they had common goals with regard to the state administration.

At the end of the seventeenth century, while engaged in military conflict with Sweden, the state first became conscious of Russia's economic and cultural backwardness relative to western Europe and began to take steps to overcome this backwardness through modernization. But the autocracy nonetheless began to reshape the country in conformity with its own ideas as to what was good for Russia and with little regard for popular sentiment. Under Peter I, the initiator of these reforms, Russia achieved great military victories, which society linked with the Petrine reforms and the autocracy's correct and far-sighted policies. Society regarded victory as the result of the reforms, as the achievement of the autocracy rather than of society or the people. As a result, the state was deemed superior to both, and the latter accepted a subordinate role. The people did not understand the reforms and protested against them—although without much energy, and still maintaining their belief in the monarchical paradigm. The only serious opposition took place in the 1770s, during the Pugachev rebellion, and even then the peasantry protested not so much against the reforms as against their consequences—the strengthening of serfdom. Two circumstances explain the weakness of popular protest: The state allowed the people to live according to the old, pre-Petrine traditions and customs while it took control of relations between the serfs and their owners. With time, the state's intervention increased, eventually leading to the Emancipation of the serfs from the landowning nobles in 1861. Thus, beginning with Peter's reign, the state became the legitimate leader and society and the people became followers. This situation was convenient for all three parties, with the exception of the small stratum of intelligentsia, and allowed the autocracy to administer the country without any special problems as long as it conducted a balanced internal policy. Most of society supported the autocracy, whereas the intelligentsia was small in number and isolated from the people.

Meanwhile, in the course of the eighteenth century and the first half of the nineteenth century, modernization affected the higher strata of society far more than the lower strata. As a result, a cultural asymmetry arose in society: a split along cultural lines, into an educated, Europeanized minority, and the people as a whole, whose way of life continued to adhere to traditional Russian values. The split between society and the people led in the mid-nineteenth century to fissures within educated society, among liberals, radicals, conservatives, and extreme rightists, with each group proposing its own solution to the social, economic, and political problems facing Russia. Playing on these contradictions, the autocracy succeeded in balancing them for some time: It depended on the extreme right and the conservatives, made concessions to the liberals, and repressed the radicals. This policy was effective enough as long as the people, predominantly the peasantry, kept silent and remained staunchly monarchist in their political worldview. However, after the abolition of serfdom, ecological and demographic pressures gave rise to a huge agrarian overpopulation in the countryside; by 1900, in European Russia, half of all rural workers were, in effect, surplus, even though there was only an extremely small landless, rural proletariat. Nor could the city and industry provide employment for these 23 million workers.[224] The peasantry subsequently awoke and began to search for an exit from this situation, which it found in the expropriation of noble land. The confiscation of all noble lands would not have fully satisfied the peasants' land hunger, for it would only have increased their landed allotment by 41 percent, whereas 3.2 times this amount would have been needed in order to eliminate overpopulation and land hunger.[225] Second, the nobles' lands were already largely under peasant cultivation. Therefore, confiscation in the best scenario would have only minimally assuaged the peasants' situation. Nevertheless, some form of expropriation (with compensation for the nobility, as the liberals insisted) undoubtedly would have prolonged the life of the monarchy. But Nicholas II did not want to abandon his traditional ally, the landowning nobility, nor did he want to make concessions to the liberals on agrarian or political questions. Instead, the government adopted the Stolypin agrarian reform, which in spite of its strategic expediency found an echo only among a third of the peasantry and provoked the dissatisfaction of the majority. As a result, the peasantry turned to the socialists, who proposed a more attractive solution to the agrarian question: revolution and the confiscation of noble land.

The working class, being in large part of peasant origin and closely linked to the village, had a fundamentally peasant mentality. For this reason, and because of serious errors in the regime's labor policy, the workers' movement could not be confined within the limits of legal trade unions. Thus, the workers too turned to the social democrats, and were inclined to decide their problems by means of revolution.

The policies of the last two emperors with respect to society were characterized by an extraordinary lack of wisdom and foresight. Step by step, these two monarchs made enemies of educated society, workers, and peasants. Their mistakes not only brought about the downfall of the monarchy but also turned the popular opposition against autocracy into a revolutionary movement against the new democratic regime—but that is another story.[226]

Notes

1. David L. Sills, ed., *International Encyclopedia of the Social Sciences* (New York, 1964), vol. 15, p. 145. The authors of the entry "The State" do not give a general definition.

2. This point of view is defended in B. B. Dubentsov, "Samoderzhavie i chinovnichestvo v 1881–1904 gg.: Politika tsarskogo pravitel'stva v oblasti organizatsii gosudarstvennoi sluzhby" (dissertation, Moscow State University, 1977), p. 53; and in E. P. Karnovich, *Russkie chinovniki v byloe i nastoiashchee vremia* (St. Petersburg, 1897), p. 4.

3. John LeDonne includes only officials with middle or higher ranks who belonged to the hereditary nobility in the Russian bureaucracy, in the eighteenth century. (See his *Absolutism and the Ruling Class* [New York, 1991], p. ix.) Hans Rogger considers officials to be only those with a rank: See Hans Rogger, *Russia in the Age of Modernization and Revolution, 1881–1917* (New York and London, 1983), p. 49.

4. Karnovich, *Russkie chinovniki*, pp. 4–5.

5. V. N. Latkin, *Uchebnik istorii russkogo prava perioda imperii* (St. Petersburg, 1909), pp. 322–339; V. G. Chernukha, *Vnutrenniaia politika tsarizma s serediny 1850-kh gg. do nachala 1880-kh gg.* (Leningrad, 1978), pp. 136–198; D. N. Shanskii, "K kharakteristike vysshikh gosudarstvennykh uchrezhdenii Rossii XVII v. (20–60-e gg.)," in N. B. Golikova, ed., *Gosudarstvennye uchrezhdeniia Rossii XVI–XVIII vv.* (Moscow, 1991), pp. 119–136.

6. N. F. Demidova, *Sluzhilaia biurokratiia v Rossii XVII v. i ee rol' v formirovanii absoliutizma* (Moscow, 1987), p. 21.

7. Chernukha, *Vnutrenniaia politika*, pp. 196–198.

8. On the development of the administrative apparatus, see A. K. Leont'ev, *Obrazovanie prikaznoi sistemy upravleniia v russkom gosudarstve* (Moscow, 1961); N. P. Eroshkin, *Istoriia gosudarstvennykh uchrezhdenii dorevoliutsionnoi Rossii* (Moscow, 1983); Golikova, ed., *Gosudarstvennye uchrezhdeniia Rossii XVI–XVIII vv.*

9. Eroshkin, *Istoriia gosudarstvennykh uchrezhdenii*; idem, *Krepostnicheskoe samoderzhavie i ego politicheskie instituty* (Moscow, 1981); A. V. Chernov, *Gosudarstvennye uchrezhdeniia Rossii v XVII veke: Zakonodatel'nye materialy (Spravochnoe posobie)* (Moscow, 1960); Latkin, *Uchebnik istorii russkogo prava*, pp. 278–426; V. M. Gribovskii, *Gosudarstvennoe ustroistvo i upravlenie Rossiiskoi imperei* (Odessa, 1912); A. N. Epifanov, *Sistema gosudarstvennogo upravleniia* (Moscow, 1908); P. A. Zaionchkovskii, *Pravitel'stvennyi apparat samoderzhavnoi Rossii v XIX v.* (Moscow, 1978); V. S. Krivenko, *Sbornik kratkikh svedenii o pravitel'stvennykh uchrezhdeniiakh* (St. Petersburg, 1884); B. I. Syromiatnikov, *Kratkii obzor i ukazanie literatury po istorii gosudarstvennoi vlasti v Rossii* (Moscow, 1913); O. Eikhel'man, *Obzor tsentral'nykh i mestnykh uchrezhdenii upravleniia Rossii* (Kiev, 1890); N. P. Zagoskin, *Nauka istorii russkogo prava: Ee vspomogatel'nye znaniia, istochniki i literatura* (Kazan, 1891). The most complete guide to the history of state institutions is E. Amburger, *Geschichte der Behör denorganisation Russlands von Peter dem Grossen bis 1917* (Leiden, 1966). See also Marc Raeff, *The Well-Ordered Police State: Social and Institutional Change Through Law in the Germanies and Russia, 1600–1800* (New Haven, 1983); George Yaney, *The Systematization of Russian Government: Social Evolution in Domestic Administration of Imperial Russia, 1711–1905* (Urbana, 1973).

10. For 1897, data on the number of ranked officials were taken from A. P. Korelin, *Dvorianstvo v poreformennoi Rossii, 1861–1904 gg.: Sostav, chislennost', korporativnaia organizatsiia* (Moscow, 1979), pp. 91, 94; evidence on office workers, from *Obshchii svod po imperii rezul'tatov razrabotki dannykh pervoi vseobshchei perepisi naseleniia, proizvedennoi 28 ianvaria 1897 goda* (St. Petersburg, 1905) (hereafter, *Obshchii svod dannykh pervoi perepisi naseleniia*), tom 2, pp. 256–259. According to the Department of the State Treasury under the Ministry of Finance, in 1905 there were 91,204 officials who received a salary of 1,000 rubles or more: See *Opyt priblizitel'nogo ischisleniia narodnogo dokhoda po razlichnym ego istochnikam a po razmeram v Rossii* (St. Petersburg, 1906), pp. xxvii, 86–87; M. V. Klochkov, *Ocherki pravitel'stvennoi deiatel'nosti vremeni Pavla I* (Petrograd, 1916), p. 428.

11. Dubentsov, "Samoderzhavie i chinovnichestvo," pp. 61, 204.

12. N. A. Rubakin, *Rossiia v tsifrakh* (St. Petersburg, 1912), pp. 61–62, 66; idem, "Mnogo li v Rossii chinovnikov," *Vestnik Evropy* (January 1910), p. 116; N. P. Eroshkin, "Chinovnichestvo," in *Bol'shaia sovetskaia entsiklopediia*, 3-e izd. (Moscow, 1978), tom 29, pp. 206–208; P. A. Zaionchkovskii, *Pravitel'stvennyi apparat samoderzhavnoi Rossii v XIX v.* (Moscow, 1978), p. 71; Marc Raeff, "The Bureaucratic Phenomenon of Imperial Russia, 1700–1905," *American Historical Review*, vol. 84, no. 2 (April 1979), p. 4.

13. V. Trutovskii, *Sovremennoe zemstvo* (Petrograd, 1914), pp. 47–48.

14. V. I. Kovalevskii, ed., *Rossiia v kontse XIX veka* (St. Petersburg, 1900), pp. 777–784.

15. I. N. Blinov, "Otnoshenie Senata k mestnym uchrezhdeniem posle reform 60-kh godov: Senatorskie revizii," in *Istoriia Pravitel'stvuiushchego Senata za 200 let: 1711–1911* (St. Petersburg, 1911), tom 4, pp. 208–209.

16. Kovalevskii, *Rossiia v kontse XIX veka*, pp. 777, 787; B. N. Mironov, "Local Government in Russia in the First Half of the Nineteenth Century: Provincial Government and Estate Self-Government," *Jahrbücher für Geschichte Osteuropas*, Bd. 42, Heft 2 (1994), pp. 161–201.

17. Trutovskii, *Sovremennoe zemstvo*, pp. 47–48. See also Terence Emmons and Wayne S. Vucinich, eds., *The Zemstvo in Russia: An Experiment in Local Self-Government* (New York, 1982).

18. Kovalevskii, *Rossiia v kontse XIX veka*, pp. 777, 787.

19. V. Ia. Laverychev, "K voprosu o vmeshatel'stve tsarizma v ekonomicheskuiu zhizn' Rossii v nachale XX v.," in I. M. Pushkareva, ed., *Samoderzhavie i krupnyi kapital v Rossii v kontse XIX–nachale XX v.* (Moscow, 1981), pp. 66–97.

20. I. Blinov, *Gubernatory: Istoriko-iuridicheskii ocherk* (St. Petersburg, 1905), pp. 355–356.

21. Karnovich, *Russkie chinovniki*, pp. 113–114. See also *Samoderzhavie i zemstvo: Konfidentsial'naia zapiska ministra finansov stats-sekretaria S. Iu. Vitte (1899) s predisloviem i primechaniiami P. N. S. pechatano "Zarei"* (Stuttgart, 1901), pp. 21–43; Paul Vinogradoff, *Self-Government in Russia* (London, 1915), pp. 57–70.

22. R. A. Fadeev, *Pis'ma o sovremennom sostoianii Rossii* (St. Petersburg, 1881), pp. 3–8, 11.

23. A. A. Polovtsov, *Dnevnik Gosudarstvennogo sekretaria* (Moscow, 1966), tom 1, p. 237.

24. V. A. Tikhonov, *Dvadtsat' piat' let na kazennoi sluzhbe* (St. Petersburg, 1912), chast' 2, pp. 21–22.

25. S. Frederick Starr, *Decentralization and Self-Government in Russia, 1830–1870* (Princeton, 1972), p. 49.

26. Rubakin, *Rossiia v tsifrakh*, p. 62; Rogger, *Russia in the Age of Modernization*, p. 49.

27. Starr, *Decentralization and Self-Government*, pp. 44–50; D. I. Mendeleev, *K poznaniiu Rossii* (St. Petersburg, 1906), pp. 67–68.

28. Demidova, *Sluzhilaia biurokratiia v Rossii XVII v.*; S. M. Troitskii, *Russkii absoliutizm i dvorianstvo XVIII v.: Formirovanie biurokratii* (Moscow, 1974); Zaionchkovskii, *Pravitel'stvennyi apparat samoderzhavnoi Rossii v XIX v.*; S.V. Mironenko, *Samoderzhavie i reformy: Politicheskaia bor'ba v Rossii v nachale XIX v.* (Moscow, 1989), pp. 28–60; Walter M. Pintner, "The Evolution of Civil Officialdom, 1755–1855," in Walter M. Pinter and Don Karl Rowney, eds., *Russian Officialdom: The Bureaucratization of Russian Society from the Seventeenth to the Twentieth Century* (Chapel Hill, 1980), pp. 369–380; D. T. Orlovsky, *The Limits of Reform: The Ministry of Internal Affairs in Imperial Russia, 1802–1881* (Cambridge, and London, 1981), pp. 104–122; M. F. Rumiantseva, "Genealogiia rossiiskogo chinovnichestva vtoroi poloviny XVIII v.: Postanovka

problemy i istochniki izucheniia," in V. A. Murav'ev, ed., *Genealogicheskie issledovaniia* (Moscow, 1994), pp. 201–221.

29. Some scholars call this "ultrabureaucracy" *(sverkhbiurokratiei)*. Pintner and Rowney, eds., *Russian Officialdom,* p. 380.

30. P. N. Miliukov, *Ocherki po istorii russkoi kul'tury,* chast' 3, *Natsionalizm i evropeizm* (Moscow, 1995), p. 337; D. S. Likhachev and G. P. Makogonenko, eds., *Istoriia russkoi literatury* (Leningrad, 1980), vol. 1, pp. 572–574; V. G. Chernukha, *Pravitel'stvennaia politika v otnoshenii pechati 60–70-e gg. XIX veka* (Leningrad, 1989), pp. 6–22.

31. M. M. Shumilov, *Mestnoe upravlenie i tsentral'naia vlast' v Rossii v 50-kh–nachale 80-kh gg. XIX veka* (Moscow, 1991), pp. 185–189.

32. L. E. Shepelev, *Aktsionernye kompanii v Rossii* (Leningrad, 1973), pp. 129–133.

33. N. E. Pushkin, ed., *Statistika aktsionernogo dela v Rossii,* vyp. 1, *Sostav direktorov pravleniia na 1897 g.* (St. Petersburg, 1897); ibid., vyp. 4, *Ezhegodnik na 1901–1902 god: Lichnyi sostav vsekh pravlenii i otvetstvennykh agentov* (St. Petersburg, 1901); V. A. Dmitriev-Mamonov, ed., *Ukazatel' deistvuiushchikh v imperii aktsionernykh predpriiatii* (St. Petersburg, 1907); *Statistika aktsionernogo dela Rossii, 1913–14 god* (St. Petersburg, 1914). See also A. N. Bokhanov, *Krupnaia burzhuaziia Rossii* (Moscow, 1992), pp. 158–159.

34. Korelin, *Dvorianstvo v poreformennoi Rossii,* pp. 101–103.

35. Others consider the penetration of bourgeois elements into the state apparatus after the Emancipation of the serfs to be insignificant: See Zaionchkovskii, *Pravitel'stvennyi apparat,* pp. 104–105, 223–204.

36. Dubentsov, "Samoderzhavie i chinovnichestvo," pp. 6–10, 204.

37. Cited in *Polnoe sobranie zakonov Rossiiskoi imperii,* sobranie pervoe (hereafter, *PSZ 1*), tom 44, chast' 2, *Kniga shtatov* (St. Petersburg, 1830); *Entsiklopedicheskii slovar' F. A. Brokgauza i I. A. Efrona,* 41 toma (St. Petersburg, 1892), tom 7, p. 823, prilozhenie, tablitsa 1.

38. Troitskii, *Russkii absoliutizm,* pp. 253–267.

39. Cited in Zaionchkovskii, *Pravitel'stvennyi apparat,* p. 45.

40. M. Weber, *Wirtschaft und Gesellschaft* (Berlin, 1964), Band 2, pp. 162–163. In more recent scholarship, the ideal bureaucrat is characterized in the same way: See F. Heady, *Public Administration: A Comparative Perspective* (New York and Basel, 1983), pp. 60–66.

41. Hans-Joachim Torke, "Crime and Punishment in the Pre-Petrine Civil Service: The Problem of Control," in Ezra Mendelsohn and Marshall S. Shatz, eds., *Imperial Russia, 1700–1917: State, Society, Opposition* (DeKalb, 1988), pp. 5–21; Demidova, *Sluzhilaia biurokratiia,* pp. 80–89, 147–189; V. O. Kliuchevskii, *Sochineniia v 8 tomakh* (Moscow, 1959), tom 6, pp. 232–238; Peter B. Brown, "Muscovite Government Bureaus," *Russian History,* vol. 42, no. 3 (1983), p. 272; George G. Weickhardt, "Bureaucrats and Boiars in the Muscovite Tsardom," ibid., pp. 331–334; Daniel B. Rowland, "Did Muscovite Literary Ideology Place Limits on the Power of the Tsar (1540s–1660s)?" *Russian History,* vol. 49, no. 2 (1990), p. 139.

42. Great changes had already taken place under Peter I: See N. I. Pavlenko, *Petr Velikii* (Moscow, 1990), pp. 434–474.

43. Ibid., p. 435.

44. *Slovar' russkogo iazyka XI–XVII vv.* (Moscow, 1975), vyp. 2, p. 170; *Slovar' russkogo iazyka XVIII veka* (Leningrad, 1975), vyp. 3, p. 144; V. I. Dal', *Tolkovyi slovar' velikorusskogo iazyka* (Moscow, 1955), tom 1, p. 197.

45. Karnovich, *Russkie chinovniki*, p. 65.

46. David L. Ransel, "Bureaucracy and Patronage: The View from an Eighteenth-Century Russian Letter-Writer," in Frederic Jaher, ed., *The Rich, the Well-Born, and the Powerful: Studies of Elites and Upper Classes in History* (Urbana, 1973), pp. 166–167.

47. Troitskii, *Russkii absoliutizm*, pp. 140–154, 223–294; *Entsiklopedicheskii slovar' F. A. Brokgauza i I. A. Efrona* (St. Petersburg, 1895), tom 14, pp. 343–344; Pavlenko, *Petr Velikii*, pp. 508–510.

48. Ransel, "Bureaucracy and Patronage," pp. 154–178.

49. Andrew M. Verner, *The Crisis of Russian Autocracy: Nicholas II and the 1905 Revolution* (Princeton, 1990), pp. 45–69.

50. G. E. Petukhov, "Administrativnaia iustitsiia v tsarskoi Rossii," *Pravovedenie* (1974), no. 5, p. 73.

51. Eroshkin, *Krepostnicheskoe samoderzhavie i ego politicheskie instituty*, p. 80.

52. Dubentsov, "Samoderzhavie i chinovnichestvo," p. 49.

53. N. M. Korkunov, *Russkoe gosudarstvennoe pravo* (St. Petersburg, 1893), tom 2, pp. 402–403.

54. Karnovich, *Russkie chinovniki*, p. 118.

55. According to the 1897 census, there were approximately 112,000 males with a higher education in Russia, excluding Poland and Finland; 57,000 of these were government officials. Cited in *Obshchii svod dannykh pervoi perepisi naseleniia*, tom 2, pp. 188–189, 198–199.

56. Karnovich, *Russkie chinovniki*, pp. 112–113; N. Flerovskii, *Tri politicheskie sistemy: Nikolai I, Aleksandr II i Aleksandr III; Vospominaniia* (Berlin, 1897), p. 21.

57. Amburger, *Geschichte der Behördenorganisation Russlands*, pp. 514–519.

58. Rossiiskii gosudarstvennyi istoricheskii arkhiv (hereafter, RGIA), fond 1375 (Reviziia senatorov D. P. Troshchinskogo i P. P. Shcherbatova Moskovskoi, Vladimirskoi, Riazanskoi, Tambovskoi, Kaluzhskoi i Tul'skoi gubernii), opis' 1, dela 1–64 (1799–1800); A. E. Nol'de, "Pravitel'stvuiushchii senat v tsarstvovanie Pavla I: Reviziia 1799g.," in *Istoriia Pravitel'stvuiushchego senata za dvesti let: 1710–1910* (St. Petersburg, 1911), tom 2, pp. 754–779; I. N. Blinov, "Otnoshenie Senata k mestnym uchrezhdeniiam do reform 60-kh gg.: Senatorskie revizii," in ibid., tom 3, pp. 616–657 and tom 4, pp. 180–214; Blinov, "Istoricheskie materialy, izvlechennye iz Senatskogo arkhiva: Reviziia senatorom Begichevym Orlovskoi gubernii," *Zhurnal Ministerstva iustitsii*, 1913, no. 4, pp. 242–268; N. M. Druzhinin, "Senatorskie revizii 1860–1870-kh godov," *Istoricheskie zapiski* (1966), tom 79, p. 39. My observations are preliminary in nature, since a systematic study of the materials from the senatorial inspections, which include thousands of complaints, would require a huge amount of effort that is beyond the capacities of a single scholar.

59. D. C. B. Lieven, *Russia's Rulers Under the Old Regime* (New Haven, 1989).

60. Richard G. Robbins, Jr., *The Tsar's Viceroys: Russian Provincial Governors in the Last Years of the Empire* (Ithaca and London, 1987).

61. Among the advocates of the first point of view are Marc Raeff (see "The Russian Autocracy and Its Officials," in Hugh McLean et al., *Russian Thought and Politics*, Harvard Slavic Studies, vol. 4 [1957], pp. 77–90); H.-J. Torke (*Das Russische Beamtentum in der ersten Hälfte des 19. Jahrhunderts* [Berlin, 1967], pp. 158–159); and Rogger (*Russia in the Age of Modernization*, pp. 44–70). Advocates of the second point of view are Starr (*Decentralization and Self-Government in Russia, 1830–1870*, pp. 128–138); Pintner and Rowney (*Russian Officialdom*, pp. 369–380); Richard S. Wortman (*The Development of a Russian Legal Consciousness* [Chicago and London, 1976], pp. 197–235; Wortman's observations relate to officials in the Ministry of Justice); Daniel Field (*The End of Serfdom: Nobility and Bureaucracy in Russia, 1855–1861* [Cambridge, 1976], pp. 51–101); W. Bruce Lincoln (*In the Vanguard of Reform: Russia's Enlightened Bureaucrats, 1825–1861* [De Kalb, 1982], pp. 102–138, 168–211; *Nikolai Miliutin: An Enlightened Bureaucrat of the 19th Century* [Newtownville, 1977]; and *The Great Reforms: Autocracy, Bureaucracy, and the Politics of Change in Imperial Russia* [De Kalb, 1990]); Sidney Monas ("Bureaucracy in Russia Under Nicholas I," in Michael Cherniavsky, ed., *The Structure of Russian History* [New York, 1970], pp. 269–281); Thomas S. Pearson (*Russian Officialdom in Crisis: Autocracy and Local Self-Government, 1861–1900* [Cambridge, 1989], pp. 1–20); David A.J. Macey (*Government and Peasant in Russia, 1861–1906: The Pre-History of the Stolypin Reforms* [De Kalb, 1987]); Francis W. Wcislo (*Reforming Rural Russia: State, Local Society, and National Politics, 1855–1914* [Princeton, 1991], pp. xiii–xvi); I. F. Gindin (*Gosudarstvennyi bank i ekonomicheskaia politika tsarskogo pravitel'stva: 1861–1892* [Moscow, 1960]); and L. E. Shepelev (*Tsarizm i burzhuaziia vo vtoroi polovine XIX veka* [Leningrad, 1981], pp. 71–82, 135–157, 193–204). See also the review of American literature of 1980s on the Russian bureaucracy: Ronald G. Suny, "Rehabilitating Tsarism: The Imperial Russian State and Its Historians; A Review Article," *Comparative Studies in Society and History*, vol. 31, no. 1 (January 1989), pp. 168–179.

62. Weber, *Wirtschaft*, Band 2, p. 165.

63. S. V. Volkov, *Russkii ofitserskii korpus* (Moscow, 1993), pp. 281–282, 355–356.

64. Dal', *Tolkovyi slovar'*, tom 2, p. 634.

65. Chernukha, *Pravitel'stvennaia politika v otnoshenii pechati*, p. 6.

66. T. V. Andreeva, "Russkoe obshchestvo i 14 dekabria 1825 g.," *Otechestvennaia istoriia*, no. 2 (1993), pp. 156–161.

67. Ia. E. Vodarskii, *Naselenie Rossii v kontse XVII–nachale XVIII veka (Chislennost', soslovno-klassovyi sostav, razmeshchenie)* (Moscow, 1977), pp. 90, 134, 192.

68. Ibid., p. 48.

69. Vodarskii, *Naselenie Rossii*, pp. 64–65, 82, 90, 134, 192; A. Bushen, ed., *Statisticheskie tablitsy Rossiiskoi imperii* (St. Petersburg, 1893), vyp. 2, pp. 267, 293; Obruchev, ed., *Voenno-statisticheskii sbornik*, vyp. 4, otdel 2, p. 40.

70. V. A. Nardova, *Gorodskoe samoupravlenie v Rossii v 60-kh–nachale 90-kh gg. XIX v.: Pravitel'stvennaia politika* (Leningrad, 1984), p. 62.

71. Between 1883 and 1886, 423,000 people had the right to participate in zem-stvo elections out of 66 million inhabitants in the 34 provinces with zemstvos (*Sbornik svedenii po Rossii 1890 goda* [St. Petersburg, 1890], pp. 48–51).

72. V. A. Nardova, "Organy gorodskogo samoupravleniia v sisteme samod-erzhavnogo apparata vlasti v kontse XIX–nachale XX v.," in *Reformy ili revoliut-siia? Rossiia 1861–1917* (St. Petersburg, 1992), pp. 57–58.

73. In accordance with official data, 3.3 percent of the population: See Minister-stvo vnutrennikh del, *Vybory v Gosudarstvennuiu Dumu tret'ego sozyva: Statis-ticheskii otchet osobogo deloproizvodstva* (St. Petersburg, 1911), pp. vii–x. See also Steven White, *Political Culture and Soviet Politics* (New York, 1979), p. 29.

74. Leopold H. Haimson, "The Parties and the State: The Evolution of Political Attitudes," in Cyril Black, ed., *The Transformation of Russian Society: Aspects of Social Change Since 1861* (Cambridge, 1960), pp. 110–111.

75. Bushen, ed., *Statisticheskie tablitsy,* vyp. 2, p. 264.

76. B. N. Mironov, "Bureaucratic or Self-Government: The Early Nineteenth-Century Russian City," *Slavic Review,* vol. 52, no. 2 (Summer 1993), pp. 251–255.

77. Hans Rogger, *National Consciousness in Eighteenth-Century Russia* (Cam-bridge, 1960).

78. P. N. Miliukov, *Ocherki po istorii russkoi kultury,* chast' 3, *Natsionalizm i obshchestvennoe mnenie* (St. Petersburg, 1903), vyp. 2, pp. 16–19; Hans-Joachim Torke, "Continuity and Change in the Relations Between Bureaucracy and Society in Russia, 1613–1861," *Canadian Slavic Studies,* vol. 5, no. 4 (1971); vol. 6, no. 1 (1972).

79. Cited in I. Trotskii, *III-e Otdelenie pri Nikolae I* (Leningrad, 1990), pp. 30–31.

80. In his memoirs, B. N. Chicherin, the well-known Russian social activist and historian, described how his studies at Moscow University during the years be-tween 1845 and 1849—when free social thought had become so difficult—made a liberal of him. See *Russkoe obshchestvo 40–50-kh godov XIX v.,* chast' 2, *Vospom-inaniia B.N. Chicherina* (Moscow, 1991), pp. 9–65.

81. P. N. Miliukov, *Iz istorii russkoi intelligentsii* (St. Petersburg, 1903); Marc Raeff, *Origins of the Russian Intelligentsia: The Eighteenth-Century Nobility* (New York, 1966).

82. Isaiah Berlin, *Russian Thinkers* (New York, 1978); Andrzej Walicki, *A His-tory of Russian Thought from Enlightenment to Marxism* (Stanford, 1979); Vladimir C. Nahirny, *The Russian Intelligentsia: From Torment to Silence* (Lon-don and New Brunswick, 1983); Theofanis G. Stavrou, ed., *Russia Under the Last Tsar* (Minneapolis, 1969), especially the articles by Robert Byrnes, Donald W. Treadgold, and Timothy Riha; V. Bogucharskii, *Iz proshlogo russkogo ob-shchestva: Obshchestvennoe dvizhenie v Rossii v pervuiu polovinu XIX veka* (St. Petersburg, 1905); E. A. Dudzinskaia, *Slavianofily v obshchestvennoi bor'be* (Moscow, 1983); B. S. Itenberg, ed., *Revoliutsionery i liberaly Rossii* (Moscow, 1990); Sh. M. Levin, *Ocherki po istorii russkoi obshchestvennoi mysli: Vtoraia polovina XIX–nachalo XX v.* (Leningrad, 1974); V. N. Rozental', "Ideinye tsentry liberal'nogo dvizheniia v Rossii nakanune revoliutsionnoi situatsii," in M. V. Nechkina, ed., *Revoliutsionnaia situatsiia v Rossii v 1859–1861 gg.* (Moscow, 1963); L. E. Shishko, *Obshchestvennoe dvizhenie v shestidesiatykh i pervoi polovine semidesiatykh godov* (Moscow, 1920); N. G. Sladkevich, *Ocherki istorii*

obshchestvennoi mysli Rossii v kontse 50-kh–nachale 60-kh godov XIX v.: Bor'ba obshchestvennykh techenii v gody pervoi revoliutsionnoi situatsii (Leningrad, 1962); N. I. Tsimbaev, *Slavianofil'stvo: Iz istorii russkoi obshchestvenno-politich-eskoi mysli XIX v.* (Moscow, 1986).

83. Leonard Shapiro, *Rationalism and Nationalism in Russian Nineteenth-Century Political Thought* (New Haven and London, 1964); Edward C. Thaden, *Conservative Nationalism in Nineteenth-Century Russia* (Seattle, 1964); *Issledovaniia po konservatizmu*, 4 toma (Perm, 1994–1997); D. Khomiakov, *Samoderzhavie: Opyt skhematicheskogo postroeniia etogo poniatiia* (Moscow, 1903); "Konservatizm v Rossii," *Sotsiologicheskie issledovaniia*, no. 1 (1993), pp. 42–61; E. L. Rudnitskaia, ed., *V razdum'iakh o Rossii (XIX v.)* (Moscow, 1996); Iu. F. Samarin and F. M. Dmitriev, *Revoliutsionnyi konservatizm: Kniga R. Fadeeva "Russkoe obshchestvo v nastoiashchem i budushchem" i predpolozheniia peter-burgskikh dvorian ob organizatsii vsesoslovnoi volosti* (Berlin, 1875); N. V. Sinitsina, *Tretii Rim: Istoki i evoliutsiia kontseptsii* (Moscow, 1997); L. A. Tikhomirov, *Monarkhicheskaia gosudarstvennost'* (St. Petersburg, 1992).

84. Charles E. Timberlake, ed., *Essays on Russian Liberalism* (Columbia, 1972); Shmuel Galai, *The Liberation Movement in Russia, 1900–1905* (New York, 1973); D. A. Andreev, "Rossiiskii liberalizm i Gosudarstvennaia Duma (Obzor anglo-amerikanskoi istoriografii)," *Vestnik Moskovskogo universiteta*, seriia 8, *Istoriia*, no. 2 (1995), pp. 16–23; A. V. Gogolevskii, *Ocherki istorii russkogo liberalizma v XIX–nachale XX vv.* (St. Petersburg, 1996); V. V. Leontovich, *Istoriia liberalizma v Rossii, 1762–1914* (Moscow, 1995); N. M. Pirumova, *Zemskoe liberal'noe dvizhe-nie: Sotsial'nye korni i evoliutsiia do nachala XX v.* (Moscow, 1977); idem, *Zem-skaia intelligentsiia i ee rol' v obshchestvennoi bor'be do nachala XX v.* (Moscow, 1986); G. Rormozer, *Krizis liberalizma* (Moscow, 1996); K. F. Shatsillo, *Russkii lib-eralizm nakanune revoliutsii 1905–1907 gg.: Organizatsiia, programmy, taktika* (Moscow, 1985).

85. Aavrahm Yarmolinsky, *Road to Revolution: A Century of Russian Radical-ism* (Princeton, 1975); Daniel R. Brower, *Training the Nihilists: Education and Radicalism in Tsarist Russia* (Ithaca and London, 1975); Adam B. Ulam, *Ideologies and Illusions: Revolutionary Thought from Herzen to Solzhenitsyn* (Cambridge, and London, 1976); Abbott Gleason, *Young Russia: The Genesis of Russian Radi-calism in the 1860s* (New York, 1980); I. K. Pantin, E. G. Plimak, and V. G. Khoros, *Revoliutsionnaia traditsiia v Rossii, 1783–1883* (Moscow, 1986); E. A. Kirillova, *Ocherki radikalizma v Rossii XIX veka: Filosofsko-istoricheskie kontseptsii 40–60-kh godov* (Novosibirsk, 1991).

86. M. I. Aronson and S. A. Reiser, eds., *Literaturnye kruzhki i salony* (Leningrad, 1929); N. L. Brodskii, ed., *Literaturnye salony i kruzhki: Pervaia polovina XIX veka* (Moscow and Leningrad, 1930); I. V. Filipchenko, "Obshchest-venno-ideinaia zhizn' v Moskovskikh literaturnykh salonakh," *Vestnik Moskovskogo universiteta*, seriia 8, *Istoriia*, no. 5 (1991), pp. 37–49; Richard Pipes, *Russia Under the Old Regime* (New York, 1974), pp. 262–265.

87. N. M. Karamzin, *Zapiska o staroi i novoi Rossii v ee politicheskom i grazh-danskom otnosheniiakh* (Moscow, 1991), pp. 48, 102, 105, et passim.

88. Tikhomirov, *Monarkhicheskaia gosudarstvennost'* (St. Petersburg, 1992), pp. 94–101, 247–254.

89. Thaden, *Conservative Nationalism*, pp. xiii, 59.

90. Anatole G. Mazour, *The First Russian Revolution, 1825: The Decembrist Movement, Its Origin, Development, and Significance* (Stanford, 1965); Marc Raeff, *The Decembrist Movement* (Englewood Cliffs, 1966); idem, *Understanding Imperial Russia: State and Society in the Old Regime* (New York, 1984), pp. 142–145.

91. Raeff, *The Decembrist Movement*; V. I. Semevskii, *Politicheskie i obshchestvennye idei dekabristov* (St. Petersburg, 1909); M. V. Nechkina, *Dvizhenie dekabristov*, 2 toma (Moscow, 1955); A. E. Presniakov, *14 dekabria 1825 g.* (Moscow and Leningrad, 1926); V. I. Semevskii, *Politicheskie i obshchestvennye idei dekabristov* (St. Petersburg, 1909); P. E. Shchegolev, *Dekabristy* (Moscow and Leningrad, 1926); G. Vernadskii, "Dva lika dekabristov," *Svobodnaia mysl'*, no. 15 (1993), pp. 82–92.

92. B. N. Mironov, *Istoriia v tsifrakh* (Leningrad, 1991), p. 82.

93. N. M. Druzhinin, *Dekabrist Nikita Murav'ev* (Moscow, 1933), pp. 303–309.

94. P. A. Zaionchkovskii, *Otmena krepostnogo prava v Rossii* (Moscow, 1968), p. 87.

95. *Arkhiv grafov Mordvinovykh* (St. Petersburg, 1910), tom 10, p. 155.

96. N. Shil'der, "Mezhdutsarstvie v Rossii s 19 noiabria po 14 dekabria," *Russkaia starina*, tom 35 (1882).

97. V. I. Krutikov, "Zakonodatel'stvo o pomeshchich'ikh krest'ianakh doreformennogo vremeni," in V. T. Pashuto, ed., *Sotsial'no-ekonomicheskie problemy rossiiskoi derevni v feodal'nuiu i kapitalisticheskuiu epokhi* (Rostov-on-Don, 1980), pp. 112–120.

98. W. Bruce Lincoln, *Nicholas I: Emperor and Autocrat of All the Russians* (Bloomington, 1978); Andreeva, "Russkoe obshchestvo," p. 156; idem, "Nikolai I i dekabristy (k postanovke problemy reform)," in A. A. Fursenko, ed., *Rossiia v XIX–XX vv.: Sbornik statei k 70-letiiu so dnia rozhdeniia R. Sh. Ganelina* (St. Petersburg, 1998), pp. 140–146; A. Kizevetter, *Istoricheskie ocherki* (Moscow, 1912), pp. 402–418, 419–502.

99. Andreeva, "Russkoe obshchestvo," pp. 159, 161.

100. The history of this schism between society and the state is clearly and convincingly described in Marc Raeff, *Understanding Russia: State and Society in the Old Regime* (New York, 1984); Nicholas V. Riasanovsky, *A Parting of the Ways: Government and Educated Public in Russia, 1801–1855* (Oxford, 1976); and Jacob Walkin, *The Rise of Democracy in Pre-Revolutionary Russia: Political and Social Institutions Under the Last Three Tsars* (New York, 1962).

101. Raeff, *Understanding Imperial Russia*, pp. 214–215, 225–226.

102. L. M. Spirin, ed., *Neproletarskie partii Rossii: Urok istorii* (Moscow, 1984), p. 3; A. I. Zevelev, ed., *Istoriia politicheskikh partii Rossii* (Moscow, 1994), p. 11.

103. N. A. Berdiaev, *Istoki i smysl russkogo kommunizma* (Moscow, 1990), pp. 31–62, 103.

104. V. G. Korolenko, *Istoriia moego sovremennika*, in Korolenko, *Sobranie sochinenii v piati tomakh* (Leningrad, 1991), tom 5, p. 254.

105. Michael Cherniavsky, *Tsar and People: Studies in Russian Myths* (New Haven, 1961), pp. 82–84, 183–184; I. V. Poberezhnikov, "Narodnaia monarkhi-

cheskaia kontseptsiia na Urale (XVIII–pervaia polovina XIX v.)," *Ural'skii istoricheskii vestnik*, no. 1 (1994), pp. 21–42; idem, "Materialy po istorii narodnoi politicheskoi kul'tury (XVIII v.)," *Ural'skii istoricheskii vestnik*, no. 1 (1994), pp. 132–146; D. I. Raskin, "Nekotorye cherty psikhologii narodnykh mass Rossii XVIII v.," in E. P. Karpeev, ed., *Nauka i kul'tura Rossii XVIII veka* (Leningrad, 1984), pp. 225–247.

106. Daniel Field, *Rebels in the Name of the Tsar* (Boston, 1976), pp. 1–29; V. G. Korolenko, "Zemli! Zemli! Mysli, vospominaniia, kartiny," *Novyi mir*, no. 1 (1990), p. 178; B. G. Litvak, *Krest'ianskoe dvizhenie v Rossii v 1775–1904 gg.* (Moscow, 1989), pp. 252–253; idem, *Perevorot 1861 goda v Rossii* (Moscow, 1991), p. 210: K. V. Chistov, *Russkie narodnye sotsial'no-utopicheskie legendy XVII–XIX vv.* (Moscow, 1967), p. 217.

107. A. A. Korinfskii, *Narodnaia Rus': Kruglyi god skazanii, poverii, obychaev i poslovits russkogo naroda* (Moscow, 1995), pp. 81–85; Tikhomirov, *Monarkhicheskaia gosudarstvennost'*, pp. 272–302.

108. Tikhomirov, *Monarkhicheskaia gosudarstvennost'*, pp. 254–274, 272–302.

109. V. Babarykin, "Sel'tso Vasil'evskoe, Nizhegorodskoi gubernii, Nizhegorodskogo uezda," *Etnograficheskii sbornik, izdavaemyi imp. Russkim geograficheskim obshchestvom* (St. Petersburg, 1853), vyp. 1, p. 20; ibid., vyp. 2, pp. 94–96, 107–109ff.

110. P. Longworth, "The Pretender Phenomenon in Eighteenth-Century Russia," *Past and Present*, no. 66 (1975), pp. 61–83; Marc Raeff, "Pugachev's Rebellion," in Robert Forster and Jack P. Greene, eds., *Preconditions of Revolution in Early Modern Europe* (Baltimore, 1970), pp. 161–200; N. V. Razorenova, "Iz istorii samozvanstva v Rossii 30-kh godov XVII v.," *Vestnik Moskovskogo universiteta*, ser. 9, *Istoriia*, no. 6 (1974), pp. 54–74; K. V. Sivkov, "Samozvanchestvo v Rossii v poslednei treti XVIII v.," *Istoricheskie zapiski*, tom 31 (1950), pp. 88–135; S.M. Troitskii, "Samozvantsy v Rossii XVII–XVIII vv.," *Voprosy istorii*, no. 3 (1963), pp. 134–146; B. A. Uspenskii, "Tsar i samozvanets: Samozvanchestvo v Rossii kak kul'turno-istoricheskii fenomen," in V. A. Karpushin, ed., *Khudozhestvennyi iazyk srednevekov'ia* (Moscow, 1982), pp. 201–235.

111. Field, *Rebels in the Name of the Tsar*, pp. 1–29.

112. B. L. Modzalevskii and Iu. G. Oksman, eds., *Dekabristy: Neizdannye materialy i stat'i* (Moscow, 1925), p. 40.

113. A. I. Klibanov, *Religioznoe sektantstvo v proshlom i nastoiashchem* (Moscow, 1973), pp. 16–23.

114. V. Ia. Bogucharskii, *Aktivnoe narodnichestvo semidesiatykh godov* (Moscow, 1911); B. S. Itenberg, *Dvizhenie revoliutsionnogo narodnichestva* (Moscow, 1965), pp. 266–360.

115. Korolenko, "Istoriia moego sovremennika," p. 254.

116. Daniel Field, "Peasants and Propagandists in the Russian Movement to the People of 1874," in *Journal of Modern History*, vol. 59, no. 3 (September 1987), pp. 415–438.

117. N. A. Troitskii, *Tsarizm pod sudom progressivnoi obshchestvennosti, 1866–1895 gg.* (Moscow, 1979), pp. 121–182.

118. R. E. Rutman, "Rabochee dvizhenie pered otmenoi krepostnogo prava," in Nechkina, ed., *Revoliutsionnaia situatsiia v Rossii v 1859–1861 gg.* (Moscow,

1962), tom 2, pp. 189–229; T. M. Kitanina, *Rabochie Peterburga 1800–1861 gg.* (Leningrad, 1991), pp. 263–279; V. Ia. Shkerin, "K kharakteristike politicheskogo i pravovogo soznaniia ural'skikh rabochikh pervoi poloviny XIX v.," in *Vlast', pravo i narod na Urale v epokhu feodalizma* (Sverdlovsk, 1991), pp. 165–179.

119. M. A. Dikarev, "Tolki naroda o skoroi konchine sveta," *Etnograficheskoe obozrenie*, kniga 21, no. 2 (1894), pp. 157–161; D. S. Sekirinskii, "Stadii formirovaniia klassovogo samosoznaniia krest'ianstva v kontse XIX–nachale XX veka (Po materialam Tavricheskoi gubernii)," in V. T. Pashuto, ed., *Sotsial'no-ekonomicheskie problemy Rossiiskoi derevni v feodal'nuiu i kapitalisticheskuiu epokhi* (Rostov-on-Don, 1980), pp. 257–260; L. M. Goriushkin, ed., *Krest'ianstvo Sibiri v epokhu kapitalizma* (Novosibirsk, 1983), pp. 162–163; A. P. Okladnikov, ed., *Krest'ianstvo Sibiri v epokhu feodalizma* (Novosibirsk, 1982), pp. 447–457.

120. P. Avrich, *Russian Rebels, 1600–1800* (New York and London, 1976); compare with B. B. Veselovskii, *Krest'ianskii vopros i krest'ianskoe dvizhenie v Rossii (1902–1906 gg.)* (St. Petersburg, 1907); idem, *Materialy po istorii krest'ianskikh dvizhenii v Rossii* (Moscow, 1923).

121. Z. K. Ianel', "Fenomen stikhiinosti i povstancheskaia organizatsiia massovykh dvizhenii feodal'nogo krest'ianstva Rossii," *Istoriia SSSR*, no. 5 (1982), p. 93.

122. L. T. Senchakova, *Krest'ianskoe dvizhenie v revoliutsii 1905–1907 gg.* (Moscow, 1989), pp. 223–228; idem, "Istoriografiia prigovornogo dvizheniia krest'ianstva v 1905–1907 gg.," in E. D. Chermenskii, ed., *Pervaia rossiiskaia revoliutsiia, 1905–1907 gg.: Obzor sovetskoi i zarubezhnoi literatury* (Moscow, 1991), pp. 58–86.

123. P. N. Pershin, *Agrarnaia revoliutsiia v Rossii*, kniga 1, *Ot reformy k revoliutsii* (Moscow, 1966), pp. 250, 271–283; A. M. Anfimov, *Rossiiskaia derevnia v gody mirovoi voiny (1914–fevral' 1916 g.)* (Moscow, 1962), pp. 339–364.

124. Tim McDaniel, *Autocracy, Capitalism, and Revolution in Russia* (Berkeley, 1988), pp. 79, 175; Robert E. Johnson, *Peasant and Proletarian: The Working Class of Moscow in the Late Nineteenth Century* (New Brunswick, 1979), pp. 67–79. On the formation of an elite of politically conscious workers, see McDaniel, *Autocracy*, pp. 164–165.

125. V. I. Startsev, *Russkaia burzhuaziia i samoderzhavie v 1905–1917 gg.* (Leningrad, 1977), pp. 109–110.

126. S. A. Stepanov, *Chernaia sotnia v Rossii (1905–1914 gg.)* (Moscow, 1992), p. 224.

127. S. A. Stepanov, "Chislennost' i sostav chernosotennykh soiuzov i organizatsii," in Iu. I. Kir'ianov, ed., *Politicheskie partii Rossii v period revoliutsii, 1905–1907 gg.: Kolichestvennyi analiz* (Moscow, 1987), pp. 193–195.

128. Stepenov, *Chernaia sotnia*, pp. 236–264; Maureen Perrie, "The Russian Peasant Movement of 1905–1907: Its Social Composition and Revolutionary Significance," *Past and Present*, no. 57 (November 1972), pp. 123–155.

129. *Minuvshee: Istoricheskii al'manakh* (Moscow and St. Petersburg, 1993), tom 14, pp. 190–196.

130. D. S. Sekirinskii, "Stadii formirovaniia klassovogo samosoznaniia krest'ianstva v kontse XIX–nachale XX veka (po materialam Tavricheskoi gubernii)," in V. T. Pashuto, ed., *Sotsial'no-ekonomicheskie problemy Rossiiskoi*

derevni v feodal'nuiu i kapitalisticheskuiu epokhi (Rostov-on-Don, 1980), pp. 257–260.

131. A. Ia. Avrekh, *Tsarizm nakanune sverzheniia* (Moscow, 1989), pp. 214–238; F. Jahn Hubertus, "For Tsar and Fatherland? Russian Popular Culture and the First World War," in Stephen P. Frank and Mark D. Steinberg, eds., *Culture in Flux: Lower-Class Values, Practices, and Resistance in Late Imperial Russia* (Princeton, 1994), pp. 131–146.

132. RGIA, f. 796 (Kantseliariia Sinoda), op. 53, d. 137.

133. I. I. Ignatovich, *Krest'ianskoe dvizhenie v Rossii v pervoi chetverti XIX veka* (Moscow, 1963), p. 447.

134. A. V. Predtechenskii, ed., *Krest'ianskoe dvizhenie v Rossii v 1826–1849 gg.* (Moscow, 1961), pp. 345, 355.

135. V. I. Semevskii, *Krest'ianskii vopros v Rossii v XVII i pervoi polovine XIX veka* (St. Petersburg, 1888), tom 2, p. 580.

136. D. I. Uspenskii, "Tolki naroda," *Etnograficheskoe obozrenie*, no. 2 (1893), pp. 183–189.

137. B. S. Itenberg, ed., *Rossiia v revoliutsionnoi situatsii na rubezhe 1870–1880-kh godov* (Moscow, 1983), pp. 161–168.

138. M. A. Rakhmatullin, *Krest'ianskoe dvizhenie v velikorusskikh guberniiakh v 1826–1857 gg.* (Moscow, 1990), p. 163.

139. Ibid., pp. 122–166.

140. S. V. Maksimov, *Izbrannye proizvedeniia* (Moscow, 1987), tom 2, p. 434.

141. RGIA, f. 1284 (Departament obshchikh del Ministerstva vnutrennikh del), op. 208, d. 480a, l. 18.

142. B. N. Mironov, *Vnutrennii rynok Rossii vo vtoroi polovine XVIII–pervoi polovine XIX v.* (Leningrad, 1981), pp. 65–66, 149, 154, 177, 214, 143–147; S. A. Arutiunov, "Innovatsii v kul'ture etnosa i ikh sotsial'no-ekonomicheskaia obuslovlennost'," in A. I. Pershits and N. B. Ter-Akoipian, eds., *Etnograficheskie issledovaniia razvitiia kul'tury* (Moscow, 1985), p. 45; B. F. Egorov and A. D. Koshelev, eds., *Iz istorii russkoi kul'tury*, tom 5, *XIX vek* (Moscow, 1995), p. 371.

143. F. Shcherbina, "Peredacha i obrashchenie narodnykh znanii," *Ustoi*, no. 5 (1885), p. 1–24.

144. V. F. Milovidov, *Staroobriadchestvo v proshlom i nastoiashchem* (Moscow, 1969).

145. N. M. Nikol'skii, *Istoriia russkoi tserkvi* (Moscow, 1931), p. 292.

146. Ibid., p. 276.

147. B. N. Mironov, *Russkii gorod v 1740–1890-e gody* (Leningrad, 1990), p. 22.

148. M. G. Rabinovich, *Ocherki etnografii russkogo feodal'nogo goroda: Gorozhane, ikh obshchestvennyi i domashnii byt* (Moscow, 1978), pp. 281–185; idem, *Ocherki material'noi kul'tury russkogo feodal'nogo goroda* (Moscow, 1988), pp. 265–269.

149. Jeffrey Brooks, *When Russia Learned to Read: Literacy and Popular Literature, 1861–1917* (Princeton, 1985), pp. 178–210; I. I. Frolova, ed., *Kniga v Rossii, 1861–1881* (Moscow, 1991), tom 3, pp. 69–86; idem, *Kniga v Rossii, 1881–1895* (St. Petersburg, 1997), pp. 305–317; A. S. Prugavin, *Zaprosy naroda i obiazannosti intelligentsii v oblasti prosveshcheniia i vospitaniia* (St. Petersburg,

1895), pp. 215–216; A. I. Reitblat, *Ot Bovy k Bal'montu: Ocherki po istorii chteniia v Rossii vo vtoroi polovine XIX v.* (Moscow, 1991); *Sbornik svedenii po Rossii za 1883 god* (St. Petersburg, 1886), pp. 44–45; *Sbornik statisticheskikh svedenii po Moskovskoi gubernii* (Moscow, 1884), tom 9, p. 150.

150. Some historians believe this to be a tradition of Russian political culture: Tibor Szamuely, *The Russian Tradition* (New York, 1974), pp. 37–48. For a review of the literature on the question of society-state interaction, see Ronald G. Suny, "Rehabilitating Tsarism," pp. 168–179.

151. Herbert J. Ellison, *A History of Russia* (New York, 1964).

152. M. I. Semevskii, *Slovo i delo, 1770–1725: Tainaia kantseliariia pri Petre Velikom* (St. Petersburg, 1885); V. Ia. Ulanov, "Oppozitsiia Petru Velikomu," in V. V. Kalash, ed., *Tri veka: Rossiia ot Smuty do nashego vremeni* (Moscow, 1912), tom 3, pp. 58–86; N. B. Golikova, *Politicheskie protsessy pri Petre I po materialam Preobrazhenskogo prikaza* (Moscow, 1957); James Cracraft, "Opposition to Peter the Great," in Mendelsohn and Shatz, eds., *Imperial Russia, 1700–1917* (DeKalb, 1988), pp. 22–36; I. L. Solonevich, *Narodnaia monarkhiia* (Minsk, 1998), pp. 427–500.

153. P. K. Alefirenko, *Krest'ianskoe dvizhenie i krest'ianskii vopros v Rossii v 30–50-kh godakh XVIII v.* (Moscow, 1958), p. 296; E. V. Barsov, "Petr Velikii v narodnykh predaniiakh Severnogo kraia," *Beseda,* kniga 5 (1872).

154. Raeff, *Understanding Imperial Russia,* pp. 97–101; A. Liutsh, "Russkii absoliutizm XVIII veka," in A. Liutsh, V. Zommer, and A. Lipovskii, eds., *Itogi XVIII veka v Rossii: Vvedenie v russkuiu istoriiu XIX veka* (Moscow, 1910), pp. 250–254.

155. Marc Raeff, ed., *Catherine the Great: A Profile* (New York, 1972); Isabel de Madariaga, *Russia in the Age of Catherine the Great* (New Haven and London, 1981), pp. 584–587; A. G. Brikner, *Istoriia Ekateriny II* (Moscow, 1991), tom 2, chast' 4; A. B. Kamenskii, *"Pod sen'iu Ekateriny . . ."* (St. Petersburg, 1992); S. A. Kniaz'kov and N. I. Serbov, *Ocherki istorii narodnogo obrazovaniia v Rossii do epokhi reform Aleksandra II* (Moscow, 1910), p. 145; A. S. Lappo-Danilevskii, *Ocherk vnutrennei politiki imperatritsy Ekateriny II* (St. Petersburg, 1898); O. A. Omel'chenko, *"Zakonnaia monarkhiia" Ekateriny II: Prosveshchennyi absoliutizm v Rossii* (Moscow, 1993).

156. M. M. Speranskii, *Plan gosudarstvennogo preobrazovaniia Rossii* (Moscow, 1905), pp. 73–74.

157. Mironov, *Russkii gorod,* pp. 91, 164; Bushen, ed., *Statisticheskie tablitsy,* vyp. 2, pp. 267, 270–271.

158. Cited in V. I. Semevskii, "M. M. Speranskii," in *Entsiklopedicheskii slovar' F. A. Brokgauza i I. A. Efrona* (St. Petersburg, 1900), tom 31, p. 192.

159. V. I. Krutikov, "Zakonodatel'stvo o pomeshchich'ikh krest'ianakh doreformennogo vremeni (1801–1860 gg.)," in Pashuto, ed., *Sotsial'no-ekonomicheskie problemy rossiiskoi derevni,* p. 113.

160. Raeff, *Understanding Imperial Russia,* pp. 147–161; Lincoln, *Nicholas I: Emperor and Autocrat.*

161. Larisa G. Zakharova, John Bushnell, and Ben Eklof, eds., *Velikie reformy v Rossii, 1856–1874* (Moscow, 1992).

162. M. Kovalevskii, *Ocherki po istorii politicheskikh uchrezhdenii Rossii* (St. Petersburg, n.d.), p. 176.

163. A. A. Mosolov, *Pri dvore poslednego imperatora: Zapiski nachal'nika kantseliarii ministra dvora* (St. Petersburg, 1992), p. 69.

164. Iu. B. Solov'ev, *Samoderzhavie i dvorianstvo v kontse XIX veka* (Leningrad, 1973), pp. 165–251.

165. Richard Wortman, "Moscow and Petersburg: The Problem of Political Center in Tsarist Russia, 1881–1914," in S. Wilentz, ed., *Rites of Power: Symbolism, Ritual, and Politics Since the Middle Ages* (Philadelphia, 1985); R. Wortman, "Nikolai II i obraz samoderzhaviia," in *Reformy ili revoliutsiia?*, pp. 18–30.

166. G. Friz (Gregory Freeze), "Tserkov', religiia i politicheskaia kul'tura na zakate starogo rezhima," in *Reformy ili revoliutsiia?*, pp. 18–30.

167. E. Trubetskoi, "Nad razbity korytom," *Ruskaia mysl'*, no. 2 (1911), pp. 191–193.

168. V. S. Diakin, *Samoderzhavie, burzhuaziia i dvorianstvo* (Leningrad, 1978), pp. 14–15.

169. Korelin, *Dvorianstvo v poreformennoi Rossii*, p. 53; A. M. Anfimov and I. F. Makarov, "Novye dannye o zemlevladenii evropeiskoi Rossii," *Istoriia SSSR*, no. 1 (1974), p. 85.

170. Gary M. Hamburg, *Politics of the Russian Nobility, 1881–1905* (New Brunswick, 1984); Roberta T. Manning, *The Crisis of the Old Order in Russia: Gentry and Government* (Princeton, 1982); Iu. B. Solov'ev, *Samoderzhavie i dvorianstvo v 1907–1914 gg.* (Leningrad, 1990), pp. 233–234, 249.

171. A. M. Davidovich, *Samoderzhavie v epokhu imperializma: Klassovaia sushchnost' i evoliutsiia absoliutizma v Rossii* (Moscow, 1975), pp. 42–52.

172. Robert F. Byrnes, *Pobedonostsev: His Life and Thought* (Bloomington, 1968), pp. 281–283; Michael D. Katz, *Mikhail N. Katkov: A Political Biography, 1818–1887* (The Hague, 1966), pp. 178–181; Thaden, *Conservative Nationalism,* pp. 38–58, 204–206. However, Wortman believes that any attempt to combine nationalist and European principles of political culture would have brought tsarism to its final collapse (Wortman, "Nikolai II i obraz samoderzhaviia," pp. 18–30).

173. Pearson, *Russian Officialdom in Crisis*; Heidi W. Whelan, *Alexander III and the State Council: Bureaucracy and Counter-Reform in Late Imperial Russia* (New Brunswick, 1982), pp. 164–244.

174. Paul R. Gregory, *Russian National Income, 1885–1913* (Cambridge, 1982), pp. 192–194; Stephan Plaggenborg, "Who Paid for the Industrialization of Tsarist Russia," *Revolutionary Russia*, vol. 3, no. 2 (December 1990), pp. 183–210; idem, "Staatsfinanzen und Industrialisierung in Russland, 1881–1903: Die Bilanz der Steuerpolitik für Fiskus, Bevölkerung und Wirtschaft," *Forschungen zur osteuropäischen Geschichte*, Bd. 44 (1990), pp. 123–339.

175. L. E. Shepelev, *Tsarizm i burzhuaziia vo vtoroi polovine XIX veka: Problemy torgovo-promyshlennoi politiki, 1861–1900* (Moscow, 1981), pp. 134–190.

176. In the 1880s and 1890s alone, the number of entrepreneurs in the upper bourgeoisie increased from just under 100,000 to 150,000 (V .Ia. Laverychev, *Krupnaia burzhuaziia v poreformennoi Rossii, 1861–1900* [Moscow, 1974], pp. 70–71).

177. Verner, *The Crisis of Russian Autocracy*, pp. 326–350.

178. B. A. Anan'ich, ed., *Vlast' i reformy: Ot samoderzhavnoi k sovetskoi Rossii* (St. Petersburg, 1996), pp. 457–479; I. V. Lukoianov, "Proekty izmeneniia gosudarstvennogo stroia v Rossii v kontse XIX–nachale XX vv. i vlast': Problema

pravovogo reformatorstva" (dissertation, Russian Academy of Sciences, Institute of Russian History, St. Petersburg, 1993).

179. Mosolov, *Pri dvore poslednego imperatora*, pp. 182–183. See also V. N. Kokovtsov, *Iz moego proshlogo: Vospominaniia 1903–1919 gg.* (Moscow, 1993), chast' 2, p. 130.

180. V. S. Diakin, ed., *Krizis samoderzhaviia v Rossii, 1895–1917* (Leningrad, 1984), p. 615.

181. Wortman, "Nikolai II i obraz samoderzhaviia," pp. 26–28; Mosolov, *Pri dvore poslednego imperatora*, pp. 175, 182–184; Diakin, ed., *Krizis samoderzhaviia v Rossii*, pp. 611, 630; R. Sh. Ganelin, *Rossiiskoe samoderzhavie v 1905 godu: Reformy i revoliutsiia* (St. Petersburg, 1991), p. 218.

182. Avrekh, *Tsarizm*, pp. 144–214, 225, 223, 233, 244–245; Spirin, *Neproletarskie partii v Rossii*, pp. 108–110, 148, 181–183; R. Pearson, *The Russian Moderates and the Crisis of Tsarism, 1914–1917* (New York, 1977); Rogger, *Russia in the Age of Modernization and Revolution*, pp. 251–271; M. F. Florinskii, *Krizis gosudarstvennogo upravleniia v Rossii v gody pervoi mirovoi voiny: Sovet Ministrov v 1914–1917 gg.* (Leningrad, 1988); Leopold Haimson, "Ob istokakh revoliutsii," *Otechestvennaia istoriia*, no. 6 (1993), pp. 3–14; V. I. Gurko, *Features and Figures of the Past: Government and Opinion in the Reign of Nicholas II* (Stanford, 1939), pp. 549–588.

183. G. Tokmakoff, *P.A. Stolypin and the Third Duma: An Appraisal of the Three Major Issues* (Lanham, 1982); Macey, *Government and Peasant in Russia*.

184. Trubetskoi, "Nad razbity korytom," pp. 191–193.

185. Riasanovsky, *A Parting of the Ways*, pp. 291–297.

186. Bushen, ed., *Statisticheskie tablitsy*, vyp. 2, pp. 276–277.

187. *Obshchii svod dannykh pervoi perepisi naseleniia*, tom 1, pp. 172–183.

188. Mosolov, *Pri dvore poslednego imperatora*, p. 202; L. E. Shepelev, *Tituly, mundiry, ordena* (Leningrad, 1991), p. 183.

189. G. V. Esipov, *Liudi starogo veka: Rasskazy iz del Preobrazhenskogo prikaza i Tainoi kantseliarii* (St. Petersburg, 1880); I. Novombergskii, *Slovo i delo gosudarevy* (Moscow, 1911); M. I. Semevskii, *Slovo i delo! 1700–1725: Tainaia kantseliariia pri Petre Velikom* (St. Petersburg, 1885); V. I. Veretennikov, *Iz istorii tainoi kantseliarii, 1731–1762: Ocherki* (Kharkov, 1911).

190. Ronald Hingley, *The Secret Police: Muscovite, Imperial Russian, and Soviet Political Security Operation* (New York, 1970); Richard Deacon, *A History of the Russian Secret Service* (New York, 1972), pp. 63–194; Ch. Ruud and S. Stepanov, *Fontanka, 16: Politicheskii sysk pri tsariakh* (Moscow, 1993).

191. "Graf A. Kh. Benkendorf o Rossii v 1827–1830 gg.: Ezhegodnye otchety III Otdeleniia i korpusa zhandarmov," *Krasnyi arkhiv*, tom 37 (1929), p. 141.

192. ibid., pp. 138–173; ibid., tom 38 (1930), pp. 109–147; I. Trotskii, *III-e Otdelenie pri Nikolae I*; Sidney Monas, *The Third Section: Police and Society in Russia Under Nicholas I* (Cambridge, 1961); P. S. Squire, *The Third Department: The Establishment and Practices of the Political Police in the Russia of Nicholas I* (Cambridge, 1968).

193. V. Zhukhrai, *Tainy tsarskoi okhranki: Avantiuristy i provokatory* (Moscow, 1991); Richard Deacon, *A History of the Russian Secret Service* (New

York, 1972), pp. 63–194; Aleksi T. Vassilyev, *The Ochrana: The Russian Secret Police* (Philadelphia and London, 1930).

194. Vassilyev, *The Ochrana*, pp. 37–62.

195. T. V. Andreeva, "Russkoe obshchestvo i 14 dekabria 1825 goda," *Otechestvennaia istoriia*, no. 2 (1993), p. 154.

196. "Graf Benkendorf v Rossii," *Krasnyi arkhiv* (1930), p. 38.

197. V. Bogucharskii, "Tret'e otdelenie sobstvennoi ego velichestva kantseliarii o sebe samom (Neizdannyi dokument)," *Vestnik Evropy*, kniga 3 (1917), p. 94.

198. S. B. Okun', ed., *Krest'ianskoe dvizhenie v Rossii v 1850–1856 gg.: Sbornik dokumentov* (Moscow, 1962), pp. 33, 35; A. M. Anfimov, *Rossiiskaia derevnia v gody pervoi mirovoi voiny* (Moscow, 1962), p. 340.

199. M. P. Pogodin, *Istoriko-politicheskie pis'ma i zapiski v prodolzhenii Krymskoi voiny, 1853–1856* (Moscow, 1874), p. 259.

200. Diakin, ed., *Krizis samoderzhaviia*, p. 611.

201. N. M. Korkunov, *Russkoe gosudarstvennoe pravo* (St. Petersburg, 1893), tom 1, pp. 361–367.

202. S. N. Pisarev, *Uchrezhdenie po priniatiiu i napravleniiu proshenii, prinosimykh na vysochaishee imia, 1810–1910* (St. Petersburg, 1909), pp. 152, 180–181, 217.

203. G. Dzhanshiev, *Epokha Velikikh reform*, 8-e izd. (Moscow, 1900), pp. 33–34, 191, 200–204, 251–257, 305–312, 516–520.

204. Ganelin, *Rossiiskoe samoderzhavie v 1905 godu*.

205. Miliukov, *Ocherki po istorii russkoi kul'tury*, tom 3, chast' 2, pp. 290–293; K. A. Papmehl, *Freedom of Expression in Eighteenth-Century Russia* (The Hague, 1971).

206. Louise McReynolds, *The News Under Russia's Old Regime: The Development of a Mass-Circulation Press* (Princeton, 1991); W. Bruce Lincoln, "The Problem of Glasnost' in Mid-Nineteenth-Century Russian Politics," *European Studies Review*, vol. 11, no. 2 (1981), pp. 171–188; Chernukha, *Pravitel'stvennaia politika v otnoshenii pechati*; Iu. I. Gerasimova, *Iz istorii russkoi pechati v period revoliutsionnoi situatsii kontsa 1850-kh–nachala 1860-kh godov* (Moscow 1974); B. S. Itenberg, ed., *Vtoraia revoliutsionnaia situatsiia v Rossii: Otkliki na stranitsakh pressy* (Moscow, 1981); G. S. Lapshina, *Russkaia poreformennaia pechat' 70–80-kh godov XIX veka* (Moscow, 1985).

207. N. Ia. Eidel'man, *Gertsen protiv samoderzhaviia: Sekretnaia politicheskaia istoriia Rossii XVIII–XIX vv. i Vol'naia pechat'* (Moscow, 1973), pp. 9–32, 349–356.

208. L. G. Zakharova, *Samoderzhavie i otmena krepostnogo prava v Rossii 1856–1861* (Moscow, 1984), p. 27.

209. Chernukha, *Pravitel'stvennaia politika v otnoshenii pechati*, pp. 6–22, 151–197.

210. *Biografiia, pis'ma i zametki iz zapisnoi knizhki F. M. Dostoevskogo* (St. Petersburg, 1883), p. 356.

211. P. A. Zaionchkovskii, *Rossiiskoe samoderzhavie v kontse XIX stoletiia: Politicheskaia reaktsiia 80-kh–nachale 90-kh godov* (Moscow, 1970), pp. 66–81.

212. Troitskii, *Tsarizm pod sudom*, p. 138.

213. Terence Emmons and Wayne S. Vucinich, eds., *The Zemstvo in Russia: An Experiment in Local Self-Government* (New York, 1982); G. A. Gerasimenko,

Zemskoe samoupravlenie v Rossii (Moscow, 1990), pp. 6–51; N. M. Pirumova, *Zemskoe liberal'noe dvizhenie* (Moscow, 1977), pp. 3–25; idem, *Zemskaia intelligentsiia i ee rol' v obshchestvennoi bor'be do nachala XX v.* (Moscow, 1986), pp. 170–230.

214. Charles E. Timberlake, "The Zemstvo and the Development of a Russian Middle Class," in Edith W. Clowes, Samuel D. Kassow, and James L. West, eds., *Between Tsar and People: Educated Society and the Quest for Public Identity in Late Imperial Russia* (Princeton, 1991) p. 178; Thomas Fallows, "The Zemstvo and the Bureaucracy, 1890–1904," in Emmons and Vucinich, eds., *The Zemstvo in Russia,* pp. 227–228.

215. William G. Wagner, "Ideology, Identity, and the Emergence of a Middle Class," in Clowes, Kassow, and West, eds., *Between Tsar and People,* pp. 149–163; A. V. Likhomanov, *Bor'ba samoderzhavie za obshchestvennoe mnenie v 1905–1907 gg.* (St. Petersburg, 1997); R. Sh. Ganelin, "S. Iu. Vitte: Pervyi predsedatel' Soveta ministrov Rossiiskoi imperii v vospominaniiakh A. A. Spasskogo-Odyntsa," in L. E. Shepelev, ed., *Ezhegodnik S.-Peterburgskogo nauchnogo obshchestva istorikov i arkhivistov* (St. Petersburg, 1997), p. 331.

216. Richard G. Robbins, Jr., *The Tsar's Viceroys: Russian Provincial Governors in the Last Years of the Empire* (Ithaca, 1987), chapter 5; V. A. Nardova, "Institut pochetnogo grazhdanstva v dorevoliutsionnoi Rossii: Pravovoi aspekt," in Fursenko, ed., *Rossiia v XIX–XX vv.,* pp. 171–182; F. A. Petrov, "Nelegal'nye obshchezemskie soveshchaniia i s'ezdy kontsa 70-kh–nachala 80-kh gg. XIX v.," *Voprosy istorii,* no. 9 (1974), pp. 33–44.

217. Avrich, *Russian Rebels, 1600–1800.*

218. Paul I ordered a yellow box placed on the wall of the winter palace in which any subject had the right to leave a petition (Deacon, *Russian Secret Service,* p. 38).

219. Ignatovich, *Krest'ianskoe dvizhenie v Rossii,* pp. 439, 441.

220. Yaney, *The Systematization of Russian Government.*

221. Boris N. Mironov, "Consequences of the Price Revolution in Eighteenth-Century Russia," *Economic History Review,* vol. 45, no. 3 (August 1992), p. 468.

222. A. L. Shapiro, "Ob istoricheskoi roli krest'ianskikh voin XVII–XVIII vv. v Rossii," *Istoriia SSSR,* no. 5 (1965), pp. 61–80.

223. Shmuel N. Eisenstadt, "Bureaucracy and Political Development," in Joseph LaPalombara, ed., *Bureaucracy and Political Development* (Princeton, 1963), pp. 96–107.

224. *Materialy Vysochaishe uchrezhdennoi 16 noiabria 1901 g. Komissii* (St. Petersburg, 1903), chast' 1, p. 249.

225. Ibid., pp. 65, 85; *Statistika zemlevladeniia 1905 g.: Svod dannykh po 50 guberniiam Evropeiskoi Rossii* (St. Petersburg, 1907), pp. 12–13, 261; S. N. Prokopovich, *Narodnoe khoziaistvo SSSR* (New York, 1952), tom 1, pp. 132–133.

226. Black, ed., *The Transformation of Russian Society.*

5

The Law: Courts, Crimes, and Punishments

Previous chapters of this study have dealt with various aspects of Russian law as they relate to the social structure and to the formation of the state, legal estates, the peasantry, the family, and other social institutions. This chapter presents a more systematic evaluation of the role and effectiveness of criminal and civil law in prerevolutionary Russian society.

Fundamental Legal Systems

As in most traditional societies, in imperial Russia three kinds of law co-existed: (1) customary law *(obychnoe pravo)*; (2) judicial law *(sudebnoe pravo)*, or the body of judicial decisions; and (3) legislative law *(zakono-datel'noe pravo)*. A judicial decision might emanate from custom or from legislation, depending on the social role assigned to the judge. In a society where customary law dominates, such as that in Russia until the eighteenth century (among the peasantry, until 1917), legal norms are not separated from social, religious, and moral norms. The law takes its form from customs, and it corresponds to the type of political and social organization in which the collective is of greater importance than the individual. The norms of customary law take shape through a collective decisionmaking process that bears an unarticulated, spontaneous character. They are not formally fixed, and it is not always easy to demonstrate their presence.

Translated by Bradley D. Woodworth, Indiana University.

Judicial law in a number of societies was also an initial source of law (an example is English law). However, the relative importance of judicial law in these societies diminished as social organs of power became more adept at working out general, abstract legal norms and as the volume and significance of this legislation grew. At the same time, the functions of judges became more and more specialized and limited. Courts increasingly became organs for the application of legal norms rather than for their creation. Judicial decisions created legal norms only when issued by a higher judicial organ competent to make a final decision in a dispute.

Whereas customary law is a spontaneous creation of law, legislation is the intentional creation of law by specialized competent organs following specialized procedures. Legislation is preestablished law, formally expressed in writing. Its contents can be set with great precision. We are dealing with legislative law when a juridical norm is established through a legalized, official process. Legislative law is universal in nature, and it is made known to society through its publication. Through this means, juridical norms are directly created.[1] Throughout the entire imperial period in Russia, both legislative and customary law (but not judicial law) were in effect. The former was implemented primarily in urban areas, and the latter in rural regions—that is to say, among the peasantry.

The following sections contain an outline of the development of legal institutions and of procedural and criminal law in Russia, as well as a number of conclusions concerning the evolution over time of civil and customary law. In particular, I examine the similarities and differences between official and customary law in the late nineteenth and early twentieth centuries. I also survey the history of criminality and the penal system in the nineteenth and early twentieth centuries and evaluate the impartiality of judicial sentences and the speed with which they were handed down. The aim of this analysis is to assess the effectiveness of Russian law. Since ancient legal norms were still in use in customary law in Russia in the late nineteenth and early twentieth centuries, the chapter also contains a brief discussion of law in Kievan Rus and in Muscovy.[2]

Criminal Law: Codes, Regulations, and Statutes

The *Sobornoe ulozhenie* (Code of Laws) of 1649 was in effect, both formally and in practice, until the introduction in 1835 of the *Svod zakonov Rossiiskoi imperii* (Code of Laws of the Russian Empire). (Although the *Svod zakonov* came into force in 1835, it was prepared in 1832 and thus is known as the *Svod zakonov* of 1832.) The fifteenth volume of this code contains legislation on criminal law. In 1845 the *Ulozhenie o nakazaniiakh ugolovnykh i ispravitel'nykh* (Code of Criminal and Correctional Punishments) was introduced. This code contains significant improvements over the 1832 code in the area of criminal law. Over the course of more than a century, the 1649 *Sobornoe ulozhenie* had been supplemented with new laws, regulations, and statutes, which had produced many contradictions. For instance, during the reign of Peter I, the *Voinskie artikuly* (Military Articles) of 1715 were an important part of the *Voinskii ustav* (Military Statute), dealing with crimes committed by those serving in the military and the punishments for such crimes. In practice, the military articles were also applied to civilian crimes, particularly those dealing with the state or with state service. Important legal documents from the reign of Catherine II include her Instruction (Russ. *Nakaz*) to the deputies of the Legislative Commission established in 1767; the 1775 *Uchrezhdenie dlia upravleniia gubernii,* which reformed the administration of provinces; the 1782 *Ustav blagochiniia* (Police Statute); and the *Zhalovannaia gramota dvorianstvu* (Charter to the Nobility) and the *Zhalovannaia gramota gorodam* (Charter to the Towns), both of 1785. After the Emancipation of 1861, the above-mentioned 1845 Code of Punishments was supplemented with the *Ustav o nakazaniiakh* (Statute of Punishments); the Code of Punishments was significantly improved upon its reissue in 1885. A new *Ugolovnoe ulozhenie* (Criminal Code) was ratified in 1903 and implemented gradually, section by section, beginning in 1904.[3] Consequently, sections of the fifteenth volume of the 1832 Code of Law, which dealt with criminal law, remained in force when not superseded by the new Criminal Code of 1903.

After the 1906 ratification by Nicholas II of the *Osnovnye zakony Rossiiskoi imperii* (Fundamental Laws of the Russian Empire)—Russia's new constitution—and the establishment of the State Duma (parliament) in the same year, the normative standards of the 1903 Criminal Code and the 1845 Code of Punishments were revised and made to conform with the constitution, and new standards were added. This revision continued until 1916, the date of the last publication of the fifteenth volume of the Code of Laws of the Russian Empire. This volume included the Code of Criminal and Correctional Punishments, with additions and corrections, as well as the Criminal Code, which was supplemented with new and additional articles.

The Principles of Criminal Law

The fundamental concepts of criminal law in Russia have undergone significant change over time. The study of their evolution is of great interest to social historians, since it reflects changes in social relations as well as in society's views toward the individual and toward criminal behavior.

The Concept of Crime

The contemporary concept of what constitutes a crime (Russ. *prestuplenie*) has both an external and an internal aspect. The external aspect is the

completion of an act forbidden by law, or an instance of legal negligence—
the failure to complete an act mandated by law. The internal aspect of a
crime is the guilt *(vinovnost')* and criminal intent of one who has broken the
law. It is only when both aspects of a crime—the external and the internal—
are present that an illegal act is considered criminal in nature and is subject
to prosecution. This concept of crime, uniting in one system both illegal action and criminal intent, has taken shape gradually over the centuries.

The notion of crime as an infraction of law was foreign to Russian criminal law from the eleventh to the thirteenth centuries. A crime then was understood as an action that was first and foremost directed against an individual and that inflicted material, physical, or moral harm. In a secondary
sense a crime was seen as a violation of social peace and tranquillity. In
some cases it was understood as an offense against the entire group to
which the offended individual belonged. We know this because in addition
to paying compensation for the losses suffered by their victims, transgres-
sors paid a fine to help buttress social order.[4]

However, the law did not distinguish between a criminal act and a civil
delict or infraction *(grazhdanskoe narushenie)*. Any violation of the law
was viewed as an infringement on the material interests of the aggrieved
party, who bore responsibility for the prosecution *(presledovanie)* of the
offender. Any criminal affair could be brought to conclusion by a reconciliation between the two sides. In the legal texts of this era, such as the
Russkaia pravda, the legal code of Kievan Rus, a criminal act was referred
to as *obida* (a personal offense), even though the word *prestuplenie* (literally, "transgression" or "infringement")—the origins of which are related
to Greek—did exist at this time in the Russian language. The word *obida*
might signify a number of different kinds of violations: an unjust act of oppression or violence, a violation of another's rights, an insult, or material
damage.[5] The word *prestuplenie,* on the other hand, referred to the violation of law or of an oath (such as the *krestnoe tselovanie,* or "kissing of the
cross"), statute, religious precept *(zapoved')*, or vow *(obet)*. *Prestuplenie*
also might signify a religious sin or transgression.[6] In general, the word
obida corresponded in Kievan Rus to what today would be thought of as
prestuplenie; hence it was favored by the lawgivers of that time. Although
prestuplenie was used in legal texts to refer to an act with both private and
public connotations *(chastno-obshchestvennoe deianie)*, the emphasis in
legal documents was on the violation of private interests rather than public or social interests.

From the fifteenth to the seventeenth centuries, the notion of what constituted a crime gradually changed, as did the language used. By the mid-
seventeenth century, as we can see from the *Sobornoe ulozhenie* of 1649, a
crime had several interpretations: a violation of the royal will, or the tsar's
decree *(narushenie tsarskoi voli)*; a violation of the legal order *(pravopori-*

adok) established by the state; an infringement of the legally protected rights of private individuals; or an act that harmed society *(antiobshchest-vennoe deianie)*. Under this new understanding of a crime, responsibility for pursuing and punishing the offender was gradually transferred from the aggrieved person to the social group or commune *(obshchina)* to which the offender belonged, as well as to the state. Whenever the state's interests were at stake in a case, the *Sobornoe ulozhenie* guaranteed the state first and absolute priority in the investigation and prosecution. It is important to note that in such cases, organs of the state not only did not close a criminal case if the aggrieved party became reconciled with the offender (a common occurrence in the eleventh to thirteenth centuries) but punished the aggrieved party for doing so. Thus the state took upon itself the function of social avenger. The expression *likhoe delo* (evil deed), instead of the word *obida,* began to be used to signify a criminal act.[7]

At the time, this phrase corresponded most closely in meaning to what we think of today as a criminal act *(prestuplenie).* Written law did not yet clearly differentiate between a criminal act and a violation of civil law. Even though the *Sudebnik* (Legal Code) of 1550 declared law the single source for defining what was right and just, the concept of crime as a violation of law was not established in the sixteenth and seventeenth centuries. Nevertheless, a public-legal understanding of crime supplanted the private-legal approach that had been dominant in the eleventh to thirteenth centuries. This was a significant achievement for criminal law in the Muscovite period (from the fifteenth to the seventeenth centuries).[8]

In legislation of the first quarter of the eighteenth century (during the reign of Peter I), a criminal act was defined for the first time as a violation of law. The concept of crime also took on the meaning of a violation of the commands of autocratic authority—that is, of an encroachment on state interests, as broadly interpreted. Peter himself understood crime as "everything that might cause harm and loss to the state" *(vse to, chto vred i uby-tok gosudarstvu prikliuchit' mozhet).* This understanding of crime was a significant step forward, since it placed the violation of law at the center of the concept of crime. In keeping with this new concept, the terminology also changed: Significantly, in Petrine legislation—the *Voinskie artikuly* of 1715—a criminal act began to be referred to as *prestuplenie.*[9] Still, the definition of crime in legislation in the time of Peter and his immediate successors did not yet admit a distinction between a criminal act and a civil delict: Relatively minor misdeeds, such as the wearing of a beard, or felling wood in state-owned forests, were treated in exactly the same terms as more serious violations, such as murder and revolt. The perpetrators of all of these acts were subject to the death penalty, for they all had violated the commands of the autocrat.[10] Thus, in practice people were punished for acts that were not explicitly forbidden by law but that infringed on state interests. Considering the contradictory nature of the law, each judge could interpret "state interests" in his own way.[11]

In her Instruction to the Legislative Commission of 1767, Catherine II further developed the concept of crime, defining it as action that was explicitly forbidden by law because it violated the common and private good *(protivorechit obshchemu i chastnomu blagu)*. From this definition, two criteria emerged by which an act was to be identified as criminal: (1) violation of the law, and (2) resulting injury both to society and to the individual. This rejection of a formalistic interpretation of crime (that is, that a violation of law was sufficient to establish criminal guilt) made it possible for a crime to be clearly differentiated from a delict. It was in her Instruction that Catherine first formulated the principle according to which everything not forbidden by law was allowed. This new understanding of crime was reflected in subsequent legislation. For example, in the *Ustav blagochiniia* (Police Statute) of 1782, a difference was drawn between a *prostupok* (misdemeanor, or infraction), which did not entail criminal punishment, and a *prestuplenie* (crime). Not all of the ideas in Catherine's Instruction were implemented, since for various reasons the Legislative Commission did not draw up a new code of laws. However, the Instruction did have a noticeable effect on the legal consciousness of educated society as well as on judicial practice.

The concept of crime as an illegal action was fixed in the fifteenth volume of the *Svod zakonov* (Code of Laws) of 1832. This concept was developed further in the 1845 Code of Punishments, approximating the contemporary definition of crime. A criminal act was defined as a punishable, illegal action, or a failure to carry out what was prescribed by the law under threat of punishment. From this it followed that both illegality *(protivopravnost')* and punishability *(nakazuemost')* as defined in the law were the most important indicators of a crime. It also followed that the punishment for a crime should precisely conform to the law. At the same time, included in the Code of Punishments was a general requirement that a crime be distinguished from a delict. In the late nineteenth and early twentieth centuries, Russian jurists still held to this definition of a crime,[12] and thus it entered the Criminal Code of 1903.

The second, internal aspect of a violation of law, as indicated above, consists of criminal negligence or inaction. This includes failure to report a planned or previously committed crime. The legal obligation to inform the Grand Prince of plots being prepared against him was first stipulated in the so-called *kresto-tseloval'nye zapisi* (literally, "records of kissing the cross"), which were written documents confirming that one had taken an oath of loyalty to the Grand Prince. Such confirmations were given by representatives of the ruling elite in the late fifteenth and the sixteenth centuries, including in the oath made to Tsar Vasilii Shuiskii in 1606. (It should be noted, however, that these confirmations of oaths did not mention what punishment was to be meted out to those who failed to report plots against the Grand Prince.[13])

The notion of criminal inaction, known in premodern Russian criminal legislation as *izvet* (denunciation or report[14]), was included in the *Sobornoe ulozhenie* of 1649. The code prescribed capital punishment for failure to report any plot or malicious intent against the tsar. The obligation to report was not applied to other intended crimes.[15] During the reign of Peter I, a new definition of criminal inaction was devised. It entailed not only failure to denounce all political crimes and acts that infringed on the state's interests, material and otherwise, but it also included remaining silent about thieves, brigands, and peasants who had fled from their owners.[16] It also included criminal inaction on the part of civil servants *(chinovniki)*, from senators to simple office clerks, who failed to deal in a timely way with circumstances such as fire, floods, crop failures, epidemics, popular disturbances, and so on.[17] In addition, the definition of political crimes and crimes against the state was broadened so that the clergy were obligated to report schemes against state interests that they heard during confessions. As a result of the law on failure to report, the number of denunciations rose in the second half of the seventeenth century. Informing became particularly widespread among the populace under the reign of Peter I.

The fear of punishment for remaining silent played a certain role in this spread of denunciations;[18] but fear alone cannot entirely account for the phenomenon. Other factors certainly were involved. First, the fact that the office of tsar was considered to be holy and the tsar himself to be God's anointed made any word of offense against the tsar (and the failure to report such) a grievous sin. Verbal offense against the tsar was all the more grave because in the seventeenth and eighteenth centuries the common folk *(prostye liudi)* believed in the magical power of words. Second, denouncers sought to identify themselves with the tsar, and thus with power and authority. The denunciation served as a means toward this end. During times of great social upheaval, or when a society's system of values is undergoing change, identification with power can help ward off uncertainty and internal instability. It is noteworthy that in the second half of the eighteenth century, denunciations began to decrease in number, and this trend continued into the nineteenth century. In my view, the decrease in denunciations was due not only to measures to discourage them taken by the government beginning with the reign of Peter III (1761–1762).[19] Of greater significance was the increasing social stability in Russia, as a result of which people felt a lesser need to identify with ruling power and authority.

The corpus delicti *(sostav prestupleniia)* for criminal inaction was broadened in the 1832 Code of Laws, in the 1845 Code of Punishments, and in the 1903 Criminal Code. These codes stipulated punishment for failure to report any intended or committed criminal offense. The codes also expanded the category of persons obliged to report such crimes to encompass the entire adult population as well as those employed in public (social) service *(obshchestvennaia sluzhba)*. Civil servants' liability for criminal inaction was confirmed in the 1811 *Obshchee uchrezhdenie ministerstv,* which defined the authority of ministers and ministry workers;[20] in the 1832 Code of Laws; in the 1845 Code of Punishments;[21] and in the 1903 Criminal Code.[22] Thus, over time, criminal inaction was interpreted more and more broadly, eventually reaching its apogee in the 1903 Criminal Code. In this document, it was interpreted not only as failure to protect political and state interests, as it had been in the second half of the seventeenth century and in the early eighteenth century, but also as failure to defend the interests of private individuals and society. Under the new Criminal Code, criminal inaction might include the most varied forms of negligence: refusal to serve as a witness or a jury member in court; failure to report a crime against a private individual; failure to report outbreaks of animal diseases or phenomena dangerous to people; and so forth. As a result of this new emphasis, a shift occurred in the legal interpretation of crimes of inaction. The demand to assist the state was now supplemented with a demand to help one's neighbor. This undoubtedly was a sign of social progress, introduced through criminal law into the legal consciousness and the life of society.

The issue of objective accountability *(vmenenie)* for a crime is closely connected with the issue of corpus delicti. Over time, Russian criminal law developed in a progressive manner also in this respect. In the Kievan and Muscovite periods, laws on criminal offenses most frequently were limited to naming the given offenses. For example, the 1649 *Sobornoe ulozhenie* prescribed for those found guilty of a first offense involving robbery *(vorovstvo)* the following: beating with the knout, cutting off of the left ear, imprisonment for two years, and confiscation of property for recompense to the injured party. After the prison term was served, the convicted person was to be sent in fetters into forced labor. For second and third offenses involving robbery, however, the punishments increased in severity. No distinctions were made for the type or extent of the robbery, nor in forms of guilt *(vina)* of the perpetrator. Analogous were the punishments for the crime of brigandage: For a first offense, the law directed that the right ear of the perpetrator be cut off, that he be imprisoned for three years and his property be confiscated, and that after prison he be subjected to forced labor. For second and third offenses, the punishment rose in severity.[23] As in the case of other crimes, no differentiation was made for the type of brigandage, nor was a concrete definition given of the crime for which one was to be punished. This lack of clarity in the definition of what constituted a particular crime paved the way for judicial arbitrariness and disregard for the principle that the punishment should fit the crime. In the eighteenth century and the first third of the nineteenth century, crimes were defined with greater and greater precision. Beginning with the 1832 Code of Laws, in the majority of cases the law not only defined all of the essential elements of a particular crime but also presented the criteria by which a given deed was to be deemed punishable. Only in cases when the corpus delicti was extremely simple and did not hold potential for juridical misunderstandings did the law simply name a given crime.[24]

Thus, the Russian concept of crime underwent a lengthy evolution. First, the definition of a criminal act developed from that of personal insult or injury *(lichnaia obida)* to that of an act that harmed society. A transformation had occurred in how crime was viewed: A personal-legal approach gave way to a public-legal one. Second, over time criminal acts were distinguished from civil delicts. Third, the notion of a criminal act developed from that of a deed that violated the royal will and the state's interests to that of an act that violated the law. Last, a criminal act was no longer seen as meriting either vengeance or mere material compensation but rather punishment of a nature strictly outlined in the law. The concept of crime was in time supplemented by the concept of criminal inaction. Over time, the increasingly precise definition of crime in general as well as of particular crimes gave judges less leeway for arbitrariness in sentencing.

As the concept of crime as an objective violation of the law developed, crime was also increasingly seen as a subjective violation of the law. In ancient times no clear distinction was made between a crime *(prestuplenie)* and a violation of the law *(pravonarushenie)*. With this understanding of crime, animals and inanimate objects, in addition to human beings, were seen as potential subjects of crime. In the ancient texts of Russian criminal law beginning with the Kievan period, there are no records of judgments made against animals for having caused a human death; but instances are known in which animals or objects were "punished" without a court ruling. For instance, in 1593 a bell was beaten with the knout and exiled from Uglich to Siberia for having been used after the death of tsarevich Dmitrii two years earlier to call together a crowd of people who then rioted. In the first third of the seventeenth century a monkey was executed in Moscow for having run into a church where it caused a disturbance.[25] The punishment of animals and inanimate objects in the sixteenth and seventeenth centuries was a survival of ancient criminal law, under which animals and objects could themselves be the subjects of a crime. Under ancient criminal law, no distinction was drawn between premeditated and unpremeditated crimes, and many important aspects of crime were not taken into account, including happenstance, carelessness, the necessity of a defense for the accused, and a lack of legal accountability *(nevmeniaemost')* for breaking the law. The legislation of the Kievan period did distinguish between premeditated and unpremeditated crimes (without using these concepts per se); but this differentiation was neither clear nor consistent and was applied only to some crimes. For instance, an act of brigandage was considered a premeditated crime, whereas a crime committed in the heat of an argument or fight, or under the influence of alcohol, was not considered premeditated. The main distinguishing characteristic of a crime, however, was material damage.

In legislation from the fifteenth to the seventeenth centuries—particularly in the 1649 *Sobornoe ulozhenie*—the distinction between premeditated and unpremeditated crimes was clear and consistent. However, only in cases of murder did it influence the severity of sentences. It was at this time that there arose the legal concepts of negligence *(neostorozhnoe deianie)*, justifiable defense *(neobkhodimaia oborona)* for an accused person, and extreme necessity *(krainiaia neobkhodimost')*. However, these notions were not yet clearly defined and differentiated, and thus were applied inconsistently. In addition, vague distinctions were made among the levels of severity of criminal activity, and members of a criminal's family were also subject to punishment. Moreover, harm or damage caused accidentally was imputed against the perpetrator equally with harm caused intentionally, for with the exception of murder, no distinction was made between premeditated and unpremeditated crimes.

The achievements made in criminal legislation in the seventeenth century were not lost during the reign of Peter I, but further progress along the same lines did not occur. For example, in the Military Articles of 1715, the division of legal violations into those premeditated and unpremeditated was still taken into account only in cases of murder. Chance, carelessness, and the necessity of a defense for the accused were recognized, but not clearly and consistently. The tendency toward establishing the guilt of the accused before a sentence was handed down, observable in the seventeenth century, was not developed further. Also, the principle of objective accountability dominated, since punishments mainly (and sometimes exclusively) depended on the objective perpetration of a crime without establishing guilt. As a result, it was possible, as before, for the innocent to be punished and for the guilty to escape punishment. Arbitrariness in judges' decisions still played a major role in legal proceedings, and punishments often did not fit the crimes.

In the second half of the eighteenth century, culpability, or criminal intent—to the degree that this notion was developed in legislation—was more and more frequently taken into consideration in legal proceedings. By the time of the creation of the 1832 Code of Laws, culpability had to be established before an act could be considered a crime. However, remnants of the exclusively objective approach to crime were long preserved in criminal legislation. For instance, in the eighteenth and nineteenth centuries all members of rural communes carried financial responsibility for those whose taxes fell into arrears; similarly, the editor of a journal or newspaper in the nineteenth century was responsible for the contents of articles published. However, these were exceptions to the rule; generally a crime was seen as a combination of an objective, illegal act together with criminal intent. The notion that culpability was a necessary component of a crime was an important achievement in criminal law, and it made courts more fair and objective.

The notion that different stages exist in the progression of a given criminal act is also important in criminal law. The Criminal Code of 1903 distinguishes between the following stages of a criminal act: intent, preparation, attempt to commit, voluntarily abandoned attempt, attempt with insufficient means, unsuccessfully completed criminal act, and completion of a criminal act. Each stage of a crime was clearly defined and had a corresponding punishment. However, Russian criminal law only gradually reached this level of development. The previous lack of differentiation of the criminal act into stages meant that the different stages were all made equal with respect to punishments and that a number of types of criminal activity were ignored. As a result, the consequences of a given criminal act were not taken into account, sometimes producing overly severe punishments; and in other cases, a criminal act begun but not completed was left completely unpunished. The notions of "attempt" and "intent" with respect to crimes appear for the first time in the 1649 *Sobornoe ulozhenie.* Whereas "attempt" is mentioned in connection with crimes both against individuals and against the state, "intent" is mentioned only with reference to political crimes. Those judged to have had clear intent *(golyi umysel)* to commit a crime were punished as if they had actually completed the crime. Threats were viewed as crimes, but punishment for them was increased if it could be shown that criminal intent truly lay behind the threat. An unsuccessfully completed crime was seen as equivalent to an attempted crime; and a botched criminal action whose damage exceeded the perpetrator's intent was seen as equivalent to an intentional, completed crime.[26]

In the eighteenth century and the first third of the nineteenth century, the conceptualization of the various stages of crime changed little. Although in her Instruction of 1767 Catherine II declared that "clear intent" was not subject to punishment, "clear intent" in connection with political crimes was punished, as previously, as if the crime had been completed. The various stages of a crime were generally seen as equivalent, and the stage had no effect on the severity of punishment. Not until the 1832 Code of Laws was the notion of the various stages of a criminal act presented more or less clearly. The conceptualization of these stages was developed further in the 1845 Code of Punishments and in subsequent legislation. The principle in modern criminal law that intent to commit a crime is not in itself a punishable offense was recognized in Russian criminal law beginning in 1845. This principle was subsequently violated on occasion, but violations were exceptions to the rule. The notion that a crime was a combination of objective (deed) and subjective (intent) aspects was of crucial importance for the differentiation in the law of the stages of a crime.

The Subject of a Crime

In the eleventh to the thirteenth centuries, the subject of crime was a free individual who committed a crime and was punished for it. This subject was a person who was conscious of his actions and who possessed free will. Since a slave *(kholop)* was not believed to possess a free will, a slave's master was seen as responsible for crimes the slave committed. In criminal law of the fifteenth to seventeenth centuries, particularly in the 1649 *Sobornoe ulozhenie,* any person, including a slave, could be the subject of a crime. Thus, equality of responsibility before the law was recognized by the mid-seventeenth century. The legal recognition of general responsibility in criminal matters represented an important step forward in social consciousness: The law acknowledged that every person, regardless of social status, possessed a free will, and that from a psychological and moral point of view, all people were equals. In part this was a result of the influence of Christianity, which began to be accepted by the peasantry only in the sixteenth to seventeenth centuries.[27] The concepts of crime and sin in many respects overlapped, and thus the Christian notion that all people are equally responsible before God for the sins they commit influenced views regarding responsibility for crimes.

Until as late as 1803 the subject of a crime in Russian criminal law was often the family, rural or urban commune, or military unit to which one belonged. For instance, in the eleventh to thirteenth centuries, when the commune was unable to locate a murderer, the entire commune paid a fine. In the fifteenth to seventeenth centuries, the entire commune paid a fine when any of the commune's police functions went unfulfilled. This could involve the harboring of runaway serfs, the committing of crimes within the territory of the commune, and other such offenses. During the reign of Peter I, all persons who were present at the commission of a crime were punished, without exception—whether a single household or an entire village. If it was proven that some unknown person or number of persons had participated in committing a crime, then the "guilty" were selected by lot—for instance, each tenth person. Responsibility of the family for a violation of the law committed by one of its members increased during this period. For instance, if a nobleman did not report on time for state or military service (which was considered a criminal offense), then his wife and children, and any other relatives living in his household, were held responsible for his failure to appear. Similarly, parents bore criminal responsibility for their children, and husbands for their wives. Group responsibility before the state was the basis for the concept of *krugovaia poruka* (collective responsibility, or collective guarantee). The family or commune, it was presumed, could not help but know if one of its members committed a crime. Of course, this seems strange to us today; but as discussed earlier, in the chapters dealing with the commune and the family, collectivism was indeed characteristic of these social groups, and for all practical purposes, there were no secrets in the commune or the family. The law took this reality into account in making all members of a collective responsible for a crime committed by one of its members.

Not until 1782 was the law making parents and children responsible for each other repealed. The principle that people are individually responsible for any criminal offense they commit was confirmed in criminal law in 1803.[28] From that time on, only the direct and immediate perpetrator of a criminal act was held responsibile for that crime; no legal entity *(iuridicheskoe litso),* including the family and the commune, could be held guilty of a criminal act. Responsibility for a slanderous *(oskorbitel'noe)* letter written on behalf of a commune was borne either by the commune *starosta* (elder) or by those who had signed the letter. The *starosta* was considered responsible for the failure of the commune to fulfill its policing duties. If a deception *(podlog)* of some sort was carried out by elected officials, they themselves were held responsible. However, the fact that juridical entities were not held responsible for criminal acts did not relieve them of responsibility for civil *(grazhdanskie)* offenses, particularly the responsibility to make recompense for damage and harm caused.

Whereas the concept of collective crime *(kollektivnoe prestuplenie)* was absent from the law of the eleventh to the thirteenth centuries, in legislation of the fifteenth to the eighteenth centuries (including the 1649 *Sobornoe ulozhenie)* all participants in a crime were held equally responsible. Punishments were not differentiated on the basis of individuals' particular roles in a collective crime, even though the law recognized different forms of complicity, such as instigation, initiation, and direct execution of a crime. The same view was taken in legislation of the eighteenth century. The question arises: If the law recognized differing forms of complicity in collective crimes, why were identical punishments meted out to participants in such crimes? There are several reasons. First, collective accountability was one of the most important principles of social relations. When a group of individuals collectively had committed a crime, it followed that all should be dealt with on the basis of collective responsibility. Second, although the notion of guilt *(vina)* did exist in legislation, the various forms of guilt were very weakly differentiated in the law. Third, until the early nineteenth century, the aim of punishment was to frighten and to edify the criminal. From the point of view of those who drew up the law, fine distinctions in punishments based on the degree of individual guilt made no sense. Finally, collective crimes generally were among the most serious crimes. Often they were of a political nature, directed against the state or against society, and undermined the existing social order *(obshchstvennyi poriadok)*. The traditional view in such cases was that it was better to punish the innocent than to let the guilty go free; thus, legislators preferred identical and harsh punishments for all involved. Evaluation of the role of individual participants in such crimes had a political rather than a juridical goal; that is, to reveal those who presented the greatest danger to the state and society.

Individual responsibility for participation in collective crimes was not formally established until the 1832 Code of Laws. But in practice, the principle was in place earlier. For example, after the Decembrist revolt of 1825, distinctions were made in the degree of guilt of direct participants in the uprising as opposed to those who had merely belonged to Decembrist societies, and the severity of punishments handed down varied accordingly. The legislation of 1832 simply confirmed what had already been the practice. It distinguished between instigators, accomplices, participants, and primary culprits, and designated different punishments for each. In the 1845 Code of Punishments these categories were defined with greater clarity and precision. Thus we may conclude that as early as the first third of the nineteenth century, the perpetrators of collective crimes were no longer viewed as undifferentiated groups. The introduction of the concepts of differing forms of guilt and individual responsibility into criminal law and the changing views toward collective crimes were indicators of significant changes in Russian society. Collective responsibility had gradually been disaffirmed. The importance of the individual was increasing in Russian society, and communal relations were being transformed into social ties among individuals rather than on the collective *(obshchina)*.

The Object of a Crime

The notion of the object of a crime *(ob'ekt prestupleniia)* underwent similarly significant change over time. This phrase refers to people, objects, and ideas toward and upon which criminal action is taken, and which are protected by the law. Not all individuals or legal entities were objects of crime. In the twelfth and thirteenth centuries, the law defended the rights only of individuals who were free and responsible before the law. Thus, the objects of crime were exclusively those endowed with full legal rights. Slaves (both *raby* and *polnye kholopy*) could not be objects of crime. The killing of a servant, therefore, was not necessarily a criminal offense. Rather, it was a civil crime of destruction of property—in this case, that of the servant's master. If a servant offended a free person, the servant could be killed by the injured party with impunity. Underage children were not objects of crime vis-à-vis their parents. Parents had the right to sell their children into slavery, to beat them, and even to kill them. During the era of blood vengeance *(krovnaia mest'),* that is, approximately until the thirteenth century, murderers were not protected by the law and thus could not be objects of crime. A thief caught in the act of stealing could be killed "like a dog."[29] In the Kievan period, religious beliefs had not yet become objects of crime either in law or in practice, even though there were incidents in which individuals who were considered to be sorcerers *(volshebniki)* were executed. Sorcerers were not executed for heresy but for the damage to society that was popularly believed to be wrought by their "magic."

In the fifteenth to seventeenth centuries, the objects of crime began to include, in addition to the rights of individuals, the social order *(obshchestvennyi stroi)* established by the state and church; laws; the orders of supreme state power *(verkhovnaia vlast');* and the dominant worldview and beliefs. At the Moscow church council of 1551 it was decided to forbid heathen rites, sorcery, magic, and *skomorochestvo* (performances by wandering minstrels or buffoons known as *skomorokhi*), and that decorum needed to be maintained in churches. Heretics began to be subject to the death penalty, and the sentence was passed down by church councils. In the 1649 *Sobornoe ulozhenie,* the death penalty was applied for the first time in cases such as blasphemy against God (the contemporary term was *khula,* or *bogokhulenie*), Christ, the Holy Virgin, the cross, and the saints. The death penalty was also passed down in cases of conversion to Islam (called *busurmanskaia vera* in the *Sobornoe ulozhenie*). In practice, blasphemy was interpreted more broadly as indicative of unbelief *(neverie)* or as a rejection of God *(otritsanie Boga).*[30] In the eighteenth century and the first half of the nineteenth, deviations in the realm of beliefs gradually ceased to be objects of legal prosecution unless they infringed on other people's rights. However, there were instances in which people were persecuted for their beliefs—for example, the Freemasons under Catherine II, and philosophers during the reign of Nicholas I.

The *Sobornoe ulozhenie* of 1649 provided for the legal protection of children, who now became objects of crime. Parents who murdered their children could be sentenced to one year's imprisonment in addition to forced ecclesiastical repentance, which involved the public admission of guilt by the parents in their parish church. Mothers who murdered an illegitimate infant faced the death penalty. For the killing of any child, the Military Statute of 1715 prescribed the death penalty—the same sentence as for the premeditated killing of an adult. The 1845 Code of Punishments and the 1903 Criminal Code preserved the principle that the murderer of a child was subject to the same punishment as the murderer of an adult, which reflected a rise in the status of children in society. Punishment was lessened, however, in cases of the murder of an illegitimate child. Although children over time became recognized objects of crime, slaves *(polnye kholopy)* did not gain such recognition until the abolition of bonded slavery *(kholopstvo)* in 1719. Women and peasants were always recognized as objects of crime.

Individuals were not generally subject to legal prosecution for acts against their personal well-being unless the rights of others were also violated. An exception to this rule was suicide. Until the reign of Peter I, individuals who unsuccessfully attempted suicide were subjected only to an ecclesiastical punishment: They were cut off from the church for a time. Suicide victims were buried outside of the boundaries of the regular cemetery and were denied a church burial. According to the 1715 Military Statute, suicide committed without evidence of mental illness was equivalent to murder. The statute proscribed an ignominious ritual for suicides: The executioner was to drag the body through the streets and bury it in a dishonorable or disgraceful *(beschestnoe)* place. Attempted suicide was punishable with the death sentence; but if the suicide attempt was judged to have been made out of pangs of conscience or in a state of delirium, the punishable was less severe.

The 1832 Legal Code prescribed penal hard labor for attempted suicide, and in cases of successful suicide the body was denied a church burial. The Code of Punishments of 1845 mitigated this punishment: Those who attempted suicide were to undertake ecclesiastical repentance. Successful suicides were not to be given a church burial, and their final wills and testaments were to be declared null and void. Suicide was not even mentioned in the Criminal Code of 1903; now neither successful nor attempted suicide entailed any punishment under secular law. However, the church refused as before to give a Christian burial to those who successfully committed suicide. As we can see, attitudes toward suicide changed over time from fanatical intolerance to a more humane view, reflecting a general movement toward a more humane society in Russia.

From 1832 to 1917, the single object of crime was the law. According to Article 1 of the 1845 Code of Punishments, "Any breach of the law by which an attempt is made upon the inviolability of the rights of supreme power and powers established by it or upon the rights or security of society or individuals is a crime." This was an enormous advance in Russian criminal law. From this time on, all persons and legal entities *(fizicheskie i iuridicheskie litsa)* were potential objects of crime, and only acts that were explicitly proscribed by law were considered crimes. This principle was consistently worked into Russian legislation in the second half of the nineteenth and the early twentieth centuries, as Russia evolved into a state governed by the rule of law *(pravovoe gosudarstvo)*. However, a serious obstacle stood in the way: The law did not protect all of the personal and political rights of individuals but only those rights that the supreme power of the state *(verkhovnaia vlast')* granted to the population and considered to be legal. Attempts to appropriate rights not granted by law were seen as criminal offenses and were prosecuted according to the law. An example is provided by the 1845 Code of Punishments. Formally, the Code of Punishments supported the principle of religious freedom *(svoboda veroispovedaniia)*, declared in the eighteenth century. The Code of Punishments divided religious faiths into four classes: Orthodoxy, other Christian confessions, heresies and schisms, and non-Christian religions. It was forbidden to convert to any faith other than Orthodoxy. Unlawful conversion was subject to punishments that varied from exile in Siberia to a sentence of hard labor for twelve to fifteen years. Written and verbal proselytism of any religion other than Orthodoxy was subject to prosecution.

The wide range of possible crimes against the state, together with the corpora delicti of these crimes, were listed in the 1832 Code of Laws and even more clearly elucidated in the 1845 Code of Punishments. Subject to criminal prosecution were all actions (and failures to act) directed against the emperor or the state or aimed at overthrowing, undermining, or changing (even by peaceful means) the existing political order. The law not only criminalized all attempts to change the structure of society but also written and oral propaganda, secret societies, the spreading of rumors, demonstrations, and riots *(bunty)*. Also actionable was any disobedience to the authorities *(vlasti)*, as well as insults and open displays of disrespect aimed at state institutions or state officials in the act of carrying out their duties. Beginning in 1867, societies of a political, nihilistic, or atheistic tendency were outlawed.[31]

Until the Great Reforms of the 1860s and early 1870s, the law did not distribute personal rights and freedoms equally among all members of the population. One's rights in a large number of areas of life were dependent on one's social estate *(soslovie)*, which could be changed only by order of the state. Thus, limitations were placed on the right to live where one chose; on the right to change one's social status *(svoboda sotsial'nykh peremeshchenii)*; on the right to choose one's profession; on the right to education; on the right to individual responsibility before the state and society; on the right to own private property; on the right to protection from the law against violations of one's place of residence; and on such rights as legal protection of life, property, and honor. Depending on the social estate to which one belonged, the law also placed limitations on freedom of conscience *(svoboda sovesti)*, the right of the accused to a defense, the right to be protected from corporal punishment, and the inviolability of personal correspondence.

The entire aggregate of personal rights, also known as civil rights *(grazhdanskie prava)*, was granted by law to the nobility, clergy, and merchant class, on the whole, by the end of the eighteenth century. (In 1832, the members of all social estates lost for a time the right to travel abroad freely.) The urban middle class *(meshchanstvo)* received these rights in the 1860s, while the peasants received them only in 1905–1906. It should be noted that even after the Great Reforms these rights were subject to certain limitations. For instance, one's personal freedom could be limited by secret police surveillance or by police interception of mail.[32] Also, freedom of religion as declared was not complete: Although all faiths were equal before the law, the right did not exist to change one's faith, with the exception that one could convert to Orthodoxy. With the exception of Jews, one's professed faith or religion no longer had any effect on one's personal rights; but as earlier, each person was obliged to belong to some faith or religion.

It was primarily those who felt no loyalty to the existing regime who suffered from these and other limitations on personal rights—in the main, individuals from among the intelligentsia. As far as political rights were concerned, criminal law protected freedom of the press (although only to a certain degree); the right to participate in elections to local courts and local organs of self-administration; and from 1864, the right to participate in elections to the zemstvos and to select juries.

More extensive political rights and democratic freedoms were granted, or rather won, for all estates simultaneously in the course of the Revolution of 1905–1907. This included freedom of speech, full freedom of the press, freedom of association and assembly, and the right to self-government and to unite in social organizations and unions. Russia also was granted a parliament possessing the power to legislate, and each person had the right to vote. Thus, before 1905–1906, the Russian populace by law had no political rights. However, when the state in the 1832 Code of Laws declared the law the only object of crime, it was not taking refuge in a ruse or engaging in subterfuge, since it was by law that the state denied political rights to members of all social estates, and personal rights to members of some estates. Consequently, the formal object of crime was indeed the law, which protected the rights of the emperor, the state, and private citizens.

To summarize, Russia between the 1830s and 1906 can be categorized only as a lawful *(pravomernoe)* state. Although after 1905–1906 Russia was de jure a state governed by the rule of law, or a *Rechtsstaat (pravovoe gosudarstvo)*, in fact it still fell short of this designation.

Accountability Under the Law

In modern criminal law, only those who are legally liable and who can be found guilty before the law can be subject to punishment for violations of the law. Individuals can be held responsible for committing a crime only when they are capable of understanding the wrongfulness of their actions. A person who has broken the law may not be legally liable as a result of a number of circumstances, such as age (being either underage or greatly advanced in years) and illness (including mental illness). Views on the influence such factors should have on legal accountability have changed over time. Let's look at how the issue of accountability was dealt with historically in Russian criminal law, beginning with the variable of age (see Table 5.1).

Until the eighteenth century, legal accountability—at least for serious criminal offenses—began at age 7. This corresponded with ecclesiastical law, which in many respects paralleled secular law.[33] Sentencing occurred on an ad hoc basis; that is, each case was dealt with individually, based on the circumstances surrounding it. Children older than 7 years were not subject to capital punishment, but they did incur other punishments commensurate with those meted out to adults, or in mitigated form.[34] In 1742 the law for the first time set the age at which full criminal responsibility began: 17 years. Individuals under the age of 17 who committed a crime were given a lashing and sent to a monastery for fifteen years of heavy labor instead of being sentenced to exile, the knout, or capital punishment.[35] Absolute nonaccountability—when individuals were subject to no specific punishment under the law but were given over to their parents for the meting out of whatever penalty the latter saw fit—was not explicitly addressed in the law of 1742. Thus, previous laws setting the age of absolute nonaccountability at 7 years remained in effect.

In 1833 the concept of conditional accountability was introduced into criminal legislation. Under conditional accountability, the court was obliged to take into account the perpetrator's "level of comprehension" *(stepen' razumeniia)* when handing down sentences to persons between 10 and 17 years of age. Depending on this evaluation the court was to determine whether the lawbreaker was to be given a reduced sentence or freed entirely from punishment. In 1845 the law set new age limits on legal accountability: unconditional nonaccountability for children under 10 years, conditional accountability for those between 10 and 14, and full accountability for those 14 and older. However, the law provided for mitigated sentences for youths between 14 and 21 years old. The law also directed that minors who were repeat offenders be held to the same level of accountability as adults. The Criminal Code of 1903 raised the age of full

TABLE 5.1 Age of Legal Accountability in Russia (various years)

Degree of Liability	1669	1742	1765	1845	1864	1903
Unconditional nonaccountability	–	under 7 yrs.	under 10 yrs.	under 10 yrs.	under 10 yrs.	under 10 yrs.
Conditional accountability	–	–	–	7–13 yrs.	10–13 yrs.	10–13 yrs.
Mitigated accountability	determined ad hoc	7–16 yrs.	10–16 yrs.	14–20 yrs.	14–16 yrs.	14–20 yrs.
Full accountability	determined ad hoc	17 yrs.	17 yrs.	21 yrs.	17 yrs.	21 yrs.

SOURCES: V. S. Nersesiants, ed., *Razvitie russkogo prava v XV–pervoi polovine XVII v.* (Moscow, 1986), p. 158; *Polnoe sobranie zakonov Rossiiskoi imperii*, sobranie pervoe, tom 11, nomer 8601; N. S. Tagantsev, *Russkoe ugolovnoe pravo: Lektsii, Chast' obshchaia* (Moscow, 1994), tom 1, p. 90.

accountability to 21; correspondingly, mitigated accountability was established for those between the ages of 14 and 21.

Vacillations in the law concerning the effect of age on criminal accountability are evidence of the influence of religion and popular *(narodnaia)* tradition on the law. According to Orthodox ecclesiastical law, children older than 7 years were allowed to repent *(dopuskalis' k pokaianiiu)* and take communion, which signified that the church considered age 7 the point at which children became accountable for their actions. Among the peasants until the early twentieth century, and until the eighteenth century among the entire population of Russia, "infancy" *(mladenchestvo)*, or childhood, continued to age 7. Until this age girls and boys were not distinguished by sex among society and were referred to as "infants" *(mladentsy)* or "children" *(deti)*. From age 7, children were distinguished by sex and by their clothing, and they began to help their parents in the household.[36] It is likely that for this reason children under age 7 were by law freed from all accountability for crimes. Under the influence of Enlightenment-era pedagogical ideas and of Catherine II herself, the age of full nonaccountability was raised in 1765 to 10 years. But the Orthodox Church, which always held firm to tradition, did not change its views concerning the age at which moral responsibility began. By demand of Russian jurists, the age of nonaccountability was confirmed at 10 years after the peasant emancipation of 1861. The church, however, held to its views and continued to admit children to repentance from age 7.

Vacillations on the part of legislators concerning the age at which full criminal accountability began were also connected with differences between secular and ecclesiastical law. Until 1774, ecclesiastical law permitted females to marry at age 12 and males at age 15. In 1774 the age at which females were allowed to marry was raised to 13. As the age at which marriage was permitted was always considered a marker of adulthood, it is natural that the church considered the age of full accountability for one's actions to begin between the ages of 12 and 15 years.[37] This view was shared by the members of all social estates, at least until the nineteenth century. For instance, in 1721, Peter I publicly declared that his daughter Elizabeth, who had just completed her twelfth year, had come of age. To signify this, Peter performed the following ritual: Having led his daughter before a gathering of retainers, Peter "cut the leading strings from the bodice of her robe [a dress of simple design—*B.N.M.*], gave them to the governess, and declared the princess to be of age."[38] The age at which one could be fully responsible for committing a criminal act was not the same as either the age at which one came of age according to both ecclesiastical and customary law, or the age when one was permitted to marry. As a consequence, the law often was not strictly followed.[39] In 1830, secular law raised the age at which one could marry to 16 for women and 18 for men;

and under the threat of criminal punishment, it forbade priests from marrying people younger than the legal age. The church obeyed, but it did not act to change formally ecclesiastical law regarding the age at which one could marry. Customary law in this regard also did not undergo change.[40]

For an extended period there was also a lack of clarity on the issue of what age marked the onset of advanced age, which gave one the right to a mitigated sentence for criminal activity. Not until 1798 did the law set the age at 70 years; persons of 70 years and older were freed from corporal punishment (including branding) and were subject only to exile. The 1903 Criminal Code preserved the privilege of mitigated punishments for those who had reached the age of 70.

Let us turn to the issue of nonaccountability for the mentally ill and those suffering from temporary mental disturbances. In the twelfth and thirteenth centuries, the law recognized two conditions that would evoke a mitigated sentence: first, *razdrazhenie* ("a fit of passion," in modern terms), and second, intoxication *(op'ianenie)*. From the fifteenth to seventeenth centuries, ecclesiastical law, which was also taken into account by the secular authorities, provided for the release from responsibility of the mentally ill (called either *besnye*, "demented," or *blazhennye*, "blissful"), who were not legally responsible even when they committed political crimes. Relatives of a mentally ill lawbreaker generally appealed to the court saying that their relative *s uma sbroden, i pro to ves' gorod znaet* ("he has departed his senses, and the whole town knows it"). This declaration would be verified; and if it was confirmed by neighbors, the individual would be exempt from punishment. If no relatives were present to intercede, then the mentally ill were sent to monasteries, like others who were unfit for work.

During the reign of Peter I, intoxication began to be considered in the law as a circumstance increasing guilt. At the same time, Petrine legislation eased punishment for violent overzealousness by officials. For instance, if in the course of punishing a subordinate an officer beat him to death, the officer's act was attributed to "a fit of passion" *(affekt)*, and punishment could be reduced to a simple fine. During Peter's reign, the mentally ill were freed from all responsibility for criminal behavior. Legislation introduced under Peter's immediate successors, however, established sentences for the mentally ill who committed especially dangerous crimes, though these sentences were handed down in mitigated form. Catherine II ended this practice, reestablishing the legal norm of nonaccountability that had existed under Peter. From that time on, the principle of the nonaccountability of the mentally ill has remained a part of Russian criminal law.[41]

The various levels of accountability for criminal activity were comparatively clearly formulated in the 1832 Code of Laws and in the 1845 Code of Punishments. The latter recognized six conditions resulting in nonaccountability: (1) insanity dating from birth; (2) insanity acquired after birth; (3) illness leading to delirium and loss of memory; (4) senility; (5) lunacy *(lunatizm)*; and (6) inability to hear or speak *(nemoglukhota)*, acquired at birth or in childhood. The first three conditions correspond to the modern concept of mental illness. The condition referred to as "lunacy" is what today is known as somnambulism.[42] Also in the mid-nineteenth century, psychiatric evaluations based on prescribed procedures came into practice. This represented a great step forward. It replaced the previous practice of questioning a lawbreaker's relatives and neighbors regarding their opinion of the lawbreaker's mental state; and judges also no longer had to rely on their own impressions of the lawbreaker when handing down sentences. The 1903 Criminal Code established new criteria for criminal nonaccountability that corresponded to the existing professional, scientific understanding of mental illness. The previously existing six conditions of nonaccountability were replaced by three newly defined conditions: (1) arrested mental development; (2) disturbance of mental activity caused by illness; and (3) states of mental incognizance or incompetence *(bessoznatel'nye sostoianiia)*, which included a number of specific circumstances under which a person was held nonaccountable. In this area Russian criminal law advanced in tandem with that in the West.[43] Medical expertise in uncovering the cause of death in cases of murder was introduced into legal practice as early as in the 1715 Military Statute.[44]

In 1782 there was a change in the way the law dealt with crimes committed under the influence of alcohol. When a crime was premeditated, intoxication was not taken into account; but in cases where the crime was unpremeditated, intoxication lessened the degree of criminal guilt. In the 1832 Code of Laws and the 1845 Code of Punishments, intoxication alleviated guilt as long as the lawbreaker did not get drunk expressly for the purpose of freeing himself from criminal responsibility. A crime committed in a state of intoxication was considered equivalent to an unpremeditated act. In the Criminal Code of 1903, intoxication was differentiated by degrees, and guilt was alleviated only in cases involving drunkenness that resulted in complete loss of control over one's behavior.[45]

Listing Corpora Delicti

The number of corpora delicti is of fundamental importance in every system of criminal legislation. In the twelfth and thirteenth centuries the number of crimes was small, and the law did not differentiate among religious crimes, crimes against the state, and other types of crimes.[46] The small number of crimes affixed in the law at this time indicates that most criminal acts were viewed and decided according to customary law, foregoing official courts. From the fifteenth to the seventeenth centuries, the nomenclature of crimes grew significantly, and in the 1649 *Sobornoe ulozhenie* a classification of crimes was presented for the first time. Four groups of crimes were listed: (1) crimes against faith and the church; (2) crimes against the state and the person of the sovereign; (3) crimes associated with one's office or official position *(dolzhnostnye prestupleniia)* and crimes against the administrative order; and (4) crimes against the rights and life of private individuals. Crimes against faith, mentioned briefly for the first time in the *Sobornoe ulozhenie,* grew tremendously in number during the reign of Peter I; and the punishments for such acts were striking for their severe brutality. For instance, converts to a non-Christian religion were punished by burning at the stake; the punishment for conversion from Orthodoxy to another Christian confession was confinement for life in a monastery; for joining a schism (within Orthodoxy), laypersons were punished with hard labor and priests with the death penalty.

The nomenclature of crimes against the state was painstakingly detailed. These crimes included insulting the sovereign and impugning his actions or intentions; and crimes associated with one's office or official position or against the administrative order. The latter included unruly, riotous conduct *(buistvo),* fistfights *(draki),* playing cards for money, gambling *(azartnye igry),* cursing in a public place, wearing overly luxurious clothing or displaying excess in one's (horse-drawn) carriage *(roskosh' v odezhde i ekipazhakh),* drunkenness, and so on. Included in the law for the first time were crimes of immoral behavior *(prestupleniia protiv nravstvennosti),* among which were listed homosexuality, bestiality, suicide, and engaging in duels. All such crimes brought harsh punishment.

This tendency of growth in the number of corpora delicti continued right up to the 1860s, indicating that the law had actively begun to regulate social life. After the peasant emancipation of 1861, the process shifted into reverse, and many corpora delicti were abolished, as is evidenced by the decrease in the number of articles in legal codices. For instance, the second edition of the Code of Punishments, published in 1857, contained 2,304 articles, whereas the third edition of the same code, published in 1866, contained 1,711 articles. The Criminal Code of 1903 contained only 687 articles; that is, 3.4 times fewer than the 1857 Code of Punishments. The abolition of many punishments and corpora delicti, the transformation of criminal legal proceedings, and the technically more advanced organization of the new legal code were factors leading to a reduction in the number of articles. This reduction was an important indicator that the all-inclusive and petty regulation of social life by means of the law was gradually being replaced by a more liberal and principled management of society.

The postreform period saw changes in the proporton of corpora delicti dealing with the interests of the state and society as opposed to those of private individuals. In the 1845 Code of Punishments[47] the corpora delicti for concrete crimes were grouped into 150 categories, containing 2,035 articles. Among these, 32 articles dealt with crimes against faith; 19, with crimes against the state; 74, with crimes against the administrative order; 175, with crimes associated with one's office or official position; 1,415, with crimes involving the interests of the state and treasury; and only 320, with crimes against the life, health, freedom, property, honor, and familial rights of private individuals. Thus, 84.3 percent of the articles dealt with defending the state and the social order, whereas 15.7 percent of the articles dealt with defending the rights of private individuals. The priority of state and public interests over private interests is clear. The nomenclature and grouping of the types of crimes in the 1903 Criminal Code differs somewhat from the 1845 Code. In the former, 25 articles deal with crimes against faith; 52, with crimes against the state and crimes against the administrative order; 51, with crimes associated with one's office or official position; 329, with crimes involving the interests of the state and treasury; and 201, with crimes against the life, health, freedom, property, honor, and familial rights *(semeistvennye prava)* of private individuals. In all, 67.3 percent of the articles in the 1903 Criminal Code dealt with defending the interests of the state and the social order, whereas 32.7 percent dealt with defending the rights of private individuals. In comparison with the 1845 Code of Punishments, the portion of articles in the 1903 Criminal Code defending the rights of private individuals increased twofold. The 1903 Criminal Code, however, was only partially implemented by 1917. On the other hand, after 1905–1906, the Criminal Code and the Code of Laws included a number of new articles defending the political rights of citizens that replaced older laws.

Conclusions based on this evidence must be somewhat tentative. However, in my view it is clear that although the defense of state interests still dominated criminal law in the early twentieth century, more attention began to be paid in legislation to the defense of private interests. This extremely important change indicates that the position of the individual had grown in significance in society and that there was a greater awareness of the need to defend private interests.

Punishments and the Penal System

The issue of punishment *(nakazanie)* is of fundamental importance in criminal law. As early as the eleventh to thirteenth centuries, there existed a rather wide selection of punishments: monetary fines, compensation for damages, denial of personal and property rights (in the language of the time, *potok i razgrablenie,* or "plunder and pillage"), banishment, imprisonment, enslavement, and various types of corporal punishment. Although the death penalty was rarely implemented, blood vengeance was permitted. If thieves caught in the act resisted arrest, they could be killed on the spot. If vengeance could not be applied, use was made of fines; if the criminal had no wealth that could be exacted, criminal punishments were used against him. The goal of punishments included the taking of vengeance, obtaining compensation for damages incurred by the victim, and extraction of material profits for use by the state. In legislation of the fifteenth to seventeenth centuries, corporal punishment and the death penalty dominated among the different types of punishment. Incorrigible criminals were sentenced to death; those deemed corrigible were subjected to corporal punishment and sent to prison. Those found guilty of petty crimes associated with their offices or official positions were dismissed from those positions. Fortunately, the majority of death sentences were not carried out, due to the ancient custom of *pechalovanie*—the right of the Orthodox clergy to petition for clemency for the accused. Those freed from capital punishment were confined for life in a monastery. The earlier functions of punishment were preserved in part, but the main goal of punishment became to frighten people and deter them from committing crimes. For this reason, punishment was very harsh.[48]

Petrine legislation introduced even harsher punishment, of which the death penalty became the primary form. In the 1715 Military Articles, capital punishment was provided for in 200 instances, whereas in the 1649 *Sobornoe ulozhenie* it was indicated in only 60. The second most commonly mentioned punishment in legislation was corporal punishment, the various types of which increased. Penal hard labor and deprivation of rights were added to the older punishments. One form of punishment that became widespread was *detsimatsia,* in which every tenth person out of a group was selected by lots for punishment. In addition, people were punished who had not been involved in a crime but who had familial ties to the perpetrator—most often wives and children. Punishments for crimes involving property were handed down in relation to the size of the loss: Minor theft merited various punishments, and the death penalty was imposed for major theft. The aims of punishment remained the same—to obtain retribution, exact material gains, instill fear, and isolate the criminal. Those convicted of crimes began to be sentenced to forced labor in factories and mines and at construction projects, and more than ever before, as oarsmen in galleys. Thrifty rulers strove to exact the maximum from prisoners. In the history of Russian criminal law, the Petrine period marks the high point of punitive severity. Criminal law under Peter was directed not only against thieves, brigands, instigators of public disturbances, and so forth, but also often against peaceful citizens who sought to preserve legal rights as they were defined in the time before Peter. Never again in tsarist Russia would the repressive organs of the state be so active in taking steps against law-abiding citizens merely because those citizens did not like the social innovations introduced by the state.

Here is an example that illustrates the repressiveness of the state under Peter: A certain court clerk *(pod'iachii)* named Dokukin added the following words to the text of the oath for the new order for royal succession, established by Peter in 1724: "I do not vouch for the unjust excommunication [*otluchenie*] and banishment from the Russian throne of the tsarevich Aleksei Petrovich [son of Peter I, executed for not following his father's policies—B.N.M.]. I do not swear, nor do I affix my name to the same, even though for this the wrath of the tsar will be poured down upon me; let His will be done, for the truth Illarion Dokukin is prepared to suffer." For this action Dokukin was tortured to death by breaking on the wheel.[49]

It is also important to note that had all punishments been carried out as indicated in the law, by the end of Peter's reign there would have remained in Russia few bureaucrats or ordinary citizens, since the death penalty was indicated for the majority of crimes. Just as in the seventeenth century, the threat of capital punishment was generally illusory; even those who drew up the laws did not intend it to be carried out. Capital punishment became a hyperbolic formula characteristic of legal language at that time. Without fail, those who complained of having been beaten described their punishment in terms like "They gave me a deadly beating repeatedly unto death" (*Bili smertnym boem do smerti mnogazhdy)*. Those who requested any sort of relief from taxes always sought to demonstrate that without relief they would die of hunger, and so on. Lawmakers who threatened the disobedient with the death penalty never assumed that this threat would actually be carried out. This general threat of capital punishment reflected the dominance of indeterminate sanctions in Petrine legislation. It also had as its goal, however, to frighten those who did not agree with the reforms being carried out under Peter.[50]

Punishments were eased under Empress Elizabeth Petrovna. On the day of the palace coup that brought her to power, Elizabeth pledged that she would repeal capital punishment. She kept her word, and unlike previous coups, this one was not accompanied by executions. High officials who had been overthrown were not tortured but simply sent into exile. Even though the laws in effect prior to Elizabeth's reign were not repealed, for all practical purposes the death penalty was not implemented; criminals were sentenced to death and then were granted clemency, or had the sentence commuted to a lesser penalty. In 1753–1754, by special royal ukases, capital punishment was replaced by "political execution" (*politicheskaia kazn'):* The person being sentenced lost all rights to property, underwent physical punishment, and then was sent into exile, to penal hard labor. This new form of extreme sanction led to the increasing use of exile to Siberia as punishment.

The easing of punishments continued under Catherine II, and during her reign only those found guilty of crimes against the state were given the death penalty. The small number of such cases, which included that of Emelian Pugachev, were considered by the Supreme Criminal Court (*Verkhnii ugolovnyi sud*) specially established by imperial manifest. Those found guilty of crimes against the state were sentenced to death on the basis of the 1649 *Sobornoe ulozhenie* and the 1715 Military Articles. However, further fundamental changes in the system of punishments were not forthcoming in the second half of the eighteenth century; and the retention of various horrific corporal punishments, including flogging to death, made the abolition of the death penalty itself something of a fiction. With the reigns of Elizabeth and Catherine II in mind, Prince M. M. Shcherbatov commented that although the light form of capital punishment—death by hanging or beheading—had been abolished in Russia, the more grievous form—death by beating—was still practiced.

Even though severe punishments remained in place in the law under Catherine II, the mass intimidation of the populace was halted. Many acts that earlier had been considered crimes against religion, the administrative order, or the state, as well as crimes of immoral behavior, began to be viewed as delicts. Some acts, such as wearing a beard or traditional Russian clothing, were no longer censured. Sentences became more lenient and corresponded more closely to the severity of the crimes committed. All of this took place gradually, and largely thanks to the liberal disposition of the empress, which was clearly expressed in her Instruction. Following Western thinkers of her time, Catherine II rejected the view that punishment was retribution. She also developed the notion that the main aim of punishment was to protect people from crimes and to decrease the damage to society caused by crime. She recommended that sentences handed down by the courts correspond to the severity of the crime, and that the courts, when determining guilt, distinguish between perpetrators' varying levels of participation in a crime. The empress proclaimed that one was responsible only for crimes one actually committed and not for the intention to commit a crime. An exception was made for the act of writing or speaking words against the person of the emperor. In Catherine's view, a lack of education and adverse social circumstances were important factors leading to criminal activity; not only was the individual responsible for his crimes, but society was as well. Thus, punishments should be more lenient and have a correctional goal. From the time of Catherine II, another important tendency is notable: Punishments directed against the life, health, or property of lawbreakers gradually gave way to punishments limiting lawbreakers' freedom—that is, imprisonment, exile, and penal hard labor.

In 1775, under Catherine II, the statute of limitations was introduced into criminal law as a general norm. Until that time, legislation contained only fragmentary and rather imprecise decrees suspending prosecution for a limited number of specific crimes after the passage of a particular period of time.[51] In accordance with the new law, ten years after the commission of a crime that had not publicly come to light during that time, the perpetrator was relieved of culpability for the crime. Suits for slander *(obida slovom)* were canceled after one year, and forms of personal injury *(obida deistviem)*, after two years. The statute of limitations initially applied to all crimes and other legal infractions; but gradually, exceptions began to be made for some crimes—in 1829 for desertion, and in 1842 for renouncing Orthodoxy. The 1845 Code of Punishments revoked the statute of limitations for crimes against the state and for murder of one's parents, and introduced a specific period of limitation for all other types of crime. According to the 1903 Criminal Code, statutes of limitations were not applied in two instances: in cases of crimes directed against the emperor, and in renunciations of Orthodoxy for another faith. The period of prescription depended on the crime committed, and varied from fifteen years for crimes punishable by death to one year for misdemeanors.[52]

Notably, sentences were not systematized until the Code of Law of 1832. Article 16 of the Code represented the first attempt to systematize sentences. Here, sentences were subdivided into ten types, based on their severity: (1) capital punishment; (2) political execution; (3) deprivation of *soslovie* (estate), family, and property rights (collectively known as *lishenie prav sostoianiia)*; (4) corporal punishment; (5) forced labor; (6) exile; (7) forced conscription; (8) imprisonment; (9) fines; (10) ecclesiastical punishment. The system of sentences in the 1845 Code of Punishments was more complex. The code outlined a hierarchy of sentences including eleven different types—four *criminal* and seven *correctional* in nature. The criminal punishments cast the offender out of society for life, whereas the correctional sentences did so only for the length of the sentence, after which the former convict could return to society. All types of criminal punishment called for the deprivation of *soslovie* (estate), family, and property rights. This meant the loss of all political, civil, familial, and property rights as well as loss of rank, honor, one's good name, all awards and medals for distinguished service, and all personal certificates and diplomas. In addition, the first type of criminal punishment called for the death sentence. The second type of punishment specified hard labor in exile for four to twenty years, or in some cases, indefinitely. The third type of criminal punishment called for exile to Siberia; and the fourth type, exile to the Caucasus. In addition to being subjected to these punishments, criminal perpetrators from nonprivileged social estates* were to be publicly whipped.

---

*Nonprivileged social estates were those whose members were subject to corporal punishment.

There were seven types or categories of correctional sentences, presented here in order of decreasing severity:

1. For the privileged social estates*, the loss of all special rights and privileges. This included the loss of rank and of awards and medals for distinguished service; removal from one's position of state service or complete banning from state service; relinquishment of one's estate to someone else's guardianship, and so on. In addition to the above, correctional sentences for the privileged social estates included exile to Siberia. For the nonprivileged social estates, correctional sentences in this category involved beating with rods (nakazanie rozgami) and forced conscription into a correctional penal battalion, with the loss of all special rights and privileges.
2. For the privileged social estates, the loss of all special rights and privileges, and exile to distant provinces other than Siberia. For the nonprivileged social estates, detention in a workhouse (rabochii dom), with the loss of all special rights and privileges.
3. For all social estates, detention in a fortress (krepost'), together with the loss of some special rights and privileges.
4. For all social estates, detention in a forced-labor prison (smiritel'nyi dom), with the loss of some special rights and privileges.
5. Exile for the privileged social estates, and for other social estates, imprisonment.
6. For all social estates, short-term detention (kratkovremennyi arest).
7. For all social estates, an official reprimand (vygovor) and a fine.

Each category or type of criminal or correctional sentence was subdivided into degrees, which numbered thirty-eight in total. For instance, the sentence of hard labor in exile was subdivided into seven degrees according to the length of the sentence and the difficulty of the labor; and exile to Siberia was divided into five degrees depending on the place of exile and the length of the period of exile. Reprimands in the presence of a judge were divided into the categories of severe, more severe, and most severe, the last being given in a public setting. Sentences depended on one's social

---

*Privileged social estates were those whose members were by law not subject to corporal punishment. The nobility and merchants of the first and second guilds were freed from corporal punishment in 1785. Priests and deacons in the Orthodox Church were given this status in 1800, and lower-level church officials received it in 1862. Those who belonged to the category of "distinguished citizens" (pochetnye grazhdane), created in 1831, were freed from corporal punishment. In 1863, members of all social estates except the peasantry were freed from corporal punishment.

estate: Noblemen, clergy, and merchants of the first and second guilds were freed from corporal punishment, and for these groups imprisonment was replaced by exile.

According to the 1832 Code of Laws, capital punishment could be handed down for crimes against the state, military crimes,* and so-called quarantine crimes *(karantinnye prestupleniia)*, which included looting and pillaging as well as other crimes committed during epidemics of plague, cholera, and so forth. The 1845 Code of Punishments repealed capital punishment for military crimes but permitted it in cases involving extraordinary crimes, such as aggravated murder and arson resulting in death and large-scale damage. Such cases were to be reviewed by a court-martial, which could use laws of wartime and thus hand down the death sentence. However, capital punishment continued to be implemented with limited frequency. After attempts were made on the life of Emperor Alexander II in 1878 and 1879, and then especially after his assassination in 1881, grievous criminal cases were handed over to courts-martial. This practice was based on a law passed after the assassination, which provided for extraordinary and reinforced protection of public order. This use of courts-martial to deal with acts of domestic terrorism became widespread and continued to the end of the old regime.

The hierarchy of sentences was simplified in the 1903 Criminal Code. Punishments were divided into eight categories: (1) capital punishment; (2) penal hard labor for a period from four years to life; (3) exile as a penal settler *(ssylka na poselenie)* for an indefinite period of time in places expressly set aside for the purpose of exile, though not to Siberia or other distant provinces; (4) detention in a correctional facility known as an *ispravitel'nyi dom*; (5) detention in a fortress; (6) imprisonment; (7) short-term detention; and (8) a fine of between 50 kopecks and 100 rubles. The formal division between criminal and correctional sentences was done away with, but the distinction in sentencing between privileged and nonprivileged social estates remained: Those from privileged estates continued to be treated more harshly than those from nonprivileged estates. When members of the nobility, the clergy, merchants, and distinguished citizens *(pochetnye grazhdane)* were sentenced to a prison term, to time in a forced-labor prison, or to hard labor and exile in Siberia, they also were deprived of their *soslovie* (estate), family, and property rights. Thus, those from privileged estates were treated more harshly than those from nonprivileged estates. Capital punishment was implemented only in cases of military crimes and crimes against the state. With the abolishment of corporal punishment as a type of

---

*Military crimes *(voinskie prestupleniia)* were defined as violations of military discipline, of military service obligations, or of military statutes.

sentence in 1863—and in 1903—and of its use on criminals from the non-privileged social estates who were then serving out their sentences—social estate ceased to be a factor in determining sentences and meting out punishment.

The average lengths of sentences were reduced: Before 1903, the length of sentences to hard labor varied from four to twenty years; but from 1903 on, the usual term of sentence was four years. Earlier, terms in the correctional facilities known as *ispravitel'nye doma* had ranged from one to ten years; after 1903, they were from six months to eight years. Correctional terms decreased from the range of three months to two years, to between two weeks and two years. However, terms of detention in fortresses, where primarily political criminals were held, were increased. Until 1903 such sentences ranged from six weeks to six years; after 1903, they ranged from two weeks to eight years. Also increased was the duration of short-term detention for minor legal violations: Before 1903, such detention could range from one day to three months; after 1903, from one day to one year. Many types of sentences were abolished entirely, including exile *(ssylka na zhit'e)* to Siberia and distant provinces (although not permanent, forced labor resettlement to such places, which remained a viable punishment); detention in the forced-labor prisons known as *smiritel'nye doma* (these facilities were now closed); full confiscation of property for those guilty of political crimes; "political execution"; forced labor to repay one's debts; forced conscription; official reprimands *(vygovory i zamechaniia)*; forced repentance in church *(tserkovnoe pokaianie)*; and forced asking of forgiveness by the offender before the offended.[53]

Let us now explore the most important types of punishment in greater detail.

Capital Punishment

Gruesome means of capital punishment were still in use in Russia in the seventeenth century and the first half of the eighteenth century. Those found guilty of certain religious offenses were burned at the stake; counterfeiters of money had molten metal poured down their throats; women who murdered their husbands were buried in the ground up to their shoulders and left without food and water until they died. Other offenders were quartered, broken on the wheel, impaled on stakes, and so on. By the beginning of the nineteenth century, two means of implementing capital punishment remained in use: beheading and hanging, and beheading occurred only rarely.

Death sentences required confirmation by the emperor. Executions were carried out publicly until 1881. After that date, executions were to be attended by officials, a physician, and no more than ten local citizens, present at the invitation of the local administration to be eyewitnesses to the execution. Executions in Russia were not the austere, ceremonial, public rituals that they were in western Europe. Only in exceptional circumstances were executions in Russia accompanied by a special ritual, such as a procession designed to heap ignominy on the condemned. Before their execution the condemned were permitted to see a clergyman of their own faith, to whom they could make confession and with whom they could partake of communion or simply pray. The clergyman accompanied the condemned to the place of execution and remained with them until the sentence had been carried out. As indicated above, in cases involving a threat to the existing social or political order, the government remanded those found guilty of crimes against the state to courts-martial. Such courts handed down sentences of capital punishment much more frequently than did the regular courts. Between 1826 and 1905, an estimated 1,397 persons were sentenced to death, of whom 64 percent were actually executed. Between 1905 and 1913, some 6,871 persons were given death sentences, of whom 43.4 percent were executed.[54]

Sentences of Disgrace

This type of sentence was widely imposed during the reign of Peter I. Sentences of disgrace can be divided into two types: moderate and severe. Moderate sentences included the loss of honor and dignity *(chest' i dostoinstvo)*, either for life or for a set period of time; lowering in rank; forced public apology; a slap in the face administered in public; and having one's name nailed to a gallows. A severe sentence of disgrace had different names at different times. Under Peter I it was called *shel'movanie*, from the verb *shel'movat'* ("to shame" or "to dishonor"). Under Peter's successors, in the eighteenth century, this type of sentence was called "public execution" *(publichnaia kazn')*, and in the nineteenth century it was called "civil execution" *(grazhdanskaia kazn')*. The sentence was accompanied by deprivation of *soslovie* (estate), family, and property rights. The severe sentence of disgrace consisted of the following ritual, established by law. On a scaffold a gallows was erected, to which was affixed the name of the offender. The hangman would break the offender's sword over his head and declare the offender to be *shel'ma* (in disgrace), and consequently, a political criminal. From the 1720s on, the deprivation of *soslovie* (estate), family, and property rights began to be called "political death" *(politicheskaia smert')*. The *oshel'movannyi*, or disgraced person, was also anathematized—excommunicated from the church—and had no recourse to any legal protection. Thus, until the 1753 replacement of capital punishment with "political execution," a person who robbed or even killed an *oshel'movannyi* was not subject to punishment. Under Catherine II, the punishment of severe disgrace was used primarily against those who committed crimes of immoral behavior; but subsequently it was also used against persons considered by law to be political criminals, as in 1864 against N. G. Chernyshevskii.

Corporal Punishment

Corporal punishment was widespread in Muscovy and was especially common during the reign of Peter I. All known methods of corporal punishment were employed, and were applied in full view of the public. For speaking disrespectfully of the tsar or speaking in an obscene manner in a church, the convicted offender's tongue was cut out; for attempting to kill one's master, a hand was cut off; for forgery and thievery, fingers were cut off; for brigandage, rebellion, and perjury, the nose or ears were cut off. Criminals were branded so that they could be easily identified. During the reign of Peter I, the more dangerous criminals had their nostrils slit; less dangerous criminals had their foreheads branded with the letter "V," for *vor* (criminal). In addition to sentences involving the mutilation of limbs, other painful punishments were meted out: beating with the knout for the most serious crimes; and for less serious crimes, beating with sticks or the lash, or in the case of soldiers, running the gauntlet. Minors and adults found guilty of less serious offenses were beaten with birch rods. The number of blows one could be sentenced to began at 500 or more and sometimes extended to infinity *(bez chetu)*—which for all practical purposes meant beating to death.

Until the beginning of the eighteenth century, corporal punishment was applied to all classes within the population equally. But in the eighteenth century, those from privileged classes successfully sought the repeal of corporal punishment against them. Motivating their opposition was the growing opinion that corporal punishment was a disgrace for those on whom it was imposed. For instance, a soldier who had undergone corporal punishment was unable to become an officer. As a result of this opposition from privileged classes, in 1785, members of the nobility, distinguished citizens *(pochetnye grazhdane)*, and merchants of the first and second guilds were exempted from corporal punishment. The clergy was granted the same privilege in 1803, followed by members of other social estates—provided they had an education. (However, beating with birch rods remained widely used until the 1860s as a form of punishment for students in elementary and secondary schools, even though children from the privileged social estates predominated in the latter.)

Over time, the severity of sentences was eased, and some forms of punishment were even abolished. For instance, the beginning of the nineteenth century saw the end of the use of the knout. (The knout was the most terrifying means of punishment, and an experienced executioner could kill a person with three blows.) The 1845 Code of Punishments established the upper limit for sentences using the lash and birch rods to 100 blows. Exceptions began to be made for the sick and the elderly. Additional measures began to be taken to protect as much as was possible the health of individuals undergoing punishment. For instance, sentences would not be carried out in extremely cold and windy conditions. Beginning in 1851, a physician was present at the carrying-out of sentences involving corporal punishment. From 1863 on, corporal punishment was greatly curtailed. Women were entirely freed from undergoing corporal punishment. For men it was retained in five cases specially stipulated by law:

1. District courts *(volostnye sudy)* were permitted to sentence peasants to up to twenty blows of the lash, a sentence that earlier had been considered appropriate only for children.*
2. With the permission of the governor of the province, prisoners were allowed to be punished with up to 100 blows of the birch rod for various violations of the established order *(ustanovlennyi poriadok)*.
3. Those serving sentences of hard labor in exile and those in exile as penal settlers could be beaten with between 100 and 300 blows of the birch rod for various violations.
4. Those serving sentences of hard labor in exile who committed an additional crime could be beaten with up to 100 blows of the lash.
5. Those serving on vessels at sea could be punished with up to five blows of the whip, and apprentices could be given between five and ten blows of the birch rod.

Not until 1903 were all forms of corporal punishment abolished for those serving sentences of exile at hard labor or sentences of exile as penal settlers. The following year, corporal punishment was abolished for all peasants, soldiers, sailors, and other categories of the population.[55]

Penal Hard Labor

In the first half of the eighteenth century, those sentenced to hard labor served their sentences primarily in European Russia, in building ships and

---

*However, there were a significant number of exceptions: Freed from corporal punishment were those peasants who had at least a secondary education; those who held public posts; those who served in the army (after the introduction in 1874 of universal military service for all social estates, approximately a third of peasant males completed service in the army); those suffering from certain illnesses; and those of 60 years of age or older (around 40 percent of the male population in the countryside).

ports, digging in mines, working in factories, and so on. For their labor they received remuneration—usually 10 percent of the income from their labor. After the abolition of capital punishment by Empress Elizabeth in 1756–1757, those sentenced to hard labor were generally sent to Siberia, where they were put to work in mines, fortresses, and factories. Between 1834 and 1844, 1,320 people were sentenced yearly to hard labor, and between 1846 and 1860, 974 yearly.[56] The system established to implement sentences of hard labor was so weakened after the Emancipation that for a period of time the sentence of hard labor for all practical purposes was not used. The reason for this was that the original punitive function of the sentence gave way to the use of convicts as a source of cheap labor. The penal hard labor system began to resemble serfdom in some respects, often functioning only to benefit those who directed it, although it was against the law to profit from penal operations.[57] After the Great Reforms, as loud protests against such abuses were voiced by public opinion and the liberal press, it became difficult to abuse the system of penal hard labor in this way, to the advantage either of various government departments or of private individuals. Thus, government departments that had hoped to acquire the labor of prisoners—such as the Ministry of War, the Ministry of Finance, and others—found that it was not in their interest to use penal labor, and instead they made use of hired labor. Beginning in the late 1860s, convicts sent into exile at hard labor in Siberia came primarily from the Perm and Orenburg provinces in eastern European Russia and from Siberia. Convicts from other regions were sent into exile and hard labor only when their families could go with them. Other criminals sentenced to hard labor were housed in special prisons in European Russia.[58] With the goal of finding a way to make use of those sentenced to hard labor, the government in 1875 opened a facility on the island of Sakhalin for penal hard labor. At the same time, those sentenced to hard labor began again to be sent to Siberia. With the rise in the number of serious crimes committed, the numbers of those sent to Siberia rose, both in absolute terms and in relation to the size of the population. At the end of the nineteenth century, some 2,000 persons were being sent into penal hard labor each year.[59]

Exile

Exile was used as a punishment as early as the Muscovite period. Until the 1750s, persons sentenced to exile were sent to distant places within European Russia. In the second half of the eighteenth century, however, convicts began to be sent primarily to Siberia, and in the nineteenth century, to the Caucasus as well.[60] Exiles were limited in their movements and activities, and they were kept under police surveillance. The status of exiles was set in law by the *Ustav o ssyl'nykh* (Statute on Exiles) of 1822 and by the

1845 Code of Punishments. Between 1807 and 1898, an estimated 876,500 persons were exiled to Siberia alone. Among these, approximately 118,500, or nearly one-seventh of the total, were sentenced to hard labor. In 1897, some 298,600 persons were serving terms in Siberia as exiles of various categories other than those at penal hard labor, and exiles made up 5.2 percent of the entire population of the region.[61]

Imprisonment and the Penal System

Imprisonment began to be used in Russia as a form of punishment in the sixteenth century. Until 1649, however, jails and prisons were mainly used as places where those under criminal investigation could be held. The use of corporal and capital punishment as the main means of sanction made it unnecessary for the government to develop a prison system. This was the case even after the 1649 *Sobornoe ulozhenie* outlined the use of imprisonment as additional punishment for forty types of crimes. No special facilities were built to serve as prisons, and sentences of imprisonment were served out generally in the cellars of monasteries, government institutions, or in small public or government buildings. Men, women, and children were held in confinement together. Until 1662, responsibility for the maintenance of prisoners was borne by the prisoners' relatives, owners (for serf prisoners), or plaintiffs. In 1662, the state began to allocate funds for the purpose. However, these funds were insufficient, and prisoners often were dependent on charity. Several prisoners, bound to each other, would be released for a day from their place of confinement in order to beg alms. Prisoners were permitted to work within the prison, earning money for themselves as tradesmen or handicraft workers. During the reign of Peter I, prisoners were put to work at government projects, but there was not enough such work to usefully occupy all prisoners.

In the 1760s, Catherine II attempted to construct a system of regular prisons, divided into several types for various types of prisoners. Apart from existing prisons, Catherine in 1775 established a special type of forced-labor prison known as *smiritel'nyi dom*. These prisons were intended for the incarceration of those found guilty of immoral conduct, which included disobedient children, parasites on society *(tuneiadtsy)*, serfs who had committed offenses, and persons who had committed sexual crimes. Beginning in 1781, workhouses were created for those who had committed crimes against property.* Those held in workhouses were

---

*Crimes against property *(prestupleniia protiv sobstvennosti)* were crimes connected with violations of the ownership rights of others, such as theft, robbery, fraud, and the like.

all held in common, shared cells and were obliged to work. In 1785, the state began to allot monies regularly for the maintenance of prisoners.

However, due to a continual shortage of funds and a lack in Russia of a centralized, separate administration for prisons, the places of incarceration instituted by Catherine were poorly organized and were unable to develop properly.[62] As earlier, the cells in most places of detention were overcrowded. Frequently, prisoners were not separated by basis of sex or age, the healthy shared cells with the ill, and prisoners were underfed and continued to have to rely on alms.[63] There were no medical care personnel in prisons; the incidence of disease was high among prisoners, and consequently, so was the death rate. The medical care that did reach prisoners was provided by the meager funds available to the Office for Public Care *(Prikaz obshchestvennogo prizreniia)* in each province, by the commune in which prisoners were registered before their arrest, and by charity.[64] The funds provided by the state for the maintenance of prisoners were never sufficient. Prison administrators continually requested that allocations for prisons be increased,[65] but the state replied that there was no money to give them. Instead, prison officials were recommended to make do with what they had or to find their own sources of income, such as prisoner labor; charity; and collections from prisoners' communes, from the owners of prisoners who were serfs, or from creditors of those who were incarcerated.[66] Prison administrators were generally able to bring their institutions into order only for short periods, when high-ranking officials, especially the emperor, were paying them visits.[67]

When the 1832 Code of Laws and the 1845 Code of Punishments made incarceration the primary means of punishment, the state met with a critical shortage of places to put prisoners. It quickly moved to develop the country's penal system. The majority of sentences handed down involved incarceration in one of the following: penal battalion, lockup center *(arestantskoe otdelenie)*, correctional facility known as *ispravitel'nyi dom*, workhouse, fortress, forced-labor prison, or prison. Conditions in the various places of incarceration differed in severity, and prisoners with similar sentences often served out their sentences in similar environments. For instance, fortresses were used to incarcerate those who had committed acts that did not involve harm to their personal honor, or dishonorable motives on their part. Such prisoners were generally held in isolation from one another and were permitted to work if they chose. Lockup centers were established in 1827 in provincial administrative centers, with the aim of providing a source of labor for improvements in these towns. The lockup centers were intended only for male prisoners of working age—primarily fugitives and vagrants sentenced to exile or to a workhouse for minor crimes. The majority of those sentenced to incarceration were held in prisons. During the summer many of these prisoners worked until eleven o'clock in the evening (or until ten o'clock in the winter), and received a paltry remuneration for this work. Prisoners who worked were permitted to have their own table and additional, modest portions of food. Those incarcerated in prisons were held in common, shared cells.

However, the system of correctional facilities outlined in the 1845 Code of Punishments failed to function as intended. Due to the shortage of forced-labor prisons and workhouses, prisoners sentenced to these facilities served their terms mainly in regular prisons and in lockup centers. However, there was also shortage of the latter. It was intended that lockup centers be established in each provincial administrative center, but this goal was not reached. In 1889 there were only 32 lockup centers, and by 1903, only one more had been added; the number of these facilities was thus two and a half times fewer than the number of provincial administrative centers. As a result of the shortage of places of incarceration, prisoners belonging to groups not exempt from corporal punishment who had been sentenced to forced-labor prisons or to workhouses were instead given between 40 and 100 blows with the birch rod. Those who were exempt from corporal punishment were sent to prisons. Since the government was unable to create a hierarchically organized penal system, it instead chose to simplify the system: In the 1880s, the workhouses and forced-labor prisons were closed, and only three types of incarceration remained—the fortress, the *ispravitel'nyi dom,* and the prison. Special arrest centers *(arestnye doma)* existed where those arrested could be detained for a period of time; these centers had sections for minors and for persons of the higher social estates. The latter, however, most frequently served their sentences in military guardhouses or within the buildings of the government department for which they worked.[68] Regulations and conditions concerning the maintenance of prisoners in these various detention facilities changed over time. Everywhere, however, four days of general incarceration were considered equal to three days of solitary confinement.

The continual increase in the number of prisons and prisoners forced the government to create in 1879 the Main Prison Administration *(Glavnoe tiuremnoe upravlenie).* This body was under the Ministry of the Interior until 1895, after which it was under the Ministry of Justice. The Main Prison Administration became the central administrative organ for all detention and prison facilities in the Russian empire. The Main Prison Administration passed a number of measures aimed at improving the penal system, but these measures did not greatly alter the conditions in which prisoners were held, and failed to turn places of detention into true correctional facilities. The main reasons for this failure were the shortage of funds and the sharp growth in the number of prisoners in the penal system as a result of increasing crime. In 1804, approximately 14,000 persons were held as prisoners in various penal institutions within Russia (excluding Finland). By 1840, the number of prisoners had risen to 17,000; by 1861, to 31,000; by 1885, to 95,000; and after a dip to 90,000 in 1900, to 169,000 in 1913. In addition to those sentenced to incarceration, prisons held exiles and those accompanying them; persons under investigation; any convicts' family members who were willing to follow and stay with the convict; vagrants; and others. These groups together totaled six to eight times the number of prisoners who had been given prison sentences. Thus, in 1804, the total number of people housed in penal institutions was 72,000; in 1840, 103,000; in 1861, 217,000; in 1868, 455,000; in 1885, 703,000; and in 1913, 899,000.[69] The increase in the number of prisons could not keep up with the rising numbers of prisoners.

Accurate statistics on the penal system in Russia are available beginning for 1879, the year in which the Main Prison Administration was founded. This new body printed yearly reports containing a detailed description of the state of the prisons and the conditions in which prisoners were being held. Before the judicial reform of 1864, there were insufficient numbers of prisons, and prisoners were held either in solitary cells or in common cells with all prisoners together; in police custody; or in small jails called *tiuremnye zamki*, which were not designed to hold criminals. The number of prisons did not figure in the statistics kept on the penal system as prominently as did the number of cells and the number of prisoners they could hold.[70] In 1879, the Main Prison Administration had under its jurisdiction 850 prisons; in 1900, 892; and in 1913, over 1,000. The number of prison spaces increased from 61,700 in 1879 to 120,000 in 1913, of which 7.2 to 7.5 percent were cells for solitary confinement. Despite the growth in the capacity of the penal system, prisons were still overflowing: In 1863–1864, the number of prisoners exceeded the capacity of prisons by 1.12 times; in the 1890s, by 1.4 times; and between 1908 and 1913, by 1.5 times.[71]

The inactivity of prisoners in many prisons was detrimental to their health. In the 1880s only about 30 percent of prisoners were occupied with some sort of work during the year, and in the first decade of the twentieth century, no more than 58 percent were working, with the number of days worked averaging between 70 and 120 days a year.[72] When reviewing the report of the governor of Pskov province for 1882, Alexander III noted the high mortality rate of prisoners at hard labor in the province and demanded an explanation. The memorandum he received in reply noted that the prisoners were not actually working but rather were being held in closed, stuffy quarters and only infrequently taken outdoors, as a result of which many were suffering from intestinal and pulmonary diseases.*

---

*RGIA, f. 1263, op. 1, d. 4330 (1883 g.), ll. 161–165.

Prisoners' inactivity had another negative result: It denied them a source of income. On the average, 31 percent of the income from a prisoner's labor was given to the prisoner; and with this money prisoners were able to eat better than they otherwise would have. Moreover, funds were remitted to prisons out of the income from prisoners' labor; and had all prisoners capable of working been given productive work, prison conditions could have been improved.

As a result of poor conditions in prisons, annual mortality rates among prisoners were high—much higher than among the population at large—and suicide rates in prisons were high as well. In the 1880s the annual mortality rate among prisoners, more than 90 percent of whom were male, was 40 to 42 per thousand, and between 1901 and 1906, 20 per thousand. For comparison, the mortality rate for the adult population (20 years of age and older) in European Russia in the 1880s was 18 per thousand, and between 1901 and 1906, 14 per thousand.[73] In the late nineteenth and early twentieth centuries approximately 40 to 50 suicides occurred for each 100,000 persons imprisoned; this rate was nearly twenty times higher than the suicide rate of the overall Russian population.[74] From 1907 to 1913, the mortality rate and the number of suicides in prisons continued to rise due to the huge influx of prisoners. From 1907 to 1912, in Russia as a whole, mortality fell to 14 per thousand, whereas the mortality rate among the prison population rose to 38 per thousand. Suicide in prisons rose to 94 per thousand prisoners, and it also rose in the country in general, judging by the numbers of suicides in the towns and cities.[75]

At the same time, it is important to note that a number of improvements were made in the penal system from 1879 to 1913. Nutrition, sanitation, and medical services were gradually improved. In the early years of the twentieth century, 67 percent of prisons had their own hospitals; the remaining prisons used existing hospitals frequented by the nonincarcerated population. The existence of prison hospitals contributed to the above-mentioned decrease in the prison mortality rate in the last two decades of the nineteenth century and the first few years of the twentieth. Significant progress was achieved also in making work available to prisoners: The number of prisoners working doubled during the period 1879–1913. Progress also was made in improving the quality of prisoners' free-time activities; in the early twentieth century, 14 percent of penal institutions had schools, 39 percent had libraries, and in 28 percent, lectures and discussion groups were held.[76] With the development of railroads and of water travel, prisoners began to be transported to prisons by train and steamship. This brought an end to their horrendous treks on foot into Siberian exile. In prisons where inmates were housed together in common cells (which made up 94 percent of all penal institutions), the regime was not excessively strict. This is borne out by the fact that between 1,500 and 2,500 prisoners managed to escape each year, of whom only about half were captured.[77]

In sum, Russia's criminal justice system underwent significant change over time. The pillars of the system in Rus were fines, compensation for losses incurred, and vengeance *(mest')*. In the Muscovite period—the fifteenth to the seventeenth centuries—and in the eighteenth century, the pillars of the system were corporal and capital punishment. In the first half of the nineteenth century, the system was centered around corporal punishment for the nonprivileged classes and incarceration for the privileged. From 1864 on, the dominant aspect was incarceration for all groups of the population. In the postreform era, new ideas penetrated the criminal justice system concerning the reeducability of prisoners and the possibility of their returning to a normal life after their sentences were served. The practice of releasing prisoners before their sentences were fully served began in 1909; and in 1910, the time prisoners spent under arrest before being sentenced began to be counted as time served against their eventual sentences. In 1913, for the first time, the sentences of convicted persons could be annulled, and all their former rights restored. From the end of the eighteenth century on, particularly after 1845, the nature of the corpus delicti for a criminal act and the hierarchy of sentences that could be handed down were of principal importance in determining a sentence. Sentencing became less rigidly pre-determined, allowing judges a degree of leeway to modify sentences in accordance with the magnitude of the crime. The latter approach is considered by jurists to be an important sign of progress in the evolution of criminal law.

The famous Russian jurist N. S. Tagantsev wrote: "In evaluating the penal system of a given epoch and a given people, one must always remember that the sensible guideline will be the system's suitability and vitality. Every penal system is worked out through the life of the people and is intended to serve the interests of that life."[78] In my view, in each step of its development, the Russian criminal justice system met the goal of protecting the legal order. It corresponded to the understanding of the law held by the overwhelming majority of Russians, and on the whole it was effectual.

The Origins of Civil Law: The Written Record

Very few early Russian sources on civil law survive today, and consequently we can only make educated guesses as we interpret the meager evidence. Widely conflicting views exist among scholars on civil law in this period. Thus, this analysis is focused on the most basic and least problematic points in the general evolution and development of the fundamental concepts of Russian civil law.

Until 1832 there was no special codex of civil law in Russia, and legal norms for governing civil matters were included in general codices of the law. No clear distinctions were made between criminal and civil law until the fifteenth and sixteenth centuries. From the mid-seventeenth century on, civil affairs were set apart in a separate sphere and regulated by special norms that were included in separate sections of general legal codices, such as the *Sobornoe ulozhenie* of 1649. The *Sobornoe ulozhenie* remained the functioning code of norms for matters of civil law until the introduction of the *Svod zakonov* (Code of Laws) in 1832, being supplemented during the second half of the seventeenth century and the first half of the eighteenth by new laws. Some of these new laws nullified, elaborated on, or added to earlier laws; others were completely new, reflecting the development of social and economic relations. The 1832 Code of Laws, which also was supplemented regularly with new laws, remained the primary source of civil law until the end of the tsarist regime. The Code of Laws was supplemented especially rapidly after Emancipation: New laws on factory workers were introduced in 1861, 1882, 1886, and 1897. Also issued were a new statute on trades and crafts; a statute on industrial factories; and standard statutes on trade, the stock exchange, bills of exchange, and commercial bankruptcy. The first procedural codex for civil law was issued in 1864.

The Subjects of Civil Law

In old Rus, only individual persons *(fizicheskie litsa)* could be subjects of the law, since the notion of a legal entity *(iuridicheskoe litso)* was unknown to the authors of the first codex of Russian law, the *Russkaia pravda.* Consequently, the earliest Russian law did not recognize crimes against the state, nor did it recognize the state's material interests. The *Russkaia pravda* made no reference to such abstract notions of civil law as "property," "possession," and "disposition of property" *(rasporiazhenie imushchestvom),* since customary law, the source of the *Russkaia pravda,* is incompatible with abstract notions, including the notion of a legal entity. All subjects are equal under customary law, and only individuals can be subjects of law.[79] Only males 15 years of age and older who were free citizens enjoyed full rights as subjects of both civil and criminal law. Women were not entirely denied the right to act in civil legal matters, but their rights were significantly limited in comparison with men's rights. In Muscovy, collective entities such as state institutions, communes *(obshchiny),* monasteries, and the like also had the right to act as a single entity in civil legal matters.

In the eighteenth century and the first half of the nineteenth century, the numbers of legal entities mushroomed. The status of legal entity was granted to municipal administrative bodies *(magistraty* and *ratushi),* educational institutions, hospitals, almshouses, trade and industrial companies, printing houses, organizations and societies of the nobility, merchant guilds *(gil'dii)*, artisans' guilds *(tsekhi)*, and other groups. Under Peter I, the age at which one attained civil rights *(grazhdanskie prava)** was raised to 20 (it was raised again in 1832 to age 21), and limitations on one's civil rights were stipulated according to one's mental health and moral status. Thus, excluded from the group of people possessing civil rights were the insane, persons placed under guardianship due to their wastefulness, and those denied by a court the right to be a subject of law. Legal contracts for such persons were concluded by their guardians. During this time the concepts of a legal entity and of corporate property began to take shape in the law. As serfdom and the system of social estates developed, limitations were placed on the civil rights of the nonprivileged estates, such as peasants (especially serfs) and burghers *(meshchane)*.

After the 1860s, all male subjects of the empire became subjects of civil law, irrespective of nationality, religion, or social estate. As before, however, women's rights were limited. The concept of a legal entity had fully solidified in legislation; legal entities were divided into the categories of public entity, private person, joint entity *(soedinenie lits)*, and institution. The legal capacity of legal entities was determined by the Senate according to the aims of each entity's activities.[80] By defining precisely the nature of legal entities and removing limitations on their formation, the law fostered their rapid increase. The number of legal entities expanded especially quickly in the form of private associations and societies; joint-stock, exchange, trade, and other such companies; museums and libraries; hospitals; and other, similar organizations. This trend reflected the growth of private and public initiative and the development of market relations in Russia.

Liability Law

In the Kievan period, pecuniary obligations arose out of contracts between parties or out of harm or injury caused by one party against another. Contracts had a sacral nature, and their conclusion was accompanied by rituals such as the affixing of signatures in the presence of witnesses; the repetition of certain formulaic expressions; the ritualistic shaking of hands, known as *rukoprikladstvo;* and so on. Rituals were particularly important in contracts concerning the sale, purchase, and exchange of goods; rituals

---

*From the eighteenth century to the early twentieth century in Russia, "civil rights" *(grazhdanskie prava)* were not political rights but rights associated with one's social estate *(soslovie)* or with the status of being a free person. Thus, for example, a nobleman who lost his civil rights lost all rights and privileges accruing to a person of noble status, as well as his freedom and property.

helped to break the ties believed to exist between an individual and a physical object. Thus, a contract alone did not determine changes in the legal status of physical things. Failure by one party to fulfill a contract gave the injured party the right to make the debtor his slave. Enforced payments could be extracted from merchants and traders who went bankrupt. In such cases, the debtor was granted an extended period in which to repay his debts, and only after this period expired was he sold into slavery.

The law recognized contracts for loans, bartering of goods, purchase and sale, pawning of goods, storage of goods, and employment. These contracts were generally concluded orally—only about 1 percent of the population in the Kievan period was literate—and as a result, they were also concluded publicly, in the open marketplace and in the presence of witnesses. Contracts thus could be contested or defended in court through oral testimony. Contracts were primarily oral until the mid-sixteenth century; written contracts were rare, and those that were drawn up concerned the acquisition of land. Contracts involving the lending of money or of goods in kind stipulated the return of the amount loaned together with an additional payment as interest. The annual rate of interest was customarily 50 percent, but the receipt of interest was limited to two years, after which a debt was considered paid. The notion of personal loans in the modern sense did not exist; those persons who failed to repay their debts generally lost their freedom until their debts were cleared.

The institutions of civil law continued to develop in the Muscovite period (the fifteenth through the seventeenth centuries). During this era, pecuniary obligations arose mainly from oral contracts, although obligations arising from harm or injury caused by one party against another also continued to exist. Many transactions, including the rental of goods to another individual and giving up items for placement in storage, were not recognized by the law without an accompanying contract; and in many cases a written contract was required. Losses suffered by a party were unrecoverable unless the suffering party could prove its case in court. A person who hired himself out as a laborer without an accompanying contract fell into debt servitude after three months' time (becoming a *kabal'nyi kholop*). The role of written contracts increased in importance over time, and contracts that dealt with large amounts of material wealth or money required notarial registration in state institutions. The conclusion of contracts lost its sacral character but gained a number of formal elements, such as set phrases for describing pecuniary obligations and the confirmation of contracts by representatives of the state. Several means were used to confirm claims to the right of property ownership. Seizure of property—the most ancient means for obtaining the right of ownership—had to be accompanied by a grant of permission *(pozhalovanie)* from the tsar, which legalized the seizure.

An important change occurred in liability law when pecuniary obligations began to be guaranteed not by the debtor's own person but rather by his property. Insolvent debtors lost their property in payment of their debts; only those who did not have guarantors for their loans or who squandered their borrowed funds (for example, through excessive drinking) were turned over to their creditors. Even when this happened, debtors were not forced into slavery *(kholopstvo)* as their counterparts in previous eras had been, but rather they were obliged to work until their debts were repaid. In the event of the death of a debtor—including those obliged to pay for inflicting insult or dishonor on another person—the debt was transferred to the debtor's wife and children, or to his servants; the notion of joint responsibility on the part of spouses, family members, and servants applied to liability law as well as to criminal law. Debts of a landlord could be recovered from his serfs, and a landlord given a sentence of flogging for insolvency (a practice known as *pravezh*) could send a serf to receive the punishment in his place. The law also lowered the level of interest on monetary loans to 20 percent per annum. Interest could not be collected longer than five years: After five years, a debt was considered repaid. The sale and purchase of real estate were limited by a number of conditions, and a landlord could alienate his landed estate only with the sanction of the state. The heirs of a person who had sold his patrimonial estate retained for forty years the right to redeem the estate back into the family's patrimony.

As a consequence of the development of serfdom, peasants had only limited contractual rights. Serfs, whose rights were particularly limited, could conclude contracts only with the permission of their masters. In 1754 the legal limit on interest on loans was lowered to 6 percent per annum, and in 1786 it was further lowered to 5 percent. Bills of exchange entered circulation with the publication in 1739 of a statute on bills of exchange, and merchants received the right to obligate themselves with bills of exchange. During the reign of Peter I, a new form of contractual relations arose—a contract of association *(dogovor tovarishchestva)*. This new type of contract made possible the creation of joint-stock companies in trade and industry. Beginning in the eighteenth century, any legal activity could be made the object of a contract. However, as the law placed so many limits on contracts and disallowed so many people from being subjects of law, the proclaimed freedom to conclude contracts rang rather hollow.

Not until the 1832 Code of Laws was liability law fully developed. This codex defined which contracts could be concluded orally and which had to be made in written form. The law stated that every legal contract was subject to fulfillment, and stipulated four means for guaranteeing contracts: sureties, forfeiture, mortgage of real estate as security, and the use of movable property as security. With few exceptions, the bartering of real estate was forbidden, although the bartering of movable property was not.

Forward contracts, by which one party obliged itself to the sale of movable property or real estate at a given price by a set date, now attained the force of law. (Such contracts had been used as early as the seventeenth century.) If one of the contracting parties was unable to fulfill its obligations, the property was subject to forfeiture for breach of contract. Forward contracts were used widely in trade, particularly in foreign trade: Foreign merchants used them to give credits to Russian merchants who delivered goods to ports.

Real estate now could be leased for periods not exceeding twelve years, and lease agreements had to be formulated in writing. As earlier, interest rates on loans of money could not exceed 6 percent per annum. The law provided for loans of movable property, but such loans had to be free of charge; the only requirement was that the loaned goods be returned on time and in the same condition as when they were loaned.

Employment contracts became widespread in the late eighteenth century and the early nineteenth. The 1832 Code of Laws, however, did little to improve this type of contract, especially with regard to peasants. In order to travel outside the commune, peasants were required to carry passports, which were issued by the state administration with the sanction of the peasant commune. Since state peasants without a passport were barred from hiring themselves out as laborers, the commune effectively had veto power over the freedom of individual peasants to work outside the commune. Proprietary peasants desiring to contract themselves out as laborers needed the permission of their master as well as a passport. A married peasant woman wanting to enter into an employment contract also had to obtain the permission of her husband; and persons who were not household heads needed the permission of their family head. Employment contracts were limited to five years.

In the first half of the nineteenth century, new types of contracts appeared, dealing with commissions, insurance, publishing, and other areas. Also introduced were copyrights, commercial rights, and proprietary rights to inventions, models, trademarks, and the names of firms. After Emancipation, the principles of bourgeois civil law penetrated Russian legislation even more deeply. Legal contracts and agreements could contain any conditions or clauses that were not in violation of law and that did not breach public order. In 1870, special statutes on joint-stock companies, insurance, and employment contracts were passed. Characteristically Russian types of contracts were retained, such as the forward contract and the *mirovaia sdelka,* in which disputants in a suit at the level of the county court *(volostnoi sud)* or court of a justice of the peace *(mirovoi sud)* came to an agreement and ended their litigation. Most frequently the form in which trans-

actions were concluded was optional, though a number of important transactions had to be made in writing and certified by a notary. The law permitted all types of contracts known in modern market economies.[81]

The freedom to enter into civil contracts led to rapid growth in the numbers of such contracts. In 1884, some 207,000 various acts, deeds, and
contracts were registered in notarial offices in Russia; 688,600 were registered in 1913—an increase of more than 330 percent. Notaries also distributed various types of information in written form *(spravki)*, the number of which (together with registered documents) grew from 357,000 in
1884 to 1,967,000 in 1913—an increase of more than 550 percent.[82]

Inheritance Law

In the Kievan period, only sons had the right to inherit. This practice ensured that property would not leave the commune, since daughters after
their weddings left to live in the commune of their husbands, whereas sons
upon marrying remained in the same commune. The rule of inheritance
along the male line is yet another piece of evidence attesting to the lack of
development of the institution of private property. The privilege of handing down property to daughters was in part used by Russia's elite—the boyars and members of boyars' retinues *(druzhinniki)*. The *druzhinniki* were
separate from the commune and had the privilege of owning private property, conditioned upon their service to the prince. In the fifteenth to seventeenth centuries, the circle of heirs, as well as the rights of testators, gradually expanded, as is evident from the increasingly common use of wills as
a means of handing down property. Any member of the family could make
a will. As a result of this expansion in their use, wills had to be drawn up
in written form. According to the *Sobornoe ulozhenie* of 1649, testators
had the right to bequeath their property as they saw fit, but only within the
limits established by law. Under the law, one could not bequeath land to
the church. Neither patrimonial estates nor estates bestowed by the tsar
could be bequeathed to persons outside the testator's clan. In the absence
of a will, property was divided among heirs in accordance with the law.
Sons who were living in their father's house at the moment of his death received equal portions of his property after the father's debts were paid
from his estate.

Women's rights of inheritance were expanded to some degree under the
Sobornoe ulozhenie: When a man had no sons or left no will, his estate
could be inherited by his daughter or his widow, if the widow had no other
means of support. After the death of the widow, the husband's property
then reverted to the possession of his clan. Widows also could inherit a
husband's landed estate if it had been purchased by the husband or
awarded to him as a result of his service. If a man did have sons, then his

daughters were ineligible to inherit from him; they were, however, granted a certain portion of the estate as a source of financial support or as a contribution to their future dowries. These changes in inheritance law had little effect on the life of peasants, however, among whom only sons had the right to inherit.

Peter I attempted in vain to introduce primogeniture among the nobility. At the insistence of the nobility, a law on inheritance introduced by Peter in 1714 was repealed in 1731, six years after Peter's death. The laws of inheritance (given the absence of a will by the deceased) were now changed. The deceased's sons had the immediate right to inheritance; if no sons were living, then grandsons were the heirs; in the absence of grandsons, then great-grandsons. If there were no heirs in the male line, then daughters (and correspondingly, granddaughters and great-granddaughters) could inherit. The existence of closer relatives precluded more distant relatives from inheriting. Inherited property was divided equally among eligible heirs of the same generation, regardless of gender. Daughters who had living brothers received by law a certain portion of the estate: one-eighth of the deceased's movable property and one-fourteenth of the real estate. The rest of the estate was then divided equally among the deceased's sons. If a deceased had no direct relatives, then collateral relatives were the inheritors, and in the absence of collateral relatives, then the deceased's parents. A surviving spouse received one-seventh of the deceased's real estate and one-fourteenth of the movable property. Adopted children inherited only property that had been purchased by their adoptive parents, and none of their ancestral (patrimonial) property. Illegitimate children had no rights of inheritance. Escheated property of the deceased reverted to the state, members of the nobility, the province, the town, or the village community, depending on the deceased's social estate.

The 1832 Code of Laws included these inheritance laws and at the same time broadened the rights of testators. Now testators could leave bequests to whomever they wished and in whatever form, with the exception that entailed estates could not be bequeathed. (Entailed estates, established by personal ukase of the emperor, ranged in size from 5 to 100,000 *desiatiny*—that is, 27 to 110,000 hectares.) The law declared as invalid wills made by minors, monks, the mentally ill, victims of suicide, and persons deprived by a court of *soslovie* (estate), family, and property rights. Also invalid were wills naming as inheritors Jews, Poles, or foreigners residing in provinces in which these groups did not have the right to possess immovable property. Beginning in 1832, in order for wills to be valid they had to be drawn up in written form, with witnesses present. After Emancipation, the bequeathing of property according to wills dominated over inheritance according to standing law; in the absence of a will, the deceased's parents were otherwise excluded from the circle of inheritors.[83]

Property Law (Veshchnoe pravo)

The norms and procedures that commonly evolved in modern civil legal systems in response to the individualization of legal subjects did not emerge in Russian legal practice until the eighteenth century.[84] This was due to the fact that private property, in the fullest sense of the word, did not exist before that time.[85] Earlier Russian law and custom did not distinguish between real estate and movable property and gave insufficient attention to the latter. All merchants, artisans, and peasants belonged to a corporate group or commune, and real estate was owned collectively by the group or commune rather than by individual members. Movable property was owned by families rather than by individuals. A certain individualization of property ownership did occur among Russia's social elite, but even for them, in the eleventh to thirteenth centuries, real estate was not considered the property of individuals but of the clan. To some degree the right of ownership one enjoyed was dependent on one's military service to the prince or to the principality. This was the case, for example, in Novgorod, where boyars were rewarded with lands for their service. Property rights could be acquired legally by the seizure—the so-called *zakhvatnoe pravo*—of goods, including land, that belonged to no one, as well as by prescription *(davnost')*, discovery *(nakhodka)*, contract, royal grant *(pozhalovanie)*, and endowment *(darenie)*.

In Muscovy, the freedom to have land at one's disposal was limited by the state for all classes of the population. Landholding existed in three forms: (1) *votchina*, or patrimonial landed estate; (2) *pomest'e*, or conditional landholding; and (3) communal *(obshchinnoe)* landholding. The owner of a *votchina* had the right to make various transactions with estate lands. A *pomest'e* was granted in exchange for service, and when that service ended, the estate reverted to the holdings of the grand prince or the tsar. Usually, however, a son would take his father's place in state service, and the *pomest'e* estate would remain in the hands of a particular family. By the mid-fifteenth century, however, both *votchina* and *pomest'e* forms of landholding were dependent on military service to the state.

Communal lands were held in the collective possession of members of a rural peasant commune or of an urban commune. These lands changed hands only among members of the given commune, and the right of supreme ownership to them was held by the state.

Movable property had acquired the characteristics of private property in a de facto sense even before the reign of Peter I; movables became private property de jure in 1714, when they were separated in a legal sense from real estate. Landed property was divided into patrimonial, awarded, and purchased estates (either of the *votchina* or the *pomest'e* type). Real estate in the form of buildings was divided into *dvory* (dwellings) and *lavki,* or buildings in which merchants and others could sell their goods. Special procedures were established for dealing with real estate of various types. In rural communes, land remained in collective possession, as it had been before.

In urban areas, there was ongoing tension throughout the seventeenth century between the landholding models of private ownership versus collective, communal possession, with neither achieving complete dominance. Private ownership predominated by the end of the century, however: Conceding to pressure from the nobility and state servitors *(sluzhilye liudi),* legislators gave obligated townspeople *(posadskie liudi)* the right to dispose of buildings that stood on land belonging to their urban communes. This included the right to sell buildings to new settlers who did not belong to the given urban commune, with the condition that a new settler pay the taxes and fulfill all of the duties and obligations that had been borne by his predecessor. This made it easier for obligated townspeople to relocate, and for persons who did not belong to the urban commune to settle on communal lands. At the beginning of the eighteenth century the rights of obligated townspeople to dispose of their own buildings and lands were further expanded.[86]

At the end of the seventeenth century and in the first half of the eighteenth, the law clearly established what kinds of property various categories of persons could own. Only those who belonged to the service class could possess land as individuals. Gradually squeezed out of the service class were those nonnobles known as *sluzhilye liudi po priboru*—state servitors recruited by contract. In terms of property rights and social status, these servitors increasingly resembled state peasants; they were organized into communes and lost the right to hold land as individuals.

An even more radical break in estate law occurred during the reign of Catherine II. Between 1762 and 1785, the nobility acquired full legal ownership of their *pomest'e* estates together with the peasants living on them. Abolished were the servitudes introduced by Peter I on noble estates, such as the right of the government to dispose of mineral resources, some types of wooded lands, and the like. In 1737, the time limit for clans to redeem former patrimonial lands was reduced from forty to three years, and the number of persons who enjoyed this right to redeem familial lands was also reduced. This change indicated a victory of the rights of individuals to landownership over those of the clan. The new rule secured the stability of rights to acquire property and made it easier for land to be purchased and sold.

In the first third of the nineteenth century, the remaining social estates, with the exception of serfs, also were granted the right to own land and other property. Ownership of significant real estate in trade and industry, such as factories, plants, facilities for trade, and other buildings in urban areas, was no longer monopolized by the urban social estate. The 1832 Code of Laws confirmed the right to private ownership of real estate, especially land, which in Russia was the main form of immovable property. The institution of private property was now completely formalized in law. Property ownership was defined as the right "exclusively, and independently of other persons, to possess, use, and dispose of property for all time and through all generations." The right to hold land as private property was extended "to all that is produced on it [the land], to all that is contained in the ground beneath it, to the water contained within its borders; that is, to everything which is a part of it."[87]

During the reign of Alexander II the freedom to hold private property was transformed from a privilege into a general legal norm for the entire population. Limitations on estate law were retained only in instances where they were necessary in order to ensure individuals' freedom of property relations, such as in the case of servitudes.[88] The government retained the right to expropriate property in the interests of the state.[89]

Family Law

From the time of the introduction of Christianity in Rus in the tenth century, church marriage *(tserkovnyi brak)* won the recognition of social elites and townspeople. However, it was only in the sixteenth to seventeenth centuries, as Christianity spread more widely throughout the population, that marriage in the church began to be practiced by the peasantry. The Christianization of the peasantry was accompanied by a prohibition of marriage between Christians and non-Christians as well as between Christians of differing confessions.[90] By law, a betrothal *(sgovor)* preceded the marriage ceremony. Among elites betrothal consisted of a written, notarial contract; among the peasants it was an oral agreement. Failure to fulfill a contract of betrothal brought with it legal action and a fine. The parties to a contract of betrothal were the parents or guardians of the future couple; the couple's own wishes were not taken into account. Among serfs, marriage occurred with the consent of landlords of the betrothed pair. When a landlord permitted a peasant serf woman to marry another landlord's peasant (which meant she would leave his estate), he received a redemption fee *(vyvod)* from the groom's landlord. After the betrothal contract was made, the parents made a payment to the eparchial church hierarch for permission for their children to be married. The church official would determine whether or not any impediments existed to the marriage. The most common impediments were consanguinity of the betrothed; too proximate a relation of godparents (persons whose godfathers or godmothers were related within four generations of each other were not allowed to marry each other); the presence of a living spouse from a previous marriage; and the age of the betrothed. An impending marriage was announced three times in the church on church holy days. After this, the wedding ceremony was held.

From this evidence, it is clear that the norms of family law were mixed with those of liability law and that marriage included characteristics of a property transaction. This indicates that at this time the family was not so much an emotional and moral union of individuals who loved and respected each other as it was an economic union. The law established the authority of the husband and father. Wives acquired the social estate of their husbands, and children that of their fathers. When a family head sold himself into bonded slavery, his wife also acquired this status, as did any children born after their father's entrance into slavery. A husband had the right to present his wife as surety for a loan or to hire her out *(otdavat' v naem)* for a period of up to five years. Fathers could send their children to a monastery or sell them into bonded slavery; but the latter right was replaced in 1649 with the right to send children into temporary servitude *(usluzhenie)*.

Despite the fact that the man was supreme in the family, in terms of property the law recognized spouses as equals, and it assigned them joint responsibility for obligations. All family property, including the wife's dowry and property belonging to the husband before marriage, was considered the common property of the family; it was managed jointly by the spouses, and after their deaths it was inherited by their children. When a marriage was childless, however, the husband was obliged to set aside a portion *(veno,* or bride-price) equal to one-third of his property; this ensured that the wife's dowry remained intact. After the death of her husband, a widow kept this portion until the husband's relatives paid her the cost of her dowry. This clearly shows that clan solidarity coexisted with family, though the former began to weaken in the second half of the seventeenth century with the rising importance of the individual and of the role of property held by individual family members.[91]

Marriages ended mainly through the death of one of the spouses. Divorce did occur, the cause of which was usually adultery. Deprivation of civil rights by court decision did not necessarily end a marriage; a wife and children carried the same legal responsibility and obligations as did the head of the family, and vice versa. In addition to adultery, grounds for divorce included incapacity of one of the spouses to maintain conjugal relations; prolonged and serious illness; departure of a spouse to a monastery or convent; and prolonged absence of a spouse from the family without contact.

Significant changes transpired in the sphere of family law in the eighteenth century. These changes concerned mainly the nobility but also urban elites.

In 1702, priority in the law was given to the wedding ceremony over the betrothal, and the fine for forfeiture was canceled in cases of refusal of one of the betrothed to wed. Thus, the religious significance of marriage was underscored, and the property aspect of the marriage transaction, which formerly predominated, became less important. An attempt in 1744 to restore sanctions for refusal to honor the betrothal agreement only resulted in the repeal of betrothal itself as an obligatory part of the marriage procedure, turning it into an optional rite of purely ceremonial and moral significance. No less important were alterations in law concerning marriage made by Peter I. In 1714 Peter raised the age at which nobles could marry. In 1722 he prohibited parents from making their children marry against their will, and he banned marriage for the mentally ill and mentally retarded. Peter also attempted to weaken traditional gender spheres by obliging women to participate with men in certain forms of public entertainment.

In 1753 the law abolished spouses' mutual responsibility for each other's debts and other obligations. According to law, a father was obliged to support any illegitimate children he might have as well as their mother, though illegitimate children could inherit from him only if specified in his will, not by standing law. However, some principles of family law from the pre-Petrine era remained in force, such as the authority of the husband over his wife and of parents over their children.

During the second half of the eighteenth century the law obligated those serving in the military and officials of various government departments to request permission from their superiors before they could be married. Beginning in 1800, officers with the ranks of general or higher were obliged to obtain permission to be married from the emperor. In 1802, parental authority over children ceased to apply to parents who had been deprived of their civil rights by a court or who had entered church orders. Parental authority over children also ended when children left the family household; this generally happened when a child married or when a son entered military service.

The 1832 Code of Laws introduced a number of changes in family law. The age at which one could enter marriage was raised to 16 years for women and to 18 for men. The law also gave women the freedom to dispose of their own property: Property that was part of a woman's dowry, that she had received as a gift, or that she had purchased or acquired by some other legal means, she could now dispose of as she desired, independently of her husband's wishes. In other respects, however, the law systematized previously enacted family legislation. Before they could marry, a couple had to obtain permission from their parents, guardians, or trustees. State officials and members of the military wishing to marry needed the permission of their superiors, and serfs required the permission of their landlords. Marriage between Christians and non-Christians was forbidden; but as early as 1712, marriages were permitted between Christians of differing confessions. A wife was obliged by law to live with her husband and to obey and submit to him. At the same time, a husband was forbidden to punish his wife; beating and otherwise maiming one's wife were criminal offenses. Grounds for divorce remained essentially the same as before: adultery; loss of civil rights by one of the spouses; the death of a spouse, absence of a spouse from the family without contact for at least five years; entry of either spouse into church orders; and incapacity of either spouse for conjugal relations, which was to be confirmed by a medical examination. For Lutherans there were additional grounds upon which a divorce could be obtained: insanity of one of the spouses, infectious disease, or a dissolute life on the part of one of the spouses. For Catholics divorce was considered indissoluble on principle. For male Muslim subjects of the empire there were no obstacles to divorce, but for Muslim women divorce was impossible.

After Emancipation, parents' permission was no longer required by law before a couple could enter into marriage, and this gave individuals greater freedom in the choice of a partner. The law also afforded couples greater freedom to divorce. The principle that spouses held property separately, as individuals, was strengthened in the law, and the independence of women from men was to some degree augmented. Still, without the permission of their husbands, married women could not accept employment, nor could they give out promissory notes or conclude other such economic transactions. Paradoxically, in the postreform period, the church strengthened its control over family and marital relations. Consequently, changes in family and marital legal matters occurred more de facto than de jure.[92]

Thus, civil law followed a long path of development. Along this path the number of subjects of the law increased as legal entities were added to individual human subjects of the law. The rights of private individuals gradually increased in all spheres of civil law, and at the expense of rights for the clan, the commune, corporative groups, and the state. Contracts and agreements acquired a concrete and individual character, and the types of contracts expanded in every way possible. In short, as civil freedoms expanded, so did the authority and rights of the individual in civil legal transactions. However, these progressive trends did not reach their logical culmination, as the rights of some people remained limited. Even to the end of the old regime, women and minors not only were significantly limited in their rights but also were insufficiently protected by the law from violence on the part of men.[93]

The Judicial System and Procedural Law in the Kievan and Muscovite Periods

In the Kievan period, judicial authority was in the hands of private individuals, corporate groups and communes, and government bodies. The juridical power of private individuals was manifested in the right of the lord to

judge his slaves and others who were dependent upon him for their liveli-
hood. The commune passed judgment for crimes committed by its members
on communal territory. The need to resolve conflicts between communes
peacefully necessitated state organs of judicial power. This power was
shared by the prince and the *veche* (popular meeting or assembly). The court
of the prince *(kniazheskii sud)* was led by the prince himself or by his counselors. At first the *veche* reviewed all types of legal suits, but gradually its
purview was narrowed to cover only cases of treason. In time, dealing with
the most serious crimes such as murder and robbery became the prerogative
of the court of the prince. Here, the most active role was played by representatives of the commune, on behalf of both plaintiffs and defendants.

The judicial process in Kievan Rus was adversarial in character. Both
sides were called "plaintiffs" *(isttsy)* or "contestants" *(soperniki)*; this
points to a lack of procedural advantages for either plaintiffs or defendants, though some exceptions were made in criminal suits. The notion
that the state could be a plaintiff in criminal cases did not yet exist, and no
distinction was made between criminal and civil procedures or between investigatory and accusatorial processes. Either side in a legal dispute could
be represented by private individuals, the family, the clan, or the commune.
Originally, the presence in court of the plaintiff and the defendant was
mandatory. In time, however, representatives were allowed to stand in for
the elderly, the ill, monks, and children. Before their court appearance, the
contestants customarily came to an agreement on the subject of the argument, on the judge, and on the date of the court hearing. At first, this
agreement was made between the plaintiff and the defendant, without the
participation of judicial powers. Later in the Kievan period, an agreement
would be reached with the participation of the judicial body to which the
defendant was appealing for assistance. However, when it was advantageous for the defendant to avoid the courts and when an agreement between him and the plaintiff was impossible, the plaintiff, with the sanction
of the state, was obliged to bring the defendant to court by force. Arrest
could be replaced by a surety *(poruchitel'stvo)*; this indicates that a high
value was placed on the freedom of the individual. If the offender could
not be found, the injured party initiated a search for him. In the case of
theft, the injured party publicly declared in the market square what possession of his was missing and what it looked like. After three days, the
possessor of the missing item was obliged to announce that he had the item
and to show that he had obtained it in an honest manner. If he could not
explain how the item in question had come into his possession, he was considered guilty and was required to compensate for the loss and pay a fine.
Anyone who was found to be in possession of an item missing for three
days had to return it and pay a fine. When it came to searching for a thief
or a murderer, it was believed that the perpetrator could be found in close
proximity to the stolen item or the murdered person. If the item or corpse

was found in a house, then the master of that house was considered guilty. If the incriminating evidence was found on the territory of a given village, then the rural commune either had to give up the guilty person, demonstrate that it was not involved in the crime, or pay a fine. If the *sled*, or "trail," of the perpetrator was lost, the search was called off.

All court proceedings were oral. The testimony of eyewitnesses, called *vidoki*, was used as evidence. Defendants also brought with them persons who could testify to their good name. These character witnesses, known as *poslukhi*, spoke on behalf of the entire commune, which then made the decision whether to clear the defendant of the charges against him or to hand down a negative judgment against him in a general communal meeting. If the oral evidence was inconclusive, resort was made to trial by ordeal *(sud Bozhii)*. The practice of *sud Bozhii* included various tests, all based on the belief that God would intervene to indicate the guilt or innocence of an accused person, or the truth in a case: ordeals involving hot iron, fire, or water; trial by combat; sacred oaths of innocence; and the casting of lots. After examining the circumstances of a particular case, the court would decide whether it was subject to *sud Bozhii,* which of the disputants would undergo a test, and what the nature of the test would be. The plaintiff who withstood the ordeal, won in combat, swore the sacred oath, or was selected in the casting of lots was thereby vindicated. Contestants in a legal dispute were permitted at any time to come to a resolution on their own—even during trial by combat.

In Muscovy as well as in Kievan Rus, judicial functions were not separated from those of administration. Justice was carried out by the same people and institutions that wielded power and carried out administrative duties—that is, by the Grand Prince (from the mid-sixteenth century on, the tsar), the Boyar Duma, and the *prikazy* (central administrative organs of various origin). Justice in the provinces was administered by representatives of the Grand Prince (later, by the tsar). These local administrators and judges, known by various names at different times, included *namestniki* (appointed to urban areas), *volosteli* (appointed to rural districts), and *voevody* (provincial governors). Representatives of the crown participated in court proceedings alongside representatives of state servitors *(sluzhilye liudi)* and of urban and rural communes. However, a number of *prikazy* specialized in fulfilling judicial functions. Thus, the *Razboinyi prikaz* *(prikaz* for brigandage, also called the *Sysknoi prikaz)* dealt with all cases involving murder, acts of brigandage, and robberies throughout Russia, with the exception of Moscow. In Moscow, judicial proceedings in all criminal affairs fell within the competence of the *Zemskii prikaz,* which oversaw the city's police and judicial affairs. The most significant political crimes were dealt with in the *Tainyi prikaz,* or *prikaz* for secret affairs. Civil affairs between noblemen were examined in the *Sudnye prikazy,* or *prikazy* for courts, the number of which varied from five at the end of the sixteenth century to only one at the end of the seventeenth century. Civil affairs between noblemen and their peasants and slaves *(kholopy)* were dealt with in the *Prikaz kholop'ego suda,* or *prikaz* for slave courts. Beginning in 1539, affairs involving murder, brigandage, and robbery were passed on for trial to criminal judicial district courts, each headed by a *gubnaia starosta* elected by the communes. The significance of the courts headed by elective officials began to decrease beginning in the mid-seventeenth century, and their official abolition in 1708 only formalized what had already occurred: the return of judicial power to the representatives of the crown—the provincial governors *(voevody).*

In Muscovy, several types of courts existed on patrimonial estates: the palace court *(dvortsovyi sud),* for trials of palace serfs; the monastery court *(monastyrskii sud),* for trials of peasants owned by monasteries; and the proprietary court *(vladel'cheskii sud),* for trials of serfs held on private estates. In contrast to the preceding, Kievan period, the judicial process on patrimonial estates was carried out by the authority of the crown. There also was a church court for cases dealing with faith and religion as well as with marital and family relations among the entire population. An ecclesiastical court existed for the clergy. Cases concerning the most serious crimes, however, were the exclusive prerogative of the crown or of the *gubnye starosty,* during the time they existed. As earlier, the various courts were not divided by levels of authority. Legal jurisdiction was determined according to place of residence. Minor criminal and civil cases were examined in communal courts in towns and villages.

An important innovation in legal proceedings occurred in Muscovy: Some trials began to emphasize an investigatory process over an adversarial one. In Kievan Rus all cases had been adversarial in nature; but in Muscovy, civil cases based on documents, and criminal cases for which there were suspects and evidence, began to be dealt with through investigatory or inquisitional procedures. Civil suits not based on documents, and criminal acts committed by unknown persons, continued to be examined according to the rules of the old, adversarial system.

Although the adversarial system was conducted in Muscovy largely as it had been in earlier times, some changes were made. For instance, the resolution of issues concerning the subject of dispute between plaintiffs and defendants and issues concerning the judge and the length of the trial was now the prerogative of the court. The disputing sides could send proxies to represent them in court; but although they could reject judges, they could not select them. Written documents and comprehensive questioning of inhabitants of the locality where the litigants lived (a practice called *poval'nyi obysk*) acquired great significance as new kinds of evidence. The only manifestations of trial by test remaining in evidence were oaths before God, the casting of lots, and combat. In the case of the latter, the contestants were permitted to hire replacements to fight in their stead. By the end of the seventeenth century, however, trial by combat had disappeared from judicial practice. Exclusively oral court proceedings had been replaced by written proceedings, and an adversarial case began with the lodging of a written complaint by the plaintiff. Failure to appear in court by either side caused the case to be terminated, with negative consequences for the side that failed to appear. Court proceedings were recorded by secretaries, called *d'iaki*. Sentences were carried out by bailiffs *(sudebnye pristavy)*. The losing side in the suit was often sentenced to flogging. Appeals of sentences were permitted.

In investigatory trials, the role of the plaintiff was assumed by the state. Evidence was not searched out by the litigants but rather by the court. The dispute between the opposing sides was turned into a matter of interrogation and confrontation; peaceful agreement between the two sides became impossible. Prior agreements made by the opposing sides had no validity in court, and plaintiffs who attempted to come to an agreement with the accused outside of the judicial process were subject to torture. Those subject to arrest could not be released on bail. Oral hearings were replaced by written proceedings, and the judicial process itself became closed to the public. Stolen goods and corpses, when found, still served as important evidence, but they no longer had the unconditional and indisputable meaning they had had earlier. At the end of the sixteenth century, personal confession became necessary in order for someone to be held accountable for a crime; torture then began to be used as the primary means of interrogation and for obtaining confessions of guilt. If evidence was conflicting, and if no confession was made, then public opinion regarding the suspect played the decisive role in determining guilt or innocence. This opinion was obtained through mass questioning of the neighbors of the accused.[94] If popular opinion was in favor of the accused, the latter was freed from punishment and released on surety to the commune. If opinion went against the accused, then the sentence was life imprisonment (instead of the death penalty, which would have been the sentence if the accused were found guilty by the court). Sentences were carried out by the state, and compensation to the aggrieved parties was replaced by the punishment of those found guilty. It should be noted that in Russia the investigatory trial, in the purest sense, never developed.[95]

The Judicial System in the Eighteenth and Early Nineteenth Centuries

Although Peter I sought through his reforms to rationalize the Russian state, a number of chaotic and contradictory judicial reforms were introduced during his reign. First, Peter sought to separate the judicial process from state administration. Toward this end he created several levels of special judicial organs that had the right to appeal to higher courts decisions made by lower courts. Second, Peter aimed to anchor judicial proceedings within the bounds of written law and to decrease the level of subjectivity in judicial decisions. Third, Peter sought to place the work of judges under the control of the office of public prosecutor, the *prokuratura*. Last, Peter wished to include the provincial nobility in the carrying out of judicial functions at the local level.

Since a number of reforms were implemented over the span of twenty-five years, and as each reform to some degree replaced its predecessor, let us examine the final result of Peter's judicial reform. Judicial institutions were divided into four levels, or *instantsii*. Municipal administrative bodies, known as *magistraty* and *ratushi*, were established as the courts of first instance for obligated townspeople *(posadskie liudi)*. For all others living in towns (apart from provincial administrative centers) and in rural areas, this role was fulfilled by lower courts called *nizhnie sudy*. For inhabitants of provincial administrative centers *(gubernskie goroda)*, with the exception of obligated townspeople, the courts of first instance were *nadvornye sudy*, or provincial-level courts. The provincial-level courts served as appellate courts *(sudy vtoroi instantsii)* for all others. The newly established College of Justice *(Iustits-kollegiia)* replaced the *prikaz* for brigandage as the higher appellate court, not only in criminal cases but also in civil affairs. The Senate established by Peter functioned as the highest appellate court (excepting appeal to the emperor himself), and it examined cases concerning crimes by high-level officials. The *Tainyi prikaz*, or *prikaz* for secret affairs, was replaced by the Privy Chancellery for Investigation *(Tainaia kantseliariia rozysknykh del)*, which was the bureau of the political police. Except for the *magistraty*, all courts had jurisdiction over all of the social estates.

Courts consisted of crown-appointed judges who had the right to fill simultaneously any additional administrative position (for example, the post of president of the provincial-level court, or *nadvornyi sud*, was filled by the crown-appointed provincial governor) and of assessors *(zasedateli)* from the local nobility. Only members of the *magistraty* were elected (by the obligated townspeople). In the provincial-level courts and in the lower courts of large towns and cities, rulings were reached collectively by the judge and the assessors. In the lower courts in small towns (which comprised the majority of such courts), judges ruled on their own. In establishing these special judicial bodies, however, Peter did not remove judicial functions from among the responsibilities of his newly created *kollegii*, or central government departments, which replaced the *prikazy*. Peter also retained the preexisting ecclesiastical and military courts.

New judicial reform followed in 1727, two years after Peter's death. The Senate, the College of Justice, and the *magistraty* were preserved, whereas the provincial- and lower-level courts were liquidated. All judicial power was restored to the crown administration—to the *kollegii;* to the provincial governors, or *voevody;* and to the *gubernatory,* or governors, who oversaw a number of provinces. This new organization of judicial administration continued until 1775.

We can summarize here the primary reasons for the failure of Peter's judicial reform. First, the idea of the separation of powers did not correspond to Russian traditions. Second, Russia lacked the large numbers of specially trained people required to make the new, specialized courts run effectively. Third, the state could not afford the resources necessary to maintain the courts. Peter sought to instill order in Russia's judicial system, but the result was increased confusion. There were amazing inconsistencies in the judicial proceedings introduced by Peter. In 1697 he directed by ukase that adversarial trials be replaced with investigatory trials, and this was confirmed in the Military Statute of 1715, which gave a detailed description of the investigatory trial. In order to minimize arbitrary rulings, judges were to be guided by the concept of formal evidence, according to which various items of evidence were assigned varying weights, measured in a point system. Judges were to collect all the evidence for and against the two sides and then evaluate their relative merit according to this point system. A personal confession was seen as the most convincing piece of evidence, and torture was used in order to extract such evidence. Torture was preceded by interrogation, which itself included threats and beatings. A confession did not free one from torture, since it was believed that torture would uncover new facts and details concerning the crime. Other forms of evidence included witnesses and documents. However, in 1723 the ukase "On the form of the court" [*O forme suda*] replaced the investigatory trial with the adversarial trial. This placed judges in a difficult position, since the Military Statute was still in full force and began to be implemented in civil trials as well. In 1725 the Senate resolved the contradiction by declaring that investigatory trials were to be used in cases of blasphemy, schisms within the Orthodox church, rebellion against the church (called *tserkovnyi miatezh*), murder, brigandage, theft, and military crimes. Other criminal offenses and all civil cases were to be resolved through adversarial trials. Also, Peter repealed the use of trial by combat and the casting of lots, thus eradicating the remnants of *sud Bozhii.* An exception was made for sacred oaths, which were still considered valid evidence.

Under Peter's immediate successors judicial proceedings underwent only minor change. Judicial organs in urban areas were supplemented in 1754 with *slovesnye sudy,* or "verbal courts," which were instituted for the resolution of minor civil suits between obligated townspeople. In Moscow, a special court was instituted at Moscow University for students and faculty. The Privy Chancellery was abolished in 1762.

Important and long-lived changes in the organization of the courts and in judicial proceedings occurred during the reign of Catherine II, who attempted to remedy the deficiencies of the courts that she had inherited from her predecessors. These deficiencies included the fact that the courts were not kept separate from state administration; that there was an excessive number of courts of varying levels; that civil and criminal cases were often mixed; and that confusion reigned in court proceedings. Courts were reformed in 1775, during the reforms of local institutions. On the levels of both district (uezd) and province, the reforms established courts for the various social estates. For the nobility, these were, at the district level, the uezdnyi zemskii sud, and at the provincial level, the verkhnii zemskii sud; for the urban social estate,* the gorodovoi magistrat and the gubernskii magistrat; and for state peasants, the nizhniaia rasprava and the verkhniaia rasprava. Courts at the provincial level were divided into courts for civil and for criminal cases; at the county level, this differentiation did not occur. The provincial-level courts served as courts of appeal for cases tried at the district level. In each province, all-estate superior courts were also established both for criminal cases (palata ugolovnogo suda) and for civil cases (palata grazhdanskogo suda), providing yet another appellate instance. Oversight of judges was carried out by procurators at the levels of the district and the province, and also by provincial governors, who were formally responsible for confirming decisions in important cases. However, since in the early nineteenth century the number of criminal cases alone exceeded 100,000 a year, it is difficult to see how provincial governors could have played any significant role in judicial affairs.

For the clergy and the military, ecclesiastical and military courts were preserved. Serfs involved in petty civil and criminal suits were judged by patrimonial or estate courts (votchinnye sudy) run by their landlord. When such peasants were involved in serious suits, however, they were judged by district-level courts. In the superior all-estate courts at the province level, judges and court counselors (sovetniki) were appointed by the crown. In the lower, province-level courts based on social estate, a chairman was appointed by the crown and assessors from the corresponding social estate. In the district-level, estate-based courts, a chairman and assessors were elected from among the nobility and the urban estate, respectively. In

---

*The urban social estate (gorodskoe soslovie) from 1775 to 1785 included merchants of the three guilds, burghers (meshchane), and artisans who were registered in urban artisans' guilds (tsekhi).

courts for state peasants, the chairman was appointed by the provincial governing board, and assessors were elected by the peasants.

In St. Petersburg and Moscow, special courts called *nadvornye sudy* were created to handle cases dealing with people who were residing temporarily in these cities. At the initiative of Catherine II, an all-estate "court of conscience" *(sovestnyi sud)* was created to deal with crimes and offenses committed by minors, the deaf, and the mentally ill. These courts also handled cases involving witchcraft; cases in which parents were hurt or insulted by their children; and crimes committed in a fit of passion, or by accident or negligence. The chairman of the court of conscience was appointed by the provincial governor, and assessors were elected by the various social estates, including state peasants. However, members of the various social estates were tried separately. The nobility judged the nobility, merchants judged merchants, and so forth.

The law not only established the composition of each court but also its jurisdiction, how suits were initiated, oversight over judges, the order of legal proceedings, and the formulation of appeals. At first, appellate review was permitted for all suits; but in 1784, appeal was limited to civil suits and to decisions in criminal suits that did not stipulate the death sentence or deprivation of civil rights. As such sentences were handed down to fewer than 10 percent of those convicted, the great majority of cases were open to appeal. Death sentences and deprivation of civil rights could be reviewed only at the initiative of a higher court and by a formal review process. Any court of the lowest instance, or district level, could initiate criminal cases not only when directed to do so by a higher court but also if a complaint was lodged by a private individual. Thus, the opportunities for appeals were rather broad. However, the frequency and number of appeals were somewhat limited by the high legal costs.[96] The Senate was the highest court of appeal for civil and criminal affairs, and the Synod was the highest appellate court for ecclesiastical affairs.

During the reign of Catherine II, a number of changes were made in judicial proceedings. In 1765 the empress directed that adversarial procedure in trials be implemented throughout Russia. In practice, however, courts used both adversarial and investigatory trials, depending on the nature of the case. Moreover, each approach contained elements of the other. Ukases issued in 1763 and 1767 restricted the use of torture to cases in which all other means for determining the truth had been exhausted. Torture could be implemented only in provincial towns and administrative centers and with the sanction of the governor. The continued, albeit limited use of torture shows that investigatory trials were still conducted during the reign of Catherine II. In 1782, new police organs *(upravy blagochiniia)* were created in towns. These bodies carried out investigations into all types of crimes. Thus, the first step was taken in removing investigations from the courts and in reducing the role of judges in trials. Estate courts remained in place, unchanged.

The judicial system created by Catherine II endured without radical change until the judicial reform of 1864, although a number of scholars believe that in the nineteenth century investigatory trials became more widespread than adversarial trials.[97] In my view, from the time of Catherine II until the 1864 judicial reform, three types of trials were in use: First, in cases of crimes against the state and other serious offenses, the investigatory trial was primarily used. Second, in the case of petty criminal and civil suits, the adversarial trial was mainly used. Third, in some instances, trials were characterized by a mixture of both the investigatory and adversarial approaches. Evidence to support this view is found in the fact that elected members of the social estates (nobility, burghers, and state peasants) functioned as assessors in the courts of first instance and in the lower-level appellate courts. This meant that judges did not hand down decisions on their own, as was usually the case in investigatory trials. According to data collected by the Ministry of Justice from 1840 to 1850, investigatory trials (also known as trials "according to form") were applied in provincial superior civil courts in only 1.2–1.4 percent of all cases. In other cases a conciliatory agreement was reached between the litigants. Rather extensive opportunities existed to appeal decisions; this too is not generally seen as compatible with the investigatory trial. In courts of first instance, the right of appeal applied to approximately 30 percent of criminal cases, and from 30 to 36 percent of civil cases. The majority of those who stood accused in criminal cases were not kept in custody during the investigation; this was the case for approximately 80 percent of defendants in the 1830s and up to 90 percent in the early 1860s.[98] In towns and cities, beginning in 1782, investigations were no longer conducted by the courts. This deprived the courts of their inquisitorial role, as judges could no longer function simultaneously as judge, investigator, and public prosecutor. Such a role for judges would not be compatible with the spirit of the ideal investigatory process. The separation of the roles of judge and of investigator shows that the adversarial character of the judicial process in Russia was not dying out but rather was continuing to develop.

Catherine's successors made several changes both in judicial organs and in legal proceedings. During the reign of Paul I, the lower-level appellate courts were abolished. These included the following: the province-level, municipal administrative bodies known as *gubernskie magistraty,* which served as courts of appeal for courts in towns and cities; the *verkhnie zemskie sudy,* or province-level courts for the nobility; and the province-level, courts for state peasants, or *verkhnie raspravy.* These bodies duplicated the work of the all-estate civil and criminal courts, the *palaty ugolovnogo suda* and the *palaty grazhdanskogo suda.* Also abolished under Paul were the county-level courts for state peasants, or *nizhnie raspravy*. The Privy Chancellery was reestablished during Paul's reign but abolished again soon after his death.

Judicial reform continued under Paul's successor, Alexander I. In 1802, torture was abolished, representatives from the social estates were given places in all courts, and autonomous courts were created in the new universities. These changes strengthened society's role in effecting justice. To be sure, in 1809, appeals for convicted persons from nonobligated social estates were banned, but in 1823, appeals were accepted for those from all social estates after the convicted person's arrival at the place where punishment was to be carried out.

In 1802 the Ministry of Justice was created and entrusted with directing all judicial departments and the office of the public prosecutor, or *prokuratura*. To make this task easier, the minister of justice also carried out the duties of the procurator general *(general-prokuror)*, who was responsible for public prosecution. At the same time, courts of commerce *(kommercheskie sudy)* were established for the purpose of sorting out disagreements in commerce and trade among merchants and between merchants and members of other social estates. The first court of commerce appeared in Odessa in 1808. The activities of these courts were placed on a firm legal footing in 1832.[99] The last (and ninth, in order) court of commerce was created in Tiflis in 1853. At the beginning of the twentieth century, only seven of these courts remained.

Important changes in the law with regard to peasants were made during the reign of Nicholas I. The 1832 Code of Laws regulated the punishments to be meted out to peasants of various categories by their owners—landlords, the state treasury, and the palace administration. In 1839, county *(volost)* and village courts *(volostnye raspravy* and *sel'skie raspravy)* were created for state peasants. These courts consisted solely of elected representatives *(vybornye)* from among the peasants themselves. The law clearly defined the jurisdiction of the court and lessened the punishments the court could impose on state peasants. These lesser punishments were introduced for serfs and palace peasants by the 1845 Code of Punishments.

The Judicial System on the Eve of the 1864 Reforms

Volost and village courts—the lower courts for state peasants—sorted out minor suits and offenses among the peasantry. They consisted of an elected village elder and two elected peasant assessors. The village court ruled in disputes involving sums of up to five rubles, and the *volost* court in disputes involving sums of up to fifteen rubles. For minor offenses these courts could mete out fines of between twenty-five kopecks and one ruble.

The lower court for patrimonial peasants was the estate or patrimonial court *(votchinnyi sud)* of the landlord. The state administration for palace peasants *(udel'nye krest'iane)* served as their lower court; the administration held legal rights over palace peasants equivalent to the rights held by landlords over their peasants.[100] Landlords and the state administration had the right to hand down the following sentences for peasants: punishment of up to forty blows with birch rods *(rozgi)*, or up to fifteen blows with larger canes *(palki)*; imprisonment in a rural jail for up to two months or in a forced-labor prison for up to three months; work in a penal battalion for a period of up to six months; forced recruitment into the army; and permanent removal from the landlord's estate as a banished criminal, and transfer to the local crown administration. The jurisdiction of the lowest-level judicial body, the communal court *(obshchinnyi sud)*, was not defined in the law; this court functioned according to custom (see Volume 1, Chapter 5).

The district-level court, or *uezdnyi sud*, was the court of first instance for everyone except those who belonged to the urban estate. Merchants refused the jurisdiction of these courts. Decisions of this court on criminal cases in which those found guilty were given correctional sentences—that is, sentences short of the loss of all civil rights—could not be appealed. Decisions of this court on civil suits involving less than thirty rubles also could not be appealed. All other cases were subject to review by a higher court. Judges to the county courts were selected by the nobility; and the court assessors, by both nobility and nonproprietary peasants. Peasant assessors, however, could participate only in cases involving peasants.

The all-estate criminal and civil courts located in each province (*palaty ugolovnogo suda* and *palaty grazhdanskogo suda*) were lower-level appellate courts. The provincial criminal court heard appeals from all courts of first instance in the given province. Approximately 40 percent of cases were reviewed by higher courts. The provincial criminal court also served as the court of first instance for crimes of official malfeasance. There was no appeal of decisions reached by the provincial criminal court except in cases involving members of the nobility. Such cases could be appealed to the imperial Senate. The all-estate civil court served as court of appeals and review for all civil cases. For cases involving 600 rubles or less, decisions reached by this court were final. Decisions in cases involving greater sums were confirmed by the Senate. The all-estate civil court was the court of first instance for suits involving landed estates within the given province, suits concerning property held by urban communes, and disputes over copyrights. The chairmen of all-estate criminal and civil courts were appointed by the crown. For cases concerning the nobility, court assessors were appointed from the nobility. For cases involving the urban estate, court assessors were likewise appointed from that estate.

The highest court in the empire for both criminal and civil cases was the Senate. Ten of its eleven departments heard appeals on judicial cases including cassation—that is, appeals on the basis of procedural violations. Among the matters that were the exclusive responsibility of the Senate were cases of official malfeasance by province-level marshals of the nobility. Departments of the Senate were located in St. Petersburg, Moscow, and Warsaw, each having jurisdiction over several provinces. Cases were decided within departments when there was unanimity among the senators. When unanimity was not reached on a case, it was given over for review to the general meeting of judicial departments, where a qualified majority was required for a decision to be made. This decision then had to be confirmed by the minister of justice. When disagreements on a case remained among senators, or if the minister of justice disagreed with the decision reached by the Senate, then the case was directed to the State Council. Senators were appointed by the emperor from among meritorious high officials, and their rank was not lower than that of privy councillor *(tainyi sovetnik)*, which corresponded to the military rank of general-lieutenant. All ministers were State Council members ex officio. Governors-general, who oversaw St. Petersburg, Moscow, and various border regions, also took part in State Council sessions when matters concerning their regions were dealt with.

The Judicial System from 1864 to 1913

The judicial reforms of 1864 fundamentally altered both the system of courts and that of judicial proceedings. The reforms included four new laws: a law on judicial administration; a law on civil procedure; a law on criminal procedure; and a statute on sentences that could be meted out by courts of the justice of the peace *(mirovye sudy)*—a new office created to deal locally with minor civil and criminal cases. The judiciary was simplified, and members of all estates were made equal before the law. The jury system was introduced, and jurors were selected by the population. Since 90 percent of the population were peasants, most juries were made up primarily of peasants. After the reforms were implemented, there were courts of only two levels, making for one appellate court in addition to the courts of first instance. Circuit courts, called *okruzhnye sudy,* were the courts of first instance, and generally there was one such court for each province. Court decisions reached with the participation of a jury were considered final and could be appealed only by cassation—that is, on the basis of procedural violations. Juries heard cases involving both full and partial deprivation of civil rights.

Decisions reached by a court without a jury could be appealed to the next echelon, the district appellate court *(sudebnaia palata),* which presided over several circuit courts, constituting a single judicial *okrug,* or district. When it served as a court of first instance, the *sudebnaia palata* heard cases concerning official malfeasance and crimes against the state. Such cases were reviewed with the participation of representatives from the estates: marshals of the nobility for cases involving nobility; a head of municipal administration *(gorodskoi golova)* for cases involving burghers; and an elected village elder *(volostnoi starshina)* for cases involving peasants. The Senate heard appeals of cassation, and it could remand a case for retrial only when the rules of judicial procedure had been violated in that case. Minor criminal cases and civil suits involving less than 500 rubles were considered by courts of justices of the peace, consisting of provincial zemstvo assembly members *(zemskie glasnye)* in rural areas, and in towns, by members of the municipal council *(gorodskie glasnye)*. The decisions of these courts could be appealed to the county conference of justices of the peace *(uezdnyi s"ezd mirovykh sudei)*. Also created was the institution of the bar *(advokatura),* which united attorneys *(prisiazhnye poverennye)* in a single corporation.[101] Judges and judicial investigators could no longer be removed from their positions, and (with the exception of justices of the peace) they were required to have a special juridical education. For the first time, the courts were fully separated from the administration, as were investigations from the courts and the police. The newly created office of the public prosecutor *(prokuratura)* was subordinate to the minister of justice, and the public prosecutor could be removed from his position.

All trials became adversarial. Secrecy in judicial affairs was replaced by openness; and behind-the-scenes manipulation of cases was replaced by public trials and hearings, together with competing sides and lawyers for each side. The principle was firmly established that justice should be carried out solely by the courts. The system of formal evidence or proofs of guilt set in place by Peter I was abolished, and the practice was ended whereby individuals could remain suspects without a court deciding on their guilt or innocence. In addition, a civil procedural code was introduced for the first time in the history of Russian law. The new code established the principle of optionality *(dispozitivnost')* and made it possible for the disputing sides themselves to determine the dates, pace, and other aspects of a trial, as in ancient Russian courts. The role of the public prosecutor in civil trials was minimized. For the fifty-year period in which the new courts existed, not one protest was made by the public prosecutor's office in civil cases. The introduction of the new civil code separated for the first time civil judicial proceedings from criminal proceedings. All imperial subjects were made equal before the courts.

The new judicial procedures were introduced gradually, and they did not reach the distant corners of Russia until 1907. Together with the general courts—which after the judicial reform were no longer based on social estate—district courts, or *volostnye sudy,* were created for the peasantry.

These courts ruled on minor criminal and civil cases according to customary law. Courts for the military and for the clergy were retained, but they were transformed along the same lines as the general civil courts.

The judicial system created by these reforms remained in place for the most part until the end of the tsarist regime, even though some changes were made in it that were not in harmony with the original principles governing the reforms. All of these changes concerned crimes against the state and were reactions to the rise and growth of the revolutionary movement, which the new judges viewed with a great deal of tolerance. Between 1871 and 1881, investigations into crimes against the state were conducted not by court investigators, as had previously been the case, but rather by the political police *(zhandarmy)*. All types of crimes against the state, as well as many crimes directed against the administrative order, were removed from the jurisdiction of juried courts and transferred to a bureau within the Senate that dealt with political crimes against the state. This Senate bureau *(Osoboe prisutsvie pravitel'stvuiushchego senata),* together with representatives of the social estates (the marshal of the nobility, the city or town mayor, and the peasant *volost* elder), formed a special tribunal called the Supreme Criminal Court *(Verkhovnyi ugolovnyi sud).* Beginning in 1879, cases involving crimes considered by the government to be the most serious were turned over to military courts, which dealt with crimes as if they had been committed in wartime, handing down the death sentence more often than not. In 1881 a statute was introduced (the Statute on Measures to Protect the State Order and Public Tranquillity) that gave the government the right to place a given locality under exceptional, reinforced protection. Courts in areas placed under such protection were made dependent upon the state administration. The state made use of this right relatively rarely, with the exception of the 1905–1907 period of revolutionary unrest, and all exceptions to the judicial statutes of 1864 were made by the government after repeated acts of terror by revolutionaries. At the same time, a number of alterations of a liberal nature were introduced into the statutes. In 1886, the rights of jurors were expanded to include the right to ask questions of those on trial and of witnesses. Beginning in 1899, an attorney had to be appointed to the *sudebnye palaty.* In 1913, the courts received the right to absolve an accused person of legal culpability *(pravo reabilitatsii).*

In 1889, the courts of the justice of the peace underwent reform, and in most locales judges to these courts began to be appointed by the state administration from among professional jurists instead of being locally elected as had earlier been the case. Introduced in the countryside at this time was the office of land captain *(zemskii nachal'nik).* This official, appointed from among the local nobility, possessed the right to act as judge and inspector of the district courts. He also had the power to hand down fines of up to six rubles and to arrest peasants for up to three days without the right of appeal. Crown-appointed municipal judges were introduced into cities and towns, paralleling the rural justices of the peace.

In 1912 the State Duma revoked the judicial authority of the land captains and restored the elective office of justice of the peace *(vybornyi mirovoi sud'ia)*. Justices of the peace were to be elected by the district *(uezd)* zemstvos. The new law also established higher rural courts *(verkhnie sel'skie sudy)* as courts of appeals for the rural district courts *(volostnye sudy)*. The higher rural court was headed by the justice of the peace, and the chairmen of the district courts served as assessors.[102]

Impartiality and the Severity of Court Sentences

In the literature published both in Russia and elsewhere, the view has become established that before the reforms of 1864, Russia's entire judicial system was malformed, and that injustice and corruption reigned in the courts. For instance, the famous prerevolutionary jurist N.V. Davydov wrote:

> Our prereform courts, created on the basis of the estate system *(soslovnost')*, secretiveness, strict formalism, an elaborate hierarchy of courts, and judicial review of cases according to this hierarchy, indeed appear to have been horrible institutions, inspiring both scorn and fear in the innocent as well as the guilty. That there was bribery and graft within the judicial organs was common knowledge. Judicial independence did not exist; judges trembled and groveled before the elite and those who wielded power. In addition to judicial officials appointed by the government, representatives of the social estates also sat in judgment in courts. They, however, brought no bright rays of justice into the dark kingdom of the courts.[103]

Those who support this view marshal the opinions of contemporaries along with anecdotes of bribery, red tape, and unjust judicial decisions. Yet in light of such revelations, the question arises: How could society and the state continue to exist at all over the course of a number of centuries if the courts were corrupt and incompetent? After all, philippics directed against the courts during the reign of Nicholas I apply even more to the courts of the preceding imperial and Muscovite eras. As we have seen, criminal law, the judicial system, and the trial process gradually improved over time. If the aforementioned criticisms of the judicial system in the nineteenth century reflect reality, then crime levels in Russia must have been very high and must have risen over time. People would have been frightened to leave their homes or to travel, and eventually, social and economic life would have become totally paralyzed. During this same period, however, Russia's emperors took walks around St. Petersburg without protective escort, life continued in its usual routine throughout the country, and there was no noticeable fear among people that they might be robbed or killed upon going out of doors at night.

How can we reconcile criticism of Russia's judicial system with reality? In order to answer this question, we need to evaluate Russian law enforcement in general, using customary indicators measuring such things as crime levels, the frequency with which crimes were exposed, the number of complaints and appeals made to higher courts regarding sentences handed down by lower courts, and the decisions made by the higher courts regarding such appeals. Since the legal system produced by the 1864 judicial reforms is considered the best produced in Russia up to that time, let us compare these indicators from the periods both before and after the introduction of the reforms.

Apprehension of Criminals.   The available data indicate that criminality in Russia in the prereform era was actually lower than levels in west European countries, and was declining.[104] Paradoxically, after the judicial reforms were introduced, the levels of crime almost continuously rose—by 1913, tripling the levels of the 1850s. Taking the ratio of the number of convicted persons to the number of those accused of crimes as an indicator of the success with which perpetrators of crimes were found and brought before a court *(raskryvaemost' prestuplenii),** then we can say that until the peasant Emancipation, crime levels tended to fall. After the Emancipation, crime levels rose: Between 1803 and 1808, perpetrators were apprehended for 44 percent of crimes; in the 1860s, 40 percent; and in the first decade of the twentieth century, 60 percent. Another indicator of the frequency with which perpetrators were apprehended might be the number of criminal cases that failed to come to trial due to insufficient evidence, because the perpetrator had fled, or for other, similar reasons. We have figures on such cases beginning in 1872: In the 1870s, such cases amounted to 60 percent of all cases; in the 1880s, 49 percent; in the 1890s, 57 percent; and between 1911 and 1913, 51 percent. These figures show that after the reforms, perpetrators were apprehended more frequently than before the reforms. This shows that criminal investigations were more efficient before the reforms than after. They also were carried out with greater speed. At the end of the nineteenth century, an investigator took up a case, on average, three weeks after the crime was committed, and completed his work within seven to eight weeks. Only 4 percent of investigations

---

*Included here are serious crimes punishable with nothing less than a prison term.

extended beyond six months, whereas between 1843 and 1848, investigations into serious criminal cases lasted on average nine months, and between 1861 and 1864, eleven months. Moreover, before the reforms, 72 percent of investigations lasted more than one year; 18 percent, between one and two years; 5 percent, two to three years; 3 percent, three to four years; and 2 percent, more than four years.[105]

Corruption. Let us consider whether claims that Russia's prereform judges were universally corrupt are justified.[106] That bribes were given and accepted rather frequently is most likely true. But was corruption so widespread that it made justice impossible, that the rich and powerful needed not fear the courts or the possibility that they would be served with sentences for crimes committed? The figures in Table 5.2 show that the portion of the population most frequently represented among those who were acquitted by the court or pardoned by the emperor were members of the legal estate of distinguished citizens *(pochetnye grazhdane).* Prominent in this group were members of the professional intelligentsia and wealthy merchants. Next in frequency among those found innocent by the courts or pardoned were members of the nobility, merchants, members of the clergy, burghers, and non-Russians *(inorodtsy).** The proportion of those found guilty and pardoned among these social groups vacillated between 43.4 and 48.1 percent—a difference of only 4.7 percent. The difference between members of the nobility and merchants was only 0.1 percent.

With respect to frequency of acquittal, a large gap separates distinguished citizens, the nobility, merchants, clergy, and burghers from peasants and retired soldiers. Last on the list, naturally, are those exiled and sentenced to penal hard labor in exile, and those who refused to reveal their identity and social origin. The fact that the merchant class is in the first and possibly the privileged group can be explained by its wealth, and thus its ability to pay bribes. The nobility is present due to its widespread network of social and other connections, as well as its ability to pay bribes. But how can one explain that generally poor groups—the clergy, the burghers, and especially the non-Russian *inorodtsy*—were also frequently acquitted? The acquittal rate of peasants, burghers, and *inorodtsy* begs explanation even more than that of the nobility, merchants, the clergy, and distinguished citizens. Most likely to have their cases referred to administrative organs and communes were those exiled to penal hard labor, followed by the *inorodtsy* and the clergy. This can easily be explained by the

---

*Those designated as members of the legal class of *inorodtsy* included the indigenous peoples of Siberia and Central Asia, the nomads of the steppe regions, the Samoyeds of the Arkhangelsk region, and the Jews.—*Trans.*

TABLE 5.2   Disposition of Criminal Defendants in Russia, for Russians and
Inorodtsy, by Defendant's Legal Estate, 1861–1864 (in percent)

a Acquitted or released by the court via pardon from the emperor
b Released, but remaining under suspicion
c Remanded to administrative or other official organ
d Sentenced to exile and hard labor
e Given correctional sentences (*ispravitel'nye nakazaniia*)
f All those found guilty (d and e combined)
g All those released by the court (a, b, and c combined)

National Status and Legal Estate	*a*	*b*	*c*	*d*	*e*	*f*	*g*
Russians							
Nobility	45.7	11.7	22.7	4.4	15.7	20.1	80.1
Clergy	44.8	11.9	26.7	3.9	13.2	17.1	83.4
Distinguished citizens	48.1	12.5	18.5	3.0	18.1	21.1	79.1
Merchants	45.6	11.8	24.9	1.1	16.6	17.7	82.3
Burghers (*meshchane*)	43.4	17.1	20.3	1.4	17.8	19.2	80.8
State peasants	36.2	15.1	21.8	1.2	25.8	27.0	73.1
Proprietary peasants	36.1	18.4	20.5	2.0	23.1	25.1	75.0
Retired soldiers	32.7	14.8	26.8	2.0	23.8	25.8	74.3
Inorodtsy*	43.9	16.0	27.0	1.6	11.6	13.2	86.9
Individuals of unknown identity	13.9	3.7	22.9	29.6	30.0	59.6	40.5
Exiles and convicts at hard labor	25.7	14.5	31.9	16.7	11.3	28.0	72.1
Totals	37.6	15.9	21.6	1.9	23.0	24.9	75.1

*Those designated as *inorodtsy* (non-Russian minorities) included the native peoples of Siberia and Central Asia, the nomads of the steppe regions, the Samoyeds of the Arkhangelsk region, and the Jews.—*Trans.*

SOURCE: *Otchet ministra iustitsii za 1861–1864 god* (St. Petersburg, 1863–1866).

need to strengthen surveillance (*nadzor*) over those formerly imprisoned, whereas cases involving *inorodtsy* had to be referred to their own native authorities, and cases involving clergy, to ecclesiastical authorities. The most severe sentences, including penal hard labor, were meted out to habitual criminals and to those whose identities were unknown. It is most interesting that these groups were dealt with more severely than were members of the nobility, members of the clergy, and distinguished citizens, and that the least likely to receive severe sentences were merchants, *inorodtsy,* and state peasants. Lighter correctional sentences were more frequently meted out to persons of unknown identity, to peasants, and to soldiers, and less often to members of privileged legal estates. As we can see, the resulting picture is complicated, and definite conclusions cannot be drawn about whether the privileged classes had advantages in the meting out of punishments.

Let us examine more closely the data in the last two columns of Table 5.2—the proportions of those found guilty and those released from punishment. Among the eleven social groups in the analysis, the group least likely to be sentenced and most likely to be released was the *inorodtsy*, 86.8 percent of whom were released after having been accused of committing a crime (see column g), followed by the clergy (82.9 percent), merchants (80.7 percent), distinguished citizens (79.0 percent), and the nobility (80.0 percent). The peasantry and retired soldiers were released less frequently and were more often punished than were the other social groups. Again, it is not apparent that the most wealthy and prominent people enjoyed special privileges.

In my view, an important factor in determining the fate of an accused person was his level of education and his ability to give clear and intelligible evidence on his own behalf. After all, until the judicial reform of 1864, all legal explanations and declarations *(ob'iasneniia)* had to be written. Under such conditions, distinguished citizens, the clergy, and the nobility had an advantage, as most members of these groups were educated or at least literate. Although merchants generally had but an elementary level of education, they were able to hire the services of legal officials known as *striapchie*, who could draw up the necessary documents. Worse off were the burghers, peasants, and *inorodtsy*. In 1857, among people older than 9 years, 77 percent of members of the nobility were literate; 72 percent of the clergy; 37 percent of the urban estates (distinguished citizens, merchants, and burghers); and 12 percent of peasants. Less than 10 percent of *inorodtsy* were literate in Russian.

The next most significant factor affecting punishments meted out to various social groups was the type of crimes each group tended to commit. Privileged persons tended to commit more crimes seen as relatively serious by legislation of the time, whereas people of lesser social and economic status generally committed more minor crimes. As a result, persons from privileged groups were given heavy sentences more often than persons from less privileged groups. The crown administration, which had the right to review judicial decisions, apparently influenced judges so that they would focus their attention on the people whom it considered the primary support of the crown and the fatherland. In cases of political and possibly other crimes as well, it seems to me that individuals from these groups were given more severe sentences than were the peasants. However, this impression has yet to be confirmed through historical research. It is also possible that jurors from among the peasantry turned a more lenient eye to crimes committed by their peers and were less forgiving of the privileged.

After the new judicial institutions were put in place, no more complaints were heard concerning the corruption of judges, but more and more public protests were made over interference in the actions of the courts on the part of the state administration. Although such complaints appear to have been fully justified, the state administration interfered only in cases involving crimes against the state. During the period from 1907 to 1913 (the only years for which parallel statistical data are available), such crimes made up less than 0.1 percent of all crimes (2,392 crimes out of 2,496,000). In reality, more crimes against the state were committed than these figures indicate, since the most dangerous cases were transferred to special military courts. Nevertheless, the majority of cases involving crimes against the state were heard in the general courts; and when defendants were placed before juries, the state administration was powerless to influence the decision of the court.

Red Tape. According to the director of the Ministry of Justice's department of statistics, E. N. Tarnovskii, from the 1870s to the 1890s, after a criminal case reached the hands of the investigator, it took an average of 7 to 8 months until a sentence was handed down.[107] However, Tarnovskii was referring to the circuit courts *(okruzhnye sudy)* and the provincial all-estate criminal courts *(grazhdanskie palaty)*. If courts of justices of the peace were included, then 2.1 months on average were required for a decision to be handed down in a criminal case in the late nineteenth and early twentieth centuries; 67 percent of such cases were resolved within 1 month; 31 percent, within 2 to 6 months; and 2 percent took 6 months or longer.[108] How long did it take for cases to be resolved in the prereform era? The majority of cases in courts of all levels were decided within a year. If a case was conclusively resolved in the court of first instance, its resolution tended to take up to one year; cases resolved in appellate courts, up to two years; and cases resolved in the Senate, the court of last resort, up to three years. According to calculations by the Ministry of Justice, from 1830 to 1840, it took approximately two years to resolve cases referred to the Senate from a court of first instance. Similar calculations were not made for later decades.[109]

A number of cases remained permanently unresolved. One reason was that judges sometimes did not have time to review cases in their entirety. This often occurred when additional information required in the case had to be obtained via correspondence, a process that sometimes lasted more than twenty years. (In bureaucratic language, this was referred to as "reasons independent of the location of the court.") Reports prepared by the minister of justice contained data on undecided cases in the courts at all levels for each year beginning with the decade 1833–1843. This information is summarized in Table 5.3.

TABLE 5.3 Proportion of Criminal and Civil Cases Remaining Unresolved After
One Year, by Judicial Instance, 1833–1864 (in percent)

Judicial Organ	1830s	1840s	1850s	1861–1864
All courts [vse sudebnye mesta]	13.6	17.0	26.3	30.8
Senate	20.6	13.3	20.1	23.9
Criminal cases	1.9	0.4	3.4	6.5
Civil cases	25.3	27.4	28.6	29.8
Provincial criminal courts [ugolovnye palaty]	10.1	10.4	15.8	17.9
Provincial civil courts [grazhdanskie palaty]	32.1	26.1	25.4	24.6
Courts of first instance – [sudy pervoi instantsii]	–	6.7	28.5	36.1
Criminal cases	–	8.3	22.0	25.6
Civil cases	–	5.8	32.0	51.3

SOURCE: Otchet ministra iustitsii za [1834–1864] god (St. Petersburg, 1835–1866).

It can be seen from the table that the portion of unresolved cases steadily increased, with the exception of cases in the provincial civil courts (grazhdanskie palaty). The total number of unresolved cases increased each year. By 1864, the total number of unresolved cases in the court system was 167,000. In 1860, each such case on average had been unresolved for 3.7 years; among cases in the Senate, 4.5 years; in the provincial criminal courts (ugolovnye palaty), 2.2 years; in the provincial civil courts, 3.5 years; and in courts of first instance, 3.5 years. In principle, criminal cases were resolved one and a half times more quickly than civil cases. It seems to me that these large numbers of unresolved cases, some of which remained so for many years, gave rise to the legend about the extraordinarily slow pace of proceedings in Russia's courts. Table 5.4 contains a breakdown of a backlog of 167,100 cases as they stood in 1863, in all courts. On average, each case had remained unresolved for 2.2 years.[110]

From the 1830s through the 1850s, the Ministry of Justice expected that 80 percent of cases, from their beginning in courts of first instance to their conclusion (in whatever court that may be, reaching as high as the Senate), would be resolved in less than five years, and that only 20 percent of cases would take more than five years.[111] An exact count shows that on average it took 2.4 years to resolve a case once it reached the Senate, and that in 1860 the average length of time a case had been sitting in the backlog of cases facing the Senate was 4.4 years. However, only 2 to 3 percent of all criminal cases were resolved in the Senate; about 40 percent of criminal cases were resolved in appellate courts; and 57 percent were resolved in courts of first instance. Taking into account the number of unresolved

TABLE 5.4   Proportion of Legal Cases Remaining Unresolved in 1863, by Years Since Initiation

More than 15 years unresolved—1.0%
10–15 years unresolved—2.3%
5–10 years unresolved—9.9%
5 years unresolved—4.1%
4 years unresolved—5.2%
3 years unresolved—8.3%
2 years unresolved—12.9%
1 year unresolved—23.0%
Less than 1 year unresolved—33.3%
Total (100%) = 167,100 cases

SOURCE: *Otchet ministra iustitsii za 1863 god* (St. Petersburg, 1865), pp. 190–191.

cases in all the various courts, we can conjecture that in the 1830s, 52 percent of criminal cases were resolved within a year. We also can conjecture that 36 percent of criminal cases were resolved within two years, and approximately 3 percent within three years. The remaining 9 percent of criminal cases—those that fell victim to bureaucratic obstruction—waited from three to nine years to be resolved. Similar calculations show that by the early 1850s, 42.0 percent of criminal cases were resolved within a year; 33.0 percent, within two years; and 2.8 percent, within three years. The remaining 22.2 percent of cases fell into backlogs, where resolution took approximately five years. Thus, on average, it took a criminal case one and one-half years to be resolved in the prereform courts from the 1830s through the 1850s; and civil cases, on average, took from two to two and one-half years to be resolved. Whereas in the 1830s only 9 percent of cases experienced significant delays, at the end of the 1850s 22 percent of cases were backlogged, and there was a rise by several years in the length of time a case remained backlogged. This created among contemporaries the largely justified sense that the courts were working more slowly than before.

Let's take a look at the causes of these delays: In the late 1850s, the Ministry of Justice began to demand that courts provide information on the reasons for delays in resolving cases. A review of data for the period 1861–1864 shows that the main sticking point in the legal defense system was the police (that is, at the level of the arrest of suspects and of police investigation), where 56 percent of criminal and civil cases were held up.[112] One contemporary who worked in the courts for a long period of time indicated that the police were the primary moving force in processing judicial matters and that the courts merely verified actions taken by the police.[113] It is not surprising that as many as two-thirds of all judicial cases became bottled up in the hands of the police.[114] The poor investigatory work performed by police is indicated by the fact that many suspects were kept imprisoned without trials for long periods of time, from a year to five years. In 1847 the Ministry of the Interior conducted a review of police institutions in 27 provinces. In only three was the level of police work found to be satisfactory. Low effectiveness, especially among police in rural areas, was rooted largely in a shortage of police personnel. Districts with populations exceeding 100,000 were sometimes provided with only five or six state officials *(statnye chinovniki)*. The few police officers who were available were overburdened with tasks of an administrative and economic nature.[115] In addition to these functions, until the introduction of the new judicial statutes, the police also were largely responsible for carrying out judicial functions in minor criminal and civil matters. This was because by law, so-called indisputable affairs *(besspornye dela)*—matters that required no further investigation—were to be resolved by the police.[116] A special investigation carried out by the Ministry of Justice in 1865 in 32 provinces found that district- and city-level police in 1863 and 1864 decided 2.6 times more civil suits than did courts of first instance and appellate courts combined, and that the police resolved tens of thousands of criminal cases—39 percent of the total number of cases processed by the courts.[117]

The second most significant bottleneck for cases were the courts of first instance. These courts suffered due to the rules for how cases moved between courts of various levels. With few exceptions, cases were to begin their movement from lower levels and gradually move to higher ones. As a result, approximately 94 percent of all criminal cases went through courts of first instance, where they were examined and screened. Up to 57 percent of cases were resolved conclusively in these courts, and 39 percent were sent on to superior appellate courts for review. A similar situation existed with civil cases. Courts of first instance played the key role in the judicial system. However, these courts were staffed with the least adequately trained and most poorly paid personnel. Moreover, there were not enough of these courts. Also, cases were dealt with by estate in courts of first instance; that is, members of each legal estate (nobility, clergy, burghers, and the peasantry) sat in judgment against other members of their own estate. This arrangement further slowed the progress of cases through the courts. In addition, the Ministry of Justice and the province-level authorities expended more care and concern on the superior appellate courts, which were located in provincial centers and were mistakenly considered to be the key level of judicial decisionmaking. The architects of the 1864 judicial reform took into account this failure to appreciate the importance of courts of first instance, and the reform abolished the previously established order for the movement of cases between the various levels of courts. This

greatly relieved the burden on judicial organs, freeing them from the re-
dundant review of cases.

Interestingly, governors of provinces only infrequently held up judicial
proceedings in the prereform period. The fifty to seventy governors in Russia in the 1830s were by law responsible for confirming yearly some
40,000 verdicts handed down in courts of first instance (60,000 verdicts
yearly, during the period from 1859 to 1863). Their contribution to judicial backlogs was small, though, as only 0.4 percent of all unresolved cases
were held up in their hands. This indicates that governors had little control
over the judicial system. Had they actually wielded control over the work
of the courts, then they would have been responsible for a far higher percentage of unresolved cases. Other government institutions also had little
influence on the work of the courts. This casts doubt on the notion, which
has become established in the literature on the history of Russia's judicial
system, that the state administration continually interfered in the work of
the courts.[118]

The slowness of judicial proceedings was well recognized by the leading
figures in the Ministry of Justice. They received a huge number of complaints about red tape in the justice system: Seven percent of the written
complaints sent to the Senate were directed against the slowness with
which judicial cases were resolved. With the help of members of the Senate, the Ministry of Justice conducted in 1848–1849 a review of the courts
in thirty-six provinces, and another review was carried out in seven
provinces in the early 1860s. These reviews revealed a picture of delays in
resolving cases, a lack of trained legal specialists, and violations in instructions to the courts.[119] The ministry devised a number of methods to try to
accelerate the course of judicial proceedings, but these efforts only succeeded in making it possible for cases to continue to be dealt with slowly,
and backlogs continued to form. The root of the problem was not in individuals, however, but in the judicial system itself, whose work was slowed
by the prescribed order for the movement of cases between the various levels of courts, by the division of legal estates, and by constant control and
surveillance on the part of higher-level courts over the work of lower-level
ones.

The extensiveness of this control can be seen from the following example. Nicholas I, who had no patience for careless state officials, himself had
to deal with bureaucratic red tape. Legal cases that at the emperor's initiative were referred to the general meeting of the Senate's departments
(Obshchee sobranie departamentov Senata) for resolution—although they
took precedence in the queue—were by no means resolved within a year.
Of the cases introduced for resolution at the emperor's personal initiative
in the 1830s (172 on average each year), only 61 percent were resolved
during the calendar year in which they were introduced. In the 1840s,

Nicholas I introduced 151 cases on average each year, and of these, 70 percent were resolved in the same year in which they were introduced. As we can see, even the emperor could only slightly speed up the progress of cases through the courts.

Complaints, Appeals, and Reversals of Verdict.   There are two primary indicators of the fairness of courts: the number of appeals to higher courts and the number of decisions that are consequently reversed as a result of such appeals. Before the judicial reforms of 1864, many Russians who were entitled to an appeal did not avail themselves of the opportunity. With the reforms in place, all bans on submitting appeals against judicial decisions were lifted. Thus, for the period both before and after the introduction of the reforms, appeals can serve as an aid to understanding the views the population held toward judicial decisions. In the prereform period, all courts reviewed the rulings of lower courts, and these reviews can serve as tests to examine the correspondence of decisions to the law. The data in Table 5.5 provide a picture that is interestingly paradoxical. Before

TABLE 5.5   Number and Disposition of Appeals in Russian Courts of First Instance and Appellate Courts, 1835–1903 (various years)

Courts of First Instance (sudy pervoi instantsii) *Before the Judicial Reforms of 1864*	*1835– 1840*	*1843– 1848*	*1861– 1864*
Criminal cases examined (thousand)	160.1	137.9	171.1
Cases with the right of appeal (thousand)	48.1	41.5	51.0
Appeals made (thousand)	1.0	1.1	1.4
Civil cases examined (thousand)	378.0	120.8	72.3
Cases with the right of appeal (thousand)	91.1	30.1	17.9
Appeals made (thousand)	5.9	4.8	5.4
Appeals granted in full by appellate courts (*sudy vtoroi instantsii*), as percentage of all cases with the right of appeal	6.5	16.1	30.2
Decisions of courts of first instance reversed on review by appellate courts, percentage	–	–	21.8
Appellate Courts (sudy vtoroi instantsii) *Before the Judicial Reform*	*1835– 1840*	*1842– 1848*	*1861– 1864*
Criminal cases examined (thousand)	42.8	47.3	55.9
Appeals made (thousand)	3.0	1.6	2.2
Appeals granted in full by the Senate (percent)	–	28.6	23.2
Civil cases examined (thousand)	23.0	52.9	80.5
Appeals made (thousand)	2.8	5.6	2.1
Appeals granted in full by the Senate (percent)	21.4	24.7	21.4

(continues)

TABLE 5.5 *(continued)*

Courts of Justices of the Peace After the Judicial Reform	1881–1885	1893–1897	1899–1903
Sentences handed down in criminal cases with the right to appeal (thousand)	1,035	–	–
Appeals made (thousand)	158	5.8	6.6
Decisions handed down in civil cases with the right to appeal (thousand)	727	–	–
Appeals made (thousand)	138	4.7	5.6
Appeals granted in both criminal and civil cases (percent)	24.3	36.7	31.4

Circuit Courts (okruzhnye sudy) and District Appellate Courts (sudebnye palaty) After the Judicial Reforms, Criminal Cases	1881–1885	1893–1897	1899–1903
Decisions handed down by circuit courts and district appellate courts (thousand)	29.8	33.0	54.5
Appeals made on decisions by circuit courts and district appellate courts (thousand)	–	16.3	33.9
Appeals granted (thousand)	–	14.6	1.7
Percent of decisions by district appellate courts that were appealed to the Senate	–	12.8	11.5
Appeals granted (thousand)	–	10.2	6.7
Appeals made to the Senate on decisions by circuit courts and district appellate courts (thousand)	2.3	1.9	2.1
Appeals granted (thousand)*	10.5	8.8	6.9

*29.1 percent of appeals in criminal cases were granted in full, as were 39.3 percent of appeals in civil cases.

SOURCES: *Sbornik statisticheskikh svedenii Ministerstva iustitsii* (St. Petersburg, 1887), vyp. 1, pp. 29, 30; *Svod statisticheskikh svedenii po delam ugolovnym v [1881–1913] godu* (St. Petersburg, 1885–1916).

the reforms, decisions were appealed relatively infrequently, and far fewer appeals were made than were allowed for by law. Appeals were made in only 2.1 to 7.0 percent of all decisions in criminal cases and in 10.6 to 15.9 percent of decisions in civil cases.

Toward the 1880s, after the peasant emancipation, the number of appeals against decisions in criminal cases handed down by all types of courts increased between four and six times. In civil suits, however, appeals were made against only 19 percent of court decisions. (This figure is calculated from data on cases dealt with by courts of the justice of the peace; corresponding data do not exist for the circuit courts and appellate courts.) The frequency with which decisions were appealed in criminal cases fell slightly between the 1870s and the period from 1899 to 1903. (For later years, no data are available). However, the frequency of such appeals never fell below that of the prereform era. If we suppose (as do most legal historians) that the frequency of appeals reflects the attitude of the population toward judicial decisions, then we must acknowledge that before the reforms people were more satisfied with court decisions in both criminal and civil cases than they were after the reforms. It is particularly surprising that the degree of satisfaction with decisions in criminal cases was significantly higher than with decisions in civil cases, despite the fact that punishments in the latter cases were less severe and that corporal punishment was abolished in 1863. After the peasant emancipation, there were significant reasons for the growth in the number of appeals: a rise in cultural and educational levels among the population; the appearance of the institution of the bar *(advokatura);* and an absence of the fear people previously felt before the courts and state administration. However, if these factors were decisive, then it remains unclear why the number of appeals against decisions in criminal cases rose more than did the number of appeals against decisions in civil cases. It is well known that the peasant population *(prostoi narod)* showed a great determination to resist when they felt their rights were being infringed on.

It is possible that one factor contributing to the growth of dissatisfaction in judicial decisions (particularly in criminal cases) after the peasant emancipation was the failure of court decisions to correspond properly with legislation on criminal affairs. As the data in Table 5.5 show, in the 1840s the Senate yearly reviewed as part of its inspection three to four thousand decisions handed down by the appellate courts for criminal cases, and five to six thousand decisions of the appellate courts for civil suits. During this process, the Senate repealed up to 29 percent of decisions in criminal cases and 25 percent of decisions in civil suits. From 1861 to 1864, the Senate repealed 23 percent of decisions in criminal cases and 21 percent of decisions in civil suits. The courts of appeal reviewed each year from 1861 to 1864 some 55,000 decisions of courts of first instance and repealed up to 22 percent of their decisions. After the introduction of the judicial reforms, court decisions could be repealed or overturned on the basis of procedural violations. As can be seen from the data in Table 5.5, such repeals were not frequent, occurring in no more than 16 percent of decisions handed down by circuit courts, 11 percent of decisions made by appellate courts, and 31 percent of decisions of courts of the justice of the peace. Decisions of the courts of appeal for criminal and civil cases (*ugolovnye palaty* and *grazhdanskie palaty*) prior to the judicial reforms were more likely to be repealed than were decisions by their postreform counterparts (*sudebnye palaty* and *okruzhnye sudy*). On the other hand, decisions by the prereform courts of first instance were less likely to be repealed than were those of the postreform courts of the justice of the peace. On the whole, decisions both before and after the reforms corresponded to the law a high percentage of the time, and therefore the issue of the legal correctness of decisions cannot explain the rise of appeals against court decisions in the postreform period.

It is therefore likely that the main cause of the rise in the number of appeals after the introduction of the judicial reforms was the failure of defendants to understand the principles by which the courts made their decisions. The courts in the postreform period handed down sentences as dictated by law, whereas the overwhelming majority of defendants and accused persons were peasants accustomed to the customary-law courts of the village. Consequently, the peasants' common understanding of justice inevitably contradicted the law, and this created dissatisfaction and caused the rise in the number of appeals against court decisions. It is no coincidence that the largest number of appeals were made against rulings by courts of the justice of the peace, which were the courts nearest the peasants, and which, like the other courts, handed down decisions according to formal, not customary law. This reasoning is confirmed by the fact that the rise in the number of appeals against sentences in criminal cases after the reforms was greater than against rulings in civil cases. The greater number of appeals against sentences in criminal cases was a result of the fact that peasants frequently turned to the village courts *(sel'skie sudy)* to resolve issues in civil cases. The village courts ruled according to customary law. In criminal matters, however, peasants had to use the courts of the justice of the peace and the circuit courts, which ruled according to official law; hence their greater dissatisfaction with decisions in criminal cases than in civil cases.

The lack of correspondence between legislation and peasants' common understanding of justice is also borne out by the fact that juries, which were predominantly made up of peasants, tended to be more lenient in their sentences than were the crown courts *(koronnye sudy)* without juries. From 1873 to 1888, courts with juries ruled to acquit in 38 percent of cases; crown courts did so in only 23 percent of cases. Around 1883, the percentage of those acquitted by juries reached its highest point—43 percent. Indicative is the case of Vera Zasulich, who on 24 January 1878 attempted to assassinate the governor of St. Petersburg, General F. F. Trepov. Zasulich was acquitted on 31 March 1878 by the St. Petersburg circuit court. Zasulich's lawyer, P. A. Aleksandrov, argued before the court that Zasulich should not be judged according to the law, which she had indisputably violated. Instead, she could be judged only by a higher moral law. "If the law," Aleksandrov said, "cannot provide for all moral, individual differences among lawbreakers, then recourse can be made to a general and innate moral sense of justice—one that suggests what is acceptable with respect to one person and what would be the utmost injustice for another." Aleksandrov's second argument concerned the nature of crimes against the state. He told the court: "The nature of crimes against the state varies. That which yesterday was considered to be a crime against the state today or tomorrow becomes a highly esteemed deed of civic valor."[120]

Zasulich's lawyer—and judging from the decision handed down, the jury as well—held to an ad hoc understanding of the applicability of the law and thus substituted a moral norm for a juridical one. This was a typical approach in customary law, and one that testifies to an insufficiently developed legal consciousness among the Russian public.[121] As a result, Zasulich, who had committed an act of terrorism, was acquitted.

Realizing that the legal consciousness of Russian society, from which juries were selected, did not conform fully to official law, the Russian government in 1884 set in place new rules for drawing up lists of potential jurors. The new rules increased among potential jurors the portion who were educated and who met the qualifications for voting in elections. Such people for the most part held the view that in handing down sentences courts should follow the law rather than emotions and moral arguments.[122] As a result of these new rules, the proportion of acquittals dropped from 43 percent of all rulings in 1883 to 36 percent in the period 1887–1891. Even though courts without juries continued to hand down more severe sentences, the difference narrowed between the percentage of acquittals handed down by courts with juries and those handed down by courts without juries. In 1883 courts with juries found for acquittal in 18 percent more cases than did courts without juries; and during the period 1894–1897, the difference was only 6 percent. Interestingly, the rate of acquittal in courts without juries in Russia was higher than the rate of acquittals in courts with juries in the West, where it ranged between 15 and 25 percent. These figures indicate that the legal consciousness of late tsarist Russian society on the whole (including the peasantry) did not fully correspond to the legislation in place in Russia. Instead, Russian legal consciousness was informed more by customary law, which was likely an important factor in the rise of appeals against court decisions after 1864.

Thus, in the postreform period, investigations were carried out with greater effectiveness, and the courts worked quickly and fairly, for the most part in accordance with official law, and were almost devoid of corruption. Though courts before the judicial reforms worked slowly, they still were relatively fair, and nearly as fair as the postreform courts. Corruption did exist before the judicial reforms, but to my mind it has been greatly overestimated in the historiography, which has uncritically accepted views of the courts presented in belletristic and journalistic accounts from the 1850s and 1860s as part of the well-meaning campaign to improve Russia's courts. Moreover, corruption in the prereform courts, it seems to me, was used mainly to accelerate the review of cases and not to escape or ameliorate punishment.

Customary Law

In the postreform period social relations were still largely governed by customary law. Customary law *(obychnoe pravo)* was used by all courts to resolve disputes in matters of trade and commerce where lacunae existed in *zakon,* or official, written law. It was also used in cases concerning inheritance, guardianship, and trusteeship among the peasantry. Customary law was used in all civil cases resolved by the rural district courts *(volostnye sudy)* that were created in 1861 for peasants. Until 1889, customary law was used in criminal cases as well. Between 1889 and 1912, civil cases before justices of the peace and land captains were also resolved on the basis of customary law in cases of lacunae in official law. Until 1887, justices of the peace had the right to judge any civil case, regardless of the stakes, "according to conscience" *(po sovesti)*, if both parties so requested. These examples show that a number of archaic legal norms were long preserved in customary law among the peasantry.

Criminal Cases Under Customary Law

As has been shown above, from the most ancient of times until 1917, all classes of Russian society were subject to the same court and the same law in cases concerning serious crimes. Cases of minor crimes and civil matters in the village were the prerogative of village courts, which used customary law in resolving them. Until the end of the seventeenth century, official law and customary law were distinguished from each other, but not significantly. However, in the eighteenth century, when Russian criminal law began to be influenced by legal systems in the West, greater and greater differences arose between official criminal law and common criminal law as practiced among the peasantry. This occurred despite the fact that the peasantry's ties with other social classes were regulated by official law and that customary law pertained only to village affairs. Russian ethnographers and jurists who after peasant emancipation seriously studied peasant life found that peasant justice, which strongly diverged from official law, resolved four out of five cases for 80 percent of the population of the Russian empire.[123]

The Concept of Crime.   Primary concepts of what constituted crime differentiated customary law of the time from official criminal law.[124] In customary law the concept of crime was associated with the religious notion of sin, with the violation of truth *(pravda)* and the laws of conscience, and with fateful misfortune *(neschast'e)*. The well-known volume of Russian proverbs collected by V. I. Dal in the mid-nineteenth century includes the following proverb: "All laws could be done away with, if only people could live in truth" *(Khot' by vse zakony propali, tol'ko by liudi pravdoi zhili)*. Proverbs always mentioned the law in negative terms. This reflected the popular legal consciousness, according to which truth, as depicted in peasant custom, was more just than was the law.[125] In the 1880s, scholar and agriculturist A. N. Engelgardt wrote:

> The Russian *muzhik* does not know of "laws" but instead honors a kind of law of God. For instance, if you apprehend a *muzhik* with a load of stolen hay, take away the hay, and give him a beating, telling him "Don't steal," it won't affect him. If a kulak buying up hemp finds in a load a handful that is soaked with water and straightaway gives the peasant a thrashing, saying "Don't deceive," the peasant won't be moved: "God's justice will prevail" *(eto vse budet po-bozheski)*, he will be thinking. In his view, the law that says that the [stolen] load of hay will bring the peasant three and a half months in jail— a law given by the lords *(pany)* "to support" the *muzhik*, the peasant says with irony—is not in keeping with God's justice.[126]

The all-peasant district courts established in the 1861 general statutes on peasant emancipation reflected a similar view of the role of law: The district court was "to judge according to conscience." In 1889, this role was confirmed by law in the Temporary Guidelines for the District Court.

In peasant legal consciousness a criminal was generally viewed as an unfortunate person, one punished by God for sins committed in the past, such as in childhood. The criminal act itself was considered the beginning of the given individual's divine punishment and his misfortune, and the criminal thus deserved sympathy. Customary law still contained the notion that a crime was a personal offense, an act of dishonor against another person. From this followed the conviction that it was up to the injured party to judge the violation against his person and property. Courts were to judge and assess punishments only for crimes that were directed against the social order. Some peasants in isolated areas still held to the ancient idea that an offense could be carried out not only against a person but also against an animal belonging to him; in other words, the object of a crime could also be an animal. Prince V. N. Tenishev, in a report to his renowned Ethnographic Bureau, recorded an incident in which a peasant had cut off half the tail of a cow belonging to another peasant, as retribution for damage the cow had done to his crops. The owner of the cow turned to the justice of the peace, asking that the perpetrator be punished for "dishonoring the heifer."[127] Additional support for the idea that a crime was considered a personal offense is provided by the custom of assessing fines (payable in vodka, money, or another medium of exchange agreed upon between the parties) in return for personal injury incurred by swindling, stealing, physical assault, insult, and the like. It was not uncommon for village courts to sentence someone found guilty of committing a criminal act to compensating twice over or even more for damage caused, while at the same time freeing the guilty from any criminal punishment. The same approach was taken in ancient Rus.[128]

As a result of their peculiar understanding of crime, peasants in postreform Russia (like those in Muscovy) viewed criminal offenses as being in the same category as civil ones. Theft, fighting, slander, failure of a son to obey his father, adultery, fraud, swindling, other amoral behavior, failure to repay debts, dishonest transactions, and even tactless behavior were all grouped together as legal violations *(prostupky)* and sins, and those who committed any such acts were subject to the same punishments. Ethnographer P. S. Efimenko recorded an instance in which a peasant girl was pursued by two different suitors, both of whom the girl promised she would marry. When the two young men found out that they were competitors, tensions flared between them. The matter was dealt with by the peasant assembly, which decided that the girl should be beaten, and the sentence was in fact carried out. Efimenko wrote: "Overall one notes that in the peasant court criminal matters are seen by the peasants to be the same as civil matters, just as was the case in ancient [Russian] law."[129] Thus, the peasants did not view crime primarily as a violation of juridical norms but rather as a violation of moral norms. Second, peasants saw crime as a personal offense. Third, crime was viewed as a misfortune and a punishment. This understanding of crime, which had faded from official Russian law in the beginning of the eighteenth century, was preserved in customary law into the twentieth century.[130] It is important also to note that customary law viewed crime primarily, if not exclusively, from the point of view of the objective damage or injury caused by the crime, and did not deal with the motives of the lawbreaker. As a result, customary law did not recognize any special circumstances mitigating guilt (with the exception of drunkenness to the point of losing consciousness, and pressure exerted by older members of one's family). Customary law lacked the very notion of legal nonaccountability.[131]

Differences existed between the understanding of crime implicit in customary law and that in official law. A number of acts that violated official law were not considered by peasants to be sins, and thus, were not viewed as crimes, even though peasants did recognize that official law held a different opinion. Such acts included begging, violation of various statutes, offending the honor of the rural police, public drunkenness, violation of rules of behavior in court, cutting down trees in state-owned forests, fraud with respect to state property, various religious crimes, incest, and others. On the other hand, not all actions that peasants viewed as wrong were considered violations under official law. Such actions included working on holidays, refusing to give alms to the poor, not participating in collective work or mutual aid in the village, or breaking the laws of church fasts. In customary law, moral violations such as drunkenness, profligacy detrimental to one's own household, and violation of the conditions of agreements (particularly with regard to hiring labor for agricultural work) were causes for punishment equal with theft, even though according to general legislation such acts did not entail legal responsibility, or if they did, they were considered only civil and not criminal violations.

Customary law was very tolerant of theft, which was widespread in peasant society. Petty theft, especially of trees or food items in the field (such as grain, vegetables, or fruit) was in many places not considered a crime. In such cases the guilty party was obliged to compensate for the damage caused or items stolen but was not subject to criminal punishment. Peasants viewed uncultivated crops, as well as water and forest timber—that is, objects that were not products of human labor—as belonging to God, and consequently, to all. Thus, felling trees in privately owned or state-owned forests and stealing from fields in small amounts and for one's own use were not considered a crime.[132] According to the calculations of the Forestry Department of the Ministry of State Properties during the period 1894–1900, in state-owned forests alone, 1,848,000 rubles' worth of trees were illegally cut down, and this was only a fraction of the overall damage inflicted by peasants on the property of others.[133] At the end of the nineteenth century, peasant youths of both sexes still engaged in ritual thievery in order to gather funds to cover the costs of their gatherings, called *posidelki*.[134] Although customary law was lenient as regards minor—and sometimes, major—thefts, peasants dealt severely with thieves who took things of vital importance to a household's economic well-being, such as a horse, farming implements, or other objects guaranteeing subsistence.

If we recall how theft was dealt with in the law several centuries earlier, we can see why such offenses became widespread and why peasants were so tolerant of them. In old Rus, theft committed with skill and cleverness was seen as an act of valor and was not subject to punishment.[135] Those guilty of theft were not given criminal punishments but only had to pay the injured party material compensation. In Muscovy, those guilty of theft were subject to criminal punishment. However, an exception was made for minor theft. The taking of small objects (for instance, from gardens) for one's own use was not considered theft, and even those guilty of outright

theft of such items were punished in a lenient manner.[136] The generally severe legislation of the Petrine era was tolerant with respect to the theft of
food, drink, or of any other item of minor value when the theft was made
out of extreme need. Theft in such cases was punished lightly, if at all. (See
the Military Statute of 1715, commentary to article 195.)[137] During Peter's
reign, for instance, there existed the right to cut down wood in forests for
one's own needs. Thus it was not at all unexpected that the 1889 Temporary Regulations for the District Court *(Vremennye pravila o volostnom
sude),* which generalized the norms of customary law, stipulated for minor
theft a sentence of only seven to thirty days. The 1885 Statute of Punishments, on the other hand, stipulated for minor theft a prison sentence of no
less than three months.

Sentences.   Under customary law, sentences were understood as retribution or as vengeance against the person who had committed a crime.[138] Although blood vengeance did not exist, attempts were made to get all
people, particularly young people, to "pay" for offenses committed. Bringing the offender to court was considered the highest form of retribution.
Once a sentence had been served, the offense was quickly forgotten. Offenses that went unpunished were long remembered, however, and
vengeance would be sought.[139]

The determination of sentences was often subjective; punishments were
handed down "according to the person" *(po cheloveku),* and "according
to the circumstances" *(po obstoiatel'stvam).* As a result, individuals could
receive different punishments for the same crime. In general, the connection between sentences and the severity of offenses was weak. When an offense was committed by a group of people, all received the same sentence.[140] In some places in Russia an ancient custom was preserved by
which the entire peasant commune was held responsible for crimes committed on its territory if the offender was not discovered or was intentionally hidden. The latter event was not uncommon, since peasants were often
reluctant to deliver up suspected offenders out of fear of retribution from
the supposed miscreant. In such cases, peasants primarily feared arson.[141]
That sentences were handed down on an ad hoc basis and that the roles
played by individuals in crimes committed by a group were ignored were
both natural results of communal ties. These ties made the systematic application of formal, indifferent juridical norms impossible. Social relations
within the commune were so interdependent, diverse, and emotionally col-
ored that it was impossible to approach legal matters in the abstract and to
resolve similar cases in the same way. In such circumstances the most sensible thing to do was to take an ad hoc approach to cases and to resolve
them by taking into account the surrounding circumstances, the moral
state of the accused, and common sense.

District courts meted out sentences of arrest and detention for up to thirty days, fines of up to thirty rubles, reprimands, and up to twenty blows with the birch rod. Corporal punishment, which was abolished for nonpeasants in 1863, was applied to peasants until 1903.[142] Corporal punishment was even applied to some who committed acts not proscribed by law, such as *bludodeianie,* or "lechery," and *razvrat,* or "debauchery."[143] In addition to the traditional use of the birch rod in administering corporal punishment, courts often passed down sentences that departed from judicial norms. For instance, on some occasions, courts gave the aggrieved party the right to strike the offender on the cheek in public.

According to customary law, after a peasant had been punished for a criminal offense, he or she was no longer subject to any sort of sanctions or limitations of rights. When a peasant was tried by a crown court and a limitation of rights was imposed in addition to the customary sentence, this limitation was not observed within the commune. However, such persons were ridiculed in the village and given nicknames corresponding to the sentences they had served. Those who had served jail sentences were called *tiuremnye* (jailbirds); those who had undergone corporal punishment were called *sechennye* (literally, whipped); those who had had to pay a fine were called *shtrafovannye* (fine-payers).[144]

The nineteenth-century ethnographers A. Efimenko and K. Kachorovskii identified a difference in the sentences handed down according to customary law from those handed down in accordance with official law. Official law was governed by the principle *suum cuique tribuer*—all must be treated equally before the law. Customary law, however, was guided by the principle *chtoby nikomu ne bylo obidno* ("let no one be offended"); in other words, sentences in customary law were tailored to restore harmony. Official, written law *(zakon)* was based on intellect and logic, whereas customary law was based on feeling. In official law, everything is objective and formal; in customary law, everything is subjective and aimed at resolving individual cases and dealing with individual people.[145]

Mob Justice.   Customary law permitted mob justice *(samosud)* in extraordinary situations, even to the extent of the killing of miscreants at the scene of the crime. Such was the fate, for instance, of arsonists, horse thieves, and sometimes other thieves caught red-handed. Mob justice was a holdover from ancient Russian law.[146] Peasants often displayed an inclination toward mob justice; official law in their view did not ensure that criminals would get their just deserts. Although mob justice was widespread in the countryside, a number of contemporary observers remarked that at the end of the nineteenth century, mob justice was dying out in some places.[147]

Civil Law and Customary Law

Customary law worked to secure law and order in the peasant village commune. Peasants' personal and property rights were limited, including their right to engage in land transactions, conclude legally binding agreements, move from place to place, leave the commune, and undertake many other actions, and by restraints on alienation. In most instances, peasants were not subjects of civil law, since by law they could not make decisions as individuals but only with the permission of their families and communes. After the Emancipation, peasants' sphere of individual rights became even more limited. In 1886, a law was introduced that significantly limited the division of peasant households into smaller units. A special law issued in 1893 forbade peasants to sell their landholdings without the agreement of the commune. Even peasants living in communes where the land was divided into individual holdings had difficulty selling their land, due to their inability to present formal proof of ownership. In 1895, the Senate declared that the land on which a peasant's house stood and the immediately surrounding yard were the property of the commune and not private property.[148] It is interesting to note that after the Emancipation some peasants who worked in towns and cities began to feel oppressed by laws and regulations concerning property relations in urban environments. In a number of instances, district courts handed down decisions in accordance with official law rather than with customary law. However, crown institutions responsible for peasant affairs were constantly overturning such decisions because they did not conform with customary law or with Senate directives on communal and familial property, or because they had declared land transactions invalid without the proper documents and notarization.[149] As a rule, the government impeded the alienation of peasant lands to other estates, regardless of the preferences of any individual peasant or group of peasants.

Property Law

As practiced within the sphere of property law, Russian customary law had several important features that give us insight into peasants' social and political behavior. Particularly important are two legal norms that contradicted official civil law. The first is the principle of the law of labor *(trudovoe pravo)*, according to which individuals could possess only what was produced by their own labor or that of their ancestors. The second contradiction with official law was the intermingling of the notions of ownership, possession, and use.[150] The peasantry on the whole did differentiate between what was "my own" and what was "someone else's," particularly with respect to movable property. But peasants did not draw clear distinctions between property ownership *(sobstvennost')* and possession *(vladenie)*, particularly concerning land and other real estate. The peasant considered as "his own" the portion of communal land of which he was temporarily in possession at a given moment, as well as the private plot of land *(usadebnaia zemlia)* that was in his permanent possession.[151]

These aspects of property law within customary law make it possible to understand peasants' claims to their noble landlords' land after Emancipation. Peasants were continually working the lands of the noble landlords. Their leasing of the land, the presence of peasant servitors on the land, and various types of rights granted to them to use landlords' property all supported the peasants' conviction that the system of law and order prevalent under serfdom was only temporary and transitional to a time when all lands held by the nobility would be transferred into peasant possession. In the peasants' view, the landlords' land had been cleared and worked by them and their forefathers; thus, the landlords were illegally appropriating the fruits of the peasants' labor. This view gave rise to frequent land seizures by peasants. It also obstructed the establishment of the notion of the inviolability of private property.[152] These aspects of property law within customary law persisted in the postreform period, despite the development of the idea of private property. The persistence of customary law ideas concerning property was not due to peasants' ignorance but rather to their longtime experience of the repartitional commune, collective responsibility, and other limitations on property rights.[153]

Liability Law

Many types of economic transactions recognized by customary law were also permissible under official law; however, due to the constraints on civil activities and civil rights among peasants, as well as to the relatively weak demand for the circulation of commodities, economic transactions were much less common in peasant villages than in urban areas. Liability law among peasants therefore contained many archaic features. As a rule, all agreements between peasants were oral; only agreements with nonpeasants were recorded. Transactions made in the peasant environment were usually accompanied by special rituals. According to official law, a transaction was considered complete at the moment when the contracting parties came to an agreement over property and price. However, peasants concluded transactions differently: The contracting parties would grasp each other's hand, and then a third person who was not a party to the transaction would strike the joined hands, thus separating them. This hand-joining ceremony was followed by a prayer in church or before icons in the peasant's home. Afterward, the buyer would give an advance on his purchase, and the seller would provide vodka for the event (a practice known as *magarich*). Even after all of this, the purchasing party could still renege on the agreement, as long as the item to be purchased was still located in the home of the seller. In this case, however, the purchaser lost the right to have his advance returned.

An animal contracted for purchase was to be delivered by the seller in person to the home of the buyer, and this act of transfer was also accompanied by a ritual. Customary law forbade the sale of property that was fundamental to the maintenance of a family's solvency. For instance, the sale of houses was forbidden without the approval of the peasant assembly. The district court could dissolve a purchase agreement if the seller was considered at the time of the agreement's conclusion to be in a state of incompetence—for instance, if he had been drunk.[154]

An agreement involving a loan of money or of objects was also, as a rule, concluded orally and without witnesses. This custom does not imply that peasants had a particularly high level of trust in each other; on the contrary, it was rooted in the fear that an outside, third party or a written agreement might harm the contracting parties—a variant of the fear of the "evil eye" *(sglaz)*. Generally, in a loan agreement, only the principal sum was repaid; but in some instances, the lender was given an additional payment, either in cash or in kind. Peasants did not see these additional payments as interest paid on the capital advanced but rather as payment for a service. These extra payments could be high. In general, however, peasants still believed, as had their forebears in the tenth to the seventeenth centuries, that if the amount borrowed was returned, the debt was paid in full.

When hiring labor, the head of a peasant household *(khoziain)* was expected to treat the laborers with consideration and not to overwork them or continually criticize, insult, or punish them. Hired laborers had the right to dissolve their work agreement at any time and to keep any money they had been paid. On the other hand, a laborer did not have the right to drink excessively, to be idle and avoid work, to be rude to his master, or to be absent from the workplace without the master's permission. Hired laborers who abandoned their workplace without permission were subject to criminal action—arrest, fine, or corporal punishment in the form of beating with birch rods.[155] Relations between peasant hired laborers and their masters thus retained some characteristics of serfdom.[156]

Inheritance Law

The customary law governing peasant inheritance practices also had its distinctive aspects.[157] First of all, written wills were almost never used by peasants. This fact testifies not only to peasant illiteracy and poverty but also to the degree to which peasant inheritance practices were tied to social and moral norms. Inheritances comprised buildings, movable property, and purchased land—all of which could be passed along only to family members. Allotment land *(nadel'naia zemlia)** could in general be passed along only to members of one's commune. Usually this land remained in the family's possession unless the children had left the household and thus were not there to claim it. Common inheritance law took into account not only blood ties but also the amount of work contributed by each male family member in creating the family's material wealth. Thus, according to common inheritance law (as opposed to official law), the property belonging to a peasant household could be inherited not only by blood relatives but by all members of the family economy, including illegitimate children, adopted children, or foster children. With the permission of the commune, household property could be divided among family members while the household head was still living, but only if the household head was not capable of directing the household economy, if he habitually drank, or if he was squandering the property of the household.

Daughters were allowed to inherit on an equal basis with sons, as long as their husbands, when they married, entered the extended family of their wives. (Such men were called *priimaki*.)[158] In the post-Emancipation period, women's inheritance rights grew, though not in all parts of Russia equally. In a number of provinces, a widow with underage children had the right to keep in her personal possession all property remaining after the death of the household head until the children reached adulthood. In the absence of collateral *(bokovye)* relatives, a childless widow had the right to inherit part or all of the household's property. (A woman's dowry, as well as property that she herself had earned, was recognized as her personal property regardless of her marital status.) However, a widow with grown children was not left entirely without inheritance: She was given a certain share of a household's property, usually one-seventh. Young, unmarried daughters generally received a portion of the inheritance at the discretion of their brothers. Daughters of a deceased household head lived with their brothers until they married, at which time they received a dowry from their brothers. Older unmarried daughters, despite their significant contribution of labor to the household, received from their brothers only a small house and enough to sustain themselves. There were large regional differences in inheritances granted to unmarried daughters. In some places, unmarried daughters received only a very small portion of the household's wealth beyond the requirements of customary law *(malaia chast' iz milosti);* in oth-

---

Nadel'naia zemlia—a special kind of land tenure that existed after the peasant emancipation. To receive these lands into their permanent possession, peasants had to pay redemption dues to the state.

ers, they received portions equal to their brothers'. Obviously, the inheritance process was undergoing change. When a deceased household head had no sons, his property (including allotment lands) usually went to his unmarried daughters, as long as these women were deemed capable of maintaining the household and paying taxes. In some places, the property of a deceased household head was divided among the widow and the daughters, in varying proportions. After the death of their mother, unmarried daughters would inherit some of the household property, but the amount they received varied greatly from area to area. Married women did not inherit property either from their deceased father or their deceased mother. As opposed to official law, customary law did not disqualify one's parents or grandparents from receiving inheritances; for instance, the personal property of a married daughter upon her death was inherited by either her mother or her father, if they were still living.[159]

Family Law

The peasant family differed in noticeable ways from other family forms, due to the fact that it was first and foremost an economic union—one that often included several nuclear families as well as a number of individuals not related to the family by blood.* All members of the extended peasant family worked to the good of the combined household economy under the direction of the household head. From this structure of family life followed many features of customary law on the family: a weakly developed concept of personal property among members of the family; the inability of family members to conclude agreements without the approval of the family head; and the right of the family head to manage the family property even though this property was formally considered to belong to all of the members collectively. The weak role of capital in the peasant household made each family member's labor even more significant. The portion of household property that family members received either upon division of the family or as an inheritance at the death of the family head depended upon their labor contribution to the family economy.[160]

Russian peasants in the early twentieth century maintained kinship ties that had been common since antiquity but that had fallen into disuse among other social estates. In addition to relationship by blood, relationship by marriage *(svoistvó)* was highly valued, as was a child's spiritual kinship with a godparent or godparents *(kumovstvo).* The adoption of children was also practiced among peasants. From ancient times, peasants

---

*Members of other social estates *(sosloviia)* generally lived in nuclear family units.—*Trans.*

also entered into a relationship called *bratanie* (also known as *pobratim-stvo* or *krestovan'e*). This relationship was formed through a special ritual of exchanging crosses worn next to one's skin. Men who entered into such relationships with each other were called "cross brothers" *(krestovye brat'ia),* and women, "cross sisters" *(krestovye sestry).**

Entrance into marriage among Russian peasants in the nineteenth century, as in previous eras, consisted of three stages: a marriage agreement, the wedding ceremony *(venchanie),* and the wedding celebration *(svad'ba).* The marriage agreement, which generally was oral, was concluded by the parents of the couple to be married. The agreement made provisions for a number of matters concerning the wedding: the wedding date; how and by whom wedding expenses would be paid; what wedding gifts would be given; the dowry; and what amount of compensation the parents of the bride would receive for the loss of their daughter's labor *(kladka,* or bride-price). The agreement also established the penalty to be paid in the event that either side reneged. Dowries were given not only by the bride's parents but also by other relatives who at some time had made use of, or profited from, her parents' property. Such relatives could include the bride's uncles, male cousins, the father of her husband-to-be, and so forth. That clan solidarity continued to be strong among peasants (although it was nearly extinct among other social estates) is clearly borne out by this participation of extended relatives in the giving of dowries, as well as by the fact that if a newly married woman suddenly died, the dowry was returned to her parents. Dowries could consist of clothing, jewelry, other valuable ornaments or decorations, money, cattle, and other movable possessions. The penalty for withdrawing from a marriage agreement could include paying all expenses incurred by the aggrieved party in preparing for the wedding as well as a payment for the disgrace caused by the cancellation.[161]

The conclusion of a wedding agreement was accompanied by symbolic acts such as a handshake, a prayer, or the drinking of vodka. The decisive voice in matters pertaining to marriage belonged to the parents, although parents increasingly took their children's wishes into account. At the end of the nineteenth century, marriage among peasants still retained more characteristics of an economic transaction than did marriage among the other social estates in Russia.

Spousal rights under peasant customary law were, in principle, the same as those observed among other social estates. They included the recognition of the supremacy of the husband, the duty of the wife and children to obey him, and so forth. In the postreform period, however, a wife who had

---

*These relationships were not contracted across gender lines.—*Trans.*

been beaten by her husband could complain to a district court. The husband might then be arrested, fined, or beaten with birch rods. Women were subject to the same sentences for violations such as disobedience, willful absence from the home, and adultery. Customary law confirmed parental power over children in its full traditional strength. For instance, when an unmarried son left without permission to work outside the household, his right to inherit the portion of the family property to which he was entitled under customary law could be denied.[162] In the postreform period, however, children who were still living with their parents had the right to own their own property obtained through inheritance, through their own labor outside the family household, or through other means.[163]

Courts and Trials

In 1861, the government established that in minor criminal and civil cases the peasantry was subject to the jurisdiction of district courts, which were to judge according to customary law. Within the commune, however, the traditional courts continued to function unofficially, including the court of the village elder *(sud starosty)* and village elders *(stariki),* or of the village elder and elected village representatives *(vybornye);* and courts made up of one's neighbors, or of the entire commune in the form of the peasant village assembly *(skhod).* In a number of regions, special judges *(sudtsy)* were selected in peasant villages. All of these unofficial judges handled affairs dealing with minor theft, insults, fights, quarrels, loss or damage of property, as well as other minor civil and criminal cases, in accordance with the norms of customary law.[164] Not infrequently, peasants preferred a trial by neighbors as quicker and more fair than the procedures in the official courts. At the same time, trial by the entire peasant village assembly was often seen as biased and under the influence of those who were most vociferous *(gorlany)* or who sought to take advantage of other peasants *(miroedy).* Moreover, in the *volost* courts, cases were often delayed and bribes were common. Peasants feared investigations carried out by state officials, and often they tried to conceal from them that crimes had been committed. In general, peasants turned to higher-level courts only in cases of "major theft and intolerable injury" *(bol'shie krazhi i nesnosnye obidy).*[165]

In 1889, *volost* courts in the central provinces of Russia were reorganized. Judges were given a set of Provisional Regulations *(Vremennye pravila)* as instructions and were placed under the authority of officials of the crown administration among the local nobility. The Provisional Regulations directed that customary law should be followed in dealing with civil suits. In criminal cases, however, judges in *volost* courts were to be guided solely by the general criminal laws, as far as the authority of these judges extended. As a result, the application of criminal customary law was significantly narrowed for peasants. (Customary law in criminal cases was still applied to the non-Russian groups that fell under the rubric of *inorodtsy*.[166]) Despite this limitation on the jurisdiction of the *volost* courts, the legal isolation *(pravovaia obosoblennost')* of peasants as a group was preserved to a significant degree by three factors. First, *volost* courts dealt mainly with civil and not with criminal law, and in civil cases the district courts were guided by customary law. Second, the reorganization of the *volost* courts did not take place in all provinces. Third, it was impossible for either the courts or the peasants to shift all at once from customary law to official law, especially since official law often did not contain provisions for certain situations that arose in peasant life. In such cases recourse was by necessity made to customary law.[167] The view is held by some that beginning in the late nineteenth century, the *volost* courts lost their former popularity among peasants, and that peasants turned to them only when absolutely necessary.[168] Such a tendency was indeed noted by contemporaries, but it should not be exaggerated.[169] Courts of the justice of the peace could not replace the *volost* courts, because the law permitted peasants to turn to the justices of the peace only in civil matters and only with the agreement of both disputants. In criminal matters peasants had recourse to the justice of the peace only concerning offenses committed beyond the boundaries of the *volost*.

Trials.   Trials in the *volost* courts were adversarial, but no lawyers were present. Peasants had to attend trials in person, or in the case of illness, a relative could act as proxy. Instances of torture, both of men and women, were recorded as late as the 1860s in Siberia and in the Urals region.[170] Although torture was unlawful, it is possible that it was used in other places as well, and in later times, but that evidence of it was concealed. In instances of theft, the injured party would announce the theft to the entire peasant settlement, and all houses would be searched in the presence of village authorities and witnesses. (Formally, this practice was also against the law.) Upon finding the stolen item or items, the injured himself was permitted to establish and carry out the punishment. It was held in peasant society that "one's own hand is master" *(svoia ruka vladyka)* and "your own court is nearer, surer, and fairer" *(svoi sud blizhe, vernee i skhodnee)*. According to an even more ancient custom *(vydacha golovoi)* that originated between the eleventh and thirteenth centuries, the victim of a crime could do what he wanted to punish the offender. This custom was forbidden by law by the sixteenth century. In general, sentences were limited to corporal punishment. In some villages, thieves were led about the streets together with the stolen item, with crowds of villagers looking on. However, by the late 1870s and early 1880s, this custom survived only in remote regions.[171]

The suspect's confession was considered the most important piece of juridical evidence. From the sixteenth century to the first half of the eighteenth, great emphasis also was placed on *polichnoe,* or eyewitness testimony. Investigations included the summoning of eyewitnesses and other, less direct witnesses, who were brought before the accused, and evidence was gathered. During difficult investigations, appeals were made to supernatural powers through recourse to sorcerers *(kolduny)* and fortune-tellers *(vorozhei).*172 Searches for a murderer sometimes included a practice known as "trial by corpse and by blood" *(ispytanie trupom i krov'iu),* in which a suspected murderer was brought before the corpse of the deceased. This practice was based on the belief that when a murderer was confronted by the body of the victim, blood would flow from the corpse.173

Throughout Russia, searches for a thief in peasant communities might involve three means. First, a special candle was lit in a church *(zabidi-ashchaia svecha).* Peasants believed that as the candle burned, the thief would begin to waste away and eventually would return the stolen item, openly or surreptitiously. The second means to catch a thief was to pray in church to St. John the Warrior. Finally, if all else failed, peasants appealed to evil spirits through the service of a sorcerer.174 The sorcerer then gathered evidence against the suspected thief through his powers of divination *(vorozhba* and *gadanie).* In particularly challenging cases, especially concerning the division of property, peasants cast lots or declared both sides guilty according to the formula "divide the sin in two" *(grekh popolam).* Evidence could consist of oaths *(prisiaga* and *bozhba),* kissing an icon, or calling down misfortunes on oneself or members of one's family as proof that one was telling the truth. If a male peasant giving an oath had had sexual intercourse with his wife the previous night, then before giving the oath he would wash in the bathhouse *(bania).* A peasant sometimes performed such ritual purification not in the bathhouse but rather by washing himself with cold water or merely by splashing water over his head and chest.175 In the unofficial village courts, investigations into criminal affairs such as theft, fighting, insults *(oskorbleniia),* and other minor civil cases most often ended with the reconciliation of the disputing parties. The aggrieved party would receive compensation from the guilty party, who instead of additional punishment would have to pay for drinks of vodka for those involved in the case.176

Although peasants were convinced that either the criminal himself or his relatives would be punished by God, they nevertheless made recourse to magic and sorcery in trying to punish criminals they could not uncover. In an effort to get a thief to turn himself in, or in order to take vengeance on him, peasants in some regions would find a footprint left by the suspect on the ground, then dig up the soil around the footprint and cast it into a fire. The belief was that this "hot track" *(goriachii sled)* would cause the thief to writhe in pain and return what he had stolen. In other areas, the footprint or track would be scattered to the wind; the track, it was believed, would find the thief and bring him before whomever he had injured. In yet other places, peasants turned to a seer *(znakhar')*, who would cast spells and perform other acts of magic. However, although peasants believed in the power of seers and sorcerers to find lost objects, they rarely turned to them for assistance, out of fear of God.[177]

Oaths, trial by one's neighbors, the use of magic, and so forth were all survivals of ancient criminal law. It must be pointed out, however, that judicial practices among the peasantry did progress. Peasants did not begin to use circumstantial evidence until around 1870 or 1880; even then, direct evidence remained the most important, and the presence of circumstantial evidence only was not considered enough to find a suspect guilty. By the beginning of the twentieth century, the casting of lots as well as the giving of oaths as evidence had gradually fallen out of use, and younger peasants made no use of them at all. Evidence in written form also became rather widely used, and torture no longer was employed as a means of gathering evidence. Peasants increasingly preferred the rural *volost* court to the village courts, and when possible, a state-administered court over the *volost* court.[178]

Peasants' Isolation from General Legal Practices

What was the basis of the isolation of the peasantry from the general practices of law and order used by other social groups in Russia? The notion of general, abstract, formally expressed legal norms was poorly developed in customary law because it went against the peasants' affinity for the actual and the concrete—an affinity that is characteristic of poorly educated people in general. For peasants, each case was different; thus, in their view, it was impossible to have selected beforehand ready-made decisions for cases. Thus, abstract legal guidelines and principles that seemed far removed from real-life, concrete conditions were not used in customary law. "Peasants have only the meagerest opportunity and aptitude for mastering the legal statutes that touch upon their lives, and for this reason they have a poor understanding of their legal rights and obligations," wrote N. Druzhinin, a nineteenth-century specialist in civil law. "The peasant has had particular difficulty in understanding legal matters because the peasant court functions solely on the basis of custom, whereas the all-estate courts functions on the foundation of law and followed procedures different from those of the peasant court."[179] In the late seventeenth century, official law was becoming more formalized and more casuistic as individual cases were being subsumed under general formulas. The very language of the law was becoming more and more abstract and rife with foreign terms, as Russian law was developing more and more in parallel with Western law. At the same time that these dramatic changes were taking place in official law, customary law among the Russian peasantry was becoming more ingrown and was assimilating less and less of what transpired in official law.

Three circumstances in particular contributed to the divergence between official law and customary law. First was the development, beginning in the early eighteenth century, of separate courts for the various social estates—in particular, for obligated townspeople *(posadskie liudi)*, who until then had been subject to the same law as were peasants and under the jurisdiction of the same court. The development in the second half of the eighteenth century and the first half of the nineteenth century of courts based on social estates corresponded with the prevailing mind-set among the populace, including the peasants, who deemed it fair that individuals should be judged by their equals.

Second, the penetration into the peasant village of new ideas, including new ideas concerning law, was hampered by low literacy levels and by pagan practices, both of which, in the opinion of ethnographers in the postreform era, significantly impeded the transformation of juridical norms among the peasantry.[180] Superstition and prejudice provided the corpus delicti for a number of crimes among peasants that had become anachronistic elsewhere in the postreform period. For example, as late as the 1870s, sorcerers in Minsk province were massacred during a cholera epidemic because peasants believed they had played a role in causing the epidemic. Peasants sometimes would take the blood of a sorcerer and perform rituals with it in order to become free of his influence. Graves were dug up with the aim of taking talismans from among the objects buried with the dead person, or from among the deceased's internal organs. Peasants believed that such talismans could help save their crops from drought as well as protect them and their families from the influence of evil forces. Superstition also motivated crimes. Those suffering from venereal diseases would rape young virgins, thinking this would free them of their illness. Those ill with fevers would sometimes engage in bestiality, believing it would cure them. Peasants would commit thefts in the belief that the stolen item would bring luck to their household; they would make false oaths at the advice of a sorcerer and out of superstitious fear of making an oath; and so on.[181]

Third, it was in the interests of the crown administration to keep the peasants separated in a legal sense from the other social estates. The state hoped that with the help of institutions such as customary law, the repartitional commune, and collective responsibility for peasant behavior, peasants could be protected from the influences of urban life and that public order could be preserved in the countryside. After the peasant emancipation of 1861, the government carried out its earlier policies with the same aim in mind—legal isolation of the peasantry—without fully realizing the peril that such isolation eventually would lead to.[182] When the *volost* courts were reorganized in 1889, the government intentionally kept them in place in Russian, Ukrainian, and Byelorussian provinces as separate courts exclusively for peasants. Only in the Baltic provinces did the government eliminate all isolation of peasant courts by introducing a general system for legal and judicial administration.[183]

The government began to realize the danger of the situation only in the early twentieth century. At this time, the government decided to purge the most obsolete juridical norms from customary law and from legislation dealing with the peasants, and to make the peasants real subjects of civil law by freeing them from the oversight of the peasant commune. Moreover, the government sought to impress upon the peasants an appreciation of private property, to inculcate in them an understanding of its importance and inviolability. During reforms that began in 1905 and continued until the outbreak of war in 1914, peasants gained the right to enter military service, or to leave the village to work or study, without asking permission of the commune or household head. Previously, peasants could be expelled from the commune if they entered civil service, were awarded an order or academic degree, or entered another social estate. Their expulsion traditionally had meant the loss of the right to communal lands. But with the new reforms, such expulsion was legally proscribed. The law now gave peasants the right to join other village communes and to acquire land in them without officially leaving their former commune. Beginning in 1906, leaving the commune became an option that could freely be exercised by all. In leaving the commune, a household head could keep the same plots that were in his possession as of the most recent repartition of communal land, and he retained the right to make use of general communal resources. The commune was obliged to honor within one month's time a request to leave the commune and to remove that household's lands from general communal holdings. If the commune did not do this, then the land captain did.

Peasants without land could leave the commune unhindered, and choosing a place of residence became the private affair of each peasant. The poll tax, collective responsibility, compulsory labor in public work projects, and compulsory work for individuals in arrears were abolished. Peasants who did not possess land had the right to acquire bills of exchange. Also abolished was the proscription against mortgaging allotment lands to private individuals or to private groups, though mortgages were allowed only as part of loans from the Peasant Land Bank. An entire village community could shift its system of land allotments from scattered strips to consolidated individual holdings by a two-thirds decision of the village assembly (when village land was under communal control) or by a simple majority decision (when land was held under the hereditary, or *podvornoe*, system).

Significant limits were imposed on the power of the land captains; they now could act only within the limits of official law, and peasants were not obliged to submit to their decisions. Peasant families could divide household lands as they themselves saw fit. Peasant rights were expanded in elections to organs of local self-government, and peasants sent their own representatives to the State Duma, created in 1905. The legal jurisdiction of the *volost* court over the peasantry was limited: If they wished, peasants could turn to courts of the justice of the peace or to other courts. Thus, the law gave peasants rights fully equal with those of other social estates. Only a third of the peasantry found the new rights and freedoms to their liking and made use of them in the period 1906 to 1915. The other two-thirds of the peasantry remained true to the principles of traditional customary law. This indicates that customary law had very strong roots in the countryside all the way up to 1917. The priority of customary law over official law and the peasants' devotion to it had been seriously undermined, but not enough to eliminate the peasantry's legal isolation.

Although the customary law of the peasantry was influenced by official law over the course of the eighteenth and the first half of the nineteenth centuries, in many respects it kept to the traditions of criminal and civil law that had prevailed throughout Russia before the eighteenth century. In a number of respects, customary law inherited the juridical norms not only of Muscovy but also of the Kievan period,[184] and thus it can serve as an important source for understanding legal practices of both these eras.[185] In other respects, however, the peasants adopted norms of official law when it was advantageous for them to do so.[186]

Customary law was not just a conglomerate of various elements but rather a distinctive *system* of law. It is difficult to share the opinion of those vigorous, early twentieth-century critics of the commune and of customary law who asserted that after Emancipation the peasantry lived in conditions where law was completely absent, and that customary law was no law at all but the power of clerks and village elders, whose ruling could be bought for a pail of vodka.[187] In answer to such accusations, one of the most knowledgeable experts on customary law, S. V. Pakhman, commented: "It is impossible to imagine a society *(obshchestvennyi byt)* that knows no system of juridical principles or rules. Mistrust and contempt [of the peasant legal system] can be justified only by the fact that until very recently our knowledge of the subject has been scanty indeed."[188] Peasants in the Russian village followed the legal norms of age-old practices of customary law. It is worth emphasizing that peasant legal norms, at least in the area of civil law, were sanctioned by official law and carried full juridical force; they were indeed customary *law,* and not merely custom and tradition.[189]

In this analysis of customary law, Russian peasant life appears somewhat more archaic than it does in other chapters of this work. This is because

customary law was not written down, and its carriers were living people—
the old men *(stariki)* of the peasant village. But even in 1917 the old men
of the village—those 60 years and older—were born as early as 1857, in an
era when serfdom still existed; and naturally these men adhered to the
norms of customary law that had then prevailed. But life moved on and left
customary law norms behind. The realities of life in Russia underwent
greater changes than can be seen from an analysis of customary law. Official law gradually made deeper and deeper inroads into peasant life. N. M.
Astyrev, who worked for three years as a *volost*-level clerk, wrote percep-
tively in an 1896 best-selling work on the peasants: "To me the district
court seems like a person sitting on two chairs, each of which is continually being shifted around underneath him in different directions. And the
two chairs are law [*zakon*] and custom [*obychai*]."[190]

Criminality in Russia in the Nineteenth and the Early Twentieth Centuries

The level of crime in a society is most indicative of that society's well-
being. In stable, traditional societies, people are tied to their place of residence and to their communities, urban life is not highly developed, and
there is strict social control. In such societies, social structures are hierarchical; there is little vertical social mobility; community ties are extensively
developed; and the needs of the community prevail over those of private
individuals. Consequently, crime levels are usually low. In industrial, urbanized societies, however, higher crime levels are more typical. Here the
population is socially and geographically mobile; public ties dominate over
communal ones; the individual's success is uppermost in the society's system of values; and people have at their disposal a great amount of freedom
and can act on their own initiative. Particularly high levels of crime are
noted, however, in societies undergoing significant cultural, social, and political change. In such circumstances the previously dominant system of
values is transformed, and a significant number of people are socially mar-
ginalized. In this respect, an evaluation of the level of crime and its dynamics in Russia from the eighteenth to the early twentieth centuries is of
great interest. Moreover, data on criminality can be used to test a number
of conclusions made in other chapters of this study. The aim of the following section of this chapter is to present a general picture of the changes in
criminality during the nineteenth and early twentieth centuries, bearing in
mind the issues discussed in other chapters.[191] Unfortunately, we do not
have a great deal of data on crime in the eighteenth century; however, the
information we do have from the first half of the nineteenth century gives
us some idea of criminality in the preceding century.

Sources on Criminality

Data on crime in Russia began to be collected on a countrywide basis in 1803, after the creation of the Ministry of Justice the previous year. Information sent from the provinces was systematized by ministry officials and included in the ministry's yearly report. From 1834 to 1868, the reports of the Ministry of Justice were published together with statistics on criminality. The reports from the years 1803–1833 and 1869–1870 are held in the Russian State Historical Archives (RGIA). The reports from 1809–1824 do not contain statistical data on crime; it is possible that from 1809 to 1818 the Ministry of Justice did not compile such data. After the completion of the 1864 legal reform, statistics on criminal activity were published yearly from 1872 to 1913 in *Svody statisticheskikh svedenii po delam ugolovnym* (Collections of Statistical Information on Criminal Affairs), which was issued separately from the report of the Ministry of Justice. From 1884 to 1913, additional data appeared in the yearly publication *Sbornik statisticheskikh svedenii Ministerstva iustitsii* (Collection of Statistical Information of the Ministry of Justice).

Thus, historians have at their disposal a good deal of information on crime in nineteenth- and early twentieth-century Russia. Moreover, the unpublished, archival resources have not yet been fully mined. For several reasons, however, it is extremely difficult to combine even the published data into a unified picture. First, from 1803 to 1913, the form in which data on crime were presented in reports and other collections of information did not remain consistent, and the data presented did not always pertain to the same geographical divisions. In addition, the system of judicial institutions in Russia was changed a number of times, most notably in the 1860s but also in 1889 and in 1912, which affected the reports as well as the collection of data on criminality. For these reasons, historians have adequate information on changes in crime levels only for certain periods, the longest of which is the twenty-year period from 1874 to 1893.

Despite the difficulties in evaluating the dynamics of criminality for the entire period from 1803 to 1913, several factors make it possible to construct a unified index on criminality during this period, with the proviso that such an index should be seen only as a general guide to criminality. First, for the period under examination, and definitely for the years 1845–1903, there existed a criminal code that did not undergo significant changes with regard to the concept of crime and the nomenclature of crimes. A new criminal code did not appear until 1903; beginning in 1904, it was introduced into practice, various sections at a time, but even by 1917 it still was not completely in force. Second, though the judicial system, judicial procedure, and procedural law were significantly reorganized under the judicial reforms of 1864, official statistics on crime both before and after the reforms included only criminal cases that were heard by the general courts. Moreover, official crime statistics used the categories of inquest, criminal case, defendant, and convicted person—all important for evaluating levels of crime.

In order to analyze imperial Russian statistical data on criminality, it is important to understand the specific definitions assigned to four key terms in Russia during the last third of the nineteenth century and the early years of the twentieth: *crime (prestuplenie), criminal case (ugolovnoe delo), defendant (podsudimyi),* and *convicted person (osuzhdennyi).* In imperial Russia as in other countries and eras, a *defendant* is a person suspected of having committed a crime, and a *convicted person* is one who has been found guilty by a court; the terms are commonly understood. However, researchers frequently confuse the terms *crime, inquest,* and *criminal case,* even though they are far from the same thing. A *crime* is an act that is directed against the currently existing legal norms and that is subject to prosecution. In Russian criminal statistics, a crime recorded by the institutions of law enforcement was called a *sledstvie,* or inquest. By law, beginning in 1864, the investigator from a given police station was informed about all crimes uncovered in the area assigned to that police station, and he initiated an inquest for each crime. An inquest essentially was simply a recorded crime; the number of inquests thus reflected the level of crime known to the institutions of law enforcement. Official police statistics on crime, as a general rule, describe a crime level lower than was the reality, since not all crimes (especially minor ones) were discovered or reported. However, in practical terms, it is impossible to accurately measure the difference between reality and what was uncovered by police. A *criminal case* signified a crime that had been exposed and investigated and had become the subject of judicial examination. Law enforcement institutions were not aware of all crimes committed, and an even smaller number of all crimes committed were subject to judicial examination. Since the number of crimes committed can never be known, the "crime level" is only hypothetical. Thus, I will henceforth label as a *crime* a violation of the law that became known to the institutions of law enforcement and for which an inquest was begun.

The yearly Ministry of Justice reports for the period 1803–1808 contain information on the total number of criminal cases reviewed by all official courts of the empire under the jurisdiction of the Ministry of Justice, and also on the number of defendants and convicted persons. From 1825 to 1870, the reports contained the same types of data, presented separately for courts of first instance and appellate courts as well as for the court of last resort—the Senate. Until the judicial reform of 1864, most criminal cases were initiated in courts of first instance, although only minor cases were conclusively resolved in these courts. In cases of serious crimes, courts of first instance handed down preliminary decisions, or opinions of the court; these cases were then directed to a court of appeal for confirmation or revision. Cases involving persons in government or public service were from their initiation heard in higher-level courts. According to my calculations, about 40 percent of all cases examined in courts of first instance were sent on to higher courts for review; fewer than 1 percent of decisions of the lower-level courts were appealed. Between 2 and 10 percent of all cases dealt with by appellate courts each year (approximately 6 percent on average) were reviewed in these courts for the first time. A very small number of cases came under judicial review or appeal before the Senate—the court of last resort. All courts sent yearly reports to the Ministry of Justice, where cases were systematized according to the level of court examining them, after which the reports were published in the *Otchet Ministerstva iustitsii* (Report of the Ministry of Justice). Since cases sent for review or appeal from a lower to a higher court were not singled out from the total number of cases, more than 40 percent of cases were counted twice in the Ministry's reports, and a very small number of cases—those that reached the Senate—were counted three times. Only after we have accounted for criminal cases appearing multiple times in the data is it possible to obtain more or less accurate indicators of criminality for the years 1803 to 1808 and 1825 to 1870.

Statistical data on criminality produced in the years from 1872 to 1913 contain additional information on crimes recorded by investigators. These data were more extensive than those given in earlier sources and were listed separately for all types of courts. In these years, all investigators were obliged to send a separate card on each new case immediately to the Ministry of Justice prior to initiating an inquest, whether any suspects had been detained or not.[192] As a result of this new procedure, a register of crimes *(uchet prestupnosti)* known to investigators and the police was created beginning in 1872. Similar data from earlier periods do not exist, although for the period 1803–1868 a reconstruction of such data might be possible. During the first five years after the implementation of the new practices in the gathering of statistics (1872–1876), some 40 percent of all inquests (i.e., the number of recorded crimes) were subject to judicial examination,[193] and this corresponded approximately to the percent of crimes that were uncovered—only approximately, since a small number of cases were closed due to a lack of information or evidence. It is generally believed that the frequency with which crimes can be uncovered improves substantially only with the introduction of technical innovations in the investigation of crimes or with a considerable increase in public law enforcement efforts. Neither occurred in Russia in the period from 1803 to 1870. Therefore, in my opinion, it is entirely possible that the correlation between the numbers of registered crimes and discovered crimes for the period from 1872 to 1876 can be applied to earlier years as well, making it possible to reconstruct the approximate number of discovered crimes for the period from 1803 to 1870.

Another difficulty in obtaining a general picture of criminality in imperial Russia arises from the periodic changes in territorial divisions; with each change, a different population was dealt with in crime figures. In order to produce comparable data, the numbers of crimes, criminal cases, defendants, and convicted persons for each year were examined with respect to the number of people living that year in the area covered by the crime register. These population figures are nearly always included in the sources. As is the custom in the field of crime statistics, the number of crimes per thousand members of the population serves as the most precise indicator of the level of crime. It should be borne in mind that for the period 1803 to 1870, the crime register covered all of imperial Russia, except Poland and Finland. For the years 1872 to 1883, the index included regions that were home to approximately 75 percent of the population of European Russia. Subsequently, the territory covered by the register continuously increased, and by 1907, the Ministry of Justice was receiving data from the entire empire, with the exception of Finland. Though crime levels varied to some degree from region to region, the crime register from 1872 to 1883 covering 75 percent of the population still gives a fairly representative picture. Data based on inference are always approximate in nature, but this does not necessarily deprive them of usefulness for the purposes of scholarly analysis.

It is also vital to note that neither before nor after the judicial reforms of 1864 did the Ministry of Justice control the activities of local village courts or of police officials in either urban or rural areas, nor did it record minor offenses dealt with by local courts and police (such as minor theft, drunkenness, fighting, and so on). Village courts were unofficial in nature until 1864. In that year, all village courts received official status as *volost* courts;* their jurisdiction included minor criminal acts among peasants that were dealt with according to customary law. Peasants living in the village could, if they desired, turn to the general courts for legal aid; but instead they preferred the *volost* court, where matters were investigated according to customary law.[194] Until the peasant emancipation, village courts for serfs were under the jurisdiction of the landlords, whereas the courts of state peasants were run by the Department of State Properties *(Departament gosudarstvennykh imushchestv)*. (In 1837 this body was renamed the Ministry of State Properties.) Courts for crown peasants were under the jurisdiction of

---

*An exception were the courts for state peasants, which became district courts in 1841.

the Crown Administration *(Udel'noe vedomstvo),* and after 1864 they were overseen by the Ministry of Internal Affairs.

The activity of village courts was significant in extent. In 1844, for example, the village courts for state peasants considered some 53,100 cases, of which only 558—about 1 percent—were transferred to general courts. In all of the general courts, approximately 22,000 criminal cases dealing with state peasants were heard, and 32,800 persons were put on trial, which was nearly two and a half times the number heard in the village courts.[195] Assuming the criminal activity of all categories of peasants was approximately the same, and taking into account that about 46 percent of all peasants were state peasants, then village courts in the 1840s reviewed about 116,000 cases throughout all of Russia, 99 percent of which consisted of minor infractions. Approximately the same situation existed in the postreform period. In 1905, for instance, village courts for the peasants in 43 provinces of Russia heard some 1,542,000 cases, which was approximately equal to the number of all committed crimes registered in the country—1,566,000.[196] Thus, if we take into account minor legal infractions in the countryside, which were dealt with independently by the police and not counted by the Ministry of Justice, then to estimate the total number of crimes both before and after Emancipation, one should double the number of crimes that were actually recorded.

The task of registering crimes, defendants, and convicted persons in a country as huge as Russia was extremely difficult, and it required an extensive system of highly trained officials, of which there were never enough. As a result, one does not expect Russian crime statistics to provide absolutely precise data, especially prior to the judicial reforms of 1864. One contemporary observer wittily remarked: "These numbers generally should be thought of as a measure of police activity rather than of the moral state of the population."[197] The data on the numbers of crimes are the least precise; figures on the number of defendants are somewhat more reliable; and the most reliable data are those on convicted persons, particularly after 1872.[198] Having become familiar with the record-keeping methods of the time and having worked with the criminal statistical records, I am convinced that these records were compiled and processed with care and that they more or less accurately reflect the main tendencies in the rate of crime in Russia in the nineteenth and early twentieth centuries. However, due to the undercounted minor legal infractions by peasants in the countryside, the overall level of crime is underestimated.

One would think that over time the state must have become more efficient at counting and registering social phenomena. If this is true in the case of crime, and in particular for the period after 1872, when changes in bookkeeping were made, then the figures given below are correct in indicating falling levels of criminality from 1803 to 1861, and consequently, an increase in the growth in the crime rate in the last third of the nineteenth and in the early twentieth centuries. However, even though real improvement in record keeping concerning crime was made after the peasant emancipation, this improvement was at least partially counteracted—on the one hand, by the growth in opportunities for criminals to conceal their crimes, which thus remained uncounted; and on the other, by a lag in the increase in size and capabilities of the police apparatus in comparison with the number of crimes being committed. Yet on the whole, the distortion caused by varying accuracy in recording crimes both before and after 1872 is hardly significant enough to render impossible a comparison of crime figures for the periods 1803–1871 and 1872–1913. Taking into account the difficulties and lack of precision in the process of recording crimes, as well as the use of methods to reconstruct information missing from the historical record, the data given below can only be considered approximate. They reflect, more or less, the primary tendencies in the development of criminality in Russia from 1803 to 1913.

The Dynamics and Structure of Criminality

Let us first examine the data on the dynamics of criminality in general. The data in Table 5.6 show that during the period of just over a century between 1803–1808 and 1911–1913, the absolute number of crimes rose nearly twelve times. When the increase in the size of the population over this time is accounted for, however, we see that the number of crimes rose 2.9 times. The number of crimes per hundred thousand persons rose during this period from 593 in 1803–1808 to 1,719 in 1911–1913. Throughout the nineteenth and early twentieth centuries, the crime level fluctuated. In general, until the Emancipation it tended to fall, whereas after the Emancipation it tended to rise. The crime level during the period from 1851 to 1860 was 87 percent of that at the beginning of the nineteenth century, whereas crime in 1911–1913 was 366 percent higher than in 1851–1860. Essentially, in the postreform period, criminality rose continuously except for a break during the 1890s. The level of crime rose during the liberal reign of Alexander I; it fell while the conservative Nicholas I was on the throne; and then under the liberal Alexander II it again rose, this time significantly—2.7 times. The level of crime stabilized during the reign of conservative Alexander III, and then rose again by 55 percent under Nicholas II. The level of crime was at its lowest under Nicholas I, when it was 13 percent lower than at the beginning of the century; and it was highest on the eve of World War I, in 1913. Criminality in Russia in 1914–1916 was 28 to 29 percent lower than in 1911–1913; but from 1916 onward, crime tended to increase.[199]

The number of criminal cases examined in the courts from 1803 to 1913 rose in absolute numbers by twenty times, and 4.8 times per hundred thou-

TABLE 5.6 The Dynamics of Criminality in Russia, 1803–1913 (various years)

a. Number of recorded crimes (*zafiksirovannye prestupleniia*) (thousand)
b. Number of criminal cases examined in courts (thousand)
c. Number of defendants (thousand)
d. Number of convicted persons (thousand)
e. Population (million)
f. Number of crimes per 100,000 persons
g. Number of criminal cases per 100,000 persons
h. Number of defendants per 100,000 persons
i. Number of convicted persons per 100,000 persons
j. Index of the increase in the number of crimes per 100,000 persons (1803–1808 = 100)

	1803–1808	1825–1830	1831–1840	1841–1850	1851–1860	1861–1870	1872–1880	1883–1889	1899–1900	1901–1910	1911–1913
a.	243	326	315	321	320	599	–	824	1,477	1,891	2,888
b.	97	130	126	128	128	239	–	–	–	1,243	1,911
c.	132	173	172	193	221	334	–	560	1,701	1,939	2,894
d.	71	111	97	73	76	102	–	397	863	985	1,484
e.	41	50	53	57	62	69	–	59	121	142	168
f.	593	652	594	563	516	868	–	1,397	1,221	1,332	1,719
g.	237	260	238	224	206	346	–	–	–	875	1,137
h.	322	346	325	339	356	484	–	949	1,406	1,365	1,723
i.	173	222	183	128	123	148	–	673	713	694	883
j.	100	110	100	95	95	146	–	236	206	225	290

(continues)

TABLE 5.6 *(continued)*

k. Index of the increase in the number of criminal cases per 100,000 persons (1803–1808 = 100)
l. Index of the increase in the number of defendants per 100,000 persons (1803–1808 = 100)
m. Index of the increase in the number of convicted persons per 100,000 persons 1803–1808 = 100)

	1803–1808	1825–1830	1831–1840	1841–1850	1851–1860	1861–1870	1872–1880	1883–1889	1899–1900	1901–1910	1911–1913
k.	100	110	100	95	87	146	–	–	–	369	479
l.	100	107	101	105	111	150	–	295	437	424	535
m.	100	128	106	74	71	86	–	389	412	401	510

SOURCES: Rossiiskii gosudarstvennyi istoricheskii arkhiv (RGIA), f. 1370 (Komitet dlia osvidetel'stvovaniia ministerskikh otchetov), op. 1, d. 7 (Vsepoddanneishii otchet ministra iustitsii za 1803 g. [henceforth, Otchet]), ll. 26–27, tablitsy f. 1341 (Pervyi departament Senata), op. 9, d. 826 (Otchet za 1804), ll. 45–47; f. 1162 (Gosudarstvennaia kantseliariia), op. 9, d. 34 (Otchet za 1805 g.), tablitsy; ibid., d. 35 (Otchet za 1806 g.), ll. 11, 76; ibid., d. 36 (Otchet za 1807 g.), ll. 73–75; ibid., d. 37, ll. 75–77; f. 1409 (Sobstvennaia ego velichestva kantseliariia), op. 1, d. 498 (Otchet za 1826 g.), ll. 325–329; ibid., dd. 500, 548 (Otchet za 1827 g.); ibid., d. 596-b (Otchet za 1828 g.), ll. 433–439; ibid., d. 643 (Otchet za 1829 g.); ibid., d. 690 (Otchet za 1830 g.); ibid., dd. 694, 771 (Otchet za 1831 g.); ibid., d. 774 (Otchet za 1832 g.); f. 1405 (Ministerstvo iustitsii), op. 521, dd. 1, 2 (Otchet za 1833); *Otchet Ministerstva iustitsii za [1834–1857] god* (St. Petersburg, 1835–1858); *Sbornik statisticheskikh svedenii Ministerstva iustitsii za [1884–1913] god* (St. Petersburg, 1887–1916), vypuski 1–30; *Svod statisticheskikh svedenii po delam ugolovnym za [1873–1913] god* (St. Petersburg, 1876–1916); V. A. Novakovskii, *Opyt podvedeniia itogov ugolovnoi statistiki s 1861 po 1871 g.* (St. Petersburg, 1891), pp. 1–63; E. N. Tarnovskii, ed., *Itogi russkoi ugolovnoi statistiki za 20 let (1874–1894)* (St. Petersburg, 1899).

sand persons. These figures reflect greater increases in the rate of prosecution than in the number of crimes. Thus, we can conclude that the frequency with which the perpetrators of crimes were apprehended rose in the late nineteenth and early twentieth centuries. Perpetrators were apprehended in 40 percent of cases before the 1870s; in the early twentieth century, the apprehension rate reached 66 percent. This success in apprehending criminals was made possible by the use of fingerprinting, photography, and more modern methods of processing information, and by increasing professionalism among detectives and improvements in investigative techniques.

The various indicators of criminality are closely related; there is a high correlation coefficient of 0.90 between the numbers of crimes, criminal cases, defendants, and convicted persons. Consequently, it is natural to expect that both the relative and absolute numbers of defendants on the whole should also rise. This is precisely what happened. But there was a substantial difference: The relative number of defendants rose more than did the relative number of criminal cases. The number of defendants per hundred thousand persons rose 5.4 times over the 111-year period from 1803 to 1913, whereas the number of criminal cases per hundred thousand persons rose 3.2 times. In the period from 1803 to 1808, the number of defendants was 36 percent higher than the number of criminal cases; and in 1911–1913, the number of defendants was 128 percent higher than the number of criminal cases. At first glance this seems to indicate a rise in the proportion of crimes committed by more than one person. It also seems to contradict the fact that the proportion of such crimes within the overall number of crimes fell across time. In 1874, crimes committed by a group made up 64 percent of major crimes; in 1894, such crimes constituted 53 percent of all major crimes; and in 1913, 47 percent. Among minor legal infractions in 1913, the proportion of crimes committed by more than one person fell to 30 percent of all crimes committed.[200] Although the proportion of crimes committed by individuals rose, there apparently was an accompanying rise in the number of crimes involving large numbers of people, such as illegal antigovernment demonstrations, strikes, religious-oriented crimes, and other forbidden political and economic actions. Despite their relatively small numbers, such cases involved a large number of defendants. An examination of the numbers of various types of crimes confirms this supposition. (See Table 5.9.)

In the last third of the nineteenth and in the early twentieth centuries, there was a rise in the number of "religious crimes,"* crimes against the

---

*Religious crimes included the desecration of graves, destruction of icons or Bibles, and other sacrilegious acts (such as giving offense to a priest as he conducted a church service, creating a disturbance in a church, or conducting an improper, un-Christian burial).

state, and crimes against the administrative order. Though these cases were relatively few in number compared to criminal cases of other types, such crimes generally were committed by groups of people rather than by individuals, which resulted in large numbers of defendants. One can surmise that the politicization of social life in Russia, and the reduction in or absence of democratic freedoms, were significant factors in the increase in the number of defendants. The number of defendants during the reign of each tsar varied, following the same trends as did the number of crimes. The end of the reign of Nicholas I saw the fewest defendants—about 350 per 100,000 persons; and the highest number of defendants was recorded in 1911–1913—1,723 per 100,000. Under Alexander II there was a significant increase in the number of defendants; in the reign of Alexander III, a slight decrease; and under Nicholas II, another marked increase. It is significant that the proportion of crimes committed by groups of people decreased in the postreform period. To my mind, this testifies to the erosion of collectivism and the increasing individualism among professional criminals, who long had related to each other as members of a community, both in prison as well as outside.

Changes in the number of convicted persons did not entirely parallel changes in other indicators of criminality. Under Alexander I, the index of the number of convictions per hundred thousand persons rose. During the reign of Nicholas I, this conviction index fell significantly; under Alexander II, it again rose rapidly—5.5 times; under Alexander III, the index continued to rise; and after a small and brief decline in the first decade of the twentieth century, it again rose sharply from 1911 to 1913. The number of convicted persons remained lower than the numbers of crimes and of defendants, indicating that the proportion of those acquitted was rising. If the high proportion of acquittals after the 1864 judicial reforms can be explained by the liberal views that prevailed in society, and consequently among juries as well, then how can one explain the even lower proportion of convictions (and correspondingly greater proportion of acquittals) *before* the reforms? Between 1803 and 1860, fewer than 52 percent of defendants were acquitted. This can hardly be explained by the occasional pardons handed down by the emperor. In my view, two factors can help explain the low percentage of convictions in the prereform period. Until Emancipation, the police had broad rights to arrest—and were inclined to do so—anyone who fell under even the slightest suspicion of having committed a crime. In the view of the police it was better to arrest someone who was innocent than to allow a guilty person to escape. There were guidelines according to which a detainee was to be released if no charge was made, but these guidelines were not followed. The result was that the number of arrests did not correspond to the number of crimes committed. Moreover, an association of professional investigators arose in Russia only in 1860, and this undoubtedly had an effect on the success with which the perpetrators of crimes were apprehended, as well as on the efficiency with which evidence was collected and the guilt (or innocence) of a suspect was proven. But the low percentage of convicted persons demonstrates the fair and impartial approach to cases by judges, who freed suspects when prosecutors could not present sufficient evidence to convict. The low percentage of convictions also indicates that although law and justice in tsarist Russia were not as developed as they were in the West, the law was far more than empty phrases, both prior to and after the implementation of the judicial reforms.

Our picture of criminality in Russia is considerably broadened when we compare the data on major crimes (those punishable by prison terms) with those on minor infractions *(melkie pravonarusheniia)*. During the period from 1803 to 1808, major crimes comprised 35 percent of all crimes, and minor crimes, 65 percent. From 1911 to 1913, major crimes represented 34 percent of all crimes, and minor crimes, 66 percent. (See Tables 5.7 and 5.8.)

As the data in Tables 5.6, 5.7, and 5.8 show, both types of crimes developed in parallel patterns: The increase in the number of major crimes per 100,000 persons for 1803–1913 was only 19 percent less than the increase in minor crimes. Both major and minor crimes rose in number during the liberal reigns of Alexander I and Alexander II and fell when the conservative Nicholas I and Alexander III were in power. Crime levels were lowest at midcentury, at the end of the reign of Nicholas I, and were highest at the end of the reign of Nicholas II. The number of criminal cases changed almost in tandem with the number of minor crimes. Perpetrators of minor crimes were apprehended more frequently than were those of major crimes, at least in the late nineteenth and early twentieth centuries. During the period 1911–1913, perpetrators were apprehended in 75 percent of petty crimes, but in only 51 percent of major criminal cases.

Table 5.9 presents important information on the structure of criminality. Before Emancipation, most crimes—69 percent—were directed against state property, and violated laws that in some way restricted personal initiative. Such crimes could be perceived, in a way, as directed against the state. Officially, these crimes were referred to as "crimes against the administrative order" *(prestupleniia protiv poriadka upravleniia)*. With rare exceptions, those who committed these types of crimes did not intend to overthrow the state or change the existing social order. Most likely, these people simply felt burdened by the many limitations upon personal initiative. Immediately after the abolition of serfdom, the proportion of this type of crime fell sharply: From 1874 to 1883, such crimes constituted only 14 percent of all crimes, and from 1899 to 1905, only 8 percent. In the period 1909–1913, the proportion of these crimes was only slightly higher: 12

TABLE 5.7   Major Crimes in Russia, 1803–1913 (various years)

a. Number of recorded crimes (thousand)
b. Number of criminal cases considered by the courts (thousand)
c. Number of defendants (thousand)
d. Number of convicted persons (thousand)
e. Population (million)
f. Number of crimes per 100,000 persons
g. Number of criminal cases per 100,000 persons
h. Number of defendants per 100,000 persons
i. Number of convicted persons per 100,000 population
j. Index of increase in number of crimes per 100,000 persons
   1803–1908 = 100 for j. through m.
k. Index of increase in number of criminal cases per 100,000 persons
l. Index of increase in number of defendants per 100,000 persons
m. Index of increase in number of convicted persons per 100,000 persons

	1803– 1808	1825– 1830	1831– 1840	1841– 1850	1851– 1860	1861– 1870	1872– 1880	1881– 1890	1891– 1900	1901– 1910	1911– 1913
a.	85	113	110	120	128	188	147	148	268	577	968
b.	34	45	44	48	51	75	71	75	115	254	476
c.	39	102	101	106	116	102	79	96	134	226	435
d.	17	55	48	35	31	41	41	67	94	135	178
e.	41	50	53	57	62	69	52	59	94	142	168
f.	207	226	208	211	206	272	283	251	285	406	576
g.	83	90	83	84	82	109	137	127	122	179	283
h.	95	204	191	186	187	148	152	163	143	159	259
i.	41	110	91	61	50	59	79	114	100	95	106
j.	100	109	101	102	100	131	137	121	138	196	278
k.	100	108	100	101	99	131	165	153	147	216	341
l.	100	215	201	197	195	156	160	172	151	167	273
m.	100	268	222	149	122	144	193	278	244	232	258

SOURCES: Rossiiskii gosudarstvennyi istoricheskii arkhiv (RGIA), f. 1370 (Komitet dlia osvidetel'stvovaniia ministerskikh otchetov), op. 1, d. 7 (Vsepoddanneishii otchet ministra iustitsii za 1803 g. [henceforth, Otchet]), ll. 26–27, tablitsy f. 1341 (Pervyi departament Senata), op. 9, d. 826 (Otchet za 1804), ll. 45–47; f. 1162 (Gosudarstvennaia kantseliariia), op. 9, d. 34 (Otchet za 1805 g.), tablitsy; ibid., d. 35 (Otchet za 1806 g.), ll. 11, 76; ibid., d. 36 (Otchet za 1807 g.), ll. 73–75; ibid., d. 37, ll. 75–77; f. 1409 (Sobstvennaia ego velichestva kantseliariia), op. 1, d. 498 (Otchet za 1826 g.), ll. 325–329; ibid., dd. 500, 548 (Otchet za 1827 g.); ibid., d. 596-b (Otchet za 1828 g.), ll. 433–439; ibid., d. 643 (Otchet za 1829 g.); ibid., d. 690 (Otchet za 1830 g.); ibid., dd. 694, 771 (Otchet za 1831 g.); ibid., d. 774 (Otchet za 1832 g.); f. 1405 (Ministerstvo iustitsii), op. 521, dd. 1, 2 (Otchet za 1833); *Otchet Ministerstva iustitsii za [1834–1857] god* (St. Petersburg, 1835–1858); *Sbornik statisticheskikh svedenii Ministerstva iustitsii za [1884–1913] god* (St. Petersburg, 1887–1916), vypuski 1–30; *Svod statisticheskikh svedenii po delam ugolovnym za [1873–1913] god* (St. Petersburg, 1876–1916); V. A. Novakovskii, *Opyt podvedeniia itogov ugolovnoi statistiki s 1861 po 1871 g.* (St. Petersburg, 1891), pp. 1–63; E. N. Tarnovskii, ed., *Itogi russkoi ugolovnoi statistiki za 20 let (1874–1894)* (St. Petersburg, 1899).

339

TABLE 5.8 Minor Crimes in Russia, 1803–1913 (various years)

a. Number of recorded crimes (thousand)
b. Number of criminal cases considered by the courts (thousand)
c. Number of defendants (thousand)
d. Number of convicted persons (thousand)
e. Population (million)
f. Number of crimes per 100,000 persons
g. Number of criminal cases per 100,000 persons
h. Number of defendants per 100,000 persons
i. Number of convicted persons per 100,000 population
j. Index of increase in number of crimes per 100,000 persons (1803–1808 = 100 for j, through m.)

	1803–1808	1825–1830	1831–1840	1841–1850	1851–1860	1861–1870	1872–1880	1883–1889	1899–1900	1901–1910	1911–1913
a.	158	213	205	200	193	411	–	676	1,242	1,314	1,920
b.	63	85	82	80	77	164	–	–	–	989	1,435
c.	93	71	71	87	105	232	–	464	1,619	1,713	2,459
d.	54	56	49	38	45	61	–	330	807	850	1,306
e.	41	50	53	57	62	69	–	59	94	142	168
f.	385	426	387	351	311	596	–	1,146	1,321	925	1,143
g.	154	170	155	140	124	238	–	–	–	696	854
h.	227	142	134	153	169	336	–	786	1,722	1,206	1,464
i.	132	112	92	67	73	88	–	559	859	599	777
j.	100	111	101	91	81	155	–	298	343	240	297

(continues)

TABLE 5.8 *(continued)*

k. The index of the increase in the number of criminal cases per 100,000 persons
l. The index of the rise in number of defendants per 100,000 persons
m. The index of the increase in the number of convicted persons per 100,000

	1803–1808	1825–1830	1831–1840	1841–1850	1851–1860	1861–1870	1872–1880	1883–1889	1899–1900	1901–1910	1911–1913
k.	100	110	101	91	81	155	–	–	–	452	555
l.	100	63	59	67	74	148	–	346	759	531	645
m.	100	85	70	51	55	67	–	423	651	454	589

SOURCES: Rossiiskii gosudarstvennyi istoricheskii arkhiv (RGIA), f. 1370 (Komitet dlia osvidetel'stvovaniia ministerskikh otchetov), op. 1, d. 7 (Vsepoddanneishii otchet ministra iustitsii za 1803 g. [henceforth, Otchet]), ll. 26–27, tablitsy; f. 1341 (Pervyi departament Senata), op. 9, d. 826 (Otchet za 1804), ll. 45–47; f. 1162 (Gosudarstvennaia kantseliariia), op. 9, d. 34 (Otchet za 1805 g.), tablitsy; ibid., d. 35 (Otchet za 1806 g.), ll. 11, 76; ibid., d. 36 (Otchet za 1807 g.), ll. 73–75; ibid., d. 37, ll. 75–77; f. 1409 (Sobstvennaia ego velichestva kantseliariia), op. 1, d. 498 (Otchet za 1826 g.), ll. 325–329; ibid., dd. 500, 548 (Otchet za 1827 g.); ibid., d. 596-b (Otchet za 1828 g.), ll. 433–439; ibid., d. 643 (Otchet za 1829 g.); ibid., d. 690 (Otchet za 1830 g.); ibid., dd. 694, 771 (Otchet za 1831 g.); ibid., d. 774 (Otchet za 1832 g.); f. 1405 (Ministerstvo iustitsii), op. 521, dd. 1, 2 (Otchet za 1833); Otchet Ministerstva iustitsii za [1834–1857] god (St. Petersburg, 1835–1858); Sbornik statisticheskikh svedenii Ministerstva iustitsii za [1884–1913] god (St. Petersburg, 1887–1916), vypuski 1–30; Svod statisticheskikh svedenii po delam ugolovnym za [1873–1913] god (St. Petersburg, 1876–1916); V. A. Novakovskii, Opyt podvedeniia itogov ugolovnoi statistiki s 1861 po 1871 g. (St. Petersburg, 1891), pp. 1–63; E. N. Tarnovskii, ed., Itogi russkoi ugolovnoi statistiki za 20 let (1874–1894) (St. Petersburg, 1899).

TABLE 5.9   Numbers and Types of Serious Crimes Recorded by Police, 1846–1913 (annual averages, various years, in thousands)

Type of Crime	1846–1857*	1874–1883**	1884–1893**	1899–1905**	1906–1908**	1909–1913**
Crimes against the public and state order	75.6	13.2	16.6	23.3	56.2	55.4
Religious crimes	6.8	1.0	1.6	1.4	1.5	5.2
Crimes against the state	0.01	–	–	2.0	2.9	2.3
Crimes by officials (sluzhebnye)	7.4	2.0	4.0	6.2	9.2	14.1
Crimes against order (protiv poriadka)	14.4	3.3	3.8	9.9	13.1	22.1
Against state property, and other similar crimes	47.0	6.9	7.2	3.8	29.5	11.7
Crimes against individuals	10.5	22.4	32.3	153.8	134.3	149.2
Murders	4.2	3.8	5.2	19.8	35.0	32.6
Sexual crimes	0.6	1.8	3.1	9.7	10.8	14.4
Assault (telesnye povrezhdeniia)	1.7	7.5	12.9	68.2	50.0	44.9
Other crimes against individuals	4.0	9.3	11.1	56.1	38.5	57.3
Crimes against private property	23.5	57.5	40.8	136.0	208.7	245.5
Robbery (grabezh, razboi)	1.6	12.3	14.1	44.8	84.4	73.1
Theft (krazha)	18.6	41.9	23.1	82.4	112.4	151.2
Fraud (moshenichestvo) and similar crimes	3.3	3.3	3.6	8.8	11.9	21.2
Total crimes against individuals and private property	34.0	79.9	73.1	289.8	343.0	394.7
Total	109.6	93.1	89.7	313.1	399.2	450.1

*Defendants in all-estate criminal courts (palaty ulogovnogo suda) and in courts of conscience (sovestnye sudy)

**Defendants in circuit courts (okruzhnye sudy) and district appellate courts (sudebnye palaty)

SOURCES: Rossiiskii gosudarstvennyi istoricheskii arkhiv (RGIA), f. 1370 (Komitet dlia osvidetel'stvovaniia ministerskikh otchetov), op. 1, d. 7 (Vsepoddanneishii otchet ministra iustitsii za 1803 g. [henceforth, Otchet]), ll. 26–27, tablitsy f. 1341 (Pervyi departament Senata), op. 9, d. 826 (Otchet za 1804), ll. 45–47; f. 1162 (Gosudarstvennaia kantseliariia), op. 9, d. 34 (Otchet za 1805 g.), tablitsy; ibid., d. 35 (Otchet za 1806 g.), ll. 11, 76; ibid., d. 36 (Otchet za 1807 g.), ll. 73–75; ibid., d. 37, ll. 75–77; f. 1409 (Sobstvennaia ego velichestva kantseliariia), op. 1, d. 498 (Otchet za 1826 g.), ll. 325–329; ibid., dd. 500, 548 (Otchet za

(continues)

TABLE 5.9   *(continued)*

1827 g.); ibid., d. 596-b (Otchet za 1828 g.), ll. 433–439; ibid., d. 643 (Otchet za 1829 g.); ibid., d. 690 (Otchet za 1830 g.); ibid., dd. 694, 771 (Otchet za 1831 g.); ibid., d. 774 (Otchet za 1832 g.); f. 1405 (Ministerstvo iustitsii), op. 521, dd. 1, 2 (Otchet za 1833); *Otchet Ministerstva iustitsii za [1834–1857] god* (St. Petersburg, 1835–1858); *Sbornik statisticheskikh svedenii Ministerstva iustitsii za [1884–1913] god* (St. Petersburg, 1887–1916), vypuski 1–30; *Svod statisticheskikh svedenii po delam ugolovnym za [1873–1913] god* (St. Petersburg, 1876–1916); V. A. Novakovskii, *Opyt podvedeniia itogov ugolovnoi statistiki s 1861 po 1871 g.* (St. Petersburg, 1891), pp. 1–63; E. N. Tarnovskii, ed., *Itogi russkoi ugolovnoi statistiki za 20 let (1874–1894)* (St. Petersburg, 1899); RGIA, f. 1405, op. 521, d. 502; M. N. Gernet, *Moral'naia statistika* (Moscow, 1922), pp. 90–97; E. N. Tarnovskii, "Dvizhenie prestupnosti v Evropeiskoi Rossii za 1874–1894 gg.," in *Zhurnal Ministerstva iustitsii*, no. 3 (1899), pp. 115–124; E. N. Tarnovskii, "Dvizhenie prestupnosti v Rossiiskoi imperii za 1899–1908 gg.," in *Zhurnal Ministerstva iustitsii*, no. 9 (1909), pp. 52–99; *Entsiklopedicheskii slovar' Russkogo bibliograficheskogo instituta Granat* (Moscow, 1922), tom 36, chast' 5, stolbtsy 629–642.

percent of all crimes. Prominent among those acts considered "antistate" *(antigosudarstvennye)* and "antisocial" *(antiobshchestvennye)* were attempts to steal or damage state property (mainly state-owned forests), white-collar crimes, and violations of the numerous regulations or statutes. Before Emancipation, crimes directed against private individuals and private property made up only 31 percent of all crimes, whereas after Emancipation they accounted for 81 to 92 percent of all crimes. Of these crimes, those against private property accounted for 21 percent before Emancipation and for between 43 and 62 percent after Emancipation. Crimes against private individuals accounted for 10 percent of crimes before and between 24 and 49 percent after Emancipation. Crimes against individuals increased from 10 percent in 1846–1857 to 49 percent in 1899–1905; immediately after the 1905 Revolution they fell to 33 percent. The number of crimes against the property of private individuals rose sharply between the years 1860 and 1880, reaching 62 percent of all crimes in the period 1874–1883. Then they fell to 43 percent by 1905. After the 1905 Revolution they again began to rise, constituting 55 percent of all crimes in 1909–1913. Thus, after the Great Reforms, crime was directed less against the social and state order and more against private persons—primarily against their property. This indicates that the central interest of hundreds of thousands of criminals (and possibly the population on the whole) had shifted away from the state and toward the individual and personal affairs.

It is extremely difficult, if not impossible, to determine shifts in the severity of crimes committed from statistics on criminality. Figures on punishments meted out can help resolve this problem to some degree. (See Table 5.10.)

TABLE 5.10 Frequency of Criminal Versus Correctional Punishments in Russia, 1834–1913 (various years, in percent)

Type of Sentence	1834– 1845	1846– 1860	1861– 1867	1874– 1883	1884– 1894	1898– 1904	1905– 1907	1908– 1913
Criminal	9.0	8.0	9.3	12.7	10.2	6.4	6.6	8.6
Hard labor	3.6	3.0	3.4	5.0	4.6	4.5	6.2	8.0
Exile	5.4	5.0	5.9	7.7	5.6	1.9	0.4	0.6
Correctional	91.0	92.0	90.7	87.3	89.8	93.6	93.4	91.3
Including prison term	47.0	42.0	68.5	59.7	49.8	61.4	62.1	59.4
Arrest, and other punishments	44.0	50.0	22.2	27.6	40.0	32.2	31.3	31.9
Total	100.0	100.0	100.0	100.0	100.0	100.0	100.0	100.0

*Figures for 1834–1867 are for sentences passed by province-level, all-estate criminal courts (*palaty ugolovnogo suda*) and courts of conscience (*sovestnye sudy*). For other years, the data are for sentences handed down by circuit courts (*okruzhnye sudy*) and district appellate courts (*sudebnye palaty*).

SOURCES: Rossiiskii gosudarstvennyi istoricheskii arkhiv (RGIA), f. 1370 (Komitet dlia osvidetel'stvovaniia ministerskikh otchetov), op. 1, d. 7 (Vsepoddanneishii otchet ministra iustitsii za 1803 g. [henceforth, Otchet]), ll. 26–27, tablitsy f. 1341 (Pervyi departament Senata), op. 9, d. 826 (Otchet za 1804), ll. 45–47; f. 1162 (Gosudarstvennaia kantseliariia), op. 9, d. 34 (Otchet za 1805 g.), tablitsy; ibid., d. 35 (Otchet za 1806 g.), ll. 11, 76; ibid., d. 36 (Otchet za 1807 g.), ll. 73–75; ibid., d. 37, ll. 75–77; f. 1409 (Sobstvennaia ego velichestva kantseliariia), op. 1, d. 498 (Otchet za 1826 g.), ll. 325–329; ibid., dd. 500, 548 (Otchet za 1827 g.); ibid., d. 596-b (Otchet za 1828 g.), ll. 433–439; ibid., d. 643 (Otchet za 1829 g.); ibid., d. 690 (Otchet za 1830 g.); ibid., dd. 694, 771 (Otchet za 1831 g.); ibid., d. 774 (Otchet za 1832 g.); f. 1405 (Ministerstvo iustitsii), op. 521, dd. 1, 2 (Otchet za 1833); *Otchet Ministerstva iustitsii za [1834–1857] god* (St. Petersburg, 1847–1858); *Sbornik statisticheskikh svedenii Ministerstva iustitsii za [1884–1913] god* (St. Petersburg, 1887–1916), vypuski 1–30; *Svod statisticheskikh svedenii po delam ugolovnym za [1873–1913] god* (St. Petersburg, 1876–1916); V. A. Novakovskii, *Opyt podvedeniia itogov ugolovnoi statistiki s 1861 po 1871 g.* (St. Petersburg, 1891), pp. 1–63; E. N. Tarnovskii, ed., *Itogi russkoi ugolovnoi statistiki za 20 let (1874–1894)* (St. Petersburg, 1899).

As can be seen from Table 5.10, the proportion of criminal punishments handed down for more serious crimes fell by 1 percent before Emancipation, and the proportion of correctional punishments handed down for less serious crimes, rose by 1 percent. More substantial changes occurred in the structure of correctional punishments: The proportion of prison terms fell by 5 percent, whereas the proportion of more lenient punishments rose by 6 percent. From the early 1860s to the early 1880s, the reverse occurred: Criminal punishments rose by 4.7 percent, and correctional punishments fell correspondingly. Within the category of correctional punishments, those of a more severe nature increased the most; the proportion of severe correctional punishments rose by 17 percent, whereas less severe ones fell by 22.4 percent. Since this significant change in the structure of punishments occurred before the judicial reforms, it can be assumed that the reforms themselves did not cause this change. In the twenty years before the 1905 Revolution (1883–1904), the proportion of criminal punishments decreased by 6.4 percent, and the proportion of correctional punishments correspondingly increased. Among correctional punishments, less severe sentences were handed down more and more frequently.

During the revolutionary years of 1905–1907, sentences increased in severity to some degree; and after the Revolution, this tendency continued. By the period 1908–1913, the proportion of criminal punishments had risen and the proportion of correctional punishments had fallen, by 2.2 percent—with no significant changes in their relative distribution. Judging from the distributional structure of these punishments, there was little change in the frequency of the most severe punishments—hard labor and exile—during the entire period of this study; and during the years 1908–1913, severe punishments were meted out with the same frequency as they had been from the 1830s to the 1850s. The rise after 1904 in the proportion of those punished by hard labor is largely connected with the repeal of exile to Siberia. However, the proportion of serious crimes (those punishable by imprisonment) among total crimes committed also was on the rise: These crimes accounted for about 45 percent of all crimes from 1834 to 1860, and for 61 percent in 1908–1913. During this same period the proportion of crimes punished with relatively mild sentences fell from 47 percent to 31 percent. In the 53 years from Emancipation to World War I, the proportion of serious crimes (those punishable by hard labor, exile, and prison) rose significantly—from 50.0 to 67.8 percent. Thus one can say that the rise in criminality was accompanied by an increasing proportion of serious crimes. A clearer picture of the degree of severity in punishments can be obtained from the data in Table 5.11, which lists the punishments meted out to 363,000 convicted persons in circuit courts *(okruzhnye sudy)* and district appellate courts *(sudebnye palaty)* during the period 1910–1913.

Factors in the Growth of Crime After Emancipation.   The significant growth in crime coinciding with the reforms of the 1860s undoubtedly indicates a connection between crime and the reforms. The acquisition by the population of civil rights, the spread of the notion of legality and respect for the individual, and greater ease in obtaining legal defense thanks to the universal introduction of courts of justice of the peace, all in a rather unexpected way, fostered the growth of crime. First, the courts of justice of the peace, established in 1866 as a venue for the review of minor criminal and civil suits, were inundated by masses of peasants and other common people. Moreover, these people brought grievances that earlier they would

TABLE 5.11   Punishments Imposed by Judges in Circuit Courts and Appellate Courts, 1910–1913

Type of Punishment	Percentage of All Punishments
Criminal punishments with loss of all rights	8.4
Exile to hard labor with no release date (*bez sroka*)	0.1
Exile to hard labor for more than 10 years	1.3
Exile to hard labor for 8–10 years	1.1
Exile to hard labor for 6–7 years	1.2
Exile to hard labor for up to 6 years	4.3
Exile as penal settler (*ssylka na poselenie*)	0.4
Corrective punishments with limitation of rights (*s lisheniem prav*)	37.3
Incarceration in a corrective facility (*ispravitel'nyi dom*) from 6 months to 6 years	0.04
Incarceration in a lockup center (*arestantskoe otdelenie*) for 2.5 years and longer	14.2
Incarceration in a lockup center for up to 2.5 years	16.0
Imprisonment for 1 year or more	3.4
Imprisonment for up to 1 year	3.7
Incarceration in a fortress for up to 6 months	0.01
Corrective punishments without limitation of rights	54.3
Imprisonment for 1 year or more	6.7
Imprisonment for up to a year	19.5
Imprisonment in a fortress for up to a year	1.3
Arrest	15.5
Fine (*denezhnoe vzyskanie*), official reprimand (*vygovor* and *zamechanie*)	8.1
Measures taken with regard to persons under age 17	2.1
Temporary forced assignment to a factory (*vremennye zavodskie sluzhby*)	0.2
Expulsion from service and other punishments	0.9

SOURCE: *Svod statisticheskikh svedenii po delam ugolovnym, proizvedennym v [1910–1913] godu* (St. Petersburg, 1913–1916).

not even have thought of taking to court—not so much because it would have been difficult earlier to obtain satisfaction or because they feared the official courts as because they often did not consider minor offenses, insults, beatings, or unfair punishments from their landlord or master to be illegal acts. With the establishment of the courts of justice of the peace, which were accessible, inexpensive, and quick to make decisions, everyone who previously had felt they lacked rights and who silently bore insult and oppression now appealed to these courts for protection and confirmation of their right to be treated with respect. Wives complained about the abusive behavior of their husbands; workers brought labor disputes into the court, complaining that their employers were dealing with them unfairly and demanding that they be punished; and so on.[201] Across Russia, courts of justice of the peace considered 1,036,000 cases yearly from 1884 to 1888; and from 1909 to 1913, they heard some 1,567,000 cases—that is, approximately 57 percent of all criminal cases and around 90 percent of all minor criminal cases.[202] A heightened sense of individual identity and a desire to defend one's personal dignity clearly were factors in the growth in the number of minor criminal cases.

The proportions of minors and of women among offenders also rose over time. From 1834 to 1913, the proportion of minors among all offenders rose from 7 to 21 percent; and the proportion of women rose from 11 to 15 percent during the same period. These increases in criminality among minors and women were in part due to the growing importance of individual identity and dignity mentioned above and also by a weakening in control over these groups by heads of families and by the commune. Given that minors (those up to 21 years of age) made up approximately 30 percent, and women, 51 percent, of the entire population, both groups exhibited a relatively small tendency toward crime. Criminality among youth, however, grew more rapidly than it did among women, which indicates that young people were more successful in escaping the control of their elders than were women in freeing themselves from the control of their husbands.

Moreover, as a result of the Great Reforms, state and corporative control over the individual was weakened. The Emancipation of the serfs widened opportunities for private initiative and enterprise. It also broadened the limits of what was allowed and fostered the development of divergent behavior patterns, including criminal behavior. This supposition is based particularly on the cyclical nature of the dynamics of criminality. As we saw earlier, the stricter and more conservative the emperor, and the more firmly he carried out domestic policies, the lower criminality tended to be. On the other hand, when a more lenient ruler, with more liberal domestic policies, was in power, criminality was higher. Contradictory, inconsistent policies, together with failures and crises such as those under Nicholas II, were accompanied by a growth in crime. Conservative policies, as a rule, were accompanied by an increase in control over people's behavior both by the state and by corporative bodies, and this served to limit divergent behaviors including criminality. When control was weakened, the long-withheld impulses to destroy what was traditional and commonly accepted burst into the open with redoubled energy, and this probably gave rise to the cyclical nature in the dynamics of criminality. Efforts by Alexander III and Nicholas II to strengthen state and corporative control over the population had only temporary and partial success. Having had a taste of freedom under Alexander II, the people of Russia did not want a return to the past, and all efforts to bring this about were met with protest and a new wave of resistance. These reactions, considered illegal under the laws of the time, produced a growth in crime.

In my view, however, the decisive factor in the growth of crime in the last third of the nineteenth century and in the early twentieth century was the destruction of the peasant commune and the urban corporative bodies— the societies of burghers and merchants and the artisans' guilds. As communal ties dissolved, social control over the behavior of individuals was weakened. This conclusion is supported by data showing the predominance of urban over rural crime, of crime in the capital cities of St. Petersburg and Moscow over that in the outlying towns, and of crime among hired laborers over that among peasant communal workers. St. Petersburg and Moscow accounted for 6.2 percent of all convicted persons in 1874, whereas only 1.6 percent of the population of European Russia lived in these two cities. Other cities and towns accounted for 24.7 percent of convicted persons, but only 8.4 percent of the population. The countryside was home to 65.4 percent of convicted persons and approximately 90 percent of the population. (The site of 3.8 percent of crimes is unknown.) Consequently, in the two capitals, the crime ratio (the percent of convicted persons from the capitals divided by the capitals' percentage of the population) was 3.9. The ratio for other cities and towns was 2.9, and for the countryside, 0.7. In 1913 the crime ratio in the capitals fell to 2.5, and in other cities and towns to 2.7; in the countryside it remained unchanged. The decrease in crime in the capitals might be explainable by the influx of peasant migrant workers *(otkhodniki)*.

The data on crime with reference to occupation and profession are revealing. If we look at the crime ratio in 1897 of various professions (the relationship between the proportion of people with a given occupation among all convicted persons, and the proportion of people with the given occupation among the entire population), we find workers at the top, with a ratio of 11.2, followed by professionals and civil servants (2.3), merchants (1.9), entrepreneurs and artisans (0.9), and finally, peasant farmers *(krest'iane-zemlepashtsy)* (0.6).[203] In the same year, 30 percent of all convicted persons came from among the 3.2 million workers. Workers, the overwhelming majority of whom were peasants by social estate, were more inclined toward criminal activity than were peasant farmers who lived in the commune. Released from the control of the commune and unaccustomed to self-control, young urbanized peasants easily gave vent to aggression and destructive impulses. The high criminality of workers also can likely be explained by their marginal status. Uprooted from the familiar surroundings and accepted behavioral standards of the village, workers were unable to adapt quickly to life in the factories and in the cities, resulting in their asocial behavior and psychological difficulties.

The fact that professionals (teachers, physicians, lawyers, and others), merchants, and entrepreneurs displayed higher crime rates than did peasants, indicates, in my view, that poverty in and of itself did not have a decisive effect on the growth of crime after Emancipation. This assumption is borne out, in particular, by the data on crime by social estate. If we look at the crime ratio of people of the various social estates (the relationship between the percentage of people of a given estate among the entire number of convicted persons, and the proportion of that estate among the entire population), we find that in 1858–1897, merchants had the highest crime ratio (2.0). Next were burghers and craftsmen (1.7), noblemen and civil servants (1.5), peasants (0.9), and finally, the clergy (0.3–0.4).[204] The peasantry, which was becoming impoverished in the last third of the nineteenth century, had a lesser propensity to commit crime than any other estate except for the clergy. This does not mean, of course, that one should not exclude poverty as a factor contributing to criminal behavior. It has been noted, for instance, that crimes against property substantially increased during and immediately after crop failures.[205] But since poverty is a constant factor in criminal behavior, it cannot explain tendencies toward change in crime rates. In the first half of the nineteenth century, poverty was widespread, but nevertheless crime rates dropped. From the second half of the 1890s to 1913, peasants saw a rise in their standard of living, and at the same time, crime levels rose very rapidly.

In my view, material wealth, or the lack of it, influenced criminality in an entirely different sense. It was not poverty but rather the striving to become rich by any means that motivated criminal activity. The increasing importance of wealth in people's system of values, and the opportunity to change one's life radically and immediately through wealth, both fostered crime. Many people of average income were drawn along this path. I. D. Putilin, head of the St. Petersburg detective force *(sysknaia politsiia)* from 1866 to 1889, noted:

How very many people are in prisons and jails, having become criminals *by chance* [emphasis in the original], and how very many "honest" people walk about freely, with heads raised proudly, honest only because not once have they been presented with temptation! Just give one hundred of these honest people the chance to take a bribe, to rob the till, or to embezzle, and I guarantee that 98 of them will do their best not to let the opportunity pass. I'll go even further: Many out of this one hundred, if presented with the right conditions, will not hesitate even . . . to commit murder.[206]

Conclusion

Official law in imperial Russia progressed toward the ideals of rule of law and the separation of judicial from administrative power. Customary law as practiced in the countryside was also evolving in this direction, but very slowly. Changes in the law led to the expansion of rights and freedoms. But these rights came at great cost to society, leading to an almost fourfold rise in criminality. Under serfdom, the strict control of the commune over its members; commune members' solidarity and their neighborly, friendly relations; and the low mobility of the population all served to restrain people with criminal proclivities and impeded their chances of escaping either popular or official justice. After Emancipation, ties within the peasant commune slowly broke down, and this inevitably led to the growth of deviant behavior in general and of criminal behavior in particular. This conclusion fully corresponds with sociologists' findings that the most significant factors in criminality invariably are deformations in people's system of values, in social relations, and in social and juridical norms, in addition to dysfunction in social institutions.[207]

Both official and customary law defended people from criminals and helped maintain social order. There was arbitrariness on the part of judges in official courts both before and after Emancipation, but it was kept more or less within the limits of the law. As a rule, sentences corresponded to legal norms over the course of the entire period of this study. We can thus conclude that on the whole, the Russian courts were fair. Because there were three judicial instances prior to Emancipation, the official courts worked very slowly. This forced interested parties to offer bribes in order to speed up the handling of their cases. Unofficial village courts worked quickly, and their sentences conformed to customary law.

Until the end of the seventeenth century, all classes of Russian society lived more or less within the same legal space. Beginning in the eighteenth century, with the development of new legislation, town and countryside began to move into separate legal spheres, giving rise to what some have called "juridical pluralism": two systems of law operating simultaneously within the borders of a single state. Each of these systems presented a rather distinctive complex of norms and institutions. The disparity between these systems was at its most critical at the end of the nineteenth century. In the early twentieth century, the government realized the danger posed by peasants' legal isolation, and steps were taken to liquidate peasant legal particularism and to establish a unified legal space in Russia. However, there was not enough time, and the ancien régime collapsed— largely because it was unable to include the peasants in the general legal order of the state. This legal isolation of the peasantry contributed greatly

to many social problems, such as overweening demands by noble landowners, insufficient patriotism, and a weak understanding of general national
interests. Thus, the 1905 Revolution, which soon followed, and indeed, the
entirety of Soviet experience (1917–1991) bear out Sergei Witte's predic-
tion, made in 1903:

> In one sense, Russia is an exception among all countries of the world. Sys-
> tematically, the people [*narod*] were raised without the notion of property and
> legality. As I see it, there is a huge question: What can an empire be that has
> a peasant population of one hundred million, among whom neither the con-
> cept of the right to own land nor the idea of the inviolability of the law has
> developed? What historical events will arise as a result of this, I cannot say at
> present, but I sense that the results will be very profound.[208]

Notes

The translator thanks Roger Leishman and Greg J. Matis for their help with
legal terminology.

1. R. Pento and M. Gravits, *Metody sotsial'nykh nauk* (Moscow, 1972), pp.
93–94; R. David, *Osnovnye pravovye sistemy sovremennosti: Sravnitel'noe pravo*
(Moscow, 1967); F. V. Taranovskii, *Entsiklopediia prava* (Berlin, 1923), pp.
360–394.

2. The literature on the history of Russian law is massive. The most extensive
and objective histories of Russian law were written before 1917. In my view the
best of these include the following: M. F. Vladimirskii-Budanov, *Obzor istorii
russkogo prava* (Kiev and St. Petersburg, 1900); V. N. Latkin, *Uchebnik istorii
russkogo prava perioda imperii (XVIII i XIX st.)* (St. Petersburg, 1909); and V. I.
Sergeevich, *Lektsii i issledovaniia po drevnei istorii russkogo prava* (St. Petersburg,
1910). From among books published in Russian I would point out two series in
particular: *Razvitie russkogo prava* (Moscow, 1986, 1992, 1994); and O. I. Chistiakov, ed., *Rossiiskoe zakonodatel'stvo X–XX vekov v deviati tomakh* (Moscow,
1984–1994). For analytical overviews of the literature on the history of law in Russia, see the following: F. I. Leontovich, *Istoriia russkogo prava*, vyp. 1, *Literatura
istorii russkogo prava* (Warsaw, 1902).

3. I. A. Isaev, *Istoriia gosudarstva i prava Rossii* (Moscow, 1994), p. 222.

4. Vladimirskii-Budanov, *Obzor istorii russkogo prava*, p. 299.

5. *Slovar' russkogo iazyka XI–XVII vv.*, vyp. 12 (Moscow, 1987), p. 49.

6. Ibid., vyp. 20 (1994), p. 61.

7. Ibid., vyp. 8 (1981), p. 249.

8. A. M. Bogdanovskii, *Razvitie poniatii o prestuplenii i nakazanii v russkom
prave do Petra Velikogo* (Moscow, 1850), pp. 91–132; A. P. Chebyshev-Dmitriev,
O prestupnom deistvii po russkomu dopetrovskomu pravu (Kazan, 1862), pp.
239–242.

9. *Polnoe sobranie zakonov Rossiiskoi imperii*, sobranie pervoe (henceforth,
PSZ 1) (St. Petersburg, 1830), tom 5, "Ukaz ot 24 dekabria 1714 g."; E. A. Skrip-

ilev, ed., *Razvitie russkogo prava vtoroi poloviny XVII–XVIII vv.* (Moscow, 1992), pp. 45–46.

10. N. S. Tagantsev, *Russkoe ugolovnoe pravo: Lektsii; Chast' obshchaia* (Moscow, 1994), tom 1, p. 33.

11. G. Lipinskii, "K istorii ugolovnogo prava XVIII v.," *Zhurnal grazhdanskogo i ugolovnogo prava,* kniga 10, p. 10.

12. Tagantsev, *Russkoe ugolovnoe pravo,* tom 1, p. 33.

13. V. S. Nersesiants, ed., *Razvitie russkogo prava v XV–pervoi polovine XVII v.* (Moscow, 1986), p. 165.

14. *Slovar' russkogo iazyka XI–XVII vv.,* vyp. 6 (1979), p. 117.

15. A. G. Man'kov, ed., *Sobornoe ulozhenie 1649 goda* (Leningrad, 1987), pp. 20–21, 145–155.

16. A. G. Man'kov, ed., *Rossiiskoe zakonodatel'stvo X–XX vekov,* tom 4, "Artikul voinskii 1715 g.," stat'i 19, 129, 136, 194, pp. 331, 350–352, 363; ibid., "Plakat o sbore podushnom 1724 g.," stat'i 10, 11, p. 208.

17. N. A. Voskresenskii, ed., *Zakonodatel'nye akty Petra I* (Moscow and Leningrad, 1945), tom 1, "General'nyi reglament ili ustav, po kotoromu gosudarstvennye kollegii postupit' imeiut, 1720 g.," p. 513; *PSZ 1* (St. Petersburg, 1830), tom 6, "Ukaz ot 27 aprelia 1722 g. o dolzhnosti general-prokurora."

18. V. I. Veretennikov, *Tainaia kantseliariia petrovskogo vremeni* (Kharkov, 1910); M. I. Semevskii, *Slovo i delo! 1700–1725: Tainaia kantseliariia pri Petre Velikom* (St. Petersburg, 1884); G. G. Tel'berg, *Ocherki politicheskogo suda i politicheskikh prestuplenii v Moskovskom gosudarstve XVII veka* (Moscow, 1912).

19. A 1762 ukase required informants to provide evidence substantiating their denunciations. Informants who could not provide evidence were subject to arrest for two days, during which time they were denied food and water. If after this period the informants still stood by their denunciations, then their testimony was taken into account. See *PSZ 1,* tom 15, ukase of 21 February 1762.

20. O. I. Chistiakov, ed., *Rossiiskoe zakonodatel'stvo X–XX vekov,* tom 6, "Obshchee uchrezhdenie ministerstv," paragrafy 279, 376, p. 122.

21. Ibid., pp. 266, 282, 286–287, 297–298, 309.

22. Ibid., tom 9, pp. 317–319.

23. Man'kov, ed., *Sobornoe ulozhenie,* pp. 118–119.

24. Tagantsev, *Russkoe ugolovnoe pravo,* tom 1, p. 79.

25. Ibid., tom 1, p. 143.

26. Vladimirskii-Budanov, *Obzor istorii russkogo prava,* pp. 329–330.

27. E. V. Anichkov, *Iazychestvo v drevnei Rusi* (St. Petersburg, 1914), p. 3; V. G. Vlasov, "Khristianizatsiia russkikh krest'ian," *Sovetskaia etnografiia,* no. 3 (1888), pp. 3–15.

28. Vladimirskii-Budanov, *Obzor istorii russkogo prava,* pp. 320, 325–326; Latkin, *Uchebnik istorii russkogo prava,* p. 491.

29. V. L. Ianin, ed., *Rossiiskoe zakonodatel'stvo X–XX vekov,* tom 1, "Russkaia pravda prostrannoi redaktsii," stat'i 1, 2, 40, 65, and 89.

30. A. G. Man'kov, *Ulozhenie 1649 g.: Kodeks feodal'nogo prava Rossii* (Leningrad, 1980), p. 199.

31. *Polnoe sobranie zakonov Rossiiskoi imperii,* sobranie vtoroe (henceforth, *PSZ 2),* tom 42, no. 44402.

32. A. F. Koshko, *Ocherki ugolovnogo mira tsarskoi Rossii: Vospominaniia byvshego nachal'nika Moskovskoi sysknoi politsii i zaveduiushchego vsem ugolovnym rozyskom Imperii* (Moscow, 1992), tom 1, pp. 151, 171; tom 2, p. 37.

33. P. Lashkarev, *Pravo tserkovnoe v ego osnovakh, vidakh i istochnikakh* (Kiev, 1889); N. S. Suvorov, *Uchebnik tserkovnogo prava* (Moscow, 1902), pp. 275–282.

34. Nersesiants, ed., *Razvitie russkogo prava*, p. 158.

35. *PSZ* 1, tom 11, no. 8601.

36. V. Dal', *Tolkovyi slovar' zhivogo velikorusskogo iazyka* (Moscow, 1955), tom 2, p. 332; *Slovar' russkogo iazyka XI–XVII vv.*, vyp. 9 (1982), pp. 183–185.

37. Tagantsev, *Russkoe ugolovnoe pravo*, tom 1, p. 90.

38. G. F. Bassevich, "Zapiski," *Russkii arkhiv*, tom 3 (1865), stolbets 569.

39. Tagantsev, *Russkoe ugolovnoe pravo*, tom 1, p. 90.

40. S. V. Pakhman, *Obychnoe grazhdanskoe pravo v Rossii: Iuridicheskie ocherki* (St. Petersburg, 1879), tom 2, p. 369.

41. Skripilev, ed., *Razvitie russkogo prava*, pp. 160–161.

42. A. V. Snezhevskii, ed., *Spravochnik nevrapatologa i psikhiatra* (Moscow, 1968), p. 427.

43. Tagantsev, *Russkoe ugolovnoe pravo*, tom 1, pp. 146–148.

44. Man'kov, ed., *Rossiiskoe zakonodatel'stvo X–XX vekov*, tom 4, stat'ia 154, p. 355.

45. Tagantsev, *Russkoe ugolovnoe pravo*, tom 1, pp. 170–172.

46. Ianin, ed., *Zakonodatel'stvo X–XX vekov*, tom 1, pp. 64–73.

47. The *Ulozhenie o nakazaniiakh ugolovnykh i ispravitel'nykh 1845 g.* consists of two sections: (1) a General Section *(Obshchaia chast')* containing 189 articles, which defines crimes, misdemeanors, guilt, sentences, and so on, and (2) a Special Section *(Osobennaia chast')* containing 2,035 articles in which individual crimes are described in greater detail. See O. I. Chistiakov, ed., *Rossiiskoe zakonodatel'stvo X–XX vekov*, tom 6, pp. 160–408.

48. On sentences prior to the eighteenth century, see the following: V. A. Rogov, *Ugolovnye nakazaniia i repressii v Rossii serediny XV–serediny XVII vv.* (Moscow, 1992); F. F. Depp, *O nakazaniiakh, sushchestvovavshikh v Rossii do tsaria Aleskeia Mikhailovicha: Istoriko-iuridicheskoe rassuzhdenie* (St. Petersburg, 1849); N. D. Sergeevskii, *Nakazanie v russkom prave XVII veka* (St. Petersburg, 1887).

49. A. Fillipov, *O nakazanii po zakonodatel'stvu Petra Velikogo v sviazi s reformoiu: Istoriko-iuridicheskoe issledovanie* (Moscow, 1891), p. 8.

50. Ibid., pp. 277, 287.

51. On this basis, a number of researchers have identified the existence of the notion of *davnost* in old Russian law. See K. Ianevich-Ianevskii, "Ob ugolovnoi davnosti," in *Iuridicheskoe issledovanie* (Moscow, 1891), pp. 1–128.

52. Tagantsev, *Russkoe ugolovnoe pravo*, tom 2, pp. 339–358.

53. *Ulozhenie o nakazaniiakh 1845 g.*, glava 2, stat'i 18–61; *Ulozhenie 1903 g.*, glava 1, stat'i 15–28. There is an extensive literature on the history of criminal law. In addition to the sources cited in the notes, see the following: O. Goregliad, *Opyt nachertaniia rossiiskogo ugolovnogo prava* (St. Petersburg, 1815); V. V. Esipov, *Ocherk russkogo ugolovnogo prava, Chast' obshchaia, Prestuplenie i prestupniki: Nakazanie i nakazuemye* (Moscow, 1904); V. A. Linovskii, *Issledovanie nachal ugolovnogo prava, izlozhennye v Ulozhenii tsaria Alekseia Mikhailovicha* (Odessa,

1847); A. V. Lokhvitskii, *Kurs russkogo ugolovnogo prava* (St. Petersburg, 1871); B. S. Osherovich, *Ocherki po istorii russkoi ugolovno-pravovoi mysli: Vtoraia polovina XVIII–pervaia chetvert' XIX v.* (Moscow, 1946); N. D. Sergeevskii, *Russkoe ugolovnoe pravo*, Chast' obshchaia (St. Petersburg, 1915); I. I. Solodkin, *Ocherki po istorii ugolovnogo prava: Pervaia chetvert' XIX v.* (Leningrad, 1961).

54. A. M. Anfimov and A. P. Korelin, eds., *Rossiia, 1913 god: Statistiko-dokumental'nyi spravochnik* (St. Petersburg, 1995), p. 400. On capital punishment, see the following: S. I. Viktorskii, *Istoriia smertnoi kazni v Rossii i sovremennoe ee sostoianie* (Moscow, 1912); M. N. Gernet, *Smertnaia kazn'* (Moscow, 1913); A. F. Kistiakovskii, *Issledovanie o smertnoi kazni* (St. Petersburg, 1896); N. D. Sergeevskii, "Smertnaia kazn' v Rossii v XVII i pervoi polovine XVIII veka," *Zhurnal grazhdanskogo i ugolovnogo prava*, kniga 9 (1884), pp. 1–56.

55. On corporal punishment, see the following: I. Gol'denberg, *Reforma telesnykh nakazanii* (St. Petersburg, 1913); N. N. Evreinov, *Istoriia telesnykh nakazanii v Rossii* (St. Petersburg, 1913), tom 1; D. N. Zhbanov, *Telesnye nakazaniia v Rossii v nastoiashchee vremia* (Moscow, 1899); M. Stupin, *Istoriia telesnykh nakazanii v Rossii ot Sudebnikov do nastoiashchego vremeni* (Vladikavkaz, 1887); A. G. Timofeev, *Istoriia telesnykh nakazanii v russkom prave* (St. Petersburg, 1904).

56. *Otchet Ministra iustitsii za [1834–1860] god* (St. Petersburg, 1835–1861).

57. Rossiiskii gosudarstvennyi istoricheskii arkhiv (hereafter, RGIA), f. 1263 (Komitet ministrov), op. 1, d. 223, ll. 224–227.

58. Tagantsev, *Russkoe ugolovnoe pravo*, tom 2, pp. 112–113.

59. *Svod statisticheskikh svedenii po delam ugolovnym, voznikshim v [1896–1900] godu* (St. Petersburg, 1900–1903). (Hereafter, *Svod svedenii po delam ugolovnym.*)

60. L. M. Goriushkin, ed., *Ssylka i katorga v Sibiri: XVIII–nachalo XX v.* (Novosibirsk, 1975); idem, ed., *Ssylka i obshchestvenno-politicheskaia zhizn' v Sibiri, XVIII–nachalo XX v.* (Novosibirsk, 1978); O. P. Podosenov, "Katorga i ssylka v Rossii v XVI–pervoi polovine XIX v." (dissertation, Moscow State University, 1971); A. D. Margolis, *Tiur'ma i ssylka v imperatorskom Rossii: Issledovaniia i arkhivnye nakhodki* (Moscow, 1995).

61. A. P. Salomon, ed., *Ssylka v Sibir': Ocherk ee istorii i sovremennogo polozheniia* (Dlia komissii o meropriiatiiakh po otmene ssylki) (St. Petersburg, 1900), prilozheniia 1–3. See also Margolis, *Tiur'ma i ssylka*, pp. 29–44.

62. RGIA, f. 1329 (Imennye ukazy i vysochaishie poveleniia Senatu), op. 4, d. 115, ll. 1–35; *Otchet Obshchestva popechitel'nogo o tiur'makh za [1819–1867] god* (St. Petersburg, 1821–1869).

63. Arkhiv S.-Peterburgskogo filiala Instituta rossiiskoi istorii Rossiiskoi Akademii nauk, f. 36 (Vorontsova), op. 1, d. 642, ll. 252–257 (1780-e gody); RGIA, f. 1286 (Departament politsii ispolnitel'noi Ministerstva vnutrennikh del), op. 2, d. 314 (1818–1826 gg.); op. 5, d. 507, ll. 1–158 (1834–1838 gg.); f. 1405 (Ministerstvo iustitsii), op. 26, d. 336 (1828 g.), ll. 1–6.

64. RGIA, f. 1286, op. 4 (1826–1834 gg.), d. 272, ll. 1–226.

65. RGIA, f. 1400 (Dokumenty unichtozhennykh del Senata i Ministerstva iustitsii), op. 1 (1757–1836 gg.), d. 171; f. 1341 (Pervyi departament Senata), op.

11 (1810 g.), d. 1164, ll. 1–61; f. 1286, op. 2 (1815 g.), d. 180, ll. 1–26; op. 2 (1817 g.), d. 247, l. 51; op. 2 (1820 g.), d. 37, ll. 1–126; op. 3 (1822 g.), d. 13, ll. 1–86; op. 4 (1829 g.), d. 664, ll. 1–169; f. 1287 (Khoziaistvennyi departament Ministerstva vnutrennikh del), op. 12 (1822 g.), d. 42, ll. 1–9; f. 1285 (Departament gosudarstvennogo khoziaistvo Ministerstva vnutrennikh del), op. 8 (1827 g.), d. 2808.

66. RGIA, f. 1286, op. 2 (1820 g.), d. 143, ll. 1–11; f. 1263, op. 1 (1822 g.), d. 291.

67. RGIA, f. 1286, op. 2 (1817–1820 gg.), d. 277, ll. 1–48.

68. Tagantsev, *Russkogo ugolovnoe pravo*, tom 2, pp. 99–274.

69. RGIA, f. 1405 (Ministerstvo iustitsii), op. 26 (1828), d. 336, ll. 4–9, 47–64; Arkhiv Russkogo geograficheskogo obshchestva (henceforth, ARGO), razriad 108, op. 1, d. 22, ll. 1–12; *Otchet Ministerstva iustitsii za [1804, 1840, 1861] god*; *Otchet po glavnomu tiuremnomu upravleniiu za [1879, 1885, 1900, 1913] god* (St. Petersburg, 1881, 1887, 1902, 1915).

70. V. N. Iuferov, "Materialy dlia tiuremnoi statistiki Rossii," in *Zapiski Russkogo geograficheskogo obshchestva po otdeleniiu statistiki*, tom 3 (1873), pp. 4–5.

71. For the years 1863 and 1864 these figures have been calculated from the following sources: *Sudebno-statisticheskie svedeniia i soobrazheniia o vvedenii v deistvie sudebnykh ustavov 20 noiabria 1864 goda (po 32 guberniiam)* (St. Petersburg, 1866), toma 1–3; *Otchet po Glavnomu tiuremnomu upravleniiu za [1890–1915] god* (St. Petersburg, 1892–1916).

72. *Ocherk razvitiia arestantskogo truda v russkikh tiur'makh, 1858–1888 gg.* (St. Petersburg, 1890); S. K. Gogel', *Arestantskii trud v russkikh i inostrannykh tiur'makh* (St. Petersburg, 1897); *Otchet po Glavnomu tiuremnomu upravleniiu za 1903 god*, pp. 112–123.

73. S. A. Novosel'skii, *Obzor vazhneishikh dannykh po demografii i sanitarnoi statistike Rossii* (St. Petersburg, 1916), p. 53.

74. *Otchet po Glavnomu tiuremnomu upravleniiu za 1915 god*, chast' 2, p. 30.

75. *Otchet o sostoianii narodnogo zdraviia i organizatsii vrachebnoi pomoshchi v Rossii za [1903–1913] god* (St. Petersburg, 1905–1915).

76. *Obzor deiatel'nosti Glavnogo tiuremnogo upravleniia 1879–1889* (St. Petersburg, 1890); N. F. Luchinskii, *Kratkii ocherk deiatel'nosti Glavnogo tiuremnogo upravleniia za pervye XXXV let ego sushchestvovaniia (1879–1914)* (St. Petersburg, 1914); *Otchet po Glavnomu tiuremnomu upravleniiu za 1903 god*, p. 142.

77. In addition to the literature indicated in the text, the following sources have been used: P. P. Bobynin, *Zapiska o nastoiashchem polozhenii tiuremnoi chasti v imperii* (n.p., 1870); M. N. Galkin-Vraskoi, *Materialy k izucheniiu tiuremnogo voprosa* (St. Petersburg, 1868); S. L. Gaiduk, "Tiuremnaia politika i tiuremnoe zakonodatel'stvo v poreformennoi Rossii" (dissertation, Institut gosudarstva i prava AN SSSR, Moscow, 1987); Dzh. Kennan, (George Kennan) *Tiur'my v Rossii: Ocherki* (St. Petersburg, 1906); *Materialy po voprosu o preobrazovanii tiuremnoi chasti v Rossii* (St. Petersburg, 1865); V. N. Nikitin, *Tiur'ma i ssylka: Istoriia, zakonodatel'stvo, administrativnoe i bytovoe polozhenie zakliuchennykh, peresyl'nykh, ikh detei i osvobozhdennykh iz-pod strazhi, so vremeni vozniknoveniia tiur'my do nashikh dnei, 1560–1880 gg.* (St. Petersburg, 1880); S. V. Poznyshev, *Ocherki tiur'movedeniia* (Moscow, 1913); *Svedeniia o deiatel'nosti Glavnogo tiuremnogo upravleniia za*

pervyi god, s 16 iiunia 1880 g. po 16 iiunia 1881 (St. Petersburg, 1881); I. Ia. Foinit-skii, *Uchenie o nakazaniiakh v sviazi s tiur'movedeniem* (St. Petersburg, 1889). See also the following bibliographies: N. F. Luchinskii, ed., *Sistematicheskii alfavitnyi ukazatel' neofitsial'nogo otdela zhurnala "Tiuremnyi vestnik" za 15 let (1893–1907)* (St. Petersburg, 1908); A. V. Borisov, *Karatel'nye organy dorevoliutsionnoi Rossii (politseiskaia i penitentsiarnaia sistemy): Bibliograficheskii ukazatel'* (Moscow, 1978).

78. Tagantsev, *Russkoe ugolovnoe pravo*, tom 2, p. 79.

79. Isaev, *Istoriia gosudarstva i prava Rossii*, pp. 16–17.

80. L. L. Gervagen, *Razvitie ucheniia o iuridicheskom litse* (St. Petersburg, 1888), pp. 88–91.

81. K. N. Annenkov, *Sistema russkogo grazhdanskogo prava*, tom 1, Vvedenie i obshchaia chast' (St. Petersburg, 1894); K. P. Pobedonostsev, *Kurs grazhdanskogo prava*, chast' 3 ("Dogovory i obiazatel'stva") (St. Petersburg, 1896).

82. *Sbornik statisticheskikh svedenii Ministerstva iustitsii, 1886 g.* (St. Petersburg, 1887), vyp. 2, pp. 106–107; *Sbornik statisticheskikh svedenii Ministerstva iustitsii, 1913 g.* (St. Petersburg, 1916), vyp. 30, pp. 391–393.

83. Annenkov, *Sistema russkogo grazhdanskogo prava*, tom 6, *Prava nasledstvennye* (1902); Pobedonostsev, *Kurs grazhdanskogo prava*, chast' 2, *Prava semeistvennye, nasledstvennye i zaveshchatel'nye*; L. I. Rudnev, *O dukhovnykh zaveshchaniiakh po russkomu grazhdanskomu pravu v istoricheskom razvitii* (Kiev, 1894); P. P. Tsitovich, *Iskhodnye momenty v istorii russkogo prava nasledovaniia* (Kharkov, 1870).

84. Nersesiants, ed., *Razvitie russkogo prava*, p. 130.

85. In the opinion of some researchers, until the mid-thirteenth century, rights of ownership in Rus were at their fullest, and not subject to limitations on the part of the state as they were in Muscovy. This view, however, has been convincingly refuted. See Vladimirskii-Budanov, *Obzor istorii russkogo prava*, pp. 517–530.

86. N. P. Zagoskin, *O prave vladeniia dvorami v Moskovskom gosudarstve: Istoriko-iuridicheskii ocherk* (Kazan, 1877), pp. 1–42.

87. *Jvod zakenov Rossiiskoi imperii* (15 vols.: St. Petersburg, 1832), tom 10, chast' 1, stat'ia 262.

88. Vladimirskii-Budanov, *Obzor istorii russkogo prava*, pp. 602–606.

89. Annenkov, *Sistema russkogo grazhdanskogo prava*, tom 2, *Prava veshchnye* (1895); Pobedonostsev, *Kurs grazhdanskogo prava*, chast' 1, *Votchinnye prava*; I. E. Engel'man, *O priobretenii prava sobstvennosti na zemliu po russkomu pravu* (St. Petersburg, 1895).

90. Vlasov, "Khristianizatsiia russkikh krest'ian," pp. 3–15.

91. Nersesiants, ed., *Razvitie russkogo prava*, pp. 152–153.

92. S. Grigorovskii, *Sbornik tserkovnykh i grazhdanskikh zakonov o brake i razvodakh i sudoproizvodstve po delam brachnym* (St. Petersburg, 1910); D. N. Dubakin, *Vliianie khristianstva na semeinyi byt russkogo obshchestva v period vremeni poiavleniia "Domostroia"* (St. Petersburg, 1880); Annenkov, *Sistema russkogo grazhdanskogo prava*, tom 5, *Prava semeinye i opeka* (1905); Pobedonostsev, *Kurs grazhdanskogo prava*, chast' 2, *Prava semeistvennye, nasledstvennye i zaveshchatel'nye*.

93. In addition to the literature indicated in the text, I also have used the following: G. L. Verblovskii, *Voprosy russkogo grazhdanskogo prava i protsessa*

(Moscow, 1896); A. Kranikhfel'd, *Nachertanie rossiiskogo grazhdanskogo prava v istoricheskom ego razvitii* (St. Petersburg, 1843); D. I. Meier, *Russkoe grazhdanskoe pravo* (St. Petersburg, 1915); G. F. Shershenevich, *Uchebnik russkogo grazhdanskogo prava* (Moscow, 1912); I. E. Engel'man, *O davnosti po russkomu grazhdanskomu pravu: Istoriko-dogmaticheskoe issledovanie* (St. Petersburg, 1901). For additional information, see the following: A. F. Povorinskii, *Sistematicheskii ukazatel' russkoi literatury po grazhdanskomu pravu*, 2-e izd. (St. Petersburg, 1904); idem, *Sistematicheskii ukazatel' russkoi literatury po grazhdanskomu pravu*, supplement (St. Petersburg, 1904).

94. V.P. [pseudonym], "Poval'nyi obysk i ochnaia stavka," *Otechestvennye zapiski*, tom 129, 3–4 (1860), pp. 127–225.

95. On legal proceedings, see I. A. Blinov, *Sudebnaia reforma 20 noiabria 1864 g.: Istoriko-iuridicheskii ocherk* (Petrograd, 1914); B. V. Vilenskii, *Sudebnaia reforma i kontrreforma v Rossii* (Saratov, 1969); I. V. Gessen, *Sudebnaia reforma* (St. Petersburg, 1905); N. L. Diuvernua, *Istochniki prava i sud v drevnei Rusi: Opyty po istorii russkogo grazhdanskogo prava* (Moscow, 1869); N. N. Efremova, *Sudoustroistvo Rossii v XVIII–pervoi polovine XIX v.: Istoriko-pravovode issledovanie* (Moscow, 1993); K. D. Kavelin, *Osnovnye nachala russkogo sudoustroistva v period vremeni ot Ulozheniia do Uchrezhdeniia o guberniiakh* (Moscow, 1844); M. G. Korotkikh, *Samoderzhavie i sudebnaia reforma 1864 g. v Rossii: Sushchnost' i sotsial'no-pravovoi aspekt formirovaniia* (Voronezh, 1994); K. P. Pobedonostsev, *Materialy dlia istorii prikaznogo sudoustroistva v Rossii* (Moscow, 1890); K. Trotsina, *Istoriia sudebnykh uchrezhdenii v Rossii* (St. Petersburg, 1851); S. Kucherov, *Courts, Lawyers and Trials Under the Last Three Tsars* (Westport, 1974); John P. LeDonne, *Ruling Russia: Politics and Administration in the Age of Absolutism, 1762–1796* (Princeton, 1984), pp. 145–202; and idem, *Absolutism and the Ruling Class: The Formation of Russian Political Order, 1700–1825* (New York and Oxford, 1991), pp. 181–238. On legal processes, see S. Barshev, "O preimushchestvakh sledstvennogo protsessa pered obvinitel'nymi," in *Iuridicheskie zapiski, izd. P.G. Redkinym*, tom 2 (1843), pp. 120–148; A. Zhizhilenko, "Obshchii ocherk dvizheniia ugolovnogo-protsessual'nogo zakonodatel'stva posle 1864 g.," in N. V. Davydov and N. N. Polianskii, eds., *Sudebnaia reforma* (Moscow, 1915), tom 2, pp. 41–69; N. Lange, *Drevne-russkoe ugolovnoe sudoproizvodstvo (XV, XVI i poloviny XVII vekov)* (St. Petersburg, 1884); V. S. Malchenko, "Obshchii ocherk dvizheniia grazhdansko-protsessual'nogo zakonodatel'stva posle 1864 goda," in Davydov and Polianskii, eds., *Sudebnaia reforma*, tom 2, pp. 70–80; I. V. Mikhailovskii, *Osnovnye printsipy organizatsii ugolovnogo dela: Ugolovno-politicheskoe issledovanie* (Tomsk, 1905); V. K. Sluchevskii, *Uchebnik russkogo ugolovnogo protsessa: Sudoustroistvo-sudoproizvodstvo po sudebnym ustavam 20 noiabria 1864 g.* (St. Petersburg, 1875); and I. E. Engel'man, *Uchebnik russkogo grazhdanskogo sudoproizvodstva* (Iurev, 1904).

96. V. A. Linovskii, *Opyt istoricheskikh rozyskanii o sledstvennom ugolovnom sudoproizvodstve v Rossii* (Odessa, 1849), pp. 217–234, 235–238.

97. Vladimirskii-Budanov, *Obzor istorii russkogo prava*, pp. 666–667.

98. See, for instance, *Otchet Ministerstva iustitsii za 1843 g.*, p. x; *Otchet Ministerstva iustitsii za 1844 g.*, p. xiii; *Otchet Ministerstva iustitsii za 1847 g.*, pp.

174–175; *Otchet Ministerstva iustitsii za 1848 g.*, pp. 136–137; and others in this series.

99. F. F. Depp, "O torgovykh sudakh," in *Zhurnal grazhdanskogo i torgovogo prava*, kniga 1 (1872), pp. 1–75; kniga 6 (1872), pp. 457–513.

100. *Istoriia udelov za stoletie ikh sushchestvovaniia, 1797–1897* (St. Petersburg, 1901), tom 2, pp. 440, 450.

101. I. V. Gessen and M. N. Gernet, *Istoriia advokatury 1864–20/XI–1914* (Moscow, 1914, 1916), toma 1–3.

102. P. N. Zyrianov, "Tret'ia duma i vopros o reforme mestnogo suda i volostnogo upravleniia," *Istoriia SSSR*, no. 6 (1969), pp. 53–55.

103. V. L. Binshtok, "Istoricheskie ocherki pravosudiia v Rossii," in V. L. Binshtok, *Iz nedavnego proshlogo* (St. Petersburg, 1896); N. V. Davydov, "Sudebnye reformy 1866 goda," in V. V. Kalash, ed., *Tri veka: Rossiia ot smuty do nashego vremeni v shesti tomakh* (Moscow, 1995), tom 6, p. 174; V. Bochkarev, "Doreformennyi sud," in Davydov and Polianskii, eds., *Sudebnaia reforma*, tom 1, pp. 205–241; Skripilev, ed., *Razvitie russkogo prava*, pp. 245–260; B. N. Syromiatnikov, "Ocherk istorii suda v drevnei i novoi Rossii," in Davydov and Polianskii, eds., *Sudebnaia reforma*, tom 1, pp. 16–180.

104. For the sake of comparison, crime levels in Russia of the 1990s are ten to fifteen times higher than they were in the period under discussion.

105. *Otchet Ministerstva iustitsii za [1843–1848, 1861–1864] god;* and *Svod svedenii po delam ugolovnym v 1897 g.*, pp. 2, 5.

106. K. Antsiferov, "Vziatochnichestvo v istorii russkogo zakonodatel'stva," *Zhurnal grazhdanskogo i ugolovnogo prava*, god 14, kniga 2 (1884), pp. 1–54; A. Tankov, "K istorii vziatochnichestva," *Istoricheskii vestnik*, god 9, tom 34 (1888), pp. 240–245; V. N. Shiriaev, *Vziatochnichestvo i likhomstvo v sviazi s obshchim ucheniem o dolzhnostnykh prestupleniiakh* (Yaroslavl, 1916).

107. E. N. Tarnovskii, "Dvizhenie prestupnosti v evropeiskoi Rossii za 1874–1994 gg.," *Zhurnal Ministerstva iustitsii*, no. 3 (1899), p. 120.

108. *Svod svedenii po delam ugolovnym v 1903 g.*, pp. 15, 20.

109. *Otchet Ministerstva iustitsii za 1839 g.*, p. ix; *Otchet Ministerstra iustitsii za 1840 g.*, p. viii.

110. *Otchet Ministerstva iustitsii za 1863 g.*, pp. 190–191.

111. *Otchet Ministerstva iustitsii za 1839 g.*, p. 9.

112. Calculated from data in *Otchet Ministerstva iustitsii za [1861–1864] god.*

113. N. M. Kolmakov, "Staryi sud: Ocherki i vospominaniia," *Russkaia starina*, no. 12 (1886), p. 527.

114. S. A. Adrianov, ed., *Ministerstvo vnutrennikh del: Istoricheskii ocherk (1802–1920)* (St. Petersburg, 1902), p. 270. On the police in the prerevolutionary era, see also E. Anuchin, *Istoricheskii obzor razvitiia administrativno-politseiskikh uchrezhdenii v Rossii s Uchrezhdeniia o guberniiakh 1775 g. i do poslednego vremeni* (St. Petersburg, 1872); A. V. Borisov et al., *Politsiia i militsiia Rossii: Stranitsy istorii* (Moscow, 1995), pp. 3–44.

115. Data on the ineffectiveness of the police on the eve of the introduction of the new judicial statutes can be found in *Materialy, sobrannye dlia Komissii o preobrazovanii gubernskikh i uezdnykh uchrezhdenii: Otdel politseiskii* (St. Petersburg, 1860–1863), chasti 1–4.

116. Engel'man, *Uchebnik russkogo grazhdanskogo sudoproizvodstva*, p. 17.

117. These figures are calculated from *Sudebno-statisticheskie svedeniia i soobrazheniia o vvedenii v deistvie sudebnykh ustavov 20 noiabria 1864 goda (po 32 guberniiam)* (St. Petersburg, 1866), toma 1–3. For figures on the unsatisfactory condition of the police on the eve of the judicial reform, see *Materialy, sobrannye dlia Komissii o preobrazovanii gubernskikh i uezdnykh uchrezhdenii: Otdel politseiskii* (St. Petersburg, 1860–1863), chasti 1–4.

118. Iu. Got'e, "Otdelenie sudebnoi vlasti ot administrativnoi," in Davydov and Polianskii, *Sudebnaia reforma*, tom 1, pp. 181–204; M. V. Dovnar-Zapol'skii, "Administratsiia i sud pri Nikolae I," *Izvestiia Azerbaidzhanskogo gos. universiteta im. V. I. Lenina*, toma 2–3 (1925), pp. 1–67.

119. *Obzor sostoianiia sudebnykh mest po 36 guberniiam, v koikh proizvedeny byli revizii* (n.p., n.d.); *Svedeniia o polozhenii sudebnogo vedomstva v guberniiakh Moskovskoi, Tverskoi, Iaroslavskoi, Vladimirskoi, Riazanskoi, Tul'skoi i Kaluzhskoi* (St. Petersburg, 1863), chasti 1, 2.

120. M. M. Vydria, ed., *Sudebnye rechi izvestnykh russkikh iuristov* (Moscow, 1958), p. 31.

121. E. P. Karnovich, "Slaboe rasprostranenie iuridicheskikh znanii v nashem obshchestve," in E. P. Karnovich, *Ocherki nashikh poriadkov administrativnykh, sudebnykh i obshchestvennykh* (St. Petersburg, 1873), pp. 1–17.

122. *Obsuzhdenie voprosa ob uchastii obshchestvennogo elementa v otpravlenii pravosudiia* (Vysochaishe uchrezhdennaia Komissiia dlia peresmotra zakonopolozhenii po sudebnoi chasti) (St. Petersburg, 1897), p. 18; *Svod svedenii po delam ugolovnym v 1897 g.*, p. 11.

123. V. V. Tenishev, *Pravosudie v russkom krest'ianskom bytu* (Bryansk, 1907), p. 4; A. A. Leont'ev, *Krest'ianskoe pravo: Sistematicheskoe izlozhenie osobennostei zakonodatel'stva o krest'ianakh* (St. Petersburg, 1914), pp. 55, 303–364; A. A. Rittikh, *Krest'ianskii pravoporiadok* (Osoboe soveshchanie o nuzhdakh sel'skokhoziaistvennoi promyshlennosti: Svod trudov mestnykh komitetov po 49 guberniiam evropeiskoi Rossii) (St. Petersburg, 1904), pp. 17–128.

124. L. [pseudonym], "Chto schitaet pravom nash narod," *Russkoe bogatstvo*, no. 8 (1884); Pakhman, *Obychnoe grazhdanskoe pravo v Rossii*, tom 1, pp. vii–xvii; P. Czap, "Peasant-Class Court and Peasant Customary Justice in Russia, 1861–1912," *Journal of Social History*, vol. 1, no. 1 (1967), pp. 149–178; S. P. Frank, "Popular Justice, Community, and Culture Among the Russian Peasantry, 1870–1900," *Russian Review*, vol. 46, no. 3 (1987), pp. 239–265; M. Lewin, "Customary Law and Russian Rural Society in the Post-Reform Era," *Russian Review*, vol. 44 (1985), pp. 1–19.

125. Dal', *Poslovitsy russkogo naroda*, pp. 245–246.

126. A. N. Engel'gardt, *Iz derevni* (Moscow, 1937), p. 56.

127. V. N. Tenishev, *Pravosudie v russkom krest'ianskom bytu*, p. 11.

128. Pakhman, *Obychnoe grazhdanskoe pravo*, pp. 402–407.

129. P. S. Efimenko, *Sbornik narodnykh iuridicheskikh obychaev Arkhangel'skoi gubernii* (Moscow, 1869), kniga 1, pp. 277–281.

130. Arkhiv Rossiiskogo gosudarstvennogo etnograficheskogo muzeia (henceforth, ARGEM), fond 7 (V.N. Tenishev), op. 2, d. 275, ll. 9–16; N. N. Zlatovratskii, *Sobranie sochinenii v vos'mi tomakh* (St. Petersburg, 1913), tom 2, pp. 27–28.

S. V. Maksimov, *Sibir' i katorga v trekh chastiakh* (St. Petersburg, 1900), chast' 1, pp. 228–229; P. S. Efimenko, *Sbornik narodnykh iuridicheskikh obychaev,* kniga 1, pp. 220–221; E. Solov'ev, "Prestupleniia i nakazaniia po poniatiiam krest'ian Povolzh'ia," *Zapiski Russkogo geograficheskogo obshchestva po otdeleniiu etnografii,* tom 18 (1900), pp. 275–300; V. V. Tenishev, "Obshchie nachala ugolovnogo prava v ponimanii russkogo krest'ianina," *Zhurnal Ministerstva iustitsii,* tom 15 (September 1909), pp. 119–158; B. M. Firsov and I. G. Kiseleva, *Byt velikorusskikh krest'ian-zemlepashtsev: Opisanie materialov Etnograficheskogo biuro kniazia V.N. Tenisheva (na primere Vladimirskoi gubernii)* (St. Petersburg, 1993), pp. 56–57; A. A. Charushin, "Vzgliad naroda na prestuplenie," *Izvestiia Arkhangel'skogo obshchestva izucheniia russkogo severa* (1912), no. 7, pp. 316–321.

131. Firsov and Kiseleva, *Byt velikorusskikh krest'ian-zemlepashtsev,* p. 59.

132. ARGO, razriad 19 (Kurskaia guberniia), delo 12, list 4 (1848 g.); P. S. Efimenko, *Sbornik narodnykh iuridicheskikh obychaev,* kniga 1, pp. 222, 227; Maksimov, *Sibir' i katorga,* chast' 1, p. 229; Firsov and Kiseleva, *Byt velikorusskikh krest'ian-zemlepashtsev,* p. 59; D. S. Fleksor, ed., *Okhrana sel'skokhoziaistvennoi sobstvennosti (Osoboe soveshchanie o nuzhdakh sel'skokhoziaistvennoi promyshlennosti: Svod trudov mestnykh komitetov po 49 guberniiam evropeiskoi Rossii)* (St. Petersburg, 1904), p. 18.

133. Fleksor, ed., *Okhrana sel'skokhoziaistvennoi sobstvennosti,* p. 122; A. N. Butovskii, "O lesoporubkakh," *Zhurnal Ministerstva iustitsii,* no. 7 (1900), pp. 111–131.

134. T. A. Bernshtam, *Molodezh' v obriadovoi zhizni russkoi obshchiny XIX–nachala XX v.* (Leningrad, 1988), p. 239.

135. B. A. Romanov, *Liudi i nravy drevnei Rusi: Istorichesko-bytovye ocherki XI–XII vv.* (Moscow and Leningrad, 1966), p. 20; Iu. I. Iudin, "Iz istorii russkoi bytovoi skazki," in A. A. Gorelov, ed., *Russkii fol'klor,* tom 15 (1975), pp. 88–89.

136. See *Sobornoe ulozhenie* (1649), glava 10, stat'i 221–222.

137. Vladimirskii-Budanov, *Obzor istorii russkogo prava,* pp. 297, 342, 355.

138. Tenishev, *Pravosudie v russkom krest'ianskom bytu,* pp. 185–192.

139. ARGEM, fond 7, opis' 2, delo 275, l. 10; opis' 1, delo 243, l. 10; Firsov and Kiseleva, *Byt velikorusskikh krest'ian-zemlepashtsev,* p. 58.

140. Firsov and Kiseleva, *Byt velikorusskikh krest'ian-zemlepashtsev,* p. 60.

141. Tenishev, *Pravosudie v russkom krest'ianskom bytu,* pp. 107–113.

142. V. Kandinskii, "O nakazaniiakh po resheniiam volostnykh sudov Moskovskoi gubernii," in N. Kharuzin, ed., *Sbornik svedenii dlia izucheniia byta krest'ianskogo naseleniia Rossii* (Moscow, 1889), vyp. 1, pp. 34–59.

143. ARGO, f. 16 (Kievskaia guberniia), d. 29, ll. 1–44.

144. P. S. Efimenko, *Sbornik narodnykh iuridicheskikh obychaev,* kniga 1, p. 238; Firsov and Kiseleva, *Byt velikorusskikh krest'ian-zemlepashtsev,* p. 62.

145. A. Ia. Efimenko, *Issledovaniia narodnoi zhizni,* vyp. 1, pp. 173–175; K. Kachorovskii, *Narodnoe pravo* (Moscow, 1906), pp. 101–102. See also Cathy Frierson, "Crime and Punishment in the Russian Village: Rural Concepts of Criminality at the End of the Nineteenth Century," *Slavic Review,* vol. 46, no. 1, pp. 55–69.

146. ARGEM, f. 7, op. 1, d. 150, l. 1; d. 242, l. 5; d. 243, l. 24; d. 515, ll. 1–11; op. 2, d. 685, ll. 1–2; M. M. Gromyko, "Territorial'naia krest'ianskaia obshchina

Sibiri," in L. M. Goriushkin, ed., *Krest'ianskaia obshchina Sibiri XVII–nachala XX v.* (Novosibirsk, 1977), pp. 89–91; O. P. Semenova–Tian-Shanskaia, *Zhizn' Ivana* (St. Petersburg, 1914), p. 101; E. Solov'ev, "Samosud u krest'ian Chistopol'skogo uezda Kazanskoi gubernii," *Zapiski Russkogo geograficheskogo obshchestva po otdeleniiu etnografii,* tom 8 (1878), pp. 15–17; Tenishev, *Pravosudie v russkom krest'ianskom bytu,* pp. 33–53; G. I. Uspenskii, *Sobranie sochinenii v 9 tomakh* (Moscow, 1956), tom 4, pp. 146–152; Steven P. Frank, "'Simple Folk, Savage Customs?' Youth, Sociability, and the Dynamics of Culture in Rural Russia," *Journal of Social History,* vol. 25, no. 4, pp. 711–736; Christine D. Worobec, "Horse Thieves and Peasant Justice in Post-Emancipation Imperial Russia," *Journal of Social History,* vol. 21, no. 1, pp. 281–293.

147. P. M. Bogaevskii, "Zametki o iuridicheskom byte krest'ian Sarapul'skogo uezda Viatskoi gubernii," in Kharuzin, ed., *Sbornik svedenii,* vyp. 1, p. 29.

148. A. P. Nikol'skii, *Zemlia, obshchina i trud: Osobennosti krest'ianskogo pravoporiadka, ikh proiskhozhdenie i znachenie* (St. Petersburg, 1902), pp. 22–23, 41–43, 53–62, 69–85.

149. Rittikh, *Krest'ianskii pravoporiadok,* pp. 11–12; P. N. Zyrianov, "Obychnoe pravo v poreformennoi obshchine," in P. A. Kolesnikov, ed., *Ezhegodnik po agrarnoi istorii* (Vologda, 1976), pp. 91–101.

150. A. Ia. Efimenko, "Trudovoe nachalo v narodnom obychnom prave," *Slovo,* no. 1 (1878), pp. 146–173; Kachorovskii, *Narodnoe pravo,* pp. 134–162.

151. Pakhman, *Obychnoe grazhdanskoe pravo,* tom 1, p. 5.

152. S. I. Shidlovskii, ed., *Zemel'nye zakhvaty i mezhevoe delo (Osoboe soveshchanie o nuzhdakh sel'skokhoziaistvennoi promyshlennosti: Svod trudov mestnykh komitetov po 49 guberniiam Evropeiskoi Rossii)* (St. Petersburg, 1904), p. 7.

153. A. Ia. Efimenko, *Issledovaniia narodnoi zhizni,* vyp. 1, pp. 183–380; S. V. Pakhman, *Obychnoe grazhdanskoe pravo v Rossii,* tom 1, pp. 1–52; E. T. Solov'ev, *Grazhdanskoe pravo. Ocherki narodnogo iuridicheskogo byta* (Kazan, 1888), vyp. 1, pp. 113–166; vyp. 2 (1893), pp. 1–57.

154. Pakhman, *Obychnoe grazhdanskoe pravo v Rossii,* tom 1, pp. 119–124.

155. Ibid., pp. 190, 196–197.

156. Pakhman, *Obychnoe grazhdanskoe pravo,* tom 1, pp. 53–447; Solov'ev, *Grazhdanskoe pravo,* vyp. 2, pp. 58–110.

157. F. L. Barykov, "O poriadke nasledovaniia i razdelov u gosudarstvennykh krest'ian po svedeniiam, sobrannym Ministerstvom gosudarstvennykh imushchestv," in *Zhurnal Ministerstva gosudarstvennykh imushchestv,* chast' 81, pp. 232–259, 353–376, 456–469 (1862) (obobshchenie obsledovaniia, provedennogo v 44 guberniiakh v 1848–1849 gg.); V. Mukhin, *Obychnyi poriakok nasledovaniia krest'ian* (St. Petersburg, 1888), pp. 111–301; Pakhman, *Obychnoe grazhdanskoe pravo,* tom 2, pp. 209–344; Solov'ev, *Grazhdanskoe pravo,* vyp. 1, pp. 51–112.

158. Isaev, *Istoriia gosudastva i prava Rossii,* pp. 216–217, 245–247.

159. Pakhman, *Obychnoe grazhdanskoe pravo,* tom 2, pp. 209–290.

160. A. Ia. Efimenko, *Issledovaniia narodnoi zhizni,* vyp. 1, pp. 1–172; Pakhman, *Obychnoe grazhdanskoe pravo,* tom 2, pp. 1–209; I. G. Orshanskii, *Issledovaniia po russkomu pravu, obychnomu i brachnomu* (St. Petersburg, 1870); Solov'ev, *Grazhdanskoe pravo,* vyp. 1, pp. 5–50.

161. Pakhman, *Obychnoe grazhdanskoe pravo*, tom 2, pp. 49–84.

162. ARGO, razriad 14, d. 73, ll. 1–21.

163. There is an extensive literature on customary law among Russian peasants. In addition to the literature cited in the text, I have made use of the following: N. K. Brzheskii, *Ocherki iuridicheskogo byta krest'ian* (St. Petersburg, 1902); S. P. Nikonov, *Krest'ianskii pravoporiadok i ego zhelatel'no budushchee* (Kharkov, 1906); P. A. Matveev, ed., *Sbornik narodnykh iuridicheskikh obychaev* (St. Petersburg, 1878), tom 1 [*Zapiski Russkogo geograficheskogo obshchestva po otdeleniiu etnografii,* tom 8 (1878)]; S. V. Pakhman, ed., *Sbornik narodnykh iuridicheskikh obychaev* (St. Petersburg, 1878), tom 2 [*Zapiski Russkogo geograficheskogo obshchestva po otdeleniiu etnografii,* tom 18 (1900)]; *Trudy etnografichesko-statisticheskoi ekspeditsii v Zapadno-russkii krai,* tom 6, *Narodnye iuridicheskie obychai* (St. Petersburg, 1872). Readers can find additional information in the following: E. I. Iakushkin, *Obychnoe pravo: Materialy dlia bibliografii obychnogo prava* (Yaroslavl, 1875–1909), vyp. 1–4; V. A. Aleksandrov, "Obychnoe pravo v Rossii v otechestvennoi nauke XIX–nachala XX v.," *Voprosy istorii,* no. 11 (1981), pp. 41–55; R. S. Lipets, "Izuchenie obychnogo prava v kontse XIX–nachale XX v.," *Trudy Instituta etnografii im. Miklukho-Maklaia,* tom 94 (1968), pp. 79–98.

164. *Trudy Komissii po preobrazovaniiu volostnykh sudov (slovesnye oprosy krest'ian, pis'mennye otzyvy razlichnykh mest i lits i resheniia volostnykh sudov, s"ezdov mirovykh posrednikov i gubernskikh po krest'ianskim delam prisutsvii)* (St. Petersburg, 1873–1874), toma 1–6; V. P. Plemiannikov, *Ukazatel' resheniiam volostnykh sudov* (Moscow, 1891); M. I. Zarudnyi, *Zakony i zhizn': Itogi issledovaniia krest'ianskikh sudov* (St. Petersburg, 1874); A. Vorms and A. Parenado, "Krest'ianskii sud i sudebno-administrativnye uchrezhdeniia," in Davydov and Polianskii, eds., *Sudebnaia reforma,* tom 2, pp. 81–174; A. A. Leont'ev, *Volostnoi sud i iuridicheskie obychai krest'ian* (St. Petersburg, 1895); Pakhman, *Obychnoe grazhdanskoe pravo*, tom 1, pp. 380–389; Tenishev, *Pravosudie v russkom krest'ianskom bytu,* pp. 70–184.

165. A. Z. [pseudonym], "O domashnem sude mezhdu gosudarstvennymi krest'ianami," *Zhurnal Ministerstva gosudarstvennykh imushchestv,* no. 3 (1846), pp. 301–310; P. S. Efimenko, *Sbornik narodnykh iuridicheskikh obychaev,* kniga 1, p. 231; N. V. Kalachov, "O volostnykh i sel'skikh sudakh v drevnei i nyneshnei Rossii," in V. P. Bezobrazov, ed., *Sbornik gosudarstvennykh znanii* (St. Petersburg, 1880), vyp. 8, pp. 1–22.

166. Tagantsev, *Russkoe ugolovnoe pravo,* tom 1, pp. 68–69; N. Druzhinin, *Iuridicheskoe polozhenie krest'ian* (St. Petersburg, 1897), pp. 298–370.

167. ARGEM, f. 7, op. 2, d. 275, l. 63.

168. Rittikh, *Krest'ianskii pravoporiadok,* pp. 119–128.

169. ARGEM, f. 7, op. 1, d. 85, l. 1.

170. T. Uspenskii, "Ocherk iugo-zapadnoi poloviny Shadrinskogo uezda," in *Permskii sbornik,* kniga 1 (1858), pp. 39–40; Gromyko, "Territorial'naia krest'ianskaia obshchina Sibiri," pp. 83–91.

171. Gromyko, "Territorial'naia krest'ianskaia obshchina Sibiri," pp. 88–89.

172. A. Pappe, "O dokazatel'stvakh v volostnom sude," in Kharuzin, ed., *Sbornik svedenii,* vyp. 1, pp. 50–62; Tenishev, *Pravosudie v russkom krest'ianskom bytu,* pp. 114–166.

173. ARGO, f. 14, d. 27.

174. P. I. Astrov, "Ob uchastii sverkhestestvennoi sily v narodnom sudo-proizvodstve krest'ian Elatomskogo uezda Tambovskoi gubernii," in Kharuzin, ed., *Sbornik svedenii,* vyp. 1, pp. 130–149; Tenishev, *Pravosudie v russkom krest'ianskom bytu,* pp. 152–153.

175. A. A. Levenstim, "Prisiaga na sude po narodnym vozzreniiam," *Vestnik prava* (June 1901), pp. 1–26; A. V. Lokhvitskii, "Sud Bozhii po russkomu pravu," *Otechestvennye zapiski,* kniga 6 (1857), otdel 1, pp. 509–520; M. N. Makarov, "Drevnie i novye bozhby, kliatvy i prisiagi russkie," in *Trudy Obshchestva istorii i drevnostei rossiiskikh,* chast' 4, kniga 1 (1828); Tenishev, *Pravosudie v russkom krest'ianskom bytu,* pp. 139–145.

176. P. S. Efimenko, *Sbornik narodnykh iuridicheskikh obychaev,* kniga 1, pp. 231–238; Gromyko, "Territorial'naia krest'ianskaia obshchina Sibiri," p. 89; N. A. Minenko, "Traditsionnye formy rassledovaniia i suda u russkikh krest'ian zapad-noi Sibiri XVIII–pervoi poloviny XIX v.," *Sovetskaia etnografiia,* no. 5 (1980), pp. 21–33 (available in English translation as N. A. Minenko, "Traditional Forms of Investigation and Trial Among the Russian Peasants of Western Siberia in the Eigh-teenth and First Half of the Nineteenth Centuries," *Soviet Anthropology and Archeology,* vol. 21, no. 3 [1892], pp. 55–79); Pakhman, *Obychnoe grazhdanskoe pravo,* tom 1, pp. 408–440.

177. ARGEM, f. 7, op. 1, d. 243, l. 42; A. A. Levenstim, *Sueverie i ugolovnoe pravo* (St. Petersburg, 1987), pp. 151–176; Tenishev, *Pravosudie v russkom krest'ianskom bytu,* pp. 152–159.

178. Astrov, "Ob uchastii sverkhestestvennoi sily v narodnom sude," pp. 132–133; P. A. Matveev, "Ocherki narodnogo iuridicheskogo byta Samarskoi gu-bernii," *Zapiski russkogo geograficheskogo obshchestva po otdeleniiu etnografii,* tom 8 (1878), pp. 38–39; Tenishev, *Pravosudie v russkom krest'ianskom bytu,* pp. 114–120; Firsov and Kiseleva, *Byt velikorusskikh krest'ian-zemlepashtsev,* p. 62.

179. Druzhinin, *Iuridicheskoe polozhenie krest'ian,* pp. 371–385.

180. E. I. Iakushkin, "Zametki o vliianii religioznykh verovanii i predrassudkov na narodnye iuridicheskie obychai i poniatiia," *Etnograficheskoe obozrenie,* god 3, kniga 9, no. 2 (1891), pp. 1–19.

181. These and many other facts concerning the influence of superstition on crime can be found in Levenstim, *Sueverie i ugolovnoe pravo,* pp. 1–176. See also Iakushkin, "Zametki o vliianii religioznykh verovanii i predrassudkov na narodnye iuridicheskie obychai i poniatiia," pp. 1–19.

182. A. A. Leont'ev, "Zakonodatel'stvo o krest'ianakh posle reformy," in *Velikie reformy: Russkoe obshchestvo i krest'ianskii vopros v proshlom i nastoiashchem* (Moscow, 1911), pp. 158–199.

183. Druzhinin, "Preobrazovannyi volostnoi sud," pp. 298–370.

184. P. S. Efimenko, *Sbornik narodnykh iuridicheskikh obychaev,* kniga 1, pp. 239–277, 281–282; P. A. Mullov, "Neskol'ko slov o materialakh dlia ob''iasneniia narodnogo iuridicheskogo byta," *Zapiski Russkogo geograficheskogo obshchestva po otdeleniiu etnografii,* tom 1 (1867), pp. 615–636; S. V. Pakhman, *O sudebnykh dokazatel'stvakh po drevnemu russkomu pravu, preimushchestvenno grazhdan-skomu, v istoricheskom ikh razvitii* (Moscow, 1851), pp. 209–212; V. I. Sergeevich, *Lektsii i issledovaniia po istorii russkogo prava* (St. Petersburg, 1883), pp. 76–97;

I. M. Snegirev, "Obozrenie iuridicheskogo byta v prodolzhenii drevnego i srednego periodov russkoi narodnoi zhizni," in *Iuridicheskie zapiski, izd. P. G. Redkinym,* tom 2 (1842), pp. 294–300.

185. A. N. Filippov, "Narodnoe obychnoe pravo kak istoricheskii material," *Russkaia mysl',* no. 9 (1886), pp. 56–71.

186. A. V. Kamkin, "Pravosoznanie gosudarstvennykh krest'ian vtoroi poloviny XVIII veka (na materialakh Evropeiskogo Severa)," *Istoriia SSSR,* no. 2 (1987), pp. 163–173; Kamkin, "Vozdeistvie krest'ianstva na zakonodatel'noe oformlenie uravnitel'no-peredel'noi obshchiny v kontse XVIII veka," in I. D. Koval'chenko, ed., *XXVI s"ezd KPSS i problemy agrarnoi istorii SSSR* (Ufa, 1984), pp. 418–423; A. A. Pushkarenko, "Pravosoznanie rossiiskogo krest'ianstva pozdnefeodal'noi epokhi," in Koval'chenko, ed., *XXVI s"ezd KPSS i problemy agrarnoi istorii SSSR,* pp. 432–439; D. I. Raskin, "Osobennosti sootnosheniia formal'no-pravovogo i real'nogo statusa krest'ianstva Rossii v XVIII v.," in Koval'chenko, ed, *XXVI s"ezd KPSS i problemy agrarnoi istorii SSSR,* pp. 423–432; P. A. Kolesnikov, "Vozdeistvie narodnykh mass na gosudarstvennoe zakonodatel'stvo v Rossii XVII–XVIII vv.," in Kolesnikov, ed., *Problemy istorii krest'ianstva evropeiskoi Rossii (do 1917 g.)* (Perm, 1982), pp. 158–174.

187. Rittikh, ed., *Krest'ianskii pravoporiadok,* pp. 17–24.

188. Pakhman, *Obychnoe grazhdanskoe pravo,* p. ix.

189. Kalachov, "O volostnykh i sel'skikh sudakh," pp. 128–148; Zarudnyi, *Zakony i zhizn',* pp. 3–50; K. I. Tur, *Golos zhizni o krest'ianskom neustroistve (po povodu raboty uchrezhdennoi pri Ministerstve vnutrennikh del Komissii po peresmotru krest'ianskogo zakonodatel'stva)* (St. Petersburg, 1898), pp. 9–18.

190. N. M. Astyrev, *V volostnykh pisariakh: Ocherki krest'ianskogo samoupravleniia* (Moscow, 1896), p. 215.

191. The history of crime in Russia was studied actively by Russian historians from the last third of the nineteenth century until the 1920s. For brief historiographical overviews, see M. N. Gernet, *Moral'naia statistika: Ugolovnaia statistika i statistika prestuplenii* (Moscow, 1922), pp. 31–38; *Kriminologiia* (Moscow, 1968), pp. 71–80; S. S. Ostroumov, *Prestupnost' i ee prichiny v dorevoliutsionnoi Rossii* (Moscow, 1960 and 1980). Progress in the study of the history of crime in tsarist Russia was made in a number of works by American historians that appeared in the 1970s and 1990s. See the following: B. F. Adams, "Criminology, Penology and Prison Administration in Russia: 1863–1917" (dissertation, University of Maryland, 1981); R. S. Sutton, "Crime and Social Change in Russia After the Great Reforms: Laws, Courts, and Criminals, 1874–1894" (dissertation, Indiana University, 1984); Steven Frank, "Cultural Conflict and Criminality in Rural Russia: 1861–1900" (dissertation, Brown University, 1987); J. Neuberger, *Hooliganism: Crime, Culture, and Power in St. Petersburg, 1900–1914* (Stanford, 1993); Steven Frank, "Narratives Within Numbers: Women, Crime, and Judicial Statistics in Imperial Russia, 1834–1913," *Russian Review,* vol. 55 (1996), pp. 541–566; J. Neuberger, "Stories on the Street: Hooliganism and the St. Petersburg Popular Press," *Slavic Review,* vol. 48 (1989), pp. 177–195; L. Shelley, "Female Criminality in the 1920s: A Consequence of Inadvertent and Deliberate Change," *Russian History,* vol. 2, no. 2–3, pp. 265–284; N. B. Weissman, "Rural Crime in Tsarist Russia: The Question of Hooliganism, 1900–1914," *Slavic Review,* vol. 37 (1978), pp. 228–242; B. F. Adams,

"Criminology in Russia," in J. L. Wieczynski, ed., *The Modern Encyclopedia of Russian and Soviet History* (Gulf Breeze, 1988), vol. 47, pp. 231–235. During the past thirty years, the history of criminality in west European countries has been studied more extensively than that in Russia. To get an idea of the work that has been done on criminality in western Europe, see this study on the historiography of criminality in eleven countries: C. Emsley and L. Knaffa, eds., *Crime History and History of Crime: Studies in the Historiography of Crime and Criminal Justice in Modern History* (Westport, and London, 1996).

192. *Svod svedenii po delam ugolovnym v 1872 g.*, pp. 1–5.

193. *Svod svedenii po delam ugolovnym v 1872 g.*, chast' 1, tablitsa 1; *Svod svedenii po delam ugolovnym v 1873 g.*, pp. 4–5; *Svod svedenii po delam ugolovnym v 1874 g.*, pp. 12–16; *Svod svedenii po delam ugolovnym v 1875 g.*, pp. 16–21; *Svod svedenii po delam ugolovnym v 1876 g.*, pp. 18–22; *Svod svedenii po delam ugolovnym v 1877 g.*, pp. 18–23.

194. I. Tetriumov, "Mirovoi sud i krest'ianskoe obychnoe pravo," *Zemstvo*, no. 26 (1882).

195. A. Z. [pseudonym], "O domashnem sude mezhdu gosudarstvennymi krest'ianami," *Zhurnal Ministerstva gosudarstvennykh imushchestv*, chast' 18 (1846), p. 301.

196. E. N. Tarnovskii, "Dvizhenie prestupnosti v Rossiiskoi imperii za 1899–1908 gg.," *Zhurnal Ministerstva iustitsii*, no. 9 (1909), pp. 52–99.

197. F. Zakharevich, "Opyt iuridicheskoi statistiki Novorossiiskogo kraia," *Zhurnal Ministerstva vnutrennikh del*, chast' 41 (1853), p. 258.

198. I. Vil'son, ed., *Ugolovnaia statistika gosudarstvennykh krest'ian po dannym za desiatiletie 1847–1856* (St. Petersburg, 1871), pp. 1–4 (*Materialy dlia statistiki Rossii, sobiraemye po vedomstvu gosudarstvennykh imushchestv*, vyp. 6); A. I. Chuprov, "Nekotorye dannye po nravstvennoi statistike Rossii," *Iuridicheskii vestnik*, no. 8 (1884), pp. 631–641; "Sudebnaia statistika Rossii," *Russkii vestnik*, tom 29 (1860), p. 301; M. Filippov, "O sudebnoi statistike v Rossii," in *Russkoe slovo* (July 1846), pp. 133–162.

199. E. N. Tarnovskii, "Voina i dvizhenie prestupnosti v 1911–1916 gg.," *Sbornik statei po proletarskoi revoliutsii i pravu*, nos. 1–4 (1918), pp. 100–122.

200. *Svod svedenii po delam ugolovnym v 1874 g.*, p. 123; *Svod svedenii po delam ugolovnym v 1895 g.*, vvedenie, p. 33; *Svod svedenii po delam ugolovnym v 1913 g.*, vvedenie, p. 19; N. M. Iadrintsev, *Russkaia obshchina v tiur'me i ssylke* (St. Petersburg, 1872), pp. 146–188.

201. There is a large literature on the courts of justice of the peace. Here are some of the more important works: *Vybornyi mirovoi sud: Sbornik statei i materialov* (St. Petersburg, 1898); *Dvadtsatipiatiletie moskovskikh stolichnykh sudebno-mirovykh uchrezhdenii 1866–1891: Obzor deiatel'nosti, vedomost' dvizheniia ugolovnykh del, lichnyi sostav* (Moscow, 1891); G. Dzhanshiev, *Epokha velikikh reform* (Moscow, 1900), pp. 428–449; M. V. Krasovskii, "O nedostatkakh nyneshnego ustroistva mirovykh sudebnykh ustanovlenii," *Zhurnal grazhdanskogo i ugolovnogo prava*, no. 4 (1885), pp. 39–64; no. 5 (1885), pp. 65–84; V. I. Likhachev, "K tridtsatiletiiu mirovykh sudebnykh ustanovlenii, 1866–1896 gg.," *Zhurnal Ministerstva iustitsii*, no. 11 (1895), pp. 1–32; no. 12 (1895), pp. 1–54; A. E. Nos, *Mirovoi sud v Moskve: Ocherk razbiratel'stva u mirovykh sudei*

(Moscow, 1869), knigi 1, 2; P. N. Obninskii, "Mirovoi institut," *Iuridicheskii vestnik,* no. 3 (1888), pp. 400–415; no. 5 (1888), pp. 106–112; P. N. Obninskii, "Mirovye sud'i i ikh preemniki," in *Sbornik pravovedeniia i obshchestvennykh znanii: Trudy iuridicheskogo obshchestva, sostoiashchego pri moskovskom universitete,* tom 5 (1895), pp. 27–68; N. N. Polianskii, "Mirovoi sud," in Davydov and Polianskii, eds., *Sudebnaia reforma,* tom 2, pp. 172–291; *S-Peterburgskie stolichnye mirovye ustanovleniia i Arestnyi dom v 1889 godu: Otchety* (St. Petersburg, 1890); *S-Peterburgskie stolichnye mirovye uchrezhdeniia 20 noiabria 1864 g.: Spravochnyi sbornik* (St. Petersburg, 1885); E. I. Tikhonov, *Volostnoi sud i mirovoi sud'ia v krest'ianskikh seleniiakh* (Kovno [Kaunas], 1873).

202. *Sbornik statisticheskikh svedenii Ministerstva iustitsii, Dopolnenie k vypuskam 1–4: Obzor deiatel'nosti sudebno-mirovykh ustanovlenii za 1884–1888 gg.* (St. Petersburg, 1887–1891); *Sbornik statisticheskikh svedenii Ministerstva iustitsii, Dopolnenie k vypuskam 1–4: Obzor deiatel'nosti sudebno-mirovykh ustanovlenii za 1909–1913 gg.* (St. Petersburg, 1912–1916).

203. These figures are calculated from data in the following sources: *Svod svedenii po delam ugolovnym v [1874, 1897, 1913] godu; Obshchii svod po imperii rezul'tatov razrabotki dannykh pervoi vseobshchei perepisi naseleniia 1897 goda* (St. Petersburg, 1905), toma 1, 2; *Chislennost' i sostav rabochikh v Rossii na osnovanii dannykh pervoi vseobshchei perepisi naseleniia Rossiiskoi imperii 1897 g.* (St. Petersburg, 1906), tom 1, p. vii. See also: M. F. Zamengof, "Gorod i derevnia v prestupnosti," in *Trudy slushatelei iuridicheskogo seminariia Moskovskogo gorodskogo narodnogo universiteta im. A.L. Shaniavskogo* (Moscow, 1913), pp. 253–308; A. Troinin, "Prestupnost' goroda i derevni v Rossii," *Russkaia mysl',* July 1909, pp. 1–28. See the remarks by contemporaries on the low level of crime and frequency of minor crimes over major ones among peasant farmers: ARGO, razriad 2 (Astrakhanskaia guberniia), d. 61, ll. 4–5 (according the calculations of the author, crime among peasants was at the level of 4.4 per thousand); I. Morachevich, "Selo Kobyl'ia Volynskoi gubernii," in *Etnograficheskii sbornik Russkogo geograficheskogo obshchestva* (St. Petersburg, 1853), vyp. 1, p. 309; A. Preobrazhenskii, "Volost Pokrovo-Sitskaia Iaroslavskoi gubernii," in *Etnograficheskii sbornik Russkogo geograficheskogo obshchestva* (St. Petersburg, 1853), vyp. 1, p. 103; Skaldin, *V zakholust'e i v stolitse* (St. Petersburg, 1870), p. 301; P. Griaznov, *Opyt sravnitel'nogo izucheniia gigienicheskikh uslovii krest'ianskogo byta Cherepovetskogo uezda* (St. Petersburg, 1880), p. 170.

204. Calculated from data in sources listed in the two preceding endnotes and from the following: *Otchet Ministerstva iustitsii za 1858 god*; A. B. Bushen, ed., *Statisticheskie tablitsy Rossiiskoi imperii* (St. Petersburg, 1863), vyp. 2, pp. 276–291.

205. E. N. Tarnovskii, "Vliianie khlebnykh tsen i urozhaev na dvizhenie prestupnosti protiv sobstvennosti v Rossii," *Zhurnal Ministerstva iustitsii,* no. 8 (1898), pp. 80–102; M. N. Gernet, *Moral'naia statistika: Ugolovnaia statistika i statistika samoubiistv* (Moscow, 1992), pp. 209–220.

206. *Prestupleniia, raskrytye nachal'nikom S.-Peterburgskoi sysknoi politsii I. D. Putilinym* (Moscow, 1990), pp. 184–185.

207. V. N. Kudriavtsev, *Sotsial'nye otkloneniia: Vvedenie v obshchuiu teoriiu* (Moscow, 1984), pp. 153–186.

208. Cited in the newspaper *Rus',* 1905, no. 191.

6

Russia and the West

From the eighteenth century to the beginning of the twentieth, Russian society underwent tremendous change. Demographically, all estates experienced a gradual transition from uncontrolled to controlled fertility, from high to low rates of mortality, and from nearly universal to somewhat diminished nuptiality. At the end of the nineteenth century, the Russian empire was in transition from a traditional to a modern pattern of population growth. Russian society also began to evidence other modern demographic trends at this time: Families became smaller, less patriarchal, and more democratic; interpersonal relations within the family grew more humane; and women and children acquired a voice in family decisionmaking.

On two occasions, Russia's social structure underwent a profound transformation: First, in the eighteenth century, with the formation of estates; and second, from the last third of the nineteenth century to the beginning of the twentieth, with the conversion of estates to classes. The structures, functions, governance, internal relations, and underlying principles of basic social institutions became more rational and formalized over time, and their activity increasingly reliant on firm juridical precepts. In other words, Russian social institutions were evolving from *Gemeinschaft* to *Gesellschaft*. Attitudes and behaviors associated with serfdom, which had permeated all of society from top to bottom at the beginning of the eighteenth century, gradually gave way to modes based on contract and law. The Russian state system also made significant progress, from an absolute monarchy at the beginning of the eighteenth century to a constitutional monarchy in the early twentieth century. From a servant of the state and an

---

Translated by Larry Holmes, University of Southern Alabama.

object of governance, Russian society became an active governing agent, thereby laying the foundation for a civil society. As early as the 1830s, Russian courts achieved a significant degree of justice; and after the juridical reform of 1864, complaints of corruption, red tape, and injustice generally ceased. Slowly but surely, the rule of law replaced that of custom. In short, the character of Russian society in the imperial period was significantly altered by the modernization of social relations.

Comparative Historical Development

From the eighteenth century to the beginning of the twentieth century, cultural, economic, and political developments in Russia followed essentially the same trends as those that had prevailed in other European countries.[1] Nevertheless, critical distinctions persisted. First, west European societies tended to eradicate local, regional, estate, and class distinctions in public and private life as they evolved toward social integration and centralization in the political, legal, and cultural realms: These societies moved away from decentralization and fragmentation according to region, estate, and class, and toward the creation of a single, unified nation. In short, the separate social classes in western Europe had consolidated into unified national populations by the 1870s.[2] In contrast, Russian society grew more fragmented socially and culturally. Earlier, at the end of the seventeenth century, Russia's social classes had been distinguished by a commonality of culture, belief, mentality, and social organization; Russian society then appeared homogeneous. However, in the centuries that followed, the distinctive social dynamics among the nobility, urban estate, and peasantry made Russian society more fragmented and asymmetrical.

At the beginning of the twentieth century, Russia's three social estates differed in their stage of development and in their structure, and occupied separate social, legal, and cultural realms, with little interaction. The peasantry, comprising a majority of the population (74 percent), lived mainly in rural communes governed largely by custom, and transmitted its cultural heritage orally. Thus the peasantry functioned as a traditional society. By the beginning of the twentieth century, the urban estate (17 percent) had evolved beyond the *Gemeinschaft* stage—although its separate strata had done so to varying degrees. The nobility and the intelligentsia of nonnoble origin (2 percent) had almost never exhibited *Gemeinschaft* tendencies, and by the early twentieth century they were abiding by the precepts of modern civil society, such as equality of opportunity, priority of merit over birth, openness, social mobility, and primacy of law. They embraced the doctrine of progress and many welcomed social change and democracy.[3]

At the beginning of the twentieth century, a social and cultural barrier divided Russia's urban areas from the countryside. City and village (15 and

85 percent of the population, respectively) had become, as it were, two distinct realms coexisting in parallel worlds; although intersecting, they nevertheless were governed by different value systems and even different laws.

In both urban and rural realms, another marked fragmentation born of modernization appeared: New classes—the bourgeoisie and proletariat—arose in the city and village; as many as 30 percent of peasants abandoned the rural commune. The bourgeoisie and a significant part of the peasantry who had broken with the commune had accepted modernization and pinned their hopes on urbanization, industrialization, and the development of market relations. In contrast, workers on the whole retained close ties to their villages, as they lacked sufficient free time in which to assimilate into factory and urban life; thus, in many respects, the proletariat bore the imprint of peasant mentality. They associated modernization with hard factory labor, separation from birthplace and family, and the destruction of their traditional way of life. They did not pin their hopes on modernization but rather dreamed of refashioning all of society, including industries and cities, along the lines of the repartitional commune. Thus, a social and cultural gap existed both in the city and in the countryside. Without much exaggeration we can say that the Russian cultural and social realms had split four ways—with respect to location (rural or urban) and to estate or class affiliation.

Three distinctive factors in Russia's historical development played a key role in bringing about this split: The slow pace of urbanization (from 1861 to 1914, urban population increased from 9.4 to 15.3 percent of the total, or by only 6 percentage points); the uneven and widely dispersed development of industry (from 1860 to 1914, only about 40 percent of all workers lived in urban areas; the other 60 percent lived in villages); and the weakly developed process of social mobility—a result of the estate paradigm's dominance in social relations and in the public's consciousness.

First, the slow rate of urbanization meant that the city had remade in its own image only an insignificant portion of the peasantry. The tardy and uneven nature of industrialization allowed the peasantry to combine agricultural pursuits with industrial ones, and traditional modes of behavior with modern ones. Limited urbanization and industrialization meant that there was little mobility among estates and that it occurred primarily in one direction—from village to city. The gradual pace of economic progress limited the extent to which new ideas and social and cultural attitudes penetrated the countryside and reduced the impact of the three powerful, dynamic forces of modernization—industrialization, urbanization, and vertical and horizontal social mobility—on Russian society and culture.

The second distinctive feature of Russia's historical development is that social changes during the imperial period occurred, in the main, asynchronously with the historical evolution of other European countries. Several developments—such as the formation of estates and urban corporations, and the transition from *Gemeinschaft* to *Gesellschaft*—began in Russia at the moment of their completion in the West. Others, such as the demographic transition, the industrial revolution, and the emergence of civil society and of representative institutions, appeared in Russia only after lengthy delays. Of course, other European countries did not experience these important social and cultural developments synchronously, either; but the periods of time separating similar developments among the various other countries of Europe were much shorter than those separating them from the same developments in Russia.

Third, the various social, economic, cultural, and political processes affected Russia differently than they did other European countries. For example, nowhere else in Europe was enserfment as extensive and intensive as it was in Russia. Even by 1917, the forces that might have mitigated serfdom and its historical consequences—that is, the forces of urbanization and industrialization, the spread of literacy, and the secularization of public consciousness—had not yet permeated Russian society. Other historical forces had generally passed Russia by or had affected it only superficially: Russian society was largely untouched by the Renaissance, the Reformation, the Counterreformation, and the scientific revolution of the seventeenth and eighteenth centuries.

These distinctive features of Russia's historical development had serious consequences. Social and cultural asymmetry created enormous tensions within Russian society and contributed to the formation of conditions conducive to the 1905 Revolution and the revolutions of 1917. And unlike the revolutions in Europe from 1789 to 1848, the last Russian revolution destroyed the vestiges of the old regime and the emerging structure of the new, modernist society. Three factors contributed to the antimodern thrust of the October Revolution: World War I; the retention by many Russian peasants and workers of traditional social institutions, customary law, and mentality; and the multinational character of the Russian empire. Repeated failures in the war effort led to the disintegration of state power, discipline, and social order, and to material shortages. The war also brought social conflict to the fore that previously had been confined—albeit with great difficulty—within distinct limits. Moreover, it allowed socialist parties to profit from wartime difficulties and to foment revolution.

Four slogans dominated the October Revolution: land to the peasantry, factories to the workers, peace to the people, and self-determination to minorities. One appeal acquired the greatest importance: the total expropriation of private property and its redistribution among urban and rural workers organized in communes, artels, and similar associations. The war's end and the overthrow of the existing state power played a secondary role, important only in removing two obstacles blocking the expropriation of private property. Thus, the revolution's chief social slogan amounted to nothing less than a summons to "black [that is, universal—B.N.M.] repartition," expressing the traditional peasant principle of "land to those who work it" in an altered form that fit the new circumstances: "private property to the laborers." If we recall the slogans of the French Revolution—"Fatherland, Liberty, Equality, Fraternity"—then the anti-bourgeois nature of the October Revolution becomes obvious. The participants in this later revolution cared nothing for the fundamental principles of bourgeois social order. Their indifference was no mere accident; for the revolution was not aimed at modernization but rather at restoring the traditional bases of life that had been trampled underfoot by increasingly rapid modernization.

The Russian empire's multinational character (a topic regretfully beyond the scope of these volumes) also hampered modernization and encouraged revolution. In Russia as everywhere else, the prevailing trends accompanying modernization—the centralization of administrative functions, courts, and law, together with economic integration—clashed with the centrifugal forces of nationalism. The modernization of the empire ran afoul of nationalism, and actually assisted its growth. Yet the October Revolution was not inevitable: It resulted from a crisis brought on by a convergence of inauspicious circumstances. Most importantly, the cultural and social schism in Russian society created the essential prerequisites for revolution.

Russia and Europe: Comparison as an Impetus to Russian Reforms

The fact that Russia lagged behind western Europe compelled its government to implement reforms that artificially encouraged some processes and stymied others. Prompted by the best of intentions, the governments of Peter I and Catherine II energetically created the estate system and police state during the eighteenth century, believing such arrangements to be the last word in European civilization. With the best of motives, Alexander II's government implemented a series of major reforms that moved ahead of Russia's needs at that moment as determined by the representatives of the peasantry and urban estate (although not by the educated portion of Russian society). Serfdom was abolished even before it had exhausted its economic and social usefulness; although many among the peasantry were clamoring for its abolition, a majority of landowners perceived the decision as ill founded and likely to prove economically ruinous. Similarly, a parliament and a constitution were introduced into Russian governance by the autocracy itself, long before the general public had the slightest inkling of the import of these institutions.

The issue is not whether Russian society needed these or other reforms. The point I wish to make is that from the beginning of the eighteenth century, when the Russian government commenced to artificially impregnate Russia with the most progressive European ideas and institutions, it was interfering with the natural, organic evolution of Russian society. Developments then under way never achieved their natural denouement; instead, other developments unfolded, the result of external stimuli. Reforms that responded to the attitudes and requirements of those in government and in educated society but not of the general public naturally affected society's upper strata to a significantly greater degree than its lower elements, and the city more than the village. These reforms exacerbated Russia's social and cultural asymmetry, deepening the split along urban and rural lines. In short, Russia experienced many of the distortions characteristic of *latecomers* to modernization.

In contrast, central and west European countries experienced a far more natural and organic transition from tradition to modernity. Nevertheless, for them, too, it was a long, painful, and difficult process, accompanied by the growth of social tensions, conflicts, and revolutions.[4] Russia's transition to modernity outpaced the populace's capacity and readiness for change, which made the process more painful. In the final analysis, forced social change produced such enormous tensions that Russia's social order collapsed, burying under its ruins the many achievements of modernization.

That said, I do not mean to imply that Russia was not or is not a European country. On the contrary, I share the opinion of those who believe that the fundamental elements of the Russian state system, social life, and popular mentality were of European origin. These elements emerged in the Kievan period and were shaped by the Byzantine inheritance, the adoption of Christianity, and the creation of a written language.[5] Over the course of several centuries, unfavorable external and internal conditions delayed their further development but neither destroyed nor replaced the basic traits of European civilization in Russia.

The contraposition of Russia to the West, or of Russia to Europe, I believe, stems from the asynchrony of social development and change in Russia and in the West. This temporal disjuncture explains why at any given moment in history Russia appears markedly different from other European countries—sometimes so much so, that their common foundation is almost indiscernible. Yet as demonstrated above, Russia experienced the same historical processes and developmental tendencies as did the West—albeit often much later. For this reason, one finds ready comparisons between Russia in its imperial period and Europe in the Middle Ages and the early modern period.[6] The similarities are especially evident when Russia is compared with central European countries such as Austria and Germany, or with the countries of eastern Europe.[7]

Comparative Social Development: From Tradition to Modernity

The Family

The transition from traditional to modern demographic trends occurred when people voluntarily began to limit the number of their offspring such that population growth ceased to threaten progress. This transition began in France in the second half of the eighteenth century, spread to a majority of European countries in the nineteenth, and ended in the main by the beginning of the twentieth century.[8] The patriarchal family, with its despotic head and submissive household members, prevailed in all European countries in the Middle Ages and early modern period.[9] Reliance on stern and systematic discipline remained the general European model for raising children until the twentieth century.[10] In contrast to historians of the Cambridge Group for the Study of the History of Population and Social Structure,[11] a number of scholars have suggested that in western Europe as in Russia, the extended and complex family preceded, or at least coexisted with, the simple or nuclear family.[12]

Social Structures

In more advanced European countries, the estate system took shape in the Middle Ages and became the basis of the social order by the end of the eighteenth century. Yet even when this system flourished in these countries, their populations did not coalesce into such neatly defined estates as nobility, clergy, urban residents, and peasantry.[13] For example, scholars have counted twenty-two social groups, subdivided into 569 subgroups, in seventeenth-century France.[14] Following its emergence as an estate from 1762 to 1785, the Russian nobility differed little from its European counterparts.[15] Except in several north European countries, the peasantry never became an estate in the full meaning of the term.[16]

Social life in medieval Europe had much in common with that in Russian cities in the seventeenth and the first half of the eighteenth centuries, and in the Russian countryside from the nineteenth century to the beginning of the twentieth.[17] An institution similar to the Russian repartitional commune was also commonplace in many European countries, and it still existed in some regions of Austria, Germany, and Norway in the eighteenth and the early nineteenth centuries. Every rural settlement in England, until the beginning of the early modern period, considered itself a *Gemeinschaft*—as did rural communities in other European countries until the eighteenth and nineteenth centuries.[18]

For a long time, in European countries as in Russia, urban and rural settlements differed little economically or socially, with the exception of large commercial centers. The overwhelming number of urban areas were small towns, each approximating a rural settlement and constituting its own *Gemeinschaft*. In the words of German historian and economist Karl Bücher (1847–1930): "This solidarity, this all-encompassing fraternity extended beyond the numerous associations, shops, guilds, and corporations formed by patricians, artisans, and apprentices. It embraced all the town's citizens in a single whole, united by an oath binding everyone 'to share a common joy or sorrow in the town or elsewhere'."[19] Fundamental differences between town and village appeared only with the full transition of cities to a market economy—in England, at the beginning of the sixteenth century, and in other European countries, in the seventeenth and eighteenth centuries. Yet even in the eighteenth century, urban residents engaged in agricultural pursuits in large cities, to say nothing of small towns.[20] Patriarchal communalism also characterized American cities in the seventeenth century.[21]

Serfdom existed in a majority of west European countries throughout the Middle Ages—albeit of a milder form than that in Russia—and its vestiges remained in evidence there, in some places, until the seventeenth or eighteenth century. In central Europe, serfdom was not abolished until the late eighteenth and early nineteenth centuries, and its consequences were felt well into the twentieth.[22]

State and Society

The Russian state system of the imperial period passed through the same stages of development as did that in other European countries, but much later and in distinctive fashion.[23] In the era of European absolutism, the concept of the state included the notion of property. The state belonged to the monarch, and many private individuals considered state institutions their private property. These people carried out their military and civil functions in such a manner that they obliterated the distinction between private and public life and between state and society. Moreover, it is difficult to distinguish the power wielded by municipal corporations (guilds and councils) over their members or by landowners over their peasants, on the one hand, from the power of the state, on the other, since these corporations and landowners possessed the juridical and administrative powers that in contemporary states belonged wholly to state institutions.

Any application of the concepts "public" and "private" to west European states in the era of absolutism presents the same difficulties as it does when applied to the Russian state of the eighteenth century and the first half of the nineteenth, when the concept of "civil rights and duties" was alien. Certain individuals and families considered their private privileges, such as immunity from taxes and military service, to be rights—purchased, inherited, or earned. The concept of "citizenship" in its modern sense was unknown, and freedom simply meant autonomy from central power.[24] When democracy emerged in European countries, the electorate was as small as it was in Russia following the formation of the State Duma. For example, in 1831, in England—the most democratic country of that time— the electorate included only 3.3 percent of the population—exactly the same as in Russia in 1910.[25]

Law

Juridical pluralism—the simultaneous operation of several legal systems in a single state—characterized Russia from the eighteenth century to the beginning of the twentieth century, and European countries in the Middle Ages and the early modern period. Legislation displaced customary law in a majority of cases only in the nineteenth century.[26] England preserved juridical dualism into the nineteenth century.[27] Like Russia before the 1860s, European countries in the preindustrial epoch experienced a low crime rate. In the second half of the nineteenth century and the beginning of the twentieth, however, differences between Europe and Russia diminished to such an extent that from 1900 to 1913 England experienced a crime rate only 1.2 times greater than Russia's; France, 1.9 times greater; and Germany, 2.4 times greater—in contrast to a rate 7 or 8 times greater, in the mid-nineteenth century.[28] The subsequent convergence in crime rates resulted from a rapid increase in crime in Russia, whereas in western Europe serious crimes actually decreased (as did minor infractions).

Religion and Mentality

The spiritual culture and mentality of Russia's imperial period approximated that of other European countries in an earlier era.[29] One striking example comes to mind. Foreign travelers in the eighteenth and nineteenth centuries observed a fundamental difference between the religious beliefs of Russians and of west Europeans. The religiosity of all Russians at the beginning of the eighteenth century and of people in all undeveloped areas until the beginning of the twentieth century featured the following elements: a poor understanding of the fundamentals of Christian belief; a substitution of a strict observance of rites and rituals for faith; the pervasiveness of superstition and prejudice (veneration of icons, pilgrimages to holy shrines, fasting, and so on); a lack of proper reverence at church during the service and the administration of the sacraments; and a pragmatic form of piety (an expectation of practical results from the observance of rites, such as a plentiful harvest, health, and success). Much the same type of religiosity characterized the inhabitants of western Europe before the Reformation; and the rural population generally, until the seventeenth and eighteenth centuries. Witch-hunts and the lynching of witches occurred in England as late as 1751.[30]

Conclusion

Traits that some have regarded as distinctively Russian had appeared previously in Europe—sometimes two, three, or more centuries earlier, albeit with variations. Nevertheless, like any country, Russia did have distinctive features brought about by religion, geography, and political and economic conditions.[31] Russia's location on the periphery of Europe, its multinational population, and the influence of its eastern neighbors reinforced these features. Russia embraced Western civilization later than other European countries. Whereas after the fall of the Roman empire most people in western Europe occupied a relatively familiar and well-delimited territory containing previously developed centers of Roman culture, Russia's historical development occurred in a largely primitive, immense, and constantly expanding space.

Early on, Russia lagged behind the rest of Europe; but this does not preclude its basic similarity to Europe in the social, economic, political, and cultural spheres. Russians and Europeans have shared common features of development, particularly in the spheres of religion, geography, and ethnicity. However, Russia developed asynchronously with other European countries. I fully share the opinion of the prominent historian P. N. Miliukov that "Russia's Europeanization was not the product of borrowing but the inevitable result of its own evolution, essentially similar to Europe's but delayed by the conditions of its historical environment."[32]

So it is that at the end of this lengthy excursion into the social history of imperial Russia we arrive at global conclusions that by and large reinforce the perspectives of earlier Russian historians. The application of modern social science techniques to the historical record has revealed much that is new about demography, the family, social interactions, state and societal institutions, the law, and so on. Yet even as this analysis refines earlier portrayals of imperial Russia, it also confirms both that Russia was profoundly European—that it shared much in common with the richly diverse, complex, and multilayered entity that emerges from the pages of historians of the Annales era and beyond—and that in quantitative and qualitative indicators of social and economic development, Russia lagged behind Europe. Although this lag placed Russia at a clear disadvantage in international power relations, it cannot be attributed to any hypothetical, peculiarly Russian moral or cultural failing; for the cultural and spiritual richness of this society, at both the popular and the elite levels, has been amply demonstrated and universally observed.

Notes

1. Johan Galtung, Erik Rudeng, and Tore Heiestad, "On the Last 2,500 Years in Western History, and Some Remarks on the Coming 500," in Peter Burke, ed., *The New Cambridge Modern History* (Cambridge, 1979), Companion Volume XIII, pp. 318–362.

2. John R. Gillis, *The Development of European Society, 1770–1870* (Washington, D.C., 1983), pp. xi–xv.

3. Ibid., pp. xv–xvi.

4. Ibid., pp. xiii–xiv; Anthony Fletcher and John Stevenson, eds., *Order and Disorder in Early Modern England* (Cambridge, 1985); Peter Laslett, *The World We Have Lost* (New York, 1965), pp. 182–209; Eugen Weber, *Peasants into Frenchmen: The Modernization of Rural France, 1870–1914* (London, 1977), pp. 485–496.

5. Tomas G. Masaryk, *The Spirit of Russia: Studies in History, Literature, and Philosophy*, 2d ed., 2 vols. (London and New York, 1955), vol. 1, pp. 1–9; Pavel Miliukov, Charles Seignobos, and Louis Eisenmann, *History of Russia*, 3 vols. (New York, 1968), vol. 1, pp. xviii–xxi, 98; Dimitri Obolensky, *The Byzantine Commonwealth: Eastern Europe, 500–1453* (New York and Washington, D.C., 1971).

6. Daniel Chirot, ed., *The Origins of Backwardness in Eastern Europe: Economics and Politics from the Middle Ages to the Early Twentieth Century* (Berkeley, 1989); Robin Okey, *Eastern Europe, 1470–1980: Feudalism to Communism* (Minneapolis, 1982); Piotr S. Wandycz, *The Price of Freedom: A History of East Central Europe from the Middle Ages to the Present* (London and New York, 1992).

7. Burke, ed., *The New Cambridge Modern History*, Companion Volume XIII; Pierre Goubert, *The Ancient Regime: French Society, 1600–1750* (London, 1973); George Huppert, *After the Black Death* (Bloomington and Indianapolis, 1989); Donald N. Pennington, *Seventeenth-Century Europe* (London and New York, 1970); Eugen Weber, *A Modern History of Europe: Men, Culture, and Society* (New York, 1971), pp. 3–36, 183–220; Galtung, Rudeng, and Heiestad, "On the Last 2,500 Years in Western History," pp. 320–329; D. M. Trevel'ian, *Sotsial'naia istoriia Anglii: Obzor shesti stoletii ot Chosera do korelevy Viktorii* (Moscow, 1959), pp. 21–121.

8. Iu. L. Bessmertnyi, "Istoricheskaia demografiia pozdnego srednevekov'ia na sovremennom etape," *Srednie veka*, tom 50 (1987), pp. 292–293; idem, *Zhizn' i smert' v srednie veka* (Moscow, 1991), pp. 222–229; A. G. Vishnevskii, *Demograficheskaia revoliutsiia* (Moscow, 1976); A. G. Vishnevskii and I. S. Kon, eds., *Brachnost', rozhdaemost', sem'ia za tri veka* (Moscow, 1979); Michael W. Flinn, *The European Demographic System, 1500–1820* (Brighton, 1981); D. O. Cowgill, "Transition Theory as General Population Theory," in Thomas Ford and Gordon F. De Jong, eds., *Social Demography* (Englewood Cliffs, 1970).

9. Katia Boh, et al., eds., *Changing Patterns of European Family Life: A Comparative Analysis of Fourteen European Countries* (London and New York, 1989); Beatrice Gottlieb, *The Family in the Western World: From Black Death to the Industrial Age* (New York and Oxford, 1993); Edward Shorter, *The Making of the*

Modern Family (New York, 1977), pp. 39–44, 54–78, 218–227; Michael Mitter-auer and Reinhard Sieder, *The European Family: Patriarchy to Partnership from the Middle Ages to the Present* (Oxford, 1982), pp. 227–234; Jean Flandrin, *Families in Former Times: Kinship, Household and Sexuality* (Cambridge, 1976), pp. 118–144; John R. Gillis, *For Better, For Worse: British Marriages, 1600 to the Present* (New York and Oxford, 1985), pp. 130–134; Lawrence Stone, "The Rise of the Nuclear Family in Early Modern England: The Patriarchal Stage," in Charles E. Rosenberg, ed., *The Family in History* (Philadelphia, 1975), pp. 13–59.

10. I. S. Kon, *Rebenok i obshchestvo* (Moscow, 1988); Bonnie S. Anderson and Judith P. Zinsser, *A History of Their Own: Women in Europe from Prehistory to the Present* (New York, 1988), 2 vols.; Philippe Aries, *Centuries of Childhood: A Social History of Family Life* (London, 1962); Lloyd DeMause, ed., *The History of Childhood* (New York, 1974); Linda A. Pollock, *A Lasting Relationship: Parents and Children over Three Centuries* (Hanover and London, 1987).

11. Peter Laslett and Richard Wall, eds., *Household and Family in Past Time: Comparative Studies in the Size and Structure of the Domestic Group over the Last Three Centuries in England, France, Serbia, Japan, and Colonial North America* (Cambridge, 1972), p. 623; Richard Wall, ed., *Family Forms in Historic Europe* (Cambridge, 1983).

12. Lutz K. Berkner, "The Use and Misuse of Census Data for the Historical Analysis of Family Structure," *Journal of Interdisciplinary History*, no. 4 (1975), pp. 721–738; Flandrin, *Families in Former Times*.

13. M. L. Bush, ed., *Social Orders and Social Classes in Europe Since 1500: Studies in Social Stratification* (London and New York, 1992).

14. D. Field, "Sotsial'nye predstavleniia v dorevoliutsionnoi Rossii," in V. S. Di-akin, ed., *Reformy ili revoliutsiia?: Rossiia 1861–1917; Materialy mezhdunarodnogo kollokviiuma istorikov* (St. Petersburg, 1992), pp. 70–78.

15. Ivo Banac and Paul Bushkovitch, eds., *The Nobility in Russia and Eastern Europe* (New Haven, 1983).

16. N. A. Khachaturian, "Frantsuzskoe krest'ianstvo v sisteme soslovnoi monarkhii," in Z. V. Udal'tsova, ed., *Klassy i sosloviia srednevekovogo obshchestva* (Moscow, 1988), pp. 103–111.

17. Frances Gies and Joseph Gies, *Life in a Medieval Village* (New York, 1990), pp. 88–105; Huppert, *After the Black Death*, pp. 1–13, 30–40.

18. G. I. Anokhin, *Obshchinnye traditsii norvezhskogo krest'ianstva* (Moscow, 1971), pp. 167, 184, 190; M. Blok, *Kharakternye cherty frantsuzskoi agrarnoi istorii* (Moscow, 1957), pp. 77–104; L. L. Kotel'nikova, "Krest'ianskaia obshchina," in Z. V. Udal'tsova, ed., *Istoriia krest'ianstva v Evrope*, vol. 2, *Epokha feodalizma* (Moscow, 1986), pp. 476–492; L. V. Kotova, "Sotsial'naia organizatsiia i soderzhanie obshchinnogo samoupravleniia v Germanii XIV–XV vv.," in Udal'tsova, ed., *Klassy i sosloviia srednevekovogo obshchestva*, pp. 150–154; V. Rosher, *Nauka o narodnom khoziaistve v otnoshenii k zemledeliiu i drugim otrasliam pervonachal'noi promyshlennosti* (Moscow, 1869), pp. 234–237; U. Dzh. Eshli, *Ekonomicheskaia istoriia Anglii v sviazi s ekonomicheskoi teoriei* (Moscow, 1897), pp. 37–48; David Hey, *An English Rural Community: Myddle Under Tudor and Stuart* (Leicester, 1974); Emmanuel LeRoy-Ladurie, *The Peasant*

of Languedoc (Urbana, 1974); idem, *The French Peasantry, 1450–1660* (Berkeley and Los Angeles, 1987).

19. K. Biukher, *Vozniknovenie narodnogo khoziaistva* (St. Petersburg, 1907), p. 165.

20. Ibid., pp. 141–166; A. K. Dzhivelegov, *Srednevekovye goroda v zapadnoi Evrope* (St. Petersburg, 1902); Eshli, *Ekonomicheskaia istoriia Anglii*, pp. 285–297; A. L. Iastrebitskaia, *Evropeiskii gorod: Srednie veka i rannee novoe vremia: Vvedenie v sovremennuiu urbanistiku* (Moscow, 1993); William Doyle, *The Old European Order, 1660–1800* (Oxford, 1990), p. 126.

21. David J. Russo, *Families and Communities: A New View of American History* (Nashville, 1974).

22. G. Knapp, *Osvobozhdenie krest'ian i proiskhozhdenie sel'skokhoziaistvennykh rabochikh v starykh provintsiiakh Prusskoi monarkhii* (St. Petersburg, 1900); F. M. Tompson, "Istoriia evropeiskikh sel'skikh obshchestv," *Tsivilizatsii,* vyp. 3 (1995), pp. 209–218; T. H. Aston and C. H. E. Philpin, eds., *The Brenner Debate: Agrarian Class Structure and Economic Development in Pre-Industrial Europe* (Cambridge, 1985); Jerome Blum, *The End of the Old Order in Rural Europe* (Princeton, 1978); Doyle, *The Old European Order,* A.D. 500–1850 (New York, 1963).

23. Richard Bendix, *Nation-Building and Citizenship: Studies of Our Changing Social Order* (Berkeley, 1977), pp. 175–211; Terrel Heady, *Public Administration: A Comparative Perspective* (New York and Basel, 1983), pp. 136–173; Derek B. Heater, *Order and Rebellion: A History of Europe in the Eighteenth Century* (London, 1964), pp. 223–229; Isabel de Madariaga, *Russia in the Age of Catherine the Great* (New Haven and London, 1981), pp. 581–588; idem, "Sisters Under the Skin," *Slavic Review,* vol. 41, no. 4 (Winter 1982), pp. 624–628.

24. Gillis, *The Development of European Society,* pp. 19–20; Iu. L. Bessmertnyi, "Sotsial'naia i gosudarstvennaia sobstvennost' v zapadnoi Evrope i na Rusi v period razvitogo feodalizma," in V. T. Pashuto, ed., *Sotsial'no-ekonomicheskie problemy Rossiiskoi derevni v feodal'nuiu i kapitalisticheskuiu epokhi* (Rostov-on-Don, 1980), pp. 21–36.

25. This is the percentage indicated in official data (see Ministerstvo vnutrennikh del, *Vybory v Gosudarstvennuiu Dumu tret'ego sozyva: Statisticheskii otchet osobogo deloproizvodstva* [St. Petersburg, 1911], pp. vii–x). Steven White and Theodore S. Hamerow give the proportion of 2.4 percent: Steven White, *Political Culture and Soviet Politics* (New York, 1979), p. 29; Theodore S. Hamerow, *The Birth of a New Europe* (Chapel Hill, and London, 1983), pp. 302–304.

26. Zh. Karbon'e, *Iuridicheskaia sotsiologiia* (Moscow, 1986), pp. 177–180 (Russian edition of Jean Carbonnier, *Sociologie juridique* [Paris, 1972]).

27. M. I. Zarudnyi, *Obshchestvennyi byt Anglii* (St. Petersburg, 1865), pp. 131–143.

28. M. N. Gernet, *Moral'naia statistika* (Moscow, 1922), pp. 50–97; "O prestupnosti v Anglii i vo Frantsii," *Biblioteka dlia chteniia,* no. 10 (1854), pp. 43–54; *Entsiklopedicheskii slovar' Russkogo bibliograficheskogo instituta Granat* (Moscow, 1933), tom 33, stolbtsy 375–378; J. S. Cockburn, "Patterns of Violence in English Society: Homicide in Kent, 1560–1985," *Past and Present,* no. 130 (February 1991), pp. 70–106; idem, ed., *Crime in England, 1550–1800* (London,

1977); Ted Robert Gurr, "Contemporary Crime in Historical Perspective: A Comparative Study of London, Stockholm, and Sydney," *Annual of the American Academy of Political and Social Science*, no. 434 (1977), pp. 114–136; Howard Zehr, "The Modernization of Crime in Germany and France, 1830–1913," *Journal of Social History*, vol. 8, no. 4 (1975), pp. 117–141; idem, *Crime and the Development of Modern Society: Patterns of Criminality in Nineteenth-Century Germany and France* (London, 1976); Clive Emsley, *Crime and Society in England, 1750–1900* (London, 1987); V. A. C. Gatrell, Bruce Lenman, and Geoffrey Parker, eds., *Crime and the Law: The Social History of Crime in Western Europe Since 1500* (London, 1980).

29. Peter Burke, *Popular Culture in Early Modern Europe* (New York, 1978); Norman Cantor and Michael S. Werthman, eds., *The History of Popular Culture to 1815* (New York and London, 1968); Kaspar von Greyerz, ed., *Religion and Society in Early Modern Europe, 1500–1800* (London, 1984); Geoffrey Scarre, *Witchcraft and Magic in Sixteenth- and Seventeenth-Century Europe* (Atlantic Highlands, 1987); Robert W. Scribner, *Popular Culture and Popular Movements in Reformation Germany* (London, 1987); Keith Thomas, *Religion and the Decline of Magic* (New York, 1971).

30. O. G. Ogeeiva, "Religioznost' russkikh liudei v pervoi chetverti XVIII veka glazami zapadnoevropeiskikh memuaristov: Iu. Iul' and Kh.-F. Veber," in A. A. Gorskii, ed., *Russkaia istoriia: Problema mentaliteta; Tezisy dokladov nauchnoi konferentsii, Moskva, 4–6 oktiabria 1994* (Moscow, 1994), pp. 102–105; Doyle, *The Old European Order, 1660–1800*, pp. 152–155; Geofrey Scarre, *Witchcraft and Magic in Sixteenth- and Seventeenth-Century Europe* (Atlantic Highlands, 1987), pp. 25, 30.

31. N. A. Khachaturian and V. M. Khachaturian, "Srednevekovaia kul'tura Rossii i zapadnoi Evropy: Identichnost' i raskhozhdenie," *Tsivilizatsiia*, no. 3 (1995), pp. 62–79.

32. P. N. Miliukov, *Vospominaniia v dvukh tomakh* (Moscow, 1990), p. 158. See also N. P. Pavlov-Sil'vanskii, *Feodalizm v Drevnei Rusi* (Moscow and Petrograd, 1923), pp. 181–186; N. Kareev, *V kakom smysle mozhno govorit' o sushchestvovanii feodalizma v Rossii: Po povodu teorii Pavlova-Sil'vanskogo* (St. Petersburg, 1910), pp. 137–145.

Index

ATE DUE